CONTEMPORARY Black Biography

ISSN 1058-1316

CONTEMPORARY

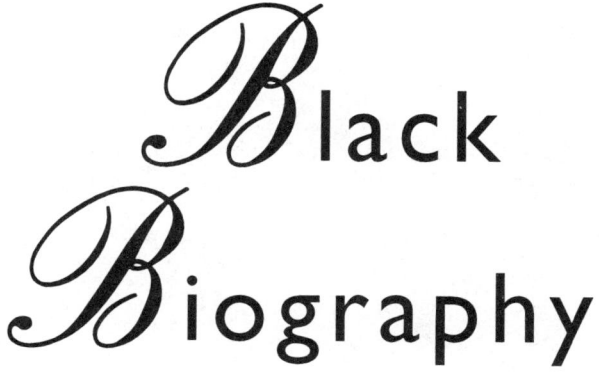
Black Biography

Profiles from the International Black Community

Volume 24

Shirelle Phelps, Editor

GALE GROUP

Detroit
New York
San Francisco
London
Boston
Woodbridge, CT

STAFF

Shirelle Phelps, *Editor*

David G. Oblender, *Contributing Editor*

Shelly Dickey, *Managing Editor, Multicultural Department*

Maria Franklin, *Permissions Manager*
Margaret Chamberlain, *Permissions Specialist*

Dorothy Maki, *Manufacturing Manager*
Stacy Melson, *Buyer*
Cynthia Baldwin, *Product Design Manager*
Gary Leach, *Graphic Artist*
Randy Bassett, *Image Database Supervisor*
Pamela A. Reed, *Imaging Coordinator*
Robyn V. Young, *Senior Editor, Imaging and Multimedia Content*
Robert Duncan, Michael Logusz, *Imaging Specialists*

Victoria B. Cariappa, *Research Manager*
Barbara McNeil, *Research Specialist*

While every effort has been made to ensure the reliability of the information presented in this publication, Gale Group does not guarantee the accuracy of the data contained herein. Gale accepts no payment for listing; and inclusion in the publication of any organization, agency, institution, publication, service, or individual does not imply endorsement of the editors or publisher. Errors brought to the attention of the publisher and verified to the satisfaction of the publisher will be corrected in future editions.

This publication is a creative work fully protected by all applicable copyright laws, as well as by misappropriation, trade secret, unfair competition, and other applicable laws. The authors and editors of this work have added value to the underlying factual material herein through one or more of the following: unique and original selection, coordination, expression, arrangement, and classification of the information.

All rights to this publication will be vigorously defended.

Copyright © 2000 Gale Group, Inc.
27500 Drake Rd.
Farmington Hills, MI 48331-3535

All rights reserved including the right of reproduction in whole or in part in any form.

Gale Group and Design is a trademark used herein under license.

Printed in the United States of America

No part of this book may be reproduced in any form without permission in writing from the publisher, except by a reviewer who wishes to quote brief passages or entries in connection with a review written for inclusion in a magazine or newspaper.

ISBN 0-7876-3248-1
ISSN 1058-1316

10 9 8 7 6 5 4 3 2 1

Contemporary Black Biography Advisory Board

Emily M. Belcher
General and Humanities Reference Librarian
Firestone Library, Princeton University

Dr. Alton Hornsby, Jr.
Professor of History
Morehouse College

Ernest Kaiser
Editor, Contributor
Retired Librarian, Schomburg Center for Research in Black Culture

Jeanette Smith
Librarian
Julia Davis Branch, St. Louis Public Library

Dr. Ronald Woods
Director, Afro-American Studies Program
Eastern Michigan University

Wendell Wray
Retired Librarian, Schomburg Center for Research in Black Culture
Retired Professor of Library Science, University of Pittsburgh

Contents

Introduction ix

Photo Credits xi

Cumulative Nationality Index 185

Cumulative Occupation Index 195

Cumulative Subject Index 216

Cumulative Name Index 249

Allen, Byron.. 1
Longstanding comedian and talk show host

Armstrong, Vanessa Bell................................ 4
Gospel singing sensation

Arrington, Richard.. 7
Birmingham's pioneering mayor

Austin, Patti.. 10
Honey-voiced veteran vocalist

Bishop, Sanford, D., Jr................................ 13
Hardworking Congressman

Boston, Lloyd... 16
Man of Style

Brown, Corrine... 18
Combative Florida Congresswoman

Brown, Lee Patrick...................................... 21
First African American mayor of Houston

Buckley, Victoria (Vikki)............................... 25
Inspirational secretary of state

Campbell, Bebe Moore................................ 28
Highly acclaimed author

Carter, Anson... 32
Hockey hero

Coleman, Donald A.................................... 35
Savvy advertising executive

Conyers, Nathan G..................................... 38
Hardworking automobile dealer

Cummings, Elijah E..................................... 41
Maryland's compassionate Congressman

Davis, Danny K... 45
"Congressional champion of liberal causes"

Davis, Ed.. 48
Pioneering automobile dealer

Devine, Loretta... 52
Veteran actress of stage amd film

Dixon, Julian C.. 56
Influential Congressman from California

Farr, Mel... 59
Superstar automobile dealer

Friday, Jeff.. 62
Keen, young film company executive

Glover, Danny... 65
Versatile actor

Hall, Elliott S... 70
Widely respected attorney and executives

Haywood, Margaret A................................. 73
Pioneering DC Superior Court Senior Judge

Herenton, Willie W...................................... 76
Popular mayor of Memphis

Hill, Oliver W... 79
Committed civil rights champion

Hilliard, Earl F... 82
"Alabama's liberal voice of Congress"

Hine, Darlene Clark..................................... 85
Distinguished African American historian

Holdsclaw, Chamique.................................. 88
WNBA's 1999 Rookie of the Year

Hutchinson, Earl Ofari................................. 91
Outspoken author and activist

Iverson, Allen.. 95
Philadelphia's player premiere

vii

Johnson, Harvey, Jr. 98
First black mayor of Jackson, Mississippi

Larkin, Barry 100
Cincinnati's sensational shortstop

Lassiter, Roy 104
Soccer sensation

Marrow, Queen Esther 107
Versatile gospel singer

Mase 110
Mellow, monotonic hip-hop rap artist

McGriff, Fred 113
Tampa Bay's sensational slugger

Newcombe, Don 116
Fearsome baseball pitcher

Painter, Nell Irvin 120
Provocative historian and author

Perkins, Tony 124
Good Morning America's Popular weatherman

Pinkston, W. Randall 128
Award-winning reporter

Powell, Bud 131
Talented and troubled jazz pianist

Pryor, Richard 136
Legendary comedic genius

Robinson, David 141
San Antonio's good-natured basketball All-Star

Silas, Paul 145
Respected basketball coach

Sisulu, Sheila Violet Makate 148
Resilent South African ambassador

Smith, Jane E. 152
Progressuve organization president

Snipes, Wesley 155
Accomplished actor

Stout,, Juanita Kidd 160
Trailblazing judge

Street, John F. 163
Outspoken mayor of Philadelphia

Tamia 167
Sultry songstress

Terrell, Dorothy A. 170
Respected company executive

Tubbs Jones, Stephanie 173
Multi-talented Congresswoman from Ohio

Watkins, Walter C. Jr. 178
Highly respected bank president

Winans, Vickie 180
Gospel singing sensation

Introduction

Contemporary Black Biography provides informative biographical profiles of the important and influential persons of African heritage who form the international black community: men and women who have changed today's world and are shaping tomorrow's.

Contemporary Black Biography covers persons of various nationalities in a wide variety of fields, including architecture, art, business, dance, education, fashion, film, industry, journalism, law, literature, medicine, music, politics and government, publishing, religion, science and technology, social issues, sports, television, theater, and others.

In addition to in-depth coverage of names found in today's headlines, *Contemporary Black Biography* provides coverage of selected individuals from earlier in this century whose influence continues to impact on contemporary life. *Contemporary Black Biography* also provides coverage of important and influential persons who are not yet household names and are therefore likely to be ignored by other biographical reference series. Each volume also includes listee updates on names previously appearing in CBB.

Designed for Quick Research *and* Interesting Reading

- **Attractive page design** incorporates textual subheads, making it easy to find the information you're looking for.

- **Easy-to-locate data sections** provide quick access to vital personal statistics, career information, major awards, and mailing addresses, when available.

- **Informative biographical essays** trace the subject's personal and professional life with the kind of in-depth analysis you need.

- **To further enhance your appreciation** of the subject, most entries include photographic portraits.

- **Sources for additional information** direct the user to selected books, magazines, and newspapers where more information on the individuals can be obtained.

Helpful Indexes Make It Easy to Find the Information You Need

Contemporary Black Biography includes cumulative Nationality, Occupation, Subject, and Name indexes that make it easy to locate entries in a variety of useful ways.

Available in Electronic Formats

Diskette/Magnetic Tape. *Contemporary Black Biography* is available for licensing on magnetic tape or diskette in a fielded format. Either the complete database or a custom selection of entries may be ordered.

The database is available for internal data processing and nonpublishing purposes only. For more information, call (800) 877-GALE.

Online. *Contemporary Black Biography* is available online through Mead Data Central's NEXIS Service in the NEXIS, PEOPLE and SPORTS Libraries in the GALBIO file.

We Welcome Your Suggestions

The editors welcome your comments and suggestions for enhancing and improving *Contemporary Black Biography*. If you would like to suggest persons for inclusion in the series, please submit these names to the editors. Mail comments or suggestions to:

The Editor
Contemporary Black Biography
Gale Group
27500 Drake Rd.
Farmington Hills, MI 48331-3535
Phone: (800) 347-4253

Photo Credits

PHOTOGRAPHS AND ILLUSTRATIONS APPEARING IN *CONTEMPORARY BLACK BIOGRAPHY*, VOLUME 24, WERE RECEIVED FROM THE FOLLOWING SOURCES:

All Reproduced by Permission: **Allen, Byron,** photograph. AP/Wide World Photos. **Arrington, Richard,** photograph by Dave Martin. AP/Wide World Photos. **Austin, Patti,** photograph. AP/Wide World Photos. **Bishop, Sanford D., Jr.**, photograph by Ron Edmonds. AP/Wide World Photos. **Brown, Corrine,** photograph by Peter Cosgrove. AP/Wide World Photos. **Brown, Lee Patrick,** photograph by Tim Johnson. AP/Wide World Photos. **Campbell, Bebe Moore,** photograph by Gene Golden. G. P. Putnam's Sons. **Carter, Anson,** photograph by Elise Amendola. AP/Wide World Photos. **Coleman, Donald A.,** photograph. Courtesy of Donald A. Coleman. **Conyers, Nathan G.,** photograph. Courtesy of Nathan G. Conyers. **Cummings, Elijah,** photograph by Roberto Borea. AP/Wide World Photos. **Davis, Danny K.,** photograph. Courtesy of Danny K. Davis. **Devine, Loretta,** photograph. Courtesy of Loretta Devine. **Dixon, Julian C.,** photograph. AP/Wide World Photos. **Farr, Mel,** photograph. Courtesy of the Mel Farr Automotive Group. **Glover, Danny,** photograph. AP/Wide World Photos. **Haywood, Margaret A.,** photograph. Courtesy of Margaret A. Haywood. **Herenton, Willie,** photograph by John L. Focht. AP/Wide World Photos. **Hill, Oliver W.,** photograph by NAACP. AP/Wide World Photos. **Hilliard, Earl,** photograph by Scott Trigg. AP/Wide World Photos. **Hine, Darlene Clark,** photograph. Courtesy of Darlene Clark Hine. **Holdsclaw, Chamique,** photograph. AP/Wide World Photos. **Hutchinson, Earl Ofari,** photograph. Courtesy of Earl Ofari Hutchinson. Middle Passage Press. **Iverson, Allen,** photograph by Beth A. Keiser. AP/Wide World Photos. **Johnson, Harvey, Jr.,** photograph by Rogelio Solis. AP/Wide World Photos. **Larkin, Barry,** photograph. AP/Wide World Photos. **Lassiter, Roy,** photograph by Lenny Ignelzi. AP/Wide World Photos. **Marrow, Queen Esther,** photograph. AP/Wide World Photos. **Mase,** photograph. AP/Wide World Photos. **McGriff, Fred,** photograph by Mark J. Terrill. AP/Wide World Photos. **Newcombe, Don,** photograph. AP/Wide World Photos. **Painter, Nell Irvin,** photograph. Courtesy of Nell Irvin Painter. **Perkins, Tony,** photograph by Steve Fenn. Good Morning America. **Pinkston, W. Randall,** photograph by Frank Micelotta. **Pryor, Richard,** photograph. AP/Wide World Photos. **Robinson, David,** photograph. AP/Wide World Photos. **Silas, Paul,** photograph. AP/Wide World Photos. **Sisulu, Sheila Violet Makate,** photograph. Courtesy of Sheila Violet Makate Sisulu. **Smith, Jane E.,** photograph. Courtesy of Jane E. Smith. **Snipes, Wesley,** photograph. AP/Wide World Photos. **Stout, Juanita Kidd,** photograph. AP/Wide World Photos. **Street, John F.,** photograph. The Office of the Mayor, Philadelphia. **Tamia,** photograph. AP/Wide World Photos. **Terrell, Dorothy A.,** photograph. Courtesy of Dorothy A. Terrell. **Tubbs Jones, Stephanie,** photograph. Courtesy of Stephanie Tubbs Jones.

Byron Allen

1961—

Comedian, talk show host, company executive

Few entertainers reach their goals in life, but even fewer make it to the big time before the age of 20. Byron Allen knew what he wanted out of life at an early age and stopped at nothing to get it. From the moment he first saw the *Tonight Show,* Allen had set his life's goal. "I decided then ... that's what I wanted to be, a comedian and a talk show host," he told Jim McFarlin of the *Detroit News.*

Allen was born Byron Folks on April 22, 1961, in Detroit, Michigan. As a small child, he would wander down to the family basement to play alone with his thoughts and dreams. "That's where I developed the creativity, the imagination," Allen told Louie Robinson in *Ebony.* But Allen learned to use his upbringing in Detroit to a greater advantage. Much of the comedy material that sends audiences into uproarious laughter draws directly upon his black, middle class family background. "Allen uses the black motif for strong material," *Variety* wrote about one of his appearances in Las Vegas. In fact, Allen uses his life as the butt of many of his jokes. *Variety* offered on example: "Confiding that he was born in Detroit's Ford Hospital, he fretted, 'I'm afraid I'll be recalled.'"

At the age of eight, when his parents separated, Byron moved to Los Angeles, California, with his mother, Carolyn Folks. It was during this time that he got his first real taste of show business. In order to support the two of them, Carolyn took a job as an National Broadcasting Company (NBC-TV) page and would often take her son with her while she worked. While mom was busy with her job, young Byron would wander over to the vacant *Tonight Show* set and host his own talk show. On one occasion "when a janitor caught him," *People* reported, "quick-thinking Byron brought the man onstage as 'the author of the wonderful book, Cleaning Up After the Stars.' A grinning Irv Johnson went through an interview for the empty house." Ironically, Johnson was in the audience when Allen made his *Tonight Show* debut several years later.

But before Allen could perform his magic for Johnny Carson, he had to prove that he had the comedic talent that was necessary for a spot on the *Tonight Show.* While visiting the sets of *Chico and the Man* and *Sanford and Son,* Allen got to meet some of the biggest television comedians of the time--Redd Foxx, Freddie Prinz, Flip Wilson, and Gabe Kaplan. In fact, Kaplan was so impressed with Allen's humor that he suggested he try

> **At a Glance...**
>
> Born Byron Folks, April 22, 1961, in Detroit, MI; son of Carolyn Folks (a TV publicist). *Education:* Attended the University of Southern California.
>
> **Career:** Comedian, actor, writer, and talk show host. Performed as comedian in numerous nightclubs, beginning 1975; worked as a comedy writer for various comedians and television shows, including *Good Times* and *Chico and the Man*, 1975-79; cohost of *Real People*, 1979-84; host and executive coproducer of *The Byron Allen Show*, 1989-92. CF Entertainment Inc, (production company), owner, currently. CF Entertainment has the Syndicated shows, *Entertainment, The American Athlete*, and next season's (fall 2000) new weekly, *Kickin' It with Byron Allen*. Selected television appearances include the *Tonight Show, Dinah, Hollywood Squares*, and the *Merv Griffin Show*; cowriter, coproducer, and costar of television movie *Case Closed*, 1988.
>
> **Addresses:** *Office*—CF Entertainment, 9903 Santa Monica Blvd., Ste 418, Beverly Hills, CA 90212.

out his routine at Los Angeles's well-known Comedy Store. "I thought it was a place where you bought jokes," Allen later told *People*, but he followed Kaplan's advice and began his stand-up comedy career.

At that point, the 14-year-old Allen devoted his whole life to school and to working on comedy routines, making sure to practice at every opportunity. One night while he was standing around the halls of NBC waiting for his mother, Allen started telling his jokes to anyone who would listen, including one of comedy star J.J. Walker's writers. The listener was so impressed with the jokes that Allen was telling that he called his boss and told him about this young comic he had found. Walker called Allen a few nights later and offered him a job on his staff of comedy writers, which at the time included David Letterman.

For the next few years Allen continued to refine his stand-up routine at various clubs around Los Angeles and to write jokes for comedians like Prinz. But Allen never let his career get in the way of his education—by the time he was 16 years old, he was working two or three shows a night while maintaining a B average at Fairfax High School. In fact he was so adamant about getting a good education that when he got a call from the talent coordinator at the *Tonight Show* during his senior year, Allen turned them down. "I was right in the middle of high school mid-term exams," he told Robinson, "and I knew that those would be the grades that the University of Southern California was going to look at, so I turned them down."

Made Network Television Debut

Once Allen got his mid-term As and was accepted at USC, he called the *Tonight Show* to say that he was ready to be on the program. On May 17, 1979, Allen made his debut on network television to the delights of Johnny, his sidekick Ed McMahon, and the studio audience. After that, the offers to write for television and to appear at clubs across the country came flooding in. But once again, Allen opted to put his education first.

There was one offer, however, that he just could not refuse. Producer George Schlatter was putting together a new show and wanted Allen to be a part of it. At first Allen thought he was going to be featured as a guest on the new prime-time informational show, *Real People*. But a few hours after meeting with Schlatter, Allen's agent called and told him that he had been offered a spot as one of the regular show hosts. Allen summed up the event for *Ebony*. "When I graduated, I had my diploma in one hand and my plane ticket in the other and I left the next day to do my first *Real People* story in Cincinnati. It was at a roller-coaster convention."

The show was a hit with the American public. In its first year it was rated as one of the top twenty shows on prime time and nominated for an Emmy Award as outstanding information series. For the next few years Allen traveled the country doing interviews with "everyday" people, including the owners of racing ducks, a walrus keeper at Sea World, a knife thrower, and Captain Sticky. But Allen was able to fulfill his commitment to education and his role as a host on the show, because most of the stories were filmed during the summer months. *Real People* was canceled in 1984, but Allen's career continued onward and upward.

From Real People to the Comedy Circuit

During his stint on network television, Allen was making appearances on *Dinah, Hollywood Squares,* and the *Merv Griffin Show*. His career as a stand-up comedian was also reaching new ground. In late 1984 Allen opened for Kenny Rogers at the Golden Nugget in Las Vegas to rave reviews. According to *Variety*, "The entire audience was mesmerized by his gurgly giggle welling up after some of his lines.... Allen's supermarket routine inspired instant response, even from the upscale crowd, but a treatise on banks was surefire. 'How come the door to the vault is always wide open, but they got the ink pens chained down?,' he questioned." It was clear that Allen had gained acceptance by both the critics and the public as a comedian. His dream of making it as a talk show host, however, would have to wait for several more years.

In the meantime Allen devoted more time to his comedy routine by making appearances on various television programs and at various night clubs. In 1988 he made his acting debut in a made-for-television movie called *Case Closed,* starring opposite Erica Gimpel and Charles Durning. As cowriter and coproducer of the film, Allen considered it a labor of love: it was the first time he was able to showcase his creativity in his own way. "I really worked hard on this project," he told *Jet,* "and I think viewers will have a lot of laughs. It's full of action, adventure, double-entendre, tongue-in-cheek and a lot of funny stuff."

Even with all the excitement that the movie gave Allen, he still hadn't fulfilled his number one career goal—to be a talk show host. "Eight years," he told McFarlin. "Eight years I've been trying to sell the same exact show: a once-a-week, one-hour talk show with comedy and music. I went around to every syndicator in the country, and they just weren't interested." But he finally found someone who was willing to take a risk.

Talk Show Premiere a Success

Working as coexecutive producer and host, Allen made a pilot episode to show to potential investors and distributors. Once the show was sold to the top three television markets in the country—New York, Los Angeles, and Chicago—others soon jumped on the bandwagon. On September 9, 1989, *The Byron Allen Show* premiered on 155 television stations, covering 96 percent of the country.

Once Allen had achieved his goal of having his own talk show, he took matters one step further by forming his own production company, BYCA Productions, and his own distribution company, BYCA Distribution. These new companies made it easier for Allen to promote other projects he was interested in, including *Jammin' 91,* a two-hour music special that counted down that year's hottest music videos and *Superstars with David Sheehan,* a weekly half-hour series devoted to interviews with major stars from the entertainment industry.

The Byron Allen show was cancelled in 1992. However, Allen launched his own production company, CF Entertainment in 1993. CF Entertainment was named after his mother Carolyn Folks. Since it's inception, CF Entertainment has launched several projects. Allen, is currently running his syndicated talk show *Entertainers,* which is now in its fifth season. *Entertainers* is seen in more than 100 markets nationally and 70 countries worldwide.

From *Entertainers* came another weekly show, *The American Athlete,* which has had guests such as Michael Jordan and Tiger Woods. Next fall Allen hopes to launch another show, *Kickin' It with Byron Allen,* which will spotlight comedians, musicians, and fashion stars in a weekly hour program. As of date, *The American Athlete* is his most popular program.

Even though Allen has taken on other projects, comedy remains his first love. But Allen is quick to point out that he is confident that the future will bring him whatever he wants. "There really isn't anything you can't do," he told Robinson. "It's just a matter of saying, 'Hey, I can do it, I *can* do it.'" Obviously, Byron Allen lives by his words.

Sources

Books

Hawkins, Walter L., *African American Biographies,* first edition supplement, McFarland & Co., 1994.

Periodicals

Broadcasting, June 17, 1991.
Broadcasting & Cable, June 1, 1998, p. 21.
Contemporary Theatre, Film, and Television, Volume 11, Gale Group, p. 12, 1994.
Detroit News, October 4, 1989.
Ebony, April 1980, June 1982.
Jet, April 25, 1988.
People, September 10, 1979, July 28, 1980.
Variety, December 19, 1984, December 21, 1988, July 12, 1989.

—Joe Kuskowski and Shirelle Phelps

Vanessa Bell Armstrong

1953—

Gospel vocalist

In the 1990s, gospel music expanded tremendously in popularity as artists such as Kirk Franklin, Yolanda Adams, and CeCe Winans turned the excitement inherent in secular musical styles to religious ends. The music shed its big-Sunday-hat image, and made inroads with the younger audiences that singers hoped to reach. Vanessa Bell Armstrong, an artist steeped in the enduring gospel traditions of Detroit's black churches, did much to blaze the trail that later artists could follow. But when Armstrong first began to merge sacred and secular in her music, she had to endure criticism from the faithful, and it may be that she has received insufficient credit for her part in creating an extremely significant musical movement.

Armstrong was born Vanessa Bell in Detroit on October 2, 1953. Her father was a minister, and she began singing in churches around the city when she was only four years old. In 1966 the gospel choir leader Mattie Moss Clark heard Armstrong sing and took her under her wing. Armstrong traveled with Clark, and under her tutelage received a gospel vocal education in some truly stellar company; among the acts with whom she appeared were the Rev. James Cleveland, the Mighty Clouds of Joy, the Clark Sisters, and the Winans.

Influenced by Aretha Franklin

Another key early influence on Armstrong's style was the singing of the most famous performer ever to emerge from Detroit's gospel scene, Aretha Franklin, and when Armstrong emerged into her own career, many observers noted a vocal resemblance between the two singers. A married woman with five children, Armstrong made her recording debut late, releasing the album Peace Be Still on the small Onyx label in 1984, when she was 31. The album, produced by Minister Thomas Whitfield, went to the top of the gospel charts.

The year 1987 marked a turning point in Armstrong's career. The success of Peace Be Still attracted the attention of big-time talent scouts, and Armstrong was signed to the flourishing r&b label Jive Records. That year, she served notice of her vocal capabilities when she edged out both Franklin and virtuoso songstress Patti LaBelle in auditions to perform the theme song of NBC television's Amen situation comedy. She also appeared in a Broadway theatrical production called Don't Get God Started. But the crucial event of the year was the release of Armstrong's Jive debut album, simply entitled Vanessa Bell Armstrong.

The album drew denunciations from fans of traditional gospel, who, according to MusicHound R&B, accused Armstrong of "backsliding" and "selling out." The source of their negative reactions was the album's stylistic foray into contemporary urban sounds, which was achieved expertly enough that one of its single releases, "You Bring Out the Best in Me," ended up as a hit on the r&b

> ## At a Glance...
>
> Born Vanessa Bell on October 2, 1953, in Detroit, Michigan; daughter of Jesse Bell, a minister. Married with five children.
>
> **Career:** Gospel vocalist. Began singing at age four in Detroit-area churches; worked with Mattie Moss Clark from age of 13; toured and sang with top gospel stars including Rev. James Cleveland, the Clark Sisters, and the Winans as a teenager; released Peace Be Still, 1984; signed to Jive label and released Vanessa Bell Armstrong, 1987; recorded theme for television comedy Amen, 1987; appeared in Broadway musical Don't Get God Started, 1987; released Wonderful One, 1990; released Chosen; 1991; released Something on the Inside, 1993; released The Secret Is Out 1995; released Desire of My Heart: Live in Detroit, 1998.
>
> **Addresses:** Label—BMG Entertainment/Verity Records, 1540 Broadway, New York, NY 10019.

charts. The song drew on a lyric device that would become a staple of both black and white contemporary gospel styles: it intentionally blurred the boundary between religious feeling and romantic love. When Armstrong employed it, though, the idea was still comparatively young.

Appeared with Oprah Winfrey

Despite the criticisms, Vanessa Bell Armstrong was a strong seller and propelled the singer's career forward. She released two more albums in the early 1990s, Chosen (1991) and Something on the Inside (1993), but after that, she took a two-and-a-half year break to appear with television talk show host Oprah Winfrey in a made-for-TV film of the novel The Women of Brewster Place; the film was widely publicized and exposed Armstrong's image to a mass audience. Armstrong's second Jive album, Wonderful One, extended her crossover experiments. It featured the duet "True Love Never Fails," recorded with jazz guitarist Jonathan Butler. In 1990 Jive attempted to cash in on the publicity surrounding Armstrong with a greatest-hits album.

When she reemerged in 1995 with the album The Secret Is Out, she stayed on top of new currents in black popular music and incorporated them into her sound. Increasingly asserting control over her own music, she hand-picked the producer for the new album, the Charlotte, North Carolina–based gospel impresario John P. Kee, known as "The Prince of Gospel," whose album The New Life Community Choir Featuring John P. Kee was one of the biggest gospel records of the middle of the decade.

The album featured an even wider stylistic mix than Armstrong had previously attempted. "It's traditional and churchy, but also hip-hop," she told Billboard. "There's the blues ... classical ... he's [Kee] just exploring my talent and challenging me all the way." Such tracks as the hip-hop–inflected "Love Lifted Me" earned Armstrong a place, along with Yolanda Adams and CeCe Winans, in a 1996 Essence magazine feature on the "divas of gospel." A reviewer for American Visions seemed both attracted and unnerved by the new energy of Armstrong's style: "I'm almost afraid to say it, but she does indeed belt out her music with such conviction that the line between gospel and contemporary is blurred. But the meaning is the same: salvation."

Affirmed Commitment to Gospel

Indeed, even as she continued to break new ground, Armstrong reaffirmed her commitment to gospel traditions. She questioned some of her label's more blatant efforts to cross her over to a secular audience, observing to Billboard, "They were trying to direct me into the secular market, and they just lost me. Fans were wondering, 'What's up, you're going secular.' But I never left. I'm gospel, and I'm not going anywhere." She continued to exert influence over secular artists—it was said that vocal diva Mariah Carey studied her singing—but she would close out the 1990s with a spectacular return to gospel basics. In 1998 Armstrong recorded Desire of My Heart—Live, recorded at the Perfecting Church in her hometown of Detroit. The album was released on the Verity label, and its release was accompanied by a video made as it was being recorded. Desire of My Heart—Live marked a homecoming and a moment of renewal for Armstrong in several ways. She wrote the album's title track, the first time one of her own compositions had been included on one of her releases, and she served as the album's co-producer. Armstrong's father, Elder Jesse Bell, was featured on the track "Labor in Vain," and Perfecting Church pastor Marvin Winans joined Armstrong and the church's choir on the barn-burning "He Is Lord." Billboard called the album "an enduring classic." Reflecting on her unheralded influence on gospel music the magazine observed, "It took a while, but the world seems to be catching up to Armstrong." Her second greatest-hits release, which appeared on Verity in 1999, gave gospel listeners the chance to survey the development of her immensely important career.

Selected discography

Peace Be Still, Benson, 1984.
Vanessa Bell Armstrong, Jive/Novus, 1987.
Wonderful One, Jive/Novus, 1990.
Chosen, Onyx, 1991.
Something on the Inside, Jive/Novus, 1993.
The Secret Is Out, Verity, 1995.
Desire of My Heart: Live in Detroit, Verity, 1998.

Sources

Books

Contemporary Musicians, volume 24, Gale, 1998.

Periodicals

American Visions, December-January 1995, p. 49.
Billboard, April 29, 1995, p. 42; May 30, 1998.
Essence, February 1996, p. 64.

Online

www.allmusic.com.

—James Manheim

Richard Arrington

1934—

Mayor of Birmingham

A bookish professor of zoology training, Richard Arrington became the first black mayor of the great Southern industrial center of Birmingham, Alabama. Reaping the rewards that came from having brought political representation to African Americans in one of the Deep South's most racially divided cities, he built a powerhouse of a political organization. Arrington vastly increased the participation of blacks at all levels of the city government, and at the height of his career wielded considerable influence in regional and national politics. Several times over his five terms in office he ran into trouble with allegations of corruption, but he consistently maintained that he had been the victim of selective targeting because of his race.

Arrington was born into a sharecropper family on October 19, 1934, in Livingston, Alabama, near the Mississippi border, but grew up and attended public schools in Fairfield, near Birmingham. He attended Birmingham's historically black Miles College, majoring in science and graduating in 1955. An honors student, he went north for a Master's program at the University of Detroit at a time when the number of blacks working toward post-graduate degrees was extremely small.

Arrington received an M.S. degree in 1957, and then decided to return to his alma mater to teach. He was part of the biology faculty and later a counselor, remaining at Miles until 1963, when he enrolled in a Ph.D. program at the University of Oklahoma.

Received Doctoral Degree

Winning a university award for outstanding work in biology, Arrington received his doctorate in 1966, and once again returned to Miles College. This time he was part of the administration, serving as an academic dean until 1970. He then took a position as executive director of the Alabama Center for Higher Education, a consortium of the state's eight historically black institutions of higher education, and remained in that post until 1979. But in the early 1970s he was drawn into his second career, one with a much higher profile.

Birmingham's name lived in infamy for much of the 1960s due to the abuses the city's police department dealt out to civil rights demonstrators; those abuses themselves formed only one chapter in a long history of

At a Glance...

Born October 19, 1934, in Livingston, Alabama; son of a sharecropper. Married; five children. *Education:* graduated from high school, Fairfield, Alabama; A.B., Miles College, Birmingham, Alabama, 1955; M.S., University of Detroit, 1957; Ph.D., University of Oklahoma, 1966.

Career: Former mayor of Birmingham, Alabama. Professor of biology, Miles College, 1957–63; academic dean, Miles College, 1967–70; executive director, Alabama Center for Higher Education, 1970–79; served two terms on Birmingham city council, 1971–79; elected mayor of Birmingham, 1979; re-elected four times; resigned before end of fifth term, 1999.

Awards: Ortenburger Award for Outstanding Work in Biology, University of Oklahoma, 1966; Man of the Year, Birmingham, 1979; numerous educational and community service awards.

Addresses: c/o City of Birmingham, 710 20th St. N., Birmingham, AL 35203.

tension between Birmingham's city government and its large black population, drawn to the city decades before by opportunities at the city's numerous steel mills. Bombings by terrorist elements of the city's white population were so common that one predominantly black area bore the chilling nickname of "Dynamite Hill," and things came to a head in 1963 with the tragic bombing of the 16th Street Baptist Church, in which four young girls were killed.

The split between the races in Birmingham has never fully healed, but the atmosphere began to improve when African Americans began to exercise their newly guaranteed right to vote; the city council's first African American member was elected in 1968. Arrington, with his already distinguished administrative record, emerged naturally as part of the city's new black political leadership, and he soon ascended to the council himself, winning four-year terms in 1971 and 1975. The Birmingham mayor's office, however, remained in white hands.

Won Mayor's Race in Squeaker

That changed when Arrington ran for mayor in 1979. His opponent was a conservative white lawyer named Frank Parsons, and the contest was breathtakingly close, with the two candidates exchanging the lead several times on election night (October 30) as the returns came in from different parts of the city. Arrington eked out a close victory, with about 10 percent of the city's white electorate crossing racial lines to support his candidacy.

"My being elected to office was very important to the city," Arrington recalled in a 1999 interview with *Jet* magazine. "It made all out citizens feel a part of it." Indeed, among Arrington's most important accomplishments during his five terms as mayor were his integration of the city payroll (blacks held 50 percent of city jobs by the mid-1990s), and above all a set of measures designed to lower tensions between the city's African-American residents and its public safety officers; black representation increased sharply in both the police and fire departments. By 1995, when Arrington ran for his last term, he had named 23 of the city's 24 department heads; 12 were black and 12 were white.

A member of numerous community organizations, Arrington also enjoyed harmonious relations with Birmingham's business community. While other American industrial cities suffered badly during the 1980s, especially those where steelmaking was an important component of the local economy, Birmingham flourished under Arrington, shedding its smokestack image and becoming a regional center for banking and health care. By 1995 the city enjoyed an expanded tax base and a budget that was both growing and balanced.

Jailed in Kickback Flap

As he racked up victory after victory, Arrington became a powerful figure in Birmingham, and even political candidates from beyond Alabama found it necessary to court his favor. His power rested on a well-oiled grassroots political organization, the Jefferson County Citizens Coalition; critics called it a machine. After the euphoria of the transfer of power to Birmingham's black majority had worn off, allegations began to surface, from both white and black observers, that an atmosphere of cronyism flourished in the Arrington administration, which held an iron grip over city contract work.

The most serious crisis connected with investigations into the activities of Arrington's circle came in 1992, when an Atlanta architect claimed that Arrington had accepted a $5,000 kickback in exchange for preference in the awarding of a city building contract. Arrington attacked the ensuing federal judicial inquiry as racially motivated, and when he refused to turn over city records pertaining to the case, he was jailed for a night. Draped in symbolic chains, Arrington led supporters in a march beginning at the 16th Street Baptist Church as he prepared to turn himself in. He eventually relented and turned over the records, and the incident barely nicked his popularity; like Detroit mayor Coleman Young, Arrington was always subject to close scrutiny from law enforcement agencies, but emerged personally and politically unscathed. He cruised to re-election in 1995.

In 1999, Arrington announced plans to write a book, and stepped down just before the end of his fifth term so that his hand-picked successor, William Bell, could run as an incumbent in the mayoral election that year. During the campaign, controversy swirled around the claim that the city government had grossly overpaid an Arrington friend for a parcel of land, and Bell's opponent, Bernard Kincaid, scored an upset victory. The city council, still in the hands of Arrington loyalists, moved to restrict Kincaid's powers, and one council representative, quoted in the *New York Times,* offered the ironic justification that "... we had a king for all those years [and] I'm not the least bit interested in having another one." Though he may have become somewhat monarchical over his years in power, Richard Arrington was a leader who brought about and oversaw fundamental change in a city at the center of America's racial divide.

Sources

Books

Hawkins, Walter L., *African American Biographies: Profiles of 558 Curren Men and Women,* McFarland & Company, 1992.

Henderson, Ashyia N., and Shirelle Phelps, eds., *Who's Who Among African Americans,* 12th ed., Gale, 1999.

Periodicals

Jet, November 6, 1995, p. 4; November 4, 1996, p. 20; August 2, 1999, p. 33.

New York Times, December 18, 1999, p. A12.

Time, February 3, 1992, p. 24.

—James M. Manheim

Patti Austin

1948—

Vocalist

A sophisticated vocalist whose style was steeped in jazz, Patti Austin enjoyed a period of stardom during the heyday of smooth, expertly produced rhythm-and blues music in the 1980s. Both before and after her period in the limelight, Austin was tirelessly active as a musician, challenging herself and her listeners with a series of acclaimed jazz albums on one hand, and achieving vocal ubiquity as a successful singer of television commercial jingles on the other. Austin has been, in short, a professional's professional.

She was born in New York on August 10, 1948, and grew up in the lap of show business. At the tender age of four she made her performing debut, singing a song called "Teach Me Tonight" on the stage of Harlem's famed Apollo Theater during an appearance by vocalist Dinah Washington, who was also Austin's godmother. Something of a child star, she appeared on Sammy Davis Jr.'s television variety show, worked on stage with such stars as Ray Bolger of The Wizard of Oz, and when she was nine she went to Europe with a group led by bandleader Quincy Jones, who would become an immensely influential figure both on Austin's own career and on the world of black popular music generally.

Toured with Harry Belafonte

Austin's first major series of appearances as a mature singer came when she was 16, when she went on tour with pop vocalist Harry Belafonte, then near the peak of his fame. This tour led to a fresh round of television appearances and to a three-year stint as a lounge singer for various international locations of the posh Intercontinental hotel chain. With this wealth of professional experience under her belt before she could even vote, it was not difficult for Austin to decide on a musical career. Recording executives and producers valued the young singer's know-how, and session-work opportunities began to flow her way.

"The first session I did was for James Brown's hit, 'It's a Man's World,' and when I got a nice juicy check from that," Austin recalled in a biographical sketch released by the Concord Jazz label. "I said, 'Hey let me do some more of this stuff.'" Austin became one of pop music's leading session musicians in the early 1970s, backing both r&b and pop vocalists such as Paul Simon, Roberta Flack, George Benson, and Cat Stevens. With her vocals

> ### At a Glance...
>
> Born August 10, 1948, in New York, New York; daughter of Gordon and Edna Austin. Education: attended high school.
>
> **Career:** Vocalist. Made debut appearance at age four with vocalist Dinah Washington, her godmother; traveled to Europe at age nine with bandleader Quincy Jones; toured with Harry Belafonte; became leading session and advertising-jingle vocalist, early 1970s; recorded debut LP, End of a Rainbow, 1976; recorded four albums for CTI label, late 1970s and early 1980s; signed with Qwest label, 1981; recorded smash Every Home Should Have One, 1981 (included single "Baby Come to Me," a duet with James Ingram); released four albums on Qwest, 1980s; signed with GRP label, 1990; signed with Concord Jazz label, 1998; signed with Intersound label, 1999.
>
> **Awards:** Academy Award nomination, with James Ingram, for "How Do You Keep the Music Playing?," 1983.
>
> **Addresses:** Booking Agent—Pyramid Entertainment Group, 89 Fifth Ave., 7th floor, New York, NY 10003. Label–Intersound, 11810 Wills Rd., Alpharetta, GA 30004

included on the soundtracks of hundreds of television commercials, Austin became one of America's most heard but least known singers.

That began to change when Austin was signed to the jazz-oriented label CTI in 1976, thanks to contacts with industry veteran Creed Taylor and Belafonte's former musical director Bill Eaton. The four albums Austin recorded for CTI helped to raise her profile in the industry and were widely appreciated by the architects of the "Quiet Storm" turn that black popular music took in the early 1980s. One of the albums, Havana Candy, was reissued in 1997 and favorably reviewed by Down Beat. The magazine pointed to "Austin's appreciation of the jazz legacy as well as her love of various pop styles.

Signed by Quincy Jones

The dawn of the 1980s brought Austin some especially high-profile session assignments: she sang on Gaucho, the rock group Steely Dan's complex exploration of the possibilities of soft rock, and, on a lighter note, appeared on the Blues Brothers album. She also enjoyed a hit single with "Razzmatazz" on Quincy Jones's Grammy-winning 1980 LP The Dude, and in 1981 was signed to Jones's Qwest label. That year, Austin's Qwest debut album, Every Home Should Have One, finally brought her stardom thanks to her chart-topping duet with James Ingram, "Baby Come to Me." The album was produced by Jones and Rod Temperton, the same team that would soon be responsible for Michael Jackson's epochal Off the Wall and Thriller albums.

"Baby Come to Me" was a perfect showcase for Austin's vocals, which had taken on an exquisite silky quality that blended nicely with the smooth instrumental textures of the period. The song drew pop as well as urban listeners in droves, and was adopted as the theme song of the television soap opera General Hospital. Austin and Ingram followed it up in 1983 with another successful duet, "How Do You Keep the Music Playing?"; part of the soundtrack of the film Best Friends, the song was nominated for an Oscar, and Austin and Ingram performed it on the Academy Awards television broadcast.

Austin's next Qwest album, Patti Austin, was released in 1984, but its assemblage of six separate producers failed to bring together a cohesive whole, and Rolling Stone complained that "except on the ballads, Austin's powerful and technically proficient voice lacks distinction." Two more albums for Qwest failed to reach the chart levels of Every Home Should Have One, and Austin's career took a dip. She was also shaken by a house fire that destroyed nearly everything she owned and came within seconds of killing her elderly parents.

Strongly Affected by Fire

The accident made Austin reexamine her priorities in life. Recalling her life atop the charts in the early 1980s in an interview with Essence, Austin said, My main concerns were looking good, the parties I would attend " and the size of the limousine that would take me to them." Her star-studded circle of associates suddenly seemed less attractive: "Yes, they were the 'happening' people—on the charts and in the news—but they were miserable in their persistent bed-hoppings. They were all doing too many drugs and too much booze. They all had lots of stuff but not much soul or heart." Austin scaled back, built a new home in upstate New York, and reconnected with some of her former jazz associates.

Austin recorded a series of albums for the GRP label in the 1990s. One of them, Love Is Gonna Getcha, reunited her with Havana Candy producer and keyboardist Dave Grusin, and included the hit "Through the Test of Time." Austin enjoyed a moderate radio presence through the decade, kept up a steady stream of television appearances, and reveled in praise from such luminaries as opera star Kathleen Battle. In 1998 she recorded the In & Out of Love album for the Concord Jazz label, and the following year moved to Intersound for Street of Dreams, a disc that allowed her to showcase her interpretations of some of her own favorite compositions. Stephen Thomas Erlewine of the music-encyclopedia website allmusic.com called the album "a fine latter-day effort from a fine singer."

Selected discography

End of a Rainbow, CTI, 1976.
Havana Candy, CTI, 1977.
Live at the Bottom Line, Epic, 1979.
Body Language, CTI, 1980.
Every Home Should Have One, Qwest, 1981.
In My Life, CTI, 1983.
Patti Austin, Qwest, 1984.
Gettin' Away with Murder, Qwest, 1985.
The Real Me, Qwest, 1988.
Love Is Gonna Getcha, GRP, 1990.
Carry On, GRP, 1991.
Live, GRP, 1992.
That Secret Place, GRP, 1994.
In and Out of Love, Concord Jazz, 1998.
Street of Dreams, Intersound, 1999.

Sources

Books

Clarke, Donald, ed., The Penguin Encyclopedia of Popular Music, Viking, 1989.
Graff, Gary, Josh Freedom du Lac, and Jim McFarlin, MusicHound R&B: The Essential Album Guide, Visible Ink, 1998.
Larkin, Colin, ed., The Encyclopedia of Popular Music, Muze UK, 1998.

Periodicals

Billboard, September 26, 1998, p. 25.
Down Beat, December 1997, p. 94.
Essence, March 1993, p. 67.
People, May 7, 1984, p. 30; May 14, 1990, p. 26.
Rolling Stone, March 29, 1984, p. 74.

Other

Additional information for this profile was obtained from www.aent.com/concord/bios/austinbio2.html; and www.allmusic.com.

—James M. Manheim

Sanford D. Bishop, Jr.

1947—

Congressman from Georgia

In 1968, as a student at Atlanta's Morehouse College, Sanford Bishop sang at the funeral of Dr. Martin Luther King Jr. Nearly thirty years later, he would take a major step toward realizing King's dream of an America where people were judged not on the color of their skin, but on the content of their character. Bishop was elected to Congress in a newly drawn district with a substantial white majority. He had been a member of the House since 1992, but the majority-African American district that had originally sent him to Congress had been struck down by the courts due to its irregular shape.

Bishop was born in Mobile, Alabama, on February 4, 1947, and grew up in a family that valued education and learning. His father, Sanford D. Bishop Sr., was an educator who became the first president of Alabama's Bishop State Community College, and his mother, Minnie, was a librarian. Bishop attended Morehouse College, which was considered one of the premier centers of African American higher education in the South. During his senior year, he was elected president of the college's student body.

Attended Emory University Law School

With sterling credentials from his years at Morehouse, Bishop won admission to the prestigious law school at Atlanta's Emory University, and distinguished himself there as well, winning scholarly awards and graduating in 1971. Along the way, he joined the U.S. Army, completing basic training at Georgia's Fort Benning and entering a ROTC program. He received an honorable discharge in 1971, and the following year, after a brief stint in New York, took up residence in Columbus, Georgia, a middle-sized city in the southwestern part of the state. Columbus had been slow to embrace the civil rights reforms of the 1960s, and the firm that Bishop founded there, Bishop and Buckner P.C., concentrated on civil rights law.

Bishop quickly put down roots in Columbus, joining several civic organizations. In 1976, at the age of twenty-nine, he was elected to Georgia's state legislature. Bishop served seven terms, and advanced to the state senate in 1990, where he sponsored bills related to job training for welfare recipients and legislative ethics. The ethics work stood Bishop in good stead in

> ### At a Glance...
>
> Born February 4, 1947, in Mobile, AL; son of an educational adminstrator and a librarian. *Education:* attended public schools in Mobile; Morehouse College, Atlanta, Georgia, B.A., 1968; Emory University School of Law, J.D., 1971. *Military service:* ROTC cadet, 1969-71. *Religion:* Baptist.
>
> **Career:** United States Representative, Second District of Georgia, member of the Democratic Party. Admitted to Georgia Bar, 1971; moved to Columbus, Georgia, and began practicing law, 1972; elected to Georgia House of Representatives, 1976; elected to Georgia state senate, 1990; elected to U.S. House of Representatives, 1992; won reelection in 1994, 1996, and 1998.
>
> **Addresses:** *Office*—1433 Longworth House Office Building, Washington, DC 20515.

1992, when the Second District's U.S. Representative, Charles Hatcher, was charged with having drawn 819 overdrafts against his U.S. House bank account. Local businessmen urged Bishop to enter the race, and he wound up second in a three-way runoff. He won both the runoff and the general election convincingly, and took his seat in Congress in January of 1993.

Aided Flood Victims

The district from which Bishop was elected was created to ensure an African American majority. It snaked through southern Georgia, and included predominantly African American neighborhoods in the cities of Columbus, Macon, Valdosta, and Albany. Such districts were intended to increase African American representation in Congress, but some observers questioned both the constitutionality and the effectiveness of such maneuvers. Many of these district boundaries were challenged in court. Bishop worked hard to aid victims of a flood that hit southern Georgia in the summer of 1994, and was convincingly reelected that November. However, in 1995, the U.S. Supreme Court threw out the existing boundaries of the Second District. Bishop's new district was more contiguous geographically, but its percentage of African American residents had declined from 57 to 39 percent.

The 1996 elections, therefore, put Bishop and fellow Georgia Democrat Cynthia McKinney in the national spotlight. While African Americans had been elected in white-majority districts before, it had never happened in the Deep South, let alone in a rural district where racist organizations such as the Ku Klux Klan had flourished. "Many black observers give Bishop little chance," *The New Republic* observed just before the election.

Bishop, however, campaigned vigorously against his Republican opponent, who ran television ads that called Bishop "shockingly liberal." Bishop tailored his political positions to put him more in tune with the essential conservatism of his district, joining the congressional group of "Blue Dog" Democrats that tried to combat the leftward drift of the national party on fiscal and social issues. He joined the National Rifle Association, and voted for Republican-proposed welfare-reform and tax-cut plans. Some African American observers condemned Bishop for these policy changes—University of Maryland political scientist Ronald Walters told the *New Republic* he could understand why some African Americans would consider Bishop a "race traitor"—but in many respects he was simply following the leader of his own party, President Bill Clinton, who took a sharp rightward tack after the losses Democrats had suffered in the 1994 congressional elections.

Downplayed Race as Campaign Issue

Bishop, who according to *The Almanac of American Politics* described himself as "a moderate conservative on fiscal issues and a 'traditionalist' on so-called family issues," fired back at his critics. "If whites can win in majority-black districts and blacks can win in majority-white districts," he told *The New Republic,* "it means we are one step closer to the magical moment when race is no longer a campaign issue." He stressed his impeccable record of constituent services, reminding both African American and white crowds that he returned to the district from Washington every weekend. Indeed, Bishop had made many friends among the district's peanut farmers as a result of his handling of the 1994 flood. His district included the home of former peanut farmer and President, Jimmy Carter. In Congress, Bishop worked to secure funds for a museum honoring Carter's years in office.

In the months before the election, Bishop was a fixture at colorful small-town events like the Big Pig Jig in the town of Vienna, Georgia. He surprised political observers by winning the election by a margin of 54 to 46 percent. Rising national prosperity trickled down to southern Georgia, and increased Bishop's margin of victory to 57–43 two years later. A member of the

House Agriculture Committee, Bishop worked across party lines to fashion a compromise that ensured the continuation of federal government subsidies to peanut growers. He has also served on the House Intelligence and Veterans Affairs Committees. Holding the position of Whip at Large in the Democratic House membership structure, Bishop's political star appeared to be on the rise.

Sources

Books

Barone, Michael, and Grant Ujifusa. *The Almanac of American Politics: 2000.* National Journal, 1999.

1997–1998 Congressional Directory: 105th Congress. United States Government Printing Office, 1997.

Periodicals

Jet, August 1, 1994, p. 12; July 29, 1996, p. 32.
New Republic, November 4, 1996, p. 18.

Other

Additional information for this profile was obtained from www.house.gov/bishop/bio.html.

—James M. Manheim

Lloyd Boston

1970(?)—

Art director, author

In the liner notes for *Miles Davis's Greatest Hits,* jazz writer George Frazier recalled a post-concert chat with Davis, the noted trumpeter and clothes horse. "He asked me how I thought he'd done. `You sounded superb. You—' But he stopped me. `No, not that,' he said. `I mean how did my suit look?'" Lloyd Boston takes the fashion of black men just as seriously, if not more so. The former Vice President of Art Direction for Tommy Hilfiger has become the preeminent authority on black men's style, the result of researching and writing *Men of Color: Fashion, History, Fundamentals,* a 256-page visual documentary the *Detroit News* called, "one of the most powerful testimonies of African American male style."

"In business, politics, sport and the arts, our influence is undeniable," Boston writes in the book's preface. "Our impact on style is no exception.... A lineage of strength and pride filters into fabrics we've sewn, standards we've twisted, traditions we've abandoned, and trends we've ignited. African American men have developed a science to dressing that has expanded the parameters for all men."

Boston's entry way into the world of fashion and the history of black male style began when he was a sophomore at Morehouse College and Tommy Hilfiger made a campus appearance. "I don't see myself represented," he told the designer, "therefore I would never buy your clothing." Hilfiger, at once taken aback and impressed with his new friend's youthful candor, offered Boston an internship and a scholarship to finish college, which he did at Rutgers University.

Boston went to work full-time for Hilfiger in 1990 rising to the position of Vice President of Art Direction. While having a hand in designing and maintaining the company's look in everything from product graphics to visual imaging, his influence can be seen in all collections of the $800 million Tommy Hilfiger label. Additionally, Boston devoted a great deal of time helping to steer the company's image through marketing, public relations, and special events while working on a variety of special projects involving the company's identity.

In Boston's spare time he began to work on *Men of Color* in an effort to legitimize the impact black men's style has had on mainstream American culture. "What better tribute to Black men's style strides over the last hundred years than a book that would bear witness for generations to come," Boston told Deborah Gregory of *Essence.* With that, Boston took to combing his grandmother's basement for old photos and visiting historically black colleges and black history museums for additional pictures and other research material.

Boston also wanted to blend his research with present-day photo shoots to accompany interviews and essays by prominent African American experts and celebrities, a tall order with his small, first-time author book advance. To raise money for the project he signed up Tommy

At a Glance...

Born c. 1969. *Education:* Attended Morehouse College; B.A., Rutgers University.

Career: Began working at Tommy Hilfiger U.S.A., Inc., 1990; appeared on the View and..., 1990s; published *Men of Color: Fashion, History, Fundamentals,* 1998; creative consultant to Tommy Hilfiger, editor-at-large for CODE magazine, 1999–.

Addresses: *Agent's office*—Faith Childs Literary Agency, Inc., 915 Broadway, Suite 1009, NY, NY 10010.

Hilfiger U.S.A., Johnny Walker Black, and Kodak as sponsors. This enabled the book to have a crisp, modern feel and features interviews with Ed Bradley, Wynton Marsalis, Samuel L. Jackson, Cornel West, Billy Dee Williams, Gregory Hines and others. The book also offers style advice.

And while at first glance, *Men of Color* may appear to be strictly about fashion, it actually says less about the clothes than the men who wear them, a point laid out by one of Boston's contributors, musician Quincy Jones, who penned the foreward.

"Despite the centuries of suppression we suffered during slavery," Jones writes, "when we weren't allowed to practice our religions, speak our languages or create our art, we somehow managed to maintain our sense of self-expression.... Whenever possible, we put our own spin on style."

"Fine vines alone have never been enough to achieve sartorial Black cool," Boston told the *New Pittsburgh Courier.* "It's always been about walking the walk, talking the talk. It's the way we break our hats, situate our jackets, lace or not lace shoes and strut on down the street.... Whether the look is tough, affluent, Afrocentric or preppie, Black men have mastered the marriage between style and attitude."

In his review for *Booklist* Vernon Ford said *Men of Color,* "reveals the substantial influence of black men on the fashion industry, if for no other reason than the rebel role that has so often been assigned to black men who couldn't find acceptance in the culture, e.g., the contributions the hip-hop style on fashion as well as music." Boston explained to Roy Campbell of the *New Orleans Times-Picayune* that finally there was "a historical document that dispels that myth that all we have influenced is street style or that black style is one style. It is more diverse. We've touched style in a unique way every day for the last two centuries."

In his introduction to the book, *Vogue* editor Andre Leon Talley suggests *Men of Color* evokes an essay on spirituals and neo-spirituals by Harlem Renaissance writer Zora Neale Hurston. Hurston asserted true spirituals are not just songs, but "unceasing variations around a theme." Boston, Talley writes, "has achieved the literary equivalent of such soulful spirituals, simultaneously celebrating the subtle nuances and setting forth a sweeping overview of a single, central theme—the undeniable stylishness of the Black man."

"For Black American men in particular," wrote Boston, "who have emerged from a history of slavery and segregation, and who continue to be stereotyped and stigmatized, clothing has always served a symbolic purpose. What we wear signals where we are and, more important, where we want to be." For his part, Boston has found his calling and is where he wants to be. Though he stepped down as Vice President at Tommy Hilfiger, he still works as a creative consultant to the designer and was named editor-at-large for *CODE* magazine in 1999. His vision for his future is unmistakably clear. "I will continue to be a purveyor of Black style," he declared to Deborah Gregory of *Essence,* "and redefine what is considered `American.'"

Sources

Books

Boston, Lloyd, *Men of Color: Fashion, History, Fundamentals,* Artisan, 1998.

Periodicals

Booklist, January 15, 1999, p. 802.
Detroit News, November 27, 1998, p. B-3.
Essence, November 1, 1998, p. 84.
New Orleans Times-Picayune, January 10, 1999, p. 4-B.
New Pittsburgh Courier, February 2, 1999, p. A-10.

—Brian Escamilla

Corrine Brown

1946—

Congresswoman

Corrine Brown, elected to the United States House of Representatives from Florida's Third District in 1992, was the first African American sent to Congress from Florida since the Reconstruction years of the nineteenth century. An outspoken and combative figure, she stood at the center of two of the most important issues affecting African American politicians during the 1990s. The use of redistricting to increase African American representation in Congress was a hotly debated issue for most of the decade. And at the end of the 1990s, Brown was subjected to an ethics investigation over her treatment of a West African millionaire who had given expensive gifts to her daughter. She became one of a number of African American elected officials whose dealings received closer-than-usual scrutiny.

A divorced mother of one, Brown was born in Jacksonville, Florida, on November 11, 1946. Graduating with a bachelor of science degree from Florida A&M University in Tallahassee in 1969, she went on to earn her master's degree in 1971, and an education specialist degree from the University of Florida three years later. Returning to her hometown, Brown taught at Florida Community College from 1977 to 1982 and then worked as a guidance counselor, a post she held until she ran for Congress in 1992. She is also the owner of the Springfield Travel Agency.

Elected to Florida House

Brown was elected to the Florida House of Representatives in 1982. She served five terms, gaining wide recognition in the Jacksonville area, and serving as a delegate to the 1988 Democratic National Convention. After the 1990 census, the Florida legislature carved out a new Third Congressional District in the northern part of the state. This district was designed to enclose an African American majority within its boundaries. Snaking through the old plantation country around the St. Johns River and Cross Creek and touching on predominantly African American neighborhoods in Jacksonville, Gainesville, Orlando, and Ocala, the Third District seemed likely to send Florida's first African American to Congress in over a hundred years, and Brown jumped at the chance to compete for this prize.

Brown faced several candidates in the 1992 Democratic

At a Glance...

Born November 11, 1946, in Jacksonville, FL; single. *Education:* Florida Agricultural and Mechanical University, Tallahassee, Florida, B.S., 1969; University of Florida, Ed.S. education degree, 1974. *Religion:* Baptist.

Career: United States Representative, Third District of Florida, member of the Democratic Party. Taught at University of Florida, 1970s; faculty member, Florida Community College, Jacksonville, 1977-82; guidance counselor, Florida Community College, 1982-92; elected to Florida House of Representatives, 1982; delegate, Democratic National Convention, 1988; elected to U.S. House of Representatives, 1992; re-elected in 1994, 1996, and 1998.

Addresses: *Office*—2444 Rayburn House Office Building, Washington, DC 20515.

primary, but the strongest opponent to emerge was a flamboyant white talk radio host from Jacksonville named Andy Johnson. Johnson, according to the *Almanac of American Politics,* called himself "the blackest candidate in the race." Brown defeated Johnson in the primary and in a two-candidate runoff, and went on to win the general election in November of 1992 by a 59 to 41 percent margin.

Combative from the start, Brown had admirers and detractors. Upon her arrival in Congress, she challenged the discriminatory treatment that minority motorists received in one of the rural counties that flanked Interstate 95, the main north-south route connecting the cities along Florida's coastline. She also worked diligently to bring economic development dollars to northern Florida. Although Brown voted mainly with the House's liberal Democratic bloc, she sat on the House Veterans Affairs Committee and was generally sympathetic to military concerns. Although the Republicans won control of the House following the 1994 congressional elections, Brown was easily re-elected.

Re-Elected Despite District Change

During the next election cycle, Brown was faced with new challenges. In 1995, the boundaries of the Third District were struck down due to their irregular shape, and the percentage of African American residents of the district declined to about 47 percent. One of the main instigators of the lawsuit that led to the redistricting was Brown's old political rival, Andy Johnson. Brown railed against the change, complaining that "[t]he Bubba I beat [Johnson] couldn't win at the ballot box [so] he took it to court," as she was quoted as saying in the *New Republic*.

Nevertheless, Brown faced a white majority smaller than those which confronted Georgia Democrats Cynthia McKinney and Sanford Bishop in the wake of the same court decision, and her district remained strongly Democratic. On Election Day in 1996, she won a convincing victory of 61 to 39 percent. Brown continued to work hard for her district, spearheading the construction of an $86 million federal courthouse in Jacksonville and using her seat on the House's Transportation Committee to set in motion various rail projects intended to alleviate central Florida's growing highway congestion. However, the most difficult challenge of Brown's Congressional tenure was yet to come.

In June of 1998, allegations surfaced that Brown's daughter Shantrel, a lawyer who worked for the Environmental Protection Agency in Washington, had received a $50,000 Lexus LS 400 automobile as a gift from an agent of a Gambian millionaire named Foutanga Sissoko. Sissoko, a friend of Congresswoman Brown, had been imprisoned in Miami after pleading guilty to charges of bribing a customs officer. Brown had worked to secure his release, pressuring U.S. Attorney General Janet Reno to deport Sissoko back to his homeland as an alternative to continued incarceration. Shantrel Brown later admitted at least the appearance of impropriety by selling the car and donating the proceeds to the African Methodist Episcopal Church's scholarship fund.

Filed Conspiracy Complaint

Brown, however, angrily denied wrongdoing. She filed a complaint of conspiracy to impede a member of Congress against two reporters from the *St. Petersburg Times* who tried to ask her about the case (the charges were later dismissed), and faxed a statement to *Editor & Publisher* magazine, which covered the controversy involving the reporters. In the statement, Brown remarked that "[i]t is unfortunate that the civil rights movement in this country must always prove itself—even defend itself when no defense should be necessary." Questions were also raised about the lack of documentation for a $10,000 donation made to Brown by the Rev. Henry Lyons, a controversial Baptist church leader who faced indictment on theft charges. Brown again denied any wrongdoing.

In the 1998 congressional election, Republicans tried to capitalize on Brown's political troubles by recruiting an African American candidate of their own. Their candidate, Bill Randall, was controversial in his own right. Much of the controversy centered around Randall's past nonpayment of taxes, and allegations that he had fathered a child out of wedlock. Although Republican heavyweights Newt Gingrich, Alan Keyes, and Christie Whitman campaigned for Randall, Brown won reelection by a margin of 55 to 45 percent.

Observers speculated that Brown had successfully weathered the political storms that had swirled around her. However, in June of 1999, the House Ethics Committee finally addressed the charges against Brown relating to Sissoko's gift to her daughter. "I am confident," Brown told the *Knight-Ridder/Tribune Business News*, "that these charges...will also be finally put to rest."

Sources

Books

Barone, Michael, and Grant Ujifusa. *The Almanac of American Politics: 2000.* National Journal, 1999.
1997–1998 Congressional Directory: 105th Congress. United States Government Printing Office, 1997.

Periodicals

Congressional Quarterly Weekly Report, January 16, 1993.
Editor & Publisher, August 1, 1998, p. 10.
Knight-Ridder/Tribune Business News, June 14, 1999.
New Republic, November 4, 1996, p. 18.

Other

Additional information for this profile was obtained from www.house.gov/corrinebrown/bio.htm.

—James M. Manheim

Lee Patrick Brown

1937—

Mayor of Houston

Lee Patrick Brown was one of the leading law-enforcement executives in the United States before Houston voters elected him as the first African American mayor in that city's history. During a long and distinguished career as head of police departments in Atlanta, New York, and Houston, Brown helped to reshape the strategies by which urban communities battled crime. He even served as America's "Drug Czar" in the Clinton administration before becoming mayor of the fourth-largest city in the nation.

Brown was born in 1937, in Wewoka, Oklahoma, a small community his parents, Andrew and Zelma, had departed by the early 1940s for the fertile San Joaquin Valley in California. There they found work in the fields as migrant workers, an enterprise in which Brown himself often participated, helping to pick grapes, cotton, or watermelon. At times the family lived in a barn, but the hardship of his early life fortified in Brown a desire to improve his lot. Enrolling at Fresno State University, he studied criminology, and before even finishing his degree had found a job with the San Jose Police Department. He spent eight years on the force, beginning as a patrol officer in 1960, and went on to work in its narcotics and vice squads as an undercover cop. In 1959 he married Yvonne Carolyn Streets, with whom he would have four children.

Snubbed Over Technicality

Brown had earned his undergraduate degree in 1961, and began taking classes toward a master's degree in sociology at San Jose State University, which he achieved in 1964. In 1968, after earning his second master's degree—this one in criminology, from the University of California at Berkeley—he applied for and was granted a leave of absence when Oregon's Portland State University hired him to create a new faculty department, the Department of Administration of Justice, in 1968. Brown returned to San Jose in 1969, and planned to run for a seat on its city council. His residency was called into question, however—during his stint in Portland, Brown had let his voter's registration expire, and because of this the San Jose city clerk disbarred him from seeking candidacy.

In 1970, Brown was awarded a Ph.D. in criminology from Berkeley, making him one of the most academical-

At a Glance...

Born October 4, 1937, in Wewoka, OK; son of Andrew and Zelma (Edwards) Brown; married Yvonne Carolyn Streets, July 14, 1959 (died, December, 1992); married Frances M. Young (a teacher), December 29, 1996; children: (first marriage) Robyn, Torri, Jenna, Patrick; (second marriage) one stepdaughter. *Education:* Fresno State University, B.S., 1961; San Jose State University, M.A. (sociology), 1964; University of California—Berkeley, M.S. (criminology), 1968, Ph.D., 1970. *Politics:* Democrat. *Religion:* Methodist.

Career: San Jose Police Department, San Jose, CA, began as patrol officer, 1960, left force, 1968; established the Department of Administration of Justice at Portland State University, Portland, OR, 1968; Howard University, Washington, D.C., professor of criminal justice, 1972-75; Multnomah County sheriff, Portland, 1975-76, director of Justice Services, 1975-78; public safety commissioner, Atlanta, GA, 1978-82; Houston Police Department, chief of police, 1982-90; New York City police commissioner, 1990-92; Texas Southern University, Houston, faculty member, 1992-93; appointed by President Bill Clinton as director of the Office of Drug Control Policy, 1993; Rice University, Houston, professor of sociology, 1996; elected mayor of Houston, 1997, re-elected to second two-year term, 1999-.

Selected memberships: National Organization of Black Law Enforcement Executives; Police Executive Research Forum; Narcotic Enforcement Officers Association; National Forum for Black Public Administrators; National Police Athletic League.

Addresses: *Office*—City Hall, 901 Bagby St., Floor 3, Houston, TX 77002.

ly astute young African Americans in law enforcement. This was also a time when the majority of urban police departments were still overwhelmingly unintegrated. The very idea that the racial makeup of a police department should reflect the community in which it serves was considered quite radical at the time.

A New Era Begins

In 1972, Brown began teaching at Washington's D.C.'s Howard University, and spent three years there. He returned to the West Coast when he was hired as sheriff of the Portland area's Multnomah County in 1975, a post in which he served one year. He continued to act as director of the county's Justice Services until 1978, when he was named public safety commissioner of Atlanta, Georgia. His four years there as head of the city's police department was a period that coincided with one of the most frightening series of unsolved murders in recent American history, the Atlanta Child Murders.

As a result of this high-profile post, Houston Mayor Kathy Whitmire hired Brown as her city's first African American chief of police in 1982. He was asked to take over a force that many African American and Hispanic community leaders had long accused of unnecessary brutality. Racism was also rampant within its ranks. During his seven years in Houston, Brown made vast improvements in the reputation, performance, morale, and crime-fighting effectiveness of the police force. A minority recruitment drive was implemented, and classes in cultural sensitivity became mandatory. Although Brown publicly supported his police force, he also ordered that "repeat offenders" in brutality complaints be dealt with harshly.

Community Policing Controversy

Brown's programs created a new era for the Houston police force. "There was an embrace by poor and moderate-income communities—that the police force was there for them," County Commissioner El Franco Lee told the *Houston Chronicle* about Brown's leadership. "It was unprecedented.' One of Brown's most ambitious attempts to initiate change, a strategy called "community policing," was met with tremendous opposition. Although Brown championed community policing as a revolutionary new way for the police and the community to join forces, it was essentially a return to an earlier era when most people knew the names of the officers who "walked the beat" in their neighborhood. The Houston plan, known as Neighborhood Oriented Policing (NOP), called for employing more police officers and assigning officers to particular neighborhoods. The officers were encouraged to acquaint themselves with people in their neighborhoods through various outreach methods.

Houston was one of the first cities to implement what would eventually become a standard urban crime-fighting strategy. Many of Brown's officers, however, opposed community policing from the start. Some claimed that NOP detracted from the focus of their job, which was to apprehend criminals, and derisively called the program "Nobody on Patrol." The plan failed to achieve a significant reduction in Houston's crime statistics, but gained currency with law-enforcement executives on a national level. By this point in his career, Brown had become increasingly active in a number of professional organizations and coalitions of other top law-enforcement executives, including the National Minority Advisory Council on Criminal Justice, the National Black Police Officers Association, and the National Association of Blacks in Criminal Justice.

As one of the leading advocates of community policing, Brown's reputation and academic credentials lent a certain credibility to the idea, and replications of Houston's NOP were soon being implemented in a number of major cities by the early 1990s. Yet his critics in Houston sometimes referred to the chief as "Out of Town Brown," since he received so many speaking and conference invitations. Moreover, his natural shyness, reserve, and tendency to deliberate on hot-button issues before speaking were sometimes misconstrued as aloofness.

Moved to Manhattan

Brown resigned from the Houston job in 1989 when New York City Mayor David Dinkins appointed him to head that city's police force. It was a department seven times as large as Houston's, with 26,000 officers, and a long history of internal troubles. While in New York, Brown was able to successfully implement a community policing program known as "Safe Streets, Safe City" program. With the support of Dinkins, Brown added a significant number of new officers to the force, recruited more women and Hispanic officers, increased street patrols, and even forced all headquarters personnel to take one day of patrol duty each week. The borough precincts also instituted "management teams" made up of officers and community leaders. Within just a few months, Brown's radical changes had resulted in the first drop in New York City crime in 36 years.

Brown's two-year tenure in New York was marked by other problems, however. After years of notorious racial incidents across the city, primarily in the rough borough sections where neighborhoods were both impoverished and uneasily integrated, tensions erupted in the Crown Heights area of Brooklyn in 1991. Members of the African American and Orthodox Jewish communities clashed violently for several days, and New York Police Department brass were criticized for their handling of the situation; much of the blame fell to Brown and Dinkins.

Became Drug Czar

Brown resigned from the New York job when his wife fell ill with lung cancer in 1992. The couple returned to Texas, where she passed away later that year. After teaching for a time at Texas Southern University in Houston, Brown was appointed by President Bill Clinton as the nation's "Drug Czar," otherwise known as the Director of the Office of Drug Control Policy. Brown took over this post, which became a cabinet-level appointment during the Clinton administration, in 1993. He worked to increase federal funds for drug-treatment and drug-prevention programs, which had been Clinton's aim as well, but found opposition in Congress to such goals. Many conservative legislators chastised the programs as handouts of tax money to drug addicts. Brown was able to pressure the Justice Department to pursue investigations into an infamous Colombian drug trafficking group, known as the Cali cartel, which resulted in several indictments. He resigned from the post in 1996, partly out of frustration with staunch Congressional opposition to his policies. "At a time when we see a rise in the use of illegal drugs by our adolescents, the proposed budget cuts in drug-fighting are wrong-headed and must be reversed," Brown stated at a news conference announcing his resignation.

Rumors began to circulate that Brown would make a bid for the Houston mayor's office. In the meantime, he took a job as a professor of sociology at Rice University. By 1997, Brown had won endorsements for his mayoral campaign from Houston's outgoing mayor as well as those of President Clinton and the Rev. Jesse Jackson. His Republican opponent was Robert Mosbacher Jr., a prominent business leader in the city as well as the son of a onetime commerce secretary in the Bush administration. After both Brown and Mosbacher failed to win a majority of votes in the November balloting, they competed in a run-off election the following month. Brown won by 16,000 votes, becoming Houston's first African American mayor.

Won Re-Election

Brown was sworn in on January 2, 1998 for a two-year term. He won re-election and was sworn in for a second term as Houston's mayor in early 2000. In his first term, Brown had instituted a number of progressive programs and new initiatives to maintain the city's record prosperity. One of his programs was based on the community policing strategy. "Super Neighborhoods" were created, which divided Houston into 88 separate districts.

Each district contained a local council that worked with representatives from City Hall to address issues specific to the area. Brown also gained the confidence of Houston citizens with his frequent Town Hall meetings across the city, and his regular "Mayor's Night In," in which people were invited to City Hall to meet with the mayor and present particular grievances. He discovered funding for after-school programs, set in motion a plan to renovate the city's three airports, and won voter and state legislative approval for a new baseball stadium for the Houston Astros. "Out of Town Brown" also made it his mission to make the city a winning contender in the race to host the 2012 Olympic Games.

Brown married Frances Young, a teacher, in 1996. He has four adult children from his first marriage, and nine grandchildren. Among Brown's numerous professional awards, he has been named both Politician of the Year by *Library Journal* in 1999, as well as Father of the Year by the National Father's Day Commission eight years earlier.

Sources

Periodicals

Corpus Christi Caller-Times, December 5, 1997.
Houston Chronicle, August 17, 1998.
New York Times, November 6, 1997.

Other

Additional information for this profile was provided by the official government web site of Houston, Texas, at http://www.ci.houston.tx.us

—Carol Brennan

Victoria (Vikki) Buckley

1947–1999

Secretary of State of Colorado

In 1994, when Victoria Buckley was elected as the Secretary of State of Colorado, she became the first African American woman to be elected to a statewide office in Colorado, as well as the nation's highest-ranking African American woman in the Republican party. Her achievement was all the more impressive because Buckley was a former welfare mother with no political experience. "Buckley was a civil servant and political nobody when she stunned the state's political establishment by winning the secretary of state election in 1994," Elaine Woo wrote in the *Los Angeles Times*. "That victory came after she had weathered many personal trials: unwed motherhood when she was 20 and three failed marriages, including one to a man who beat her even while she was pregnant."

Although Buckley's first term as secretary of state was controversial, she managed to win a second term in 1998. Just seven months into her second term, however, Buckley died of a heart attack at the age of 51. In the days following her death, politicians from both parties praised Buckley for achieving success against the odds. "Her rise from a single parent on welfare to secretary of state was remarkable and something in which her family and friends can take great pride," Treasurer Mike Coffman was quoted as saying in the *Denver Post*. Colorado Governor Bill Owens told CNN.com, "She overcame many challenges in life and achieved high office through determination and hard work."

Victoria Buckley, the daughter of Charles and Rubye Buckley, was born on Nov. 2, 1947, in Denver, Colorado. Her interest in politics first surfaced when she was just a child attending Cheltenham Elementary School. She ran for, and won, a seat on the school's student council by using the slogan, "Don't be icky. Vote for Vikki."

After graduating from East High School, Buckley planned to go into the Peace Corps, and then attend college. These dreams were cut short, however, when she found out she was pregnant. "My boyfriend said, 'It couldn't be mine,' and that was the end of him,'" Buckley wrote later in the article "Against All Odds," for the *Ladies Home Journal*. After giving birth to a son, Ian, Buckley lived on welfare for 18 months while attending trade school. In 1968, she graduated from the Sieble School of Drafting and Engineering with an associate's degree. Buckley would later attend the University of Colorado, Denver and Metropolitan State College.

Buckley initially worked as a draftsperson for Humble Oil before deciding to pursue a career in public service. In 1974, she was hired as a state government clerk in the secretary of state's election division. By this time, her first son was in school, but her second child, JeVon, was still a toddler—so Buckley brought him into the office with her. "I'd put him in a playpen while I did my work," she was quoted as saying in the *Denver Post*. Buckley later had one more son, Kahlin.

At a Glance...

Born Victoria Buckley, Denver, CO, Nov. 2, 1947; died of a heart attack, July 14, 1999. daughter of Charles and Rubye Buckley; married three times, last marriage to T. R. Newsome, a private investigator, Dec. 30, 1994; children: Ian Charles, JeVon Franklyn, and Kahlin DeLaney. *Education:* Sieble School of Drafting and Engineering, associate's degree, 1968; attended the University of Colorado-Denver and Metropolitan State College (Denver). *Politics:* Republican.

Career: Humble Oil, draftsperson, 1969-70; Opportunities Industrialization, director, 1971-73; Public Service Careers, office manager, 1973-74; Colorado Secretary of State Office, administrative officer, 1974-94, secretary of state, 1994-99.

Member: Stand Up for Kids, director, 1993-99; Feed the Homeless, volunteer director, 1994; Kids Voting, honorary chair; National Association of Secretaries of State.

Buckley advanced steadily through the ranks at the secretary of state's office until, by 1993, she was deputy secretary of state. That year, Secretary of State Natalie Meyer announced that she would not run for re-election. Buckley decided to run for the office, despite the fact that she had no political experience.

According to Mark Obmascik and Mark Eddy of the *Denver Post,* "Her statewide race for secretary of state in 1994 combined work and luck." During her campaign, Buckley was able to capitalize on her background. In speech after speech, she used her life story as an example of the Republican dream of success through hard work and self-sufficiency. As a result, she won the Republican party nomination over four opponents, including a former state legislator and other political insiders.

At first, Buckley trailed in the polls behind the Democratic candidate, Sherrie Wolff. Just days before the election, however, Wolff's campaign ran into trouble when she had an ugly dispute with her former boss, Senator Ben Nighthorse Campbell. Wolff threatened to sue Campbell if he dropped her from the payroll after the election. Both of the city's major newspapers, the *Denver Post* and the *Rocky Mountain News,* abruptly withdrew their endorsements of Wolff, backing Buckley instead.

On election day, Buckley won by a substantial margin of 57 to 36 percent. "It was one of the few times in my life that I cried like a baby," she was quoted as saying in the *Denver Post.* By winning the election, Buckley had become the first African American woman elected to a statewide office in Colorado, and the nation's highest-ranking African American woman in the Republican party.

In Colorado, the secretary of state's office supervises corporate filings, state election reports, and bingo regulation. During her campaign, Buckley had stressed that she would improve the level of customer service offered by the office. She initially won praise for returning $9 million to the state treasury from office fees.

Within a few years, however, critics began to complain that the secretary of state's office was poorly run. Her decisions to disqualify two candidates for office were overruled by judges. Two initiatives made it on the ballot by default, because all of the signatures could not be verified within the specified time limit. Other errors included misspelled candidate names and incorrect placements on the ballot.

Despite the criticism, Buckley chose to run for re-election in 1998. She trailed her opponent, Ric Bainter, for most of the campaign. In addition, the *Denver Post* did not endorse her. "The secretary of state's office has been beleaguered ever since Republican incumbent Victoria Buckley was elected in 1994," the *Post's* editorial board wrote. "...While a likeable woman, Buckley lacks efficiency and management skill. We have reluctantly concluded that the office situation has deteriorated to the point where it cannot be repaired under her stewardship."

On election day, however, Buckley narrowly managed to defeat Bainter by a margin of 49 percent to 45 percent. Part of her last-minute strategy was to cast her vote while wearing a Denver Broncos jersey, which struck a populist chord among Colorado's many football fans. It was a controversial tactic. Some county elections officials had warned against candidates wearing sports apparel, because one of the issues on the ballot asked voters whether or not they would provide funds to build a new football stadium for the Broncos.

In January of 1999, on the day Buckley was sworn into office for her second term, she was hospitalized for arrhythmia. Arrhythmia is a condition in which the heart beats too fast or too slow. She was treated and released from the hospital after six days.

Buckley's second term in office was as controversial as her first. After she awarded a lucrative consulting contract to her campaign adviser, who was also a close friend, her office became the subject of a state investigation. Her reaction to the shootings at Columbine High School in Littleton, Colorado also sparked criticism. Although she delivered a eulogy at the funeral of Isiah Shoels, an African American athlete who was one of the victims, she also spoke at the National Rifle Association's annual meeting, which was held in Denver two weeks after the shootings. Buckley was the only state constitutional officer to address the group, which had cut short the meeting amid anti-gun protests.

Partly because of her impassioned speech to the NRA, Buckley began to build a reputation in the national Republican party. She even began to consider the possibility of making a run for the presidency. According to Elaine Woo, writing in the *Los Angeles Times,* "she [Buckley] was considered a bright light on the national Republican scene and was expected to play a role in the upcoming Republican National Convention."

While Buckley was a staunch Republican, she was not afraid to go against the party when her principles demanded it. In 1999, she refused to appear in a pamphlet aimed at African American voters because she felt that it treated her as a token. "Vikki believed African-Americans should have a seat at all tables, Democrat and Republican," Joe Rogers, Colorado's lieutenant governor and one of the nation's highest-ranking African American politicians, was quoted as saying in the *Denver Post*—but as full, not token members.

On July 13, 1999, Buckley's estranged husband, Todd Newsome, found her collapsed on the floor of her southeast Denver home. By the time she was discovered, she had suffered irreparable brain damage. She died the following day. Buckley was given a state funeral, which included a procession to the state capitol led by the governor, lieutenant governor, and a bipartisan group of legislators and officials. The Southern Christian Leadership Conference sent a letter of condolence signed by Martin Luther King III, while the first vice president of the NRA, Kayne B. Robinson, spoke at the funeral ceremony.

In the days following her death, many Colorado politicians spoke publicly about Buckley's abilities and influence. "I have lost a good friend and Colorado has lost a leader," Lieutenant Governor Joe Rogers told the *Denver Post*. "She was a role model, mentor, and friend to my entire family....She was simply an elegant woman." "Few of us have risen from so little to so much," Governor Bill Owens was quoted as saying in the *Denver Post*. "Vikki Buckley showed us that we are that much closer to living the American creed that we are all created equal."

Sources

Periodicals

Denver Post, Sept. 27, 1998; Nov. 4, 1998; Apr. 30, 1999; June 9, 1999; July 14, 1999, p. 1A; July 15, 1999, P. 1A, 14A, 15A; July 21, 1999, p. 1A, 1B; July 22, 1999, p. 1B.
Jet, Aug. 2, 1999, p. 17.
Los Angeles Times, July 17, 1999, p. A18.
New York Times, July 16, 1999.

Other

Additional information for this profile was obtained from www.cnn.com, July 15, 1999.

—Carrie Golus

Bebe Moore Campbell

1950—

Journalist, author

Bebe Moore Campbell is establishing a reputation as an important African American writer of both fiction and nonfiction. In her books and numerous pieces for periodicals, Campbell probes the complexities of relationships between spouses, parents and children, and members of communities caught in the grip of racism. Both her memoir, *Sweet Summer: Growing Up With and Without My Dad,* and her novels, *Your Blues Ain't Like Mine* and *Brothers and Sisters,* drew praise from literary critics. *Washington Post* correspondent John Katzenbach, for instance, commended Campbell for her "thoughtful, intelligent work," adding that the author "has a strong creative voice and will probably only improve."

Campbell was born in 1950 and grew up influenced by the civil rights battles of the 1950s and 1960s. She turned to journalism in 1976 as a means to express her own frustrations and describe her own discoveries, and within a few years was a regular contributor to *Ebony, Essence,* and several major urban newspapers. It is through her book-length writings, however, that she has found the best means to explore themes and concerns that resonate throughout her life. "Campbell has a storyteller's ear for dialogue and the visual sense of painting a picture and a place that make [fiction] sing," noted Veronica Chambers in the *Los Angeles Times Book Review.* "She has the grown-up maturity to point out right from wrong, yet at the same time she never forgets how a child might see things--whether the child be the black boy who knows he's going to die or the white boy who kills because it is what his father wants him to do."

A Childhood of "Sweet Summers"

Campbell's parents divorced when she was an infant. Only months later, when she was still less than a year old, her father, George Moore, was permanently disabled in a severe automobile accident. Campbell spent most of the year with her mother and grandmother in Philadelphia, where her mother earned a living as a social worker. Summers, however, were the province of her dad, who would drive from his home in North Carolina to retrieve his daughter for an extended vacation with his family. As Alexis Moore remarked in the *Philadelphia Inquirer,* Campbell's summers "brought into her life the masculine element deeply craved, if only dimly under-

At a Glance...

Born in 1950 in Philadelphia, PA; daughter of George and Doris Moore; married twice, second husband's name Ellis Gordon, Jr. (a banker); children: one daughter, one stepson. *Education:* University of Pittsburgh, B.A., c. 1968.

Career: Public school teacher, 1970-76; author: *Sweet Summer: Growing Up With and Without My Dad,* 1990; *Your Blues Ain't Like Mine,* 1992; *Brothers and Sisters,* 1994; *Singing in the Comeback Choir,* 1998; commentator for National Public Radio.

Addresses: c/o The Putnam Publishing Group, 200 Madison Ave., New York, NY 10016.

---

stood, by a 7-year-old who could have 'died from overexposure to femininity,' a girl who lived in 'a world of no morning stubble, no long johns or Fruit of the Loom on clotheslines ... no beer in the refrigerator, no ball game on TV, no loud cussing.'"

Campbell was tempted to write about her youth in response to the debate about the importance of two-parent involvement with children. "Studies show that girls without that nurturing from a father or surrogate father are likely to grow up with damaged self-esteem and are more likely to have problems with their own adult relationships with men," the author told the *Philadelphia Inquirer.* "I think it's very important at this time for black people to see that there are fathers, despite divorce, that stuck around and were responsible. We know in the black community, or come to expect, that mothers stick around and are responsible. And it's not that I don't give my mother credit for doing that. I do. But it's very important at this point that we can look at some black male images that we can be proud of and to inspire some men who aren't doing what they are supposed to be doing."

Campbell's memoir *Sweet Summer* describes the nurturing she received not only from her father, but also from other important male role models--a school teacher, a minister, and a neighbor. She also reminisces about the mother and grandmother who raised her during the school year, a pair of women she calls "the Bosoms" for their protective yet powerful presence in her life. A *Philadelphia Inquirer* reviewer concluded: "While *Sweet Summer* is infused with experience unique to African American culture, it speaks to the universals of human experience: the confusion and excitement of awakening sensuality, the inevitable disillusionment that children face when it comes to parents, the ways men view women and women view men. The author omits nothing, from the most complex and vital relationships of her life to her political awakening during the shining possibilities and harsh realities of the civil rights movement. Campbell weaves fictional techniques and the rhythms of black speech into a fresh, funny and knowing saga that will intrigue those unfamiliar with our idioms and amuse those who grew up with them."

Campbell graduated from the Philadelphia High School for Girls and attended the University of Pittsburgh, where she majored in early childhood education. She became a teacher in 1970 and worked for several years in that profession. Then--in a watershed moment--she took a writing course with well-known African American author Toni Cade Bambara in 1976. The course excited Campbell more than teaching, and she began to submit articles to magazines and newspapers.

Social Journalist, Successful Novelist

Campbell's idea of writing a memoir came to her as early as 1977, when her father died in an automobile accident. Before she published that work, however, she finished another. It was *Successful Women, Angry Men: Backlash in the Two-Career Marriage,* a nonfictional account of the conflicting expectations between working women and their partners. Campbell drew from her own experiences as well as those of dozens of other two-career couples in order to penetrate the subject. The author told the *Philadelphia Inquirer* that she made many striking discoveries during her research for the book. "A lot of women are stunned by what they regard as the price of success," she said. "Men understand hard work, the politics of business, the reasons for having a drink with the boss, the reality of moving when the company says to move. Women are stunned to find out how hard it is to be successful--the hours required, the adjustments.... A lot of women are turned off and burned out.... I would ask [women] to consider the significance of the amorphous thing called success. I would ask them to define success, to be clear on how much success they want, how badly they want it, what it would take for them to get it."

Tragic Inspiration

Campbell was only five years old when a young teenager named Emmett Till was discovered in Mississippi's Tallahatchie River, the victim of a brutal murder. People of color all over America followed the Till story and the subsequent trial of three white men, who were all acquitted by a white jury. *Washington Post* contributor Mae Ghalwash observed that as Campbell grew up in Philadelphia, "the youth [Till] drifted in and out of her own conversations." Her mother, aunts, and uncles talked about the case. Campbell told the *Boston Globe* that Till "was a very real ghostlike presence in my life and in the lives of a lot of blacks. He catapulted us into civil rights. He died, he was murdered, in August (1955), and Rosa Parks refused to move on the bus in Birmingham the next month, in September. Emmett Till wasn't only murdered but brutally disfigured. It was worse than a lynching. Lynchings were anonymous. But this was personal. This trial got into the newspapers. The trial was ugly."

That tragic episode inspired Campbell to write her first novel, *Your Blues Ain't Like Mine*. Based only loosely on the Till case, Campbell's novel tells the story of Armstrong Todd, a fifteen-year-old Chicago native who loses his life during a summer visit to rural Mississippi. The tale not only explores Todd's fate after he mutters a few words of French in the presence of a white woman, but it also charts the fortunes of his fictitious murderers in the decades following the incident. Ghalwash wrote: "In a span of about three decades, *Blues* explores a tangle of racial issues. Campbell probes deep into the psychological and sociological pressures of the segregated South that lead to racial prejudice and ultimately to violence." The book traces the possible repercussions of aggressive acts and culminates in the emergence of what Campbell calls the "new enemy of African Americans today--gang wars." The reviewer added: "What happened to the killers of Armstrong Todd is not unlike the fate of the accused murderers of Emmett Till. Although they are acquitted by an all-white jury, their lives crumble into poverty, fear and miserable marriages. Thus Campbell's message: If society withholds justice, life doesn't."

Your Blues Ain't Like Mine was first published in 1992, and within months Campbell was being hailed as an important new voice in African American letters. *Newsday* essayist Francine Prose noted that the book "spans the turbulent decades and upheavals of our country's recent history, from the passionate commitment of the civil rights movement to the divisiveness and confusion surrounding the Vietnam War to the contemporary inner-cityscape.... We finish Campbell's novel eager to see what she will write next, and even more eager to believe in her vision of recovery and repair." *Emerge* magazine reviewer Karen Taylor concluded that Campbell's first novel "ranks with such classic works as Ralph Ellison's *Invisible Man*, Toni Morrison's *The Bluest Eye*, and Alice Walker's *Meridian*."

Campbell published her second novel, *Brothers and Sisters*, in 1994. This novel was set in Los Angeles following the riots that occurred after the Rodney King verdict. The plot of *Brothers and Sisters* revolves around two women, one African American and one white. Despite the fact that they have greatly differing opinions regarding issues such as affirmative action, white privilege, and the criminal justice system, the two women become friends. The novel focuses on the intricacies of the interactions between the two women. *Brothers and Sisters* appeared on the *New York Times* best-seller list and was widely hailed by critics. Christopher John Farley praised the novel in *Time:* "Writing with wit and grace, Campbell shows how all our stories–white, black, female–ultimately intertwine." *Ms.* reviewer Retha Powers commended Campbell for her "astute observations about the subtleties of race and race relations in the U.S." In the *Knight-Ridder/Tribune News Service,* Campbell explained the reason why she wrote *Brothers and Sisters:* "We've got to start getting past stereotypes, and anger, and fear, if we're going to have any semblance of racial harmony in this country. We have to make color our joy, not our burden."

> "We've got to start getting past stereotypes ... if we're going to have any semblance of racial harmony in this country. We have to make color our joy, not our burden."

In 1998, Campbell published a new novel entitled *Singing in the Comeback Choir*. The plot of the novel focuses on a woman who sacrifices a career as a singer to raise her granddaughter, who grows up to become a successful businesswoman. The grandmother eventually gets another chance to resurrect her singing career. *Singing in the Comeback Choir* is an uplifting tale that conveys the message that it is never too late to pursue one's dreams. As Campbell told *Jet,* the novel illustrates that "with support and with love and commitment, a second chance is possible, if you are willing to work at it....Anybody can have a second chance."

Campbell lives in Los Angeles with her husband, Ellis Gordon, Jr., and is the mother of two children. She has also served as a commentator for National Public Radio's "Morning Edition." Her literary work has also appeared in the *New York Times, Washington Post, Los Angeles Times, Ebony, Essence, Ms., Black En-*

terprise, and other periodicals.

Selected writings

Successful Women, Angry Men: Backlash in the Two-Career Marriage, out of print.
Sweet Summer: Growing Up With and Without My Dad (memoir), Ballantine, 1990.
Your Blues Ain't Like Mine (novel), Putnam, 1992.
(Contributor) *Wild Women Don't Wear Blue: Black Women Writers on Love, Men and Sex,* edited by Marita Golden, Doubleday, 1993.
Brothers and Sisters, (novel), Putnam, 1994.
Singing in the Comeback Choir, (novel), Putnam, 1998.

Sources

Boston Globe, October 26, 1992, p. 32.
Chicago Tribune, October 25, 1992, p. 5; February 19, 1993, p. 1.
Emerge, February 1993, p. 69.
Jet, March 30, 1998, p. 39.
Knight-Ridder/Tribune News Service, November 2, 1994, p. 1102.
Los Angeles Times Book Review, September 6, 1992, p. 3.
Ms., September/October 1994, p. 78.
Newsday (Long Island, NY), August 20, 1992, p. 62; September 27, 1992, p. 34.
Philadelphia Inquirer, April 30, 1987; June 11, 1989, p. F-4; August 1, 1989, p. E-1; December 27, 1992, p. F-3.
San Francisco Chronicle, September 20, 1992, p. 7.
Time, October 17, 1994, p. 81.
Washington Post, October 10, 1992, p. D-1, D-10.

—Anne Janette Johnson and David G. Oblender

Anson Carter

1974—

Professional hockey player

Anson Carter was born on June 6, 1974 in Toronto, Ontario and would go on to change the face of his sport by excelling in the National Hockey League (NHL). He grew up in the Scarborough section of Toronto as the middle child of three in the Carter family. His parents Horace and Valma emigrated from Barbados. He started playing hockey seriously at the age of eight—a rather late start for a kid growing up in Canada. By the time he reached high school many of his peers had drifted to other sports, but Carter stuck with hockey. He had decided to become a doctor and thought that hockey would be an excellent way for a Canadian kid to get into one of the top colleges in the United States. Carter followed his plan and received a scholarship to play hockey at Michigan State University (MSU) in 1992. Although he did enroll in the pre-med program, Carter's plans soon changed when he began to excel at his sport.

Carter Makes His Mark

Throughout his career at MSU he continued to improve. From the 1992-93 season to the 1995-96 season Carter made a name for himself in the Central Collegiate Hockey Association (CCHA). Tom Newton, who was then- an assistant at MSU, told Joe LaPointe of the *New York Times* that Carter "was a businessman at the rink" who "worked hard and pushed himself, forced himself to get better." He was twice named a CCHA First Team All-Star and made the second team once. In 1994-95 Carter was named Second Team All-American and was a finalist for college hockey's top prize, the Hobey Baker Trophy. In 1992 the Colorado Avalanche—at that time the Quebec Nordiques—had drafted him in the tenth round of the NHL's amateur draft. Carter knew coming out of college that he would have little chance of making it in a lineup that was packed with veteran stars so he asked Colorado to trade him. Carter told Terry Frei of the *Denver Post* about his situation: "They were one of the deeper organizations in terms of young talent. I'm pretty fortunate he (Colorado General Manager) made that trade. He could have buried me in their minor-league system, and I could have been there for a couple of years. I'm thankful he gave me a chance to move on to Washington, where I got a chance to play in the NHL." On April 3, 1996 Carter was traded to the Washington

At a Glance...

Born Anson Carter, June 6, 1974 in Toronto, Ontario; son of Horace and Valma Carter; *Education:* attended Michigan State University.

Career: Drafted by the Quebec Nordiques, 1992; starred at Michigan State University, 1992-96; traded to the Washington Capitals, 1996; traded to the Boston Bruins, 1997; second-line forward for the Bruins, 1997-.

Awards: Central Collegiate Hockey Association All-Star, 1993-95; second team All-American and finalist for the Hobey Baker Trophy, 1995.

Addresses: *Residences*—Boston, MA and Toronto, Canada; *Mailing*—c/o the Boston Bruins, One Fleet Center, Suite 250, Boston, MA 02114-1303.

Capitals.

On to the NHL

Carter began the 1996-97 season in Portland, Maine playing for the Capitals' American Hockey League (AHL) team, but he was not in the AHL for long. After 27 games Carter had totaled 38 points and was promoted to the Capitals. Once in Washington, Carter found it tough to break into the lineup. He also injured his thumb and missed an additional five games. After playing 19 games with the Capitals, Carter, known as a scorer throughout most of his career in hockey, had only made three goals. But two of those goals came on February 24 against the Boston Bruins, a team that must have been impressed with his efforts. On March 1, 1997 Carter was in a restaurant when he heard on the television that he had been traded as part of a six-player deal to the Bruins. The little-known rookie was thought to be a throw-in on the part of Washington, but Bruins' scout Gerry Cheevers knew differently. He told *Sports Illustrated's* Kostya Kennedy about seeing Carter play in Portland: "He skated stronger than anyone else, and every time he was in a collision, he came out on top. We had a few players we needed to get from Washington to give up the players we gave up. Anson was at the top of our list." Carter played 19 games for the Bruins and finished off his tumultuous rookie season scoring eight goals and tallying five assists for his new club. He went into the 1997-98 season finally comfortable with a team where he would be given a chance to play. Carter played in 78 games in his sophomore season and tallied 43 points. More importantly the young hockey player had found a home. He told LaPointe of the *New York Times* about his adjustment to Boston: "I came in with an open frame of mind, just like I did when I went to school... The people here in Boston, they couldn't have treated me better then I've been treated so far. I've been treated with a lot of respect and class."

A Bright Future

He was starting to attract attention around the league as one of the top young prospects in hockey, and he knew it. The following season he refused to sign a contract with the Bruins. Instead of signing what he thought to be a less-than-adequate deal, Carter started the season with Utah of the International Hockey League. After missing the first 12 games of the 1998-99 season, Carter signed a two-year $1.5 million contract. Despite missing the first part of the season and then 15 games with an ankle injury, Carter quickly gave the team its money's worth. He recorded 40 points including 24 goals in 55 games. He finished second on the team with six game-winning goals and was instrumental in the Bruins drive through the playoffs. Carter scored three goals in six games of the playoffs including a game-winner over the Carolina Hurricanes in double-overtime. Boston's Hall-of-Fame defenseman and captain Ray Bourque spoke to Kennedy of *Sports Illustrated* about Carter's overall game: "The bigger the game, the better he plays. He's got the whole package: speed, strength, moves and vision. He can be scary. And because he lives right and prepares himself, he's going to get better." Carter came off his breakthrough playoff performance with another great start to the 1999-2000 season. In just 38 games, Carter totaled 30 points to become a leader on the Bruins' young team. He leads off the ice and in the community also. Carter is active around Boston and has even created a program called "Carter's Corner." He buys six tickets and the club buys six more for each Bruins home game and distributes them to youth groups around the Boston area.

The man who was traded twice before his rookie season seems to have found a home in Boston, which has in the past had a reputation for being a difficult place to play for black athletes. Carter told Frei of the *Denver Post* that the swap with the Capitals that brought him to Bean Town has worked out just fine: "Whenever you're involved in a trade of that magnitude, you know you're getting a chance to play. You don't want to let the G.M. down after you're traded like that. A lot of fans were upset here... But I'd like to think the fans are happy with the trade now."

Sources

Periodicals

The Denver Post, April 3, 1999.
The New York Times, May 11, 1999.
Sports Illustrated, October 4, 1999.

Online

http://www.bostonbruins.com/bios/carter_a.htm.
http://nhl.com/players/car608774.htm.

—Michael J. Watkins

Donald A. Coleman

1952—

Advertising executive

Donald Coleman Advertising, Inc. (DCA) never shied away from being known as an African American agency. In one DCA print ad, the caption under a photo of a cup of coffee read, "How do you take your advertising? Well, if you want it to be successful, you take it rich and full-bodied. And if you want it to be strong, you take it Black." The company's founder and C.E.O., Donald Coleman, wouldn't have it any other way. Coleman started his career in advertising by working for big, general-market agencies in Detroit and Chicago, but quickly made moves to launch an agency that was tailored specifically for minorities. While in his thirties, Coleman established what would become the third largest African American-owned advertising agency in the United States. DCA is noted for its Kmart, General Mills, Ameritech, and DaimlerChrysler ad campaigns, among many others. Coleman also demonstrated his foresight in multicultural marketing when he headed up a national alliance of marketing firms targeted at African Americans, Hispanics, and Asians.

Coleman may never have gone into advertising if his football career had not been cut short by injuries. A former linebacker for the University of Michigan, New Orleans Saints, and New York Jets, Coleman was permanently sidelined in 1977 due to a series of knee injuries. He'd already earned his B.A. at the University of Michigan and an M.B.A. in marketing from Hofstra University in Hempstead, New York, so Coleman was able to fall back on his education. In 1977, he began his career in advertising at Lintas Campbell-Ewald in Warren, Michigan. Lintas Campbell-Ewald was a major, general-market firm, and had little interest in Coleman's observations of the incredibly underserved African American and Hispanic markets. Coleman, who rose to the position of vice president and management supervisor at Lintas Campbell-Ewald, decided he wanted to learn everything about the industry. In 1985, he moved to Chicago to accept a position as senior vice president for Burrell Advertising, an African American-owned company.

A Diverse New Agency

In 1988, Coleman moved back to Detroit and opened Donald Coleman & Associates (DCA). He was also able to lure away some of the more talented staff from Lintas

At a Glance...

Born Donald Alvin Coleman on January 11, 1952 in Toledo, OH; son of Augustus and Dorothy Bowers Coleman; married Jo Moore on October 5, 1976; children: Kelli. *Education:* University of Michigan, B.A., 1974; Hofstra University, M.B.A., 1976.

Career: Vice president, Lintas Campbell-Ewald Advertising, 1977-85; senior vice president, Burrell Advertising, 1985-87; president and C.E.O., Donald Coleman Advertising, Inc., Southfield, MI, 1988-.

Member: NAACP; American Association of Advertising Agencies, 1988; advisory committee, Reggie McKenzie Foundation, 1988; National Association of Market Developers, 1989; executive board, Adcraft Club of Detroit; board of directors, Alma College; board of directors, Charles H. Wright Museum of African American History; board of directors, Children's Center of Michigan.

Awards: Advertising Agency of the Year, PRAME, 1997; Black Enterprise Advertising Agency of the Year, *Black Enterprise* magazine, 1998.

Addresses: *Office—* Donald Coleman Advertising, Inc., 26555 Evergreen Rd., 18th Floor, Southfield, MI, 48076.

Campbell-Ewald and Burrell. By 1995, DCA had Domino's Pizza, Chrysler, and General Mills on its client roster, and was seen as a first-tier advertising agency. In 1998, DCA was the third largest African American-owned ad agency in the United States, trailing only Burrell in Chicago and UniWorld Group in New York City. "No one else has graduated from a black agency, started their own business and then become a rival to that former employer," Ken Smikle, president of Target Market News, a research firm that tracks African American consumers, told *Black Enterprise* about Coleman, "That's important because it suggests that the next generation of black-owned ad agencies is in good hands." Cassandra Hayes of *Black Enterprise* added: "The agency's ability to meld innovative creative product with clever business strategy serves as a lead for the next generation of black advertising firms." It was that blend of creative and business talent that earned DCA *Black Enterprise's* 1998 Advertising Agency of the Year award. "They (DCA) have the ability to blend sophistication and hipness in their creative approach," Smikle told *Black Enterprise*.

DCA seeks to capitalize on the brand awareness of African Americans without pandering to racial stereotypes. Coleman's agency tries to "present an intelligent African-American image and mindset in everything we do," W. Juan Roberts, a senior vice president and creative director at DCA, said in an interview with *Black Enterprise*, "We stay away from 'the ghetto'." In her article in *Black Enterprise*, Cassandra Hayes defined "the ghetto" as "the hip-hop, finger-popping, singing, dancing, and dunking ads that have been laid before African-American consumers for so long."

Brand-Name Recognition

Chrysler, now known as DaimlerChrysler, first started working with DCA in 1994. DCA was in charge of minority advertising, promotions, and special events for the Neon, Cirrus, Intrepid, and Jeep vehicles. Chrysler's selection of DCA for its minority advertising proved to be a wise choice. The company's share of the African American automotive market increased from 13.8 percent in 1994 to 17.9 percent in 1996. "We had to show African Americans that these cars fit their lifestyles," Coleman told *Black Enterprise* in reference to Chrysler.

In 1997, DCA earned the business of the Kmart Corporation and its numerous Kmart and Super Kmart retail stores. Kmart hired DCA as a specialty agency to focus marketing on African American shoppers. Kmart declared it's commitment to meeting the needs of African American consumers, and Coleman remarked in the *New York Beacon* that he was excited to provide his services to a major retailer.

Worked Tirelessly for Clients

Coleman's business acumen is simple. "It's to learn everything about the client, strategically attack the competition, establish product identity, and grow the client's business," he remarked in an interview with *Black Enterprise*. That philosophy has made DCA the fastest-growing African American advertising firm. In order to become better identified as an advertising agency, Coleman elected to change the firm's name from Donald Coleman & Associates to Donald Coleman Advertising, Inc.

In 1999 DCA joined True North Diversified Companies, under its New America Strategies Group (NASG), the company's multicultural offshoot. True North gained a

49 percent interest in DCA, and named Coleman as the head of NASG. The merger gave DCA the resources of the largest multicultural marketing-firm network in the U.S. and NASG added DCA to its billings, which would increase to about $200 million. NASG also boasted that it was the only partnership with the resources to target the African American, Hispanic, and Asian markets simultaneously. In an interview with *Black Enterprise,* Coleman remarked that he was pleased with the merger: "This network represents a new and compelling model with the potential to create a strong link between the mainstream advertisers and America's growing multicultural communities. The credibility and experience we are providing now will make corporate America more comfortable in addressing multiculturalism. It's going to be a lot easier for companies to get involved in these markets through us because we are all working together."

Although many general-market agencies have started ethnic-market "boutique" agencies to try to compete for African American advertising dollars, Coleman never had an interest in seeking out general-market accounts. Instead, he focused on developing the African American and multicultural markets, which represent his agency's greatest strength. "Why would I jump into that shark tank [developing general-market accounts] when I'm dealing with the fastest-growing ethnic segment that my general-market competition knows nothing about?" Coleman told *Black Enterprise.*

Sources

Periodicals

Black Enterprise, June 1998, p. 164; December 1999.
Business Wire, September 1, 1999.
New York Beacon, May 21, 1997.

Other

Additional information for this profile was provided by Donald Coleman Advertising, 1999.

—Brenna Sanchez

Nathan G. Conyers

1932—

Automobile dealer

Nathan Conyers worked as a successful attorney for a number of years, but couldn't resist the desire to become an entrepreneur. He went on to own Detroit's only African American-owned dealership and the oldest African American-owned dealership in the United States. From his parents, Conyers learned to be self-sufficient, responsible, and committed. John Sr. and Lucille Conyers also stressed the merits of personal and professional success to Conyers and his older brother John Jr., who went on to become a U.S. Congressman. Conyers is known as a standout among African American businessmen, and has received many professional accolades.

Conyers graduated from Wayne State University law school in 1959, after a stint in the army. As an attorney, he worked for the Small Business Administration and Veteran's Administration until he set up his own private practice from 1965 to 1969. He also served as a special assistant to the Attorney General for the State of Michigan. In 1969, he became a senior partner at Keith, Conyers, Anderson, Brown & Wahl, P.C., but decided to become a businessman in 1970.

A Good Time for Business

During the early 1970s, Detroiters were trying to rebuild the city from the devastation of the 1967 riots, and many of Detroit's white residents and business owners were fleeing. Ford Motor Company Chairman Henry Ford also wanted to increase the number of minority-owned dealerships in the company. Conyers's timing was perfect when Hetche Motors, a white-owned Ford dealership, went up for sale just as Ford Motor Company was looking to increase minority involvement. Conyers told *Black Enterprise* in an interview that he imagined a Ford executive in 1969 saying to himself, "I'll put a black dealer there, and they'll sell cars like hotcakes." Conyers was determined to become that dealer.

With $400,000 in capital and financing from Ford, Nathan and John Conyers Jr. bought Hetche Motors in 1970 and renamed it Conyers Ford. The dealership became Ford's fourth African American-owned dealership, and Michigan's first African American-owned dealership. Conyers credited his late father with giving he

At a Glance...

Born Nathan George Conyers July 3, 1932 in Detroit, MI; son of John Sr. and Lucille Conyers; married Diana Callie Howze, 1956; children: Nancy, Ellen, Susan, Steven, Peter. *Education:* Wayne State University, L.L.B., 1959. *Military service:* U.S. Army, 1953-55.

Career: Closing attorney, Small Business Administration, 1963-64; closing attorney, Veteran's Administration, 1964-65; attorney, private practice, 1965-69; special assistant, Attorney General, State of Michigan, 1967-70; partner, Keith, Conyers, Anderson, Brown & Wahls, P.C., 1969; president, Conyers Riverside Ford, 1970-; president, Supreme Ford, 1991-93.

Selected awards: Commitment to Excellence Award, Howard University School of Business and Public Administration; Business Achievement Award, Booker T. Washington Business Association, 1990; Dealership of the Year, *Black Enterprise,* 1995; 25 Year Award, Ford Motor Company, 1996; North American Customer Excellence Award, Ford Motor Company, 1998; *Time Magazine* Quality Dealer Award, 1999.

Selected memberships: NAACP; Y.M.C.A.; American Civil Liberties Union; Greater Detroit Chamber of Commerce; Greater Detroit Area Hospital Council; Blue Cross/Blue Shield of Michigan; Diversitech.

Addresses: *Office*—Conyers Riverside Ford, 1833 E. Jefferson, Detroit, MI 48207.

and his brother the incentive to own their own business. "He challenged us from early childhood that one day, regardless of what we were doing, wherever we might be, we were all going to come together and create a family business," Conyers told *Black Enterprise.* Nathan and John Jr. were both successful attorneys at the time. A coin toss decided that Nathan would run the dealership. "John Jr. pulled out a coin and said, 'I'll tell you what. Let's flip and see who's going to leave what they're doing,'" Conyers related to *Black Enterprise.* Nathan Conyers became sole owner of the dealership in 1979.

Conyers admitted in an interview with *Black Enterprise* that the time had been right for an African American-owned dealership because government bodies were supportive of minority entrepreneurs. By the late 1980s, African Americans were encountering greater resistence. "A number of bankers feel that life is just more comfortable not dealing with blacks," Conyers told writer Faye Rice in an interview with *Fortune*. During the late 1980s, 90 percent of the participants in Ford Motor Company's dealer development program were African Americans. This statistic indicated that African American-owned dealerships were getting started mostly with the manufacturer's help, not with loans from outside lenders. However, Conyers told *Black Enterprise*, adversity can be a positive incentive for minorities. "If you increase the odds," he remarked, "it increases the will to succeed."

Conyers watched with dismay as the neighborhood around his West Grand Boulevard dealership deteriorated. His clientele was almost exclusively African American, and consisted of people who knew his family. This loyal customer base and a strong commitment to the city of Detroit contributed greatly to Conyers's success. In 1984, Conyers moved his dealership to the edge of downtown Detroit, near the Detroit River, and renamed it Conyers Riverside Ford. After an awkward period of adjustment to the new environment, Conyers tailored his sales staff and marketing to downtown office workers and commuters. He promoted the merits of his service department, figuring that if people trusted the dealership to fix their old cars, they'd feel confident buying their new ones there. He also sought out government contracts, which aided the company during tough economic times.

Conyers is known for his commitment to his community and to education. He provides financial support to his old neighborhood grade school, and gave local community college students a crash course in minority entrepreneurship. "Commitment goes beyond a dollar," he told Karen Dumas in a *Michigan Citizen* interview. "Although financial contributions to organizations are imperative to the community of their efforts, it is equally important that one get involved with attacking those same issues on a daily and ongoing basis."

A Family Affair

Conyers Riverside Ford is a family-owned and operated business. All of Conyers's five children are involved in the dealership. His eldest son Steven is general sales manager, daughter Nancy and son Peter are business managers, and daughter Susan is a former manager. His daughter Ellen, an attorney, handles the dealership's contracts and collections and looks forward to owning her own dealership. Conyers is extremely proud of his dealership's success. "Pride is an understatement," Conyers told Jourdan C. Harper of the *Michigan Chronicle*. "This is the real African-American dream—and a realistic one for all to embrace and realize for themselves."

> "If you increase the odds, it increases the will to succeed."

Conyers appreciates the importance of African Americans handing down family businesses to the next generation. "The issue of succession is a whole new issue for black businesses now that we have them in some number," he said in an interview with *Black Enterprise*. He also has a plan in place that qualifies one of his children to be on the dealer agreements "so that if something happens to me, they could step into the business." Conyers told *Black Enterprise* he hopes one day that each of the Conyers children will have a dealership of their own, creating a family-owned string of dealerships.

Conyers's commitment to the African American community extends beyond his own family and automobile dealership. He has served as a mentor for other African Americans, many of whom are women, who left jobs at Conyers Riverside Ford to head their own dealerships. "I would not be a dealer today were it not for Nathan Conyers," Wendell Barron, president of the Michigan Automobile Dealers Association and owner of Campus Ford in Okemos, Michigan, told the *Detroit Free Press*.

Accolades for Conyers

When Conyers Riverside Ford appeared on the first *Black Enterprise* magazine "BE 100" list of the nation's largest African American businesses, it was one of 13 automobile dealerships. Twenty-five years later, Conyers is the only automobile dealer to have been selected for every annual list, and is the only one of the original 13 dealerships that is still in business. Another media mogul tipped her hat to Conyers in 1998. Television talk show host Oprah Winfrey celebrated her birthday by inviting him onto her show to give away an F-150 Ford truck. Conyers has received commendations from former President Jimmy Carter, Detroit Mayor Dennis W. Archer, and the Detroit City Council. Ford Motor Company awarded him its prestigious 25 Year Award on the 25th anniversary of his dealership. He also was given keys to the cities of Atlanta, New York, Chicago and Detroit. In 1990, Conyers accepted the Businessman of the Year award from Detroit's Booker T. Washington Business Association (BTWBA). BTWBA President Nicholas Hood III told writer Michael Goodin of *Crain's Detroit Business* that the award "is a way of expressing our support and encouragement" for Conyers. In 1999, he was selected from more than 20,500 dealers nationwide to be awarded *Time* magazine's Quality Dealer Award. Later that year, Conyers became the owner of a Jaguar Motorcar franchise, becoming only the second African American to own a Jaguar dealership.

Sources

Periodicals

Automotive Executive, September 1998.
Black Enterprise, June 1995, p. 134; June 1997, p. 104.
Crain's Detroit Business, July 30, 1990, p. 4; May 10, 1999, p.3.
Detroit Free Press, February 6, 1998, p. 1F.
Fortune, August 14, 1989, p. 68.
Michigan Chronicle, May 23, 1995.
Michigan Citizen, 1997, p. A1.

Other

Additional information for this profile was provided by Conyers Riverside Ford.

—Brenna Sanchez

Elijah E. Cummings

1951—

Congressman from Maryland

Elijah E. Cummings has been a member of the United States Congress since 1996 when he took over the Baltimore-area House seat vacated by Kweisi Mfume, who resigned from Congress to become president of the National Association for the Advancement of Colored People (NAACP). Representing a heavily African American and mostly urban district that includes many economically distressed neighborhoods, Cummings has taken a special interest in urban problems and the concerns of the poor. "I will continue to speak up for those whose voices are rarely, if ever, heard, and stand up for those who cannot stand up for themselves," Cummings said after his 1996 as quoted by Deborah Kalb in *Congressional Quarterly*.

Cummings was born in 1951 in Baltimore, one of seven children of a working class parents who had moved to Baltimore from rural South Carolina. His father, Robert, was a Davidson Chemical plant employee. Cummings spent his early years living in rented houses in the southern part of Baltimore. When he was 12, his family bought a house in the Edmondson Village section of West Baltimore. At Baltimore City College High School, Cummings was president of the senior class. After graduating from high school in 1969 he enrolled at Howard University in Washington, D.C., one the nation's leading traditionally Black colleges. At Howard, Cummings served as sophomore class president, student government treasurer, and student government president. Leaving Howard in 1973 with a Phi Beta Kappa honor society key and a bachelor's degree in political science, Cummings entered the University of Maryland Law School from which he received a law degree in 1976. He then began a private law practice in Baltimore. Cummings continued to practice law with the firm of Cummings and Dashiell until entering Congress in 1996.

Cummings entered the Maryland House of Delegates in 1983, representing a mostly African American district in the southern part of West Baltimore. As a member of the Maryland state legislature, Cummings quickly proved himself a rising star. After just one term in Annapolis, he was elected chairman of the Maryland Legislative Black Caucus. Cummings spent much of his time seeking improvements in health care and educational opportunities for his urban constituents. He also worked with businesses to bolster economic development in his dis-

> **At a Glance...**
>
> Born on January 18, 1951 in Baltimore, MD, the son of Robert (a chemical plant worker) and Ruth Cummings; married to Joyce Cummings (separated); two children. *Education:* Howard University, B.A., 1973; University of Maryland Law School, J.D. 1976. *Politics:* Democrat. *Religion:* Baptist.
>
> **Career:** Practicing attorney in Baltimore, 1976-96; member of Maryland House of Delegates, 1983-96; Speaker Pro-Tem of Maryland House of Delegates, 1995-96; member of U.S. House of Representatives from Maryland's seventh district, 1996-; columnist for the *Baltimore Afro-American*, 1996-.
>
> **Organizations:** Member of the Maryland Bar Association, 1976-; Morgan State University Board of Regents; Baltimore Area Council of the Boy Scouts of America, board of directors; Baltimore Zoo, board of trustees; Dunbar-Hopkins Health Partnership, executive board.
>
> **Addresses:** *Home*—Madison Park, West Baltimore, MD. *Office*—District: 3000 Druid Park Drive, Baltimore, MD 21215. Washington: 1632 Longworth House Office Building, Washington, DC 20515.

trict, and played a fundamental role in banning liquor advertisements from inner-city billboards. During his years in the Annapolis legislature, Cummings honed his political skills and earned a reputation as a consensus builder. He served as vice chair of the Constitutional and Administrative Law Committee and vice chair of the Economic Matters Committee, and in 1995 became the first African American to be named Speaker Pro-Tem, the second highest position in the House of Delegates.

Kweisi Mfume's announcement of his intention to resign from the U.S. House of Representatives in early 1996 to take over as head of the NAACP resulted in a record-breaking 32 candidates (twenty-seven Democrats, five Republicans) entering the race to fill the vacated seat from Maryland's seventh Congressional district, a crescent-shaped area that runs from downtown Baltimore, through the western part of the city, and into suburban Baltimore County. The seventh district, which is about 70 percent African American, includes many poor West Baltimore communities, though it also encompasses Johns Hopkins University, the Baltimore Museum of Art, several gentrified urban neighborhoods, and the lower middle class suburbs of Randallstown and Catonsville. Mfume had held the seventh district seat since 1987. For 16 years prior to that the seventh district, then entirely within the city of Baltimore, was represented by Parren Mitchell who, in 1971, became Maryland's first African American member of Congress.

Included among the 27 candidates in the special Democratic primary election held in March of 1996 were five members of the Maryland state legislature, five ministers, an engine mechanic, a psychiatrist, and several businessmen. Cummings' notoriety as a state lawmaker made him a strong contender in the crowded field. He gained important endorsements from the Baltimore Building and Construction Trades Council, state senate majority leader Clarence Blount, the *Baltimore Afro-American* and *Baltimore Sun* newspapers, and from community leaders in suburban areas. He was also able to raise more money than any other candidate, an estimated $450,000, and mounted a print and television advertising campaign that emphasized economic issues. Herbert C. Smith, a Western Maryland College political science professor who specializes in Baltimore politics, told Paul Valentine of the *Washington Post* that Cummings did "a good job of putting together coalitions...including both black and white political clubs" during his election bid.

Cummings won 37 percent of the vote in the Democratic primary, running far ahead of second place finisher Frank M. Reid III, a prominent minister and the stepbrother of Baltimore Mayor Kurt Schmoke. Reid garnered 24 percent of the vote. In the April 1996 special election Cummings easily beat Republican Kenneth Kondner, winning 81 percent of the vote to Kondner's 19 percent. The April special election only decided who would fill out Mfume's term, so Cummings faced Kondner again in the November 1996 regular general election. This time, Cummings defeated his GOP rival by an even wider margin and won his own two-year term in Congress. In 1998, Cummings was easily reelected to a second term. Maryland's seventh district is heavily Democratic, and Cummings is likely to follow his predecessors Mfume and Mitchell in receiving no strong reelection opposition during his tenure in Congress.

As a new member of Congress, Cummings was struck by the highly partisan nature of debate. This contentious atmosphere was very different from that of the Maryland legislature, where legislators worked together without much regard to party affiliation. "I just did not expect the partisanship to the degree it is...And it gets kind of vicious, too...on both sides. It saddens me," Cummings told Valentine in April of 1997. In his first speech on the House floor in April of 1996 Cummings called for greater cooperation between Democrats and Republicans. "Our world would be a much better world and a much better place if we would only concentrate on the things we have in common instead of concentrating on our differences. It is easy to find differences, very easy. We need to take more time to find common ground," Cummings told his fellow lawmakers as quoted by Philip D. Duncan and Christine C. Lawrence in *Politics in America 1998*. Despite the ill-will between parties, Cummings has gained the respect of members on the other side of the aisle, including Representative Wayne T. Gilchrest, a Republican from Maryland's Eastern Shore. Gilchrest told Valentine that Cummings is "a gentleman and a professional."

Education is a high priority on Cummings' agenda and he has made an effort to visit every school in his district in order to gain information from the educational front lines. Cummings is a strong supporter of public education and opposes voucher programs that would help defray the cost of private school tuition. "Quality public education is necessary to improve our children's lives and to ensure that their futures remain bright," Cummings said in a statement included in his office website. Cummings believes it is very important that schools in minority communities be connected to the Internet. "We must bring the twenty-first century into every classroom in America. Technological literacy is essential to succeed in the new economy...African-Americans, historically concentrated in agriculture, personal service, and blue-collar occupations, are now disproportionately displaced in the emerging Information Age...Now is the time to commit to helping underserved minority schools. The longer we wait, the wider the gap between these kids and the kids who are technology-fluent expands," Cummings said in speech to the House in February of 1997 as quoted in *Politics in America 1998*.

A resident of the Madison Park neighborhood of West Baltimore, Cummings has been robbed at gunpoint and his home and car have been burglarized. His personal experience has made Cummings especially aware of crime. He opposes the death penalty and believes that dealing with the social conditions that foster criminal behavior is the most effective way to prevent crime. As a member of the Maryland state legislature, Cummings helped establish a "Boot Camp" program to address the needs of juvenile offenders. To prevent domestic violence, which he also believes is primarily caused by adverse social conditions, Cummings joined Representatives John Conyers of Michigan and Constance Morella of Maryland in sponsoring the Violence Against Women Act of 1999. Cummings believes that his father set an example in regard to coping with the frustrations that lead to domestic violence. In a May 1999 column for the *Baltimore Afro-American*, Cummings recalled how his father would often sit quietly in the car for a hour or so before entering the house after a hard day at the chemical plant — "It worked. During my forty-eight years on this earth, I have never heard my father raise his voice to my mother. He understood what is required to be a gentle man."

> "I will continue to speak up for those whose voices are rarely, if ever, heard, and stand up for those who cannot stand up for themselves."

Drug abuse plagues many areas of the seventh district, and Cummings supports needle exchange programs that distribute clean needles to intravenous drug users in the hope of preventing the spread of HIV. He does not believe that such programs condone or increase illegal drug use. In 1997, Cummings introduced the HIV Prevention Outreach Act which called for an end to ban on federal funding of needle exchange programs. "I am fully aware that the idea of exchanging clean syringes for used needles make some of my colleagues in Washington uncomfortable [but] the bottom line is that giving clean needles to addicts will save lives. Not only the lives of the intravenous drug user, but also the men, women, and children who are involved in their lives," Cummings said in an August 1997 press release.

In 1998, Cummings led members of the Congressional Black Caucus on a tour of two of Baltimore's drug rehabilitation centers and an AIDS outpatient clinic. The Baltimore visit came soon after a Centers for Disease Control study showed that African Americans, who make up 12 percent of the U.S. population, account for more than 40 percent of all new HIV infections. "As a leader in the Black community, I am deeply concerned about this new information. This new data highlights an issue we must urgently address. As a member of the Congressional Black Caucus, I am dedicated to supporting increased funding for AIDS education and research," Cummings stated in a July 1998 press release.

Cummings co-sponsored the Traffic Stops Statistics Study Act of 1999, which called for documentation of the extent to which police are influenced by race when conducting traffic stops. "Thousands of people of color are the victims of DWB – driving while Black...The practice of unjustly stopping, humiliating, searching, and arresting people of color on our highways has escalated," Cummings was quoted in a press release as telling the House. In his column for the *Baltimore Afro-American,* Cummings wrote that "as a member of Congress, and as an African- American male, I cannot tolerate the practice of stopping and searching American citizens for no reason other than their race."

The investigation into President Bill Clinton's relationship with White House intern Monica Lewinsky absorbed much of the attention of Congress in 1998. Cummings was the only member of the Maryland Congressional delegation to vote against release of the Starr Report which offered lurid details of Clinton's affair with Lewinsky. Cummings joined with many other House Democrats in maintaining the case against Clinton went beyond the Constitutional power of the national legislature. "The framers of the Constitution did not entrust this House with the power to impeach the president of the United States in order to establish this body as a court of personal morality...We should be leaving personal and moral sanctions to the courts, the branch of government where they properly belong. And we should be doing the job we were elected to do. The wisdom of history, not the passions of this moment, must guide our actions," Cummings said in a speech on the House floor as quoted in the *Washington Post.*

Cummings is an active member of Baltimore's New Psalmist Baptist Church. In his spare moments Cummings enjoys jogging, reading, and spending time with his two daughters. He keeps in touch with the concerns of the residents of his district by holding "Town Hall Meetings" where constituents can meet with him to discuss issues. Cummings has also organized five community input groups or "Round Tables," which assist him in developing solutions to the problems facing the district. Cummings told Valentine that his mission in Congress is "to be the voice of the people who put their faith and trust in me."

Sources

Books

Barone, Michael, and Grant Ujifusa. *Almanac of American Politics 1998.* Washington, DC: National Journal, 1997.

Duncan, Philip D. and Christine C. Lawrence. *Politics in America 1998.* Washington, DC: Congressional Quarterly, 1997.

Periodicals

Baltimore Afro-American, May 1, 1999; May 8, 1999.
Congressional Quarterly, March 9, 1996, p. 647; April 20, 1996, p. 1070
Ebony, January 1997, p. 65.
Washington Post, February 25, 1996, p. B5; April 17, 1996, p. D5; April 24, 1997, Maryland Weekly sect., p 1, 3; September 12, 1998, p. A15; December 20, 1998, p. A42.

Other

Additional information for this profile was obtained from Cummings' website (www.house.gov/cummings).

—Mary Kalfatovic

Danny K. Davis

1941—

Congressman from Illinois

A survivor of the "council wars" that plagued Chicago's combative and racially divided city government, Danny Davis emerged in the 1990s as one of the leaders of the city's large and influential African American community. In 1996, after two previous attempts, he was elected to the U.S. Congress. Far from mellowing politically, Davis continued as a staunch advocate of government social programs, and proved surprisingly effective in protecting some of them against the budget-cutters who flourished in the Republican-dominated Congress of the 1990s.

Davis was born in Parkdale, Arkansas, on September 6, 1941, the son of a cotton farmer. He graduated with a B.A. degree from Arkansas Agricultural, Mechanical, and Normal College, now the University of Arkansas at Pine Bluff, in 1961, and moved to Chicago's West Side shortly thereafter, landing a job as a postal clerk. Davis pursued a career in education, teaching and serving as a guidance counselor in Chicago's public schools during the 1960s. In 1968, Davis received a master's degree from Chicago State University. Married with two children, he has established deep roots within his West Side community, and serves as a deacon of the New Galilee Missionary Baptist Church.

Became Health Care Administrator

A strong commitment to his community prompted the idealistic Davis to switch careers, putting him on a path that would ultimately lead him into politics. He became a health care administrator at the community level, serving as director of training at the Martin Luther King Neighborhood Health Center between 1969 and 1971, and then once again laying the educational groundwork for further advancement in the field; he earned a Ph.D. degree from the Union Institute in Cincinnati in 1977. Davis had already become the executive director of the Westside Health Center, a post he held until 1981. He has served as president of the National Association of Community Health Centers.

Davis combined his health care career with a commitment to grassroots community organizing, founding and becoming president of an organization called the Westside Association for Community Action. A run for the Chicago City Council was the next logical step. Davis was elected in 1979 as alderman of the Twenty-Ninth

> **At a Glance...**
>
> Born September 6, 1941, in Parkdale, AR; son of a cotton farmer; married to Vera; children: Jonathan, Stacey. *Education:* Arkansas A., M. & N College, B.A., 1961; Chicago State University, M.S., 1968; Union Institute, Ph.D., 1977. *Religion:* Missionary Baptist.
>
> **Career:** United States Representative, Seventh District of Illinois, member of the Democratic Party. Clerk, Chicago Post Office, 1961-65; teacher, Chicago Public Schools, 1962-68; became director of training, Martin Luther King Neighborhood Health Center, 1969; became executive director, Westside Health Center, 1975; elected to Chicago City Council, 1979; backed Mayor Harold Washington in "council wars," early 1980s; elected as Commissioner, Cook County Board, 1990; ran for mayor of Chicago, 1991; elected to U.S. House of Representatives, 1996-.
>
> **Addresses:** *Office*—1222 Longworth House Office Building, Washington, DC 20515.

Ward, a district on the city's western edge. He served on the council through some of its most turbulent years, emerging as a key ally of Mayor Harold Washington, who was elected on a groundswell of African American support in 1983 and became Chicago's first African American mayor. Finding that Washington's initiatives were frustrated by entrenched whites who controlled the council, Davis received an education in the difficulty of bringing about political change through established channels.

With an eye to the future, Davis challenged veteran U.S. Representative Cardiss Collins twice in primary elections, in 1984 and 1986. He was unsuccessful both times, but in 1990 was elected to the Cook County Commission. He ran for mayor of Chicago in 1991 against the extremely popular Richard Daley Jr. Although he lost the election, Davis broadened his name recognition, and went on to build his influence within the Chicago-area Democratic Party. In 1992, he became a state co-chair of Bill Clinton's successful campaign for the presidency. Clinton, in return, named Davis to the board of directors of the National Housing Partnership, and he continued to serve on the county commission.

In 1996, Collins finally retired, and Davis entered a ten-way race for the Seventh District Congressional seat. A campaigner with a booming voice and a stately personal presence that contrasted favorably with the other, more flamboyant candidates in the race, Davis offered a liberal platform that called for increased spending on urban concerns and health care, and for a rise in the federal minimum wage to $7.60 an hour. Running, according to *The Progressive*, on a slogan of "jobs, justice, equality, and peace," Davis called for cuts in defense spending and argued for the maintenance of affirmative action programs, a favorite target of Republicans. He also led journalists on tours of Chicago's public housing projects during the Democratic National Convention. Davis won the primary by a margin of 13 percentage points over his nearest competitor, and cruised to victory in the general election in his overwhelmingly Democratic district.

Among the most liberal members of the House—in addition to his long-standing Democratic affiliation he also maintains ties with a small left-wing organization called the New Party—Davis might have been expected to have his influence severely circumscribed in the Republican-dominated House of the late 1990s. But Davis brought his considerable persuasive skills to bear on his fellow House members. He voted against a 1997 tax-cut bill, arguing, according to the *Almanac of American Politics*, that "[w]e cannot have a great, civilized and humane nation without paying the cost; if all we can do is cut, cut, cut, all that we will get is blood, blood, blood." On that issue and on many other votes, Davis ended up in the minority.

However, on other issues, Davis enjoyed more success. He worked with the House Transportation Committee leadership on a bill to increase funding for services that would transport inner-city workers to suburban jobs. This issue gained importance in the late 1990s as the economy flourished and suburbs grew dramatically. Inner-city workers, many of whom did not own a car, were unable to commute to jobs that often went unfilled. Davis sponsored new funding for neighborhood health care centers, and worked with fellow Chicago Representative Bobby Rush to secure emergency help for the perennially strapped Chicago Housing Authority.

Challenged Supreme Court Hiring Practices

During the late 1990s, Davis took a strong stand on several controversial issues. He vigorously opposed the charter school movement, and was quoted by the *Almanac of American Politics* as saying that it was "a sinister move to dismantle public education." In 1998, Davis was the first to point out that the U.S. Supreme Court had employed very few minority lawyers on its staff of clerks. Although this situation went virtually unchanged, Davis earned national recognition within progressive circles. That same year, Davis took the lead in resisting Republican-inspired budget cuts aimed at home-improvement loans for low-income Americans and at summer jobs programs for urban youth. "Having them [young people] on our streets instead of working is a crazy plan that is detrimental to their futures and to our communities," Davis told *Jet*. At the turn of the century, American liberalism had found a vigorous new champion in Danny Davis and, with his record of ambition and accomplishment, he seemed to be a politician to watch for years to come.

Sources

Books

Barone, Michael, and Grant Ujifusa. *The Almanac of American Politics: 2000*. National Journal, 1999.

1997–1998 Congressional Directory: 105th Congress. United States Government Printing Office, 1997.

Periodicals

Ebony, January 1997, p. 64.
Jet, April 8, 1996, p. 40; August 3, 1998, p. 32.
Progressive, November 1996, p. 25.

Online

Additional information for this profile was obtained at www.house.gov/davis/.

—James M. Manheim

Ed Davis

1911–1999

Automobile dealer

Ed Davis was the first African American to win a franchise to sell new cars. Davis had been a successful used-car seller in Detroit in the 1930s before he signed on with the Studebaker Automobile Company to sell their cars. In the early 1960s, he achieved another historic first by becoming the country's first African American to own and operate a new-car franchise from one of the "Big Three" automakers. Davis faced tremendous obstacles as an African American businessperson in an era before workplace integration, fairness in commercial lending practices, and minority dealer-development programs. Still, he prospered through perseverance and a scrupulous attitude toward his customers, and indeed became one of Detroit's leading citizens. Just a few months before his death, Davis was honored with a special dinner held in conjunction with the North American International Auto Show, and was inducted into the Automotive Hall of Fame—again, becoming the first African American to achieve this honor.

Davis was born in 1911 in Shreveport, Louisiana, where he was one of ten children. His father was a food jobber for oil-pipeline construction workers with the Standard Oil Co., which was a large-scale daily catering job. His father purchased the produce and meat from local farmers, and did much of the cooking himself. "The fact that he was his own boss was the greatest influence, I believe, in motivating me eventually to get into business for myself," Davis wrote in his 1979 autobiography, One Man's Way. "…I realized that real power and true economic freedom came frcm developing self-reliance and independence."

Moved to Detroit as a Teen

Though Davis's family prospered, his early life in Louisiana was marked by other hardships. His mother died when he was ten, and discrimination and random violence against African Americans was common in the South of the era. Davis's father owned a 500-acre farm and a Ford Model T, which fascinated him as a youngster. "It got me interested in mechanics," Davis told Detroit Free Press reporter Lisa Jackson. "How a car worked was more fascinating to me than the actual car itself." As a teenager, he convinced his father to allow him to move north to Detrcit, where an aunt lived, in order to attend better, unsegregated public schools. Davis was able to gain entrance to the city's most prestigious public high school, the academically rigorous Cass Technical High School. He hoped to become an accountant, but was discouraged when he learned that there were almost no African Americans in the field at the time.

A tinkerer by nature, Davis convinced the owners of a car-repair garage to hire him, which they initially did in exchange for his bus fare. The owners of the garage instructed Davis to look busy doing janitorial work when

> **At a Glance...**
>
> Born February 27, 1911 in Shreveport, LA; died on May 3, 1999, in Detroit, MI; son of Thomas H. (a food jobber) and Hester (Bryant) Davis; married Mary Agnes Miller, late 1930s. *Education:* attended Wayne State University.
>
> **Career:** Worked as a mechanic in a garage and as operator of a car wash business, both in Detroit, early 1930s; worked in the foundry and then the machine shop in a Dodge Motor Company factory; salesperson at Merton L. Lampkins Chrysler-Plymouth, Highland Park, MI, 1936-38; opened Davis Motor Sales in Detroit, 1938; became a Studebaker new-car dealer, 1940-56; Victory Loan and Investment, co-founder, 1940, and president; opened Davis Chrysler-Plymouth in Detroit, 1963; City of Detroit Department of Street Railway Systems (DSR), manager, 1971-74; business consultant, 1974-94.
>
> **Awards:** Named Michigan's Small Businessman of the Year, 1966; inducted into the Automotive Hall of Fame, 1999.

customers were in the garage, and not to appear to be working on any cars. Eventually they hired him for wages that rose to $12 a week—a good salary for a 16-year-old—during the worst years of the Depression, but he eventually lost the job when the owners could no longer afford to keep any employee. Next, Davis approached the owner of a gas station and convinced him to let him wash cars there for money. The owner agreed with some reluctance, but after a month realized that Davis was making more money than his gasoline business. He then tried to renegotiate the rates they had agreed upon, but Davis refused.

Snubbed by Colleagues

One of Davis's car-wash customers was a man named Lampkins, who was a supervisor at a local factory operated by the Dodge automobile company. When he heard of Davis's plight, Lampkins offered him a job in the foundry—a dangerous, arduous position, and one of the few open to African Americans in the auto industry at the time—which he accepted. He shoveled pig iron into huge blast furnaces for a few weeks when Lampkins and another manager, who both seemed to appreciate Davis's dedication to any task he undertook, gave him a job in the plant's machine shop. When Lampkins's son opened a car dealership, Davis was invited to become a salesperson there, for it was thought that the business might attract more African American customers if they had an African American salesperson on staff. Davis began working part-time at Merton L. Lampkins Chrysler-Plymouth in Highland Park, a small city inside north-central Detroit, in 1936, but kept his Dodge plant job for a year until he thought it safe to quit.

As he wrote in his autobiography, *One Man's Way*, Davis became one of only three African Americans selling cars in Detroit in 1936. His sales-floor colleagues at Lampkins snubbed him from the start, and he was not allowed to conduct his business with customers in the showroom when they were present. "So you know what I did? I got an office upstairs, and I bought really nice furniture," Davis said in the *Detroit Free Press* interview with Jackson. It was actually the parts showroom, but African American customers soon began flocking to Davis. "Every day, more people came to buy cars from me," he recalled. "Every day, that mean secretary had to lead people up to my office. Drove her crazy."

In time, the other salesmen and even Mert Lampkins himself began to resent the amount of money Davis was making, and they often made derogatory remarks. With the money he saved Davis opened his own business, Davis Motor Sales, in 1939. It was a used-car lot on East Vernor Avenue, on Detroit's lower east side and in the heart of its African American business district. Davis would arrive at the lot each morning at 5:30 to clean it. His business was a success nearly from the start. "I had the opportunity of operating in a neighborhood that not only held opportunities, but was congenial to me," Davis wrote in *One Man's Way*. In "those days," he noted, "most blacks spent their money where they lived."

Won a Studebaker Franchise

Davis's business was soon thriving to such a degree that it attracted the attention of one of the Detroit representatives for the Studebaker automobile company. In July of 1940, Davis's lot became a Studebaker new-car dealership. Although his business experience and financial success had been met with approval by the company, becoming a new-car dealer involved a great deal of personal investment. Davis was unable to obtain financing from any bank, and had to risk his entire savings to pay for his first delivery of cars to the showroom. He managed to stay in business during the difficult years of World War II—no new cars were manufactured for a time—but prospered in the years after the war, when Studebakers enjoyed a surge in sales.

The Studebaker Company went out of business in 1956, so Davis returned to selling used cars on his lot. Despite this setback, he fully expected to obtain another new-car franchise from a more successful automaker. He contacted the Big Three automakers, and was offered a Plymouth-DeSoto dealership. Within a few months, however, his phone calls were not returned and he learned that other dealers in the area had threatened to quit if he was awarded a franchise. By this time Davis had become a prominent local business leader, and was appointed by Detroit's mayor to head the Community Relations Commission in 1953, a civil-rights watchdog group that tried to end segregation in the city's public-housing projects.

Active in Democratic Politics

Davis had also founded, along with four other African American businessmen, the Victory Loan and Investment Company, which made loans to the African American community. For a time in the late 1950s, Davis worked with a local white Ford dealer as a vice-president, but his success in this job was rewarded with both official and covert discrimination. Because of his opposition to what was euphemistically called "urban renewal"—the wholesale government condemnation of some of the city's poorest neighborhoods, Davis became increasingly active in politics during the late 1950s. New low-income housing communities were created, but the homes were often poorly constructed and the areas became riddled with crime. In Detroit, many of the condemned homes were owned by African Americans who had worked in the auto factories for years and managed to purchase their own home; they were the working poor, and the small home was all that they possessed. "I think we are paying the social price today," Davis wrote in the late 1970s about this policy. "Urban renewal has turned men and women bitter at the loss of their homes, destroyed their sense of security, and confused and frustrated them," he wrote in *One Man's Way*. "How can anyone expect peace in the inner city under such circumstances? No wonder these people became wary of buying another home and working to keep it looking nice, when they knew that a lifetime of hard work and saving could be swept away by government edict."\

A freeway was also slated to be built on Vernor, which meant that Davis would soon be forced to shut his doors and relocate. But in 1963, a chance occurrence at a business dinner changed his fortunes. A friend of Davis's asked the president of the Chrysler Corporation why his company did not have any African American new car dealers. The executive replied that Chrysler was looking for qualified businessmen of any race. The friend then introduced him to Davis and, four months later, Davis Chrysler-Plymouth opened for business. Those four months, however, were fraught with long, difficult negotiations with company sales executives, who requested that Davis obtain an extraordinary amount of bank financing, and then quizzed him on how he and his sales and service force would deal with white buyers.

Eight Years of Success

Davis received a good deal of local press when Davis Chrysler-Plymouth opened its doors on Dexter and Elmhurst on Detroit's west side in late 1963. He was the first African American to be awarded a new-car franchise from one of the "Big Three," as the top three automakers of General Motors, Ford, and Chrysler were once known. "It was one of the proudest moments of my career," the *Detroit News* quoted Davis as saying. "The auto companies (had) kept turning me down, but then they realized they were missing out on sales in that neighborhood." The dealership, like all of Davis's other businesses, enjoyed excellent sales from the start. As in the past, however, other dealers snubbed him at sales gatherings and company events. He also realized that some of these dealers were even conspiring to undersell him.

But Davis persevered, and won a loyal clientele for his honest practices. He also became active in the neighborhood, and bought a sound truck painted with the slogan, "Good Citizenship is Our Business Too." With three dozen other merchants, Davis founded the Dexter Boulevard Redevelopment, Inc., which was dedicated to improving the neighborhood and encouraging business growth in the area. Davis's wife, whom he married in the late 1930s, was also extremely active in community work. A pianist by training, Mary Agnes Davis had returned to college to earn a social work degree. In 1966, Davis was named Michigan's "Small Businessman of the Year."

The riots that devastated large tracts of Detroit commercial property in the summer of 1967 did not damage Davis's dealership, but they did forever alter the business climate in Detroit. Suddenly, job opportunities for African Americans at white-owned businesses became more available, and Davis had a hard time retaining his staff. Vandalism, rising insurance costs, and problems with the unionized sales force forced Davis to close his business in 1971. Still active in community improvement efforts, Davis began a training program for entrepreneurs and managers, and became the manager for Detroit's Department of Street Railway Systems (DSR), the city's mass-transit authority, in October of 1971. Davis found the department riddled with inefficiency and waste. The DSR's own employees wouldn't even ride the system because service was so bad. Davis took over a public agency, with 2,300 employees and over a thousand buses, that had been losing money for five years. During his three years on the job, he improved the financial situation for the DSR, tried to boost employee morale and performance, and even hired the city's first female bus drivers.

After Davis retired, he spent the next 20 years serving as a consultant to minority auto dealers and other African American business owners. He also tried unsuccessfully to gain a Cadillac dealership from General Motors. Davis wrote extensively about affirmative action and minority hiring practices in the last chapter of his book, *One Man's Way*. "Too often, minorities are hired to meet minority quotas within individual companies, and these companies have no intention of letting them succeed," Davis asserted in *One Man's Way*. "Minorities who are capable of being promoted and doing a good job should be given consideration for promotion in positions throughout their organization, not just promotion into an isolated spot or department especially designated for special groups. This is racism as its worst."

During the late 1970s, when Davis published his memoirs, there were only 30 African American-owned car dealerships in the United States. Twenty years later, there were over 600. Davis formally retired in 1994, a year after the National Association of Minority Automobile Dealers created a Pioneer award and established a scholarship fund, both in his name. In early 1999, he became the first African American to be inducted into the Automotive Hall of Fame. "It turned out that I opened many doors," Davis told the *Detroit Free Press* at the induction ceremony. " I didn't plan for it, but I guess it did happen. I'm proud of it."

Selected writings

One Man's Way (autobiography), Ed Davis Associates, 1979.

Sources

Periodicals

Detroit Free Press, January 7, 1999, p. 11A; January 31, 1999; May 4, 1999.
Detroit News, May 4, 1999; November 12, 1999.

—Carol Brennan

Loretta Devine

1953—

Actress

Soft-spoken, dreamy-eyed Loretta Devine is a big-boned beauty who is instrumental in changing the way African American females are viewed on stage, television, and screen. *Ebony* writer, Lisa Jones Townsel, includes Devine as one of the "beautiful big women who continue to make significant strides." Although she debuted on Broadway in 1977 in "Hair" and tasted a large dose of success in 1982 with her role in the Broadway blockbuster "Dreamgirls," Devine was not a household word until 19 years after she first appeared on Broadway when her role in the movie "Waiting to Exhale" earned her the 1996 Image Award for "Outstanding Supporting Actress in a Motion Picture." Diane Haithman, a writer for the *Los Angeles Times* confirms that "Devine, a theater, film, and television veteran is probably best known for her role as a sensible single mom Gloria in the 1995 movie "Waiting to Exhale," or in Broadway's "Dreamgirls" in the mid-1980s."

Loretta Devine, daughter of laborer, James Devine and beautician, Eunice O'Neal Devine was born in Houston, Texas on August 21, 1953. She worked her way through Brandeis University. According to Haithman, "Devine, who comes from a 'large, poor' Houston family... is a graduate of the University of Houston" and "received her master's degree in fine arts from Brandeis University, working as a teacher and a dorm supervisor to help pay for her studies." Devine wasted no time launching her career.

Launch from Phase I to Phase II

In 1977, she landed the role of Dionne in the hit musical "Hair." Four years and at least 14 stage productions later, Devine was cast as Lorell Robinson, in "Dreamgirls," at the Imperial Theatre in New York City in 1981. Although some would consider "Dreamgirls" to be the play that launched Devine's career, she attributes it to her performance in another play five years later. In an article written by Emory Holmes II for the *Los Angeles Times*, Devine says it was George C. Wolfe's play, "The Colored Museum" in 1986, that "really did project her career into the next phase." Holmes quotes Devine as saying, "I had just finished doing 'Dreamgirls,' and the talk of the town around New York was that there was this new show coming. I read the script and said 'Oh my God, I will never get a chance to do this.' But I auditioned for

At a Glance...

Born Loretta Devine, August 21, 1953, in Houston, TX. *Education:* BA, Speech/ Drama Educ., Univ. of Houston, 1971; MFA , Theater Arts: Brandeis Univ., 1976; Studied acting with Ed Koven and Improvisation with Gary Austin.

Career: Julia C. Hester House, youth prog. dir. and activity coord., 1971-72; founder of Hester House Players and Hester House Dancers, 1971; Black Arts Center, Houston, dir. of theater dept., 1972-74; Ethnic Arts Center Players, founder, 1972-74; Instructor in English and Dorm Supervisor at Brandeis Univ, 1974-76; TX Southern Univ., instructor, 1974; Harvard Univ., instructor,1975-76; worked in repertory theater, Rhode Island, 1977. Credits include, stage: *Big Deal,* and *Dreamgirls;The Colored Museum,* and *Spunk; A Midsummer Night's Dream, The Hot Mikado, East Texas Hot Links, The Rabbit's Foot,* and *Lady Day at Emerson's Bar and Grill.* Television: *Jackie's Back! (1999), Funny Valentines (1999), "The Pjs" (1999), The Parkers (1999), Introducing Dorothy Dandridge (1999), Clover (1997),Rebound: The Legend of Earl "The Goat" Manigault (1996), The American Clock (1993), Reasonable Doubts (1991), "Sugar and Spice"* (1990), *Parent Trap III (1989), The Murder of Mary Phagan (1988), Murphy Brown (1988), "A Different World" (1987), The Colored Museum (1986).* Motion pictures: *Operation Splitsville (1999), Book of Love (1999), Lillie (1999), Urban Legend (1998), Down in the Delta (1998), Love Kills (1998), Hoodlum (1997), Lover Girl (1997), The Price of Kissing (1997), The Preacher's Wife (1996), Waiting to Exhale (1995), The Hard Truth (1994), Amos & Andrew (1993), Caged Fear (1992), Livin' Large (1991), Little Nikita (1988).*

Selected awards: Best Actress Award nomination, NAACP, 1988; Best Supporting Actress Award, NAACP, 1990; Image Award "Outstanding Supporting Actress in a Motion Picture" (Waiting to Exhale), 1996.

Addresses: *Agent*—Writers and Artists; 11726 San Vicente #300; Los Angeles, CA 90049

the La La part, and I got it. I was so amazed, because La La is so broad and huge compared to what I thought my personality was at the time. My agents were so upset because I chose this, making absolutely no money, and I had no idea that it would be the sort of thing that pivoted my career from where I was into the next phase." As a result of her performance in "The Colored Museum," Devine told Holmes, "I got a chance to go to London. I got a chance to come out here to L.A. to do the play." And from that I got my first pilot for television, 'Sugar & Spice.'"

Since that time, she has not only become a familiar face on stage, television, and in motion pictures, but she has also become a familiar voice. Diane Haithman describes Devine as having a "...breathy, little-girl voice that belies her statuesque physique." Devine's unmistakably identifiable voice got her the role of Muriel Stubbs, wife of Thurgood (voiced by Eddie Murphy) in Murphy's controversial animated TV series, "The PJs" in 1999.

Sexy and Respectable

Loretta Devine's success opened doors for African American actresses who previously may have felt they had to be pencil-thin and light-skinned to make a mark in Hollywood. In fact, the role that won Devine the "Image Award for Outstanding Supporting Actress in a Motion Picture" was Gloria, in "Waiting to Exhale." Devine actually "gained 30 pounds for the role of a woman who struggled with weight along with her relationships with men." Says Haithman, who notes that Devine "has since lost" the 30 pounds. Traditionally, it was never the heavier set or darker-skinned woman who got the sexy roles, but when Gloria (Loretta Devine) says 'good-bye' and walks away from her new neighbor (handsome Gregory Hines) in a scene in "Waiting to Exhale," she turns and notices he is watching her, then changes her walk to a sexy strut as she goes on her way. As noted in *USA Today,* Devine's prize-winning role also demonstrated that a black woman can play a sexy role that is respectable. "Unlike three of the movie's four principle characters, many (upscale black women) don't flaunt their bodies, fornicate, or commit adultery." The *USA Today* article goes on to say, "That's why there was so much applause for Gloria, played nicely by Loretta Devine... who doesn't sleep around and still ends up with heartthrob (Gregory) Hines."

Ellen Futterman, Entertainment Editor of the *St. Louis Post-Dispatch* says Devine believes the movie captures the essence of sisterhood regardless of race. Devine told Futterman, "The problems these women are dealing with are problems for a lot of women. How can I get all of these other things in my life right and still be so off when it comes to men? Unfortunately, the way our society is, it's hard to feel total and complete if you're a woman and you don't have a man." Devine, a single woman herself, lives in Culver City. According to Diane Haithman, in the 1998 *Los Angeles Times* article, Devine "maintains a long-distance relationship with a man who lives in Alabama."

Keeping Busy

Jack E. White, of *Time Australia*, says he can "remember the 1950s, when blacks were so rarely on television that the mere sight of one was enough to produce pandemonium," in his neighborhood. "'Colored on TV,' someone would shout from the front porch," He said "all normal activity ceased as everybody within earshot rushed to the nearest set for a moment of electronic racial solidarity." Devine was just a baby in diapers back then, but today black actresses continue to struggle to find decent roles and keep busy, even proven talent like Devine. There is no doubt that Devine is one of the most talented actresses of her time. She has won numerous awards for her performances, including the 1996 Image Award for "Outstanding Supporting Actress in a Motion Picture" for her performance in "Waiting to Exhale." For the African American actress, unfortunately, winning awards does not guarantee adequate work. "Actresses perennially complain of lack of work," says Bob Ivry of *The Record* "And the roles they do get usually fall into the girlfriend-wife-mother category, playing second fiddle to men. As bad as things are for women in general, for black women it's downright scary." Ivry goes on to say that except for "...three films from the '98 roster — 'Beloved,' 'Down in the Delta,' and 'Why Do Fools Fall in Love' ... African American women weren't even a blip on the big screen in 1998. Devine appeared in one of those three films, "Down in the Delta."

Bob Ivry says that "for every Cuba Godding Jr. who goes from 'Boyz N the Hood' to an Oscar for 'Jerry Maquire,' there are a dozen talented black actors who can't find enough work, especially women." In fact, Ivry gives the example of Dorothy Dandridge who was "the first African American female to be nominated for a best actress Oscar..." Yet, tragically, Ivry goes on to say that Dandridge's "life fell apart after she could no longer find enough work." Another example is given by John Stark of *People* who says that the actress who rose to fame with her role as the maid, Prissy, in "Gone With the Wind," Butterfly McQueen, "spent eight years in Hollywood, but returned to Harlem in the late 1940s after being discouraged by the roles she was offered." Half a century later, veteran actress Leslie Uggams (starred in the award-winning TV mini-series "Roots") who, according to Janice Gaston of *The Tampa Tribune*, "was nominated for an Emmy." has a problem finding work. "Nowadays, she sings with symphonies." Says Gaston, who quotes Uggams as saying, "acting roles are hard to come by." Gatson goes on to say that "the declining number of black people on television disappoints 56 year-old Uggams" who "has been performing since she was six."

One reason for the struggle to find work was given by actress Halle Berry, who played the leading role in the movie portraying the life story of singer, dancer, actress "Dorothy Dandridge." Devine played the mother of Dorothy Dandridge in the movie. "The industry has a hard time considering us for roles unless the script says 'black woman,' 'black man'." Ivry quotes Berry as saying. "If it just says 'woman' or 'man,' they don't even think of us." Berry goes on to say that her struggle is "to get them to think of us just as people, not always make us black people. We're people first."

Devine's Love for the Theater

The multi-talented Devine's ability to perform on stage as well as on TV and in films cannot guarantee that she will always find suitable work, however, it does allow her more choices than many other African American actresses. This, along with her obvious love for the theater, is probably the reason Devine, after being featured on TV and in movies, has not abandoned the stage. According to Diane Haithman of the *Los Angeles Times*, Loretta Devine helped "Black Artists Network Development (BAND) make the big leap to producing its first play (*'Blues for an Alabama Sky'* by Pearl Cleage)". Devine is very active in Los Angeles community theatre. In the article, Haithman noted that Devine "is dedicated ... to nurturing a black theater company in Los Angeles." Haithman quoted Devine as saying, "A black theater is important, because I think that's what gives longevity to the careers of actors who go on and on— Samuel Jackson, Denzel Washington, all of those people came from very strong theater backgrounds."

How She Does It

Sherri A. McGee of *Essence* writes that for Devine, "time away from daily demands is a ritual." McGee quotes Devine as saying, "I have this small place in my house that serves as a meditation room." McGee says Devine "retreats to her miniature haven for morning prayer, to write in her journal, and to pen poetry." McGee goes on to say that "Devine also frees her mind by engaging in hobbies that are both meditative and creative," and quotes Devine as saying, "I'm constantly painting the walls and fixing things up. I retiled my entire bathroom and hand-dyed my carpet."

"...People think this is an easy career. There is a lot of fun, and there are a lot of rewards, but there are a lot of ups and downs to it." Devine told Diane Haithman. Devine's point is confirmed by one of her 'Waiting to Exhale' co-stars, actress Lela Rochon, who told Ellen Futterman, she "went from a year and a half... of nothing to ... having all these wonderful scripts and choices. As an actress, all you want are choices. As a black actress, you never have choices." Another of Loretta Devine's "Waiting to Exhale" co-stars, actress Angela Bassett, gives Ann Oldenburg and Susan Wloszczyna of USA Today one of the reasons for this. "We know the history that black women are not considered beautiful--they are considered sexual but not beautiful." says Bassett, who makes the point that she "couldn't wear ... braids 10 years ago going up for the nurse on 'Loving.' Not that it was a big thing," continues Bassett, "but it would affect people. I would have to wear my hair straight. It's only hair, and everybody's different ... we should applaud differences."

The multi-talented Devine, who is also a writer, knows that more scripts written by black writers, will mean more work for black actresses. Devine is the author of "Managing the Hunks," an unsold television pilot. "For a young person interested in... acting as a career," Devine told Haithman, "I would advise them to try to become as well trained as possible, and to be as family oriented as possible, or have some emotional center ... And get as much training as you can, this will help you make the choices and do whatever it is you want to do." Devine continues to make wise choices which not only keep her career rising to new heights, but gives encouragement and sets examples for actresses who may fall victim to negative, stereotypical typecasting.

Sources

Periodicals

Ebony February 1997, p 162,
Essence, October 1999, p. 21.
Los Angeles Times, February 1, 1998, p. 46; May 2, 1999, pp. 75.
Newsday, The Marvin Kitman Show, January 11, 1999, pp. B23.
People, December 1, 1986, pp. 69.
The Record (Bergen County, NJ), September 20, 1998, pp. y01; February 21, 1999, pp. y01.
St. Louis Post-Dispatch, December 22, 1995, pp. 01D.
Tampa Tribune, August 17, 1999, pp. 1.
Time Australia, January 15, 1996, p. 62.
USA Today, December 22, 1995; December 29, 1995.

—Sadie Mungro

Julian C. Dixon

1934

Congressman from California

An institution in California politics, Julian C. Dixon has been a consistent voice speaking out for minorities in the United States House of Representatives. Beyond that, as chairman of the House Ethics Committee during the high-profile scandal that led to the resignation of Speaker of the House Jim Wright in 1989, he was instrumental in maintaining the dignity of the House in the midst of intense partisan wrangling. An effective politician who has rarely been challenged at the polls, Dixon was emerging by the end of the twentieth century as one of the most powerful lawmakers in the United States.

Dixon was born in Washington, D.C., on August 8, 1934, but moved to California as a young man, graduating from Dorsey High School in Los Angeles in 1953. Serving in the Army from 1957 to 1960, he rose to the rank of sergeant, and, like many other ambitious young African Americans of his day, found in the newly integrated military the key to future advancement in civilian life. Following his discharge from the Army, Dixon attended Los Angeles State College (now California State University at Los Angeles), and graduated with a bachelor of science degree in 1962.

Practiced Law

Dixon earned a law degree at Southwestern University in Los Angeles in 1967, and remained a practicing attorney in Los Angeles for several years. In 1972, he ran a successful campaign for a seat in the California State Assembly, serving three terms and rising to the post of chairman of the Assembly's Democratic caucus. Dixon also developed a friendship with assemblyman Henry Waxman, a relationship that would prosper after both were elected to the U.S. Congress and Waxman emerged as a forceful Democratic party leader on a variety of domestic issues. In 1978, when incumbent Democratic Representative Yvonne Burke left Congress to run for the post of California Attorney General, Dixon was a natural choice to succeed her in what was then California's 28th Congressional District.

As the Democratic leadership realized that Dixon was, in the words of the *Almanac of American Politics,* "a team player with high ethics and a discreet style," he was tapped for a series of hot-seat political roles. Dixon performed brilliantly in each role, and by the time he emerged from his baptism in national government, he

> ### At a Glance...
>
> Born August 8, 1934, in Washington, DC; grew up in Los Angeles; married to Betty; one child. *Education:* Los Angeles State College, B.S., 1962; Southwestern University, Los Angeles, LL.B. law degree, 1967. *Military service:* U.S. Army, 1957–60. *Politics:* Democratic.
>
> **Career:** United States Representative, 32nd District of California; practiced law in Los Angeles, late 1960s and early 1970s; elected to California State Assembly, 1972; elected to U.S. House of Representatives, 1978; chair, rules committee, Democratic National Convention, 1984; chair, House Ethics Committee, presided over hearings implicating House Speaker Jim Wright, late 1980s; oversaw District of Columbia finances, 1990s.
>
> **Addresses:** *Office*—2252 Rayburn House Office Building, Washington, DC 20515.

had become a well-entrenched political veteran. Dixon's first challenge occurred during the contentious 1984 Democratic National Convention, in which the Rev. Jesse Jackson mounted a series of widely publicized challenges to the party's delegate-selection procedures. Dixon, appointed chairman of the convention's rules committee, managed Jackson's insurgency expertly, insuring that it never got out of hand before national television cameras.

Chaired Ethics Committee

More significant was Dixon's assignment as chairman of the House Ethics Committee, just as the ethical quagmire that ensnared the powerful House Speaker Jim Wright ballooned from a single botched book deal to a barrage of 69 separate accusations of violating House rules. Chief among Wright's pursuers was the man who would become House Speaker in the Republican landslide of 1994, Georgia Representative Newt Gingrich, an aggressive, highly partisan lawmaker with an eye cast firmly toward his own ambitions. In the midst of this rancorous atmosphere, which in *Ebony*'s words "thrust Dixon, almost as much as Wright, in the forefront of one of the most politically compelling controversies of the decade," Dixon proved to be a stabilizing influence. He earned the trust of committee members on both sides of the aisle, and eventually permitted the orderly emergence of the evidence that sealed Wright's political fate.

After he surmounted these challenges, Dixon began to receive coveted committee posts within the U.S. House of Representatives. He moved from the Ethics Committee to the Permanent Select Committee on Intelligence, an important behind-the-scenes player in setting U.S. national security policy. By the end of the 20th century, with the Democrats in the minority, Dixon had become the ranking minority member of the committee. He also began to advance through the ranks of the Appropriations Committee, which was a coveted assignment because of the committee's direct control over the federal government's purse strings. As part of his duties for this committee, Dixon was given another sensitive and difficult task—he became chairman of the subcommittee overseeing the perennially mismanaged and fiscally crisis-ridden District of Columbia.

Changed Position on D.C. Government

At first, Dixon was sympathetic to the District's government, one of the largest in the country under African American administration. However, after the regime of flamboyant mayor Marion Barry ended with Barry's imprisonment for several years on drug-related charges, Dixon changed his position. In 1995, he demanded the privatization or federal takeover of several of the city government's functions. "He has tried to get the District to make the changes on its own," explained a Dixon staffer quoted in the *Los Angeles Times*. "He wanted to give them every opportunity to get their own house in order. They didn't, and it just pains him."

By the late 1990s, Dixon was able to use his increasing influence to benefit his Los Angeles district (after the 1990 redistricting it became the 32nd District), a multicultural, predominantly middle-class section of the city's west side with a small African American majority. He emerged as a chief backer of the city's slowly coalescing subway system, and worked to mitigate the effects of 1990s defense spending cuts upon Southern California's numerous defense contractors, making loan money available to the small businesses associated with them. Dixon has been in the forefront of efforts to reimburse local communities for the costs of imprisoning and processing undocumented aliens, a hot-button issue for many Californians.

On national issues, Dixon has generally been a reliably liberal voice over his two decades in Congress. He has supported President Bill Clinton on such issues as the failed Republican effort to override his veto of a law prohibiting so-called "partial birth" abortions. Firmly entrenched in his Congressional seat, Dixon refused pleas from Democratic movers and shakers to run for the Los Angeles County Board of Supervisors, and later for mayor of Los Angeles. As a senior member of the House Appropriations Committee, Dixon is part of the inner circle of national power and influence.

Sources

Books

Barone, Michael, and Grant Ujifusa. *The Almanac of American Politics: 2000.* National Journal, 1999.

Hawkins, Walter L., *African American Biographies,* McFarland & Co., 1992.

1997–1998 Congressional Directory: 105th Congress. United States Government Printing Office, 1997.

Periodicals

Ebony, December 1989, p. 144.
Los Angeles Times, March 24, 1995, p. A3.

Other

Additional information for this profile was obtained at www.house.gov/dixon/bio.htm.

—James M. Manheim

Mel Farr

1944—

Automobile dealer

As president of the Mel Farr Automotive Group, Mel Farr owns the largest African American-owned automobile dealership group in the United States, according to *Black Enterprise* magazine's annual rankings. Farr, who was once a pro football player for the Detroit Lions, oversees a chain of Ford, Lincoln-Mercury, and Toyota dealerships spread across five states with over $600 million in sales. Farr also presides over one of the most successful car dealership chains in the country, and holds the top spot on *Black Enterprise*'s list of Industrial/Service companies in its annual rankings of African American-owned businesses. Farr entered the automobile business at a time when there were only a handful of new-car dealerships owned by African Americans and Hispanics, and has been credited with paving the way for increased minority ownership among domestic car dealers. He credited his skills as a professional athlete for his future success as an automobile dealer. "It takes an extreme amount of effort to go out there and apply your training on the football field," Farr told Burt Herman in the *Detroit Free Press* in 1997. "It takes an extreme amount of effort to be an African American and be very successful at this thing."

A Gridiron Star

Farr was born in 1944 in Beaumont, Texas where his father, a truck driver, eventually owned and operated his own used-car lot. His mother was a domestic worker who tried in vain to keep her sons from roughhousing. However, Farr and his brother willfully ignored her pleas to keep away from touch football games, and both would soon emerge as talented high school players. Farr was a standout at Herbert High, and won a football scholarship to the University of California at Los Angeles. He began his career at UCLA in 1963, and was twice named to the All-American team. Farr left UCLA before graduating to pursue a pro career, and he became the Detroit Lions' number-one draft pick in 1967.

After relocating to the Motor City, Farr was signed to a three-year, $94,000 contract. He quickly demonstrated his value to the Lions, who were owned by members of the Ford family, scions of the automotive dynasty. In his first season, Farr was named the National Football League's Rookie of the Year, and was selected to the Pro Bowl. Following the stunning successes of his rookie season, Farr attempted to renegotiate his contract.

At a Glance...

Born 1944, in Beaumont, TX; son of a car dealer and a domestic worker; married since the mid-1960s; wife's name, Mae; children: Mel Jr., Michael, Monet. *Education:* Attended the University of California at Los Angeles, 1963-66; University of Detroit, B.S., 1970.

Career: Played pro football for the Detroit Lions, 1967-74; affiliated with Ford Motor Company's Minority Dealer Development Program, Dearborn, MI, 1968-75; became co-owner of Cook-Farr Ford, Oak Park, MI, 1975, became sole proprietor of Mel Farr Ford, 1978.

Addresses: *Office*—Mel Farr Automotive Group, 24750 Greenfield Rd., Oak Park, MI 48237.

However, the Lions refused to negotiate. "I got $500 for being Rookie of the Year," Farr told Hiawatha Bray in *Black Enterprise.* "That's all."

Hired by Ford

Realizing that his career as a pro athlete would eventually come to an end, Farr went back to college and earned a bachelor of science degree in 1970 from the University of Detroit. When he was a teenager, Farr often spent weekends scouting junkyards for good deals for his father's used-car dealership, or by assisting in other ways. "The car business has been in my blood all my life," Farr told the *Detroit Free Press* in 1997. When the Ford Motor Company offered him a choice of two off-season jobs, doing public-relations work for Ford's racing division or a lower-paying post with its recently created minority dealer development program, Farr opted for the latter. He spent the next several years in the development program. "As an African-American, I could see being an auto dealer," Farr told Herman in the *Detroit Free Press.* "As an African-American, I could not see being a coach in the National Football League, because there weren't any."

There were also very few African American new car dealers in the late 1960s. Ford's minority dealer development program aimed to correct this imbalance within its ranks. It offered a training program with classes and on-the-job experience at a dealership, and Farr, having completed the program himself, then recruited candidates for it. The company then provided financing to program graduates so that they could open their own sales franchises. Working for Ford during the off-season also helped Farr in his athletic career. "I thought it made me a better football player," Farr told Bray in *Black Enterprise.* "I had that fulfillment of learning something else, so I could go out and play with reckless abandon. If I got hurt, I knew I could do something else."

Indeed, Farr's years on the gridiron began to catch up with him, and he was often sidelined with injuries. During his career with the Lions, Farr continually saved money so that he could purchase his first dealership. Upon his retirement from pro football in 1974, Farr approached the executives of the minority dealer development program and expressed his desire to start his own business. Ford executives, however, felt that he still lacked the necessary experience, and so Farr went into business with a mentor, John Cook. With a $40,000 investment, the two men opened Cook-Farr Ford in Oak Park, a suburb of Detroit.

Nearly Folded

The location selected by Farr and Cook had been the site of two failed car dealerships, and their business partnership soon became untenable. He and Cook disagreed over marketing strategies, and Farr was eventually able to buy Cook's share of the business in 1978. However, he soon realized that he had made a mistake. "I thought I was buying a profitable business," Farr told Bray in *Black Enterprise,* but instead found "I had bought a company that was on the verge of bankruptcy." Still, he became just one of over two dozen African American new car dealers in the country at the time.

Farr and his new business were soon faced with several other daunting challenges: oil prices in the United States rose dramatically, Ford produced few of the fuel-efficient economy cars that customers demanded, and a massive recession overtook the Michigan economy. As plant closings and layoffs became widespread, new car sales plummeted in the Detroit area. In 1980, Farr could barely meet his payroll. He was forced to lay off half of his staff, and brought his teenage sons in to help with the janitorial work on nights and weekends. Fortunately, Farr was able to borrow funds from the Small Business Administration and from the Ford Motor Company that enabled him to stay in business.

"Mel Farr, Superstar"

During these lean years, Farr and his dealership became known for the company's inventive television ads. In the first series, Farr put himself in a Superman-style cape and flew over his dealership while trumpeting its bargains in a rapid-fire voice-over. He called himself "Mel Farr, Superstar," and advertised his "Farr better deals." He wrote, directed, starred in, and edited the low-budget, comic ads himself, which became a hit with local television audiences. "I was hanging on by my fingernails," Farr told *Chain Store Age Executive*. "I had to make myself known." Another series of ads, which starred a popular Detroit Lions player at the time, Billy Sims, also helped to boost sales.

In 1986, Farr opened his second dealership, a Lincoln-Mercury franchise in another suburb. His brother Miller managed the dealership, and both of Farr's sons also grew into the business. Farr became a Toyota dealer during the late 1980s, but only after several years of haggling with the import automaker. His Bloomfield Hills, Michigan dealership was only the fifth African American-owned Toyota sales franchise in the United States.

A Top Dealer

Farr went on to acquire or launch dealerships in New Jersey, Ohio, Maryland, and Texas. He also began his own financing company, Triple M Financing, to help low-income buyers who did not qualify for a car loan from the Ford Motor Credit Corporation. His son, Mel Jr., runs the Cincinnati area dealership. Another son, Michael, manages the flagship showroom in Oak Park, and several other relatives are also employed by the company. With his wife Mae, whom he married in the mid-1960s, Farr also has a daughter, Monet.

Farr keeps his father's original business license for his used-car lot in Beaumont, dated July 8, 1960, above his desk. Named Auto Dealer of the Year in *Black Enterprise* magazine in 1992, Farr has steadily held the top spot in the magazine's annual rankings of African American dealerships—twenty years after he opened for business, there were over 600 minority-owned dealerships in the United States. In 1997, the Mel Farr Automotive Group was ranked 46th among all of the nation's top 100 auto dealers, according to *Crain's Detroit Business,* and is consistently listed on *Black Enterprise*'s list of the Top 100 black-owned businesses in the country.

In addition to his stellar pro football career and his tremendous financial success in an industry where minority representation has been hard-won, Farr can also boast one other claim to fame: he sang backup on the Marvin Gaye hit "What's Going On." He and another Lions player, Lem Barney, were playing golf one day with the famous Motown singer when he came up with the melody; Farr and Barney liked it and urged Gaye to record it, but Gaye told them he would only do it if they helped out. "I guess I've done a little bit of everything—a lucky guy," Farr told Herman in the *Detroit Free Press.*

Sources

Black Enterprise, June 1992, p. 154; June 1999, pp. 131-138.
Chain Store Age Executive with Shopping Center Age, December, 1997, p. 68.
Detroit Free Press, November 2, 1997; May 11, 1999.

—Carol Brennan

Jeff Friday

1964(?)—

Film company executive

Even before Jeff Friday was named president of UniWorld Films in 1999, he was known throughout the business world as a skilled marketer and successful entrepreneur. His passion for films and filmmaking led him to the UniWorld Group, the nation's largest minority-owned and operated advertising and communications company in 1997. As executive director and producer of the Acapulco Black Film Festival, co-sponsored by UniWorld, Friday helped launch an annual, week-long celebration of black cinema that is getting worldwide recognition after only a few years. In 1999 the company began UniWorld Films, a division designed to market and promote black films as well as assisting filmmakers and movie studios in designing promotional campaigns targeted to African Americans.

Friday's marketing career followed impressive educational pursuits which included graduating cum laude from Howard University and earning his MBA from the Leonard Stern School of Business at New York University in 1987. From there Friday went to work at Bristol Myers International where he developed new markets in Latin America and the Caribbean. It was Friday's next job that showcased his talent for recognizing the kinds of marketing strategies that spoke to the values and desires of African American consumers.

Understanding the Audience

In 1989 Friday joined Schiefflin & Sommerset, the importers of such fine wines and spirits as Moet & Chandon, Tanqueray, and Dom Perignon. It was Friday who developed promotions which increased demand by black consumers. "The key things are understanding the audience, their sensitivities, their intricacies, their dynamics and their purchasing button," Friday explained to Jason Elias of *Upscale*, about his skill in pinpointing his audience. He later used those skills on behalf of the Mingo Group as Vice President of Promotions and Event Marketing in directing new product initiatives for Tyco Toys.

In 1996 Byron Lewis, chairman of the UniWorld Group, decided to create a black film festival in response to the complaints that, as he told Caryl Lewis of the *Newark Star-Ledger,* "Hollywood doesn't make movies that show a balanced view of the black life experience." That notion coupled with the fact that the Acapulco Convention and Tourist Board was encouraging African American dollars to seek their way to the resort town, initiated the Acapulco Black Film Festival. Lewis recruited Friday to executive produce and Warrington Hudlin, founder and executive director of the Black Filmmakers Foundation, to co-sponsor with the UniWorld Group.

The UniWorld Group first achieved recognition three decades earlier by pioneering the marketing of feature films and soundtracks to black audiences beginning with the soundtrack to *Shaft* by Isaac Hayes in 1972. Other film projects included *Glory, Boyz N the Hood, Malcolm X, Dead Presidents* and *Amistad.* Additionally,

At a Glance...

Born c. 1964 in New York, New York. *Education:* Graduated cum laude from Howard University; MBA from the Leonard Stern School of Business at New York University, 1987.

Career: Developed new markets in Latin America and the Caribbean for Bristol Myers International, c. 1987; joined Schiefflin & Sommerset, importers of fine wines and spirits, 1989; joined Mingo Group as Vice President of Promotions and Event Marketing in directing new product initiatives for Tyco Toys, c. 1990s; appointed executive director and producer of the Acapulco Black Film Festival, 1997–; named president of UniWorld Films in 1999; initiated BlackFilmFestAmerica 2000, a national tour of independent black films.

Addresses: *Office*—UniWorld Films, 100 Sixth Avenue, 6th Floor, New York, NY 10013.

UniWorld markets consumer goods to African Americans for a host of clients which include AT&T, Burger King, Colgate-Palmolive, Pepsi-Cola, Pfizer and others.

Acapulco Black Film Festival

The first Acapulco Black Film Festival took place in July of 1997 and screened nine films, held panel discussions and culminated in what would be the highlight of that and future festivals, the awards ceremony. Thirty black film professionals were nominated in five categories and special artistic achievement awards went to actor and director Bill Duke and the actress, Halle Berry. "This is a dream come true," Friday told Caryl Lucas of the *Newark Star-Ledger.* "There's a huge sense of satisfaction that an idea which started less than a year ago had come into fruition."

The success of the first and subsequent film festivals prompted the UniWorld Group to become more involved in everyday world of marketing black films. To that end, they initiated a new division, UniWorld Films and installed Friday at the president.
"This division will allow us to focus our energies to impact the film community in a variety of ways," Friday told *Business Wire.* "From providing alternative venues for independent Black films, to creating opportunities for industry professionals to network, to encouraging African Americans to make movies, UniWorld Films will seek to bridge the gaps that exist between the Black creative community and the film industry."

Byron Lewis told *Business Wire* "This new arm of UniWorld will provide [Jeff] the room and resources to effectively realize the goals we've set and elevate our involvement in the film industry to new levels." Friday echoed Lewis, telling Jason Elias of *Upscale,* "My expertise is in marketing as well as filmmaking," Friday explained to Jason Elias of *Upscale.* "So, not only do we have an understanding of black consumers, but we also understand the film business. When we combine these two strengths, we're a unique force in the business.... I was excited about this position because it's a chance for me to create some opportunities and to be a trailblazer."

Black Cinema Café and More

In addition to the film festival, Friday has initiated other programs to promote black films. One is BlackFilmFestAmerica 2000, a national tour designed to bring independent films to a larger audience. Another is the Black Cinema Café, a monthly event in New York City which spotlights emerging filmmakers. "The overall goal of the Café is to...build the commercial market for black independent films," Friday told K.D. Shirkani of *Daily Variety.* This event, initiated by Friday and Reggie Scott, started small but has grown in popularity.

"The first time we screened a film," Friday reminisced to Brett Kelly of *New York,* "we invited nine people over and had cocktails and talked about the movie and had a really good time. But by the third one, we had 37 people in my house, and I looked at Reggie and said, `This is ridiculous!'" The screenings were then moved to a SoHo coffeehouse and in January of 2000 the Black Cinema Café began residence as part of the Cinematek program at the Brooklyn Academy of Music.

"It's combining the best elements of a test screening and a cocktail party," Friday told Kelly. "We just want to build a commercial market. It's very experimental. It may not work. Maybe America doesn't want to see independent black films, but I'm not satisfied that anyone has explored it enough to answer that question yet. And we're committed to answering the question."

"Over the next five to ten years, I'd like UniWorld Films to be a couple of things," Friday told Elias of *Upscale.* "I'd like us to be a one-stop shop for anyone interested in marketing a film to ethnic audiences. Not that our expertise is limited to ethnic audience, but that's our specialty. I'd also like the Acapulco Black Film Festival to be the pre-eminent international film festival for black filmmakers around the world; I don't mean African Americans, but blacks from all countries and continents."

Sources

Periodicals

Black Enterprise, February 28, 1999, p. 28.
Business Wire, November 30, 1998; June 18, 1999.
Daily Variety, January 6, 2000.
Michigan Citizen, December 26, 1998, p. B-2.
New York, January 17, 2000, p. 60.
New York Times, January 9, 2000, p. XIV-14.
Sister 2 Sister, October 1999, p.6.
Source, July 1999, p. 116.
Star-Ledger (Newark), July 6, 1997.
Tennessee Tribune, December 16, 1998, p. 4-B.
Upscale, May 1999, p. 28.

—Brian Escamilla

Danny Glover

1948—

Actor

In an industry that offers limited screen opportunities for African Americans, Danny Glover managed to be one of the busiest actors at work in the 1980s and the 1990s. He began on the stage in the late 1970s and within ten years had made a successful transformation to the screen, starring in some of the biggest films of the 1980s and 1990s, including *Places in the Heart, Witness, The Color Purple, Lethal Weapon,* and its sequels, *Lethal Weapon 2, Lethal Weapon 3,* and *Lethal Weapon 4*. His stage career had also been quite successful and was highlighted by his acclaimed role in the 1982 award-winning Broadway play *"Master Harold"... and the Boys;* Glover also has made frequent appearances on television. The talented actor has displayed great diversity in the roles he has tackled and is regularly noted for his empathetic treatment of the characters he has portrayed.

Born in rural Georgia and raised in California, Glover had early ambitions to become an economist, but was exposed to acting while a politically active student at San Francisco State University in the late 1960s. "My [acting] interest began simultaneously with my political involvement," Glover explained to Aldore Collier in *Ebony*. "My acting is also an extension of my involvement in community politics, working with groups like the African Liberation Support Committee, tutorial programs.... All of these things, at some point drew me into acting." While in college he obtained roles in several plays by Amiri Baraka, who had traveled to San Francisco to stage new theater productions aiming for a fresh perspective as part of the Black arts movement. "I did activist roles in many of the plays," Glover told Collier. "I felt I was making a statement in the plays."

Gained Stage Experience

In addition to his stage experience Glover studied acting formally while in college, yet did not pursue it as a career until years later. After graduation he continued his political activism by working within city government and was employed for five years as an evaluator of community programs for the Mayor's Office in San Francisco. He continued to dabble in local theater, however, and eventually decided that his calling was to be an actor, not a bureaucrat. Glover studied at the American Conserva-

At a Glance...

Born in 1948 in Georgia; raised in San Francisco, CA; married wife Asake (a jazz singer) c. 1972; children: Mandisa. *Education:* Graduated from San Francisco State University, late 1960s; also studied at the American Conservatory of Theatre and with the Black Box Theatre Company.

Career: Actor, 1977-. Researcher for Mayor's Office, San Francisco, late 1960s-early 1970s. Stage credits include *The Island, Sizwe Bansi Is Dead, "Master Harold"...and the Boys, The Blood Knot,* and *A Lesson From Alloes,* all by Athol Fugard, and *Suicide in B Flat,* by Sam Shepard. Film credits include *Escape from Alcatraz,* 1979; *Chu Chu and the Philly Flash,* 1981; *Iceman,* 1984; *Birdy,* 1984; *Places in the Heart,* 1984; *Witness,* 1985; *Silverado,* 1985; *The Color Purple,* 1985; *Lethal Weapon,* 1987; *Bat 21,* 1988; *Lethal Weapon 2,* 1989; *To Sleep With Anger,* 1990; *Flight of the Intruder,* 1991; *A Rage in Harlem,* 1991; *Pure Luck,* 1991; *Grand Canyon,* 1992; *Lethal Weapon 3,* 1993; *The Saint of Fort Washington,* 1993; *Bopha!,* 1993; *Angels in the Outfield,* 1994; *Maverick,* 1994; *Operation Dumbo Drop,* 1995; *Gone Fishin',* 1997; *Switchback,* 1997; *Antz,* 1998; *The Prince of Egypt,* 1998; *Beloved,* 1998; *Lethal Weapon 4,* 1998. Television performances include *Many Mansions,* PBS-TV; *A Raisin in the Sun,* American Playhouse, PBS-TV, 1989; and *Lonesome Dove,* CBS-TV, 1990.

Awards: Theatre World Award, 1982, for performance in *"Master Harold"...and the Boys;* honorary doctorate, Paine College, 1990; MTV Movie Award for *Lethal Weapon 3,* 1993; Image Award nomination for *Bopha!,* 1993; inducted into the Black Filmmakers Hall of Fame, 1998..

Addresses: *Home*—San Francisco, CA; *Office*—c/o Warner Brothers, 4000 Warner Blvd. Burbank, CA 91522.

---

tory of Theatre and the Black Box Theatre Company, moonlighted as a taxi driver, and quickly amassed a great amount of stage experience. He appeared in South African anti-apartheid playwright Athol Fugard's *The Island* and *Sizwe Bansi Is Dead* at the Eureka Theatre in San Francisco and the Los Angeles Actors Theatre, and later at New York City's Roundabout Theatre in Fugard's *The Blood Knot.* He also performed in Sam Shepard's *Suicide in B Flat* at the Magic Theatre in San Francisco and played Shakespeare's Macbeth at the Los Angeles Actors Theatre.

In 1982 Glover received recognition for his performance in Fugard's three-person *"Master Harold" ... and the Boys,* which premiered at the Yale Repertory Theatre in New Haven, Connecticut, and eventually moved to Broadway. Glover's performance as Willie, a good-hearted waiter whose white friend turns on him and a fellow African American waiter in a vicious barrage spurred by self-hatred, won him a Theatre World Award as one of the most promising new talents of 1982. *Master Harold* was praised by the *New York Times's* Frank Rich as one of the best and most well-written plays of recent times, which, he speculated, "may even outlast the society that spawned it—the racially divided South Africa of apartheid." Rich noted that "as the easygoing Willie, Mr. Glover is a paragon of sweet kindliness—until events leave him whipped and sobbing in a chair, his low moans serving as forlorn counterpoint to the play's main confrontation."

Earned Film Respect

Glover's performance in *Master Harold* was seen by film director Robert Benton, who cast Glover in the role of Mose in his 1984 film, *Places in the Heart.* Although the role originally called for an older man, Benton was so impressed with Glover's reading for the part that he had the script rewritten. Glover portrays an African American hobo-farmer who helps to save the farm of a Southern white widow played by Sally Field; for character reference Glover drew upon the many years of his youth spent on his grandparents' farm in Georgia. He told Lisa Belkin in the *New York Times* that in playing Mose he continually looked to the image of his grandfather "picking cotton and trusting in God." Glover was more profoundly influenced, however, by the tragedy of his mother's death in an automobile accident days before he went to work on the film. "She was with me in so many ways," he told Charlene Krista in *Films in Review,* especially in the film's poignant farewell scene. "I mean, she was there when I gave the handkerchief to Sally.... I think as actors, we probably would have found ways to get what we wanted, but what happened with my mother gave us the thrust. At a time I was mourning, it gave me strength."

Places in the Heart was nominated for best picture, as was the next film Glover appeared in, 1985's *Witness,* a romance-thriller set amid the Amish communities of Pennsylvania. *Witness* provided Glover the opportunity to create a completely different type of character--a dapper ex-police officer turned murderer. Also in 1985 Glover appeared in Lawrence Kasden's acclaimed western, *Silverado,* playing the role of Malachi, an African American cowboy-hero. Glover told Belkin that feedback from the role, especially from children, reinforced for him the importance of his image as an African American screen actor. "I've run into black kids who flash their two fingers at me like guns and who say, 'This ought to do' or 'I don't want to kill you and you don't want to be dead,'" he remarked, citing two of his lines from the film. "They're watching me. That's a responsibility."

Mister Stirred Controversy

The following year Glover appeared in *The Color Purple,* which provided one of his most complex roles and certainly his most controversial. In the Steven Spielberg-directed film based on Alice Walker's Pulitzer Prize-winning novel, Glover plays Mister, a southern widower who marries a young woman Celie (Whoopi Goldberg). Not only does he cruelly separate Celie from her beloved sister, but he intercepts and hides her sister's letters over a number of years. Mister is an abusive husband who exploits Celie ruthlessly, openly carrying on a love affair with a sultry blues singer named Shug. *The Color Purple* was protested by the NAACP, which felt the film typecast African American characters in stereotypical roles—in particular, Glover's Mister, which allegedly projected a negative image of African American men as violent and insensitive. Glover, who'd been criticized by some friends and relatives in the South, held that the character accurately depicted life in the early 1900s. "I hear the criticism," he told Belkin, "... [and] prefer to remember the reaction of older black women who say, 'That's the way it was.'" Glover nonetheless understood the disapproval and explained his character in a broader context. "Mister was an adequate representation of one particular story," he told *People.* "He's a product of his past and his present and I think we showed that he has some capabilities for changing." Glover's empathy with the reprehensible Mister translated onto the screen in a manner that was noted by many critics. Donald Bogle in *Blacks in American Films and Television* wrote that Glover "gave a tightly drawn, highly charged performance of a man who's both brute and simp," while Janet Maslin of the *New York Times* said that Glover "somehow makes a very sympathetic villain."

In 1987 Glover teamed up with screen idol Mel Gibson for the biggest movie hit of the year, the comic-action film *Lethal Weapon.* In it Glover portrays Roger Murtaugh, a homicide detective and dedicated family man, whose partner is a reckless--to the point of suicidal--officer named Martin Riggs (Gibson). Glover's stable character serves as a successful counterpoint to Gibson's crazed persona; their rapport made the movie a blockbuster at both the box office and with critics. Roger Ebert in *Roger Ebert's Movie Home Companion 1988 Edition* claimed that although Glover had important film roles in the past, his performance in *Lethal Weapon* "makes him a star. His job is to supply the movie's center of gravity, while all the nuts and weirdos and victims whirl around him." Two years later Glover and Gibson teamed up again for the equally successful *Lethal Weapon 2.* "Like its predecessor, *Lethal Weapon 2* is well-written and competently acted," noted Paul Baumann in *Commonweal.* "It's blood-drenched fluff, but there is real chemistry between these two accomplished actors."

Glover's performance in the little-noticed 1990 Charles Burnett film, *To Sleep With Anger,* has been judged by some critics to be among his best. Glover played a superstitious and manipulative man from the Deep South who pays a visit to old friends who have become a middle-class African American family in Los Angeles. Slowly but surely, Harry works to stir up simmering disputes within the family, which eventually come to a head. David Ansen wrote in *Newsweek* that "Glover, in what may be the best role of his film career, makes [Harry] an unforgettable trickster, both frightening and a little pathetic." Terrence Rafferty in the *New Yorker* noted that Glover turns in "an elegantly suggestive performance."

Maintained Sense of Responsibility

Throughout the diverse roles of his career, Glover has been aware of his responsibility as a role model for African Americans. Echoing the political activism of his earlier days, Glover was quoted as saying in *Jet:* "I've always felt my experience as an artist is inseparable from what happens with the overall body of Black people.... My sitting here now is the result of people, Black people and people of good conscience in particular, fighting a struggle in the real world, changing the real attitudes and the real social situation." This awareness results in a special discretion regarding the roles he plays. "I have to be careful about the parts I take," he told Belkin. "Given how this industry has dealt with people like me, the parts I take have to be political choices."

Following his role in *To Sleep With Anger,* Glover

starred as Commander Frank "Dooke" Camparelli in the 1991 action-adventure thriller *Flight of the Intruder*. That same year, he appeared in the films *A Rage in Harlem* and *Pure Luck*. He also earned praise for his portrayal of Simon, the diligent and moral tow-truck driver in the well-received 1992 film *Grand Canyon*. In 1993, Glover reprised his role as Roger Murtagh in *Lethal Weapon 3*, the third installment of the enormously popular action-adventure series. In the film, Murtagh teams with his partner Martin Riggs (played by Mel Gibson) to track down an ex-cop turned gun smuggler. *Lethal Weapon 3* earned Glover an MTV Movie Award. He also starred as Jerry, a homeless man who shows a mentally handicapped youth how to survive on the streets of New York in *The Saint of Fort Washington*. Also in 1993, Glover received an Image Award nomination for outstanding lead actor in a motion picture for his role as Micah Mangena in the film *Bopha!* Mangena is a black South African policeman who is torn between his duty to the state and the plight of his people who are suffering from the repression of apartheid. Glover received another Image Award nomination in 1993 for outstanding actor in a telefilm or miniseries for his work in *Queen*.

In 1994, Glover starred in the family feature film *Angels in the Outfield*. The film was a remake of a 1951 film and featured Glover as George Knox, the hot-tempered manager of a losing baseball team. Chris Hicks of the *Deseret News* remarked that the film's success at the box office was due to "the presence of Danny Glover and some razzle-dazzle special effects in its presentation of heavenly intervention....Glover is blustery in the film's first half and saintly in the second, naturally lending heft to the light material." That same year, Glover had a small role as a bank robber in *Maverick*, which starred Mel Gibson and Jodie Foster.

In 1995, Glover starred opposite Ray Liotta and Denis Leary in the Disney family film, *Operation Dumbo Drop*. The film centers around three Green Berets stationed in Vietnam who accept a mission to parachute an elephant into a remote jungle region in time for a ceremonial ritual. Reviews of the film were generally unfavorable. In his review of *Operation Dumbo Drop*, Zachary Woodruff of the *Tucson Weekly* wrote, "neither kids nor adults are likely to get too wrapped in the picture's strained Vietnam-era story, the shrill friction between Danny Glover and Ray Liotta, Denis Leary's one-note sardonic performance or anything else." However, a review of the film on the *Movie Snapshot* website remarked, "The "trunk and cheek" sarcasm and subtitles will be lost on younger audiences, but older kids will want to see 'Dumbo' fly."

In 1997, Glover teamed with another *Lethal Weapon* co-star, Joe Pesci, in the comedy *Gone Fishin*. Glover and Pesci play two slow-witted buddies who go on a long-awaited fishing trip to the Everglades and experience a series of mishaps during their trip. *Gone Fishin'* was a box-office dud and was mercilessly panned by critics. Clarissa Cruz of *The Providence Phoenix* wrote, "*Gone Fishin'* is one of the most mindlessly banal so-called comedies ever made. The movie tries to recreate the hackneyed buddy film formula, ala Cheech and Chong, but ends up more like a painfully interminable episode of *Three's Company*." Remington Dahl, in a review of the film on *www.movie-reviews.com* remarked, "*Gone Fishin'* places its every hope on the possibility that Glover and Pesci can rekindle their endearing *Lethal Weapon* chemistry. It never happens."

Glover also landed a role in the 1997 suspense thriller *Switchback*, which tells the story of the hunt for a serial killer in Texas. In the film, Glover plays Bob Goodall, a mysterious stranger who drives a Cadillac with an interior decorated with photos of nude women. Mark Caro of the *Chicago Tribune* reacted favorably to Glover's development of Goodall, "The director gets a big assist from his cast, particularly Glover, who digs into his ambiguous character with the same kind of gusto he brought to Charles Burnett's *To Sleep With Anger*." Caro also praised the film, calling *Switchback*, "well made, well acted and occasionally subtle." However, Frank Gabrenya of the *Columbus Dispatch* was less enthused with Glover's performance, "Glover recycles his suspicious house guest from *To Sleep With Anger*, complete with slippery charm and earthy laugh. The old pro is fun to watch, but his effort is wasted on a character who makes no sense outside the world of thriller stereotypes."

In 1998 Glover served as the voice of Barbatus, a grizzled soldier ant, in the highly acclaimed animated film *Antz*. He also provided the voice of Jethro in another animated film, *The Prince of Egypt*. Glover also starred opposite Oprah Winfrey in the film *Beloved*, which was based on a novel by Toni Morrison. Five years after the third *Lethal Weapon* was released, Glover and Mel Gibson were paired for yet another sequel, *Lethal Weapon 4*. Initial reaction to the idea was dubious. Critics doubted that the storyline could be freshened up, and pointed to the actors' advancing age as an unbelievable element in the plot. An *Entertainment Weekly* writer remarked, "[Gibson and Glover are] still very attractive men, to be sure, but it's distracting to worry about their coronary health while they're being battered and shot at in the course of a day's work. Shouldn't they just cash out and discuss pension plans?" Audiences did not agree with this assessment, as *Lethal Weapon 4* surpassed the opening-weekend revenues of the previous three *Lethal Weapon* sequels, reaping $34 million upon release. Glover capped a tremendously successful 1998 by being inducted into the Black Filmmakers Hall of Fame. He was also appointed Goodwill Ambassador for the United Nations Development Program.

Glover is pragmatic about his career, recognizing that an actor is only as good as his last work and that the next good part may be a long time coming. As he told Kevin Powell in *Essence,* "I want to feel that I made choices that empowered me and substantiated me as a human being. My career is going to be here and gone. But I'm always going to be a human being. And I want to look myself in the mirror and say that I was the human being I wanted to be."

Sources

Books

Bogle, Donald, *Blacks in American Films and Television: An Illustrated Encyclopedia,* Simon & Schuster, 1988.

Ebert, Roger, *Roger Ebert's Movie Home Companion 1988 Edition,* Andrews, McMeel & Parker, 1987.

People Weekly Magazine Guide to Movies on Video, edited by Ralph Novak and Peter Travers, Macmillan, 1987.

Periodicals

Chicago Tribune, October 31, 1997.
Columbus Dispatch, October 31, 1997.
Commonweal, October 6, 1989.
Deseret News, July 15, 1994.
Ebony, March 1986.
Entertainment Weekly, July 17, 1998; July 24, 1998.
Essence, July 1994.
Films in Review, April 1985.
Gentleman's Quarterly, July 1989.
Jet, March 17, 1986; April 6, 1987; October 31, 1988; September 18, 1989; March 5, 1990.
Maclean's, November 19, 1990.
Newsweek, October 22, 1990.
New Yorker, November 5, 1990.
New York Times, May 5, 1982; May 6, 1982; May 16, 1982; December 18, 1985; January 26, 1986.
People, March 10, 1986.
The Providence Phoenix, June 5-12, 1997.
Tucson Weekly, August 17, 1995.

Other

Additional information for this profile was obtained from the Movie Snapshot website at www.moviesnapshot.com; and a review by Remington Dahl on www.moviereviews.com.

—Michael E. Mueller and David G. Oblender

Elliott S. Hall

1938(?)—

Automobile executive

Elliott S. Hall is commonly referred to as "Ford's man in Washington" in his role as vice-president of governmental affairs for the Big Three automaker, a position he has held since 1987. He was the first African American to become a vice-president at the company, but prior to this juncture in his career, Hall enjoyed a distinguished career as a prominent attorney in Detroit. His name was even mentioned frequently as a possible successor to Detroit's longtime mayor, Coleman A. Young, during the 1980s. However, Hall has excelled in his high-profile, powerful Washington job and has become active in numerous civic affairs in the nation's capital, as he once had in his hometown. "You'd have to search high and low to find someone who didn't respect him," said the man who eventually succeeded Young, Dennis Archer, of Hall in a *Detroit News* interview in 1985. "He has a tremendous amount of integrity."

Hall was born in the late 1930s in Detroit, the second youngest of eight children. His father was a steelworker employed at the Ford company's Rouge River plant, for many years the largest industrial complex in the world. As a teenager, he sold newspapers and attended Chadsey High School on the city's west side, where he excelled only on the track team. Poor grades caused him to graduate 267th among his 313 senior classmates, who nevertheless voted him Most Likely to Succeed. Hall then became the first person in his family to attend college, earning a bachelor's degree from Detroit's Wayne State University, where he worked in the school library for minimal wages. One summer, he wanted to apply for a temporary job at one of the auto plants, but his father cautioned him about working in the industry. "I wanted to get a summer job," at the Rouge plant, Hall recalled in an interview with *Black Enterprise* writer Karen D. Gutloff. "My dad said no. He was afraid I'd start making money at Ford and not continue school."

Black Panther Lawyer

After earning a law degree from Wayne State, Hall began his career as an attorney in the mid-1960s defending civil-rights cases. His name first appeared in the local media in 1970 when he successfully defended members of the local Black Panther Party who had been involved in a shoot-out with Detroit police; the incident occurred during an era of tense race relations in the city, and Hall was one of a number of rising African American attorneys and civil-rights activists renowned for their leftist beliefs and battles against a white political establishment. In 1972, he was elected to head the Detroit chapter of the National Association for the Advancement of Colored People (NAACP)—at a time when it was the biggest chapter of the organization in the country—and was also active in a local group, the United Black Coalition. His prominence led to his appointment by Coleman Young, Detroit's first African American mayor, in the first months of his mayoral administration in

At a Glance...

Born c. 1938, in Detroit, MI; son of a steelworker and Ethel Hall; first marriage to Evelyn Hall ended in divorce; married Shirley Robinson Hall (a special-projects fundraiser for the Detroit Symphony Orchestra), c. 1970; children: (first marriage) Lannis, Frederick; (second marriage) Tiffany. *Education:* Received bachelor's and law degrees from Wayne State University.

Career: Began career as an attorney in Detroit, 1965; corporation counsel for the city of Detroit, 1974-75; attorney in private practice, 1975-83; Wayne County Prosecutor's Office, chief assistant prosecutor, 1983-85; Dykema Gossett Spencer Goodnow and Trigg (law firm), Detroit, partner, 1985-87; Ford Motor Company, vice-president of governmental affairs, 1987-; served as president of the United Black Coalition and the Detroit chapter of the National Association for the Advancement of Colored People (NAACP), early 1970s.

Awards: Distinguished Alumnus Award, Wayne State University Law School.

Addresses: *Office*—Ford Motor Company, 1350 I St. NW, Washington, DC 20005-3323.

1974. Young named Hall as the city of Detroit's corporation counsel, a job in which he suddenly found himself in charge of forty lawyers. Hall, his former rival in the election as head of the NAACP post, told the *Detroit Free Press*'s Ed Boyer at the time, "will make an excellent corporation counsel because he has guts, imagination, and access to a lot of good legal minds." With his connections, Hall announced plans to encourage some of Detroit's top law firms into providing advisory help for the embattled city, which faced numerous problems at the time. "Some law firms have made a lot of money from handling city business," Hall told Boyer in the *Detroit Free Press*. "I think they're willing to repay the city by providing free legal help."

Hall's appointment was part of a new era in the city of Detroit that was ignited by Young's election—once the lawyer against Detroit police officers in the much-publicized Black Panther case, Hall was now the Police Department's lawyer. He also planned to make the department more aggressive, not just a defensive body working to protect the city in the array of cases filed against it, and also told the *Detroit Free Press* that he wanted the department to begin filing suits against landlords who refused to rent to African American tenants, for instance. He vowed to return to private practice some day, but said he was happy to work for the public good for a time. "I'm a committed cat," Hall told Boyer. "I don't know where I got the bug from. I was born and raised here in Detroit, and everything I've got out of life I got out of this city."

Founded Own Firm

Disappointingly, Hall spent less than a year on the job, and it was a year fraught with problems with the administration and press. "I was accustomed to making my own decisions," Hall said of his brief stint in an interview with the *Detroit News*'s Brenda Ingersoll Gave in 1985. "And the confines of being a department head became unpleasant." Hall returned to private practice, and eventually founded his own firm in Detroit. In 1983, he became the first African American chief assistant prosecutor for Wayne County, of which Detroit is the seat. His tenure in this high-profile job was marked by one notable, yet noble failure. Following a rash of shootings, Hall put forth a proposal to ban the sale and possession of handguns in Detroit in an effort to curb violent crime. However, the city administration and the general public, many of whom kept a legally obtained weapon for protection, soundly rejected the idea.

During the 1980s Hall was considered a viable mayoral candidate to succeed Coleman Young, who would go on to an unprecedented five four-year terms. But Hall, like many other prominent younger leaders in Detroit, vowed never to run against the man who had done so much for his career and for Detroit in general. In a 1985 interview with the *Detroit News,* Hall asserted that "I would never, ever run against the mayor. He's been too good to me."

Historic First at Ford

During the mid-1980s, Hall became a full partner at a top Detroit law firm, Dykema Gossett Spencer Goodnow and Trigg. His skills in the courtroom attracted the attention of Ford executives when he represented a half-dozen of the company's executives who had been charged with unfairly conspiring to oust one of their own. The case was thrown out of court in 1986 as contrary to law, a ruling credited to Hall's persuasive argument before the bench. In late 1987, he became vice-president of governmental affairs for Ford, the first African American to be hired at such a level at the company. He moved to Washington with his wife, a Democratic Party activist, and young daughter. (Hall also has two sons by his first marriage.) Hall's move was viewed by some former colleagues and associates from

Detroit with a bit of skepticism, for had made his career as the quintessential attorney, not corporate legal executive. "Sure, I agonized a bit," Hall told Marcia Stepanek of the *Detroit Free Press* about his decision. "But the agony was over leaving Detroit."

> "I've got to give something back. There are too many of my brothers and sisters out there who do not have what I've been fortunate enough to acquire—an education and a series of decent places to work."

One of Hall's first challenges was to help extricate, without losing money, Ford's investment in a South African automaker. American companies were barred from doing business in South Africa as a result of official sanctions in protest of its harsh apartheid laws, which kept the country's black majority in abysmal poverty. Hall, on behalf of Ford, argued that the company's onetime payment of $61 million would preserve nearly 5,000 jobs at the South African Motor Corporations plant, many of them held by black workers. Hall earned some criticism from friends back in Detroit from his civil-rights days, but as he told the *Detroit News*'s Bryan Gruley, he viewed his new role at Ford as a means to achieve common good on a higher level. Admittedly, Hall told Gruley, he once opposed lobbying as "perhaps not quite ethical," earlier in life, but now stood on the other side of the political fence. "One of the things you learn when you grow older ... is that many elements have to exist in this system," Hall remarked. "Ford employs 104,000 people, GM employs over 300,000. These businesses exist in our democratic system. They feed people, they feed families, they contribute to institutions."

An Important Washington Player

In the interview with Gutloff in *Black Enterprise,* Hall explained the purpose of his job as Ford's vice president for governmental affairs. "Due to the immense size of Ford Motor Co., there is rarely a time when there is no legislation pending in the U.S. Congress that does not impact in some way on company activity," Hall said. "It is our job to prevent passage of legislation that adversely impacts the company and to encourage legislation that would enhance the economic growth and competitiveness of the auto industry." Hall's duties involve meeting with members of Congress and their staff; he also has had the ear of the President, officials from the National Highway Traffic Safety Administration and the Environmental Protection Agency, and doles out money from Ford to political action committees. His lobbying efforts have involved battling environmentalist and consumer-safety lobbying forces over pending gas-mileage and safety regulations for the auto industry, as well as working to improve the trade balance with Japan. Hall's office, staffed by 26 lawyers, aides, and other associates, also oversees the leasing of Ford luxury vehicles to local politicians and White House staff members.

In Washington, Hall is known as a bridge-builder, not a hardball player like many top lobbyists for some of the nation's most powerful corporations. "This town is about credibility," Hall told *Black Enterprise*'s Gutloff. "I've found that having a relaxed, informed demeanor is more effective than the high-pressure, 'I gotta have your vote, you've got to do this for me.' I give a congressman or senator both sides of an issue. But of course, I tell them why they should choose my side."

A political future back in Detroit seems unlikely for Hall, who sat on a District of Columbia committee charged with revamping the city's troubled public-school system. He is also a member of the board of the Washington Performing Arts Society, the National Symphony Orchestra, as well as the Federal City Council, a private group of prominent Washingtonians. Such involvement continues Hall's longtime commitment to social and economic justice, though it plays out on a different field than defending Black Panthers in court. "I figure I've got to give something back," Hall told Gutloff in *Black Enterprise.* "There are too many of my brothers and sisters out there who do not have what I've been fortunate enough to acquire—an education and a series of decent places to work."

Sources

Periodicals

Black Enterprise, June 1993, p. 308.
Detroit Free Press, April 17. 1973; May 9, 1974; May 13, 1974; October 17, 1988, p. 3C.
Detroit News, June 23, 1985; September 23, 1987.

—Carol Brennan

Margaret A. Haywood

1912—

Judge

The Honorable Margaret A. Haywood, senior judge of the Superior Court of the District of Columbia, is perhaps best known for her work as counsel in the epochal Thompson Restaurant case, which went to the U. S. Supreme Court and resulted in the decision that ended segregated restaurant operation in the District of Columbia. On June 23, 1973, while she was an associate judge of the Superior Court of the D.C., she was elected the first female to head the United Church of Christ and the first African American woman to lead a major U. S. denomination.

Born Margaret Austin in Knoxville, Tennessee on October 8, 1912, Haywood is the only child of Mayme F. and Jonathan William Austin. While Margaret was still a girl, the family moved to D.C., where her father was serving as financial secretary of a large fraternal order. Hanging around this office is where she plodded at typing practice and developed an interest in becoming a lawyer. Haywood credits her father for having inspired her interest in law. Her father was associated with the late Attorney Benjamin Gaskins and former Judge Walter C. Hueston, and she spent evenings after school around their offices. Not only was she intrigued by legal operations, but mastered typing and the operation of other office machinery.

The most influential person in Haywood's life was her father, Jonathan William Austin, who died in 1959. He encouraged her to attend Cardozo High School. Haywood was one of the first pupils to attend Cardozo High School studying business. Later, it was also her father who encouraged her to attend the Robert H. Terrell Law School in Washington, D.C.

After getting her degree from Terrell Law School in 1940, Haywood gave five years service as a volunteer teacher at Terrell. The Terrell Law School was organized by practicing attorneys who gave voluntary services as instructors, however, it had accreditation problems because of the lack of full-time professors. It was eventually phased out as black law students were admitted to other institutions.

Before beginning her law practice, the attractive Haywood, nic-named "Peggy," was able to work in secretarial positions because of the strong typing skills she developed in her father's law office. In 1942, she began

At a Glance...

Born Margaret Austin, October 8, 1912, in Knoxville, Tennessee. Divorced. Children: Geraldine H. Hoffman. *Education:* Robert H. Terrell Law School, 1940

Career: Senior Superior Court Judge. General Practice Attorney, 1940-72; DC Council, Member 1967-72; Superior Court District of Columbia, Associate Judge, 1972-82; Senior Judge 1982-

Awards: Cited Lambda Kappa Mu, Outstanding Sorority of Year, 1947, 1968, 1972; National Association for the Advancement of Colored People Trophy, 1950; one of America's Outstanding Women, National Council of Negro Women, 1951; elected to Afro-American Newspaper Honor Roll, 1951; Sigma Delta Tau, Outstanding Professional Service, 1957; National Bar Association Award, 1968; Woman of Year, Oldest Inhabitants, 1969; Woman Lawyer of Year, Women's Bar Association, 1972; DC Women's Commission, Trophy, Hall of Fame Inductee; Washington Bar Association, Charles Hamilton Medallion of Merit for Contribution to Jurisprudence, 1980; Honorary Degrees: Elmhurst College, Humanics, 1974; Carleton College, DHL, 1975; Catawba College, DL, 1976; Doane College, DL, 1979; Numerous other awards and honorary degrees.

Addresses: *Office*—Senior Judge, Superior Court of the District of Columbia; 500 Indiana Avenue NW, 5520, Washington, DC 20001. *Home*—100 Coast Blvd., La Jolla, CA 92037-4601.

practicing law with the noted firm of Houston, Houston, and Hastie. In April of 1954, Haywood was selected as 'Woman of Achievement For the Year' by the Barristers Wives of Washington, D.C.

Before receiving the award from the Barristers Wives, Haywood had already won several awards and trophies. In 1951, she was recognized as "One of America's Outstanding Women" by the National Council of Negro Women. She has since won numerous awards and honorary degrees for her outstanding work as an attorney and for her community involvement. Her awards include, the 1968 "National Bar Association Award," the 1972 "Woman Lawyer of Year, Women's Bar Association," the "DC Women's Commission, Trophy, Hall of Fame Inductee," and the 1980 Washington Bar Association, Charles Hamilton Medallion of Merit for Contribution to Jurisprudence" among many others.

In May of 1945, Margaret A. Haywood was sworn in as an Associate Judge of the Superior Court of the District of Columbia by Chief Justice Harlan Fiske Stone. *The Pittsburgh Courier* quoted Haywood as saying, "That was the most thrilling experience I have ever known." After Haywood had been practicing law for 25 years, she was named by President Lyndon B. Johnson to the post of D. C. Councilwoman. In reference to the D. C. Council appointment, *The Washington Post* quoted Haywood as saying, "I feel I am part of history." Haywood's first inkling that she was being considered for the post came from President Johnson himself. She was ushered into the President's office at the White House, and the first thing President Johnson asked Mrs. Haywood was how long she had lived in Washington. *The Washington Post* quoted Haywood as saying, "I was so nervous, I couldn't count. I just told him I was 55 years and I'd lived in the District since I was eight. He just grinned at me and said I'd lived here 47 years. He knew his arithmetic, all right."

Busy Schedule

Haywood had an intense feeling about keeping her work current, she preferred having meals sent to the office or grabbing a sandwich at a snack bar and eating while driving rather than spending time eating in a restaurant. In addition to her busy work schedule, Haywood is known to be very active in the community. She has served as president of the Gamma Delta Epsilon (legal) Fraternity, president of the Theta Chapter, Lambda Kappa Mu, Business and Professional Women's Sorority, second vice president of the Washington Bar Association, and active with the Washington Urban League and in numerable other community programs."

Haywood's church life has not suffered because of her busy schedule. In fact, she has managed to compliment one with the other. She is chair of the governing committee of the institute of church and society of the Greater Washington Council of Churches, a group whose role she describes as "acquainting church members with public issues where moral positions should be explored." stated the Washington Post. One such issue was the Administration's Reorganization plan for the District. As a result of her church committee's study, a communication was forwarded to the President, approving the plan and urging that he go forward with it. *The Washington Post* quoted Haywood as saying, "We did say, however, that our goal is still home rule, but this was a step in the right direction." On June 23, 1973, Margaret Austin Haywood was elected the first woman to head the United Church of Christ and the first African American female to lead a major U. S. denomination."

Loved by Superiors, Peers, and Subordinates

Haywood's "sweet" personality is an asset, causing people of all walks of life to be fond of her. When Haywood went to L'Enfant Plaza for the ceremony dedicating the 10th Street Overlook site as Benjamin Baneker Park, she was greeted with a fond kiss by the mayor; and also received cheery welcomes by her fellow platform guests at the ceremony. An even more revealing glimpse of the kind of person Margaret Haywood really is, comes when she enters the U. S. District Court record office where she is hailed good-heartedly by the clerks and other staffers. According to an article in the *Evening Star and Daily News,* when Haywood left her post as a Washington Metropolitan Area Transit Authority board member fellow subway agency directors gave her a fond farewell. The article says that one of the farewell gifts Haywood received was a piece of the original Metro track--the piece of track was a one-inch cross-section, suitable for keeping on one's desk.

Even a person like Haywood, who seems to be able to get along with most people has had to deal with racism. When asked about Congresswoman Shirley Chisholm's comment that "she has suffered more discrimination as a woman than racial discrimination," Haywood told *The Washington Post,* "I was my father's 'little boy,' so my whole outlook may have been different from that of the average girl. I have never called on men to make a difference in their proceedings because I was present. For two years I was the only woman in my law classes and the guys just thought of me as one of the fellows. In my ... years of law practice, there may have been occasions of discrimination from fellow lawyers or judges, but they would have to have been very limited." Haywood admits her experience may not be the norm, and added, "I respect this as being unusual, because in many instances women have felt differential treatment. Racially, of course, I have felt discrimination much more so than any against women."

In her paper, entitled "The Modern Challenge to Women in Law," Haywood writes, "...no lawyer who is a woman, fails in awareness that while the problems of her community really are more largely human than merely racial, yet racism contributes so dangerously to inhumanities that it is folly to let it exist!! ...she (the woman lawyer) then must take her case to the community. She becomes, as public servant and public spirited citizen, advocate of the community--for it and against it--for its improvement and against its self-destruction."

Housewife and Mother Too!

With all Haywood's career and community activities, it's hard to believe she was just as busy at home. During the height of Haywood's career, along with her many professional obligations, she successfully maintained a happy home for her husband and daughter. Haywood usually does the cooking at home on Sundays and holidays, and is a wiz with a backyard grill. She gourmet cooks with seafoods, meats, and casseroles. When time permits, Haywood also enjoys sewing and apparently is quite good at it. Haywood once used a gift of Chinese silk to make herself an outfit to wear to a banquet.

Age has not stopped Haywood's activity, nor her achievements. As recently as 1991, Haywood was one of the recipients of "the annual 'Women of Achievement' award from the D.C. Federation of Business & Professional Women Inc. Today, at age 88, The Honorable Margaret A. Haywood maintains an office in Washington, D. C. and also works in La Jolla, California, where she now lives.

Sources

Book

Stuber, Irene, *Women of Achievement and Herstory,* Episode 329, June 23, 1995.

Periodicals

Capitol Spotlight, April 22, 1954.
Evening Star and Daily News, July 14, 1972.
Pittsburgh Courier, February 2, 1946
Washington Afro-American, January 1, 1972, June 9, 1945.
Washington Post, 1968, 1971, 1991.

—Sadie Mungro

Willie W. Herenton

1940—

Mayor of Memphis

In 1991, Willie W. Herenton made history when he was elected mayor of Memphis, Tennessee. Memphis—the city where Rev. Martin Luther King Jr. was assassinated in 1968—had never previously elected an African American mayor. According to an article about Herenton in *Ebony* magazine, "His victory has gone a long way toward changing the long-standing view of Memphis as 'a backward, backwater, riverboat town' whose black residents were often described as not sophisticated enough to unite behind one black candidate."

As mayor, Herenton promised to bring about a new era of racial cooperation and economic progress. "This is truly the dawn of a new era, an era that will move this city toward unprecedented unity and prosperity for all our city," he told *Ebony*. "We are going to reach new plateaus in human understanding; we're going to experience tremendous economic growth, and we're going to change the national image of this city." Seven years after Herenton was elected, Jonathan Scott, writing in the *Memphis Business Journal,* praised him as a "consummate politician" and "chief lobbyist for the city," while also working "to address those social and economic issues too long ignored by others, such as inner city revitalization, affordable housing, and minority business development."

Chosen Memphis School Superintendent

Herenton was born on April 23, 1940 in Memphis. His parents separated when he was a child, and he and his sister were raised by his mother and grandmother. The family was poor, and as a young man Herenton helped to support the family by chopping and picking cotton. Initially, he had hoped to become a professional boxer like his idols, Joe Louis and Sugar Ray Robinson. While Herenton later became a Golden Gloves champion, he decided to give up boxing to pursue a career in education.

After graduating from high school, Herenton worked his way through LeMoyne College in Memphis, earning a B.A. in 1963. Later that year, he became an elementary school teacher in the Memphis City School System. Meanwhile, he continued to pursue his graduate studies, earning an M.A. from Memphis State University in 1966. In 1967, at the age of 28, Herenton became the

At a Glance...

Born Willie W. Herenton, April 23, 1940, in Memphis, TN; married Ida Jones; children: Errol, Rodney, and Andrea. *Education:* LeMoyne-Owen College, B.S., 1963; Memphis State University, M.A., 1966; Southern Illinois University, Ph.D, 1971.

Career: Memphis City School System, elementary school teacher, 1963-67, elementary school principal, 1967-73, deputy superintendent, 1974-78, superintendent, 1979-92; City of Memphis, mayor, 1992-.

Awards: Rockefeller Foundation Fellow, 1973; Horatio Alger Award, 1988; honorary doctorates from Rhodes College and Christian Brothers College.

Memberships: National Board of Directors of the Urban League, Junior Achievement, National Executive Board of the National Conference of Christians and Jews, Rotary Club, Economic Club of Memphis.

Addresses: *Home*—Memphis, TN. *Office*—Mayor, City of Memphis, 125 Mid-America Mall, Ste. 200, Memphis, TN.

youngest elementary school principal in Memphis. In addition to his administrative duties, he also worked toward a PhD from Southern Illinois University, a goal he achieved in 1971. From 1973 to 1974, Herenton was a fellow of the Rockefeller Foundation.

In 1974, Herenton became deputy superintendent of the Memphis City School System. Five years later, he was appointed superintendent, becoming the first African American to hold this position. In both 1980 and 1984, *Executive Educator Journal* named Herenton as one of the top 100 school administrators in the United States and Canada. In 1988, he was given a Horatio Alger Award, in recognition of his dedication to community leadership, individual initiative, and commitment to excellence. According to the Horatio Alger Award's website, Herenton was "a role model for more than 100,000 youths in his system, the majority of whom are black. Herenton is seen as a symbol of what they can achieve."

The following year, Herenton established a pioneering program that permitted seven inner-city schools to close, then reopen with hand-picked staffs and greater autonomy. Before the pilot program began, some of the schools had annual teacher turnover rates of 50 percent. By the end of the program's third year, this figure had dropped dramatically. Herenton's innovative program won national attention.

Elected Mayor of Memphis

In 1991, after 12 years as school superintendent, Herenton announced that he would run for mayor of Memphis. Although almost 60 percent of the city's 645,000 residents are African American, Memphis had not previously elected an African American mayor, unlike other southern cities such as Atlanta, Georgia, and Birmingham, Alabama. For this election, various African American groups pulled together, holding neighborhood summit meetings and organizing the first African American People's Convention in April of 1991. The 5,000 delegates overwhelmingly nominated Herenton as the consensus candidate for the African American community.

On October 3, 1991, the day of the election, there was a record turnout among African American voters. Herenton managed to defeat nine-year incumbent Richard Hackett by a mere 142 votes—the closest election for mayor in the city's history. "As I travel across this city, I see black folks with their heads held high," Herenton was quoted as saying in *Ebony*. "There's a new look. A new talk of self-esteem, and that's what makes me feel good." Herenton pledged to fight racism and poverty, while encouraging tourism and exploring new initiatives in crime prevention, education, and housing.

In 1995, Herenton announced that he would run for re-election. In his campaign, he touted his accomplishments as mayor: the city's improved financial position, the recruitment of several major companies to the city, new and renovated housing for low-income residents, downtown redevelopment, and improved race relations. As the election approached, a second term for Herenton seemed assured. According to a poll by the *Commercial Appeal* (Memphis), held a few weeks before the election, three out of four Memphis residents approved of his job performance. "The big uncertainty about the Oct. 5 election: What percentage of registered voters will vote?" Susan Adler Thorp wrote in the *Commercial Appeal*. "The big certainty: Mayor W.W. Herenton will be re-elected." On election day, Herenton won 74 percent of the vote—including a large percentage of white voters— and soundly defeated his three opponents.

In his second term, Herenton continued his struggle to

bring economic investment into the city. "For the past two years, we've experienced $1 billion in capital investment and about 10,000 new jobs have been created annually. So Memphis has a bustling economy," Herenton told Jonathan Scott of the *Memphis Business Journal* in 1998. Still, Herenton told Scott, he was concerned about more than just economic issues. "We've made some gains, but we still have a long way to go," he was quoted as saying in the *Memphis Business Journal*. "While the economic growth of the city has been moving forward, I'm also concerned about quality of life issues such as housing, crime, and education." Herenton has fought to bring a permanent Grammy Award museum to Memphis, and to revitalize the deteriorating neighborhoods near its historic downtown.

Fought Difficult Campaign

In 1999, Herenton declared that he would seek a third term as mayor. This time, he was challenged by Joe Ford, a member of a well-known political family in Memphis, as well as 13 other opponents. Blake Fontenay, writing in *The Commercial Appeal,* described the run-up to the election as "one of most contentious and expensive campaigns in the city's history." Herenton managed to win 46 percent of the vote, 20 percentage points more than Ford, his closest competitor. According to an editorial published in the *Commercial Appeal,* "Mayor Willie Herenton's impressive—and surprisingly easy—re-election victory has provided a solid foundation on which he can plan his third term, as well as an encouraging expression of solidarity among Memphis voters. Herenton assembled a winning coalition that was not limited by geography, race, political party or demographics."

Herenton has gained a reputation as a tough negotiator, who puts the needs of his city first. "I view myself as being desirous of working harmoniously with all government officials as long as they do the right thing," he was quoted as saying in the *Memphis Business Journal.* "I will never compromise on what is in the best interest of this city just to get along...."

Herenton has received numerous awards for outstanding public service, including honorary doctorates from Rhodes College and Christian Brothers College. He has served on several corporate boards, including Promus Companies and First Tennessee National Corporation. He has also served on the National Board of Directors of the Urban League, Junior Achievement, and the National Executive Board of the National Conference of Christians and Jews. He has devoted time to many civic and service organizations such as March of Dimes, United Way, the Rotary Club, the Boy Scouts and the Economic Club of Memphis. Herenton is divorced, and has three children, Errol, Rodney, and Andrea.

Sources

Periodicals

Commercial Appeal (Memphis), Oct. 8, 1999; Oct. 10, 1999; Oct. 19, 1999; Oct. 24, 1999; Oct. 6, 1995; Oct. 5, 1995; Oct. 2, 1995; Sept. 24, 1995; Sept. 3, 1995.
Ebony, March 1992, p. 106.
Memphis Business Journal, March 9, 1998; June 1, 1998.

Other

Additional information for this profile was provided by the mayor's office, City of Memphis.

—Carrie Golus

Oliver W. Hill

1907—

Attorney

Oliver Hill was still a young man when he realized that the most effective way to achieve an equal footing for African Americans was through the legal system. He went to law school and blazed a trail virtually unparalleled in the history of the civil rights movement. In 1948, Hill became the first African American elected to the Richmond City Council since Reconstruction. "Oliver Hill is one of the pioneer civil rights lawyers of our age," Ronald L. Plesser said in 1994. Plesser, the section chair of the Individual Rights and Responsibilities, was announcing Hill's selection as the recipient of that year's Thurgood Marshall award from the American Bar Association. "His lifetime commitment to achieving equal rights through law positively affected the direction of the entire nation at a crucial time in our history."

Born Oliver White Hill in Richmond, Virginia in 1907, Hill had an early fascination with the role of law in society as it related to African Americans. While at Howard University, he and other students realized there was no hope of attaining equal rights through the U.S. Congress. That branch of government clung to the 1896 Supreme Court decision in *Plessy vs. Ferguson,* a case that stated that the provision of "separate but equal" facilities for African Americans did not violate the Thirteenth and Fourteenth amendments, amendments which outlawed slavery after the Civil War.

Attended Law School

The *Plessy vs. Ferguson* decision led to the creation of Jim Crow laws, which institutionalized racial separation in schools, public facilities and transportation. "So our only hope was to go back through the courts and get the courts to reinterpret and correct the mistake made in 1896," Hill said at a program celebrating the 40th anniversary of *Brown vs. Board of Education,* and excerpted in *Human Rights.* "And that is the reason I went to law school." While attending the Howard University School of Law, Hill became friends with a fellow student, Thurgood Marshall, who would become the lead attorney in the *Brown* case and a future Supreme Court Justice.

Hill began his law practice in 1934 and was one of the few African American lawyers in the South. Many of his cases were race related, and Hill was involved in litiga-

At a Glance...

Born Oliver White Hill on May 1, 1907 in Richmond, VA; son of Olivia Lewis White-Hill and William Henry White II; married Beresenia Walker, September 5, 1934; children: Oliver White Hill, Jr. *Education:* Howard University, AB, 1931; Howard University School of Law, JD, 1933.

Career: Attorney, Roanoke, Virginia, 1934-36; law practice, Richmond, Virginia, 1939-61; elected to Richmond City Council, 1948-50; worked on *Davis vs. County School Board of Prince Edward County* (Virginia), one of the five cases the Supreme Court combined into their 1954 decision of *Brown vs. Board of Education,* 1951-54; named to committee on government contract compliance, 1952; FHA, assistant to commissioner, 1961-66; partner and founder, Hill, Tucker & Marsh, 1966–.

Selected awards: Chicago Defender Merit Award, 1948; Howard University Alumni Award, 1950; Omega Man of the Year, Omega Psi Phi, 1957; National Bar Association, Lawyer of the Year, 1959; Judicial Council of National Barr Association, 1979; NAACP Legal Defense and Educational Fund, The Simple Justice Award, 1986; The Justice Thurgood Marshall Award, 1994; Oliver Hill Day in Roanoke, VA, 1995; Oliver Hill Courts Building in Richmond, VA, 1996.

Addresses: *Home*—3108 Noble Ave., Richmond, VA 23222.

tion involving voting rights and equal access to housing and public facilities. In 1947 Hill ran for the Virginia House of Delegates, the lone African American in a field of 18 candidates seeking seven seats. Hill fell 190 votes short. "Had he been nominated and then elected in November," the *New York Times* reported at the time, "Mr. Hill would have been the first [black] to occupy a seat in the General Assembly since the session of 1889-1890."

Elected to Richmond City Council

The following year Hill sought political office again, this time as a candidate for the Richmond City Council. Hill's quest was successful and he became the first African American to be elected in Richmond in 52 years. Hill placed ninth in a field of 29 candidates for nine vacant seats and finished ahead of some white candidates. In a *New York Times* editorial, the election was hailed as "a good omen for the South." The article continued, "That the candidate is an educated person and a young man is especially important, for from the age of thirty-one, he can look forward to long years of service to his people and to his community as a whole."

In 1950, Hill lost his bid for reelection to the Richmond City Council and returned to his private law practice. In 1951 another council member resigned to take a job outside of Richmond, and the all-white council had to decide who would replace him. Hill was mentioned as a possible replacement, but his increasingly outspoken views against segregation had sparked opposition within the council and the white community. In a move that angered Richmond's 40,000 African Americans, the council chose a former white council member to fill the vacant seat.

By this time, Hill was actively assisting the National Association for the Advancement of Colored People in their lawsuits against the state of Virginia. These lawsuits demanded improved educational facilities for African American children. Hill eventually became the leading attorney in the case of *Davis vs. County School Board of Prince Edward County* (Virginia), one of five cases that the Supreme Court combined into their 1954 decision of *Brown vs. Board of Education.* That decision, which overturned *Plessy vs. Ferguson,* was the culmination of nearly 20 years of hard work.

Involved in Landmark Court Case

"Two or three of us, including Thurgood Marshall, wanted to do something about segregation from the get-go in the 1930s," Hill recalled at the *Brown* symposium. "We had to educate judges and the white and black public as to what we were trying to do.... We were careful with our cases. We never carried a case to the Supreme Court that we didn't have well documented. Anything weak, we passed aside." The *Brown* decision, which integrated public schools throughout the United States, was a landmark case that helped to set the civil rights movement in motion. In overturning *Plessy vs. Ferguson,* the Supreme Court ruled that education was an essential element of modern life and that the doctrine of "separate but equal" was unconstitutional. Hill and his colleagues then went to work implementing the Court's decision, which was a difficult task because the state of Virginia had taken steps to dismantle the public school system rather than desegregate. Hill again took to the courtroom to ensure that the state's public school system would remain intact and become integrated. Forty years later, on the occasion of Hill's acceptance of the Marshall Award, James E. Coleman, Jr. of the American Bar Association remarked, "By using the courts, rather than physical resistance, to fight desegregation, Virginia made civil rights lawyers' work much more difficult....If the state's strategy had succeeded, desegregation would have taken much longer."

Following his efforts to desegregate Virginia's public schools, Hill returned to private practice and established the law firm of Hill, Tucker & Marsh in 1966. He continued to work for civil rights causes throughout his career. In 1994, 40 years after the *Brown* decision, Hill lamented the state of race relations in America in a *Human Rights* interview, "I can't understand why Americans are willing to send their children—black and white—to foreign lands to fight, and sometimes die, to preserve the American concepts of freedom, democracy, and civil rights when at the same time these same Americans are unwilling to undergo an occasional inconvenience or suffer a slight financial loss to help break down racial barriers and racial discrimination in *this* country."

Sources

Human Rights, Spring 1994, p. 12; Summer 1994, p. 6.

Life, September 27, 1948, p. 47.

New Republic, April 9, 1951, p. 7.

New York Times, August 7, 1947, p. 23; June 10, 1948, p. 16; June 12, 1948, p. 14; October 1, 1948, p. 22; June 15, 1950, p. 27; January 11, 1952, p. 13; August 11, 1955, p. 43.

—Brian Escamilla

Earl F. Hilliard

1942—

Congressman from Alabama

Earl Hilliard rose steadily through Alabama's political ranks to become the state's first African American representative in the U.S. Congress since the Reconstruction era. An idealist whose official biography states that "he has seen first-hand the difference one person can make to effectuate positive change," Hilliard has been an unabashedly liberal voice in Congress. Several times the target of inquiries into his handling of legislative funds over his long career, he has consistently denied any wrongdoing. A proven vote-getter, Hilliard has surmounted such ethical questions and convinced his constituents of his commitment to their well-being.

A lifelong Alabama resident, Hilliard was born in the steel-making center of Birmingham on April 9, 1942, and was educated in the city's public schools. He came of age during, and his thinking was fundamentally shaped by, the ascendancy of civil rights activism during the early 1960s. Jet magazine quoted Hilliard as saying that "[i]f it hadn't been for Martin Luther King's march across the Edmund Pettus Bridge in Selma, I wouldn't have been a congressman." Hilliard received the finest education that the nation's historically black institutions had to offer. He graduated from Morehouse College in 1964. Three years later, Hilliard earned a law degree from Howard University.

Admitted to Alabama Bar

Hilliard returned home to Birmingham, and was admitted to the Alabama bar in 1968. He flirted with several careers before settling into the life of a Birmingham attorney. Hilliard taught at Birmingham's Miles College during the 1967–68 school year, and then worked for two years as an assistant to the president of Alabama State University. During this period he took courses that led him to yet another advanced degree, a masters in business administration from the Atlanta University School of Business, which he received in 1970. In addition to earning many of his impressive educational credentials in Atlanta, Hilliard met his wife Mary, a teacher and public school administrator, there. The couple's two children have both followed in their father's footsteps and become attorneys.

Becoming a partner in the Birmingham law firm of Hilliard, Jackson, Little & Stansel, Hilliard also prac-

> **At a Glance...**
>
> Born April 9, 1942, in Birmingham, AL; married to Mary; children: Alesia, Earl Jr. *Education:* Morehouse College, B.A., 1964; Howard University, J.D. 1967; Atlanta University School of Business, M.B.A., 1970. *Religion:* Baptist.
>
> **Career:** United States Representative, Seventh District of Alabama, member of the Democratic Party. Attorney; admitted to Alabama Bar, 1968; practiced law in Birmingham, 1970s; elected to Alabama House of Representatives, 1974; became first chairman of Alabama Black Legislative Caucus, 1975; elected to Alabama State Senate, 1980; elected to U.S. House of Representatives, 1992; re-elected 1994, 1996, and 1998; member of Agriculture and International Relations committees.
>
> **Addresses:** *Office*—1314 Longworth House Office Building, Washington, DC 20515. *Home*—1625 Castleberry Way, Birmingham, AL 35214

ticed law on his own. The political bug bit him as the voter registration drives of the 1960s began to bear fruit, and low-level political offices became accessible to African Americans across the South. Hilliard ran a successful campaign for the Alabama House of Representatives in 1974. The following year, he became the fledgling Alabama Black Legislative Caucus's first chairman. In 1980, Hilliard won election to the Alabama State Senate.

In the Alabama legislature Hilliard gained a reputation as a sharp floor tactician, once marshaling the votes for a pension bill while the bill's opponents had gone out to eat dinner. He served as chairman of the Judiciary Committee and the Commerce, Transportation, and Utility Committee, and began to build the track record of constituent services that would help to further his career. He shepherded through the legislature a bill to create a horse-racing track in Birmingham, and working tirelessly to increase the state's meager educational funding. Outside of the legislature, Hilliard maintained his ties to educational institutions, serving as a trustee at Miles College and Tuskegee Institute. In 1990, the *Birmingham News* raised questions about Hilliard's use of campaign funds for business purposes. Hilliard denied the allegations, and no action was taken.

Elected to Congress

After the 1990 census, redistricting carved out a new Seventh Congressional District with the intent of guaranteeing an African American majority. Its irregular boundaries encompassed predominantly African American neighborhoods in Birmingham and Montgomery, together with some of the old plantation counties of the Black Belt (the name refers to the area's characteristic soils rather than to the racial composition of its population). In 1992 the district's white incumbent declined to run for re-election, and Hilliard threw his hat into the ring along with three other candidates. He was able to expand his appeal beyond his Birmingham base, coming in first in the primary and squeaking by with a razor-thin margin of 50.5 to 49.5 percent in a runoff election. Hilliard's opponent questioned the vote count, but did not challenge the result, and Hilliard went on in November to win easily in this overwhelmingly Democratic district.

Having served notice of his orientation by running on a platform favoring nationalized health care along the lines of the Canadian system, Hilliard has taken consistently liberal stands in Congress, although he voted in favor of a constitutional amendment banning the burning of the U.S. flag. He used his leverage with the federal Justice Department to raise questions about continuing civil rights abuses in Alabama, and argued in favor of federally financed reparations to the descendants of slaves. "It's often said that you can't fault the offspring of slaveholders," he was quoted as saying by *The Almanac of American Politics*. "I would say that's incorrect because [some of] the offspring are still living off the wealth created by the labor of my ancestors."

Restored Ferry Service

Hilliard made headlines when he took action to redress an injustice connected with an unusually visible reminder of Alabama's civil rights conflicts. The small, predominantly African American town of Gees Bend, which is in Hilliard's district, had once been connected by ferry with the nearby cities of Camden and Selma. White residents of these cities, who were enraged by the participation of Gees Bend's citizens in Selma's historic civil rights protests, cut off the ferry service in 1962. Residents of Gees Bend were forced to make an eighty-mile round trip by car in order to purchase basic necessities. Hilliard obtained a $456,000 federal transportation grant that restored ferry service. He also secured for Alabama three of the federal government's "enterprise zones," which used tax incentives to encourage businesses to locate in depressed areas.

Hilliard has not been without his critics during his years in Congress. In 1995, according to the *New York Times*, he was tagged with the dubious distinction of being Congress's "most frequent flyer" on overseas trips. It was also revealed in 1998 that the percentage of campaign funds Hilliard had received that year was the third highest of any congressional candidate. With several relatives of key local politicians on his payroll, Hilliard's use of office funds also came under scrutiny. In October of 1999 the Republican-dominated House Ethics Committee opened an investigation into Hilliard's activities, but he seemed unconcerned; "I thought this matter was over," he was quoted as saying in *Insight on the News*. Seventh District voters, who had proven themselves satisfied with Hilliard's performance, seemed likely to agree.

Sources

Books

Barone, Michael, and Grant Ujifusa, *The Almanac of American Politics: 1994,* National Journal, 1999.
Barone, Michael, and Grant Ujifusa, *The Almanac of American Politics: 2000,* National Journal, 1999.
Henderson, Ashyia, and Shirelle Phelps, eds., *Who's Who Among African Americans,* 12th ed., Gale, 1999.
1997–1998 Congressional Directory: 105th Congress. United States Government Printing Office, 1997.

Periodicals

Insight on the News, October 25, 1999, p. 34.
Jet, February 5, 1996, p. 40.
New York Times, June 4, 1995, p. 1/13.

Other

Additional information for this profile was obtained from www.house.gov/hilliard/bio.htm.

—James M. Manheim

Darlene Clark Hine

1947—

Historian, author, educator

Darlene Clark Hine is a pioneering scholar in the field of African American women's history. She has written three award-winning books on African American women's history, and edited a two-volume encyclopedia, *Black Women in America,* the first major encyclopedia on the subject. Hine is considered to be a leading expert on the subject of race, class, and gender in American society. As the John A. Hannah Professor of History at Michigan State University in East Lansing, Hine helped to establish a new doctoral field in comparative African American history, one of the first of its kind. She has co-edited a 16-volume series on African American history in the United States, *Milestones in African American History,* as well as numerous anthologies.

In her academic work, Hine seeks not only to explore African American history, but also to redefine the discipline of history itself. "To me, the historical profession is still too caught up with the wealthy and the influential in political, social, and cultural arenas, who actually number only a very small minority of the human population," Hine told Roger Adelson of the *Historian.* "...Because so few of the new social historians have included black women, who remained at the very bottom of the ladder in the United States, we continue to lose much understanding and wisdom."

Influenced by Civil Rights Movement

Hine was born in Morley, Missouri, on February 7, 1947, the oldest of four children of Levester Clark, a truck driver, and Lottie Mae (Thompson) Clark, a homemaker. When she was three- years-old, her parents moved north to Chicago in order to obtain better jobs, while Hine remained behind with her grandparents. Her grandmother was an early influence in Hine's life. As she told Roger Adelson of the *Historian,* "my maternal grandmother early observed that I was 'smart,' and she saw to it that the rest of the family neither discouraged my reading nor dampened my curiosity."

When she was nine years old, Hine left Missouri to join her parents on the west side of Chicago. From that point until she graduated from high school, her weekly routine was the same: weekdays she went to school, Sundays to church, and Saturdays to the public library. "Every Saturday I checked out five or six books to take me

At a Glance...

Born Darlene Clark, Morley, MO, February 7, 1947; daughter of Levester Clark, a truck driver, and Lottie Mae (Thompson) Clark, a homemaker; married William C. Hine, 1970 (divorced 1974), Johnny E. Brown, 1981 (divorced, 1986); children: one daughter, Robbie Davine. *Education:* Roosevelt University, BA, 1968; Kent State University, MA, 1970, PhD, 1975. *Politics:* Democrat. *Religion:* Baptist.

Career: South Carolina State College, Orangeburg, SC, assistant professor of history and coordinator of black studies, 1972-74; Purdue University, West Lafayette, IN, assistant professor, 1974-79; associate professor, 1979-85; professor of history, 1985-87, interim director of Africana Studies and Research Center, 1978-79, vice provost, 1981-86; Michigan State University, East Lansing, MI, John A. Hannah Professor of History, 1987-

Selected awards: Outstanding Book Award, Gustavus Myers Center of Human Rights, 1990; Letitia Woods Brown Book Award, Association of Black Women Historians, 1990; Outstanding Reference Source Award, American Library Association, 1994; Zora Neale Hurston-Paul Robeson Award, National Council for Black Studies, 1995.

Selected memberships: American Historical Association; Association for the Study of Afro-American Life and History; Southern Historical Association; Southern Association for Women Historians.

Addresses: *Home*—East Lansing, MI. *Office*—Department of History, 301 Morrill Hall, Michigan State University, East Lansing, MI 48224.

through the week," she was quoted as saying in the *Historian*.

After graduating from Crane High School as valedictorian, Hine was offered a full scholarship to Chicago's Roosevelt University, where she began undergraduate work in 1964. During her freshman year, Hine discovered that she was pregnant; her daughter, Robbie Davine, was born that summer. "With my baby daughter to support and educate, I became more determined than ever to be a success," Hine told Adelson.

While she had originally planned to become a microbiologist, Hine began to develop an interest in African American history during her years at Roosevelt. As an undergraduate, she attended meetings of the Black Panthers and Nation of Islam, read books published by independent black presses, and attended lectures by eminent African American scholars. "Hearing black activists refer so often to history, seeing the black culture of the past and present celebrated by Chicago artists, and reading so many new works penned by black authors helped convince me that I should major in history," Hine remarked in the *Historian*.

The civil rights struggles of the 1960s also made her aware of the kind of history that was commonly taught in American schools—and the possibility that she could someday change the definition of "history." "When I was searching for some way to make a contribution to the whole movement for social justice, I came across the Black Panther Party's Ten Point Program," Hine was quoted as saying in the PBS documentary program, *Shattering the Silences: Minority Professors Break into the Ivory Tower*. "It was the fifth point that really struck me. The fifth point said we want a true education for our people. And I said, wow! That's it!"

Wrote Pioneering Books

After graduating from Roosevelt, Hine was awarded a graduate fellowship to attend Kent State University in Ohio. As a student at Kent State, she was present when the National Guard fired on student protesters in 1970. "I almost shut down emotionally, intellectually. It didn't make any sense. I went into exile into the library," she was quoted as saying in *Shattering the Silences*.

In 1972, Hine accepted a position as assistant professor of history and coordinator of African American studies at South Carolina State College in Orangeburg. During this time, she worked on her doctoral dissertation, which was later published as her first book, *Black Victory: The Rise and Fall of the White Primary in Texas*. "It reflects my concerns with the antecedents to the modern civil rights movement," Hine remarked in *Contemporary Authors*.

In 1974, Hine took a job as assistant professor at Purdue University, in West Lafayette, Indiana. She rose steadily through the ranks at Purdue, becoming an associate professor in 1979 and a full professor in 1985. Hine also held two administrative positions: interim director of Africana Studies and Research Center from 1978 to

1979, and vice provost from 1981 to 1986.

During her tenure at Purdue, Hine began to focus on African American women's history—a development that came about in an unorthodox manner. In 1980, she received a phone call from Shirley Herd, president of the Indianapolis section of the National Council of Negro Women. Herd wanted to commission Hine to write a history of African American women in Indiana. At first, Hine was uninterested. As she recalled in *Shattering the Silences,* she initially told Herd, "'...you cannot call up a historian and order a book the way you would drive up to a Wendy's and order a hamburger. We historians do not work like that.' And Mrs. Herd was undaunted." Hine eventually agreed to look at the papers that Herd's organization had collected: letters, diaries, church bulletins, newspaper clippings, receipts, and legal documents. The papers revealed an unknown story: how black women had raised money to found and maintain churches, schools, settlement houses, and clinics. Using the information provided by Herd, Hine published a book, *When the Truth Is Told: Black Women's Community and Culture in Indiana, 1875-1950.*

> "I hope that I can continue to give voice to people who otherwise would be ignored or forgotten, or rendered invisible and dismissed as unimportant."

"Historians can write a history of anything or anyone," Hine was quoted as saying in *Shattering the Silences,* "but the key is the historian must decide that thing, event, person or group is worthy of investigation. And apparently no one had ever thought black women were worth studying." After the publication of *When the Truth Is Told,* Hine received a grant from the National Endowment for the Humanities to set up the Black Women in the Middle West Project, an archive of information on African American women. In 1985, Hine co-edited a book about these sources, *Black Women in the Middle West: A Comprehensive Research Guide, Illinois and Indiana.*

Published Encyclopedia on African American Women

In 1987, Hine accepted the position of John A. Hannah Professor of History at Michigan State University in East Lansing, Michigan. Since then, she has published two more books, *Black Women in White: Racial Conflict and Cooperation in the Nursing Profession, 1890-1950* (1989), and *Speak Truth to Power: The Black Professional Class in United States History* (1996). In addition to her academic writing, Hine edited a 16-volume series called *Milestones in African American History* (1993) designed for middle- and high-school students. Also in 1993, Hine edited a two-volume encyclopedia, *Black Women in America.* "The encyclopedia is intended to place a stone in the shoe of every American historian," Hine remarked in *Contemporary Authors.* "The encyclopedia will make it difficult, if not impossible, to exclude black women and their deeds, contributions, and experiences...."

At Michigan State, Hine worked with other history professors to establish a new doctoral field in comparative African American history, encompassing African, African American, Latin American, Caribbean, and southern U.S. history. "This is one of the most exciting things that I'm doing within the larger field of African American history at present," Hine told the *Historian.* In 1997, Hine published the book *Hine Sight,* a collection of 14 of her most significant articles and essays. The book not only made her work more accessible, Hine told the *Historian,* but also served " to trace the evolution of my thinking about black women as historical subjects." She remarked further, "I hope that I can continue to give voice to people who otherwise would be ignored or forgotten, or rendered invisible and dismissed as unimportant," Hine told Adelson. "If I can...impress upon the historical profession how important it is to talk to those people who do not leave written records, but who have remembrances and have influenced generations and people all over the globe, then I feel that my career is worthwhile."

Sources

Books

Contemporary Authors, volume 143, Gale Research, 1994.

Periodicals

The Historian, Winter 1995, pp. 259-74.

Other

Additional information for this profile was obtained from a transcript of the PBS documentary *Shattering the Silences: Minority Professors Break into the Ivory Tower* at www.pbs.org/shattering/hine.html.

—Carrie Golus

Chamique Holdsclaw

1977—

Professional basketball player

The pioneering women's professional basketball player Nancy Lieberman-Cline summed up her feelings with a single word when asked about Chamique Holdsclaw by the Knight-Ridder/Tribune News Service in 1997: "What I'm saying is, 'Yikes.'" On the strength of her four-year college basketball career at the University of Tennessee, sportswriters searched for superlatives to describe Holdsclaw's abilities; she was thought to be not just a great player, but someone who was fundamentally changing women's basketball. In 1999, her first year in the pros, she disappointed no expectations. Holdsclaw has often been compared to male basketball superstar Michael Jordan, who has expressed admiration for Holdsclaw's skills.

Chamique Holdsclaw (her first name is pronounced shuh-MEEK-wah, and she is known by the nickname "Meek") was born on August 9, 1977, and raised in New York City. Her family was never well off, and the financial strains became severe when her parents went their separate ways. When she was eleven, Chamique went to live with her grandmother, June, in a housing project in the Queens borough neighborhood of Astoria. In her grandmother's home she found a warm, stable environment; years later at the University of Tennessee, when she had to contribute to a listing of team members' parents, she entered her grandmother's name.

Joined Team as Freshman

The religious upbringing Holdsclaw received from her grandmother was strong; her lifelong jersey number of 23 refers not to any sports figure or tradition, but to the Bible's Twenty-Third Psalm ("The Lord is my shepherd…"). But it still left her time to play basketball at a neighborhood court, where the local schoolboys set male pride aside and clamored for her to join their teams. She had the nickname "Flat Out" because she would flat out drop anything to play basketball. By the end of the eighth grade, approaching her mature height of six feet, two inches (with size 14 feet), Holdsclaw could throw a basketball the length of the court, and Vincent Canizzaro, coach of one of the nation's top girls' basketball programs at New York's Christ the King High School, put her in his team's varsity lineup during her freshman year.

At a Glance...

Born August 9, 1977; mother's name Bonita; raised from age 11 in Queens, New York, by grandmother June Holdsclaw. *Education:* Graduated from Christ the King High School, New York, New York; graduated from University of Tennessee, Knoxville, Tennessee, 1999.

Career: Professional basketball player with Washington Mystics of WNBA league. Led Christ the King High to four consecutive state championships; led team to national championships for three of four years at Tennessee, 1996-98; became Tennessee's all-time leading scorer; drafted by Washington Mystics in first round, 1999; signed six-figure endorsement deal with Nike, 1999; named WNBA Rookie of the Year, 1999.

Awards: Numerous awards include selection for Associated Press All-America team, 1996-97, 1997-98, and 1998-99; named four consecutive years to Kodak All-American team; won Sullivan Award as nation's best amateur athlete, 1999.

Addresses: *Team office*—c/o Washington Mystics, MCI Center, 601 F Street NW, Washington, DC 20001

Canizzaro's judgment proved sound when Holdsclaw led the Christ the King team to four consecutive state championships; the team lost only four games during her entire career there. "We've been blessed with a lot of great players," Canizzaro told *Sports Illustrated*, "but she has to be the best." In her last year, Holdsclaw averaged 25 points a game, and found herself the object of heavy recruitment from college programs. Her grandmother, a native Southerner, nudged her toward the University of Tennessee, partly out of admiration for Tennessee coach Pat Summitt.

Summitt, who became a second strong female presence in Holdsclaw's life over her four years at Tennessee, was as immediately bowled over by her new protegee as Canizzaro had been. Holdsclaw, who played the position of forward, was named Southeastern Conference Player of the Week in her very first week of play at Tennessee, as she averaged nearly 13 points a game over her first three games. 12 games into Holdsclaw's freshman season, Summitt praised her as potentially the best player ever to come to Tennessee, a perennial powerhouse in women's college basketball.

Led Team to Championship

Holdsclaw had a sensational freshman year, averaging 18.6 points a game and becoming the only woman ever named college Player of the Week by the ESPN cable-television sports network during one particularly torrid stretch. Summitt honed Holdsclaw's competitive instincts, taking Holdsclaw to task for her initial relaxed attitude in the face of the occasional loss, but eventually becoming the kind of strong yet nurturing guiding force Holdsclaw needed. At the season's end, Holdsclaw was named to a women's All-America squad sponsored by the Kodak corporation, the only freshman to be so honored. Injured in the finals of the Southeastern Conference tournament, she bounced back, and Tennessee romped to the National Collegiate Athletic Association (NCAA) championship.

That year's worth of accomplishments by itself would have brought major prestige to any basketball player, but for Holdsclaw it was only the beginning. That NCAA championship would be the first of three that Tennessee would win during her college career. "The Tiger Woods of women's basketball is here," observed John Smallwood of the Knight-Ridder Tribune News Service, "and Holdsclaw may very well take the game to another level." Holdsclaw eventually became Tennessee's all-time leading scorer and rebounder, and in her senior year won the Sullivan award as the best amateur athlete in the United States.

Neither the biggest nor the most physically powerful woman in the game, Holdsclaw had uncanny mental strength, consistently summoning incredible energy in clutch situations. "Some people compete when it's convenient," Nancy Lieberman-Cline told *Time* magazine. "Chamique steps up when the team needs her." A typical performance came in January of 1999, when Holdsclaw scored 25 points to lead the Lady Volunteers to an away-game victory over arch-rival Connecticut, dealing that team its first loss at home in 54 games.

Signed Nike Deal

As Holdsclaw neared the end of her time at Tennessee, speculation about her future ran hot and heavy in the nation's sports press. With her camera-friendly looks and a disarming manner often described as humble, Holdsclaw has been expected to reap huge financial rewards not just from her work on the basketball court, but also through endorsement deals and the like. She had already been approached about a movie deal; filmmaker Spike Lee had wanted to cast Holdsclaw in his college basketball story *He Got Game* (whose title, with gender altered, provided the headline for many a Holdsclaw newspaper story). NCAA rules did not allow that, but once her final season was over, the marketing of Chamique Holdsclaw began. She agreed to a five-year contract with Nike, Inc., that was easily the largest ever signed by a female athlete; it promised to bring her an annual income in six figures before she even picked up a basketball. She also announced plans to join the Nickelodeon television network as an on-air sports personality.

> She had the nickname "Flat Out" because she would flat out drop anything to play basketball.

Holdsclaw was the only college player selected in the first round of the Women's National Basketball Association (WNBA) draft. Though she had expressed a desire to return home to New York, she was drafted by the Washington Mystics. Her first-year performance was as remarkable as ever: she averaged 16.9 points per game (good for a ranking of sixth in the league), started 31 of 32 games, and was named the WNBA's Rookie of the Year. Whether Holdsclaw could become the female Michael Jordan remained to be seen, but she was well on her way.

Sources

Periodicals

Jet, September 20, 1999, p. 48: May 24, 1999, p. 46.
Interactive Sports Wire, May 14, 1999.
Knight-Ridder/Tribune Business News, May 14, 1999.
Knight-Ridder/Tribune News Service, March 31, 1997.
Newsweek, March 15, 1999, p. 63.
Sporting News, April 7, 1997, p. 17.
Sports Illustrated, December 2, 1996, p. 100.
Time, March 22, 1999, p. 95.

—James M. Manheim

Earl Ofari Hutchinson

1945—

Author, journalist

Whenever the American media has provided coverage of the social issues and concerns facing African Americans, it is quite likely that Earl Ofari Hutchinson has offered his opinions. Hutchinson is a political analyst, social critic, author, and nationally syndicated columnist. He has lectured at universities and has also appeared on talk shows and radio and television discussion programs.

Learned From His Father

Hutchinson was born on October 8, 1945 in Chicago, Illinois. His father was a postal worker who went into real estate after retirement. His mother had been a talented seamstress who made clothes for family, friends and neighbors. Hutchinson's parents were loving and nurturing, and took he and his sister to church regularly.

Hutchinson's father was a role model who taught his son by example. In his 1992 book, *Black Fatherhood: the Guide to Male Parenting,* Hutchinson told the story of a family trip to California. During the trip, he learned a valuable lesson. "Each evening, as dusk began to settle, my father pulled into a filling station. He took a small blue-covered book from the glove compartment and carefully circled an address in it." His father's blue book held the names of motels or private homes where African Americans could find lodging. Due to segregation, many motels and restaurants refused to serve African Americans. Hutchinson noted in *Black Fatherhood,* "I did not realize it at the time, but my father was giving me a lesson in the art of black survival."

Hutchinson received a bachelor of science degree in sociology from California State University, Los Angeles in 1969. Following graduation, he worked for a radio station in southern California for about ten years. He went on to earn a masters degree in humanities from California State University, Dominguez Hills in 1989. Hutchinson began a doctoral program in sociology at Cornell University. However, he transferred to Pacific Western University and received his doctorate in 1991.

In 1982 Hutchinson began a subscription newsletter, *Ofari's Bi-Monthly,* which discussed political and social issues. He published this newsletter for 12 years. Hutchinson had never considered journalism as a career option. Instead, he wanted to be a teacher. In an

> ### At a Glance...
>
> Born October 8, 1945 in Chicago, IL; son of Earl Hutchinson, a postal worker, and Nina (Brown) Hutchinson; wife's name Barbara (Bramwell) Hutchinson; children: Fanon and Sikivu. *Education:* California State University, Los Angeles, B.S. sociology, early 1970s; California State University, Dominguez Hills, M. Hum., 1989; Pacific Western University, Ph.D. sociology, 1991.
>
> **Career:** KPFK Radio, Pacifica, CA, 1974-82; author of *The Myth of Black Capitalism,* 1970; *Let Your Motto Be Resistance,* 1974; *Black Fatherhood: Guide to Male Parenting,* 1992; *Black Fatherhood II: Black Women Talk About Their Men,* 1994; *The Assassination of the Black Male Image,* 1994; *Blacks and Reds: Race and Class in Conflict, 1919-1990,* 1995; *Betrayed: a History of Presidential Failure to Protect Black Lives,* 1996; *Beyond O.J.: Race, Sex, and Class Lessons for America,* 1996; *The Crisis in Black and Black,* 1998.
>
> **Awards:** Outstanding Book Award, Gustavus Myers Center for the Study of Human Rights, 1995, 1997; Best Published Article in a Series, Parts 1 and 2, National Association of Black Journalists, 1997.
>
> **Member:** Black Journalists Association. Coalition Against Media Exploitation.
>
> **Addresses:** *Office*—Author/Journalist, Middle Passage Press, 5517 Secrest Drive, Los Angeles, CA 90043.

interview with *Contemporary Black Biography,* Hutchinson spoke about his entry into the world of journalism. "I backed into it. The week after I finished my degree work at Cornell, I was talking to a friend at the old *Los Angeles Free Press* and, in passing, he indicated they needed a piece analyzing black nationalism. I agreed. He liked it. A few days later, he told me that one of his staff writers had quit and they needed a temporary replacement. Well, as they say, the rest is history."

Published Books On Black Issues

Hutchinson went on to write for several newspapers and magazines, including the *Chicago Tribune, Los Angeles Times, San Francisco Chronicle, Black World, Ebony, Essence, Newsday, Nation, Harper's,* and *Emerge.* In 1965 he edited *The Black Book,* a book of African American quotes which was published by the Radical Education Project of Detroit, Michigan. Hutchinson's first book, *The Myth of Black Capitalism,* was published by Monthly Review Press in 1970. Two years later, *Let Your Motto Be Resistance; the Life and Thought of Henry Highland Garnet* was published by Beacon Press of Boston. Hutchinson's book, *Black Fatherhood: The Guide to Male Parenting,* examined the challenges that African American fathers face while raising their children in contemporary African American society..

In *Blacks and Reds: Race and Conflict, 1919-1990,* Hutchinson explored the links between African Americans and communism during the 20th century. The book detailed how the Communist Party in America had attempted to win the support of African Americans. Paul Robeson, an African American actor and singer, was greatly admired in both African American and white communities in the 1940s. On one occasion, he made comments that seemed to praise communism. These comments caused Robeson to fall out of favor with the American public, and he was called upon to testify before the House Un-American Activities Committee. Journalist W.E.B. DuBois, who had worked for the NAACP, also supported the Communist Party. In addition to DuBois and Robeson, Hutchinson related how the Communist Party in America had influenced other prominent African Americans, including Malcolm X, Stokely Carmichael, and Eldridge Cleaver.

In *The Assassination of the Black Male Image,* published by Middle Passage Press in 1994, Hutchinson discussed his views on how the African American male is portrayed by the media in a consistently negative fashion. He also examined the perceptions of American society toward African American men, and called for greater respect and understanding. Hutchinson originally published *The Assassination of the Black Male Image* himself, and sold 30,000 copies before signing with the publishing house Simon & Schuster. The book was a tremendous success, and was eventually released in paperback. In its review of *The Assassination of the Black Male Image, Kirkus Reviews* remarked, "He [Hutchinson] argues that the overwhelming mass media image of black men is of evil incarnate, and that Americans—including many black women—are ready to pounce any time a black man slips up, from O.J. Simpson to Michael Jackson to Clarence Thomas to Louis Farrakhan." Hutchinson also argued that racism, poverty, gangs, drugs, family roles, and male-female relationships are among the greatest challenges facing

African American males.

Commented on Social Issues

During the year-long murder trial of former football star and television commentator O.J. Simpson, Hutchinson served as a media trial analyst for MSNBC and KCBS-LA. In 1996, he wrote the book *Beyond O.J.: Race, Sex, and Class Lessons for America*. The book discussed the O.J. Simpson trial and its social implications. Lillian Lewis, in a review for the American Library Association, noted that "Hutchinson offers compelling comparisons of recent cases involving white and black male defendants with similar charges, yet with disparate dispositions. Not only were the white males treated differently by the courts for the same crime .... Hutchinson is seemingly building a strong case for the view of the black male as a menace to society ...."

In his 1998 book, *The Crisis in Black and Black,* Hutchinson discussed several topics dealing with social issues and prominent African Americans such as Clarence Thomas, O.J. Simpson, and Louis Farrakhan. A reviewer for the American Library Association remarked, "Hutchinson's style and candor provide an excellent commentary on ... contemporary issues. He begins each chapter with the scientific approach of stating an opinion and raising the questions to debate. After a brief and engaging analysis, including statistics, the chapters end with a final comment that dispels and challenges the opinion."

In addition to his career as an author and journalist, Hutchinson was the co-director of the Sherrice Iverson Justice Fund and an official spokesperson for the mother of Sherrice Iverson, a seven-year-old child who was murdered in a Las Vegas casino in 1997. In his online column for *Davey D*, Interview/Analysis, Hutchinson remarked, "Strohmeyer [the man convicted of Iverson's murder] is middle-class and white. Iverson is African-American, and her parents are working class. This virtually guarantees that it will be a highly charged trial in which race, income and public attitudes often determine legal fairness." He also noted in his online *JINN* magazine column for the Pacific News Service that, "The murder of Sherrice Iverson is a near textbook example of indifference, insensitivity, and disdain toward black victims, no matter how young and innocent."

As director of the National Alliance for Positive Action, Hutchinson has voiced his desire to have the word "nigger" eliminated from the Merriam-Webster dictionary. The National Alliance for Positive Action, which was founded by Hutchinson, is a multi-ethnic public issues advocacy group whose mission statement, in part, is to "promote justice and fairness for America's dispossessed." Merriam-Webster officials told Knight-Ridder Newspapers that, "We do not believe we can make offensive words go out of existence by leaving them out of the dictionary. People do not learn these words from the dictionary nor would they refrain from using them if we left them out." Hutchinson disagreed and remarked to the Knight-Ridder/Tribune News Service that, "a word as emotionally charged as 'nigger' can reinforce and perpetuate stereotypes." The word is defined in the 1996 edition of *Webster's* as: 1. A black person—usually taken to be offensive. 2. A member of any dark-skinned race—usually taken to be offensive. 3. A member of a socially disadvantaged class of persons. The NAACP also gave its opinion, stating that the definition needed to be changed from "a black person or member of any dark-skinned race," to simply a derogatory word and not one that was another name for African Americans. Hutchinson said in his *JINN* column, "If the word must be dictionary defined—and several dictionaries have deleted it—it should be 'deracialized' and defined simply as 'a racially derogatory term applied to African-Americans.'"

In his work for the Coalition Against Media Exploitation, Hutchinson was able to convince President Clinton to pardon African American sailors who were court martialed in the 1940s for refusing to load ammunition onto Navy ships following an explosion. This incident occurred during World War II, when mostly African American sailors were ordered to load live ammunition onto Navy ships bound for the Pacific theater. At the Port Chicago Naval Magazine near San Francisco, an explosion on July 17, 1944, killed 320 men and injured almost 400. The African American sailors who survived were ordered to continue loading ammunition onto the ships. However, 50 sailors refused to obey the order because they were afraid that another explosion would occur. These sailors were accused of disobeying an order, court martialed, convicted of mutiny, and jailed. In December of 1999, President Clinton granted a pardon to one of two known surviving sailors, 80-year-old Freddie Meeks.

As director of the Coalition Against Media Exploitation, Hutchinson openly criticized the lack of African American actors and producers both in television and the movies. He told *Jet* magazine, "African Americans are still mostly invisible on and especially off-screen in Hollywood." Hutchinson accused television producers of segregation when one network announced that it would put most of its African American-themed programs into a single time block. He also challenged network executives who believed that white viewers would not watch

African American oriented television shows. Hutchinson noted that the success of African American sitcoms from the 1970s and 1980s, such as *The Cosby Show,* were due to the fact that they appealed to viewers of all races.

> "I'm a writer. That has always been the emphasis—I'm first a writer, second a writer, tenth, twentieth a writer."

Hutchinson has a syndicated column that appears in over 150 newspapers nationwide. He is also a columnist for the *Los Angeles Daily News,* and his writings are often published in the *Los Angeles Times.* He is a regular commentator for Pacifica National News, and writes for Pacific News Service. In regard to his future plans, Hutchinson told *CBB,* "I'm a writer. That has always been the emphasis—I'm first a writer, second a writer, tenth, twentieth a writer. I would like to see essentially my place established as a leading authority, or to be recognized in many circles as a prominent and even cutting edge issues person, to influence opinions, to help make changes in public policy."

Selected writings

The Myth of Black Capitalism, 1970.
Let Your Motto Be Resistance; the Life and Thought of Henry Highland Garnet, 1972.
Black Fatherhood: the Guide to Male Parenting, 1992.
The Assassination of the Black Male Image, 1994.
Black Fatherhood II: Black Women Talk About Their Men, 1994.
Blacks and Reds: Race and Class in Conflict, 1919-1990, 1995.
Betrayed: a History of Presidential Failure to Protect Black Lives, 1996.
Beyond O.J.: Race, Sex, and Class Lessons for America, 1996.
The Crisis in Black and Black, 1998.

Sources

Books

Hutchinson, Earl Ofari. *Black Fatherhood: The Guide to Male Parenting,* Middle Passage Press, Los Angeles, 1995, p. 133-134.

Periodicals

Essence, April 1996, p. 140.
Jet, December 14, 1998, p 12.
Kansas City Star, (Missouri) December 24, 1999, p. A-1, A-6.
Knight-Ridder/Tribune News Service, October 16, 1997.

Other

Additional information for this profile was obtained from www.daveyd.com/earlchasepol.html ; a 1995 American Library Association review of *Beyond O.J.: Race, Sex, and Class Lessons for America* at www.amazon.com; a 1996 *Kirkus* Associates review of *The Assassination of the Black Male Image* at www.amazon.com.; a 1998 American Library Association review of *The Crisis in Black and Black* at www.amazon.com; an Author Biography Media Sheet from Middle Passage Press; a Coalition Against Media Exploitation Media Release published at www.theafrican.com; JINN, Pacific News Service, September 26, 1997 and August 18, 1998 columns at web site www.pacificneews.org/pacificnews/jinn; and an interview with *Contemporary Black Biography* on January 6, 2000.

—Sandy J. Stiefer

Allen Iverson

1975—

Professional basketball player

Allen Iverson, perhaps the quickest player ever to play in the National Basketball Association (NBA) was born on June 7, 1975 in Hampton, VA. His mother Ann Iverson was a teenager and was deserted by Iverson's father. Soon after her son was born, Ann Iverson's mother died, leaving the young mother and son to fend for themselves. Iverson grew up in severe poverty in a house that sometimes had no electricity or water. Sports offered an outlet for the immensely gifted young athlete and he excelled in football, baseball, and basketball. Though he is arguably the best player in the NBA today, Iverson told Leigh Montville of *Sports Illustrated* that basketball was not his first choice: "I always figured I was going to go to one of those big football schools. Florida State. Notre Dame. Football was my first love. Still is. I was going to go to one of those schools and play both. I just loved running the option, faking, throwing the ball, everything about football. I didn't even want to play basketball at first. I thought it was soft. My mother's the one who made me go to tryouts. I thank her forever. I came back and said 'I like basketball, too.'" Iverson cruised through high school doing just well enough in the classroom to stay eligible for sports. In his senior year he led Bethel High School's football team to a state championship. He was excelling in basketball also until the night of February 13, 1993. Iverson and some friends were at a bowling alley when a fight broke out which then escalated into a brawl divided along racial lines. Of the 50 or so participants involved in the fight, only four black teenagers were charged—one of them Iverson. Though video of the incident did not show Iverson at all and he testified that he left the bowling alley when the brawl started, two other witnesses said that he threw a chair at a woman. The 17-year-old was tried as an adult and sentenced to five years in prison for maiming by mob.

Iverson went to jail for four months before the governor of Virginia commuted his sentence under the condition that he not play organized sports until he graduated from high school. Two years later his conviction was overturned by the State Court of Appeals. Though the incident is erased from his legal record, it made him even more determined to succeed for his family. Iverson told *Sports Illustrated's* Rick Reilly about his motivation: "I knew I had to succeed for them. People would say, 'Man, that's a million-to-one shot to make it to the NBA,' but I'd say 'Not for me it ain't.' 'Cause if I didn't succeed,

At a Glance...

Born Allen Ezail Iverson, June 7, 1975 in Hampton, VA; son of Allen Broughton and Ann Iverson (a factory and shipyard worker); children: Tiara and Allen II; *Education:* Attended Georgetown University.

Career: Iverson starred in football, basketball, and baseball at Bethel High School, 1990-93; Iverson was arrested and convicted after a bowling alley brawl. Served four months in prison before Virginia governor commutes his sentence, 1993; star point guard for Georgetown University, 1994-95, 1995-96; first player chosen in the NBA draft by the Philadelphia 76ers, 1996; sentenced to two years probation after police found marijuana and a handgun in his car; switched from point guard to shooting guard, 1997; led team to playoffs, 1998-99.

Awards: Big East Rookie of the Year, 1995; Big East Defensive Player of the Year, 1995, 1996; first team AP All-American, 1996; NBA Rookie of the Year, 1997; All-NBA first team, 1999.

Addresses: *Residence*—Philadelphia, PA; *Mailing*—c/o The Philadelphia 76ers, 3601 South Broad St., Philadelphia, PA 19148.

well, I don't wanna think about it. I thought, for all the sufferin' they've done, they need me to make it. They oughta have some satisfaction in life." Iverson suddenly became serious about school and worked all the way through the summer at a rigorous learning center to make up his lost class work.

Iverson at Georgetown

After high school, Iverson attended Georgetown University. The freshman would earn the Big East Rookie of the Year award after leading his team with 20 points and 4.5 assists per game. His sophomore season was better. He drove the Hoyas to a 29-8 record, averaging 25 points, 4.7 assists, and 3.5 steals per game. Iverson, who started 66 of 67 games as a Hoya, was also named Big East Defensive Player of the Year in 1994 and 1995 and named an Associated Press (AP) First Team All-American in 1995. Despite his success and enjoyment of college life, after two years at Georgetown he knew it was time to leave. His family was still living in poverty back in Hampton, and he now had a daughter Tiara to think about. His sophomore season at Georgetown would be his last in college.

NBA Rookie of the Year

On June 26, 1996 Iverson was the first player selected in the NBA draft by the Philidelphia 76ers. He signed a $9.4 million contract and set his sights on becoming the best player in the NBA. If he was not the best on the court in his first season, Iverson quickly established himself as one of the most exciting players in the league. His crossover dribble proved to be so explosive that the NBA issued a memo to referees across the league addressing one individual player's single move. Iverson had to change his crossover dribble slightly to avoid travelling but that did not diminish his achievements. He led his team and all NBA rookies in points (23.5), assists (7.5), steals (2.07), and in minutes played (40.1) per game. His coach Johnny Davis told Montville of *Sports Illustrated:* "He's as quick with the ball as anyone in the history of the league. He's a combination of Isiah Thomas and Tiny Archibald. Fast guys in this league, he makes them look as if they're slow. He has a level beyond their quickness." Iverson was named Rookie of the Year and was the Most Valuable Player (MVP) in the Rookie All-Star game during the NBA's All-Star weekend. Despite his success, Iverson came under some harsh criticism. His penchant for taking off-balanced shots, sometimes before looking for teammates, coupled with a poor shooting percentage for a point guard (.416), and his turnovers, prompted some to label him selfish—especially among the leagues old guard. Charles Barkley called him "Me-Myself-and-Iverson." His loyalty to the shoe company Reebok, which erected a 40-foot mural of Iverson in downtown Philadelphia, prompted his next coach Larry Brown to openly question his devotion to the 76ers. And then the league fretted about Iverson's image. Instead of suits and ties, the 20-year-old opted for baggy pants, mountains of jewelry, and do-rags—like many other young people of his generation. The league even questioned his choice of friends who remained with him from his days in Hampton. But Iverson told *Sports Illustrated's* Montville that his loyalty would remain firm: "The NBA can't pick my friends. When I was struggling growing up, no running water in my house, the electric lights turned off, these were the guys who were with me. They grew up with me. I'm not going to turn my back on them now. Not many people were always angels as they grew up. These are the guys who won't always be telling me how great I am. They know me."

Off-Season Controversy

The league and other critics seemed to be proved

correct in the off-season after Iverson's rookie year. Iverson was on his way to record a rap song at a local Richmond recording studio; a man offered to drive him there, and Iverson fell asleep around midnight on the way there. Police pulled over Iverson's car after it was clocked at 93 miles per hour and allegedly found marijuana and a handgun in the Mercedes. Iverson was arrested but all charges were dropped after he was given two years probation with monthly drug tests and 100 hours of community service. Iverson told *Sports Illustrated's* Reilly about the incident: "That was so stupid. It was such poor judgment ... If that car had crashed, I'd have put my family right back where they'd come from. From then on, I decided I gotta be smart."

> "I'll do anything to help this team win, I don't care what it is. I'll do anything it takes to get a championship. I think coach Brown knows what it takes to get there."

Iverson vowed to put his past behind him and even hired two bodyguards to help him make better decisions socially. The 76ers brought in veteran coach Larry Brown to help tutor Iverson as a pointguard. Though the two had their moments of frustration, Iverson improved his game. He led Philadelphia in every offensive category and finished eighth in the league in scoring with 22 points per game and eleventh in minutes played with 39.4 a game. He scored in double figures in 74 of his 80 games and improved his shooting percentage to .461. Though the 76ers improved in the 1997-98 season, coach Brown thought the team and its star pointguard could do better. The following season, he switched Iverson from point guard to shooting guard to relieve some of the pressure of bringing the ball up court. Even though he played against taller opponents, Iverson and his team had a breakout year. Iverson led the NBA in scoring with 26.8 points per game and in minutes played. He was named to the All-NBA first team and scored in double figures in 46 of 48 games. The season was not without controversy, though, when Iverson was on the bench and Brown told him to go back in during an April second game; Iverson cursed at having been held out of the game for so long, and Brown sat him for the rest of the contest. Iverson then missed the following game citing a hamstring injury. But ironically the incident seemed to help relations between the two stubborn men. Iverson apologized and later told *Sports Illustrated's* Michael Bamberger: "Coach and myself, we've come a long way. We started off rocky. Now we're friends." More importantly the 76ers finished the lockout-shortened season 28-22 and made the playoffs. The sixth-seeded Philadelphia team proceeded to defeat the third-seeded Orlando Magic three games to one. Iverson dominated the series averaging 28.3 points a game during the first round. Though Philadelphia was swept by the Indiana Pacers in the following round, Iverson had returned playoff basketball to Philadelphia.

Iverson approached the 1999-2000 season as a seemingly different individual. Fresh off his post-season success and a new six-year multimillion dollar contract, Iverson has left the bodyguards and much of the controversy behind him. He finds himself more concerned with his two children now, and instead of two bodyguards, he often travels with his mother. He also has become fully committed to his team telling Ken Berger of the Associated Press, "I'll do anything to help this team win, I don't care what it is. I'll do anything it takes to get a championship. I think Coach Brown knows what it takes to get there."

Sources

Books

Schmidt Jr, Charles E., *Allen Iverson*. Chelsea House Publishers: Philadelphia, PA. 1998.

Periodicals

The Los Angeles Times, October 10, 1999.
Sports Illustrated, December 9, 1996; March 9, 1998; May 24, 1999.

Online

http://www.nba.com/playerfile/bio/allen_iverson.html.

—Michael J. Watkins

Harvey Johnson, Jr.

1947(?)—

Mayor of Jackson, Mississippi

In 1997, Harvey Johnson, Jr. was elected the first African American mayor of Jackson, Mississippi. The capital city of Mississippi, Jackson has 200,000 residents, of whom about 60 percent are African American. During the civil rights years, the city gained infamy as the place where civil rights leader Medgar Evers was gunned down, and where campaigners were routinely beaten, falsely arrested, and murdered.

According to Kevin Chappell, writing in Ebony, Johnson's election was a substantial step in the healing process: "In a city—still considered by some to be one of America's most racially divided towns—and in a state with a steep history of bigotry and intolerance, Johnson's mayoral victory in June served as a resounding notice that there is indeed a New South desperately trying to live down a stubborn reputation that has dogged it for at least the last 30 years." Johnson, who was a teenager during the tumultuous civil rights era, remembers those years well. Still, while Mississippi has significant racial problems, he told Kevin Chappell of Ebony, "...so do other states. We are improving as far as understanding each other. We have made progress, but there continues to be more progress that has to be made."

Johnson was born in Vicksburg, Mississippi, the only child of a garbage collector and a cleaner. "My mother and father were older when I was born," he told Ebony, "so I remember always being 50 years younger than the people I was around." After graduating from high school, Johnson attended Tennessee State University. There he met Kathy Ezell, who would become his wife. Johnson then pursued graduate studies at the University of Cincinnati. He had initially planned to stay in Cincinnati and go to law school, but was persuaded to come back to Mississippi at the urging of his father. According to Ebony, Johnson's father told him, "Boy, you ought to go to Jackson to get a job."

Johnson returned to Mississippi in 1972, where he found a job as a community planner in the governor's office, even though he had no experience in the field. In his wide-ranging career, Johnson has been as a political science professor at Jackson State University, a state tax commissioner, a commissioner on the powerful Mississippi Gaming Board, and a political commentator on a local television station.

In 1993, Johnson made an unsuccessful run for mayor.

> ### At a Glance...
>
> Born c. 1947 in Vicksburg, MS; son of a garbage collector and a cleaner; married Kathy Ezell; children: Harvey III, Sharla. *Education:* Tennessee State University, University of Cincinnati.
>
> **Career:** Jackson State University, professor; Mississippi Gaming Board, commissioner; City of Jackson, Mississippi, mayor, 1997-.
>
> **Addresses:** *Home*—Jackson, MS. *Office*—P.O. Box 17, Jackson, MS, 39205.

Undaunted, he tried again four years later, running on a platform of racial and economic unity. A Democrat, Johnson upset the incumbent, Kane Ditto, to earn the right to face the Republican candidate, Charlotte Reeves, who hoped to become the city's first female mayor. His opponents tried to dig up dirt on him, Johnson joked to Kevin Chappell of *Ebony*, "but the handles on their shovels weren't long enough." He was elected in June of 1997 with an overwhelming 70 percent of the vote. "We have come a mighty long way in this city," Johnson told a crowd of cheering supporters on election night (quoted as saying in the *New York Times*). "We're going to have to forge some common ground in this city."

Johnson told Kevin Chappell of *Ebony*, that his plans for Jackson included creating a strong business class to provide quality jobs for the city's residents, increasing the tax base, and providing money to improve services in the city. He also wanted to foster the African American business community, hoping to change Jackson's identity and bring new respect to the city. Johnson planned to model the success of Atlanta's African American mayor, Maynard Jackson, who helped to transform that city into the capital of the New South. "As mayor, I want to be known as a man of integrity who conducts his affairs in a dignified way, one who is able to bring together a lot of people to build the city and make it a shining example of how a great city is run," Johnson told *Ebony*. "There can't be a lot of rhetoric. There has to be action. There has to be more than just talk from a black guy in a suit calling himself mayor. And I'm planning to do that." He also hoped to change the reputation of his home state. "Because you come from Mississippi, you are somehow considered backwards, and that's not the case," Johnson was quoted as saying in *Ebony*. "The state gets a bad rap given its history, but I hope my election gives people here something to be proud of."

Johnson's tenure as mayor has not come without criticism. Buddy Bynum, writing in *Mississippi Business Journal,* faulted Johnson for not cooperating with the county government, and for welcoming controversial Nation of Islam leader Louis Farrakhan to Jackson. "Coming into his own as mayor of the state's largest and in some ways most complex city, Johnson seems to be facing more problems than solutions," Bynum wrote. "His problems seem to have gotten worse, not better."

In his 1999 state of the city address, called "Building the Best of the New South," Johnson touted his accomplishments since his election two years earlier. The foundation of his plan was improving basic city services, "such as picking up trash, maintaining streets, repairing a crumbling infrastructure, enhancing efficiency and customer service, and putting our fiscal house in order," Johnson told the city council, according to a transcript of the speech. Johnson also detailed his efforts to revitalize the city's downtown, and to bring investment into Jackson. "The city of Jackson is experiencing tremendous business growth," he was quoted as saying in the transcript. "Estimated capital investment from business growth and expansion within the city is just over $12 million, and brings with it an estimated 291 jobs."

Johnson's plans for the rest of his term included improvements to the city's infrastructure, programs for youth, and crime-fighting initiatives. He also touted the city's first "millennium activity," a Civil Rights Driving Tour of Jackson, which would acknowledge the important civil rights events that happened there. "The achievements of this past year," Johnson was quoted as saying in the transcript, "have provided the foundation and momentum needed to build the Best of the New South as we move into the next century."

Sources

Periodicals

Ebony, August 1997, p. 76.
New York Times, June 5, 1997.

Other

Additional information for this profile was obtained from "Building the Best of the New South," the state of the city address by Mayor Harvey Johnson, Jr. Available at www.city.jackson.ms.us/Govt/cityaddress.html.

—Carrie Golus

Barry Larkin

1964—

Professional baseball player

Barry Louis Larkin was born on April 28, 1964 in Cincinnati, Ohio and would grow up to become one of that city's favorite sons and one of Major League Baseball's most productive players. Although Larkin grew up in an athletic family, his parents made sure that their children were well-rounded. On holidays, the Larkins often spent their time with the elderly or at homeless shelters. Larkin attended Moeller High School and starred in football, baseball, and basketball. After graduating in 1982, Larkin attended the University of Michigan where he twice led the Wolverines to the College World Series. In his three years at Michigan, Larkin compiled a .361 batting average and was the first baseball player to be twice named Most Valuable Player (MVP) of the Big Ten. He was also named First Team All-American in 1984 and 1985. After his junior year at Michigan Larkin decided to turn professional and, barely a month after his college career ended, the Cincinnati Reds made him their first-round draft choice with the fourth overall selection. Larkin immediately reported to Vermont in the AA Eastern League and helped to lead the team to a championship.

On to the Majors

The following season, Larkin was sent to Cincinnati's AAA ball club in Denver. He took the American Association by storm, batting .329 and hitting ten home runs. He was named to the American Association's All-Star team, and won the league's MVP, and Rookie of the Year awards. All of these accolades attracted the attention of the Reds. Larkin was called up to the Cincinnati Reds on August 13, 1986. Because he arrived in Cincinnati before any of his luggage, he played his first major league game wearing shorts, a batting glove and spikes that he borrowed from his new teammates. Despite this rough start, Larkin knocked in a run for his first major-league at-bat. He would go on to bat .306 with 14 runs batted in (RBI) in the last 24 games of the season. Despite a great major-league start, Larkin battled injuries in 1987 that included a hyper-extended knee. In 1988, Larkin batted .296 and earned the first of ten trips to the All-Star Game. He also led the major leagues by striking out only 24 times in 652 times at bat. In 1989, Larkin seemed destined for a tremendous season. At the All-Star break, he was third

> ### At a Glance...
>
> Born Barry Louis Larkin, April 28, 1964 in Cincinnati, OH; son of Bob (a chemist) and Shirley (a community activist); married; children: Brielle D'Shea, Cymber Nicole, DeShane Davis. *Education:* attended the University of Michigan.
>
> **Career:** Played football, basketball, and baseball at Cincinnati's Moeller High School, 1979-82; played baseball for the University of Michigan, 1983-85; drafted in the first round (fourth overall) by the Cincinnati Reds, 1985; played in Denver, CO at the AAA level, 1986; shortstop for the Cincinnati Reds, 1987-.
>
> **Awards:** Big Ten MVP and First-Team All-American, 1984-85; American Association MVP and Rookie of the Year, 1986; National League All-Star, 1988-91, 1993-97; Silver Slugger award winner, 1988-92, 1995-96, 1998; Gold Glove winner, 1994-96; National League MVP, 1995; finalist for the Branch Rickey "Service Over Self" award, 1996, 1998; Reds official team captain, 1997.
>
> **Addresses:** *Home*—Orlando, FL; *Office*—c/o The Cincinnati Reds, 100 Cinergy Field, Cincinnati, OH 45202.

in the National League in batting with a .340 average. Larkin was also named to the All-Star team. However, during an exhibition skills competition, he tore the medial collateral ligament in his elbow. His brilliant season was finished.

In 1990, Larkin and the Reds enjoyed a remarkable season that was capped by a World Series sweep of the Oakland A's. Larkin was named to his third consecutive All-Star game and, on four occasions, had hitting streaks of ten games or more. He finished the season with a .301 average and was healthy throughout the Reds run for the pennant. In the World Series, Larkin batted .353 and was named the Reds Most Valuable Player. The following year Larkin batted over .300 for the third year in a row, became a member of the National League All-Star team for the fourth consecutive year, and won the Reds' MVP Award. He also hit 20 home runs, which at that time tied a Reds record for homers in a season by a shortstop. Larkin's 69 RBIs led all National League shortstops during the 1991 campaign, in spite of the fact that he was sidelined for three weeks with elbow problems.

Prior to the 1992 season, the Reds made Larkin one of the highest-payed players in baseball by signing him through the 1996 season for $25.6 million. Before signing the new contract with the Reds, Larkin nearly left the team. Following the team's fifth place finish in 1991, Larkin spoke out publicly about what he perceived as the organization's lack of desire to win. He also hinted that he might leave the club via free agency. Larkin told the *Associated Press*, "Throughout the years, I've been kind of vocal about questioning the commitment to winning here. The things that happened this off-season showed me that this team does want to win. This is the kind of situation I want to be in." The team's decision to re-sign Larkin paid dividends immediately as he batted .304 and led all National League shortstops with 78 RBIs in 1992. These accomplishments came after one of Larkin's slowest career starts. He was batting only .179 when he sprained his knee on April 15, and went on the disabled list four days later. When he was activated on May 8, Larkin played 128 of the next 129 games. In 1992 he also started a long association with the Caring Team of Athletes, Inc., donating money to the charity each time he hit safely in a game.

Larkin started the 1993 season on an ominous note. He hurt his thumb before the second game of the season, although fans did not notice that Larkin was hurt. He was voted onto the All-Star team as a starter for the first time and finished the season with a .315 average. As the season wore on, Larkin's injury worsened. He went on the disabled list on August 5th and his thumb was placed in a cast 11 days later, thus ending a promising season. In 1994, Larkin finished the year with a batting average below .300 for the first time in five seasons. Because a players strike ended the season early, Larkin did not have time to overcome his slow start at the plate. However, he was named to the All-Star team for the sixth time and won his first Gold Glove.

The Most Valuable Player

The 1995 season became a milestone for Larkin. The perennial All-Star was named the National League's Most Valuable Player and led his team to the playoffs. Early in the season, Larkin summed up his game for Frank Lidz of *Sports Illustrated*, "I consider myself an amoeba man. I'll assume any shape to help the team. If the team needs someone to lead by example, I do that. If it needs someone to steal, I do that. If it needs someone to bunt or move a runner from second to third, I do that." Larkin started off the 1995 season quickly, hitting safely in 12 straight games from April 26 to May 9. In May of

1995, he batted .326 with two home runs and 18 RBIs. On the eighth of June, a pitch hit Larkin on the hand. He needed stitches on the back of his thumb and missed six games. After returning to the lineup, Larkin's bat was silenced and he went into a seven-for-62 slump. His batting average plummeted from .353 to .278. Larkin then went on a 13-game hitting streak. By the end of the 1995 season, Larkin was sixth in the National League in batting average (.319), second in stolen bases (51), fifth in runs (98), ninth in on-base percentage (.394), and tenth in hits (158). He also made only 11 errors in 544 appearances at shortstop, and won his second consecutive Gold Glove. Larkin summed up his season for Ross Newhan of the *Los Angeles Times* in typical understated fashion, "I played my game this year. This year it was critiqued, and people appreciated it for what it was. Because we were able to win, they spoke about it more often." Larkin also started his second All-Star game, and led the Reds to the National League Championship Series against the Los Angeles Dodgers. After the season Larkin signed another deal with the Reds, again making him one of the highest-paid players in baseball. Larkin followed up his MVP season with a sterling 1996 campaign. He hit 33 home runs and stole 36 bases to become the first shortstop in the history of the major leagues to join the 30/30 club. In addition to career-highs in home runs, Larkin established new personal highs in runs scored (117) and RBIs (89). He led the Reds in each of those categories and finished second in hits (154) with a .298 batting average. Larkin was acknowledged by the fans as the premier shortstop in the National League by being voted to start in the All-Star game for the third consecutive year. He also excelled on the defensive side of the diamond, earning his third Gold Glove at shortstop.

The Captain Takes Over

In 1997, Larkin was named the first official captain of the Cincinnati Reds since 1988. However, he battled injuries during the entire season, and appeared in only 73 games. Larkin developed Achilles tendon problems in his left foot, and a bone spur on his left big toe. He twice received cortisone injections so that he would be able to play. Despite his injuries, Larkin hit .317 for the season, and was named the National League Player of the Week in late May after hitting .583 with three home runs and six RBIs. He was also voted to start in the All-Star Game, but was unable to play due to injuries. Larkin was on the disabled list from mid-June until August first with a strained left calf. His season ended in September when he underwent surgery to correct problems with his left heel. Off the field, Larkin's Caring Team of Athletes, Inc. donated $25,000 to schools in Kentucky which were decimated by flooding.

Larkin's season got off to a rocky start in 1998. After appearing in just two spring training games, he underwent surgery to repair a bulging disc in his neck. There were also rumors that he might be traded as Cincinnati slashed $15 million from its payroll in an effort to save money and develop younger players. Larkin stayed with the team and returned to the lineup on April 7, 1998. In his first 25 games, he hit a paltry .169. Following this slow start, Larkin hit .336 the rest of the season to finish with a .309 average—leading all National League shortstops in batting average, home runs (17), and RBIs (72). Trade rumors involving Larkin continued to persist. At one point in the season, Larkin told his agent to ask for a trade to a contending team. When the Reds traded Bret Boone, perhaps the organization's most promising young player, following the 1998 season, Larkin expressed his frustration to Paul Daugherty of the *Cincinnati Enquirer,* "I want to win. I don't want to pay out the string. I don't want to be a coach. It's about winning, not about wanting to be here or there. If I have a chance to win here, great. If I don't, move me...It's not about me. It's about winning." Larkin was heavily criticized by the Cincinnati fans and media for his statement.

> "I consider myself an amoeba man. I'll assume any shape to help the team."

As the 1999 season began, Larkin remained with the Reds and served as a role model for younger players. Larkin told Daugherty of *The Cincinnati Enquirer* about the motivation behind his earlier comments, "I don't know if it was a matter of being mad. It was a matter of not knowing what was going on and being the captain of the team. It was having teammates calling me and asking what's going on and not being able to give them an answer." During the 1999 season, Larkin appeared in a career-high 161 games and posted a .293 batting average with 12 home runs and 75 RBIs. He also led the Reds to within one game of the National League playoffs, where they finished behind the New York Mets on the last day of the season. By the end of the 1999 season, Larkin had played in 1,707 games, knocked out 1,884 hits, hit 168 home runs, batted in 793 RBIs, and compiled a career average of .299. The only question that remained about Larkin's career was whether or not he would be a future inductee into baseball's Hall of Fame. For Reds fans, however, there is no doubt about Larkin's value to the city. As teammate Mark Sweeney told Chris Haft of the *Cincinnati Enquirer,* "Barry, he's Cincinnati."

Sources

Periodicals

The Cincinnati Enquirer, March 1, 1999 (Two articles).

The Los Angeles Times, January 20, 1992; November 16, 1995.

Sports Illustrated, June 12, 1995.

Other

Additional information for this entry was found on the worldwide web at http://www.majorleaguebaseball.com and http://www.cincinnatireds.com

—Michael J. Watkins

Roy Lassiter

1969—

Professional soccer player

Roy Lassiter was born on March 9, 1969 in Washington, D.C. and grew up to be one of the United States' most recognizable soccer players. The man who would star in his own Nike commercial started out humbly, not even being heavily recruited by the traditional college soccer powers. After high school he attended Lees McRae Junior College and was named Junior College All-American on the strength of a 21-goal season. He transferred to North Carolina State and made an immediate impact. In 1990 he led the Atlantic Coast Conference (ACC) in goals scored and points with 40 and was named to the All-Conference team. In his senior year, he scored 22 goals in 23 games. He was named All-Conference again, but because there was no professional soccer league in the United States at the time, his only options for a career in his sport were to play in a league abroad or to make the US National Team.

After graduating from college, Lassiter pinned all his hopes on making the U.S. squad; and the high-flying forward seemed to have a good chance. During one of his first practices, though, Lassiter was tackled from behind and his left ankle was broken. His chances with the National Team and perhaps his career in soccer were over.

A Brush with the Law

Not only did Lassiter break his ankle in the spring of 1992, his parents also divorced. Now he found himself with no job and plenty of time on his hands. The young man who suddenly had no career and very little guidance at home began to associate himself with the wrong kind of friends—spending his time partying and hanging out. In 1990, Lassiter had pleaded guilty to misdemeanors for breaking and entering, larceny, and credit card fraud. After a short time of idleness, Lassiter was committing crimes again. Lassiter and separate acquaintances broke into a house on May 23 and then another on July 8, 1992. The value of what Lassiter stole added up to $26,500. Though Lassiter's life seemed to be on the slide, physically he was improving and soon after the July robbery he left the country to play soccer in the Costa Rican First Division. Lassiter played the 1992-93 season in Turrialba, the 1993-94 season with Carmelita, and the 1994-95 season with Alajuela. In his third season in Costa Rica, Lassiter led his team to a second-place finish and scored 17 goals. He was named "For-

At a Glance...

Born Roy Lassiter, March 9, 1969 in Washington, D.C.; married with a son: Ariel Daniel; *Education*: Graduated in 1992 from North Carolina State.

Career: Starred at North Carolina State, 1989-91; played in Costa Rican First Division, 1992-92, 1994-95; began career in Major League Soccer (MLS) with the Tampa Bay Mutiny, 1996; traded to D.C. United, 1998; traded to the Miami Fusion, 1999.

Awards: Junior College All-American, 1988; All-Atlantic Coast Conference, 1990-91; named "Foreigner of the Year" in the Costa Rican First Division, 1995; MLS Golden Boot Award, MLS AT&T Best Eleven, 1996; MVP of CONCACAF Champions Cup, 1998; tied for the MLS lead in goals scored, 1999; leads MLS in career goals scored, 1996-99; made 29 appearances with three goals for U.S. National Team, 1992-99.

Addresses: *Residence*—Raleigh, N.C.; *Office*—c/o The Miami Fusion, 2200 W. Commercial Boulevard, Suite 104, Fort Lauderdale, FL 33309.

eigner of the Year" in Costa Rica. His success abroad was improving his game so that he was finally receiving attention on the U.S. National Team. He was also receiving attention from the police. After a detective read about Lassiter's game-winning goal in an international competition, the detective arrested him when he returned to the United States on August 8, 1995. He missed his first court date and was forced to surrender his passport. Lassiter, who was going to spend the 1995-96 season with the Brazilian club Santos, was forced to give up his chance to play for the legendary Brazilian side. A day after Lassiter scored the game-winning goal for the United States in a match against Saudi Arabia, he was sentenced to a month in jail. He was also sentenced to a ten-year suspended prison sentence, 200 hours of community service, a $500 restitution fine, and a $1,600 fine for court costs. The sentence was particularly embarrassing to Lassiter as he changed immensely in three years. His career was going along well, he had married and had a son by this time, and he had become a born-again Christian. His defense attorney Spurgeon Fields told the Associated Press: "He [Lassiter] is extremely remorseful. He has never denied doing this. It was just one of those things where he knew he had done wrong, but had changed his way of life and wanted to get this behind him."

Coming to America

His legal problems behind him, Lassiter stayed in his home country to join the fledgling American soccer league—Major League Soccer (MLS). He was signed by the Tampa Bay Mutiny. In his first season with the club, Lassiter led MLS in scoring with 27 goals in 30 games. Besides winning the Golden Boot as the league's top scorer, Lassiter received international recognition after the season when he was loaned to Genoa, a club in Italy's Seria B. After playing only four games in Italy, Lassiter returned to the United States and signed a three-year deal with the Mutiny, which made him one of the league's highest-paid players. Lassiter had another productive season for Tampa Bay in 1997 scoring ten goals in 24 games, but the following season, Lassiter seemed to hit the wall. After six games with Tampa Bay in 1998, he had no goals. The club, frustrated with its star's lack of production, traded him to league-dynasty D.C. United. In his first game with his new team, Lassiter scored his first goal of the season. He would score in 12 of his first 15 games with his new team including a hat trick against D.C. rival, the Chicago Fire. Lassiter's then coach Bruce Arena commented on his new forward's impact on the team for *Sports Illustrated's* Grant Wahl: "Here you have a black American born in Washington, D.C., who comes back and happens to be fluent in Spanish. Plus he's been scoring goals. If we had to write a job description for a forward to match up with us, he'd fit the bill."

International Glory

Late in the 1998 season, Lassiter again made his mark on the international scene in the CONCACAF Champions Cup. In addition to its regular season in MLS, D.C. United was competing in an international tournament for championship clubs throughout North America, Latin America, and the Caribbean. Lassiter drove his team to become the first U.S. club to ever win the CONCACAF Championship Cup. In the quarterfinals against Joe Public of Trinadad and Tobago Lassiter scored four goals. In the semifinals of the competition, Lassiter scored both his team's goals as United defeated CSD Leon of Mexico 2-0. After D.C. United defeated Mexican champion CD Tolvea for the final victory, Lassiter was named the Most Valuable Player of the Champions Cup. Back in the US, Lassiter helped his team reach the MLS Championship Series, but the team lost to the Chicago Fire.

In 1999, Lassiter had another standout year. The 30-year-old forward kept up his scorching scoring pace and finished the season tied for the first in goals (18). In the playoffs, Lassiter tallied three goals and one assist and D.C. United won its third MLS Cup in four years. But the season did not end on a happy note for Lassiter. Midway through the 1999 campaign, D.C. United made a trade with the Miami Fusion. The Washington, D.C.—based team sent a current player, a draft pick, and a player to be named later to Miami. All season Lassiter was rumored to be that player to be named later. And he was. After United's MLS Cup victory, Lassiter was shipped to the Fusion on November 23. The trade left a bitter taste as Lassiter explained to Brook Tunstall of the *Washington Times:* "When the deal first went down and I heard my name came up, I went to (D.C. United management) and they said not to worry, that I wasn't going anywhere. But I kept hearing the rumors, and I asked them again about two or three weeks ago and they wouldn't tell me anything. They lied to me. They knew all along they were going to trade me and they lied." After the trade, Lassiter even said that he might not report to Miami unless he receives a raise in line with his talents—which are prodigious. Though his status for the 2000 season was up in the air, his place as one of the most productive and exciting players in American soccer history is secure. At the end of the 1999 season, Lassiter had scored 73 goals and added 25 assists in his four seasons in MLS. He holds the league record in all-time goals and points (171), has appeared in three MLS All-Star games, and was named to the AT&T "Best 11" Team after the 1997 season.

Sources

Periodicals

Sports Illustrated, August 3, 1998.
The Sporting News, August 14, 1998.
The Washington Times, November 25, 1999.

Other

Additional material for this entry was found on the worldwide web at www.dcinited.com/theteam/players/lassiter.htm.
http://www.soccertimes.com.
http://www.socceramerica.com.

—Michael J. Watkins

Queen Esther Marrow

1943(?)—

Gospel vocalist

If your mother names you "Queen," you better have the class and dignity to live up to it. Gospel singer Queen Esther Marrow has proven throughout her illustrious career that she is worthy of the name. She has sung for four presidents, Pope John Paul II and the British royal family, and has performed with Bob Dylan, Harry Belafonte, Lena Horne, Ray Charles and Oscar the Grouch. As a member of the Harlem Gospel Singers, Marrow has touched millions with a high-spirited gospel-fest that blends jazz, blues and R&B. "The word 'gospel' means good news," she explained to Monte Young of *Newsday*. "I don't see myself trying to reach young people so much that I lose what I have to say about the gospel. I keep traditional music with an underneath sound of contemporary. If you believe what you are saying in your message, then you are not selling yourself out."

Marrow was born in Newport News, Virginia, and was raised by her grandparents on a farm outside of town. Although it was her mother who christened her "Queen," it was Marrow's grandmother who gave her the inner strength that this regal moniker evokes. A devoted churchwoman, she eventually lead young Esther through the doors of the United House of Prayer for All People.

Influenced by the Church

"As soon as I could walk she was taking me off to the local Apolistic church," Marrow told John Crace of the *Independent*. "And I loved it. I loved the Bible stories and I loved the singing. I can remember playing on the swing in the back yard singing the Lord's Prayer to myself. When I was eight, I joined the choir." The church band that played with the choir consisted of five trombones, a tuba, a trumpet, a saxophone, a bass drum and a cymbal hit with a coat hanger.

It was while singing with the choir that Marrow first felt the power of gospel music. As she matured, she was further inspired by the voice of legendary gospel singer Mahalia Jackson coming through her radio. "When I first heard Mahalia sing, it changed my life," Marrow told Hazel Smith of the *New York Beacon*. "I knew that I had to reach for the fervent messages in her songs and try to match the vocal power that this wonderful woman possessed. She was my inspiration."

At a Glance...

Born Queen Esther Marrow in Newport News, Virginia, c. 1943.

Career: Began singing in church choir as a child; sang with Duke Ellington and his Orchestra at the first sacred concert in San Francisco, 1966; toured with the Ellington band, 1966-70; performed as part of Dr. Martin Luther King's "World Crusade," 1966; performed at the Kennedy Center to honor Dr. King's widow, Coretta Scott King, 1968; performed on Broadway in the musicals, *Comin' Uptown* and *It's So Nice To Be Civilized*, and appeared as Auntie Em in *The Wiz*, c. 1972-76; starred in George Faison's national touring production of *Sing Mahalia, Sing*, c. 1977; portrayed the mother of Oscar the Grouch on *Sesame Street*, c. early 1970s; appeared in the film, *The Last Dragon*, 1985; wrote, produced and starred in the musical *Truly Blessed*, 1990; formed the Harlem Gospel Singers, 1991; toured with the Harlem Gospel Singers, 1992–.

Awards: Nominated for three Helen Hayes awards for *Truly Blessed*.

Addresses: *Office*—BB Promotion, L7, 7a, Mannheim, Germany D-68161.

Sang for Duke Ellington

Following her graduation from high school, a thirst for big city life led Marrow to New York where she lived with her aunt and found work at a manufacturer in the garment district. An impromptu performance of "Happy Birthday" for her boss so impressed him, that he introduced her to a friend who knew Duke Ellington. A few weeks later, Marrow auditioned in Ellington's Harlem apartment. "I sang "How Great Thou Art" in his living room," Marrow told Paula Span of *The Washington Post*. "Billy Strayhorn was playing the piano. After Duke listened—he was a person who didn't talk much—he looked up and said, 'It was good.'"

Ellington hired Marrow to sing at the first of his sacred concerts, which took place at Grace Cathedral in San Francisco in 1966. "I still get goose bumps about the actual performance," she recalled to *USA Today*. "It was a Saturday evening, and the sun [was] shining through the stained-glass windows. When I turned and looked at Johnny Hodges playing that solo on "Come Sunday," tears were streaming down his face. The band had on white jackets, and I had on a white dress. It was so beautiful, and I can see it like yesterday."

Marrow went on tour periodically with Ellington and his band for the next four years and received a formal musical education from the great bandleader. "He expanded my musical being. He taught me that what you feel inside of you, you can't stifle it—you have to let it grow," she told Lisa Raushchart of the *Washington Times*. "If you feel it, work on it and you can do it." In 1999, Marrow reprised her performance of "Come Sunday" at the Washington National Cathedral to commemorate what would have been Ellington's 100th birthday. "When Marrow sang, 'I don't mind the gray skies/cause they're just clouds passing by,'" *Washington Post* writer Richard Harrington remarked, "she embodied the yearning and hope at the heart of the black church, as well as the personal faith and optimism so central to Ellington himself."

When not singing with the Ellington band, Marrow joined Dr. Martin Luther King's "World Crusade," which was a series of civil rights rallies. The tour's Chicago rally featured Marrow's idol, Mahalia Jackson. "That night on stage, she put her arms around me, said 'Come on, baby, we're going to sing'—I thought I was in seventh heaven." She also toured with Harry Belafonte around this time and, following the assassination of Dr. King in 1968, performed at the Kennedy Center to honor his widow, Coretta Scott King.

Returned to Gospel Music

Although she was a gospel singer, Marrow also sang in jazz clubs. This transition proved to be a difficult one for her. "One gets the impression," John Wilson wrote in a 1971 nightclub review in the *New York Times*, "...that she is working under wraps, muffling her individuality to try to conform to the routine expectations of a nightclub audience." Marrow also recognized the problem and decided to focus on gospel. "I made up my mind to do gospel music, that I couldn't serve two [masters]," she told Young of *Newsday*. "It had to be one or the other. I was brought up in the church, and gospel is really all I know."

During the 1970s, Marrow branched out into other areas of show business. She performed on Broadway in the musicals, *Comin' Uptown* and *It's So Nice To Be Civilized*, and appeared as Auntie Em in *The Wiz*. She also starred in choreographer/director George Faison's national touring production of *Sing Mahalia, Sing*. On television, Marrow portrayed the mother of Oscar the Grouch on *Sesame Street*.

The 1970s offered Marrow an array of opportunities, but she experienced difficult times during the 1980s. Although she appeared in the film, *The Last Dragon*, and sang on two Bob Dylan albums during the middle of the 1980s, work opportunities were scarce. Unable to find sustainable work in entertainment, Marrow took sales jobs at Saks Fifth Avenue and Bloomingdale's and worked as a toll-taker at the New Rochelle exit of the New York State Thruway. "There were times I'd get despondent, down in the mouth," she admitted to Paula Span of the *Washington Post,* but she would tell herself, "...[just] because I don't have a record deal doesn't mean I'm not good."

Wrote and Produced a Musical

Marrow's positive attitude and self-confidence gave her the courage to write, produce and star in the musical *Truly Blessed* in 1990. Based on the life of Mahalia Jackson, the show appeared on Broadway and toured both nationally and in Europe. Although the reviews of *Truly Blessed* were mixed, the production earned three nominations for the prestigious Helen Hayes Award.

In 1991 Marrow and her manager, Roseanne Kirk, met German music impresario Michael Brenner. Brenner shared the two women's vision for a new kind of gospel show that would examine and celebrate gospel music and its influence on jazz, blues, R&B and pop. Because Europe had long championed African American music, Marrow formed the Harlem Gospel Singers and toured the continent in 1992. "I really can't tell you why I haven't had the same success here [in the United States] that I've had in Europe," she remarked to Young. "It bothers me to a certain extent. But I feel it will [come], all in due time. It's all in God's plan and it will happen."

After eight years in existence, Marrow and the Harlem Gospel Singers had performed for more than two million people in Europe, including Pope John Paul II. John Crace of the *Independent* described a typical concert in Berlin. "The audience was made up of everyone from smacked-out students to well-heeled 50-somethings, and by the end of the show every single one of them is on their feet, dancing." Buoyed by their success in Europe, Marrow and the Harlem Gospel Singers began to tour the United States in 1999.

Marrow's performances in the United States were as successful as those in Europe. "The show has the energy of a dozen revival meetings, the power of a couple of locomotives and the sheer joy of what feels like all humanity," extolled William Triplett of the *Washington Post.* Initially the show was called *Inspiration* but Marrow changed the named to *Higher and Higher,* after the old Jackie Wilson hit, a rendition of which the group performs. "We're giving you inspiration automatically," she told James Sullivan of the *San Francisco Chronicle*. "Higher and higher is where we want to take the people."

Selected discography

Live at Philharmonic Hall-Cologne.
Live in Paris.
Happiness, 1999.

Sources

Daily Telegraph (London), February 21, 1998.
Independent (London), February 6, 1998, p. 18.
New York Beacon, May 21, 1997, p. 20.
New York Times, June 21, 1971, p. 37; April 23, 1990, p. C-13.
New Yorker, May 7, 1990, p. 83.
Newsday (New York), May 27, 1998, p. B0; May 1, 1999, p. D-4.
San Francisco Chronicle, August 22, 1999, p. 40.
San Francisco Examiner, August 26, 1999.
USA Today, April 29, 1999, p. 2-D.
Village Voice, May 8, 1990, p. 111.
Washington Post, January 31, 1999, p. G-1; February 5, 1999, p. C-1; April 30, 1999, p. C-1.
Washington Times, February 14, 1999, p. D-1.

—Brian Escamilla

Mase

1977(?)—

Hip-hop rap artist

Barely out of high school, Mason Durrell Betha, a.k.a. Mase, found his way into one of the most successful entertainment circles of the 1990s—Sean "Puffy" Combs' Bad Boy Entertainment. Mase ended up signing with the label and going on to appear on dozens of hit records for artists like chart-topping pop singer Mariah Carey, veteran Tina Turner, and hip-hop brethren like the Notorious B.I.G. He appeared on songs that achieved success on the hip-hop, R&B, pop, and Billboard charts. Mase was seen by critics as Combs' protege, and Combs referred to Mase as "my little brother." When he did release his first record, *Harlem World,* on Bad Boy, it debuted at No. 1 on the Billboard 200 chart and went quadruple platinum. Although Mase's songs ranged from uplifting hip-hop dance tracks to menacing hard-core raps, he always thanks God—and Combs—for his success. In 1999, just before the release of his second solo album, *Double Up,* the young and successful rapper announced his retirement from music and his dedication to God.

Born in Jacksonville, Florida, Mase and his family moved to the heart of New York City's Harlem when he was five years old. He divided his time between school, church, and basketball. When he got involved in the Harlem street life a little too heavily for his mother's comfort, she sent him back to Jacksonville for two years. Mase returned to Harlem to graduate the Manhattan Center for Science and Mathematics in 1994, and then attend the State University of New York at Purchase on a basketball scholarship. He quit his second year to pursue his career in music. "She wasn't okay with that at all," Mase told *Rolling Stone* writer David Fricke of his mom. "But she always respected my decisions, and I just told her that this is my dream."

Combs' Cuddly Star

Mase, then struggling to make it as Mase Murder, traveled to Atlanta, Georgia, to meet noted producer Jermaine Dupri. Instead, at a party hosted by Dupri, he met Combs. Mase rapped for him on the spot and Combs asked him to join the Bad Boy "Family" of recording artists. Combs first had Mase rapping on a song by Bad Boy group 112, then on pop diva Mariah Carey's "Honey," Notorious B.I.G.'s "Mo' Money Mo' Problems," and Comb's "No Way Out." Although he had

> ### At a Glance...
>
> Born Mason Durrell Betha c. 1977 in Jacksonville, FL. *Education:* graduated, Manhattan Center for Science and Mathematics, 1994; studied at State University of New York at Purchase.
>
> **Career:** Rapper, Bad Boy Entertainment, 1997-99.
>
> **Awards:** Quadruple-platinum award for four million in sales of *Harlem World*.
>
> **Addresses:** *Office*—Bad Boy Entertainment, 1540 Broadway, 30th Floor, New York, NY 10036.

no release of his own yet, Mase was becoming a familiar face to fans—he appeared in more than six high-rotation music videos. On the 1997 MTV Video Music awards, Mase joined the Bad Boy Family and veteran rocker Sting to perform "I'll Be Missing You," a tribute to the Notorious B.I.G.—who was gunned down outside a Los Angeles club in 1997.

Mase is known for his sound, which is monotonic, slow and mellow. *Rolling Stone* writer Fricke wrote that Mase's rapping has "sleepy, unforced authority." *Village Voice* writer Robert Christgau defined Mase's sound as a "phlegmatic, just-woke-up drawl." *Harlem World* executive producer Deric "D-dot" Angelettie told *Rolling Stone*, that Mase "says things in such a manner where it's real street but also real easy to understand. That's a knack few MCs have." Mase is also recognized for his unthreatening demeanor. While most rappers strove to be known as hard, "gangsta" street characters, Mase eagerly displayed his child-like charisma. Christgau called him the "cuddliest rapper ever," and Mase told *Spin*'s Sia Michel that he wanted to be the "black Barney," referring to the purple dinosaur and children's television star.

Hit Big with *Harlem World*

1997's *Harlem World*, aside from going quadruple platinum and debuting at #1 on the Billboard 200 chart, earned approval from critics. A smash hit, Christgau wrote that the record's success may have even been a surprise to Mase and to Bad Boy. "Suddenly, he saw his debut album debut at No. 1, which was a given," Christgau wrote, "and then maintain for a second week, which wasn't."

Once he achieved financial success, Mase sought to help those who weren't as fortunate as he. The athletic director at Laurinburg Institute in North Carolina asked Mase's former coach Richard Pagan to head up a girls basketball team at the school. Pagan picked some of the most talented players from Manhattan's Riverside Church League and moved them to the North Carolina school. Mase footed the $10,000 tuition, books, and board for each of the nine girls. "Coach Pagan and Riverside Church were always there for us and providing us with positive alternatives to running the streets, that I felt it was my job to assist them in supporting the girls here," Mase said in an interview with Jumoke R. Gamble of *Newsday*. "... I'm trying to create an opportunity for kids in New York to up their chances in life." In exchange for Mase's support, each girl got a "Harlem World" tattoo on one arm.

More Than a Song

"Harlem World" is a concept that goes beyond the title of the rapper's first solo release. It's the name of the first group he put out on his new label, All Out Records, under Dupri's So So Def label, in March of 1999. Mase's twin sister Stason "Stase" Betha appeared on Harlem World's first release, *The Movement*. Also, Harlem World means "sharing where I'm from and mapping out where I'm looking to go," Mase said in *Newsday*.

In 1999, the month before the scheduled release of his second album on Bad Boy, *Double Up*, Mase announced that he would retire from music to follow God. "I'm grateful for all the blessings bestowed on me that were a result of my music career," Mase said in a Bad Boy press release. "Now it's time for me to serve God in His way. The Lord sends you messages when He's ready and not necessarily when we are." He reportedly had plans to get involved helping inner-city kids, while also considering pursuing a psychology degree, preaching, and travel. To promote the record for Bad Boy, Mase agreed to speaking engagements only, and would not do any performances. He told *USA Today*, "I just felt like my work as a rapper is done."

Selected discography

Harlem World, Bad Boy, 1997.
"Feel So Good," Bad Boy, 1997.
"Lookin' at Me" [US CD/LP Single], Bad Boy, 1998.
"Lookin' at Me" [US CD5/Cassette Single], Bad Boy, 1998.
"What You Want [#1]," Bad Boy, 1998.
"What You Want [#2]," Bad Boy, 1998.

Double Up, Bad Boy, 1999.
"Lookin' at Me" [Australia CD Single], BMG International, 1999.
"All I Ever Wanted," BMG International, 1999.

Appears on

Tribe Called Quest, *Beats, Rhymes and Life,* Jive, scratching, 1996.
Turner, Tina, *Wildest Dreams,* Virgin, drum programming, 1996.
One Twelve, *112,* Bad Boy, rap, 1996.
Holiday, Tasha, *Just the Way You Like It,* MCA, rap, 1997.
Winans, Mario, *Story of My Heart,* Motown, rap, 1997.
McKnight, Brian, *Anytime,* Mercury, rap, 1997.
Carey, Mariah, *Butterfly,* Columbia, vocals, 1997.
Winans, Mario, *Don't Know,* Motown, Rap, remixing, 1997.
Dupri, Jermaine, *Jermaine Dupri Presents: Life in 1472,* So So Def, 1998.
Bad Boy's Greatest Hits, *Bad Boy's Greatest Hits,* Bad Boy, rap, 1998.
Total, *Kima, Keisha & Pam,* Bad Boy, 1998.
South Park, *Chef Aid: The South Park Album,* Columbia, vocals, 1998.
Carey, Mariah, *#1's,* Sony, backround vocals, 1998.
DJ Clue, *Professional,* Def Jam, rap, 1998.
Turner, Tina, *Wildest Dreams [Bonus CD],* EMI, drum programming, 1998.
Harlem World, *Movement,* Sony, producer, executive producer, 1999.

Sources

Periodicals

Jet, May 17, 1999, p. 22.
Newsday, January 14, 1999, p. A78.
Newsweek, June 21, 1999, p. 77.
Rolling Stone, January 22, 1998, p. 27; February 5, 1998, p. 20.
Village Voice, December 16, 1997, p. 95.

Other

Additional information for this profile was obtained from Bad Boy Entertainment publicity materials, 1999, and from a profile of Mase at http://www.ubl.com/ubl_artist.asp?artistid=24162&p_id=p+++276343

—Brenna Sanchez

Fred McGriff

1963—

Professional baseball player

Fred McGriff's ability to hit home runs has amazed and delighted baseball fans throughout his career. The Tampa Bay Devil Rays first baseman will start his 15th year in baseball at the start of the 2000 season. In that time, he has compiled career statistics that are comparable to those achieved by players enshrined in Major League Baseball's Hall of Fame. McGriff has enjoyed a career that many major league baseball players only dream of, while conducting himself with a calm professionalism.

Humble Beginnings

Taken in the ninth round of the free agent draft by the New York Yankees in 1981, McGriff was traded the following year to the Toronto Blue Jays. That transaction marked the beginning of his workmanlike approach to professional baseball. He toiled in the minor leagues for six seasons, averaging .249 and demonstrating a potential for greatness. After paying his dues in the minors, McGriff eventually graduated to the big leagues. He would quickly make the most of this opportunity.

McGriff was named to Toronto's major league roster in 1986. To improve his hitting abilities, he sought the advice of Blue Jays manager and former slugger Cito Gaston. Gaston taught McGriff to be more patient at the plate, and helped him to overcome his fear of left-handed pitchers. This guidance paid off handsomely for McGriff. After hitting his first major league home run off of Boston pitcher Bob Stanley on April 17, 1987, McGriff quickly established himself as a home run threat. He went on to hit 20 home runs during the 1987 season, which set a club record for rookies.

In 1988, McGriff continued to develop at the plate and replaced Willie Upshaw as Toronto's regular first baseman. He enjoyed a stellar 1988 season. McGriff finished second in the American League with 34 home runs, and second in slugging percentage (.525) and extra-base hits, with 73. He also lead American League first basemen with a nearly flawless .997 fielding percentage.

McGriff's assault on American League pitching continued in 1989 as he led the American League with 36

At a Glance...

Born on October 31, 1963 in Tampa, FL; married to Veronica; children: Erick and Ericka.

Career: Drafted by the New York Yankees on June 8, 1981 in the ninth round of free-agent draft; played for the Toronto Blue Jays, 1982-90; San Diego Padres, 1990-93; Atlanta Braves, 1993-97; Tampa Bay Devil Rays, 1998-.

Awards: Holds major league record for most grand slam home runs in consecutive games with two, 1991; First player in modern era to win a home run title in both the American and National Leagues, with 36 homers in the AL (1989) and 35 in the NL (1992); named Most Valuable Player in All-Star Game, 1994.

Addresses: *Office*—Tampa Bay Devil Rays, Tropicana Field, 1 Tropicana Drive, St. Petersburg, FL 33705.

---

home runs. This was an especially impressive feat because McGriff battled a slump at the end of the season and did not hit a home run during the last 24 games of the season. On June 5, 1989, he hit a two-run blast against the Milwaukee Brewers that marked the first home run in Toronto's new ballpark, the Sky Dome. He also drew a total of 119 walks, a Toronto Blue Jays record.

Traded to San Diego

In 1990, McGriff enjoyed another successful season. He hit .300 for the first time in his career and ranked fourth in the American League in home runs with 35. He also reached a career-high in hits (167), and had three two-home run games against Boston, Cleveland, and California. Following the conclusion of the 1990 season, McGriff was traded to the San Diego Padres.

During McGriff's first season in San Diego, he smacked 31 homers and batted in 106 runs. In August of 1991, he hit grand slams in back-to-back games. McGriff became only the third National League player in the 20th century to accomplish this rare feat. His second consecutive grand slam was hit off of Jim Deshaies, who hadn't allowed a grand slam in his five full major league seasons. Former Blue Jays teammate Lloyd Moseby summed up McGriff's talent in a 1989 *Sports Illustrat-*

ed article, "Fred...has a good eye and power, a combination you don't see too often anymore. And the power. You know that highlight reel that shows the Willie Mays catch and then switched to the fan, who grabs his head with his hands in amazement? Fred McGriff does that to you when he hits a home run."

McGriff continued to shine in San Diego, thanks to his strong bat and an even stronger chemistry with his teammates. In 1992, McGriff and teammate Gary Sheffield became an intense one-two punch for the Padres. That year, the duo formed the National League's best home run combination. McGriff batted .286 with 35 home runs, while Sheffield hit .330 with 33 homers. For the second time in three seasons, McGriff led his league in home runs. Despite his consistently stellar performances, he remained humble. As McGriff told Ralph Wiley of *Sports Illustrated*, "You know what I always dreamed? I dreamed of being a ballplayer. I guess all kids dream that, don't they? But you know, I dreamed that dream even when I was awake. Now when I hit some of my longest home runs, I don't even swing hard. How I do it, I don't know. But baseball will humble you real quick. I stay prepared for that." In addition to Sheffield, McGriff teamed with Tony Fernandez and future Hall of Famer Tony Gwynn to anchor San Diego's formidable offense. The four men, who were eventually dubbed The Four Tops, continually punished opposing pitchers. As the Padres entered the final week of the 1992 season, each of The Four Tops was hitting over .300.

McGriff began the 1993 season with the Padres. He belted 18 home runs and batted in 46 runs before being traded to the Atlanta Braves during mid-season. The move to Atlanta did not adversely affect his performance at the plate. McGriff blasted another 19 home runs and batted in 55 runs for the Braves, finishing the year with a career-high 37 homers.

McGriff smacked 34 home runs for the Braves in 1994, making him just the ninth player in baseball history to hit more than 30 home runs in seven consecutive seasons. By doing so, he joined the elite company of Hall of Famers Babe Ruth, Lou Gehrig, Jimmie Foxx, Ralph Kiner, Mickey Mantle, Eddie Matthews, Hank Aaron, and Mike Schmidt. In addition to hitting 34 home runs, McGriff was named to the 1994 National League All-Star team. He earned the All-Star Game's Most Valuable Player award when he hit a game-tying homer off of Lee Smith in the ninth inning to lead the National League to a 10-9 win. On June 7, 1994, he hit a career-high five RBIs in one game against the San Francisco Giants. During the last 10 games of the season, he hit seven home runs and batted in 13 runs. At the end of the

1994 season, McGriff placed fourth in the National League in homers (34), RBIs (94), total bases (264) and slugging percentage (.623).

During McGriff's next three seasons with the Atlanta Braves, he hit 27, 28 and 22 home runs respectively. In 1996, he achieved a personal milestone by hitting his 300th home run. By finishing that year with 28 home runs, McGriff achieved his 10th straight, 20-plus home run season.

Returned Home

Following the end of the 1997 season, McGriff was traded to the expansion Tampa Bay Devil Rays. The trade to the Devil Rays marked a homecoming for McGriff, who was born and raised in Tampa. He lived only four blocks from Al Lopez Field, the former spring training home of the Cincinnati Reds. "I can't remember going to my first game," McGriff told Riley. "I mean, I was always at a baseball game. I lived at ball games. I always loved the game."

McGriff, who was born on October 31, 1963, is the youngest son of Eliza and Earl McGriff. Along with his other siblings, sisters Sandra and Terrie and brothers Michael and Dexter, McGriff received a great deal of love and guidance from his parents. "Freddie's well adjusted," Earl McGriff told *Sports Illustrated,* "They all are. We let our children produce at their own speed. We didn't push them. We didn't hold them back. There are no bad children, only bad parents."

Sources

Periodicals

Jet, August 1, 1994, pg. 50.
Sports Illustrated, May 8, 1989, pg. 34; June 15, 1992, pg. 36.
The Sporting News, June 20, 1994, pg. 8.

Other

Additional material for this essay was found on the Internet at http://www.sportingnews.com and http://espn.go.com/mlb/profiles/profile/3579.html.

—John Horn

Don Newcombe

1926—

Professional baseball player

Don Newcombe is the only man in baseball history to win all three of the sport's major awards, winning Rookie of the Year, the Cy Young award, and Most Valuable Player. While he got his start in the Negro Leagues, it wasn't long before he followed Jackie Robinson into Major League baseball, where he was one of the first four African Americans to play in the major leagues during the late 1940s. In his prime, Newcombe was one of the most feared pitchers in baseball and is considered one of the best-hitting pitchers of all time.

Newcombe was born June 14, 1926 in Madison, New Jersey to Roland and Sadie (Sayers) Newcombe. One of five children, he was nine years old when his older brother managed a semiprofessional baseball club. Newcombe took batting and pitching practice there, but it wasn't until a few years later in junior high school that he played both football and baseball. He preferred baseball to football, but when Newcombe attended Jefferson High School in Elizabeth, New Jersey, there was no baseball team.

Started in Negro Leagues

In 1942, Newcombe joined the U.S. Army. However, because he was only 16 years old at the time, he was released. He joined the Navy in August of 1943, but was discharged a month later. Newcombe had planned to be a truck driver, and never seriously considered baseball as a career option. He tried out with the Newark Eagles, which was a Negro League team, and signed a contract in 1943. He posted seven wins and five losses as a pitcher in 1944. The following year, Newcombe proved that he was also an excellent hitter. He posted a 14-4 record, and was named to the Negro National League All-Star team. In October of 1945, Newcombe pitched at Ebbetts Field in Brooklyn. It was the first time that he had faced white big league players. He pitched three scoreless innings before leaving the game with a sore elbow. Newcombe's performance impressed Clyde Sukeforth, a scout for the Brooklyn Dodgers. He invited Newcombe to try out for the team. The tryout was successful, and Newcombe was signed to the Dodgers' Class B farm team at Nashua, New Hampshire along with catcher Roy Campanella.

At a Glance...

Born Donald Newcombe, June 14, 1926, in Madison, NJ; wife's name Freddie; children: Gregory and Evit. *Religion:* Methodist.

Career: Played for Newark Eagles in Negro Leagues beginning 1944 season; signed by the Dodgers organization and assigned to Class B New England farm team at Nashua, NH in 1946; promoted to AAA team, Montreal Royals, in 1948; promoted to Brooklyn Dodgers in 1949. Was a starting pitcher most of his Major League career; director of community relations with Los Angeles Dodgers.

Awards: Negro National League All Star Team, 1945; National League All Star Team, 1949; National League Rookie of the Year, 1949; National League All Star Team, 1950; National League All Star Team, 1955; Cy Young award, 1956; Most Valuable Player, 1956; Honorary Doctorate, Daniel Webster College 1997.

Addresses: *Office*—Director, Community Relations, c/o Los Angeles Dodgers, Dodger Stadium, 1000 Elysian Park Drive, Los Angeles, CA 90012.

Branch Rickey, the owner of the Dodgers and the man who is credited with integrating major league baseball, tried to have Newcombe and Campanella assigned to the Class A affiliate in Danville, Illinois. However, league officials refused to accept them and threatened to shut down the league if they were forced to integrate.

Newcombe did not know what to expect when he and Campanella arrived in Nashua. Segregation and racism were still the norm in the United States at the time, and African Americans were often barred from many hotels and restaurants. Newcombe would tell *The Telegraph* (Nashua) over fifty years later, "When Roy Campanella and I came to Nashua in 1946....We were embarking on a mission. This was a mission in Nashua that was helping to revolutionize the game of baseball, that was going to impact on black people all over the world....It was in April of 1946, and the graciousness of how we were accepted here really shocked us." Both men were pleasantly surprised that they did not experience racial prejudice during their time in Nashua.

In 1947, which was Newcombe's second season in Nashua, he compiled a record of 19 wins and 6 losses.

He pitched 223 innings, and struck out 186 batters. He also led the New England league in wins and strikeouts. That same year Jackie Robinson, who would become the first African American to play in the major leagues, was transferred from the Dodgers' minor league team in Montreal to the major league club in Brooklyn, New York. In 1948, Campanella and pitcher Dan Bankhead joined Robinson in Brooklyn. Newcombe, however, remained in Nashua.

Newcombe was called up to the Brooklyn Dodgers in 1949, but not before he nearly walked out of baseball for good. In 1948, Newcombe was promoted from Nashua to the Montreal team. However, he was eager to play for the Brooklyn Dodgers and he began to believe that owner Branch Rickey would never promote him. Newcombe decided to quit baseball, and left Montreal. Three days later, he called Montreal general manager Buzzie Bavasi and asked to be reinstated to the team. Bavasi agreed to Newcombe's request, and he remained in Montreal until 1949. At the time, Newcombe did not realize that Rickey was gradually adding African American players to the major leagues in a "stair-step" plan, so as to avoid problems with other Dodger players and fans.

Played Integrated Baseball

Newcombe joined the Brooklyn Dodgers in May of 1949, and compiled a record of 17 wins and eight losses. He struck out 149 batters in 244 innings and had a 3.17 earned-run average. He also pitched 32 consecutive scoreless innings, and won the National League Rookie of the Year award. Reflecting on the year of 1949, Newcombe told Art Rust, Jr. in *Get That Nigger Off the Field*, "I was the first black pitcher ever to take the mound in a Major League World Series game. At the time I remember I had a double set of feelings: a modicum of fear about the Yankee dynasty we were playing and that I was only a rookie." Newcombe also told Rust about his debut with the Newark Eagles, "I didn't have a dream back in 1944 that I would be pitching against the Yankees in the 1949 series. Back in 1944 there was no way that a kid from the ghetto in Elizabeth, New Jersey, could ever think along those lines." While pitching in the fourth game of the 1949 World Series against the New York Yankees, Newcombe gave up a home run to Tommy Henrich. The Yankees won the game 1-0, and went on to win the series. Despite the loss, Newcombe was considered one of the best pitchers in the major leagues.

During the early 1950s, Newcombe was drafted into the army and served during the Korean War. Although he was nearing the end of his eligibility for the draft, Newcombe related to *The Telegraph,* (Nashua, New Hampshire) that he was told that the American public needed to see that baseball players did not receive special treatment. Following his discharge, Newcombe resumed his baseball career. After a shaky start, he returned to form and enjoyed a remarkable season in 1955. That year, Newcombe was named to the National League All-Star team and ended the regular season with the National League's best pitching record. He also faced the Yankees again in the World Series, losing the first game in his only World Series start. However, the Dodgers went on to defeat the Yankees in seven games. The following year, Newcombe again led National League pitchers with a 27-7 record. He compiled a .794 winning percentage, striking out 139 batters while walking only 46. Newcombe also captured both the Most Valuable Player award and the Cy Young award.

Tired of Segregation

Despite the tremendous success that Newcombe enjoyed, he grew tired of the segregation that was prevalent in the United States during the 1940s and 1950s. Until 1954, Newcombe and other African American players had to stay in segregated hotels during road trips. These hotels were not nearly as comfortable as those enjoyed by their white teammates. They were often not air conditioned, and the food was of poor quality. Newcombe told Rust in *Get That Nigger Off the Field* that he complained to Jackie Robinson that he had had enough, "I've just spent two years in the Army fighting for my flag, for my country. I'm not going to live like a substandard human being anymore unless somebody can tell me why I've got to live like that." Robinson agreed, and they both went to the hotel and talked with the manager about the situation. They were told that as long as they didn't use the swimming pool they could stay in the hotel. "Eventually Jackie, I, and Roy Campanella moved into all the hotels with the team on a regular basis and incidents like these became part of baseball lore," Newcombe told Rust.

Newcombe often appeared lethargic and seemed unwilling to work hard. However, former Dodger Jim Gilliam told Rust, "Everyone thought he [Newcombe] was a lazy pitcher, but actually Don was the hardest-working pitcher around." One of Newcombe's former opponents, Chicago Cubs shortstop Ernie Banks, told Rust, "A lot of fans have asked me who's the toughest pitcher I had to face in the majors. I would say Don Newcombe. He had tremendous drive. He loved competition, was a winning-type pitcher....He had great control, and he could hit like hell; he was the type of man everybody would like to be like."

In 1957, Newcombe struggled throughout the season and finished with a mediocre record of 11-12. He was traded to the Cincinnati Reds during the 1958 season. In 1959, Newcombe finished the season with a 13-8 record and 3.16 ERA for the Reds. The following year, he was traded to the Cleveland Indians and posted a dismal 6-9 record. Upon completion of the 1960 season, Newcombe retired from baseball.

Throughout most of Newcombe's career, he waged a battle against alcoholism. As Steve Daly of *The Telegraph* remarked, "[the alcohol was] an evil which, though it may have been an attempt to help him deal with the hatred and racism around him, essentially cost him his career." Newcombe sought the help of Alcoholics Anonymous, and has stayed sober for many years. In his work as director of community relations for the Los Angeles Dodgers, Newcombe travels around the country to speak about alcohol and drug dependency. He told Mike Lupica in *Esquire,* "Everybody wants to do something about the drug problem in sports, but they just sort of wink at the main drug, which is alcohol." Newcombe specializes in drug and alcohol awareness and prevention programs. He also served as a spokesman for the National Institute on Drug and Alcohol Abuse, a presidentially appointed position.

Newcombe's battle with alcoholism and his work in alcohol abuse prevention prompted him to file suit against Coors brewing company over an ad for George Killian's Irish Red beer that appeared in a 1994 issue of *Sports Illustrated*. According to an Associated Press release, Coors admitted that the ad had been based on a newspaper photo of Newcombe pitching in the 1949 World Series. In the suit, Newcombe claimed that people would recognize him in the ad, even though his facial features, uniform number, and team insignia were not visible. The judge did not allow the suit to go to trial, however, claiming that the picture in the advertisement did not bear a strong enough resemblance to Newcombe.

In addition to his work for the Dodgers organization, Newcombe is active in several causes, including The Paralysis Project, the Starlight Foundation, the Wiesenthal Center, and the City of Hope. He also had a pediatric wing named for him at the White Memorial Hospital in 1997. He has also sought to have a national holiday declared in honor of Jackie Robinson. On a spring day in 1997 in Nashua, New Hampshire, Newcombe was honored with an honorary doctorate by Daniel Webster College and was also honored by the city of Nashua for his contributions to the integration of baseball. In his typically modest fashion, Newcombe told *The Telegraph,* "Jackie Robinson means everything to Don Newcombe. Don Newcombe could not have the life he's had and the life he has today without him. Wherever he is, I thank him."

Sources

Books

Rampersad, Arnold. *Jackie Robinson,* Alfred A. Knopf, 1997.

Rust Jr., Art. *Get That Nigger Off the Field,* Book Mail Services, 1992, pp. 110, 112, 125.

Periodicals

Esquire, June 1988, p. 54.

Other

Additional material for this profile was obtained from the Los Angeles Dodgers Web site at www.acmewebpages.com/dodgers and www.dodgers.com.

The Telegraph, (Nashua, New Hampshire) April 17, 1997 at www.nashuatelegraph.com/Archive/Sports/Dodgers/dalynewk.htm.

The Sporting News at www.sportingnews.com/features/jackie/newcombe.html.

—Sandy J. Stiefer

Nell Irvin Painter

1942—

Historian, educator, author

Nell Irvin Painter is a noted historian and author who specializes in late 19th and early 20th century American history. She is particularly interested in the experiences of African Americans, women, and the poor and working classes, people who have traditionally been excluded from positions of power. Her books include an examination of African American migration to Kansas during the 1870s, a narrative history of the United States from the end of Reconstruction through World War I, and a biography of legendary feminist and abolitionist Sojourner Truth. Painter explained to Randall Rothenberg of the *New York Times Book Review* that her historical subjects "are not the 'dispossessed!' They're most Americans! It's like calling blacks or women 'special interests.' I'm talking about the lives and concerns of the majority!" Painter's vibrant personality, provocative writing style, meticulous research methods, and wide range of interests have earned her a reputation among her colleagues as a force to be reckoned with. Thadious M. Davis, an English professor at Brown University, told Karen J. Winkler of *The Chronicle of Higher Education.* "What always strikes me about Nell is her intellectual energy and curiosity. That makes her move into new areas – but it's also exhausting."

Painter was born in Houston, Texas in 1942. When she was an infant, her parents moved to Oakland, California. In the early 1940s, California offered well paying defense industry jobs and was less racially segregated than Texas. "Overall it was freer and easier. For one thing, we didn't have to sit on the back of the buses. We went to stores. You could try on hats, or clothes or dresses or anything you wanted to. And that was mostly forbidden in Houston," Painter's mother, Dona Irvin, told Randall Kenan in *Walking on Water.* Following the end of World War II Painter's father, Frank Irvin, became an administrator in the department of chemistry at the University of California at Berkeley. Her mother was a housewife who later became an educational personnel officer.

Traveled Abroad

As a teenager, Painter attended Oakland Technical High School and was active in youth programs at the Downs Methodist Church. She maintained a good academic record, and welcomed opportunities to aug-

At a Glance...

Born on August 2, 1942 in Houston, TX, daughter of Dona McGruder (a personnel officer) and Frank Edward Irvin (a chemist); married Colin Painter, 1965, married Glenn R. Shafer, 1989- . *Education:* University of California at Berkeley, B.A., 1964; University of California at Los Angeles, M.A., 1967; Harvard University, Cambridge, MA, Ph.D., 1974; also attended the University of Bordeaux, France, 1962-63, and the University of Ghana, 1965-66.

Career: University of Pennsylvania, assistant professor, 1974-77; University of North Carolina at Chapel Hill, associate professor of American and Afro-American history, 1978-80, professor of history, 1980-88; Princeton University, professor of history, 1988–91, Edwards professor of American history, 1991-; author of *Exodusters: Black Migration to Kansas After Reconstruction,* 1976; *The Narrative of Hosea Hudson: His Life as a Negro Communist in the South,* 1979; *Standing at Armageddon: The United States, 1877-1919,* 1987; *Sojourner Truth: A Life, A Symbol,* 1996.

Awards: Radcliffe Institute Fellowship, 1976-77; John Simon Guggenheim Foundation Fellow, 1982-83; Black Alumni Club, University of California, Berkeley, Alumnus of the Year, 1989; American Antiquarian Society, Peterson Fellowship, 1991; National Endowment for the Humanities Fellow, 1992-93.

Addresses: *Office—*Princeton University, History Dept., Princeton, NJ, 08544-1017.

ment her formal studies with reading, travel, and visits to museums, concerts, and theatrical performances. As a student at the University of California at Berkeley, Painter majored in anthropology in order to pursue her interest in the culture of Africa and the African Diaspora. She did not take courses in American history, believing that historical approaches of the time failed to adequately address the actualities of American life, especially with regard to racial issues. Painter spent the summer of 1962 in Nigeria as a part of an American student program that was designed to assist in raising the standard of living in various African countries. From Nigeria, Painter traveled to France and spent her junior year at the University of Bordeaux. She then returned to Berkeley to complete her undergraduate studies.

After receiving her bachelor's degree, Painter traveled to Ghana to attend a post-baccalaureate program at the University of Ghana's Institute of African Studies. While in Ghana, she was exposed to historical scholarship that included studies of imperialism, class consciousness, and the economic aspects of political issues. Painter's experiences in Ghana sparked a newfound interest in history. She returned to the United States and earned a master's degree in history at the University of California at Los Angeles in 1967. Painter then enrolled in a doctorate program at Harvard University, in part because her parents encouraged further education and were willing to pay for it. While at Harvard, she gradually shifted her focus from African to American history. "I don't think Harvard ever knew just how little history I knew. I'm sure my spotty background has a lot to do with my odd pattern of writing history: I've never been properly formed as a historian," Painter told Winkler.

Obtained a Doctoral Degree

Painter's doctoral dissertation examined the post-Civil War migration of freed African Americans from the South to settlements in Kansas. These former slaves settled in Kansas to escape racist laws that were put in place by state legislatures in the South. "The freedpeople's struggle was against what they saw as actual or effective reenslavement. And in fact, the forces ruling their states after Reconstruction did set about constructing a set of laws that would make and keep nearly all of them a powerless, immobilized, landless agricultural work force. The impulse to flee came from the conditions that freedpeople lived in and that they anticipated for the future...First and foremost, this is a study of the grass roots that seeks to delve into and explain the meaning of economic and political emancipation for the masses of Southern Blacks after the Civil War," Painter wrote in the introduction to *Exodusters: Black Migration to Kansas after Reconstruction,* a book version of the dissertation originally published in 1976 and reprinted with a new introduction in 1986.

Following completion of her doctoral studies in 1974, Painter accepted a teaching position at the University of Pennsylvania. Although she proudly acknowledged that she had obtained the position through the help of affirmative action, Painter believed that it had little bearing on her qualifications for the job. "Admitting that you have been helped by affirmative action is usually tantamount to admitting deficiency. To hear people talk, affirmative action exists only to employ and promote the otherwise unqualified, but I don't see it that way at all...I had worked hard as a graduate student and had written a decent dissertation. I knew foreign languages, had traveled widely and had taught and published. I thought I had been hired because I was a promising young historian," Painter wrote in an article published by the *Knight-Ridder/Tribune News Service,* adding that "Without affirmative action, it never would have occurred to any large, white research university to consider me for professional employment, despite my qualifications."

Became an Author

In her second book, *The Narrative of Hosea Hudson,* Painter recounted the experiences of an African American steel worker who was a union organizer and Communist Party operative in Alabama from the 1930s through the 1950s. The book, which Painter wrote after sifting through hours of taped interviews with the semiliterate Hudson, is an "oral biography" which resembles the slave narratives of the 19th century. "I wanted to write southern social history using Hudson's life as an illustration...He is a unique informant, an expressive representative of the unlettered workforce that built the new urban South and peopled its cities," Painter wrote in the book's introduction. Critics enthusiastically embraced *The Narrative of Hosea Hudson.* "Moving, fearful and funny, Hudson and Painter's *Narrative* is as valuable an American life as has ever been wrested from anonymity," wrote Benita Eisler in *The Nation.* Painter's own political views fall short of Hudson's radical activism. "I'm not a real leftist. As a kind of wishy, washy liberal, I feel my doing is my writing," Painter explained to Rothenberg.

In her 1987 book *Standing at Armageddon: The United States, 1877-1919,* Painter examined the impact of industrialization on the American working class. "In the forty-two years this book covers, the United States traded the fears and struggles of a mostly rural, fundamentally agrarian society for the fears and struggles of one that was largely urban and industrial," Painter wrote in the book's preface, adding that "My central concern is politics, which is where and how citizens of a democracy express public concerns. But I have not written a political history in the sense that historians have defined the genre...This is mostly a hybrid political-labor history, but it also pays attention to social changes such as the temperance crusade and the entry of women into political life." In his review of *Standing at Armageddon* for the *New York Times Book Review,* historian Charles Tully wrote that Painter lets "the leaders of American popular movements speak for themselves. She offers a narrative of politics emphasizing swings from prosperity to depression, transformations of American capitalism, successive Presidential campaigns and Presidencies, major social movements and their issues...She does dispel any thought that unruly protest is un-American, that the normal state of the American polity from the 1870s to the 1920s was civic obedience or that absorption of Americans in the pursuit of material gain in those years made them immune to appeals for radical action."

Painter firmly believes that African American women, because they must contend with both race and gender issues, occupy their own special position in American society. According to Painter, African American women have been marginalized by a white-dominated women's movement and a male-dominated African American civil rights struggle. "Because black women have been harder than men to fit into cliches of race, we often disappear...Disregarded or forgotten or, when remembered, misconstrued, the symbolic history of black women has not functioned in the same way as the symbolic history of black men. If the reality of the Scottsboro boys and other black men accused of rape showed that the charge was liable to be false and thereby tempered the stereotype, the meaning of the history of black women as victims of rape has not yet penetrated the American mind," Painter wrote in the essay "Hill, Thomas, and the Use of Racial Stereotype," which is included in her 1992 book *Race-ing Justice, En-gendering Power: Essays on Anita Hill, Clarence Thomas, and the Construction of Social Reality.*

Painter's interest in the effects of race and gender inspired her to write a biography of the 19th century abolitionist and feminist, Sojourner Truth. She claimed that the idea to write a biography of Truth came from Truth herself. "Sojourner came to me and told me to write it. I hadn't decided what my next project would be. I heard a voice saying, 'Write about me!' And it was her voice," Painter explained to Jill Petty of *Ms.* Writing the book, *Sojourner Truth: A Life, A Symbol,* was a difficult task for Painter. It was hard to assemble facts about Truth's life because she had spent the first 30 years of her life in slavery, and few accounts of slave life were recorded. Also, since Truth was illiterate, she did not leave any dairies or letters that could provide a glimpse into her life. Painter spent much of the book exploring how Truth was used, both during her life and after her death, as a symbol and how the meaning of that symbol has changed over the years. She told Petty that in recent decades the complexities of Truth's personality have been "flattened out by whites and blacks to create this strong, unafraid, sassy black woman. In place of a heroic, vulnerable, and brilliant individual, we've created an icon to suit our own needs." Painter has little regard for the alterations to Truth's character. "In the obituaries that appeared after her death [in 1883], one word kept coming up: intelligent. Today's stereotype of black women is one of militance. It's angry, sassy, castrating, but not intelligent....[which] takes away a part of our humanity," Painter told Donna Britt of the *Washington Post*.

Painter's biography of Truth was well received by most reviewers. Brenda E. Stevenson of *Emerge* called the book "an important contribution to American history, a stimulating monograph about a fascinating woman." Loretta H. Campbell in *QBR: The Black Book Review* declared that the book is "a biography that yields not only insight into the real life and the symbolism of Sojourner Truth, but into her family, community, and colleagues."

In 1997, when Congress agreed to relocate a statue of three white 19th century suffragists— Lucretia Mott, Elizabeth Cady Stanton, and Susan B. Anthony— from the basement of the Capitol to the more prestigious Capitol Rotunda, Painter gave her support to a campaign by the National Political Congress of Black Women (NPCBW) to halt the move. Led by C. DeLores Tucker, the NPCBW objected to the statue because it did not include Sojourner Truth, the leading African American suffragist of the 19th century. They charged that the absence of Truth implied that the women's suffrage movement was an entirely white undertaking. As Painter told Britt, a statue that included Truth would acknowledge "that black women existed in the nineteenth century, and not just as victims."

Painter's study of the visual representations of Sojourner Truth spurred her interest in her next project, which is a study of the concepts of beauty and how they are developed by and transmitted to society. Painter explained to Petty, "I want to enter this raging discussion of beauty, and whether or not beauty is simply determined by genetics, as many people are now arguing. What about the impact of fashion, ideology, social movements, and photography, the medium through which we usually consume beauty? Isn't it a bit more complicated than having 'symmetrical features?'"

Painter has taught history at Princeton University since 1988, after nearly a decade at the University of North Carolina at Chapel Hill. She married Glenn R. Shafer, a professor of business, in 1989. An earlier marriage to Colin Painter, a teacher of linguistics, ended in divorce. Her spare time activities include swimming and knitting. Despite being a respected historian, Painter admitted that she sometimes feels uncomfortable, "Maybe that's a reaction to always feeling that I'm on display. People ask me what it's like to be an educated black person. It's tiring – I feel like I'm always being judged," she told *The Chronicle of Higher Education*.

Sources

Books

Kenan, Randall. *Walking on Water: Black American Lives at the Turn of the Twenty-First Century*. New York: Knopf, 1999.

Notable Black American Women, Book I. Jessie Carney Smith, editor. Gale Research, 1992.

Race-ing, Justice, En-gendering Power. Toni Morrison, editor. New York: Pantheon Books, 1992.

Periodicals

Black Issues in Higher Education, November 3, 1994, p. 24.

Chronicle of Higher Education, September 13, 1996, p. A18-19.

Emerge, October 31, 1996, p. 74.

Journal of Blacks in Higher Education, Autumn 1996, p. 127-129.

Knight-Ridder/Tribune News Service, February 15, 1995, April 5, 1995.

Ms., January-February 1997, p. 78.

New York Times Book Review, September 22, 1996, sect. 7, p. 29.

QBR: The Black Book Review, February 28, 1997, p. 16.

Washington Post, September 15, 1996, Book World, p. 9; May 2, 1997, p. B1.

—Mary Kalfatovic

Tony Perkins

1959(?)—

Television personality

Tony Perkins became a nationally recognized personality when he joined ABC as one of the pillars of Good Morning America's (GMA) on-air staff as part of the successful effort to boost that show's ratings in 1999. ABC management recognized in Perkins the talent and charm his fans and coworkers in Washington D.C., had appreciated for the prior decade and a half, during which he was a local radio and television celebrity. His style, humor, and warmth have touched audiences—locally in Washington, D.C. and nationally on ABC—and proved to be of great value to the broadcast operations for which he has worked, as his pleasant nature, gentle spirit, and comic wit draw viewers.

Born with a Microphone in His Hand

Tony Perkins was born in New York City to Constance Bellamy Perkins and Tommy Perkins. The couple met in a shoe store in New York, where Tommy Perkins worked. Perkins's father was employed in several varying occupations after he and Perkins's mother were married and settled in the South Bronx. When Perkins was five, he, his parents, and younger brother, Scott—who as an adult went on to work for CNN as an art director—moved to Washington, D.C., where Tommy Perkins worked as a promotions representative for WDCA-TV. He became well-known in the community for his work in promoting musical and theatrical events, and he became involved with the Southern Christian Leadership Conference during the 1960s as well. Perkins commented about his father's career in an article appearing in the *Washington Post* by Lloyd Grove, "You name it, he pretty much did it. He was what they now call and entrepreneur, but back then they didn't have a word for it."

When Perkins was 11, his parents divorced. Going back to her maiden name, Constance Bellamy was employed as a telephone operator and night clerk at the post office. Struggling financially, the family could only afford to live in the poorer neighborhoods of D.C. Gradually Bellamy was able to elevate the family a bit economically and moved herself and her sons into a trailorpark in Alexandria, Virginia, and later to a townhouse.

Perkins's mother recognized in her son at an early age

> ### At a Glance...
>
> Born Anthony Perkins in New York City, c. 1959; married Rhonda in 1994. *Education:* American University, B.A., communications.
>
> **Career:** Desk assistant, ABC News, Washington, D.C., early 1980s; radio producer and on-air personality, *The Donnie Simpson Show*, WKYS-FM, Washington, D.C., 1985-92; stand-up comedian, various clubs and campuses in eastern United States, 1985-92; television producer and host, *DC 20 Breakaway*, WDCA-TV, Washington, D.C., 1986-88; comedy writer and performer, *Comic Strip Live*, WTTG-TV, Washington, D.C., 1989; radio show co-host, *The Morning Crew*, WKYS-FM, Washington, D.C., 1992-93; television weatherperson, *Fox Morning News*, WTTG-TV (Fox affiliate), Washington, D.C., 1993-97; news co-anchor, *Fox Morning News*, WTTG-TV, Washington, D.C. 1997-99; weatherperson, *Good Morning America*, ABC, New York City, 1999-.
>
> **Selected awards:** Emmy Award, 1988.
>
> **Addresses:** *Office*—Good Morning America, ABC, 147 Columbia Avenue, F1 6, New York, NY 10023-5900.

a calling into the spotlight. She remarked to Grove, "Anthony always had a microphone in his hand, or whatever resembled a microphone, even before he could talk. He would imitate the game shows on television. In fact, he took his first steps walking to the TV set during the old 'Price Is Right' show." Later, in high school, Perkins displayed confidence and skills in leadership. A student of strong academic achievement, he was also a sort of star in school extracurricularly as leader of the video club, honors society, and student newspaper. Overall he was extremely popular among his classmates. However, among the small group of African American students, he was sometimes ridiculed as acting white. Perkins' explained the situation in the *Post* article, "There was a feeling that if you were doing the things I was doing, you were kind of leaving your own community and living in the quote unquote 'white world.' That bothered me quite a bit and was difficult to deal with. There were times when there was an attitude towards me that was not the friendliest. You know, 'What are you trying to do, act white?'..." Perkins graduated from Mount Vernon High in 1977.

Perkins's father, known throughout his life as a charming, outgoing person, committed suicide in 1992. He was in his early fifties. He was survived by his sons Tony and Scott and three daughters he had during two marriages following his marriage with Perkins's mother. He described to Grove the hardship of getting through the kind of grief his father's death brought on, "I don't think anyone ever fully gets over something like that. It was a pretty shattering experience.... It's difficult to talk about because I don't think there's anything that you can really say that conveys the sadness and grief and the anger and all the different emotions you go through....one of the things that's been difficult for both my brother and me, and for the family, is that during these last several years there's been a certain degree of success which has been very, very exciting. And I know that my dad would be thrilled...."

Success on the Airwaves of Radio and Television

After graduating from the American University with a bachelor of arts in communications, Perkins landed a job with *ABC News'* Washington bureau as a desk assistant. Perkins first met Charlie Gibson, with whom he would later work with on *Good Morning America*, during his tenure at the Washington desk. Gibson offered a reminiscent anecdote in the *Post* article, recalling, "Tony was a very bright, very amusing young fellow." Gibson and Perkins only worked together briefly at the Washington desk, but Gibson was deeply impressed with Perkins's production and writing skills. When Gibson left Washington to join the *GMA* team in New York, Perkins had already left ABC to work in radio. Gibson contacted Perkins to contract production work from him. "And he very politely said no," Gibson detailed, "'Why not?' And Tony said, 'Because I want to be on the air....'"

In 1985 Perkins joined the locally popular *The Donnie Simpson Show* on WKYS-FM in Washington. Remaining with the show until 1992, Perkins amused and impressed listeners with his comic sharpness, speed, and brilliance. Donnie Simpson lauded him as "very funny." he explained to Grove, "...and he allowed me to be funny. Most of the time with comedians, if there are two of them in a room, they're always trying to get off the last line. But Tony always gave me room...." As well as performing on the radio show, Perkins wrote and produced comedy spots for which the show was so highly rated. In 1992 Perkins left *The Donnie Simpson Show* to be a cohost of *The Morning Crew* radio show on the same station.

While working his day job at WKYS, Perkins performed stand-up comedy, touring the eastern club and campus circuit. Perkins recalled the sense of accomplishment he felt when he read his first comedy review in a Baltimore paper, "...it called me a black Johnny Carson, which to me was high praise. There was some 'black material,' but I really didn't do what a lot of the black comics at that time did—you know, 'I got roaches in my apartment' and all that kind of thing." Like Carson, Perkins did not reveal much personal information in his comedy.

Perkins was active in the field of broadcasting in various other ways as well while simultaneously working for WKYS. He wrote and performed for *Comic Strip Live* on WTTG-TV. Between 1986 and 1988, he produced and hosted *DC 20 Breakaway* for WDCA-TV, for which he won an Emmy Award in 1988.

In 1993, Perkins left WKYS and joined the *Fox Morning News* on Channel 5 in Washington, D.C., as the weather forecaster. His entertaining delivery of the weather news brought him even greater notoriety in Washington. In 1997 he began co-anchoring *Fox Morning News*, which entailed broadcasting the news, interviewing notable personalities, reviewing movies, and delivering feature stories. When Shelley Ross, executive producer of *Good Morning America,* viewed a piece about the Scottish Tourist Board on Perkins's resume tape, she was moved by good laughter into offering him the position as *GMA's* weatherperson. She explained to Grove how impressed and amused she was by Perkins's humor, "Once I saw Tony in a kilt, and I saw those knobby knees, I just knew he had to be ours. I've had a couple of conversations with him and he brings warmth, comfort and family feelings—and that's really what this broadcast is about." Perkins's colleagues a Channel 5 were disappointed to see him leave the station for *GMA. Fox Morning News* anchor Lark McCarthy revealed to Grove, "Between my sobs, I have to say that I'm sorry to see him go." The day news of Perkins's departure from channel 5 was announced to viewers, Perkins reported receiving 84 voicemail messages from fans expressing their enjoyment of his work.

Joins the *GMA* Revival Team

When Perkins's mother received word of his move to the national celebrity as *GMA's* weather personality, she treated the change as "very natural" for her son. According to Grove, she viewed it as "his calling." Perkins himself, however, nevertheless felt a bit anxious over the move up to a national show and over the mandate by ABC management that he be part of a force to turn viewers from the number-one rated *Today Show* on NBC to the third-spot *GMA*. Perkins expressed his anxiety this way in the Grove article, I'm thinking thoughts of 'Good Morning America,' ABC, what this means, what's it going to be like and all that kind of thing. I think the anticipation makes me pretty nervous. I'm anxious. I really am." In an earlier *Washington Post* article, however, he expressed more confidence, " [ABC is] obviously going to be putting a lot of time, attention, and effort into the show. The show has obviously seen better days, but clearly their focus is to get it back on track. What folks are about to see is a new energy at 'GMA.' If I didn't believe this I wouldn't be leaving this very good situation at WTTG to go there."

Good Morning America had been struggling since the mid-1990s in the ratings due to strong competition from the *Today Show's* new look and format. ABC imposed a few on-air personality shifts that did not bring about the desired results in ratings advancement. In 1997 ABC management ousted longtime host Joan Lunden, replacing her with Lisa McRee, who did not previously have a national presence on the tube, and in 1998 Charlie Gibson was replaced by Kevin Newman, formerly the news anchor for *GMA.* Weatherperson Spencer Christian was the only celebrity left from the old guard, but he opted to leave and take a position with a station in San Francisco. Shortly prior to Christian's departure, McRee and Newman were dumped from the show. Management warmed up to Gibson again and brought him back to the show with Diane Sawyer as co-host, a television personality with deep and wide national admiration among America's viewership. Shortly after Gibson and Sawyer were in place, ratings increased by one percent.

With Christian's absence, finding a weatherperson that could measure up to Christian's charm and warmth was critical. ABC announced the addition of Perkins to the *GMA* on-air team in January of 1999. On March 8, 1999, he was in place in front of the weather map. He was also given the responsibility of travelling throughout the United States to interview community leaders and notables and to bring to the airwaves special features on various American communities and events.

By April of 1999, *GMA's* ratings were up by 23 percent since January. Finding on-air personalities that Americans would feel comfortable inviting into their homes at such an intimate time of the day—the morning—, albeit via the television set, was crucial. ABC News President David Westin explained that Perkins, along with Gibson and Sawyer, contributes to making the show comfortable and enjoyable for Americans to watch in the morning. He admitted to Grove in February, "...we are trying to recast 'GMA' in part along the lines of what once was a truly great show, smart and warm. When it comes to Tony, both of those adjectives apply. He is smart, very good with people, very warm and very comfortable." Commenting on Perkins's ability in reacting quickly in a humorous, light way, as he did during his career as a radio personality, Westin added, "He's very quick on his feet."

Sources

Periodicals

Jet, May 3, 1999, p. 15.

Washington Post. January 21, 1999, p. C07; February 19, 1999, p. C01; April 13, 1999, p. C01.

Other

Additional information for this profile was obtained from a biography on Tony Perkins on Good Morning America's website at www.abcnews.go.com/onair/GoodMorningAmerica/perkins_tony_bio.html.

—Melissa Walsh

W. Randall Pinkston

1950—

Broadcast journalist

He has crisscrossed the world and the United States. Randall Pinkston, or Pinkston, as he simply calls himself when he picks up his desk phone, has covered numerous top stories during the 1990s for CBS News. Among these stories were: a devastating earthquake in Turkey; the Albanian refugee crisis in Kosovo and U.S. military involvement in the Balkans; Saddam Hussein's refusal to permit U.N. inspectors to go into Iraq; the American intervention in Haiti; the Susan Smith trial; the Freemen siege in Montana; the Unabomber story; and indentured servitude in America.

Since 1994, Pinkston has been a correspondent for CBS News in New York City. He has appeared at regular times on the *CBS Evening News* and *CBS News Sunday Morning* and has taken part in other CBS News broadcasts, among them *48 Hours*. Yet while one can find numerous references to Dan Rather on the Internet, there is little personal information available about Pinkston, and one senses he wants to keep it that way. Pinkston, a modest man who does not list his awards among his achievements, is an outstanding investigative reporter.

Pinkston won an Emmy Award in 1996 for Outstanding Investigative Journalism. He also won the Edward R. Murrow Award for his reports in the *CBS Reports* documentary "Legacy of Shame," which was inspired by Edward R. Murrow's 1960 CBS documentary, "Harvest of Shame." In the documentary, Pinkston spoke with a teenaged migrant farm worker trapped in a camp until he could pay off his "debt obligations" to his "crew leader" just for transporting him to the fruit fields. "Legacy of Shame" aired in 1995 and dealt with the continuing exploitation of migrant farm workers in places like Florida and Phoenix, El Paso and Clarendon County, South Carolina.

One writer gave the documentary a mixed review. John Leonard wrote in *New York,* "Dan Rather reminds us that we have been here before, feeling bad about migrant farm workers, and will probably be back again in another decade or so, to wince and deplore....These periodic conscience-stricken inquiries into indentured servitude are almost a CBS franchise....What's more, for *Legacy,* [Rather's] got Randall Pinkston to do the legwork. It's a nervy Pinkston, waving tax forms and

At a Glance...

Born W. Randall Pinkston, March 3, 1950, in Yazoo County, MS; married Patricia McLain (a certified public accountant), 1982; children: Ada Randall Pinkston, Rolanda Johnson, Kathleen Johnson. *Education:* Millsaps College, B.A. in history, 1973; University of Connecticut Law School, J.D., 1980.

Career: Anchor and reporter, WLBT-TV, 1971-74; announcer, WJDX-FM Radio, 1969-71; urban affairs director, general assignment reporter, producer of a daily public affairs program, WJXT-TV, 1974-76; reporter, anchor, producer of public affairs programs and specials, WFSB-TV, 1976-80; reporter, WCBS-TV, 1980-90; White House correspondent, CBS News' Washington, DC bureau, 1990-94; correspondent for *CBS Evening News* and *CBS News Sunday Morning*, CBS News, New York, 1994-.

Member: National Association of Black Journalists, Abyssinian Baptist Church, Wesleyan Alumni Association, University of Connecticut Law School Foundation.

Addresses: *Home*—Teaneck, NJ. *Office*—CBS News, 524 West 57th Street, New York, NY 10019.

federal regulations, who confronts the growers, their lawyers, their cops, their goons....*Legacy*, personalizing a social problem, is old-fashioned network television journalism at its storytelling best."

Pinkston also was on the scene to cover the death of Princess Diana and the TWA Flight 800 disaster. He was awarded two Emmys in 1997 and 1998 for his coverage of these stories. Also, in 1999, he was co-honored with a third-place prize for his participation in an interview with Betty Shabbazz's daughter on the *CBS Evening News with John Roberts*. Before coming to New York, Pinkston worked in the CBS News bureau in Washington, DC, where he signed on with the network as a White House correspondent in 1990. He spent a lot of time reporting on the Persian Gulf War on *CBS This Morning* and CBS Radio. Pinkston spent two years at the White House covering President George Bush and the president's trips abroad. He was first to broadcast the story when President Bush became ill while dining with the Japanese prime minister Miyazawa.

Prior to reporting for CBS News Pinkston reported for WCBS-TV, the station owned by CBS in New York, from 1980 until 1990. While working for WCBS-TV Pinkston covered the American political scene, including the 1984 and 1988 presidential campaigns of Jesse Jackson in New York, the 1988 Democratic National Convention in Atlanta, and several gubernatorial and Senatorial campaigns in New Jersey. Pinkston was made WCBS-TV's New Jersey correspondent in 1989 and he garnered two Emmy Awards for his reporting there.

After a report on teenage drunk driving, Pinkston won the Public Service Award from the Greater New York Safety Council and the Outstanding Journalist Award by Black Citizens of Fair Media in 1983. His reporting helped to pave the way for changes in New York State's drunk driving laws. Pinkston also did a series for WCBS-TV on the absence of government care for the mentally ill and physically challenged. For his work on the series, he received honors from the Scripps-Howard Foundation, the New York State Associated Press Broadcasters Association, and the Council of Churches of the City of New York.

From 1976 until 1980 Pinkston juggled several jobs at WFSB-TV, the CBS branch in Hartford, Connecticut. He served as a reporter, anchor and producer of public affairs programs and specials. From 1974 to 1976 Pinkston worked for WJXT-TV, the CBS affiliate in Jacksonville, Florida, as an urban affairs director, general assignment reporter and producer of a daily public affairs program. Pinkston began his career in Jackson, Mississippi as an anchor and reporter at WLBT-TV, from 1971 to 1974, and as an announcer at WJDX-FM, from 1969 to 1971.

Pinkston was born on March 3, 1950, in Yazoo County, Mississipi. He studied at W.H. Lier High School in Jackson, Mississippi, then attended Wesleyan University in Middletown, Connecticut. He also took part in the Michele Clark Fellowship program at Columbia University. Pinkston traveled south to Jackson, Mississippi to attend Millsaps College, where he graduated in 1973 with a B.A. in history. He traveled north again to study at the University of Connecticut Law School, where he received his J.D. degree in 1980. He and his wife, Patricia McLain, and their daughter and two stepdaughters, live in Teaneck, New Jersey.

Sources

Books

Directory of Blacks in the Performing Arts, Scarecrow Press, 1990.

Periodicals

CBS Evening News with Dan Rather—Weekend Edition, "Death of a Princess."
CBS Reports: "Legacy of Shame," July 20, 1995, pp. 1-21.
Imaging America, April 1-15, 1997.
Media Watch, January 1995.
New York, July 24, 1995, p. 46.

Other

Additional material for this profile was obtained through Randall Pinkston and CBS News; and through the Internet at http://ink.yahoo.com/bin/query?p=%22randall+pinkston%22+and+%22cbs%22&hc=0&hs=0; http://entertaindom.ultimatetv.com/news/bn/98/shows/08/0805excellenceawards.html; Lanier High School, Jackson, Mississippi; and CBS newscasts.

—Alison Carb Sussman

Bud Powell

1924–1966

Jazz pianist and composer

A founding genius of bebop piano during the 1940s, Bud Powell's musical contributions helped define modern jazz music. Absorbing the lessons of European concert music, jazz pianists such as Art Tatum and Thelonious Monk, and the music of alto-saxophonist Charlie Parker, Powell's unique style served as a catalyst for modern jazz keyboard. An epitome of the tortured genius, Powell experienced psychological afflictions, intensified by substance abuse and electroshock treatments, which cut short a brilliant career. Because of Powell's personal travails, jazz writers have often overlooked his monumental musical achievements. Never forgotten by fellow musicians for his contributions, he spent his last years in Paris and New York City suffering from mental illness which limited him to playing occasional club dates and concerts. Under the honorary guardianship of French jazz aficionado Francis Paudras, he formed a friendship that served as the basis for the 1986 film *Round Midnight*.

Born in New York City on September 27, 1924, Earl "Bud" Powell began playing piano at six years of age, and subsequently received seven years of formal pianistic training. Powell's musical family included his father William, a talented stride pianist, brother William Jr., a violinist and trumpeter, and a younger brother Richie who became the pianist in the famed Clifford Brown/Max Roach Quintet. After dropping out of Dewitt Clinton High School at the age of 15, Powell played Coney Island clubs and Harlem nightspots such as actor Canada Lee's Chicken Coop. As a teenager he first heard jazz, and fell under the influence of pianist Billy Kyle, a member of bassist John Kirby's band who hailed from the school of Earl Hines. As jazz pianist Billy Taylor asserted in *Swing to Bop*, Kirby played a style that contained many "pre-bop" elements that helped bridge swing with modern jazz.

Mentored with Thelonious Monk

During the mid-1940s Powell met Thelonious Monk, the innovative composer and house pianist at Minton's Playhouse, one of Harlem's premiere birthplaces of bebop. After Monk first took him to Minton's, Powell was urged by the older keyboardist to perform among the other visiting musicians who constituted the core of New York City's bebop scene. As Thomas Owens asserted, in *Bebop: The Music and Its Players*, "There was a symbiotic relationship between Monk and Bud Powell," that benefitted Powell in an informal instruction by his older counterpart. According to musicians like drummer Kenny Clarke, Monk gave Powell many of written arrangements because he believed the younger pianist was the only one capable of playing his work. Powell's exceptional musical skills also astounded another member of Minton's bebop circle, Miles Davis who, in his memoir *Miles,* recalled that "Bud Powell was one of the few musicians I knew who could play, write, and read all kinds of music."

At a Glance...

Born Earl Rudolph "Bud" Powell, September 27, 1924, in New York City, New York; son of William Powell (a pianist) and Pearl Powell; married Frances Barnes; children: daughter Celia Barnes; married Audrey Hill 1953.

Career: At fifteen dropped out of high school to play local clubs; 1942-1944 performed with the band of Charles Melvin "Cootie" Williams; performed on New York City's 52nd Street with various jazzmen; recorded with Charlie Parker and Dexter Gordon in 1946; 1949-1951 recorded as trio leader for Blue Note and Verve labels; 1953 appeared at Jazz at Massey Hall concert in Toronto, Canada; between 1953 and 1957 performed with a trio at New York City's Birdland; in 1956 performed in a trio with Charles Mingus and Elvin Jones; toured of Paris with "Birdland 56" concert package; performed at the Club Saint Germain in Paris 1957; moved to Paris in 1959, where until 1964, he recorded and performed at clubs and concert dates throughout Europe; during tenure in Paris usually performed in a trio with Kenny Clarke and Peirre Michelot; returned to New York City in 1964 and 1965 occasionally performed at Birdland.

Awards: The Schaeffer Award.

Like numerous other young jazzmen of the 1940s, Powell fell under the influence of alto-saxophonist Charlie Parker. As Thomas Owens asserted in *Bebop: The Music and Its Players,* "Powell was one of 'Bird's children' as surely as were any saxophonists of the time. He, more than any other early bebop pianist, transferred Parker's melodic vocabulary and phrasing to the piano." But as Gary Giddins asserted in the liner notes to *The Genius of Bud Powell,* "it would be a mistake to assume that Powell did nothing more than adopt Parker's percepts to the piano." As Giddins added, "The surface of his music seems frequently to be a mask made up of be-bop acrobatics, convoluted triplets, and flashy chromatic runs. Lurking below, however, is a confluence of emotions, ranging from self-lacerating ferocity to an elegant benignity more associated with [pianist] Teddy Wilson." Powell's close friend, Francis Paudras, also countered the notion that Powell simply translated Parker's music into the pianisitic idiom. Privy to tapes of Powell's playing recorded during the mid 1930s, Paudras, in his memoir *Dance of the Infidels,* asserted that the pianist's style had already possessed modernist elements and that it matured as a result of an independent vision which absorbed numerous musical sources.

Apart from the younger bebop innovators, Powell's most profound musical influence was Art Tatum, a virtuoso pianisitic talent whose music combined the elements of stride, swing, and European concert music. As pianist Erroll Garner explained in *Notes and Tones,* "To me Bud was the second greatest thing to Art Tatum....Bud came along later and added to what Tatum had....He was another Tatum, only much more modern." In summation of Powell's impact on bebop pianists, writer Whitney Baillet wrote in his book, *American Musicians II,* that during "the mid-1940s, Powell who came out of Kyle and Tatum, hypnotized a new generation of pianists. His single-note figures....particularly at up tempo....were nervous, hard, driven," which revealed "a coarse quick-wittedness."

Between 1943 and 1944 Powell, while still a teenager, performed and recorded with the band of trumpeter Cootie Williams, who served as his legal guardian. "When I was with Cootie Williams in 1944," recounted Powell in *Dance of the Infidels,* "I did most of the arrangements for the band 'cause I was the only one who could write music." Through Powell's insistence, Williams' band recorded Monk's classic ballad "Round Midnight." By the mid 1940s, Powell's musicianship found him abundant work on New York City's famed 52nd Street with musicians such as Dizzy Gillespie, Don Byas, Dexter Gordon, J.J. Johnson, and Sid Catlett. In 1946 he recorded sessions for the Savoy label with Dexter Gordon, and the following year with Charlie Parker which yielded the sides "Donna Lee" and "Chasin' the Bird." That same year, Powell recorded Monk's "Off Minor" nine months before its composer.

In the midst of establishing a music career, Powell suffered from physical and mental ailments. Withdrawn and aloof, Powell possessed a complex personality, and his penchant for alcohol only increased his unstable condition. In January of 1945, he received a blow on the head from a Philadelphia policeman, and was arrested for disorderly conduct. Powell received only superficial treatment for his head wound, and was often plagued with severe headaches. He was admitted to Bellevue for mental health treatment, and was subsequently confined to Creedmore Psychiatric Center.

Brilliant Trio Leader

Following his release from Creedmore, Powell recorded with the Blue Note label. Created from recording sessions held between 1949 and 1951, the album *The Amazing Bud Powell Volume I* showcased such Powell classics as "Bouncin' With Bud," "Dance of the Infidels," and "Un Poco Loco." Between 1950 and 1951, Powell also recorded for the Verve label. These sessions were featured on the album *Genius of Bud Powell*. Accompanied by bassist Ray Brown and Buddy Rich, Powell cut the sides "Tea For Two," "Hallelujah," and "Parisian Thoroughfare." The remaining solo piano numbers, recorded in February of 1951, included the original compositions "Oblivion," "Dusk in Sandi," and Hallucinations."

Arrested on a trumped up narcotics charge in 1951, Powell was placed in Bellevue's psychiatric ward. He was then admitted to Pilgrim State Hospital, where he underwent electroshock treatment before being transferred to Creedmore. Although Powell would still produce brilliant performances his playing, like his troubled personal life, became increasingly unpredictable. After his release from Creedmore in February of 1953, the State of New York declared Powell legally incompetent. Oscar Goodstein, owner of New York City's famed Birdland nightclub, became Powell's guardian and provided him with steady musical work. As bassist George Duvivier, who played with Powell at Birdland, related in his autobiography, *Basically Speaking,* "When I joined [Powell], he was already in the latter years of his career, and slowly deteriorating mentally. It was sad. There were nights when it was pure genius....We had no communication - only the music." Despite his increasing illness, Powell continued to record many fine Blue Note sides. His playing on sessions held in 1951 and 1953 which constitute *The Amazing Bud Powell Volume 2,* reveal a brilliant instrumentalist on such numbers as "Night in Tunisia," and the original compositions "Parisian Thoroughfare" and "Glass Enclosure," a piece which Powell claimed to describe his taste for drink.

Personal Troubles Increased

On May 15, 1953, Powell performed with the quintet of Parker, Gillespie, Mingus, and Roach at the Jazz at Massey Hall concert in Toronto, Canada. Recorded by Mingus and released on the Debut label, the date included a quintet release and a Powell trio performance, *The Amazing Bud Powell at Massey Hall*. On March 4, 1955, Powell was reunited with Parker, Mingus and Gillespie for a concert at Birdland. While on stage Powell insulted the saxophonist, who was ill. The two men began to exchange curses. Powell pounded his fists on the keyboard, and left the club. Eight days after the concert, Charlie Parker died in a New York City apartment. After Parker's death, Powell and Mingus formed a trio with drummer Elvin Jones. After Mingus' departure from the group in 1956, Jones continued to perform with Powell. In *Notes and Tones*, Jones, though in awe of Powell's musicianship, told the book's author Art Taylor that he "always had the impression that Bud had been hurt so much. He was like a delicate piece of china. I think he was an extremely sensitive person, a very beautiful person. I think he was a genius in what he was doing. His ideas about modern music were revolutionary."

Lived in Paris

The State of New York revoked Powell's need for legal guardianship in 1956, a decision that allowed him to travel to Europe as part of a package jazz tour, "Birdland 1956." During his short stay, he performed with a trio at a Paris nightclub, the St. Germain. In 1957, Powell returned to the St. Germain and received a hero's welcome. Jazz aficionado Francis Paudras, who was in attendance that evening, recounted in his memoir *Dance of the Infidels,* "The music he played was elusive but so appealing, and in it I felt his suffering." Powell recorded the Blue Note album, *The Scene Changes,* in 1958 with Taylor and bassist Paul Chambers, an effort that recaptured some of his earlier brilliance. Booked for an engagement at the Blue Note in Paris, Powell, accompanied by his girlfriend Buttercup and her young son Johnny, left for France in 1959.

While at the Blue Note, Powell performed with a resident trio comprised of drummer Kenny Clarke and Pierrre Michelot. Nicknamed the Three Bosses, the trio, noted Clarke's biographer Mike Hennesey in *Klook,* marked "the golden age of jazz in Paris and the presence of Kenny Clarke and Bud Powell at the Blue Note....was unquestionably a key factor in the high level of jazz activity in the French capital." While living in Paris Powell often embarked on European tours, and made guest appearances with visiting American musicians. In 1959, he sat in with Art Blakey's Jazz Messengers at the Theatre des Champs-Elyees. The following year, Powell appeared as a guest with Charles Mingus' band at the Antibes Jazz Festival. This concert was later captured on the Atlantic album, *Mingus Live at Antibes*. In the recording's liner notes, Robert Palmer wrote, "The pianist is in a deliberate mood here, phrasing in a blocked-out, infinitesimally behind-the-beat manner that brings forth the Powell-Monk relationship to mind. His style is leaner and less like a steamroller than in his earlier years, and there are a few occasions when his articulation is not all it could be, but these are the kind of quibbles only a pedant would take seriously. The man is playing music of a very high order." In 1960, Powell participated in a live recording with legendary tenor saxophonist Coleman Hawkins and, the following year, recorded with a trio for the Mystic Sound label.

While in Paris, Powell did not find a respite from his personal troubles. His bouts with alcoholism and its unpredictable effects alarmed fellow artists and club owners. Saxophonist Jackie McLean, in *Jazz Masters of the Forties,* related how "all Paris knows Bud - when I say Paris, I mean all the jazz people and artists, and they know its not a good idea to give Bud anything to drink....One glass of brandy can completely flip him around. I've never seen juice affect anyone like that." Under the harsh dominance of his girlfriend Buttercup, who garnished his wages, Powell was given doses of an anti-schizophrenic drug that nearly incapacitated him. In 1962 Francis Paudras, who had struck up a friendship with Powell, discovered that his friend had been admitted to a psychiatric ward in Paris. After securing Powell's release, Paudras served as his honorary guardian. Powell's troubled life in Paris is recounted in Paudras's memoir, *Dance of the Infidels,* which details Powell's troubled existence, and his effort to look after the welfare of a musician whose brilliance he ranked with Debussy and Ravel. Paudras's memoir subsequently inspired Bertrand Tavernier's 1986 film *Round Midnight,* in which the main character, played by Dexter Gordon, emerged as a composite of Powell and saxophonist Lester Young.

In May of 1963, Powell provided the piano accompaniment for Dexter Gordon's album *Our Man in Paris.* Powell's performances with Kenny Clarke and Pierre Michelot, described by Ira Gitler in *Jazz Masters of the Forties,* revealed "a flowing line of improvisation, even if the old fire is not there." In 1963 Powell contracted tuberculosis and, in October of that year, Oscar Goodstein held a Birdland benefit concert to help pay for the ailing pianist's medical expenses. Although he had planned to come to America for a brief visit, Powell left Paris in 1964 and never returned. As Tyler Stovall commented, in his study, *Paris Noir,* "Paris helped restore Bud Powell but could not save him...."

Last Years In America

Accompanied by Paudras, Powell arrived in New York on August 1, 1964. Powell played an extended engagement at Birdland where, in March of 1965, he appeared at a concert commemorating the tenth anniversary of Charlie Parker's death. During the summer of 1965, Powell discovered that he had severe liver damage. He continued to perform, but his musical skills were severely reduced. On July 31, 1966, Powell died in New York City's Kings County Hospital. An estimated 5,000 people lined the streets to bid farewell to Powell as his body passed in funeral procession. The procession was led by a Jazzmobile on which Barry Harris and Lee Morgan played Monk's "Round Midnight," "Dance of the Infidels," and "Bud's Bubble."

As jazz writer Ira Gitler noted in his work *Jazz Masters of the Forties,* "Despite the deterioration suffered by Bud Powell through his many and varied encounters with illness, his mark has been ineradicably stamped on the music of his native country." As the founder of an entire school of modern jazz piano, Powell's music has inspired musicians such as Bill Evans and Cecil Taylor. He remains an important influence for all who perfrom post-bebop acoustic jazz piano.

Selected discography

The Amazing Bud Powell Vol. I, Blue Note,
The Amazing Bud Powell Vol. 2, Blue Note,
The Genius of Bud Powell, Verve, 1950, reissue 1988.
Jazz at Massey Hall Vol. Two, Bud Powell Trio, Debut (recorded 1953) reissue Original Jazz Classics, 1991.
Strictly Powell, RCA, 1957.
Swingin' With Bud, RCA, 1958.
The Scene Changes, The Amazing Bud Powell, Blue Note, (recorded 1958) reissued 1987.
Portrait of Thelonious Monk, Columbia, 1961.
The Complete Bud Powell on Verve, Verve, 1994.
The Complete Blue Note (C-D Box set), Blue Note 1994.
Jazz Profile, Blue Note 1997.
Young Bud, Indigo, 1999.

With Others

The Quintet, Jazz at Massey Hall, Debut (recorded 1953) reissue 1989.
Dexter Gordon, Our Man in Paris, Blue Note (recorded 1963) 1987.
Mingus at Antibes, Atlantic, 1976, reissued 1994.

Sources

Books

Baillett, Whitney, *American Musicians II: Seventy-One Portraits in Jazz,* 1996, p. 455.
Berger, Edward, *Bassically Speaking: An Oral History of George Duvivier,* The Scarecrow Press, 1993, p. 91.
Davis, Miles, with Quincy Troupe, *Miles, The Autobiography,* Simon & Schuster, 1990, p. 60.
Hennesey, Mike, *Klook: The Story of Kenny Clarke,* University of Pittsburgh Press, 1990, p. 152.
Gitler, Ira, *From Swing to Bop: An Oral History of the*

Transition of Jazz in the 1940s, Oxford University Press, 1985, p. 103.

Gitler, Ira, *Jazz Masters of the Forties,* Collier Books, 1966, pp. 110-130.

Notes and Tones: Musician-to-Musician Interviews, expanded edition, Da Capo, 1977, p. 225.

Owens, Thomas, *Bebop: The Music and Its Players,* Oxford University Press, 1995, p. 146.

Paudras, Francis, *Dance of the Infidels: A Portrait of Bud Powell,* translated from the original French by Rubye Monet English translation edited by Warren Bernhardt, Da Capo, 1998.

Stovall, Tyler, *Paris Noir: African Americans in the City of Light,* Houghton Mifflin, 1996, p. 241.

Other

Additional information for this profile was obtained from the liner notes by Robert Palmer to *Mingus at Antibes,* Atlantic Records, and the liner notes by Gary Giddins to *The Genius of Bud Powell,* Verve Records.

—John Cohassey

Richard Pryor

1940—

Comedian, actor, writer

In the 1970s and 1980s Richard Pryor was one of America's top comedians, an actor, writer, and stand-up artist whose irreverent albums sold in the millions. Pryor mined both personal and social tragedy for his comic material and peppered his appearances with outrageous language and adult humor. Even at the peak of his popularity, however, he suffered the dire consequences of drug and alcohol abuse--a heart attack, a suicide attempt, and the onset of multiple sclerosis. Since the early 1990s, he has lived a reclusive life in his Bel Air home, reportedly unable to walk and rarely seeing any but a small cadre of friends.

One of Pryor's ex-wives, Jennifer Lee, told *Premiere* magazine: "Richard's so isolated from the human race. When you're with him now, you feel a kind of solitude you don't even feel when you're by yourself." Pryor's is indeed the tragic story of a talented personality who took a path of self-destruction, a comic who could draw laughs from his own misfortunes but who was powerless to change his habits until the damage had been done. *Premiere* correspondent David Handelman theorized: "Like many celebrities, Pryor turned to drugs in part out of insecurity about his fame. But he had the added guilt trip of being perhaps the most successful black man in a country of disenfranchised blacks."

Pryor was not the first African American comedian to succeed as a stand-up comic. He followed in the footsteps of Bill Cosby and Dick Gregory, among others. He became unique--and a pioneer in his own right--when he created a bold new comedy of character, turning African American life into humorous performance art without softening either the message or its delivery. He could glide effortlessly from portraying an elderly wino to mimicking a cheetah poised to bag a gazelle. With an astounding repertoire of accents and body lingo, Pryor often played a predator one moment and a victim the next. His was a comedy forged from life's tragic moments.

Pryor's audience included a number of comics who have since risen to fame. "I just dreamed about being like Richard Pryor," Keenen Ivory Wayans told *Premiere*. "Pryor started it all. He's Yoda. If Pryor had not come along, there would not *be* an Eddie Murphy or a Keenen Ivory Wayans or a Damon Wayans or an Arsenio Hall-- or even a [white comedian like] Sam Kinison, for that matter. He made the blueprint for the progressive

At a Glance...

Born Richard Franklin Lennox Thomas Pryor, December 1, 1940, in Peoria, IL; son of LeRoy and Gertrude (Thomas) Pryor; married and divorced five times; children: Renee, Richard, Jr., Rain, Elizabeth. *Military service:* U.S. Army, 1958-60.

Career: Comedian, actor, and writer. Has appeared in over forty films, including *Lady Sings the Blues,* 1972; *Uptown Saturday Night,* 1974; *Silver Streak,* 1976; *Bingo Long and the Traveling All-Stars and Motor Kings,* 1976; *Blue Collar,* 1978; *The Wiz,* 1978; *Richard Pryor Live in Concert,* 1979; *Stir Crazy,* 1980; *Bustin' Loose,* 1981; *Live on Sunset Strip,* 1982; *Some Kind of Hero,* 1982; *The Toy,* 1982; *Superman III,* 1983; *Brewster's Millions,* 1985; *Jo Jo Dancer, Your Life Is Calling,* 1985; *See No Evil, Hear No Evil,* 1989; *Harlem Nights,* 1989; and *Another You,* 1991. Guest and host of numerous television shows, including *The Tonight Show* and *Saturday Night Live.* Star of *The Richard Pryor Show,* 1977. Author or co-author of screenplays, including *Blazing Saddles,* 1974; *Car Wash,* 1976; *Silver Streak,* 1976; *Blue Collar,* 1978; *Stir Crazy,* 1980; and *Jo Jo Dancer, Your Life Is Calling,* 1985.

Selected awards: Emmy Award, 1973, for *Lily;* Writers Guild Award and American Academy of Humor Award, both 1974, for *Blazing Saddles;* five Grammy awards for best comedy albums; Emmy Award nomination and Image Award nomination for *Chicago Hope,* 1996; Hall of Fame Award, National Association for the Advancement of Colored People, 1996; recipient of the first Mark Twain Prize, 1998.

Addresses: *Agent*—c/o Tri-Star Pictures, 3400 Riverside Dr., Burbank, CA 91505.

thinking of black comedians, unlocked that irreverent style."

A Tragic Background

Bill Cosby told *People* magazine: "For Richard, the line between comedy and tragedy is as fine as you can paint it." Given Pryor's background, it is not surprising that he entwined comedy and tragedy so brilliantly. He was born in Peoria, Illinois, in December, 1940, to an unwed mother. He has always claimed that he was raised in his grandmother's brothel, where his mother worked as a prostitute. His parents, LeRoy and Gertrude Pryor, married when he was three, but the union did not last. Ultimately he chose to live with his grandmother, who was not shy about administering beatings.

At the height of his fame, Pryor declared that he had no bitterness about his unconventional upbringing. He revealed to *People* that his mother "wasn't very strong, but she tried. At least she didn't flush me down the toilet, like some." He added: "The biggest moment of my life was when my grandmother was with me on the *Mike Douglas Show.*" On the other hand, Pryor's former bodyguard and spiritual adviser Rashon Khan told *Premiere* that Pryor was sometimes sexually abused in his childhood environment and was often "exposed to a lot of crazy stuff." Khan suggested that these childhood traumas helped set the stage for Pryor's drug abuse even before he became established in his career. "The problem that Richard was having with Richard was what happened when he was a kid," Khan said. "It created a void so big, it didn't matter how famous he got."

In school, Pryor was often in trouble with the authorities. His one positive experience came when he was eleven. One of his teachers, Juliette Whittaker, cast him in a community theater performance and then let him entertain his classmates with his antics. Years later, Pryor gave Whittaker the Emmy Award he earned writing comedy for a Lily Tomlin special.

Pryor was expelled from high school after striking a teacher. He never returned. Instead, he sought work in a packing house and then, in 1958, joined the army. He spent his two-year hitch in West Germany, once again clashing with his superiors. Pryor returned home to Peoria in 1960, married the first of his five wives, and fathered his second child, Richard Pryor, Jr. His first child, daughter Renee, was born three years earlier.

Early Career Moves

The owner of a popular African American nightclub in Peoria gave Pryor his first professional opportunity. By the early 1960s the comedian was performing on a circuit that included East St. Louis, Youngstown, and Pittsburgh. Then, in 1963, Pryor decided to move to New York City. He settled briefly in Greenwich Village, where he performed an act with strong similarities to Bill Cosby's. Pryor told *People:* "I'll never forget going up to Harlem and seeing all those black people. Jesus, just knowing there were that many of us made me feel better."

Pryor broke into television in New York City in 1964 when he appeared on a series called *On Broadway Tonight*. Other offers followed, including a couple from *The Ed Sullivan Show* and the *Merv Griffin Show*. Pryor pulled up stakes and moved to Los Angeles, where he supported himself with bit parts in movies such as *The Green Berets*, starring John Wayne, and *Wild in the Streets*, a teen-exploitation film. He also continued to play to live audiences, especially in Las Vegas showrooms. "In his early days there was a lot of Bill Cosby in Richard's act," Cosby himself noted in *People*. "Then one evening I was in the audience when Richard took on a whole new persona--his own, in front of me and everyone else. Richard killed the Bill Cosby in his act, made people hate it. Then he worked on them, doing pure Richard Pryor, and it was the most astonishing metamorphosis I have ever seen. He was magnificent."

Fame Brought Its Own Troubles

By the late 1960s Pryor was already indulging in one hundred dollars worth of cocaine a day. While his new, more personal act found followers, it also alienated the management in Las Vegas. Pryor clashed with landlords and hotel clerks, was audited by the Internal Revenue Service for nonpayment of taxes between 1967 and 1970, and was sued for battery by one of his wives. He disappeared into the counterculture community in Berkeley, California, and did not work for several years. Then he resurfaced in 1972 with a new stand-up act and a supporting role in the film *Lady Sings the Blues*, a drama for which he earned an Academy Award nomination.

Pryor also contributed his writing talents to other comics. He wrote bits for *The Flip Wilson Show* and *Sanford and Son* and helped Mel Brooks to write the classic Western film comedy *Blazing Saddles*. In 1973 he earned an Emmy Award for the special *Lily*, starring Lily Tomlin. That provocative show also proved a vehicle for Pryor, when he teamed with Tomlin for a skit about a raggedy black wino and a prim, "tasteful lady."

In 1976, Pryor wrote and starred in *Bingo Long and the Traveling All Stars and Motor Kings*. He made a bigger splash, however, in the film *Silver Streak*, a mixture of comedy and suspense that centers on a murderous train ride. Even though he had only a supporting role in this 1976 release starring Gene Wilder, Pryor earned the bulk of the critics' attention. The film grossed $30 million at the box office, and it opened new venues for the versatile Pryor.

Lonely at the Top

Pryor was at the height of his form as a live comedian by the late 1980s. He had earned Grammy Awards for the 1974 album *That Nigger's Crazy* and the 1976 work *Bicentennial Nigger*. Both of the albums went platinum in sales. In all, Pryor earned five Grammy Awards for best comedy album, but the 1979 movie *Richard Pryor Live in Concert* remains his "indisputable moment of glory," to quote Handelman. In the *New York Times Magazine*, James McPherson claimed that Pryor was creating a whole new style in American comedy, a style born more of the theater than of traditional humor. The characters, McPherson wrote, "are winos, junkies, whores, street fighters, blue-collar drunks, pool hustlers--all the failures who are an embarrassment to the black middle class and stereotypes in the minds of most whites. The black middle class fears the glorification of those images and most whites fear them in general. Pryor talks like them; he imitates their styles.... He enters into his people and allows whatever is comic in them, whatever is human, to evolve out of what they say and how they look into a total scene. It is part of Richard Pryor's genius that, through the selective use of facial expressions, gestures, ... speech and movements, he can create a scene that is comic and at the same time recognizable as profoundly human."

Some of those "profoundly human" comedy scenes were based on unhappy events in Pryor's life. He had a serious heart attack in 1978 and underwent yet another divorce after a violent episode on New Year's Eve that culminated in his riddling his wife's car with bullets. These two grave incidents are given the full comic treatment in *Richard Pryor Live in Concert*. At a point in the act, Pryor "becomes" his heart itself during the attack, with asides from other parts of his body. He also "becomes" his ex-wife's car under attack.

The theme would be recreated two years later after an even more dangerous event. By 1980 Pryor was freebasing cocaine, using volatile ether to help light the drug for smoking. No one is clear about exactly what happened on June 9, 1980. At first, Pryor claimed the fire was started during the freebasing process. Later, he stated that he poured rum on himself and set himself on fire. At any rate, he nearly burned himself to death, suffering severe injuries to half his body. Early reports told of his untimely death, but he survived and underwent an anguishing rehabilitation.

The healing process did not speak to his addiction, however. He took painkillers in the hospital and returned to freebasing when he was released. Nevertheless, he began to see the fatal consequences of drug use, and this attitude is evident in his final concert movie, *Live on Sunset Strip*. The film contains the well-known Pryor routine about his accident, his drug use, and his stay in the hospital. *New York* magazine contributor David Denby called *Live on Sunset Strip* "a perfect entertainment." The critic added: "Richard Pryor works directly with the life around him, and he digs deeper into fear and lust and anger and pain than many of the novelists and playwrights now taken seriously. Like any great actor, he dramatizes emotion with his whole body, but his mind is so quick and his moods so volatile, he's light-years ahead of any actor delivering a text. Working from deep inside his own experience and understanding of what a human being is and is capable of, he can shake you to your roots."

A Second Chance

Live on Sunset Strip was released in 1982. The following year Pryor made concerted efforts to clear his system of drugs and alcohol. He joined a rehabilitation program and worked with other addicts to overcome his problems. He also tackled a project that was daring indeed--he co-wrote, directed, and starred in the 1985 film *Jo Jo Dancer, Your Life Is Calling*. A thinly veiled autobiography, *Jo Jo Dancer* stars Pryor as a comedian who relives his life immediately following a near fatal accident. Critics praised the intentions of the movie-- especially the fact that Pryor hired African American workers for every aspect of the production--but the film was not a hit. *Detroit Free Press* critic Catherine Rambeau, for instance, cited the work for its "honorable premise," but faulted it for a "lack of focus."

Los Angeles Times reviewer Peter Rainer speculated that, as far as movies in general are concerned, Pryor "seems to have taken a wrong turn." A number of Pryor's movies did brisk business at the box office, but in Rainer's words, they led Pryor "into creative oblivion." Films such as *The Toy, Brewster's Millions, Stir Crazy,* and *Bustin' Loose* show a Pryor who "is resignedly bland.... Anything malign or threatening has been bleached out," to quote Rainer. Pryor's ex-wife Jennifer Lee told *Premiere:* "Don't bother looking for a pattern to Richard's movies.... He's lazy, he took the money, he doesn't care."

Fans Remained Loyal

Others held greater respect for Pryor, however. Eddie Murphy asked Pryor to co-star in the 1989 movie *Harlem Nights* and a huge comedy concert in Pryor's honor. Commenting in *Premiere* on the restrictive social atmosphere that existed during Pryor's rise to fame, comedienne Lily Tomlin expressed astonishment over his ability to achieve anything at all. "Richard lost jobs, was blackballed and everything else," Tomlin said, "because people thought he was too hard to deal with or incorrigible or out of control. Now people's careers are *built* on drug use or rehab. And I can't imagine anything happening to Eddie Murphy like what's happened to Richard. Richard paid the price for using language on the stage, ... and Eddie has been celebrated for it. And I don't think Eddie would ever be conflicted the way Richard was about playing [Las] Vegas, playing white clubs with white managers and taking white money. It was a different consciousness."

The pioneer of that change in consciousness is now in retirement. Pryor was diagnosed with multiple sclerosis, a degenerative disease that attacks the central nervous system, in 1986. He has also experienced further heart trouble, and has had triple bypass surgery. Although he is still sharp mentally, multiple sclerosis has robbed Pryor of his ability to speak clearly and he is confined to a wheelchair. Pryor's physical limitations and frail, gaunt appearance are a great source of frustration for him. One of Pryor's closest friends, Paul Mooney, told the *Knight Ridder/Tribune News Service*, "He [Pryor] has always been the life of the party. He does not like people seeing him like this, and he does not like being like this." In an ironic twist, multiple sclerosis may have actually extended Pryor's life. Jennifer Lee remarked to the *Knight Ridder/Tribune News Service,* "I think he is grateful, in a strange way, that this sickness is extending his life. We are always joking about it. I mean, where do you think he would be now if he were able to get into his car and take off? He'd probably be off getting into more trouble."

In 1998, Pryor received the first Mark Twain Prize in celebration of American humor in a ceremony at the John F. Kennedy Center for the Performing Arts in Washington, D.C. Over 2,000 guests, including Whoopi Goldberg, Robin Williams, Chris Rock, Morgan Freeman, Richard Belzer, Tim Allen, and Damon Wayans, attended the ceremony. The ceremony featured video clips of some of Pryor's most famous comedic moments interspersed with comments and tributes from comedians and actors who were influenced by Pryor. Although he was unable to rise from his chair, Pryor graciously accepted the award with a whispered "Thank you." In a written statement that was quoted in *Jet,* Pryor wrote: "I feel great about accepting this prize. It is nice to be regarded on par with a great white man–now that's funny. Seriously, though, two things people throughout history have had in common are hatred and humor. I am proud that, like Mark Twain, I have been able to use humor to lessen people's hatred!"

Pryor's ill health does not detract from the body of work he has left behind, though--a half dozen million-selling albums, two classic concert videos, several creditable dramatic performances, and--of course--the daring live routines with their uncensored social and psychological commentary. *Progressive* contributor Michael H. Seitz noted that Pryor grounded his comedy "on human feelings, often the most intimate sort." Handelman concluded: "Even though his best work had nothing to do with one-liners, Pryor is unquestionably still the most important and influential stand-up comedian of the past 25 years. Using raw street language, he [turned] black American life into breathtaking one-man theater, his rubbery face, multioctave voice, and lithe body physicalizing every situation." As Damon Wayans told *Jet*, "If [a comedian] hasn't copied from Richard Pryor, then you're probably not funny. Like Michael Jordan has defined the game of basketball, Richard Pryor has defined stand up comedy."

Selected discography

That Nigger's Crazy, Reprise, 1974.
Bicentennial Nigger, Warner Bros., 1976.
Live on Sunset Strip, Warner Bros., 1982.
Greatest Hits, Warner Bros.
Is It Something I Said?, Reprise.
Wanted, Warner Bros.

Sources

Books

Contemporary Literary Criticism, Volume 26, Gale, 1983.
Contemporary Theater, Film, and Television, Volume 3, Gale, 1986.

Periodicals

Commonweal, May 7, 1982.
Detroit Free Press, May 2, 1986.
Ebony, July 1986.
Entertainment Weekly, October 11, 1991.
Film Comment, July-August 1982.
Jet, November 9, 1998.
Knight Ridder/Tribune News Service, January 15, 1999.
Los Angeles Times, May 2, 1986; November 24, 1989.
New York, March 29, 1982.
New York Times, January 9, 1977; May 2, 1986; May 18, 1986.
New York Times Magazine, April 27, 1975.
People, March 13, 1978.
Philadelphia Inquirer, January 26, 1992.
Premiere, June 1991; January 1992.
Progressive, June 1982.

—Anne Janette Johnson and David G. Oblender

David Robinson

1965—

Professional basketball player

David Robinson, future NBA Hall-of-Famer and leader of the San Antonio Spurs, was born in Key West, Florida on August 6, 1965. He was the second child of Ambrose and Freda Robinson. Since Robinson's father was in the Navy, the family soon moved to Virginia Beach, Virginia where Robinson excelled in school and in most sports except basketball. He was 5 feet, 9 inches tall in junior high school so he tried basketball, but he soon quit. Robinson attended Osbourn Park High School in Manassas, Virginia just outside of Washington D.C., where Robinson's father was working as an engineer after retiring from the Navy. By his senior year in high school he was 6 feet, 7 inches tall, but he had not played organized basketball. When the coach added the tall senior to the basketball team, Robinson earned all-area and all-district honors but generated little interest among college basketball coaches. Basketball was not his first priority anyway, getting an education was. With an SAT score of 1,320 out of a possible 1,600, Robinson could go to any school he chose, and he chose the United States Naval Academy.

Robinson entered the Naval Academy in the fall of 1983. Not only did Robinson have to deal with the rigors of the Naval Academy, but he had to learn to play college basketball. In his freshman year he did not start a single game and averaged 7.6 points and four rebounds a game. But the next year Robinson's height and ability in basketball would change dramatically. Robinson grew to be 6 feet, 11 inches tall and began to dominate on the basketball court. Robinson led the Midshipman to a 26-6 record, a Colonial Conference Title, and into the second round of the NCAA tournament for the first time in 25 years. Robinson averaged 23.6 points and 11.6 rebounds per game, and blocked 128 shots. Robinson performed so well that he finally allowed the thought of playing in the NBA to enter his mind. But after graduating from the academy, he would still owe the Navy five years of service. Because of this long-term commitment he seriously considered transferring after his sophomore year, but he decided to stay when Navy officials hinted at reducing his obligation after graduation.

In his junior year Robinson led the Naval Academy to the Great Eight of the NCAA tournament and was named to the Associated Press (AP) 1986 All-American Team. Robinson averaged 22.7 points and 13 rebounds per game. But he really dominated on the defensive end.

> **At a Glance...**
>
> Born David Robinson, August 6, 1965 in Key West, FL; son of Ambrose (an engineer) and Freda Robinson; married with children: David Jr. and Corey. Education: graduated from the United States Naval Academy.
>
> **Career:** After one year of high school basketball Robinson attended the Naval Academy and played basketball all four years, 1983-84, 1986-87; the first overall selection in the NBA draft of the San Antonio Spurs, 1987; served two additional years at Kings Bay Naval Base, 1988-89; participated in the Olympic Games, 1988, 1992, 1996; starting center for the San Antonio Spurs, 1989-.
>
> **Awards:** Associated Press All-American, 1985-86, and 1986-87; Naismith and Wooden Awards as the College Player of the Year, 1987; NBA Rookie of the Year, 1989-90; NBA All-Defensive First Team, 1990-91, 1991-92, 1994-95, and 1995-96; NBA Defensive Player of the Year, 1991-92; All NBA First Team, 1990-91, 1991-92, and 1994-95; All NBA Second Team, 1993-94, and 1997-98; All NBA Third Team, 1989-90, and 1992-93; NBA's Most Valuable Player, 1994-95; Named by the league as one of its 50 Greatest Players in NBA History, 1996; Eight-time NBA All-Star, 1990-98.
>
> **Addresses:** Residence—San Antonio, TX; Mailing—c/o The San Antonio Spurs, 100 Montana, San Antonio, TX 78203-1031.

After three seasons Robinson had set NCAA records for most shots blocked in a game (14), most shots blocked in a season (207), and most career shots blocked (372). Robinson's 207 blocks were more rejections than every team in the NCAA except Louisville, which won the national championship in 1986.

In his senior season, Robinson was named the only unanimous selection on the AP's All-American Team and won the Naismith Award as the College Player of the Year. Robinson graduated from the Naval Academy in the spring of 1987 and almost immediately he was the first player selected in the NBA draft by the San Antonio Spurs. The Spurs drafted Robinson knowing that he would not be available until the 1989-90 season. Robinson reported to the Kings Bay Naval Submarine Base and worked as an engineer. He also played on the United States' national team. Robinson participated in the Pan Am Games in 1987 and in the Olympic Games in Seoul, South Korea, where the U.S. team finished a disappointing third.

The Admiral in the NBA

In May of 1989 Robinson was discharged from the Navy. Robinson went from being a solitary engineer to the glamour of the NBA and a starring role in his own Nike commercial. His impact on the Spurs was phenomenal. The year before San Antonio posted a 21-61 record and in Robinson's first year the team improved 35 games to finish at 56-26. Robinson ended the season tenth in the league in scoring with a 24.3 average, second in rebounding averaging 12 per game, and third in blocked shots with 3.89 per game. Robinson was named to the All-Star Game, was All-NBA third team, and was the unanimous Rookie of the Year. In his first year Robinson led his team to a Midwest Division title and into the second round of the playoffs.

The following season Robinson again played in all 82 games and bettered his statistics from the previous year. He not only made the All-Star team but was also first team All-NBA and a member of the All-Defensive team. Robinson was the only player in the league to finish the season in the top 10 in four statistical categories. He finished first in rebounding (13 a game) and second in blocked shots (3.90 a game). Despite his individual achievements the Spurs were eliminated in the first round of the playoffs. Two years into his career, he seemed to be on top of the world, but just the opposite was true. Robinson told Sports Illustrated about his state of mind after the 1991 season: "What surprised me was that I wasn't happy. Here I had everything I ever wanted—I had graduated from a good school, had a good family behind me, was doing things I never dreamed I'd do—and I wasn't happy at all. I looked at myself, and I didn't like the person I was becoming. I felt I was so important. I had selfishness and arrogance." Robinson's solution was to commit more fully to Christianity. He also became more settled marrying Valerie Hoggat, a woman he had met in 1988 while he was serving in the Navy.

Robinson continued to improve in his third season despite an injury that forced him to miss the last part of the season. Robinson tore a ligament in his hand and missed all the games after March 16. Robinson became only the third player in NBA history to finish the season in the top ten in scoring (seventh), rebounding (fourth), blocked shots (first), steals (fifth), and field-goal percentage (seventh). For the third time Robinson made the All-Star team and was again named All-NBA first team and the Defensive Player of the Year. Robinson also played in his second Olympic games winning the gold medal in Barcelona with the first Dream Team. After the injury the previous season, Robinson took on a massive workload in the 1992-93 season. He played in all 82 Spurs games and broke the franchise record for minutes played with 3,211. The star center played more than 40 minutes in 41 games. During this marathon season, Robinson was typically excellent, starting for the Western Conference All-Star Team and for the year averaging 23.4 points, 11.7 rebounds, 3.22 blocks, and 1.55 steals per game. In the post season the Spurs advanced to the Western Conference semi-finals before losing to the Phoenix Suns in six games.

Robinson Wins the MVP

For the 1993-94 season, the Spurs brought in rebounding sensation Dennis Rodman, which allowed Robinson to concentrate more on offense. He responded by leading the NBA in scoring, averaging 29.8 points per game. Robinson averaged 40.5 minutes per game and finished second in the voting for the league's Most Valuable Player (MVP). Robinson also made a fifth straight All-Star appearance and led his team to a 55-27 record. Still there were whispers that the intelligent, religious, young center who listened to classical music could never lead his team to an NBA championship. Isiah Thomas, the Detroit Pistons Hall-of-Fame point guard, commented on this perception in an article in Sports Illustrated: "David Robinson has always been nice, and their team has always been nice. But do you want a bunch of guys who are nice all the time, or do you want to win championships? If Dennis can keep David angry, they could make it out of the West." Rodman would not help enough as the Spurs lost in the first round of the playoffs.

Robinson seemed to answer his critics during the 1994-95 season winning the NBA's MVP award. Robinson showed the all-around quality of his game averaging 27.6 points, 10.8 rebounds, and 3.23 blocks per game. He led the Spurs to the best regular season record in the NBA (62-20) and a number one seed throughout the playoffs. San Antonio moved through the first two rounds of the post-season, but lost in the conference semi-finals to the Houston Rockets and the 1993-94 MVP Hakeem Olajuwan. Robinson told Sports Illustrated about the turnaround from winning the MVP award to being bounced from the playoffs: "I don't think there's any worse feeling for an athlete than to feel inadequate. These are the times when you really have to love the game, when you realize you were six games away from a title, and now you have to start over again. I just stayed home for a few days. The kids give you perspective."

> "Everybody thinks the trophy and the ring are the ultimate things, but as valuable as they are, they're just things. They'll wind up on a shelf somewhere, but the experience of winning them, the journey, will be right here in my heart forever."

Despite his disappointment, in 1995-96 Robinson almost equaled his accomplishments from the previous MVP year. He made All-NBA and All-Defensive First Teams and made the All-Star game for the seventh consecutive time. After a seven-year career filled with every sort of accolade except post-season success, Robinson was finally bitten by the injury bug during the 1996-97 season. He missed his first 18 games with a lower back strain, and then after six games back in the lineup, Robinson broke his foot and missed the rest of the season.

The 1997-98 season marked the arrival of highly-regarded rookie Tim Duncan. Robinson came back strong from his year off and battled through a concussion and nagging injuries in both knees to be named an All-Star and second team All-NBA. Despite missing some games and a reduction in playing time, Robinson still averaged over 20 points and 10 rebounds per game. As he approached his tenth season in the league, Robinson had accomplished about as much as an individual player could accomplish--including being named one of the 50 greatest players in NBA history. He had homes in San Antonio and Aspen, Co. and his family had now grown to include two sons, David Jr. and Corey. Off the court he had established the David Robinson Foundation, his own charitable organization, helped an entire grade at a San Antonio school pay for college, and is active in feeding the homeless through a problem called "Feed My Sheep." He also founded the Ruth Project that provides diapers and baby food for needy families. In short, he had done it all—except win a championship.

The Top of the Mountain

To win the championship, Robinson was asked to do

something he hadn't done since he was a freshman at Navy—play a supporting role rather than be the man. The coach asked his former franchise player to focus more on the defensive end of the court and allow Duncan to take over as the scorer. Robinson told Sports Illustrated's Phil Taylor that the adjustment was difficult: "It grinds on everything in me that's competitive—my ego, my pride, everything. I've always been the focus here. To feel as though I'm not anymore is difficult, very difficult. I look at my numbers, and they look so strange. I used to laugh at the guys who averaged only 12 points and 10 rebounds. Anybody could average 12 and 10. But now I find myself in that position." When the Spurs, which were one of the favorites to win the championship, started 6-8, many, including Robinson himself, questioned the strategy. But the Spurs kept to the game plan and then stormed through the rest of the season running up a 42-6 record to the NBA finals. During the playoffs Robinson averaged 15.6 points, 9.9 rebounds, 2.35 blocks, and 35.3 minutes per game. In the NBA finals against the New York Knicks, Robinson pushed his playoff numbers even higher. He averaged 16.6 points, 11.8 rebounds, and 3.0 blocks per game. The Spurs went out and beat the Knicks in five games and the man known as "The Admiral" led his team to the NBA Promised Land. But still he kept the title in perspective as he explained in an article he wrote with Phil Taylor of Sports Illustrated: "Everybody thinks the trophy and the ring are the ultimate things, but as valuable as they are, they're just things. They'll wind up on a shelf somewhere, but the experience of winning them, the journey, will be right here in my heart forever."

Sources

Books

Miller, Dawn M., David Robinson: Backboard Admiral (The Achievers). Lerner Publications Co.: N.Y., 1991.

Periodicals

Sports Illustrated, March 7, 1994; April 26, 1996; April 12, 1999; July 13, 1999.

Other

Additional information for this profile was obtained from http://nba.com/playerfile/bio/david_robinson.html.

—Michael J. Watkins

Paul Silas

1943—

Professional basketball coach

Paul Silas is perhaps best remembered by professional basketball fans as one of the fearsome quintet that brought the National Basketball Association (NBA) championship back to Boston after several years of ownership by the Boston Celtics' arch-rivals, the New York Knicks. As a forward, Silas was a powerful player who dominated opposing players in the rough-and-tumble zone under the net, and he is still ranked as one of the top rebounders—players who gain control of the ball after a missed shot—in the history of the NBA. After his retirement as an active player in 1980, Silas stayed active in the game, and the beginning of his tenure as head coach of the Charlotte Hornets in 1999 seemed to promise future success.

Silas was born in Prescott, Arkansas, on July 12, 1943, but spent much of his youth in Oakland, California. He attended McClymonds High School, a large institution on the city's east side with strong sports traditions; other famous McClymonds alumni included longtime Boston Celtics center Bill Russell and baseball stars Vada Pinson and Frank Robinson. Silas moved on to Creighton University in Omaha, Nebraska, and graduated in 1964.

Excelled at Creighton

During his time at Creighton, Silas's all-around skills and the power of his game began to mark him as a future professional standout. One of only six players in National Collegiate Athletic Association (NCAA) history to average both over 20 points and over 20 rebounds per game in a single season—a distinction he shares with such stellar company as Julius Erving, Bill Russell, and Artis Gilmore—Silas compounded this achievement by repeating it in all three years of his varsity career. He remains the NCAA record holder for most rebounds in a three-year career (when Silas played college basketball it was unusual for freshmen to play at the varsity level), and holds the rank of sixth overall.

Other aspects of Silas's collegiate career caught the attention of pro scouts. He led the NCAA in rebounds in 1963 with his average of 20.6 per game, and his extraordinary 38 rebounds during a game on February 19, 1962 still rank eighth on the all-time list. In the 1964 draft, Silas was selected by the St. Louis Hawks in the second round, as the 12th pick overall of the hundreds of players who began their NBA careers that year.

> **At a Glance...**
>
> Born July 12, 1943, in Prescott, AR; married to Carolyn; children: Donna, Paula, Stephen. *Education:* graduated from Creighton University, Omaha, Nebraska, 1964.
>
> **Career:** Professional basketball player and coach; drafted by the St. Louis Hawks, 1964; forward: St. Louis (later Atlanta), Hawks, 1964-69; Phoenix Suns, 1969-72; Boston Celtics, 1972-76; Denver Nuggets, 1976-77; Seattle Supersonics, 1977-80; head coach, San Diego Clippers, 1980-83; assistant coach, New Jersey Nets, 1988-89 and 1992-95; assistant coach, New York Knicks, 1989-92; assistant coach, Phoenix Suns, 1995-97; asst. coach, Charlotte Hornets, 1997-99; head coach, Charlotte Hornets, 1999–.
>
> **Addresses:** *Office*—c/o Charlotte Hornets, One Hive Dr., Charlotte, NC 28217.

Except for a short stint with the minor-league Wilkes-Barre Barons, Silas remained with the Hawks for five seasons.

Silas was traded to the newly-established Phoenix Suns in 1969, where he remained until 1972. A consistent player whose performance tended not to vary widely over his entire career, he notched his single best season with Phoenix during the 1971-72 campaign, scoring 1403 points and averaging 17.5 points per game. Silas also logged 3,082 minutes of playing time that year, a personal high. During his 16 seasons in the NBA, he was almost always a member of his team's starting lineup.

Played on Celtics Championship Teams

The Suns traded their emerging star to the Boston Celtics in September of 1972. Following the end of the 1973-74 regular season, Silas found himself in the thick of a hotly contested NBA championship series against the New York Knicks, the team that had displaced the Celtics as the league's perennial powerhouse in the early 1970s. The Celtics brought the championship crown back to Boston, as Silas, in the words of *The Modern Encyclopedia of Basketball*, "outmuscled the Knicks forwards." In addition to his shooting and rebounding skills, Silas was also a talented defensive player. Silas was named to the NBA's All-Defensive first team in 1975, after making the second team in 1971, 1972, and 1973. He made the first team again in 1976, and helped to lead the Celtics to another league championship.

Silas was traded to the Denver Nuggets in 1976, and to the Seattle Supersonics the following year. He helped lead these teams to the playoffs each year until his retirement in 1980. A two-time NBA All-Star (in 1972 and 1975) and a past president of the NBA Players' Association by the time he retired, Silas had amassed an impressive record. By 1980 Silas ranked ninth on the NBA's all-time list of top rebounders, and he remained in 14th place as of 1999. When he retired, Silas was also ranked seventh in number of games played, having taken to an NBA court 1,254 times.

Following the end of his playing career, Silas was hired as the coach of the San Diego Clippers, a perennial cellar dweller that had hired a succession of coaches during its brief existence. Initially, Silas was hired as a player-coach, but he decided to end his playing career to focus on coaching. Silas remained at the helm for three years, but injuries, including one to Clippers center Bill Walton, plagued the team. The Clippers' won-lost record dropped to 17–65 during the 1981–82 season. Although the Clippers record improved to 25–57 the following season, Silas was fired in the spring of 1983.

Returned to NBA

A married father of three, Silas spent several years away from the NBA. He eventually hosted an annual corporate basketball tournament to benefit youth organizations in his home area of Westchester County. Silas returned to coaching in 1988 as an assistant with the New Jersey Nets. After one season, he took a coaching job with the New York Knicks, only to return to the New Jersey Nets in 1992. During this time, he had the opportunity to work with two of the NBA's finest coaches of the 1990s, the Knicks' Pat Riley and the Nets' Chuck Daly. In 1995, Silas became a top assistant with the Phoenix Suns, for whom he had played a quarter century before. In 1997, he accepted an assistant coaching position with the Charlotte Hornets.

Early in 1999, the Hornets were struggling with a 4–11 record under coach Dave Cowens. Cowens resigned, and Silas was named as interim head coach. He promptly turned the team's fortunes around. Under Silas's leadership, the Hornets compiled a 22-13 record and narrowly missed the Eastern Conference playoffs. The Hornets' management rewarded Silas by removing the interim designation from his title, and named him as the team's head coach. Silas appeared to be well on his way to adding another chapter to a distinguished basketball career.

Sources

Books

Broussard, Mark, and Brendan Roberts, eds., *The Sporting News Official NBA Register,* 1999–2000 ed., Sporting News, 1999.
Broussard, Mark, and Craig Carter, eds., *The Sporting News Official NBA Guide,* 1999–2000 ed. Sporting News, 1999.
Hollander, Zander, *The Modern Encyclopedia of Basketball,* Dolphin, 1979.

Periodicals

Jet, May 31, 1999, p. 48.
New York Times, April 23, 1999, p. D3.

Other

Additional information for this profile was obtained from http://www.nba.com/hornets/bios/coach.html

—James M. Manheim

Sheila Violet Makate Sisulu

1948—

South African ambassador

Sheila Sisulu is the first black person to represent South Africa as the country's ambassador to the United States. She is also the first woman to hold this post and was appointed by President Nelson Mandela in 1999, just before he handed over the reins of power to his successor, President Thabo Mbeki. Sisulu planned to continue fostering bilateral relations between the United States and her homeland.

Sisulu has devoted her attention to the educational and social problems facing post-apartheid South Africa. She was a teacher who became a staunch advocate for underprivileged and uneducated black students. With the dawn of black majority rule in South Africa during the mid-1990s, Sisulu was able to secure appointments overseas. This enabled her to locate international sources of financial support that will help to foster greater educational opportunities for a new generation of black South Africans.

Ruled by Apartheid

For Sisulu, the long journey to a South African ambassadorship began on the outskirts of Johannesburg, in the Southwestern Native Township known as Soweto. Her parents, a former salesman and factory seamstress, operated a store in Soweto. By the time Sisulu was five years old, South Africa's apartheid system was firmly entrenched. Blacks and whites lived in separate communities, sought medical treatment in segregated hospitals, and worked in occupations deemed appropriate by the government. In 1955 the Minister of Native Affairs, Hendrik Frensch Verwoerd, implemented a segregated educational system throughout South Africa.

Sisulu faced many obstacles as a result of South Africa's segregated educational system. For instance, schools for black students were confronted with a chronic shortage of textbooks and other materials. Some classrooms had 60 or more students, which made personal attention from a teacher rare. Homework was often done by candlelight, since Soweto had no electricity.

Soon after Sisulu began school her older brother, who was an anti-apartheid activist, warned their parents that tanks, soldiers and police would be raiding the township

At a Glance...

Born c. 1948 near Johannesburg, South Africa; married to Mlungisi Sisulu; three children. *Education:* University of Lesotho, Botswana and Swaziland, BA, 1974; University of the Witwatersrand, bachelor's degree in education, 1990.

Career: South African Committee for Higher Education, 1978-88; National Coordinator for Educational Opportunities, South African Council of Churches (SACC); Educational Coordinator for the African Bursary Fund, SACC, 1988-91; director of the Joint Enrichment Fund, 1991-94; Special Advisor to the Minister of Education, 1994-; Consul-General at the South African Consulate-General, New York, 1997-99; South African ambassador to The United States of America, 1999-.

Awards: Allan Pfier Fellowship Fund, 1989; Nedbank Femina Woman of the 90s, 1993; South African Women for Women Education Award, June, 1998.

Addresses: *Office*—The Embassy of South Africa, 3051 Massachusetts Ave NW, Washington, DC, 20008.

---

school on the following day. Alarmed, Sisulu's parents kept her home from school. This proved to be a serious miscalculation, since the police announced that any students who were absent from school on the day of the raid would not be allowed to return. Six long months would pass before Sisulu was allowed back in school.

Despite these challenges, Sisulu was a good student. When she was 12 years old, her life took an unexpected turn. After it was discovered that Sisulu had been molested by a teacher, her parents sent her to a boarding school, St. Michael's School for Girls, in neighboring Swaziland. Freed from the inequities of South Africa's segregated educational system, Sisulu received a sound education based on the British system. The teachers at St. Michael's were also much better trained than those at her former school.

When school recessed for the summer, Sisulu returned home to South Africa and was reintroduced to the humiliations of apartheid. Having spent time outside of the country, the separate train coaches, drinking fountains, and other public facilities in South Africa were deeply shocking to Sisulu. On her 16th birthday, she received her government-issued passbook. Black South Africans were required to carry this passbook at all times. "That pass was almost my branding," Sisulu told *Ebony*, "...to have it was to identify me as a second-class citizen in the country of my birth."

Sought a New Career

Soon after receiving her passbook, Sisulu vowed to pursue a career that would give her an opportunity to help bring an end to the apartheid system. She enrolled at the Lesotho campus of the University of Lesotho, Botswana and Swaziland, and graduated with a bachelor's degree in English and philosophy in 1974. Sisulu returned to South Africa and took a job as a teacher in the public school system. However, after three months on the job, she earned the equivalent of $275. Sisulu decided that she must pursue a different career. She worked briefly as a secretary and a personal assistant for a bakery. Sisulu then accepted a position at a life assurance company, becoming a personal assistant to a public relations officer. This job proved to be unsatisfying as well.

By the mid-1970s, Sisulu was in her mid-twenties. She was highly educated and socially conscious, but lacked a fulfilling career. During this period in her life, she fell in love and got married. Her husband, Mlungisi, was the son of Walter and Albertina Sisulu, both of whom were central figures in the struggle for equal rights. As an ardent civil rights supporter herself, Sisulu had great admiration for her new in-laws. Walter Sisulu was well-known among black South Africans, and had been a friend of Nelson Mandela since the 1940s. Together, they had founded the Youth League of the African National Congress (ANC) and supported the goals of *Umkhonto we Sizwe,* the ANC's military wing. Mandela and Sisulu were both accused of sabotage in 1963, and spent more than 20 years in the notorious Robben Island prison. Because of her own civil rights activities, Albertina Sisulu was placed under house arrest. Since she was not allowed to leave to attend her son's wedding, the ceremony was held in a tent across the road from her home. She was able to view the ceremony from her driveway.

In 1974, Sisulu took a job as a teacher for the South African Committee for Higher Education (SACHED) a non-governmental agency catering both to people with special needs and black students who were seeking an escape from South Africa's inferior black schools. In 1976, the South African government issued an edict declaring that all classes must be taught in Afrikaans, which is the language spoken by most white South Africans. This edict led to riots throughout Soweto and other black townships. To combat this edict, Sisulu taught a class designed to help black students pass the A-level examinations, which was required for high school graduation and entrance to college. All of the students who took Sisulu's class passed the examinations. Sisulu also realized that there were many students in rural areas that did not have access to regular schooling or intellectual stimulation. To assist these students, Sisulu established a children's magazine and headed the student services division of a local distance-learning college.

In 1988, Sisulu accepted a position with the South African Council of Churches (SACC). The SACC appealed to Sisulu because it was an organization that openly opposed apartheid, and was unintimidated by threats of government harassment. Also, it backed the student demonstrators who protested South Africa's unequal educational system. During Sisulu's years with the SACC, the organization became increasingly emboldened and learned to use the media to expose the horrors of apartheid to the outside world. Due, in part, to the efforts of the SACC, international disapproval of all apartheid policies soared. The South African government retaliated by deporting all clergy who supported the anti-apartheid movement, banning all public statements from anyone supporting the SACC, and launching a military crackdown against the demonstrators.

The SACC openly acknowledged that they could not defeat the government's military forces. However, they embarked on a strategy that was guaranteed to sway world opinion in their favor. The SACC ensured that every funeral of a demonstrator killed by the government became a media event. Scheduled graveside demonstrations were consistently reported by the media. This strategy worked magnificently and, by the end of the 1980s, the apartheid regime was showing signs of weakening.

Sisulu left the SACC in 1991, and accepted a position with the Joint Enrichment Project (JEP). From its establishment in 1986, the JEP had been an organization looking ahead to the days when the anti-apartheid struggle was won. Rather than the political concerns of the present, its main concern was the future of young black South Africans who had rejected government education in favor of protest. The JEP understood that these young people needed guidance if they were to be rescued from an uncertain future. Not only did they require an academic education—they also desperately needed mentors who could be positive role models, and who could help with decision making techniques and conflict resolution. They needed renewed faith in values based on family traditions, rather than on the violence and fatalism to which many of them had succumbed. Above all, they needed a safe place where they could be prepared for the fast-approaching days of black majority rule.

Sisulu was selected to lead this daunting task. Armed with a new bachelor of education degree from the highly-regarded University of the Witwatersrand, and new ideas garnered from a four-week inspection tour of American schools, she was pleased to accept this challenge. Sisulu also commissioned a research project on the disadvantaged youth of South Africa. In cooperation with the Community Agency for Social Enquiry, an independent research and training organization, this project was published in 1993, under the title *Youth, Education and Work*. As Sisulu had suspected, the report indicated that extensive reform was necessary, so that all South African students might benefit from the same educational advantages.

By the mid-1990s, the long-awaited end to apartheid had come to pass. Along with all other adult South Africans, Sisulu had the privilege of voting for the government of her choice. As she told *Ebony*, this experience made her feel "like a bride." The election of Nelson Mandela as president of South Africa opened new opportunities to Sisulu.

Sisulu became South Africa's Consul-General in Washington, D.C. in 1997, and was charged with the task of helping to secure foreign investment in the South African economy. In 1999, Sisulu was appointed as South Africa's ambassador to the United States. As ambassador, she represented the face of a new South Africa that is freeing itself of apartheid, a place where people of all races may one day succeed according to their abilities.

Sources

Books

Truscott, Kate, *Youth, Education and Work*, Johannesburg, University of the Witwatersrand, 1993.

Periodicals

Boston Globe, October 7, 1990, p. 84.
Chicago Tribune, May 30, 1999, Perspective, p. 3.
Ebony, October, 1999, p. 190;
Guardian, (London) October 10, 1995, p. 6.

Other

Additional information for this profile was obtained from http://archive.iol.co.za/Archives/1998/9811/26/

sonn.2411.html; http://archive.iol.co.za/Archives/1997/9705/31/satsheila.html; http://www.interlog.com/-saww/sisulu.htm; and http://222.southafrica.net/reference/ambisisulu.html

—Gillian Wolf

Jane E. Smith

1946—

Organization executive, social activist

In February of 1998, Jane E. Smith took over as president and chief operating officer of the National Council of Negro Women (NCNW). Founded in 1935 by educator Mary McLeod Bethune, the NCNW is a coalition of organizations and a political lobby group representing an array of African American women's organizations including National Women of Achievement, Trade Union Women of African Heritage, the National Bar Association Women Lawyers Division, and 20 college sororities. The NCNW also has 250 community based sections of its own with 60,000 members. In total, the NCNW is connected to over four million women either through direct membership or membership in an affiliated organization. The mission of the NCNW is to advance opportunities and the quality of life for African American women, their families and their communities.

Smith succeeded Dorothy I. Height, a well-known civil rights activist, who was NCNW president for 40 years. Height now serves as chair of the NCNW executive committee and president emertia and continues to play an important role at the council. Smith took office with the intention of continuing Height's bold, proactive style.

"Dr. Height is progressive, she's a risk taker. She steps out there on issues that she believes in. You don't tell Dr. Height what to do, she does what's right. I am the exactly same way," she told Junious R. Stanton of the *New Pittsburgh Courier*.

Smith was born and raised in Atlanta. Her father, Harvey Smith, was a dentist and her mother, Lavada Johnson Smith, taught kindergarten at local public schools. Smith received a bachelor's degree in sociology from Atlanta's Spelman College, then went on to earn a master's in sociology at Emory University in Atlanta, and a doctorate in education and public policy from Harvard University in Cambridge, Massachusetts. She is eager to dispel the notion that the NCNW is a "ladies' club" that represents the interests of only educated, middle class African American women. "I belong to a whole lot of women's organizations that I won't name, but the closest that I've come to grass-roots identification is the National Council of Negro Women," Smith told Victoria Valentine of *Emerge*.

Smith has spent much of her career in the non-profit sector. In 1981 to 1991 she was managing director of

At a Glance...

Born on July 27, 1946 in Atlanta, GA; daughter of Harvey B. (a dentist) and Lavada Johnson (a teacher) Smith. *Education:* Spelman College, Atlanta, GA, bachelor's degree in sociology; Emory University, Atlanta, GA, master's degree in sociology; Harvard University, Cambridge, MA, doctorate in education and social policy.

Career: INROADS/Atlanta and INROADS/Detroit, managing director, 1981-91; Martin Luther King Center for Nonviolent Social Change, director of development, 1991-94; The Atlanta Project of the Carter Center, director, 1994-98; National Council of Negro Women, president and chief operating officer, 1998-.

Member: Phelps-Stokes Fund, board of directors; National Summit on Africa, board member; Knoxville College, board of trustees; National Advisory Board of Reading is Fundamental; Black Leadership Forum; National Women's Business Council.

Awards: NAACP, Atlanta Chapter, Roy Wilkins Image Award, 1997.

Addresses: *Office*—National Council of Negro Women, Inc., 633 Pennsylvania Ave. N.W., Washington, DC 20004.

INROADS/Atlanta and INROADS/Detroit, career development organizations for minority students. Smith considers the development of leadership skills among young African American women as one of the most important goals of the NCNW, and believes that fostering attitudes of authority among young African American women is fundamental to achieving this goal. The NCNW has created the Dorothy I. Height Leadership Institute, which conducts workshops and other training programs for emerging and established leaders in national, community, and student organizations. "Now, I'm a Spelman College graduate, and I pick up the same sense in the Dorothy I. Height Leadership Institute as I do at Spelman College. Never at Spelman College did we say that we are trying to correct some numbers or fill spots that men now have. We produce women to be leaders for the century in this country, period. And the Dorothy I. Height Leadership Institute is the same way. We will produce women who will be leaders in this country, in the communities, in the states, across the country, and in doing so we will correct the disparity," Smith explained to Valentine.

In 1991, Smith became director of development at the Martin Luther King, Jr. Center for Non-Violent Social Change in Atlanta, where her duties included fundraising and strategic planning for domestic programs. She then served as director of The Atlanta Project (TAP), an urban initiative created by former President Jimmy Carter. As director of TAP, a program of the Carter Center, Smith worked to improve the quality of life on the neighborhood level and developed an agenda based on community and corporate partnerships.

The appointment of Smith, who is more than 30 years younger than her predecessor, marked an effort by the NCNW to rejuvenate its image and bring fresh blood into the organization. "There is a generational difference and I bring something to the table," Smith told Stanton. Smith feels it is especially important for the NCNW to reach out to young women and point out to them the advances that can be made by collective action. Smith sees high-tech communication as key to reaching younger women. "These young women want to talk to each other on the Internet. They want to do e-mail. They want to learn about the council on the Internet. So, we are going to find a way to be progressive and current with technology to spread that word, harness the power, have impact on policy in the way that Mrs. Bethune could never foresee, really that Dr. Height could never conceive, that Jane Smith couldn't conceive. I had no idea when I finished college that we would be here where we are in terms of communication today. It's incredible. That's the challenge and that's the horizon that we must go...These young women need us as much as we need them. We need to make special efforts and we are making special efforts around the eighteen to about forty-five year old to get them. First of all they have so much more energy than I do. I need them," Smith explained to Stanton.

One of the priorities of the NCNW is to foster the economic empowerment of African American women. Although traditional civil rights initiatives such as affirmative action and racial integration are still important, Smith believes that economics should be at the forefront of the NCNW agenda. "Black women are indicating that they're more interested in owning their own and running their own [businesses]," she told Valentine. The NCNW has established the Economic and Entrepreneurial Development Center (EEDC), which provides women with the technical assistance they need to set up and run their own business. The EEDC also encourages economic development as a means of combating poverty among African American women. EEDC participants gain access to tested economic development program models, gather information about federal, state, and local resources available to minority communities, and are provided with mentoring and internship opportunities.

Smith told Valentine that the NCNW has made its own "statement of economic control" with its Fund for the Future, a campaign that was designed to raise $30 million to support NCNW programs, establish an endowment, and help pay for the NCNW's new headquarters on Pennsylvania Avenue in Washington, D.C. Smith's appointment to the NCNW's executive board was due, in part, to her experience as a fund-raiser. She is also the first NCNW president to be appointed. Previous presidents were elected.

With regard to social and political issues, Smith does not believe that African American women need to put race ahead of gender. "One of the things that I had said to my feminist friends is that the African-American experience in this country brings so much to the feminist position that when I come into a room, I bring all of me as an African-American who is also a feminist...I think a woman is a feminist when she believes women can be equal participants in leadership positions that are related to quality of life in this country. I have decided that I will call myself a feminist. I am not afraid of that word," Smith told Valentine.

Smith serves on the U.S. Department of Housing and Urban Development's Community Builders National Advisory Board. She also represents the NCNW on the National Women's Business Council. She is the mother of two sons and has three grandsons.

Sources

Periodicals

Atlanta Journal Constitution, *March 10, 1993, p. A11.*
Emerge, *March 1998, p. 26-29.*
Jet, *December 29, 1997, p. 4.*
New Pittsburgh Courier, *August 4, 1999, p. A6.*
Washington Afro-American, *December 13, 1997, p. A1.*
Washington Post, *September 13, 1998, p. B1.*

Other

Additional information for this profile was obtained from the National Council of Negro Women website at www.ncnw.com.

—Mary Kalfatovic

Wesley Snipes

1962—

Actor

Before reaching the age of 30, actor Wesley Snipes was recognized as an important new figure in his field. His picture has graced the cover of *Newsweek* and *Jet* magazines, and *New Yorker* magazine critic Pauline Kael dubbed him one of the most impressive members of a new generation of American actors. Snipes came to be considered one of the chief players in the film industry and an enduring, mesmerizing talent.

Snipes was born on July 31, 1962, in Orlando, Florida. His father, an aircraft engineer, and his mother, Marian, then a teacher's aide, divorced a year after his birth. His mother then moved him and two of his seven siblings to the South Bronx section of New York, where he spent his childhood honing negotiating skills. Snipes stood 5 feet 5 inches tall when in high school--he eventually grew 6 more inches--and substituted bravado, boldness, and charm for height at that time, which in turn served as a solid foundation for his adult life.

Snipes's aunt Della Saunders entered him in talent shows when he was a child. One of those led to a minor role in the off-Broadway play *The Me Nobody Knows* when Snipes was 12 years old. Frequent auditions and basketball practice kept him busy in high school, and his competitive nature helped ensure that he would fare well academically. His keen interest in dance led him to enroll in New York's High School of the Performing Arts, known for its strong dance department. Snipes was content there, so two years later, when his mother decided to move the family back to Orlando, the teenager complained bitterly. He had become a regular at the local pool hall and was so good at the game that he made money hustling pool. His mother decided it was time for a change of atmosphere.

Seeds of Raw Talent

After attending a multiethnic elementary school in the South Bronx, and then the High School of the Performing Arts, Snipes suddenly found himself in a predominantly African American public school in Orlando, and his fast-paced style was at odds with Southern sensibilities. In an interview with *Washington Post* contributor Jay Mathews, Snipes described how he felt when he first went to Orlando: "They're just moseying along, like lemonade on the porch on a Sunday afternoon, and

At a Glance...

Born July 31, 1962, in Orlando, FL; son of an aircraft engineer and a teacher's aide; married, 1985 (divorced, 1990); children: Jelani (son). *Education:* State University of New York at Purchase, B.A., 1984.

Career: Actor in motion pictures, stage plays, and on television, 1985—. Selected stage appearances include *The Me Nobody Knows, The Boys of Winter, Death and the King's Horsemen,* and *Execution of Justice.* Also appeared in HBO's *Vietnam Story,* 1987, *America's Dream,* 1996, and Michael Jackson's music video *Bad,* 1987. Film appearances include roles in *Wildcats,* 1985, *Streets of Gold,* 1986, *Major League,* 1989, *King of New York,* 1990, *Mo' Better Blues,* 1990, *New Jack City,* 1991, *Jungle Fever,* 1991, *White Men Can't Jump,* 1992, *The Waterdance,* 1992, *Passenger 57,* 1992, *Boiling Point,* 1993, *Demolition Man,* 1993, *Rising Sun,* 1993, *Drop Zone,* 1994, *Sugar Hill,* 1994, *To Wong Foo, Thanks for Everything, Julie Newmar,* 1995, *Waiting to Exhale,* 1995, *The Fan,* 1996, *Murder at 1600,* 1997, *One Night Stand,* 1997, *U.S. Marshals,* 1998, *Down in the Delta,* 1998, *Blade,* 1998.

Awards: Cable television's ACE Award for best actor for his performance in *Vietnam Story;* Best Actor award for *One Night Stand,* Venice Film Festival, 1997.

Addresses: *Agent*—Dolores Robinson, 335 North Maple Road, Suite 250, Beverly Hills, CA 90210.

you're like, yo, I can't stand this. Let me outta here."

The drama department of Jones High School in Orlando soon took his mind off of what he had left behind when they started casting for *Damn Yankees.* Snipes was given a warm reception in the theater department and wasn't modest when it came to letting it be known that he had attended the High School of the Performing Arts. He earned spending money in high school by joining a city-sponsored drama troupe called *Struttin' Street Stuff* and performed puppet shows in parks and schools for up to $70 a week. Around the same time, he also won an award for his one-man show playing Puck, a character from William Shakespeare's comedy *A Midsummer Night's Dream,* and had a successful run playing Felix Ungar in *The Odd Couple.*

Snipes told Stephen Holden of the *New York Times:* "Moving to Florida was the best thing that could have happened to me. A lot of the cats I grew up with in the South Bronx found themselves in sticky situations." Karen Rugerio, Snipes's drama teacher at Jones High, told the *Washington Post:* "He was always very focused. If you criticize the work of someone at that age, they often get upset, but Wes would always listen very carefully, wanting to learn how he could do it better."

Shaped by Experiences in College

When it came time for college, Snipes auditioned for the State University of New York at Purchase's esteemed theater arts program and was readily accepted, receiving a Victor Borge scholarship. As Snipes explained to Larry Rohter of the *New York Times,* he fell into acting through the urging of others who saw that he was a natural. "I really wanted to be a singer and dancer," he said, "and I still have a latent passion for that. When I see Alvin Ailey or Chuck Davis or Forces of Nature, I'm sitting there saying 'I could have been up there.'"

Snipes was one of only four African American students in the theater arts department at SUNY Purchase, and he told *Ebony* magazine that it was a disconcerting experience: "I felt like mold on white bread.... What saved me was being exposed to Malcolm X." The emphasis on African American pride found in the writings of Malcolm X helped Snipes weather a confusing period in his life: an African American man coming of age while surrounded by whites. He became a Muslim for a short time, starting in the second semester of his freshman year, then abandoned the faith three years after he graduated. He revealed to Randolph: "A brother of mine used to say 'When you're drowning, grab onto a log to keep afloat. But don't hold on to the log when the boat comes by. Get on the boat and bring your butt on back home.' So Islam for me was the log to make me more conscious of what African people have accomplished, of my self-worth, to give me some self-dignity."

While in college, Snipes auditioned for Harry Belafonte's movie about break-dancers called *Beat Street* and realized that in addition to applying standard acting techniques, he also had to draw more from his own life-experience on the street. He didn't land a part in the movie, but it was a learning experience for him. Although Snipes was never given the role of leading male in any of the university productions--in spite of his obvious talents and experience--after he left college to pursue professional work, he quickly became a leading man who was very much in demand. David Garfield, an acting teacher at SUNY Purchase, told the *Los Angeles Times* that Snipes was "obviously gifted. He was extremely funny, he could do straight drama, he could sing and he would stop shows with the dance numbers he had choreographed. He also exhibited a strong black consciousness even then."

Steady Climb to Fame

Snipes met his wife while a senior in college, and they married a year after he graduated in 1984. He took a job installing telephones in New York, and that same year a casting director who had spotted him at a university drama convention contacted him for Goldie Hawn's football parody *Wildcats* after the first choice actor didn't work out. Then, along with Matt Dillon and Andrew McCarthy, Snipes procured a leading role in John Pielmeier's off-Broadway play *The Boys Of Winter,* about the ravaging effects of the Vietnam War on U.S. soldiers, and followed with a role in the Lincoln Center production of Wole Soyinka's *Death and the King's Horsemen.* After this, true to his flexible nature, he put on spike heels to portray drag queen Sister Boom-Boom in Emily Mann's Broadway play *Execution of Justice.* Mann told the *Los Angeles Times:* "I remember when he auditioned. I had never seen a man put on high heels and walk that way and all of us said 'That guy is going to be a star.'"

Because Snipes pursued an interest in martial arts, and because he has the natural grace and balance of a dancer, he was well-cast as an athlete. In 1986, Snipes portrayed a boxer in the film *Streets of Gold.* Then he experienced a short lull in his career, so he turned to other pursuits for his livelihood. Therapeutic massage and parking cars were two of the things Snipes tried in 1987 before landing a role in HBO's *Vietnam Story.* He eventually won the cable industry's ACE Award for best actor for his work in *Vietnam Story.*

In 1987, Snipes also appeared in Michael Jackson's *Bad* video, and this cameo role changed the course of his fate. Snipes portrayed a gang leader who shoved Michael Jackson up against a wall, and in doing so, caught the attention of director Spike Lee and *New Jack City* co-screenwriter Barry Michael Cooper. Lee commented to *Premier* magazine's Ralph Rugoff that Snipes "was so real, Michael Jackson must've been scared to death."

Vietnam Story was followed by a part in the 1989 baseball comedy *Major League*--he turned down a smaller part in Lee's *Do the Right Thing* for this role--and later a minor role in the drug warfare film *King of New York.* Around the same time, Snipes and his wife had a son named Jelani. The couple divorced in 1990. That same year, Snipes portrayed a jazz saxophonist named Shadow Henderson in Lee's *Mo' Better Blues,* holding his own opposite Academy Award winner Denzel Washington. Snipes told Randolph: "I just wanted to go in, do a good job, and not let Denzel blow me off the screen." In preparation for his role as a saxophonist, Snipes watched tapes of John Coltrane and other jazz legends and visited a variety of the jazz clubs in New York City. A proficient mimic, Snipes memorized scales and fingering for all of the music played in the film.

An Established Leading Man

The role of Harlem drug baron Nino Brown in the 1991 film, *New Jack City,* was also written with Snipes in mind after his appearance in the video *Bad.* Directed by Mario Van Peebles, *New Jack City* grossed $22.3 million at the box office within its first three weeks--a tribute to the powerful screen presence of Snipes. *New Jack City* was designed to be an anti-drug and anti-violence gangster film, but a spate of shootings and violence erupted briefly at some theaters across the country after it opened. Some of the eruptions were due to the fact that few theaters were showing the film at first, and those that were sold out quickly, leaving dozens of frustrated people--usually teenagers--outside of the theater without tickets. Rohter noted: "Indeed, Mr. Snipes now finds himself in the peculiar position of fending off arguments that his portrayal (of drug lord Nino Brown) may have been too effective." Commenting in the *Los Angeles Times* about the theaters where outbreaks occurred, Snipes asserted: "They oversold the showings by 1,500 tickets and the theater owners didn't give their money back. The same thing would happen with a Menudo concert, or the Rolling Stones."

Landed Leading Roles

Because of Snipes's outstanding performance as Shadow in *Mo' Better Blues,* Lee decided to cast him as Flipper Purify in *Jungle Fever,* a controversial film about interracial romance, and wrote the part with Snipes in mind. Snipes told the *New York Times* that Lee had said to him on the last day of shooting *Mo' Better Blues:* "Be ready for the next one, because I got something great for you." In *Jungle Fever,* released in June of 1991, Snipes portrayed a married architect having an affair with his white secretary-an affair that ended due to economic and cultural differences between the lovers and their conflicted families. The film was a vehicle for Lee's views on interracial relationships, and

Snipes told Hilary De Vries of the *Los Angeles Times:* "I don't know if the film is an argument for racial purity. I think it's about how color-conscious this society really is."

Snipes followed *Jungle Fever* with a leading role in Ron Shelton's 1992 release *White Men Can't Jump,* a movie about street basketball featuring Snipes and *Cheers* actor Woody Harrelson as urban hoop hustlers. The on-screen chemistry between the two stars helped make *White Men Can't Jump* one of the season's top moneymakers, and through his performance, Snipes solidified his place in American film. As he pointed out in *Entertainment Weekly,* "Rarely have you seen a young black male in this type of powerful position, who can basically make or break a project."

Following *White Men Can't Jump,* Snipes began work on Neil Jamenez's *The Waterdance,* which won several awards at the 1992 Sundance Film Festival. In the film, he portrayed one of a group of hospitalized paraplegics and quadriplegics. To research his role, Snipes spoke with patients at rehabilitation centers to understand their physical limitations and to glean emotional insight as well.

In mid-1992, Snipes appeared in the action/adventure film *Passenger 57.* The film featured Snipes as a security agent and martial arts expert named John Cutter. Cutter is a passenger on a plane that is hijacked by terrorists, and he uses his skills and intelligence to save his fellow passengers. Stephen Holden of the *New York Times* critiqued Snipes's performance: "As an action hero, Mr. Snipes belongs to the school that plays it cool and tongue-in-cheek. Consistently underplaying his part, he strolls through the role with a glint in his eye that seems to acknowledge that the movie is really a live-action cartoon."

The following year, Snipes starred in *Boiling Point* as a U.S. marshal who tracks down a sociopathic con artist. He also starred opposite Sean Connery in a film adaptation of Michael Crichton's novel, *Rising Sun.* Snipes and Connery play two detectives who are called upon to investigate the murder of a prostitute during the opening of a new skyscraper in Los Angeles. Although reviews of the film were mixed, many critics lauded Snipes's performance. "Snipes, as the bewildered-innocent half of the detective team..., has the trickier role and brings it off flawlessly: his confusion is necessarily comic, but he never seems a buffoon, " remarked Terrence Rafferty of the *New Yorker.* Also in 1993, Snipes teamed with Sylvester Stallone in *Demolition Man.* As Simon Phoenix, Snipes portrayed a criminal who escapes from prison after being cryogenically frozen for 36 years. In order to recapture Phoenix the authorities turn to John Spartan, a police sergeant who was also cryogenically frozen. The film centers around the battles between Phoenix and Spartan, who is played by Stallone, in the fictional city of San Angeles. Again, Snipes received rave reviews for his performance. John Anderson of *New York Newsday* remarked: "Snipes, the villain you can't quite bring yourself to hate, turns out to be the kind of natural comedian Stallone will never be."

In 1994 Snipes landed the role of Roemello Skuggs, a drug dealer who seeks an escape from his violent world, in the film *Sugar Hill.* That same year he starred as Pete Nessip in *Drop Zone,* a film about a U.S. marshal who enters the world of professional skydiving to destroy a terrorist group and avenge the death of his brother. Along with John Leguizamo and Patrick Swayze, Snipes played a drag queen in the 1995 comedy *To Wong Foo, Thanks for Everything, Julie Newmar.* In the film, the three men portray drag queens who are on their way to a beauty pageant when their car breaks down in a small town. Stranded, the three men become involved in the lives and problems of the town's inhabitants. In 1995, Snipes also played the role of James in the highly acclaimed film adaptation of Terry Mcmillan's novel *Waiting to Exhale.*

In 1996, Snipes starred in the action thriller *The Fan.* Snipes appeared in the role of Bobby Rayburn, a star baseball player who is stalked by an overzealous fan, played by Robert DeNiro. The fan becomes psychotic after Rayburn falls into a batting slump, and kidnaps Rayburn's young son. That same year, Snipes narrated and served as the executive producer of the documentary *John Henrik Clarke: A Great and Mighty Walk.* He also landed the role of George Du Vaul in the movie *America's Dream,* which aired on HBO.

Snipes maintained a presence on the big screen in 1997. In the film *Murder at 1600* Snipes starred as Harlan Regis, a detective who is called upon to investigate a murder at the White House. Critics generally gave the film poor reviews. Although Roger Moore of *Journal Now* called the premise of the film "preposterous," he noted that Snipes as Harlan Regis is "properly jaded, efficient, and annoyed." Susan Wloszczyna of *USA Today* remarked that *Murder at 1600* is "a fairly diverting game of whodunit, like a big screen version of *Clue,* until it sinks into routine thriller antics and wraps up preposterously." Snipes also appeared as Max, a successful ad executive who travels from his home in Los Angeles to New York to visit a friend who is dying of AIDS, in the film *One Night Stand.* While in New York, Max has an affair with a stranger and begins to question the meaning of his life. Although *One Night Stand* generally received poor reviews, Snipes received a best actor award for his work in the film at the 1997 Venice Film Festival.

In 1998, Snipes teamed with Tommy Lee Jones and Robert Downey Jr. in the action thriller *U.S. Marshals*. In the film Snipes played the role of Sheridan, a man who is falsely accused of murdering two government agents. As Sheridan tries to clear his name, he is pursued by U.S. Marshal Sam Gerard (Tommy Lee Jones) and his assistant John Royce (Robert Downey, Jr.) The film received mixed reviews. Snipes also appeared in *Down in the Delta,* a film directed by poet Maya Angelou. The film was produced by Snipes's production company, Amen Ra Films, and aired on Showtime. Snipes also played a half-human, half-vampire who tries to save humanity from a race of vampires in the film *Blade*. Michael O'Sullivan of *The Washington Post* remarked that the film's "stomach-turning special effects, bone-crunching martial arts, and cynical humor will more than satisfy any action-film addict's need for a fix of eye-popping escapist adrenaline." Charles Taylor of *Salon Magazine* noted that *Blade* "in no way resembles a good movie, but its combination of music-video bombast, goth-rock sensibility, high-tech industrial production design, cold-blooded glossy magazine visuals, high-fashion club culture, horror movies, blaxploitation movies, Hong Kong movies, and comic-book nihilism make it diverting trash." In addition to his starring role, Snipes was also the producer of *Blade*.

Through hard work and perseverance, Wesley Snipes has become one of the country's most successful African American actors. However, Hollywood stardom can also lead to enormous pressure. "It's a stressful life," Snipes told Lynn Norment of *Ebony,* "It has benefits and perks, but it's highly stressful. The more you do and the more money you make, the more stress there is." To cope with the stresses of his daily life, Snipes has developed a deeply-rooted spirituality. As he remarked to Norment, "I think that's the only way I've been able to survive."

Sources

Periodicals

Atlanta Constitution, August 7, 1990.
Boston Globe, June 7, 1991.
Ebony, November 1997.
Entertainment Weekly, September 27, 1991; April 10, 1992.
Journal Now, April 18, 1997.
Los Angeles Times, April 13, 1991; May 19, 1991; June 29, 1991.
Newsweek, April 22, 1991; June 10, 1991.
New York Newsday, October 8, 1993.
New York Times, August 24, 1990; March 8, 1991; March 27, 1991; June 7, 1991, November 6, 1992.
New Yorker, July 26, 1993.
Premiere, July 1991.
Rolling Stone, August 22, 1991.
Salon, August 20, 1998.
USA Today, December 1, 1998.
Washington Post, June 7, 1991, April 21, 1998.

—B. Kimberly Taylor and David G. Oblender

Juanita Kidd Stout

1919–1998

Judge

Juanita Kidd Stout started her career as a small-town music teacher. She went on to become the first African American woman to be elected as a judge in the United States. Stout made history a second time by becoming the first African American woman to be appointed to the Pennsylvania Supreme Court. The former music teacher became fascinated with law, and ultimately became well-known and respected as a judge for her bravery, her passion for justice, and her commitment to education.

Stout was born Juanita Kidd on March 7, 1919 in Wewoka, Oklahoma, to Henry and Mary Chandler Kidd. Having studied piano since she was five years old, she left Oklahoma at the age of 16 to attend Lincoln University in Lincoln, Missouri, for two years. Kidd was forced to leave Oklahoma to attend an accredited school because schools in her home state would not admit African Americans. After earning a music degree from the University of Iowa in 1939, she taught music at Booker T. Washington High School in Seminole, Oklahoma. She then taught at Sand Springs, near Tulsa, Oklahoma, where she met her future husband, Charles Otis Stout. He was a history and Spanish teacher and boys' counselor there. Because she weighed only 88 pounds and was smaller than many of her students, Kidd sent her unruly pupils to Stout for discipline. For a year, the two spent time together outside the classroom, singing, playing piano, and playing bridge. When World War II erupted, Stout went into the Army and Kidd moved to Washington D.C. with a friend and worked as a secretary. Although the couple had never discussed marriage, Stout proposed to Kidd on his first leave from the Army. She accepted, and they were married on June 23, 1942.

Aspired to a Legal Career

Stout began to study law at Howard University, but soon transferred to Indiana University, where her husband was doing doctoral work. She earned her Doctor of Jurisprudence degree from Indiana in 1948. Stout remained at Indiana and, in 1954, received a master of laws degree with a specialty in legislation.

It was in Washington, D.C., where Stout's law career began in earnest. In 1950 she took a job as secretary to

At a Glance...

Born Juanita Stout March 7, 1919 in Wewoka, OK; daughter of Henry and Mary Chandler Kidd; died August 21, 1998 of leukemia in Philadelphia, PA; married Charles Otis Stout (deceased), June 23, 1942. *Education:* University of Iowa, B.A., 1939; Indiana University, J.D., 1948, L.L.M., 1954.

Career: Music teacher, Booker T. Washington High School, Seminole, Oklahoma, c. 1939-41; music teacher, Sand Springs, Oklahoma, c. 1941-42; administrative assistant, Honorable W. H. Hastie, U.S. Court of Appeals for Third Circuit, Philadelphia, 1950-55; chief, Appeals, Pardons & Paroles Division, District Attorney's Office, Philadelphia, 1956-59; assistant district attorney, City of Philadelphia, 1956-59; judge, Commonwealth of Pennsylvania, 1959; justice, retired, Pennsylvania Supreme Court, 1989; senior judge, Pennsylvania Court of Common Pleas 1989-98.

Awards: Jane Addams Medal, Rockford College, 1966; inducted into Oklahoma Hall of Fame, 1981; inducted into the Oklahoma Women's Hall of Fame, 1983; Distinguished Daughter of Pennsylvania, 1988; Gimbel Award for Humanitarian Services, Medical College of Pennsylvania, 1988; Justice of the Year, National Association of Women Judges, 1988; Sandra Day O'Connor Award, Philadelphia Bar Association, 1994; Thurgood Marshall Award, National Bar Association, 1994; honorary doctor of laws degrees: Ursinus College, 1965, Indiana University, 1966, Lebanon Valley College, 1969, Drexel University, 1972, Rockford College, 1974, University of Maryland, 1980, Roger William College, 1984, Morgan State University, 1985, Fisk University, 1989; honorary doctor of human letters degree, Russell Sage College, 1966, Delaware State College, 1990.

William Hastie, a prominent African American lawyer. Hastie was soon appointed by President Harry S. Truman to the U.S. Court of Appeals in Philadelphia—making Hastie the first African American appellate court judge in U.S. history. Stout accompanied Hastie to Philadelphia, and served as his administrative secretary.

In 1954, Stout began her own private law practice. Two years later, she accepted a position as assistant district attorney for the city of Philadelphia. Stout continued her private practice even after she was promoted to Chief of Appeals, Pardons and Paroles Division of the District Attorney's Office. In September of 1959, Stout was appointed as a judge of the municipal (county) court by Pennsylvania Governor David L. Lawrence, making her the first African American woman to sit on the bench in Philadelphia. Two months later, she was elected by a two-to-one margin to a ten-year term, becoming the first elected African American female judge in the United States. In 1969, Stout became the first African American woman to be elected to the Common Pleas Court.

In 1963, Stout was sent by President John F. Kennedy to attend the independence celebration in Kenya as a special ambassador. In 1967, Lyndon B. Johnson sent her back to Kenya on a speaking tour. As a participant in a State Department cultural exchange program, she toured six African countries.

Tough on Juvenile Offenders

During the mid-1960s, Stout garnered national attention for her tough sentencing of juvenile offenders. Because of her stature on the court, she often received death threats from gang members. Stout refused to be bullied, however, and continued to speak out publicly against gang violence. Stout's reputation as a tough, but fair, judge earned her a feature in *Life* magazine entitled "Her Honor Bops the Hoodlums."

Stout was raised in a family environment that promoted education and achievement. Having earned advanced degrees, she was a staunch advocate for education. "She loved her roots," one colleague told the *Philadelphia Tribune*, "She loved her family and was a great admirer of education. When she had a defendant, she would extol the virtues of education, the wonders it could accomplish. She always put that as a requirement for probation." In the same article, Rev. Shirley Hilton, whom Stout referred to as the "daughter she never had," agreed. "She never stopped promoting education," Hilton remarked. "Everyone who passed her way got an earful about the importance of education."

In 1988, Stout's husband passed away. That same year, she became the first African American woman in the United States to be appointed to a state Supreme Court. In 1989, having reached the Pennsylvania Supreme Court's mandatory retirement age of 70, she was forced to retire. Stout returned to the Common Pleas Court as a senior judge in the homicide division. In 1993, she presided over the trial in absentia of Ira Einhorn.

Einhorn was convicted of the 1977 murder of his girlfriend, Holly Maddux, and was living as a fugitive in France.

Indifferent to Accolades

The anteroom of Stout's courtroom was covered with cartoons. She chose to decorate her walls with legal cartoons instead of the many plaques, awards, commendations and medals that she received through the years. "She (Stout) does not need rewards to reinforce, to give; she is truly a generous person," Audrey C. Talley, co-chair of the Philadelphia Bar's Women in the Profession Committee, told the *Philadelphia Tribune*. "She will do as she has done and will continue to do it without recognition." Stout received very special recognition in 1981 when her home state of Oklahoma, a state whose colleges refused to admit African Americans, inducted her into its Hall of Fame. She often cited this honor as one of her greatest achievements.

Although modest, Stout did acknowledge her place in history. "Looking back, I guess that I have (done historic things)," she told the *Philadelphia Tribune*, "but when I was doing these things I did not know that I was being a pioneer. I just did them because I wanted to." Stout has been a role model for other African American women. "There are many African-American women who look to her," Talley told the *Philadelphia Tribune*. "Without question, her accomplishments are significant. Her accomplishments are not just significant for the Philadelphia community. She made a number of firsts for the nation."

Stout's influence transcends the history books. In a story recounted by the *Philadelphia Tribune*, Stout was stopped on the street by a woman she did not know. The woman had once served on a jury in Stout's court, and she told Stout that she had inspired her to switch careers. The woman had returned to college, finished law school, and passed the bar exam. Even those tried, convicted, and given long sentences by Stout thanked her for her legal "insight," the story said.

Stout's tremendous success can be attributed to her love for her chosen profession. "Let me tell you one thing," she told the *Philadelphia Tribune*, "99 percent of the reason I am working is that I love the job and I think that I can do some good. I cannot understand how a person can work eight hours a day or more at a job that they do not like. I love my job. I just love the law. I enjoy it."

On August 21, 1998, Stout died of leukemia at Thomas Jefferson Hospital in Philadelphia. Although she had not heard cases for seven months, she was expected back on the bench in September of that year. Immediately after Stout's death, she was lauded for her many achievements. Philadelphia Bar Association Chancellor Mark Aronchick praised Stout in the *Philadelphia Tribune* as "a giant in our justice system." In the same article, Philadelphia Mayor Ed Rendell said Stout was "a true champion for justice and a role model for thousands of Philadelphians." According to the *Philadelphia Tribune*, a few days before she died, Stout told her close friend Shirley Hilton, "I'm ready to go home."

Sources

Periodicals

Jet, September 7, 1998, p. 52.
New York Times, August 24, 1998, p.15.
Newsday, August 24, 1998, p. A33.
Philadelphia Tribune, October 14, 1994; August 25, 1998, p. 1A.

Books

Epic Lives: One Hundred Black Women Who Made a Difference, edited by Jessie Carney Smith, Visible Ink Press, Detroit, 1993.

—Brenna Sanchez

John F. Street

1943—

Mayor of Philadelphia

In 1999, John F. Street became only the second African American elected mayor of Philadelphia, the fifth largest city in the United States. The former lawyer and longtime local gadfly had enjoyed a dynamic quarter-century in Philadelphia city politics, and his career seemed emblematic of a changing of the guard inside American urban politics: Street was a 1960s-era radical who vociferously fought his way into the system, and then worked from within to change it. Along the way, Philadelphia city changed as well—from a blighted hotbed of racial tension to an energetic, prosperous, and effortlessly integrated city. Street's election victory was a close one, but observers deemed the reformed rebel an ideal leader for the new millennium. "May all Philadelphians, and all who wish the city well, take heart from the vitality, commitment and humility John Street showed at his inauguration," a *Philadelphia Inquirer* editorial declared the day after he was sworn in.

Street, who was 56 years old on his inauguration day, grew up during the 1940s and 1950s on a working farm outside Conshohocken, Pennsylvania, an area not far from Philadelphia. His father, who worked in a brick factory, leased the farm with another family, and Street and his two older brothers, James Jr. and Milton, put in long hours to keep it profitable. "When we came home from school, we had to work our farm," Street told James McBride in the *Philadelphia Inquirer*. "There were cows to feed, chickens to feed. I first drove a tractor when I was 9." Street's parents were devout Seventh Day Adventists, and he and his brothers grew up according to the strict tenets of the church, which prohibited the use of alcohol and tobacco and observed the Sabbath on Saturday. An active member of the church throughout his teens, Street even served as president of a youth group, the Missionary Volunteer Federation. He remained involved with the Seventh Day Adventists beyond his college years.

Grew Disillusioned with Church

Despite the suggestion of a teacher at Conshohocken High who tried to dissuade him from a college education—remarking that perhaps he was better suited for vocational training—Street left Pennsylvania in 1961 to

At a Glance...

Born c. 1943; son of James Sr. (a farmer and brick manufacturing plant employee) and Elizabeth Street; married Carolyn Robinson, mid-1960s (divorced); married Helen Street, late 1960s (divorced); married Naomi Post (an attorney); four children. *Education:* Oakwood College, B.A., 1964; Temple University Law School, J.D., 1975.

Career: Worked on his family's farm as a teenager, and as a manual laborer in the South in the early 1960s; substitute teacher, cab driver, and street vendor in Philadelphia in the late 1960s and early 1970s; attorney in private practice, Philadelphia, 1975-80; elected to Philadelphia City Council, 1979; re-elected four times and named president of the Council, mid-1990s; elected mayor of Philadelphia, 1999-.

Addresses: *Office*—Mayor's Office, Philadelphia City Hall, 1 South Broad Street, Philadelphia, PA 19107.

attend Oakwood College, a Seventh Day Adventist school for African Americans in Huntsville, Alabama. He left home carrying three money orders for his $150 tuition, a $5 bill, and a bag lunch for the train trip. Street remained in Alabama after classes recessed for the summer, earning money through manual labor jobs for his living expenses the following year. The racism that he experienced firsthand in the South during the early 1960s caused him some dissatisfaction with his church; Seventh Day Adventist elders avoided politics, and were detached from the civil-rights fray of the era, unlike other sects with large numbers of African American members.

After he earned his degree from Oakwood in 1964, Street married briefly, but by 1966 had moved to Philadelphia. He drove a cab, worked as a substitute teacher, married a second time and started a family. He also began working with his brother Milton, who sold hot dogs as a street vendor and had become increasingly involved in community issues. Yearning for a career in the law, Street applied to Philadelphia's Temple University Law School. His applications were annually rejected because of his education at Oakwood College, which school officials deemed insufficient. One day in 1972, the director of minority admissions at Temple bought a hot dog from a vendor on Broad Street. "This guy with a scraggly beard and a big old Afro wearing five sweatshirts hands me my hot dog and then says, 'Hey. Why can't I get in that law school?'" the administrator, Carl F. Singley, told *Philadelphia Inquirer* staff writers Karen E. Quinones Miller and Cynthia Burton.

Singley told Street that he would look into the matter, and Street was then asked to make a personal appearance before the Law School's admissions committee; his forthright manner and sincerity impressed them, and he was admitted. After he graduated in 1975 and passed the Pennsylvania bar, Street began his own private practice, specializing in criminal law, but he often took on cases without charging his clients (known as *pro bono* work) when he felt the merits of the issue were worthwhile. Instead of feeling as if he was making a positive difference in the world, however, Street grew dejected by the nature of his profession. Once, he achieved a hard-won acquittal for a client, and then a few months later the same man was charged in a triple slaying. "I remember thinking that I worked so hard all of my life, I really struggled to get an education, and I applied all that I learned to this case, and now three people are dead because of it," he told Miller and Burton in the *Inquirer*.

Became a Rabble Rouser

Street's brother, Milton, had become a well-known figure in Philadelphia, partly as a result of his challenges to the city's tough new vending ordinances. Street helped with Milton's boisterous organized demonstrations, and soon both were regular visitors at Philadelphia City Council meetings. Their activism began to include housing and community issues; they gained a groundswell of grass-roots support in their charge that the current City Hall was ineffectively using the federal funds awarded to the city for urban improvement.

Milton Street ran for a seat in the Pennsylvania state legislature in 1978 and won the election. Inspired by his brother's success, Street made a bid for a seat on the City Council the following year, representing north central Philadelphia and much of Center City—and defeated three other challengers. Just a few days after he took office in January of 1980, he was pulled over by the police while driving on a street in his council district, and a license plate check revealed unpaid parking tickets totaling more than $900. Taken into custody, Street was transported to the station house in a police van.

By this time, Street had already been plagued by financial woes that would continue to dog his career. However, he did not let these personal problems detract him from his duties to his constituents, nor did he use his position to obtain preferential treatment. Prior to his election, Street had never earned much money in private practice, and found himself in arrears to the city for taxes and utilities, the Internal Revenue Service, and even Temple University. "I just wasn't a person who cared or worried about a lot of personal amenities or all that," *Philadelphia Inquirer* Robert Zausner quoted Street as saying. "I spent almost no time accumulating any personal wealth."

Chastised Abscam Defendants

But for Street, the antagonistic newcomer challenging the entrenched Philadelphia political system, his entry into municipal politics was blessed, in the first month in office, by the advent of Abscam. In this Federal Bureau of Investigation sting operation, Philadelphia's powerful City Council president, George Schwartz, and two other council members accepted large amounts of cash from FBI agents posing as wealthy Arab sheikhs hoping for political favors. Street immediately called for their resignation, but the three managed to hold on to their seats until the investigation was final, and a virtual war inside council chambers ensued over the next few months—with Street leading the opposition in a most vociferous manner. In one memorable session, Street conducted a three-hour harangue against Schwartz. "You come here every week and arrogantly sit by, and you went over to the Barclay, and you took the cash," Street recalled about this infamous day in a 1984 interview with *Philadelphia Inquirer* reporter James McBride. "Then you . . . come in here every day acting like you did nothing, like those newspaper reports were just, you know, something that somebody plucked out of thin air..."

Yet Street's most famous moment during his long tenure on the council came one day in 1981, when its new president ruled that the body would not vote on a bill to rescue the city's financially troubled school district. "I'm tired of this and I'm fired up, because I got a lot of children out there who are looking to me," Street fumed, according to the McBride article. "Everybody knows that the overwhelming majority of students in the public school system are black. We're black. It's a black public school system . . . and white people in this council are not going to tell me that I can't put my bill in." He then declared that if he couldn't introduce his bill, then no one else could introduce any further legislative matters either. Street then seized the stenotype tripod in the chambers. A council member grabbed him from behind, while another, Francis Rafferty, sucker-punched him; Street broke free and wrestled Rafferty to the ground. The brawl made the national news.

Street said he learned two lessons that day: "One, that I could pick a 250-pound man up above my head," he told Miller and Burton in the *Inquirer* interview, "and two, that if I wanted to be an effective leader, I would have to learn how to approach people in a way that they could accept, and not take offense." Vowing to improve his attitude and his reputation, Street began to polish his conciliatory skills on the council, and the strategy paid off, both for his political career and his constituency. "I know exactly why I was elected," he told McBride in 1984 after voters returned him to the council job. "My job is not to complain about the conditions of North Philadelphia. My job is to do something about it. My job is to be a part of the council, so that people who have heretofore been shut out of the process are part of the process and reap the benefits."

A Respected Leader

Throughout the 1980s, Street continued to earn a reputation as one of the hardest working members on the Philadelphia City Council. He regularly put in 12-hour days, and used his legal background to school himself on municipal law, Philadelphia's city charter, local ordinances, council procedural rules—in general, how to challenge the system through its own means. The area of Philadelphia that Street represented, and where he and his family lived, was one of the most disadvantaged areas in the city; unemployment was 38 percent in the mid-1980s in some sections of his district, and an estimated 40 percent of residents lived below the poverty level when he was first elected. Street's own home was broken into several times, and his vehicles stolen or vandalized on other occasions. During his years on the council, Street worked to win community development funds and secured minority hiring contracts. The need for adequate housing was one of his top priorities. Street's district contained 67,000 residential tracts, 11,000 of which were vacant at one point. Behind the scenes at City Hall, he convinced his colleagues on the city council to support a radical piece of legislation. This legislation affirmed the rights of squatters, and allowed them to occupy and rehabilitate abandoned homes within a one-year time-frame. "It's the piece of legislation for which I take the greatest pride," Street told the *Inquirer* in 1984. "The development and concept of that represents the most creative solution to the housing problem I've seen in my years as a housing activist."

By the time a new mayor took office in 1992, the city of Philadelphia was in dismal financial shape. As a respected member of the city council, Street's political skills were courted by the new mayor, Ed Rendell. "Hoping to avoid the rancor that had plagued previous administrations, Rendell made Street part of every important decision in City Hall, shared patronage jobs, and heaped praise on him," Miller and Burton wrote in the *Inquirer* article. "The two met every Tuesday morning—in Street's office." In return, Street supported the mayor's political agenda and schooled himself in municipal matters. Over the next few years, Rendell secured wage concessions from the city's powerful unions, tightened the budget, and sought new business development for Philadelphia. By the time Street was elected city council president in the mid-1990s, Philadelphia had pulled back from the brink of financial ruin, and the coalition between Rendell and Street was considered a key factor in that comeback.

Bid for Top Job

In 1999, Street resigned as city council president to run for mayor. Rendell, barred by the city charter from seeking a third term, endorsed Street's candidacy. There were also four other Democratic contenders and one Republican contender for the office. Street edged out the other Democrats in the primary election and faced Sam Katz, a white Republican and municipal finance expert, in the general election. As the campaign heated up, it was feared that voters in the city might indeed choose its first Republican mayor since 1947. Street obtained the support of prominent Democrats such as Senator Edward Kennedy of Massachusetts and President Bill Clinton, who made a stop in Philadelphia to stump for him. "Above all, in debate after debate, Street delighted in simply announcing that his opponent was a Republican, a fact Katz hardly advertised," wrote Francis X. Clines in the *New York Times*. "Street fairly gloated in counting on this city's deep history of party loyalty." Registered Democrats in Philadelphia outnumbered Republicans by a four-to-one margin.

The mayoral election was extremely close, with Street winning by a mere 8,000 votes. In his inaugural address in early January of 2000, he vowed to continue his fight against urban blight and for improved educational opportunities for Philadelphia's students. "Any community that fails its children can never call itself a success," the *Philadelphia Inquirer* quoted him as saying. As the mayor of the nation's fifth-largest city, Street faced battles with the state legislature on several key issues, including funding for education. He also noted that his election to the mayor's office had won him a whole new crowd of admirers, many of whom came to him in the weeks after the election as he planned his administration and told him, "We weren't for you, but we are willing to support you now," Street told the *Philadelphia Inquirer*.

Street, who has three grown children from his second marriage and an 11-year-old son with his third wife, lawyer Naomi Post, is a longtime fitness fanatic who once forced a newspaper reporter to endure a 17-mile bike ride at a fast clip in order to conduct an interview. Less than a month after taking office, Street appeared on the *Oprah Winfrey* show after a magazine poll found Philadelphians to be the most overweight urban residents in the United States. He told the talk show host that he planned to establish a fitness czar's office in his administration. "We are sedentary. We don't exercise enough. We really do have to create a movement," Street told Winfrey, according to *Philadelphia Inquirer* writer Monica Yant.

Sources

Periodicals

New Republic, November 1, 1999, pp. 13-14.
New York Times, May 13, 1999; May 19, 1999; May 20, 1999; November 3, 1999; November 4, 1999.
Philadelphia Daily News, January 26, 1980, p. 2.
Philadelphia Inquirer, March 18, 1984; April 18, 1999, p. A1; May 7, 1999, p. A1; January 3, 2000; January 4, 2000; January 20, 2000.

—Carol Brennan

Tamia

1975—

Vocalist

Tamia was born Tamia Nee Washington in Windsor, Ontario, Canada on May 9, 1975. The precocious Tamia began performing early. She began studying music and drama when she was only ten years old. While performing in the musical 'Godspell' she wanted to improve her voice, so she began working with vocal coach Eugene Davis (Freeman). While working with Davis, Tamia began singing in the choir at the Church of God in Christ--a church near the McDougall Street Projects where she grew up.

It was not long before the gifted young singer began receiving recognition for her talent. Tamia made several appearances in local theater and choral concerts before winning Canada's prestigious YTV Vocal Achievement Award in 1993 and the Steve Ross Music Scholarship at the American Achievement's Annual Salute to Excellence in 1994. John Vacratsis, director of the arts program at Walkerville Collegiate Institute in Windsor, recruited Tamia to the school when she was in eighth grade. Vacratsis had seen her perform in community musicals, such as 'The Little Shop of Horrors,' and was blown away.

In 1994, Tamia accepted the Steve Ross Music Scholarship at the American Academy of Achievement's Annual Salute to Excellence in Las Vegas. She became an overnight success in the music industry when she was nominated for a Grammy in 1996. The most unusual thing about Tamia's career is that she already had three hits before ever releasing a solo album.

Tamia was exposed to music at an early age by her mother and stepfather, Barbara Washington Peden and Frederic Peden, and has impressed millions with her sultry sounds and stirring duets. She enjoys a wide range of music, especially ballads. She told *Teen,* "I don't care about labels--country music, rock music, it's the way it makes me feel that counts." Naturally witty, comical, talented ... and a bundle of energy, is how *Ebony Man* describes Tamia, who has three younger brothers Tajhee, Tiras, and Trajan. Creativity is another characteristic of Tamia. She told Mark Scheerer of *CNN,* "I used to staple two paper plates together and put rice in them to make a tambourine..."

Tamia's hometown of Windsor is a small factory town in western Ontario. Its population is also very ethnically

> **At a Glance...**
>
> Born Tamia Washington, May 9, 1975, in Windsor, Ontario, Canada; married Grant Hill, July 24, 1999. *Education:* Walkerville Collegiate Institute.
>
> **Career:** Singer and actress. Hit song, "You Put A Move On My Heart," was featured on Quincy Jones' album *Q's Jook Joint*, 1995; recorded the hit song "Slow Jams" with Babyface, also on *Q's Jook Joint*, 1995; recorded the hit song "Missing You" for the *Set It Off* soundtrack with Chaka Khan, Gladys Knight and Brandy; released her first solo album, *Tamia*, 1998; recorded "Spend My Life With You," with Eric Benet on his album, *A Day In The Life*.
>
> **Awards:** Youth TV (YTV) Vocal Achievement Award (Canada), 1993; Steve Ross Music Scholarship, 1994; Grammy nomination for Best Female R&B Vocal Performance for "You Put A Move On My Heart," 1996; Grammy nomination for Best R&B Performance by a Duo for "Slow Jams," 1996; Grammy nomination for "Missing You," on the *Set It Off* soundtrack.
>
> **Addresses:** *Agent*—Elektra Entertainment, 75 Rockefeller Plaza; New York, NY 10019-6908.

diverse. Tamia, who has an African American mother and a white father, told *Mic Check* that she "had the best of both worlds," and added "that she's related to most of the black people in Windsor.... My family comes in all shades from really light to very dark."

Became a Star

Music has always played a prominent role in Tamia's life. As a young child living in Ontario, she was first exposed to the Motown sound. Tamia told *Essence*, "My mother and five sisters would sing like they were the Supremes to entertain me." The early presence of music in her life helped to plant the seeds that would sprout into superstardom.

Many young people dream of meeting a big music executive, impressing them with a song, then skyrocketing to fame. In Tamia's case, her dream came true when she sang at a birthday party for Luther Vandross that was hosted by her manager, Brenda Ritchie. One of the guests, music legend Quincy Jones, took note of Tamia and was moved by the passion in Tamia's voice when he saw her perform.

Jones contacted Ritchie, and offered Tamia the opportunity of a lifetime. "Quincy had a song on his album that he had tried six or seven singers for, and they couldn't do it." Ritchie told *The Record*, "He asked Tamia and she did it." Jones also invited Tamia to Los Angeles to appear on his album, *Q's Jook Joint*. Tamia remarked in *Essence*, "Can you imagine being 18 years old in the vocal booth with Quincy Jones waiting for you to sing his song? What an experience!" This recording session with Jones was the spark that ignited her career.

Recorded Hit after Hit

Tamia won a Grammy nomination for "You Put A Move On My Heart" in the Best Female R&B Vocal Performance category in 1996. The song was the first single on Quincy Jones' album, *Q's Jook Joint*. "You Put A Move On My Heart" established Tamia as a major new recording star. Songwriter extraordinaire, Babyface, then asked her to perform a duet with him, which would also be featured on Jones' album. Babyface chose Tamia to share the spotlight with him on *Jook's* second single, the romantic duet "Slow Jams," which earned them a Grammy nomination for Best R&B Performance by a Duo. Tamia also collaborated with Chaka Khan, Gladys Knight, and Brandy on the song "Missing You" for the *Set It Off* soundtrack. "Missing You" was later nominated for a Grammy. All of these hits were released before her debut album, *Tamia*, hit the stores in 1998.

Tamia has worked with some of the music industry's greatest artists, including Quincy Jones, Chaka Khan, Gladys Knight, Babyface, Brandy, R Kelly, Eric Benet, Daryl Simmons, Mario Winan, and many others. She is treated as a peer by other recording stars. "I've fallen victim to seeing people on TV and thinking that's how their personalities are. I think you just kind of put them on a higher level, and when you meet them, you realize they're just like you ... It's all still kind of weird to me to have people acknowledge me as a peer," Tamia stated in *Ebony Man*.

Tamia is a spiritually grounded person, and has handled her phenomenal success well. "She hasn't changed a bit," Vacratsis told the *Detroit Free Press*. He added, "she was always kind of a little devilish; always smiling, full of energy ... and other than the fact that she drives a much bigger car now, it's like talking to the same old Tamia." She handles her success by keeping things in perspective. As Tamia told *Essence*, "Los Angeles is like Disneyland. When I go home to Windsor, my mom is like,

'Clean your room, and don't forget to do the dirty dishes!'"

Tamia is grateful to those who have helped her to stardom, including Quincy Jones. She told *Ebony Man,* "he [Jones] introduced me to the world ... I felt very honored to have him take time out of his busy schedule. He's one of the most humble people you'll ever meet, and he has everything going for him." Tamia has had her share of doubters and critics, but has been able to impress the right people at the right time. Being nominated for three Grammy awards before the release of her debut album has increased the pressure on Tamia. As she remarked to *The Atlanta Journal and Constitution,* "That's when having Quincy Jones introduce you to the music world is not such a great thing... because people tend to listen to you harder — and judge harder. Man, the expectations!"

Married Grant Hill

On July 24, 1999, after a three-year courtship, Tamia married basketball superstar Grant Hill. She surprised Hill at the wedding when she sang 'Colour of Love,' a tune recorded by Celine Dion. Tamia first met her future husband in Detroit when she served as a judge at a singing contest. Hill told *Jet,* "I just found somebody that I'm real compatible with. When we first started seeing each other that first two or three months, I kind of knew that this was the one. I've dated a few people but never really had that chemistry. But when I first met my fiancee it was like we'd known each other for a long time. So I'm ready to settle down. It's a sign of maturity." When asked about her marriage, Tamia remarked to Deborah Gregory in *Essence,* "I'm not one for flowers and stuff, but I love staying in bed all day with Grant, relaxing, and watching movies together. That's what I find romantic."

Working with the likes of Quincy Jones and numerous other music legends has taught Tamia that making an album is not all fun and games. As she told *Ebony Man,* "I thought that you just got up on the microphone and sang. There's a lot that goes into getting that person onstage, contract negotiations, and then there's the technical work." She added in *Essence,* "It got to the point where I just stopped telling people when my album was coming out. I'd record a lot of songs, write a few, then throw them all away and start again! Finally I had to let go and let God in on the process."

Tamia's debut album was very successful. It featured several hits, including "So Into You" and "Imagination," which was produced by Jermaine Dupri. Tamia told *Ebony Man,* "I really believe that it's not about your voice. It's the anointing that God puts on your voice that separates you." Her manager, Brenda Ritchie, recalled in *The Record* that when she first heard Tamia sing "she had the voice of an angel... Immediately, you just know upon listening to her that she is going places."

In addition to her career as a recording artist, Tamia has appeared as a model in Tommy Hilfiger ads. In 1997, she made her acting debut in the film *Speed II: Cruise Control.* Following the release of her debut album, Tamia signed a recording contract with Elektra Records.

Sources

Periodicals

Atlanta Journal and Constitution, April 16, 1998.
Detroit Free Press, July 23, 1999.
Ebony, October 1998, p. 50.
Ebony Man, June 1996, p. 30.
Essence, March 1998, p. 60; February 2000, p. 60.
Jet, September 6, 1999, p. 60.
Mic Check, April 1998, p. 24.
New York Beacon, June 25, 1997.
The Record, May 11, 1998, p. 9.
Seventeen, December 1996, p. 127.
Teen, November 1998, p. 53.

Other

Additional information for this profile was obtained from a *CNN* interview with Mark Scheerer on August 7, 1998, and *Lycos Music: RollingStone.com,* January 2000.

—Sadie Mungro

Dorothy A. Terrell

1945—

Business executive

Dorothy Terrell has impressed her contemporaries in the field of global technology with her intuition for technological trends and ability to manage the creation of high-growth technology businesses. She has been recognized for her outstanding achievements and management skills while working at some of the world's most prominent corporations in the technology industry, including Digital Equipment Corporation, Sun Microsystems, Inc., and Natural MicroSystems Corporation. Her leadership and hard work have earned her several notable distinctions in the corporate and technological spheres.

Pursued the Liberal Arts

Terrell was born in 1945 and raised in Hallandale, Florida, in a community segregated between African Americans and whites. Her father was a gardener, and her mother was a cashier and housekeeper. Although neither of Terrell's parents graduated from college, they strongly encouraged her and her siblings to get an education. Terrell explained that in her community, there were few educated African American role models that represented various professional disciplines. Elaborating on this observation to Maria Shao of the *Boston Globe,* Terrell noted that the highest position she and her peers saw an African American holding in Hallandale during the 1940s and 1950s was most likely that of high school principal. Terrell's street was the dividing line between her own African American community of Hallandale, Florida, and the white community of Hollywood, Florida. She recalled to Shao, "My life was in Hallandale. I knew it was segregated. Very seldom did I go across the street. It was a different world."

After graduating from Florida A&M University in 1966 with a bachelor of arts degree in English, Terrell became a guidance counselor with the U.S. Jobs Corps program in Maine. She welcomed the opportunity both to work outside of her native Florida, and interact with many different kinds of people. Terrell admitted to Shao, "I learned a lot about life on that job." After receiving valuable vocational training and experience with the Jobs Corps, Terrell moved to Boston to pursue a career as a counselor, and later an administrator, at a social services center called the Opportunity Industrialization

At a Glance...

Born Dorothy A. Terrell, Hallandale, FL, 1945, married Albert Brown; children: Dorian. *Education:* Florida A&M University, B.A., English, 1966.

Career: Guidance counselor, Job Corps, 1966-67; counselor and administrator, Opportunity Industrialization Center and the Massachusetts Office for Children, 1967-76; manager of employee relations, Digital Equipment Corporation, 1976-84; plant manager, Digital Equipment Corporation, 1984-91; president, SunExpress, Inc. of Sun Microsystems, 1991-97; vice president for corporate operations and president of the services group for Natural Microsystems, 1998-.

Selected awards: Distinguished Alumni Award, Florida A&M University, 1995; "20 Women of Power and Influence in Corporate America," *Black Enterprise* magazine, 1997; Directors' Choice Leadership Award of the National Women's Economic Alliance Foundation, 1997; a subject of "The Wizards and Their Wonders: Portraits in Computing, an exhibit of the Computer Museum in Boston, 1997; "Top 50 Women Line Managers in America," *Executive Female* magazine; "Top Ten Business Marketer," *Business Marketing* magazine.

Member: The Boston Club; The Committee of 200; The Commonwealth Institute; director of Boston Computer Museum; member of board of directors of: General Mills, Inc.; Sears, Roebuck and Company; Herman Miller, Inc.; National Housing Partnership Foundation, Massachusetts Technology Development Corporation.

Addresses: *Office*—Natural Microsystems, 100 Crossing Blvd., Framingham, MA 01702.

Center. While working there, she gained additional experience in human resources management and participated on a business advisory council with representatives from local Boston companies. Following her tenure at OIC, Terrell took a job with the Massachusetts Office for Children. While on the Boston-area business advisory council, Terrell met representatives of Digital Equipment Corporation, who offered Terrell a position in their human resources department. Terrell soon decided that she was ready to move out of employment in the public sector.

Confronted Technological Change

Terrell took her management expertise to Digital Equipment Corporation in 1976, where she was appointed as human resources manager at a plant in Westminster, Massachusetts. Because she possessed a big-picture sense for company procedure and production, Terrell was offered a management position over an entire facility. In 1984, she became plant manager of a factory that produced keyboards in Roxbury, Massachusetts. Terrell reminisced about that career opportunity in a 1998 article in the *Journal of New England Technology*, "Me and Ken (Olsen, DEC's founder) were the only ones with an overall view because of the unique position of being group manager human resources for manufacturing, engineering and market organizations. However, when they asked me to run the low-end manufacturing in Boston, I laughed ... but it was not such a drastic transition. It played to my strengths rather than weaknesses. They needed someone to pull together a team."

Terrell's expertise in managing employees led to another promotion with Digital, this time to a silicon wafer plant in Cupertino, California. Although she had not received formal technological training, Terrell gained knowledge as she worked in the industry. It was a daunting challenge for a person without technological experience to manage a group of engineers. Terrell explained in the *Journal of New England Technology* that the position required intense energy and hard work to become a successful leader of the facility, commenting, "I damn near killed myself and a few other people, but I did it and it was the most challenging job I ever had." Digital colleague, Joseph Zeh, revealed his admiration for her to Shao, "Engineers got to like her. She pulled the right people together. She is a good judge of expertise and character." Prior to leaving Digital in 1991, Terrell turned Digital's Interconnect Packaging Group from a zero-yield business into a highly productive and sophisticated technology and manufacturing operation. Terrell's success in managing Digital's Cupertino plant was admired throughout the industry. She had been selected to relocate to London to work in a marketing position for Digital, when Sun Microsystems offered her the challenging opportunity of developing Sun's new international catalogue and telemarketing venture known as SunExpress. Scott McNealy, Sun's CEO, sought Terrell for the position after receiving recommendations from several Sun employees who had worked with her at Digital. Former colleagues praised her as an outstanding manager and leader. McNealy was convinced that Terrell had the type of personality and temperament that would suit her well at Sun. He told Shao that she had "a triple play combination—smart, experienced and your managers would enjoy working with that person." Terrell was soon recognized as an integral part of SunExpress's rapid success. She served as the leader of nearly 20 employees in the United States and later managed revenues of hundreds of millions of dollars. With Terrell's skilled leadership, SunExpress brought in $160 million in sales in its first year. By 1994, Terrell quadrupled the after marketing catalog product line and expanded its distribution to Europe and Japan. In 1996, Terrell and her team founded and developed Sun's electronic commerce venture. Over time, SunExpress became a $300 million unit of Sun Microsystems with 300 employees worldwide. In 1997, Terrell led the consolidation of SunExpress with its parent company, even though it eliminated her position as president.

After taking a break from corporate life to spend time with her family, Terrell accepted a position as senior vice president for corporate operations and president of the services group for Natural Microsystems, a global telecommunications corporation based in Framingham, Massachusetts. The company is a leading provider of computer telephony platforms and a pioneer in telecommunications innovation and standards, offering products such as Internet voice and fax systems, voice response workflow systems, and Web-based call centers. Terrell welcomed the opportunity to lead the operation into a period of substantial international growth. The chief executive officer of Natural Microsystems and former Lotus Development Corporation CEO, Robert P. Schechter, was pleased to recruit a proven leader like Terrell. According to Ronald Rosenberg of the *Boston Globe,* Schechter praised Terrell as having "...proven ability to build a profitable services business and to provide operations leadership in a rapidly growing technology-intensive environment...." She entered the position with the formidable task of leading several Natural Microsystems organizations, including: operations, manufacturing, procurement, logistics, human resources, and information technology. Terrell was also charged with building a new Services Group, called Natural Edge, for Natural Microsystems and its business partners. She designed the program to offer additional support and consulting services to equipment manufacturers. Ralph Gillespie, a former Digital colleague, offered this appraisal of Terrell to Shao, "I would think of Dorothy as being a manager first.... She doesn't walk around thinking about being black. She thinks about being a manager." In the *Journal of New England Technology,* Terrell appraised herself as a manager, "The talent I have is bringing people together, making things happen."

Terrell is married to Albert Brown. The couple have a daughter, Dorian, who was born in 1987. From 1988 to 1994, the family lived in Saratoga, California. During this time, Terrell commuted back and forth to the Boston area, where she would spend about two weeks out of each month. The family relocated to Boston in 1994.

Sources

Periodicals

Black Enterprise, April 1987; August 1991.
Boston Globe, July 25, 1994; February 18, 1998.
Journal of New England Technology, November 9, 1998.

Other

Additional information for this profile was obtained from www.the.commonwealth.mass.com/about_us/spokespeople_bios/dorothy_terrell.html, January 17, 2000; and www-gsb.stanford.edu/advisorycouncil/acterrell.html, January 17, 2000.

—Melissa Walsh

Stephanie Tubbs Jones

1949—

Congresswoman from Ohio

Stephanie Tubbs Jones claims that when she was young, her mother described her as a quiet, rather introverted little girl, one who was content to play by herself with her dolls on the steps of her house. Her warm, engaging smile and dancing eyes, however, belie the confident, dynamic woman who easily commands an audience and has emerged to take the political scene in Cleveland, Ohio by storm, garnering 74% of the vote in her district in 1998 to win its Congressional seat and thrust her into the national political arena.

Stephanie Tubbs Jones was born on September 10, 1949 at Booth Memorial Hospital in Cleveland, OH. The third and youngest daughter of Mary and Andrew Tubbs. Tubbs Jones was raised in Cleveland's Glenville neighborhood, a stable area of predominantly working-class people which produced, according to Tubbs Jones, some of the best and the brightest working in the city today. Her home life, too, was solid and secure. While her father worked as a skycap for United Airlines, her mother, Mary, remained at home with Stephanie and her two older sisters, returning to work as a cook in a college fraternity house when Stephanie entered kindergarten. As Tubbs Jones reflected in an interview with CBB, "I had a great childhood, and I never wanted for anything. My parents were loving and nurturing and made me think that I could do anything. If I couldn't do it, I didn't know that I couldn't." To this day, Tubbs Jones explains that her mother is her mentor. As she explained to Tracy Bean of Kaleidoscope Magazine, "My mother is strong, determined, ever-faithful, and grounded in her faith ... One of the most valuable lessons I've learned [from her] is never forgetting that I am a woman ... I use [that] fact to my advantage and allow that fact to help me."

Planted Seeds of Social Activism

Tubbs Jones still fondly recalls her early years of education. From kindergarten through the sixth grade, she attended Miles Standish Elementary School and participated in its major works program, a program designed for gifted children. Thus, for instance, she began to study French in the third grade, a pursuit she continued into college. Tubbs Jones still vividly remembers the names of each of her first teachers, some of whom remain friends. Upon graduating from Miles Standish, Tubbs

At a Glance...

Born Stephanie Tubbs in Cleveland, OH on September 10, 1949, daughter of Mary (a homemaker, eventually a cook at a Case Western Reserve Univ. fraternity house) and Andrew (a skycap for United Airlines); married Mervyn L. Jones in 1976; son Mervyn Jones born in 1983. *Education:* Case Western Reserve University, BA, Sociology, 1971, JD, 1974.

Career: Assistant General Counsel, Equal Opportunity Admin., Northeast OH Regional Sewer District, Cleveland, 1974-76; Asst..Cuyahoga County Prosecutor, Cuyahoga County Prosecutor's Office, 1976-79; Trial Attorney, Equal Employment Opportunity Commission, Cleveland District Office, 1979-81; Judge, Cleveland Municipal Court, 1982-83; Judge, Cuyahoga County Court of Common Pleas, 1983-91; Cuyahoga County Prosecutor, 1991-99; U.S. Representative, 11th District, Ohio, 1999-.

Selected memberships: Congressional Black Caucus; Baltic Caucus; Census Caucus; Women's Caucus; Bar: Supreme Court of the U.S., Sixth Circuit Court of Appeals; Northern District of OH, Federal District Court; Supreme Court of OH; Natl. District Attorneys Assn.; OH Prosecuting Attorneys Assn.; American Bar Assn.; Cleveland Bar Assn.; Natl. Council of Negro Women; Bd. of Trustees, Community Re-Entry Program; Bd. of Trustees, Bethany Baptist Church, Cleveland; Delta Sigma Theta Inc.

Selected awards: MLK Jr. Award, Case Western Reserve Univ. School of Law, Cleveland, OH, 1974; Collinwood High School Hall of Fame, Cleveland, 1994; OH Democrat of the Year, OH Democratic Party, 1994; Black Professional of the Year, Black Professional Assn., 1995.

Addresses: *Office*—1516 Longworth Building, Washington, D.C. 20515; 3645 Warrensville Center Road, Suite 204, Shaker Heights, OH 44122.

Jones entered Collinwood High School. There she excelled, earning ten academic and athletic awards during her graduation ceremony. Concurrently, she was active with Future Teachers of America, the girls' chorus, the school newspaper, Spotlight, and with the Student Council of Christian and Jews. Through this organization Tubbs Jones began to tackle issues of race relations in her school community, revealing a commitment to social justice which she has pursued ever since. Thus, even though racial disturbances plagued Collinwood and its surrounding neighborhoods during her high school years, at times forcing her and fellow African American students to be escorted out of school, such events did not dampen her overall high school experience but instead, energized her to act.

Tubbs Jones' activism continued during her college and law school years. As she recounted to CBB, she accepted a full scholarship to Case Western Reserve University (CWRU) in Cleveland for several reasons: her father had told her that "blacks don't get to go to Case and so if you get in you should go there", and also because she did not like the restrictive curfew at Morris Brown College in Atlanta, GA, which her older sister attended. While at CWRU she founded the African American Students Association and tirelessly campaigned for the acceptance of more minority students and the hiring of additional minority faculty while concurrently promulgating the idea of "relevant education" and school-to-work programs. She also strove to promote greater involvement by the university within the local community.

A sociology major with a minor in psychology, Tubbs Jones believed that she was going to "cure the ills of society" upon graduation, as she told CBB. However, her focus altered greatly after she enrolled in a course in the Black Studies Program during her senior year. Entitled "Law As It Relates to the Black Community," the class was taught by the late Judge Charles W. Fleming, who at the time was a prominent trial lawyer and defense attorney. Through Fleming Tubbs Jones not only met people of color who were practicing law, but she was also encouraged to apply to law school herself. Thus, in 1971 Tubbs Jones entered Case Western Reserve University School of Law on another scholarship. At that time very few women, let alone women of color, attended law school, and Tubbs Jones has commented that, with poor scores on the LSAT, she herself was an "affirmative action child." Continuing her undergraduate efforts, Tubbs Jones assumed a leadership role in the Black American Law Student Association and fought to bring more African American students and faculty to the school.

Throughout law school, Tubbs Jones worked as a law clerk for the Northeast Ohio Regional Sewer District and remained with the district as the assistant general counsel and equal opportunity administrator following her graduation in 1974. However, she yearned to try courtroom cases and after applying three times was hired to work as an assistant prosecutor in the Cuyahoga County Prosecutor's Office in Cleveland in 1976. From 1979 until 1981 she continued her time in the courtroom as a trial attorney with the Equal Employment Opportunity Commission in Cleveland, trying a wide variety of discrimination cases.

Elected Into Public Office

In 1979, moreover, Tubbs Jones and several close friends worked together on a mutual friend's political campaign. When their candidate won, the group of friends vowed to work for the election of one among them. They discussed the importance of having persons of color serve on the municipal bench, and Tubbs Jones was chosen as their favored candidate for a judgeship. In January of 1981, then, she filed for election as a judge on the Cleveland Municipal Court. In November of 1981, at the age of 31, Tubbs Jones was elected with 33 percent of the vote among a field of five candidates, and she has been in elected life ever since.

After only 15 months, then-Ohio Governor Richard Celeste appointed Tubbs Jones to the Court of Common Pleas, making her the first African American female to serve on the Court of Common Pleas in the state of Ohio. After winning election to the bench in 1984 and again in 1988, Tubbs Jones was asked by the Democratic Party in July of 1990 to replace Judge Mary Cacioppo on the ballot for the Ohio Supreme Court who had been forced to withdraw due to health problems. Despite the short lead time and despite running against Republican incumbent Justice J. Craig Wright, who had twice as much funding as she herself commanded, she almost won the November statewide election, losing by only three percentage points.

Needless to say, this race gained Tubbs Jones ever more attention from the Ohio Democratic Party. As Mary Mihaly of Cleveland Magazine explained, "Party leaders knew they had a vote-getter in their ranks." In 1990 John Corrigan, the Cuyahoga County prosecutor for the previous 34 years, retired, and Tubbs Jones was drafted by a cross-section of the party to run for his position. Following a ten-day campaign Tubbs Jones won the party election by 31 votes to become not only the first female prosecutor in Cuyahoga County but also the first African American prosecutor in the state of Ohio and the only African American female prosecutor in a major metropolitan area in the United States. But, as she told Mihaly, "I don't glory in being first ... I hope I don't see myself being last." Capitalizing on her success, she won the general election in 1992 with a resounding 70 percent of the vote and was reelected again in 1996. Jones had truly proven to be a masterful politician.

As Cuyahoga County prosecutor, Tubbs Jones directed a staff of 230 employees, including 150 attorneys, that handled approximately 36,000 legal cases each year. At the time, it was Ohio's busiest prosecutor's office, dealing with 28 percent of the criminal cases in the state presided over by the most judges (34) in the most municipalities (59). Not only did she oversee these activities, but she also served as legal counsel for all elected officials, judges, and the county's nine library systems.

In this role Tubbs Jones was particularly concerned about the welfare of children in her community and earned recognition for her pursuance of deadbeat parents. As she told Bean, she also valued the contributions she made to the fair prosecution of criminal cases and the assistance that she provided to help women enter this traditionally male profession. "When I came into office," she noted, "there were ten female attorneys in [the] office. Now [in 1998] there are more than 50." She also computerized the department and began supplemental training both for her staff and for law-enforcement agencies across the county. "They have to know the law if they want to do a good job," she explained to Mihaly.

Elected to House of Representatives

After seven years in office, Tubbs Jones decided to build upon her previous electoral success and enter the national political scene. When Louis Stokes, the only African American congressperson in the state of Ohio, decided not to seek reelection in 1998, Tubbs Jones mounted a campaign for his seat. As might be expected, her platform focused on those key issues which had always consumed her: the protection of children and the improvement of education for all; safe, affordable child care; the safety of neighborhoods; the extension of affirmative action for minorities and women; and the protection of social security and health care for seniors and families. After gaining 51 percent of the vote among a field of five candidates in the primaries, she dominated the slate in the general election: with 52.1 percent of her support coming from business and 33.5 percent from labor, she won 79 percent of the vote to become the next United States congressperson from Ohio's 11th District.

While in office Tubbs Jones has sought to address the issues which she raised during her campaign. Given the broad socio-economic diversity of the district which she represents, she has focused on economic development and a strong educational system, issues which connect and are powerfully relevant to her entire constituency. Towards this end, Tubbs Jones has energetically worked as a member of the banking and small business Congressional committees. Thus, for example, she helped to secure funding for the redevelopment of a local shopping center with an emphasis on minority businesses. She also coordinated a Small Business Conference in Cleveland in September of 1999 which sought to provide resources to local entrepreneurs. Free and open to the public, the conference addressed such topics as creating a business, business growth, women entrepreneurs, financing a business, and e-commerce. Tubbs Jones is also committed to a decent minimum wage and to a patient's Bill of Rights, which passed the House of Representatives but, much to her chagrin, did not clear the Senate in 1999.

In addition to broad economic issues, Tubbs Jones has also embraced social concerns as well. Of critical importance to Tubbs Jones is the wellbeing of children, and her positions clearly reflect her experience on the bench and in the prosecutor's office. For instance, she does not favor treating juveniles as adults. "If we can't rehabilitate adults in prison," she told CBB, "how do we think we can rehabilitate juveniles there?" Concurrently she is the original sponsor of the Child Abuse Protection and Enforcement Act of 1999, which uses common sense enforcement reforms to protect children from abuse and neglect. The CAPE Act, as it is known, will provide child protection service organizations access to funds to train child protection workers. Rather than increasing federal spending or imposing unfunded mandates on states, all the money that the act allocates originates from forfeited assets and bail bonds and fines paid to the government. Noted Tubbs Jones in an October 1999 news release, [B]y providing better funding for Child Advocacy Centers and training for child care providers, we can help protect our children more effectively and deal with any abuse in an effective manner." The legislation also calls for greater access to criminal conviction records for child protection workers and law enforcement officials so as to ensure that abused children are sent to safe adoption and foster homes.

Tubbs Jones is further passionate about the need for gun control legislation. She has cosponsored several initiatives seeking to make guns safer, to restrict the sale of weapons through loopholes to existing laws, and to limit the types of guns available for purchase. As she expressed in an April 1999 news release, "We regulate cribs, food, and prescription drugs, we should regulate the manufacture and use of guns ... As leaders we must address the issue of violence in schools and homes. If we ignore this responsibility and do not debate these bills on their merits we are letting down our youth and future generations of Americans."

In analyzing her freshman year in Congress, Tubbs Jones was frustrated by the House of Representatives' failure to pass legislation raising the hourly minimum wage by one dollar per hour. As the States News Service commented, she was "also frustrated that the House spent too much time debating needless partisan legislation rather than dedicating more attention to substantive issues." But such disappointments have not curbed Tubbs Jones' enthusiasm nor her commitment to public service. With economic development, health care for all Americans, gun control legislation, and the completion of a patient's Bill of Rights all on her plate for the coming session of Congress, she will continue to press to meet the needs of her district. She would be happy, she remarked to CBB, if Congress could resolve even one of these key issues.

At the same time Tubbs Jones struggles to balance the demands of her professional life with the joys and demands of home. Actually, she told CBB, "You truly don't balance; you prioritize " Such a routine is not new for Tubbs Jones. In fact, just 12 days after she was sworn in as a judge on the Court of Common Pleas, her son, Mervyn, was born. As a congresswoman Tubbs Jones travels weekly between Washington, D.C. and her home in Cleveland, sharing household responsibilities and the care of her son with her husband, Mervyn, whom she married in 1976. Her husband, she has noted, has always been particularly supportive of her career. As she recounted to CBB, when she first ran for office she decided to use both her maiden and married names, thereby assuming the public name of Tubbs Jones. Afraid of offending her husband, he only responded, "whatever will get you elected, honey!

Tubbs Jones never envisioned a career in elected service and saw her only public service within the realm of social work. And yet her ride has been remarkable. At the State of the Union Address in 1999, President Bill Clinton shook her hand and addressed her by name, a thrilling experience for her. In January of 2000, moreover, she filed the delegate petitions for Al Gore's presidential campaign--and filed her own petitions to retain her Congressional seat in the 2000 election. Tubbs Jones is not yet ready, however, to consider the next step beyond this election, where she faces a challenge from fellow Democrat Gerald Hinkley. "I don't know what I want to do when I grow up," she confessed to Bean--but the lack of clarity about the future does not reveal any lack of direction. Rather, she explained to CBB, "I just got here [into Congress] ...

Seniority means everything. If I move too quickly, I don't have a chance to see what that means." Meanwhile, she looks forward to a Democratic majority in the House of Representatives, which will broaden her experiences and provide more committee responsibilities.

Proud of her accomplishments, Jones does not dismiss them lightly. As she remarked to Mihaly, she sees herself not as a woman who has it all, but as one who has "been blessed, like I've been given the opportunity to do whatever I want to do ... I believe God has blessed me--and I believe He can take away the gifts He's given me if I don't watch it."

As Tubbs Jones looks back over her 50 years, she admitted to CBB: "I think I've accomplished a lot in my 50 years. I don't know whether there is something else after this or not. I am blessed never to have thought about the next step because before I had to think about it, God just swept me up and said, 'OK, girlfriend, you're in charge, time to do something else.' This might be it. I don't want to be in public life until I am 70 or 80 years old. My favorite thing it do is sail. I would love to have a boat, sail around the world, live in a tropical area, and be on the water. But never say never. I am happy with this so far."

Sources

Periodicals

Cleveland Magazine, March 1993, pp. 30-33, 102-103, 105.
Dallas Morning News, March 29, 1998.
Kaleidoscope, Special Women's Issue 1998, pp. 24-25.

Other

Additional information for this profile was obtained from an interview with Contemporary Black Biography, January 6, 2000; and from press releases from the Office of Congresswoman Stephanie Tubbs Jones, April 27, 1999; May 28, 1999; September 22, 1999; October 4, 1999; October 20, 1999; October 27, 1999; November 18, 1999. States News Service, December 24, 1998; August 23, 1999; October 14, 1999; November 22, 1999.

Online

Web Site, Ohio Legislative Black Caucus.Web Site, Jones for Congress.

—Lisa A. Weitzman

Walter C. Watkins, Jr.

1946(?)—

Bank president

When Walter C. Watkins became president of the Detroit branch of one of the country's largest banks in 1998, he became the first African American to head the top bank in the city. Watkins had been with the National Bank of Detroit since his graduation from college, and his elevation from executive vice president to president was considered a sign that the new parent company possessed a good deal of confidence in its local management team.

Relocated to Detroit

Born in the mid-1940s in Nashville, Watkins grew up in Tennessee, where his first exposure to the financial world came with his father's job as a courier for a Nashville bank. He graduated from Fisk University, Nashville's historic African American college, in 1968 with a degree in business administration. In order to find work, Watkins was forced to move north because he realized that few financial institutions in the South would hire an African American for a career-track position. He had already spent a summer in Detroit working at one of the factories operated by the Chrysler Corporation, and he was accepted for a slot in the management training program at what was then called the National Bank of Detroit. Watkins arrived in 1968 with few possessions. "I had no car, no apartment," Watkins told Lorene Yue in the *Detroit Free Press*. "I just showed up with my shirts on hangers."

Watkins completed the management training program and began his rise through the ranks of the company. He became a branch manager in the early 1970s at a bank on Detroit's east side, and was promoted to loan officer, where he worked with minority business owners large and small. It was a time in the city when African Americans were making tremendous gains in Detroit's political, cultural, and economic life. "It's safe to say that there are more opportunities today for minorities, but there's still a long way to go," Watkins told the *Detroit Free Press* in 1975. After earning a master's degree in business administration from Wayne State University in Detroit, he was promoted to a vice-president post at NBD in 1980, and three years later was made group head of the institution's Midwest banking division. Watkins rose to first vice president in 1985, and a year later, became the second African American member of the Detroit Golf Club, an exclusive, formerly segregated private club whose first African American member was Detroit's mayor, Coleman A. Young.

Rose Through the Ranks

In 1988, Watkins was named head of NBD's Eastern group, but in 1992 he took on a more crucial role in NBD's Michigan operations as head of the Detroit East Regional Banking Center. In 1994, with a merger in the works between NBD and First Chicago Bank, the company elevated him to director of the southern

> ### At a Glance...
>
> Born c. 1946, in Nashville, TN; married to Harriet; children: two daughters. *Education:* Fisk University, B.A., 1968; Wayne State University, M.B.A., 1977.
>
> **Career:** Began career at National Bank of Detroit as a management trainee, 1968, became branch manager, 1972, promoted to vice-president, 1980, group head in the Midwest banking division, 1983, first vice president, 1985, head of NBD's Eastern group, 1988, senior vice president, 1994; First Chicago NBD, executive vice president and head of Michigan regional banking, 1997-98, president, 1998—.
>
> **Addresses:** *Office*—Bank One, 611 Woodward Ave., Detroit, MI 48226.

metropolitan regional banking division. With that promotion, Watkins also became a member of NBD's senior management group in Michigan. Two years after the formal creation of First Chicago NBD in 1995, Watkins became executive vice president and head of Michigan regional banking, a position he held from 1997 through the end of 1998. In this capacity, he was responsible for all Michigan branches of the bank and the welfare of employees.

When Banc One of Columbus, Ohio, merged with First Chicago NBD in the fall of 1998, yet another bank was created: Bank One Corp., one of the five largest banks in the United States. Watkins was named Detroit president to succeed retiring NBD executive Tom Jeffs. Although Bank One's company headquarters would be in Chicago, Watkins's role in maintaining a strong and vital corporate presence for the institution in Detroit was unchanged. His new duties would include dealing with legal and regulatory compliance issues, and he was now answerable to a team of bank officers in Chicago. With the merger, Watkins became a member of the management roster of the fourth-largest bank holding company in the United States. Holding assets of $264 billion, Bank One was also the largest issuer of Visa cards in the world.

A Capable Leader

The subsuming of NBD, a fixture in Detroit since 1933, was part of a new wave of bank acquisitions and mergers that were leaving few homegrown financial institutions independent, especially those that served urban markets. Bernard Parker, co-chair of the Detroit Alliance for Fair Banking, told Yue in the *Detroit Free Press* that his group was initially wary about the merger of First Chicago NBD and Banc One, but in the end was pleased about Watkins's promotion to president. The Alliance, a community watchdog group that works to ensure fairness in banking and lending practices for Detroit residents, feared that the new bank's operations in Detroit would be relegated to a lesser status now that it was part of a much larger national bank headquartered elsewhere. But after meeting with representatives from Bank One, the Alliance's concerns abated and were replaced by faith in Watkins as leader and symbol of a new era. Parker said Watkins was ideally suited for the job of overseeing what would become one of Banc One's largest markets in the country. His presidency, the Alliance chair remarked to the *Detroit Free Press*, conveyed the idea that "African Americans can do more than just community relations. I think he is really going to become a role model." Watkins's predecessor at NBD agreed. Tom Jeffs was happy to be handing over his duties to someone who knew the Detroit market so well. "It's always a source of real comfort to know that if you are leaving that you are leaving the keys to someone you've worked with for a long time, who isn't a stranger; somebody who is really well-known and liked in this organization and Walt meets all of those tests really well," Jeffs told Yue in the *Detroit Free Press.*

Watkins planned to continue NBD's program, operated in conjunction with the Detroit Alliance for Fair Banking, to provide small-business loans, mortgages, and community development funds for Detroit. Banc One pledged a total of three billion dollars to fund the program. "This is not a charitable contribution, these are good loans, and it's good business," Watkins told *Detroit Free Press* writer Molly Brauer. He also sits on the boards of several corporate and community groups, including the Health Alliance Plan, Downtown Detroit Development Authority, Detroit Works Partnership, and the Urban Bankers Forum. The father of two grown daughters, he lives in the Detroit suburb of Livonia with his wife, Harriet.

Sources

Periodicals

Crain's Detroit Business, *September 28, 1998, p. 3.*
Detroit Free Press, *November 25, 1975; July 5, 1986; June 26, 1998; October 10, 1998.*

—Carol Brennan

Vickie Winans

1953(?)—

Gospel vocalist

Although she rose to fame partly as a member by marriage of gospel music's most famous family, Vickie Winans has carved out an independent identity, musically and personally. Dubbed "the hardest working woman in gospel music," according to the *Detroit News,* Winans was a fixture of the gospel concert scene at the end of the 1990s, making more than 200 appearances a year. Her sense of humor and gutsy, down-to-earth stage persona, effectively displayed on a pair of top-selling live albums, were continuing to attract new fans to her recorded offerings and above all to her religious message. "My main, number one goal in life is that everybody be reached with the message of Jesus Christ," she told the *Detroit Free Press.*

A native of Ecorse, Michigan, just south of the gospel-drenched city of Detroit, Winans was born around 1953 (interviews from early 1999 in the *Detroit News* and *Detroit Free Press* each list her age as forty-five). Her full maiden name was Vivian Bowman, and her mother, Mattie Bowman, was a singer well known in local gospel circles. All twelve Bowman children (eight girls and four boys) were exposed to gospel music at the Pentecostal church the family attended, the International Gospel Center in Ecorse, and others besides Vickie became involved in music; her brother Tim Bowman is a noted gospel guitarist with a jazz-flavored style, and two of her sisters followed in their mother's footsteps as church musicians.

Sang in Bathtub

Despite all the emphasis on church music, it was in quite a different place that her vocal ability really got noticed. In a *Detroit Free Press* interview, Winans recalled a bathtub singing contest with her sisters that ended when one sister ran to tell their mother that "Vickie can sing for real, for real." She sang solos at church, accompanied by her brother on the guitar. One day, her singing attracted the attention of someone who was able to appreciate the depth of her abilities, and was in a position to do something about it.

The Rev. Marvin Winans, pastor of Detroit's Perfecting Church, was a member of the Grammy-winning group of gospel-singing brothers, The Winans. Several generations of Winans family members had become successful gospel performers, and the family had risen to the top levels of the gospel scene in a city with a great deal of strong competition. The Winans style was spiritual, emotional, rooted in traditional styles but also open to popular influences. And when Marvin Winans heard Vickie Bowman sing, she noted an immediate reaction: "When I saw him, I knew that I had him," she told the *Free Press.*

That turned out to be true in more ways than one: Vickie Bowman, in addition to becoming Marvin Winans's

> ### At a Glance...
>
> Born Vivian Bowman c. 1953; raised in Ecorse, Michigan, near Detroit; mother a gospel singer; one of 12 children; daughter of Mattie Bowman. Married Rev. Marvin Winans, a gospel singer and pastor; later divorced; two children. *Religion:* Pentecostal.
>
> **Career:** Gospel vocalist. Discovered by Rev. Marvin Winans; released debut album, *Be Encouraged,* 1985; released *Total Victory,* 1989; released *The Lady,* 1991; 1992 song "I'm Hooked" incorporated rap elements; released *Vickie Winans,* 1995; released *Live in Detroit,* 1997; released *Live in Detroit, Vol. 2,* 1999; released *Share the Laughter* gospel comedy disc, 1999; album *Woman to Woman* slated for release, 2000.
>
> **Awards:** Nominated for five Grammy awards.
>
> **Addresses:** *Office*—Viviane, Inc., 6689 Orchard Lake Rd., #256, West Bloomfield, MI 48322.

musical protegee, also became his wife. Her recording career, launched in 1985 with the album *Be Encouraged* on the Light label, by her own admission took off as a result of the influence of the Winans family, but she stood out as a performer from the start. After several releases in the late 1980s, which did well enough to merit an *At Her Best* collection, Winans struck off in several new directions. Her 1992 song "I'm Hooked" was an early example of the incorporation of rap into gospel music, and she appeared in several stage musicals; one of them, called *The First Lady,* told the story of a minister's wife who is faced with the challenge of taking over her church congregation after her husband's death.

Divorced from Marvin Winans

In a way, the musical's plot was a harbinger of the challenges Winans herself would face in the next stage of her career, for as a result of her divorce in the mid-1990s from Marvin Winans, she was forced to take charge of her own career and define herself apart from the Winans musical style and promotional empire. "It was a very hurting experience," she told the *Free Press.* "Both of us took it for granted that everything was OK. But, you know, after a while, it don't even matter whose fault it was." On top of the emotional stress, she suffered health problems: diabetes, and ulcerated vocal cords that required surgery.

She found solace by turning to her own creativity. "It was a difficult time for me, and so I sang songs that would bring me through the trying times," Winans told the *Detroit News.* Winans took control of her own business affairs (she handles her bookings and PR through her own firm, Viviane, Inc.), and came through her time of trials as a stronger performer than she had been as part of the Winans family circle. Channeling the emotions engendered by her divorce into such songs as "Long as I Got King Jesus," Winans began to make waves with her live appearances, and capitalized on them with the release of her 1997 album *Live in Detroit,* recorded at the city's Straight Gate Church.

Live Album Enjoyed Strong Sales

That album sold over 200,000 copies, a strong success by gospel standards; it remained on *Billboard* magazine's Top 40 Gospel Albums chart as of the summer of 1999. It spawned a follow-up, *Live in Detroit II,* which had a more upbeat mood than its predecessor. I'm healed and I'm celebrating," Winans told the *Detroit Free Press.* "I'm in my groove now. The Lord has defined me and showed me what I'm here to do." The album was accompanied by a concert video featuring Winans's mother, and individual videos of songs from the album gained considerable airtime on cable-television gospel programs.

The large crowds that greeted Winans at promotional events for *Live in Detroit II* made an auspicious beginning for an ambitious jump in the intensity of her career. Two more Winans albums followed in quick succession, each displaying a different side of her personality and exposing listeners to her considerable versatility. The most unusual project was *Share the Laughter,* one of the few comedy recordings in the history of black gospel; the album included such Winans stage routines as "Y'All Raggedy Too?" and "Daddy Can't Sing." "People Think I'm funny, but I'm not just being funny," Winans explained to the *Free Press.* Laughter is universal and laughter is good medicine. The Bible says, 'A merry heart does good like medicine'" (Proverbs 17:22). Slated for release as of early 2000 was the third leg of the Winans trilogy, *Woman to Woman,* a set of gospel and inspirational songs aimed at women who were trying to survive periods of adversity in their lives. Winans had done just that, and emerged as a gospel star.

Selected discography

Be Encouraged, Light, 1985.
Total Victory, Light, 1989.

The Lady, MCA, 1991.
The Best of All, CGI/Light, 1991.
Vickie Winans, CGI, 1995.
Live in Detroit, CGI, 1997.
Live in Detroit, Vol. 2, CGI, 1999.
Share the Laughter, CGI, 1999.
Woman to Woman, CGI, 2000.

Sources

Books

Graff, Gary, Josh Freedom du Lac, and Jim McFarlin, *MusicHound R&B,* Visible Ink, 1998.

Periodicals

Billboard, November 20, 1999, p. 41.
Detroit Free Press, April 12, 1990, p. C1; May 6, 1991, p. E2; June 11, 1999, p. C1.
Detroit News, June 23, 1999.

Online

http://www.allmusic.com
http://www.capitalentertainment.com
http://www.timbowman.com/bio.html
http://www.vickiewinans.com

—James M. Manheim

Cumulative Indexes

Cumulative Nationality Index

Volume numbers appear in **bold**.

American
Aaron, Hank **5**
Abdul-Jabbar, Kareem **8**
Abernathy, Ralph David **1**
Abu-Jamal, Mumia **15**
Adams Early, Charity **13**
Adams, Floyd, Jr. **12**
Adams, Oleta **18**
Adams, Yolanda **17**
Adkins, Rutherford H. **21**
Agyeman, Jaramogi Abebe **10**
Ailey, Alvin **8**
Al-Amin, Jamil Abdullah **6**
Albright, Gerald **23**
Alexander, Archie Alphonso **14**
Alexander, Joyce London **18**
Alexander, Margaret Walker **22**
Alexander, Sadie Tanner Mossell **22**
Ali, Muhammad **2, 16**
Allen, Byron **3, 24**
Allen, Debbie **13**
Allen, Ethel D. **13**
Allen, Marcus **20**
Allen, Tina **22**
Amos, John **8**
Amos, Wally **9**
Anderson, Jamal **22**
Anderson, Marian **2**
Andrews, Benny **22**
Andrews, Bert **13**
Andrews, Raymond **4**
Angelou, Maya **1, 15**
Ansa, Tina McElroy **14**
Archer, Dennis **7**
Arkadie, Kevin **17**
Armstrong, Louis **2**
Armstrong, Robb **15**
Armstrong, Vanessa Bell **24**
Arrington, Richard **24**
Asante, Molefi Kete **3**
Ashe, Arthur **1, 18**
Ashford, Emmett **22**
Ashford, Nickolas **21**
Ashley-Ward, Amelia **23**
Austin, Patti **24**
Avant, Clarence **19**
Ayers, Roy **16**
Badu, Erykah **22**
Bailey, Radcliffe **19**
Bailey, Xenobia **11**
Baker, Anita **21**
Baker, Dusty **8**
Baker, Ella **5**
Baker, Gwendolyn Calvert **9**
Baker, Houston A., Jr. **6**
Baker, Josephine **3**
Baker, Thurbert **22**
Baldwin, James **1**
Bambara, Toni Cade **10**
Banks, Jeffrey **17**
Banks, Tyra **11**
Banks, William **11**
Baraka, Amiri **1**
Barboza, Anthony **10**
Barden, Don H. **9, 20**
Barkley, Charles **5**
Barrett, Andrew C. **12**
Barry, Marion S. **7**
Barthe, Richmond **15**
Basie, Count **23**
Basquiat, Jean-Michel **5**
Bassett, Angela **6, 23**
Bates, Daisy **13**
Bates, Peg Leg **14**
Baugh, David **23**
Baylor, Don **6**
Beals, Jennifer **12**
Beals, Melba Patillo **15**
Bearden, Romare **2**
Bechet, Sidney **18**
Beckford, Tyson **11**
Belafonte, Harry **4**
Bell, Derrick **6**
Bell, Robert Mack **22**
Bellamy, Bill **12**
Belle, Albert **10**
Belle, Regina **1**
Belton, Sharon Sayles **9, 16**
Ben-Israel, Ben Ami **11**
Benjamin, Regina **20**
Bennett, Lerone, Jr. **5**
Berry, Bertice **8**
Berry, Halle **4, 19**
Berry, Mary Frances **7**
Bethune, Mary McLeod **4**
Bickerstaff, Bernie **21**
Biggers, John **20**
Bing, Dave **3**
Bishop Jr., Sanford D. **24**
Black, Keith Lanier **18**
Blackwell, Unita **17**
Blanks, Billy **22**
Blige, Mary J. **20**
Bluford, Guy **2**
Bluitt, Juliann S. **14**
Bolden, Charles F., Jr. **7**
Bolin, Jane **22**
Bond, Julian **2**
Bonds, Barry **6**
Bontemps, Arna **8**
Booker, Simeon **23**
Borders, James **9**
Bosley, Freeman, Jr. **7**
Boston, Lloyd **24**
Bowe, Riddick **6**
Bowser, Yvette Lee **17**
Boyd, John W., Jr. **20**
Boyd, T. B. III **6**
Boykin, Keith **14**
Bradley, Ed **2**
Bradley, Thomas **2, 20**
Brandon, Barbara **3**
Brandon, Terrell **16**
Brandy **14**
Braugher, Andre **13**
Braun, Carol Moseley **4**
Braxton, Toni **15**
Brimmer, Andrew F. **2**
Briscoe, Connie **15**
Brock, Lou **18**
Brooke, Edward **8**
Brooks, Avery **9**
Brooks, Gwendolyn **1**
Brown, Charles **23**
Brown, Corrine **24**
Brown, Donald **19**
Brown, Elaine **8**
Brown, Erroll M. **23**
Brown, James **22**
Brown, Jesse **6**
Brown, Jim **11**
Brown, Lee Patrick **1, 24**
Brown, Les **5**
Brown, Marie Dutton **12**
Brown, Ron **5**
Brown, Sterling **10**
Brown, Tony **3**
Brown, Wesley **23**
Brown, Willie L., Jr. **7**
Brown, Zora Kramer **12**
Brunson, Dorothy **1**
Bryant, Kobe **15**

Bryant, Wayne R. **6**
Buckley, Victoria (Vikki) **24**
Bullard, Eugene **12**
Bullock, Steve **22**
Bumbry, Grace **5**
Bunche, Ralph J. **5**
Burke, Selma **16**
Burnett, Charles **16**
Burrell, Thomas J. **21**
Burris, Chuck **21**
Burroughs, Margaret Taylor **9**
Burton, LeVar **8**
Busby, Jheryl **3**
Butler, Leroy III **17**
Butler, Octavia **8**
Butler, Paul D. **17**
Butts, Calvin O., III **9**
Byrd, Donald **10**
Byrd, Michelle **19**
Byrd, Robert **11**
Cadoria, Sherian Grace **14**
Caesar, Shirley **19**
Cain, Herman **15**
Callender, Clive O. **3**
Calloway, Cab **14**
Camp, Kimberly **19**
Campbell, Bebe Moore **6, 24**
Campbell, Bill **9**
Campbell, E. Simms **13**
Campbell, Tisha **8**
Canada, Geoffrey **23**
Cannon, Katie **10**
Carew, Rod **20**
Carroll, Diahann **9**
Carson, Benjamin **1**
Carson, Julia **23**
Carson, Lisa Nicole **21**
Carter, Anson **24**
Carter, Betty **19**
Carter, Cris **21**
Carter, Mandy **11**
Carter, Regina **23**
Carter, Stephen L. **4**
Carver, George Washington **4**
Cary, Lorene **3**
CasSelle, Malcolm **11**
Catlett, Elizabeth **2**
Chamberlain, Wilt **18**
Chambers, Julius **3**
Chapman, Jr., Nathan A. **21**
Chappell, Emma **18**
Charles, Ray **16**
Chase-Riboud, Barbara **20**
Chavis, Benjamin **6**
Cheadle, Don **19**
Chenault, Kenneth I. **4**
Chideya, Farai **14**
Childress, Alice **15**
Chisholm, Shirley **2**
Christian, Spencer **15**
Christian-Green, Donna M. **17**
Chuck D **9**
Clark, Celeste **15**
Clark, Joe **1**
Clark, Kenneth B. **5**
Clark, Patrick **14**
Clark, Septima **7**
Clark-Sheard, Karen **22**

Clarke, Hope **14**
Clarke, John Henrik **20**
Clash, Kevin **14**
Clay, William Lacy **8**
Clayton, Constance **1**
Clayton, Eva M. **20**
Clayton, Xernona **3**
Claytor, Helen **14**
Cleage, Pearl **17**
Cleaver, Eldridge **5**
Cleaver, Emanuel **4**
Clements, George **2**
Cleveland, James **19**
Clifton, Lucille **14**
Clinton, George **9**
Clyburn, James **21**
Coachman, Alice **18**
Cobbs, Price M. **9**
Cochran, Johnnie L., Jr. **11**
Cohen, Anthony **15**
Colbert, Virgis William **17**
Cole, Johnnetta B. **5**
Cole, Nat King **17**
Cole, Natalie Maria **17**
Coleman, Donald A. **24**
Coleman, Leonard S., Jr. **12**
Coleman, Bessie **9**
Colemon, Johnnie **11**
Collins, Albert **12**
Collins, Barbara-Rose **7**
Collins, Cardiss **10**
Collins, Marva **3**
Coltrane, John **19**
Combs, Sean "Puffy" **17**
Comer, James P. **6**
Cone, James H. **3**
Connerly, Ward **14**
Conyers, John, Jr. **4**
Conyers, Nathan G. **24**
Cook, Samuel DuBois **14**
Cook, Suzan D. Johnson **22**
Cook, Toni **23**
Cooper, Anna Julia **20**
Cooper, Cynthia **17**
Cooper, Edward S. **6**
Cooper, J. California **12**
Cornelius, Don **4**
Cosby, Bill **7**
Cosby, Camille **14**
Cose, Ellis **5**
Cottrell, Comer **11**
Cowans, Adger W. **20**
Crawford, Randy **19**
Crew, Rudolph F. **16**
Crockett, Jr., George **10**
Cross, Dolores E. **23**
Crothers, Scatman **19**
Crouch, Stanley **11**
Crowder, Henry **16**
Cullen, Countee **8**
Cummings, Elijah E. **24**
Cunningham, Evelyn **23**
Cunningham, Randall **23**
Currie, Betty **21**
Curry, George E. **23**
Curry, Mark **17**
Curtis-Hall, Vondie **17**
Dandridge, Dorothy **3**

Daniels-Carter, Valerie **23**
Darden, Christopher **13**
Dash, Julie **4**
Davidson, Jaye **5**
Davidson, Tommy **21**
Davis, Allison **12**
Davis, Angela **5**
Davis, Anthony **11**
Davis, Benjamin O., Jr. **2**
Davis, Benjamin O., Sr. **4**
Davis, Danny K. **24**
Davis, Ed **24**
Davis, Miles **4**
Davis, Ossie **5**
Davis, Piper **19**
Davis, Terrell **20**
Dawes, Dominique **11**
Dawkins, Wayne **20**
Days, Drew S., III **10**
Dee, Ruby **8**
Delaney, Beauford **19**
Delany, Bessie **12**
Delany, Sadie **12**
Delany, Samuel R., Jr. **9**
Dellums, Ronald **2**
Devers, Gail **7**
Devine, Loretta **24**
Dickens, Helen Octavia **14**
Dickerson, Ernest R. **6, 17**
Dickey, Eric Jerome **21**
Diggs, Charles C. **21**
Diggs-Taylor, Anna **20**
Dinkins, David **4**
Divine, Father **7**
Dixon, Julian C. **24**
Dixon, Margaret **14**
Dixon, Sharon Pratt **1**
Dixon, Willie **4**
Doby, Sr., Lawrence Eugene **16**
Dodson, Howard, Jr. **7**
Donegan, Dorothy **19**
Dorsey, Thomas **15**
Douglas, Aaron **7**
Dove, Rita **6**
Dove, Ulysses **5**
Downing, Will **19**
Dr. Dre **10**
Draper, Sharon M. **16**
Dre, Dr. **14**
Drew, Charles Richard **7**
Drexler, Clyde **4**
Driskell, David C. **7**
Driver, David E. **11**
DuBois, Shirley Graham **21**
DuBois, W. E. B. **3**
Ducksworth, Marilyn **12**
Duke, Bill **3**
Duke, George **21**
Dumars, Joe **16**
Dunbar, Paul Laurence **8**
Duncan, Tim **20**
Dungy, Tony **17**
Dunham, Katherine **4**
Dupri, Jermaine **13**
Dutton, Charles S. **4, 22**
Dyson, Michael Eric **11**
Early, Gerald **15**
Edelin, Ramona Hoage **19**

Cumulative Nationality Index • 187

Edelman, Marian Wright **5**
Edley, Christopher **2**
Edmonds, Kenneth "Babyface" **10**
Edmonds, Terry **17**
Edmonds, Tracey **16**
Edward, Melvin **22**
Edwards, Harry **2**
Edwards, Teresa **14**
Elder, Lee **6**
Elders, Joycelyn **6**
Ellerbe, Brian **22**
Ellington, Duke **5**
Ellington, E. David **11**
Ellison, Ralph **7**
Elmore, Ronn **21**
Epps, Omar **23**
Erving, Julius **18**
Esposito, Giancarlo **9**
Espy, Mike **6**
Eubanks, Kevin **15**
Europe, James Reese **10**
Evans, Darryl **22**
Evans, Faith **22**
Everett, Francine **23**
Evers, Medgar **3**
Evers, Myrlie **8**
Faison, George **16**
Farmer, Forest J. **1**
Farmer, James **2**
Farr, Mel, Sr. **24**
Farrakhan, Louis **2, 15**
Fats Domino **20**
Fattah, Chaka **11**
Fauntroy, Walter E. **11**
Fauset, Jessie **7**
Favors, Steve **23**
Feelings, Tom **11**
Fielder, Cecil **2**
Fields, Cleo **13**
Fishburne, Larry **4, 22**
Fitzgerald, Ella **1, 18**
Flack, Roberta **19**
Frazier, E. Franklin **10**
Frazier, Joe **19**
Freeman, Al, Jr. **11**
Freeman, Charles **19**
Freeman, Harold P. **23**
Freeman, Marianna **23**
Freeman, Morgan **2, 20**
French, Albert **18**
Friday, Jeff **24**
Fudge, Ann **11**
Fulani, Lenora **11**
Fuller, Charles **8**
Fuller, S. B. **13**
Fuller, Solomon Carter, Jr. **15**
Gaines, Ernest J. **7**
Gaither, Alonzo Smith (Jake) **14**
Gantt, Harvey **1**
Garnett, Kevin **14**
Garrison, Zina **2**
Gary, Willie E. **12**
Gaston, Arthur G. **4**
Gates, Henry Louis, Jr. **3**
Gates, Sylvester James, Jr. **15**
Gaye, Marvin **2**
Gayle, Helene D. **3**
Gentry, Alvin **23**

George, Nelson **12**
Gibson, Althea **8**
Gibson, Johnnie Mae **23**
Gibson, Josh **22**
Gibson, Kenneth Allen **6**
Gibson, William F. **6**
Giddings, Paula **11**
Gillespie, Dizzy **1**
Gilliam, Frank **23**
Gilliam, Sam **16**
Giovanni, Nikki **9**
Gist, Carole **1**
Givens, Robin **4**
Glover, Danny **1, 24**
Glover, Nathaniel, Jr. **12**
Glover, Savion **14**
Goines, Donald **19**
Goldberg, Whoopi **4**
Golden, Marita **19**
Golden, Thelma **10**
Goldsberry, Ronald **18**
Gomes, Peter J. **15**
Gomez-Preston, Cheryl **9**
Goode, Mal **13**
Goode, W. Wilson **4**
Gooden, Dwight **20**
Gooding, Jr., Cuba **16**
Gordon, Ed **10**
Gordone, Charles **15**
Gordy, Berry, Jr. **1**
Goss, Tom **23**
Gossett, Louis, Jr. **7**
Gourdine, Simon **11**
Graham, Lawrence Otis **12**
Graham, Stedman **13**
Gravely, Samuel L., Jr. **5**
Graves, Denyce **19**
Graves, Earl G. **1**
Gray, F. Gary **14**
Gray, William H. III **3**
Green, Al **13**
Green, Dennis **5**
Greene, Joe **10**
Greenfield, Eloise **9**
Gregory, Dick **1**
Gregory, Frederick D. **8**
Grier, Pam **9**
Grier, Roosevelt **13**
Griffey, Ken, Jr. **12**
Griffith, Mark Winston **8**
Grimké, Archibald H. **9**
Guillaume, Robert **3**
Guinier, Lani **7**
Gumbel, Bryant **14**
Gumbel, Greg **8**
Gunn, Moses **10**
Guy, Jasmine **2**
Guy, Rosa **5**
Guy-Sheftall, Beverly **13**
Guyton, Tyree **9**
Gwynn, Tony **18**
Hailey, JoJo **22**
Hailey, K-Ci **22**
Hale, Clara **16**
Hale, Lorraine **8**
Haley, Alex **4**
Haley, George Williford Boyce **21**
Hall, Elliott S. **24**

Hall, Lloyd A. **8**
Hamblin, Ken **10**
Hamer, Fannie Lou **6**
Hamilton, Virginia **10**
Hammer, M. C. **20**
Hammond, Fred **23**
Hampton, Fred **18**
Hampton, Henry **6**
Hampton, Lionel **17**
Hancock, Herbie **20**
Handy, W. C. **8**
Hannah, Marc **10**
Hansberry, Lorraine **6**
Hansberry, William Leo **11**
Hardaway, Anfernee (Penny) **13**
Hardison, Bethann **12**
Hardison, Kadeem **22**
Harkless, Necia Desiree **19**
Harper, Frances Ellen Watkins **11**
Harrell, Andre **9**
Harrington, Oliver W. **9**
Harris, Alice **7**
Harris, Barbara **12**
Harris, E. Lynn **12**
Harris, Eddy L. **18**
Harris, Jay T. **19**
Harris, Leslie **6**
Harris, Marcelite Jordon **16**
Harris, Monica **18**
Harris, Patricia Roberts **2**
Harris, Robin **7**
Harsh, Vivian Gordon **14**
Harvard, Beverly **11**
Harvey, Steve **18**
Haskins, Clem **23**
Hastie, William H. **8**
Hastings, Alcee L. **16**
Hathaway, Donny **18**
Hawkins, Coleman **9**
Hawkins, Erskine **14**
Hawkins, La-Van **17**
Hawkins, Steven **14**
Hawkins, Tramaine **16**
Hayden, Palmer **13**
Hayden, Robert **12**
Hayes, Isaac **20**
Hayes, James C. **10**
Hayes, Roland **4**
Haynes, George Edmund **8**
Haynes, Marques **22**
Haywood, Margaret A. **24**
Hedgeman, Anna Arnold **22**
Height, Dorothy I. **2, 23**
Hemphill, Essex **10**
Hemsley, Sherman **19**
Henderson, Gordon **5**
Henderson, Wade J. **14**
Hendricks, Barbara **3**
Hendrix, Jimi **10**
Henry, Aaron **19**
Henson, Matthew **2**
Henson, Matthew **2**
Herenton, Willie W. **24**
Herman, Alexis M. **15**
Hernandez, Aileen Clarke **13**
Hickman, Fred **11**
Higginbotham, A. Leon, Jr. **13**
Hightower, Dennis F. **13**

Hill, Anita 5
Hill, Bonnie Guiton 20
Hill, Calvin 19
Hill, Grant 13
Hill, Janet 19
Hill, Jessie, Jr. 13
Hill, Lauryn 20
Hill, Oliver W. 24
Hilliard, David 7
Hilliard, Earl F. 24
Himes, Chester 8
Hinderas, Natalie 5
Hine, Darlene Clark 24
Hines, Gregory 1
Hinton, William Augustus 8
Holder, Eric H., Jr. 9
Holdsclaw, Chamique 24
Holiday, Billie 1
Holland, Endesha Ida Mae 3
Holland, Robert, Jr. 11
Holmes, Larry 20
Holyfield, Evander 6
Hooks, Benjamin L. 2
hooks, bell 5
Hope, John 8
Horne, Lena 5
House, Son 8
Houston, Charles Hamilton 4
Houston, Cissy 20
Houston, Whitney 7
Howard, Desmond 16
Howard, Juwan 15
Howlin' Wolf 9
Hrabowski, Freeman A. III 22
Hudlin, Reginald 9
Hudlin, Warrington 9
Hudson, Cheryl 15
Hudson, Wade 15
Huggins, Larry 21
Hughes, Albert 7
Hughes, Allen 7
Hughes, Langston 4
Hughley, D.L. 23
Humphrey, Bobbi 20
Humphries, Frederick 20
Hunt, Richard 6
Hunter-Gault, Charlayne 6
Hurston, Zora Neale 3
Hutchinson, Earl Ofari 24
Hutson, Jean Blackwell 16
Hyman, Phyllis 19
Ice Cube 8
Ice-T 6
Iceberg Slim 11
Ingram, Rex 5
Innis, Roy 5
Irving, Larry, Jr. 12
Iverson, Allen 24
Jackson, Alexine Clement 22
Jackson, George 14
Jackson, George 19
Jackson, Isaiah 3
Jackson, Janet 6
Jackson, Jesse 1
Jackson, Jesse, Jr. 14
Jackson Lee, Sheila 20
Jackson, Mahalia 5
Jackson, Mannie 14

Jackson, Maynard 2
Jackson, Michael 19
Jackson, Reggie 15
Jackson, Samuel L. 8, 19
Jackson, Sheneska 18
Jackson, Shirley Ann 12
Jacob, John E. 2
Jakes, Thomas "T.D." 17
James, Daniel Jr. 16
James, Etta 13
James, Juanita 13
James, Rick 19
James, Sharpe 23
Jamison, Judith 7
Jarreau, Al 21
Jarvis, Charlene Drew 21
Jeffries, Leonard 8
Jemison, Mae C. 1
Jenifer, Franklyn G. 2
Jenkins, Beverly 14
Jenkins, Ella 15
Jimmy Jam 13
Joe, Yolanda 21
John, Daymond 23
Johnson, Beverly 2
Johnson, Charles 1
Johnson, Charles S. 12
Johnson, Earvin "Magic" 3
Johnson, Eddie Bernice 8
Johnson Jr., Harvey 24
Johnson, Jack 8
Johnson, James Weldon 5
Johnson, John H. 3
Johnson, Michael 13
Johnson, Norma L. Holloway 17
Johnson, Robert 2
Johnson, Robert L. 3
Johnson, Robert T. 17
Johnson, Virginia 9
Johnson, William Henry 3
Jones, Bill T. 1
Jones, Bobby 20
Jones, Carl 7
Jones, Cobi N'Gai 18
Jones, Elaine R. 7
Jones, Elvin 14
Jones, Ingrid Saunders 18
Jones, James Earl 3
Jones, Lois Mailou 13
Jones, Marion 21
Jones, Quincy 8
Jones, Star 10
Joplin, Scott 6
Jordan, Barbara 4
Jordan, June 7
Jordan, Michael 6, 21
Jordan, Montell 23
Jordan, Vernon E. 3
Josey, E. J. 10
Joyner-Kersee, Jackie 5
Joyner, Matilda Sissieretta 15
Joyner, Tom 19
Julian, Percy Lavon 6
Just, Ernest Everett 3
Justice, David 18
Kani, Karl 10
Karenga, Maulana 10
Kearse, Amalya Lyle 12

Keith, Damon J. 16
Kelly, Patrick 3
Kelly, R. 18
Kendricks, Eddie 22
Kennedy, Adrienne 11
Kennedy, Florynce 12
Keyes, Alan L. 11
Khan, Chaka 12
Khanga, Yelena 6
Kilpatrick, Carolyn Cheeks 16
Kimbro, Dennis 10
Kincaid, Jamaica 4
King, B. B. 7
King, Barbara 22
King, Bernice 4
King, Coretta Scott 3
King, Dexter 10
King, Don 14
King, Gayle 19
King, Martin Luther, Jr. 1
King, Martin Luther, III 20
King, Yolanda 6
Kirby, George 14
Kirk, Ron 11
Kitt, Eartha 16
Kitt, Sandra 23
Knight, Gladys 16
Knight, Suge 11
Komunyakaa, Yusef 9
Kotto, Yaphet 7
Kountz, Samuel L. 10
Kravitz, Lenny 10
Kunjufu, Jawanza 3
L.L. Cool J 16
La Salle, Eriq 12
LaBelle, Patti 13
Lafontant, Jewel Stradford 3
Lampkin, Daisy 19
Lane, Charles 3
Lane, Vincent 5
Langhart, Janet 19
Lankford, Ray 23
Larkin, Barry 24
Larsen, Nella 10
Lassiter, Roy 24
Latimer, Lewis H. 4
Lawless, Theodore K. 8
Lawrence, Jacob 4
Lawrence, Jr., Robert H. 16
Lawrence-Lightfoot, Sara 10
Lawrence, Martin 6
Lawson, Jennifer 1
Leary, Kathryn D. 10
Leavell, Dorothy R. 17
Lee, Annie Francis 22
Lee, Canada 8
Lee, Joie 1
Lee-Smith, Hughie 5, 22
Lee, Spike 5, 19
Leffall, LaSalle, Jr. 3
Leland, Mickey 2
Lemmons, Kasi 20
Leon, Kenny 10
Leonard, Sugar Ray 15
Lester, Julius 9
Levert, Gerald 22
Lewellyn, J. Bruce 13
Lewis, Byron E. 13

Cumulative Nationality Index

Lewis, Carl **4**
Lewis, David Levering **9**
Lewis, Delano **7**
Lewis, Edmonia **10**
Lewis, Edward T. **21**
Lewis, John **2**
Lewis, Reginald F. **6**
Lewis, Shirley A. R. **14**
Lewis, Terry **13**
Lewis, Thomas **19**
Lincoln, Abbey **3**
Little, Benilde **21**
Little Richard **15**
Little, Robert L. **2**
Locke, Alain **10**
Lofton, Kenny **12**
Logan, Onnie Lee **14**
Long, Nia **17**
Lorde, Audre **6**
Lott, Ronnie **9**
Louis, Errol T. **8**
Louis, Joe **5**
Love, Darlene **23**
Love, Nat **9**
Lover, Ed **10**
Lowery, Joseph **2**
Lucas, John **7**
Lymon, Frankie **22**
Lyons, Henry **12**
Lyttle, Hulda Margaret **14**
Mabley, Moms **15**
Madhubuti, Haki R. **7**
Madison, Joseph E. **17**
Major, Clarence **9**
Mallett, Jr., Conrad **16**
Malone, Annie **13**
Malone, Karl A. **18**
Manigault, Earl "The Goat" **15**
Manley, Audrey Forbes **16**
Marable, Manning **10**
Marrow, Queen Esther **24**
Marsalis, Wynton **16**
Marshall, Bella **22**
Marshall, Paule **7**
Marshall, Thurgood **1**
Martin, Louis E. **16**
Mase **24**
Massenburg, Kedar **23**
Massey, Walter E. **5**
Master P **21**
Mathis, Johnny **20**
Maxwell **20**
Mayfield, Curtis **2**
Maynard, Robert C. **7**
Maynor, Dorothy **19**
Mays, Benjamin E. **7**
Mays, Willie **3**
McBride, Bryant **18**
McCabe, Jewell Jackson **10**
McCall, Nathan **8**
McCarty, Oseola **16**
McCoy, Elijah **8**
McCray, Nikki **18**
McDaniel, Hattie **5**
McDonald, Audra **20**
McDonald, Erroll **1**
McDonald, Gabrielle Kirk **20**
McDougall, Gay J. **11**

McEwen, Mark **5**
McGee, Charles **10**
McGriff, Fred **24**
McGruder, Robert **22**
McKay, Claude **6**
McKay, Nellie Yvonne **17**
Mckee, Lonette **12**
McKinney, Cynthia Ann **11**
McKinnon, Isaiah **9**
McKissick, Floyd B. **3**
McKnight, Brian **18**
McMillan, Terry **4, 17**
McNair, Ronald **3**
McNair, Steve **22**
McNeil, Lori **1**
McPhail, Sharon **2**
McQueen, Butterfly **6**
Meek, Carrie **6**
Meredith, James H. **11**
Mfume, Kweisi **6**
Micheaux, Oscar **7**
Millender-McDonald, Juanita **21**
Miller, Bebe **3**
Miller, Cheryl **10**
Mills, Florence **22**
Mingus, Charles **15**
Mitchell, Arthur **2**
Mitchell, Brian Stokes **21**
Mitchell, Corinne **8**
Mitchell, Russ **21**
Monica **21**
Monk, Thelonious **1**
Moon, Warren **8**
Moore, Melba **21**
Moore, Shemar **21**
Moorer, Michael **19**
Morgan, Garrett **1**
Morgan, Joe Leonard **9**
Morgan, Rose **11**
Morial, Marc **20**
Morrison, Toni **2, 15**
Morton, Joe **18**
Moses, Edwin **8**
Moses, Gilbert **12**
Moses, Robert Parris **11**
Mosley, Walter **5**
Moss, Carlton **17**
Moss, Randy **23**
Moten, Etta **18**
Motley, Constance Baker **10**
Mourning, Alonzo **17**
Moutoussamy-Ashe, Jeanne **7**
Mowry, Jess **7**
Muhammad, Elijah **4**
Muhammad, Khallid Abdul **10**
Murphy, Eddie **4, 20**
Murray, Cecil **12**
Murray, Eddie **12**
Murray, Lenda **10**
Muse, Clarence Edouard **21**
Myers, Walter Dean **8**
N'Namdi, George R. **17**
Nanula, Richard D. **20**
Napoleon, Benny N. **23**
Naylor, Gloria **10**
Ndegéocello, Me'Shell **15**
Nelson, Jill **6**
Neville, Aaron **21**

Newcombe, Don **24**
Newton, Huey **2**
Nicholas, Fayard **20**
Nicholas, Harold **20**
Nichols, Nichelle **11**
Norman, Jessye **5**
Norman, Maidie **20**
Norman, Pat **10**
Norton, Eleanor Holmes **7**
Notorious B.I.G. **20**
O'Leary, Hazel **6**
O'Neal, Shaquille **8**
O'Neil, Buck **19**
Oglesby, Zena **12**
Ogletree, Jr., Charles **12**
Owens, Jesse **2**
Owens, Major **6**
Pace, Orlando **21**
Page, Alan **7**
Page, Clarence **4**
Paige, Satchel **7**
Painter, Nell Irvin **24**
Parker, Charlie **20**
Parker, Pat **19**
Parks, Bernard C. **17**
Parks, Gordon **1**
Parks, Rosa **1**
Parsons, James **14**
Parsons, Richard Dean **11**
Patrick, Deval **12**
Patterson, Floyd **19**
Patterson, Frederick Douglass **12**
Payne, Allen **13**
Payne, Donald M. **2**
Payton, Benjamin F. **23**
Payton, Walter **11**
Peck, Carolyn **23**
Peete, Calvin **11**
Peete, Holly Robinson **20**
Pendergrass, Teddy **22**
Peoples, Dottie **22**
Perez, Anna **1**
Perkins, Edward **5**
Perkins, Tony **24**
Perrot, Kim **23**
Person, Waverly **9**
Petry, Ann **19**
Pickett, Bill **11**
Pinchback, P. B. S. **9**
Pinkett, Jada **10**
Pinkney, Jerry **15**
Pinkston, W. Randall **24**
Pippen, Scottie **15**
Pippin, Horace **9**
Pleasant, Mary Ellen **9**
Poitier, Sidney **11**
Porter, James A. **11**
Poussaint, Alvin F. **5**
Powell, Adam Clayton, Jr. **3**
Powell, Bud **24**
Powell, Colin **1**
Powell, Debra A. **23**
Powell, Maxine **8**
Powell, Mike **7**
Pratt, Geronimo **18**
Price, Frederick K.C. **21**
Price, Glenda **22**
Price, Hugh B. **9**

Price, Kelly 23
Price, Leontyne 1
Primus, Pearl 6
Prince 18
Pritchard, Robert Starling 21
Procope, Ernesta 23
Prothrow-Stith, Deborah 10
Pryor, Richard 3, 24
Puckett, Kirby 4
Quarles, Benjamin Arthur 18
Quarterman, Lloyd Albert 4
Queen Latifah 1, 16
Raines, Franklin Delano 14
Ralph, Sheryl Lee 18
Ramsey, Charles H. 21
Rand, A. Barry 6
Randall, Dudley 8
Randle, Theresa 16
Randolph, A. Philip 3
Rangel, Charles 3
Rashad, Ahmad 18
Rashad, Phylicia 21
Raspberry, William 2
Rawls, Lou 17
Razaf, Andy 19
Reagon, Bernice Johnson 7
Reason, J. Paul 19
Reddick, Lawrence Dunbar 20
Redding, Otis 16
Redmond, Eugene 23
Reed, Ishmael 8
Reese, Della 6, 20
Reeves, Rachel J. 23
Reid, Irvin D. 20
Rhames, Ving 14
Rhodes, Ray 14
Rhone, Sylvia 2
Ribbs, Willy T. 2
Ribeiro, Alfonso 17
Rice, Condoleezza 3
Rice, Jerry 5
Rice, Linda Johnson 9
Rice, Norm 8
Richardson, Nolan 9
Richie, Leroy C. 18
Richmond, Mitch 19
Riggs, Marlon 5
Riley, Helen Caldwell Day 13
Ringgold, Faith 4
Roach, Max 21
Roberts, Marcus 19
Roberts, Robin 16
Roberts, Roy S. 14
Robeson, Eslanda Goode 13
Robeson, Paul 2
Robinson, Bill "Bojangles" 11
Robinson, David 24
Robinson, Eddie G. 10
Robinson, Frank 9
Robinson, Jackie 6
Robinson, Max 3
Robinson, Patrick 19
Robinson, Rachel 16
Robinson, Randall 7
Robinson, Sharon 22
Robinson, Smokey 3
Robinson, Spottswood W. III 22
Robinson, Sugar Ray 18

Roche, Joyce M. 17
Rochon, Lela 16
Rock, Chris 3, 22
Rodgers, Johnathan 6
Rodman, Dennis 12
Rogers, John W., Jr. 5
Roker, Al 12
Rolle, Esther 13, 21
Rollins, Jr., Howard E. 16
Ross, Diana 8
Rowan, Carl T. 1
Rowell, Victoria 13
Rudolph, Wilma 4
Rupaul 17
Rushen, Patrice 12
Russell, Bill 8
Russell, Herman Jerome 17
Russell-McCloud, Patricia A. 17
Rustin, Bayard 4
Saar, Alison 16
Saint James, Synthia 12
Samara, Noah 15
Sampson, Charles 13
Sanchez, Sonia 17
Sanders, Joseph R., Jr. 11
Sapphire 14
Savage, Augusta 12
Sayles Belton, Sharon, 9, 16
Scott, Robert C. 23
Scott, Sr., Wendell Oliver 19
Sengstacke, John 18
Shakur, Tupac 14
Sharpton, Al 21
Sheffield, Gary 16
Sherrod, Clayton 17
Shipp, E. R. 15
Silas, Paul 24
Simmons, Ruth J. 13
Simone, Nina 15
Simpson, O. J. 15
Simpson, Valerie 21
Sinbad, 1, 16
Singletary, Mike 4
Singleton, John 2
Sinkford, Jeanne C. 13
Sister Souljah 11
Slater, Rodney E. 15
Sleet, Moneta, Jr. 5
Smaltz, Audrey 12
Smiley, Tavis 20
Smith, Anna Deavere 6
Smith, Barbara 11
Smith, Bessie 3
Smith, Clarence O. 21
Smith, Emmitt 7
Smith, Jane E. 24
Smith, John L. 22
Smith, Joshua 10
Smith, Roger Guenveur 12
Smith, Tubby 18
Smith, Will 8, 18
Smith, Willi 8
Sneed, Paula A. 18
Snipes, Wesley 3, 24
Sowell, Thomas 2
Spaulding, Charles Clinton 9
Spikes, Dolores 18
Sprewell, Latrell 23

St. Jacques, Raymond 8
Stallings, George A., Jr. 6
Stanford, John 20
Stanton, Robert 20
Staples, Brent 8
Staupers, Mabel K. 7
Steele, Claude Mason 13
Steele, Shelby 13
Stephens, Charlotte Andrews 14
Steward, Emanuel 18
Stewart, Alison 13
Stewart, Kordell 21
Stewart, Maria W. Miller 19
Stewart, Paul Wilbur 12
Stokes, Carl B. 10
Stokes, Louis 3
Stone, Chuck 9
Stone, Toni 15
Stout, Juanita Kidd 24
Strawberry, Darryl 22
Street, John F. 24
Stringer, C. Vivian 13
Sudarkasa, Niara 4
Sullivan, Leon H. 3
Sullivan, Louis 8
Sweat, Keith 19
Swoopes, Sheryl 12
Swygert, H. Patrick 22
Sykes, Roosevelt 20
Tamia 24
Tanner, Henry Ossawa 1
Tate, Eleanora E. 20
Tate, Larenz 15
Taulbert, Clifton Lemoure 19
Taylor, Billy 23
Taylor, Charles 20
Taylor, Kristin Clark 8
Taylor, Meshach 4
Taylor, Regina 9
Taylor, Susan L. 10
Taylor, Susie King 13
Terrell, Dorothy A. 24
Terrell, Mary Church 9
Thigpen, Lynne 17
Thomas, Alma 14
Thomas, Clarence 2
Thomas, Frank 12
Thomas, Franklin A. 5
Thomas, Isiah 7
Thomas, Rufus 20
Thomas, Vivien 9
Thompson, Tazewell 13
Thurman, Howard 3
Thurman, Wallace 16
Till, Emmett 7
Tillman, George, Jr. 20
Tolliver, William 9
Toomer, Jean 6
Towns, Edolphus 19
Townsend, Robert 4, 23
Tribble, Israel, Jr. 8
Trotter, Monroe 9
Tubbs Jones, Stephanie 24
Tubman, Harriet 9
Tucker, C. DeLores 12
Tucker, Chris 13, 23
Tucker, Cynthia 15
Tucker, Rosina 14

Cumulative Nationality Index

Turnbull, Walter **13**
Turner, Henry McNeal **5**
Turner, Tina **6**
Tyree, Omar Rashad **21**
Tyson, Cicely **7**
Tyson, Neil de Grasse **15**
Uggams, Leslie **23**
Underwood, Blair **7**
Unseld, Wes **23**
Upshaw, Gene **18**
Usher **23**
Usry, James L. **23**
Utendahl, John **23**
Van Peebles, Mario **2**
Van Peebles, Melvin **7**
Vance, Courtney B. **15**
VanDerZee, James **6**
Vandross, Luther **13**
Vanzant, Iyanla **17**
Vaughan, Sarah **13**
Vaughn, Mo **16**
Vereen, Ben **4**
Vincent, Marjorie Judith **2**
Von Lipsey, Roderick K. **11**
Waddles, Charleszetta (Mother) **10**
Wagner, Annice **22**
Walker, A'lelia **14**
Walker, Albertina **10**
Walker, Alice **1**
Walker, Cedric "Ricky" **19**
Walker, Herschel **1**
Walker, Madame C. J. **7**
Walker, Maggie Lena **17**
Walker, T. J. **7**
Wallace, Michele Faith **13**
Wallace, Phyllis A. **9**
Wallace, Sippie **1**
Ward, Lloyd **21**
Warfield, Marsha **2**
Warner, Malcolm-Jamal **22**
Warwick, Dionne **18**
Washington, Booker T. **4**
Washington, Denzel **1, 16**
Washington, Dinah **22**
Washington, Fredi **10**
Washington, Grover, Jr. **17**
Washington, Harold **6**
Washington, Laura S. **18**
Washington, MaliVai **8**
Washington, Patrice Clarke **12**
Washington, Val **12**
Wasow, Omar **15**
Waters, Ethel **7**
Waters, Maxine **3**
Watkins, Levi, Jr. **9**
Watkins, Perry **12**
Watkins, Shirley R. **17**
Watkins, Walter C. **24**
Watson, Johnny "Guitar" **18**
Wattleton, Faye **9**
Watts, J. C., Jr. **14**
Watts, Rolonda **9**
Wayans, Damon **8**
Wayans, Keenen Ivory **18**
Weathers, Carl **10**
Weaver, Robert C. **8**
Webb, Veronica **10**
Webb, Wellington **3**

Webber, Chris **15**
Wells-Barnett, Ida B. **8**
Wells, James Lesesne **10**
Welsing, Frances Cress **5**
Wesley, Dorothy Porter **19**
Wesley, Valerie Wilson **18**
West, Cornel **5**
West, Dorothy **12**
West, Togo D., Jr. **16**
Westbrook, Peter **20**
Wharton, Clifton R., Jr. **7**
Wheat, Alan **14**
Whitaker, Forest **2**
Whitaker, Mark **21**
Whitaker, Pernell **10**
White, Barry **13**
White, Bill **1**
White, Jesse **22**
White, Lois Jean **20**
White, Michael R. **5**
White, Reggie **6**
White, Walter F. **4**
Whitfield, Fred **23**
Whitfield, Lynn **18**
Wideman, John Edgar **5**
Wilder, L. Douglas **3**
Wiley, Ralph **8**
Wilkens, Lenny **11**
Wilkins, Roger **2**
Wilkins, Roy **4**
Williams, Anthony **21**
Williams, Bert **18**
Williams, Billy Dee **8**
Williams, Daniel Hale **2**
Williams, Doug **22**
Williams, Evelyn **10**
Williams, George Washington **18**
Williams, Gregory **11**
Williams, Hosea Lorenzo **15**
Williams, Joe **5**
Williams, Maggie **7**
Williams, Mary Lou **15**
Williams, Montel **4**
Williams, O. S. **13**
Williams, Patricia J. **11**
Williams, Paul R. **9**
Williams, Robert F. **11**
Williams, Samm-Art **21**
Williams, Serena **20**
Williams, Vanessa L. **4, 17**
Williams, Venus **17**
Williams, Walter E. **4**
Williams, William T. **11**
Williams, Willie L. **4**
Williamson, Mykelti **22**
Wilson, August **7**
Wilson, Cassandra **16**
Wilson, Flip **21**
Wilson, Nancy **10**
Wilson, Phill **9**
Wilson, Sunnie **7**
Wilson, William Julius **20**
Winans, BeBe **14**
Winans, CeCe **14**
Winans, Marvin L. **17**
Winans, Vickie **24**
Winfield, Dave **5**
Winfield, Paul **2**

Winfrey, Oprah **2, 15**
Wolfe, George C. **6**
Wonder, Stevie **11**
Woodard, Alfre **9**
Woodruff, Hale **9**
Woods, Granville T. **5**
Woods, Tiger **14**
Woodson, Carter G. **2**
Woodson, Robert L. **10**
Worrill, Conrad **12**
Wright, Bruce McMarion **3**
Wright, Louis Tompkins **4**
Wright, Richard **5**
X, Malcolm **1**
Yoba, Malik **11**
Young, Andrew **3**
Young, Coleman **1, 20**
Young, Jean Childs **14**
Young, Whitney M., Jr. **4**
Youngblood, Johnny Ray **8**

Angolan
Bonga, Kuenda **13**
Savimbi, Jonas **2**

Bahamian
Ingraham, Hubert A. **19**

Batswana
Masire, Quett **5**

Belizian
Jones, Marion **21**

Beninois
Hounsou, Djimon **19**
Kerekou, Ahmed (Mathieu) **1**
Mogae, Festus Gontebanye **19**
Soglo, Nicéphore **15**

Bermudian
Gordon, Pamela **17**
Smith, Jennifer **21**

Brazilian
da Silva, Benedita **5**
Nascimento, Milton **2**
Pelé **7**
Pitta, Celso **17**

British
Abbott, Diane **9**
Campbell, Naomi **1**
Christie, Linford **8**
Davidson, Jaye **5**
Henry, Lenny **9**
Jean-Baptiste, Marianne **17**
Julien, Isaac **3**
Lindo, Delroy **18**
Pitt, David Thomas **10**
Seal **14**
Taylor, John (David Beckett) **16**

Burkinabé
Somé, Malidoma Patrice **10**

Burundian
Ndadaye, Melchior **7**

Ntaryamira, Cyprien **8**

Cameroonian
Kotto, Yaphet **7**
Milla, Roger **2**

Canadian
Bell, Ralph S. **5**
Fuhr, Grant **1**
Johnson, Ben **1**
McKegney, Tony **3**
O'Ree, Willie **5**
Reuben, Gloria **15**
Richards, Lloyd **2**

Cape Verdean
Evora, Cesaria **12**

Chadian
Habré, Hissène **6**

Costa Rican
McDonald, Erroll **1**

Cuban
León, Tania **13**
Quirot, Ana **13**

Dominican
Charles, Mary Eugenia **10**
Sosa, Sammy **21**

Dutch
Liberia-Peters, Maria Philomena **12**

Ethiopian
Haile Selassie **7**
Meles Zenawi **3**

French
Baker, Josephine **3**
Baldwin, James **1**
Bonaly, Surya **7**
Noah, Yannick **4**
Tanner, Henry Ossawa **1**

Gabonese
Bongo, Omar **1**

Gambian
Jammeh, Yahya **23**

Ghanaian
Annan, Kofi Atta **15**
DuBois, Shirley Graham **21**
Jawara, Sir Dawda Kairaba **11**
Nkrumah, Kwame **3**
Rawlings, Jerry **9**
Rawlings, Nana Konadu Agyeman **13**

Guinea-Bissauan
Vieira, Joao **14**

Guinean
Conté, Lansana **7**
Touré, Sekou **6**

Guyanese
Beaton, Norman **14**
Jagan, Cheddi **16**

Haitian
Aristide, Jean-Bertrand **6**
Auguste, Rose-Anne **13**
Charlemagne, Manno **11**
Christophe, Henri **9**
Danticat, Edwidge **15**
Jean, Wyclef **20**
Pascal-Trouillot, Ertha **3**
Pierre, Andre **17**

Italian
Esposito, Giancarlo **9**

Ivorian
Bedie, Henri Konan **21**
Houphouët-Boigny, Félix **4**

Jamaican
Ashley, Maurice **15**
Belafonte, Harry **4**
Ewing, Patrick A. **17**
Fagan, Garth **18**
Garvey, Marcus **1**
Johnson, Ben **1**
Marley, Bob **5**
McKay, Claude **6**
Morrison, Keith **13**
Patterson, Orlando **4**
Patterson, P. J. **6, 20**
Perry, Ruth **19**
Tosh, Peter **9**

Kenyan
Kenyatta, Jomo **5**
Mazrui, Ali A. **12**
Moi, Daniel **1**

Liberian
Fuller, Solomon Carter, Jr. **15**
Perry, Ruth **15**
Sawyer, Amos **2**
Taylor, Charles **20**

Malawian
Banda, Hastings Kamuzu **6**
Muluzi, Bakili **14**

Malian
Touré, Amadou Toumani **18**

Mozambican
Chissano, Joaquim **7**
Machel, Graca Simbine **16**
Machel, Samora Moises **8**
Mutola, Maria **12**

Namibian
Mbuende, Kaire **12**
Nujoma, Samuel **10**

Nigerian
Abacha, Sani **11**
Achebe, Chinua **6**
Arinze, Francis Cardinal **19**
Azikiwe, Nnamdi **13**
Babangida, Ibrahim **4**
Fela **1**
Obasanjo, Olusegun **5, 22**
Olajuwon, Hakeem **2**
Onwueme, Tess Osonye **23**
Rotimi, Ola **1**
Sade **15**
Soyinka, Wole **4**

Puerto Rican
Schomburg, Arthur Alfonso **9**

Russian
Khanga, Yelena **6**

Rwandan
Bizimungu, Pasteur **19**
Habyarimana, Juvenal **8**

Senegalese
Diop, Cheikh Anta **4**
Diouf, Abdou **3**
Mboup, Souleymane **10**
N'Dour, Youssou **1**
Sané, Pierre Gabriel **21**
Sembène, Ousmane **13**
Senghor, Léopold Sédar **12**

Sierra Leonean
Kabbah, Ahmad Tejan **23**

Somali
Ali Mahdi Mohamed **5**
Iman **4**

South African
Biko, Steven **4**
Buthelezi, Mangosuthu Gatsha **9**
Hani, Chris **6**
Luthuli, Albert **13**
Mabuza, Lindiwe **18**
Makeba, Miriam **2**
Mandela, Nelson **1, 14**
Mandela, Winnie **2**
Masekela, Barbara **18**
Masekela, Hugh **1**
Mathabane, Mark **5**
Mbeki, Thabo Mvuyelwa **14**
Nyanda, Siphiwe **21**
Nzo, Alfred **15**
Ramaphosa, Cyril **3**
Sisulu, Sheila Violet Makate **24**
Thugwane, Josia **21**
Tutu, Desmond **6**

Sudanese
Bol, Manute **1**
Wek, Alek **18**

Tanzanian
Mkapa, Benjamin **16**
Mongella, Gertrude **11**
Mwinyi, Ali Hassan **1**
Nyerere, Julius **5**
Rugambwa, Laurean **20**

Togolese
Eyadéma, Gnassingbé **7**
Soglo, Nicéphore **15**

Trinidadian
Carmichael, Stokely **5**
Guy, Rosa **5**
Primus, Pearl **6**

Ugandan
Museveni, Yoweri **4**

Upper Voltan
Sankara, Thomas **17**

West Indian
Innis, Roy **5**
Kincaid, Jamaica **4**
Staupers, Mabel K. **7**
Pitt, David Thomas **10**
Taylor, Susan L. **10**
Walcott, Derek **5**

Zairean
Kabila, Laurent **20**
Mobutu Sese Seko **1**
Mutombo, Dikembe **7**
Ongala, Remmy **9**

Zambian
Kaunda, Kenneth **2**

Zimbabwean
Mugabe, Robert Gabriel **10**
Chideya, Farai **14**
Nkomo, Joshua **4**

Cumulative Occupation Index

Volume numbers appear in **bold**.

Art and design
Allen, Tina **22**
Andrews, Benny **22**
Andrews, Bert **13**
Armstrong, Robb **15**
Bailey, Radcliffe **19**
Bailey, Xenobia **11**
Barboza, Anthony **10**
Barnes, Ernie **16**
Barthe, Richmond **15**
Basquiat, Jean-Michel **5**
Bearden, Romare **2**
Biggers, John **20**
Brandon, Barbara **3**
Brown, Donald **19**
Burke, Selma **16**
Burroughs, Margaret Taylor **9**
Camp, Kimberly **19**
Campbell, E. Simms **13**
Catlett, Elizabeth **2**
Chase-Riboud, Barbara **20**
Cowans, Adger W. **20**
Delaney, Beauford **19**
Douglas, Aaron **7**
Driskell, David C. **7**
Edwards, Melvin **22**
Ewing, Patrick A. **17**
Feelings, Tom **11**
Gantt, Harvey **1**
Gilliam, Sam **16**
Golden, Thelma **10**
Guyton, Tyree **9**
Harkless, Necia Desiree **19**
Harrington, Oliver W. **9**
Hayden, Palmer **13**
Hope, John **8**
Hudson, Cheryl **15**
Hudson, Wade **15**
Hunt, Richard **6**
Hutson, Jean Blackwell **16**
John, Daymond **23**
Johnson, William Henry **3**
Jones, Lois Mailou **13**
Kitt, Sandra **23**
Lawrence, Jacob **4**
Lee, Annie Francis **22**
Lee-Smith, Hughie **5, 22**
Lewis, Edmonia **10**
McGee, Charles **10**
Mitchell, Corinne **8**
Morrison, Keith **13**
Moutoussamy-Ashe, Jeanne **7**
N'Namdi, George R. **17**
Pierre, Andre **17**
Pinkney, Jerry **15**
Pippin, Horace **9**
Porter, James A. **11**
Ringgold, Faith **4**
Saar, Alison **16**
Saint James, Synthia **12**
Sanders, Joseph R., Jr. **11**
Savage, Augusta **12**
Serrano, Andres **3**
Shabazz, Attallah **6**
Simpson, Lorna **4**
Sleet, Moneta, Jr. **5**
Tanner, Henry Ossawa **1**
Thomas, Alma **14**
Tolliver, William **9**
VanDerZee, James **6**
Walker, A'lelia **14**
Walker, Kara **16**
Wells, James Lesesne **10**
Williams, Billy Dee **8**
Williams, O. S. **13**
Williams, Paul R. **9**
Williams, William T. **11**
Woodruff, Hale **9**

Business
Abdul-Jabbar, Kareem **8**
Ailey, Alvin **8**
Al-Amin, Jamil Abdullah **6**
Alexander, Archie Alphonso **14**
Allen, Byron **24**
Amos, Wally **9**
Avant, Clarence **19**
Baker, Dusty **8**
Baker, Ella **5**
Baker, Gwendolyn Calvert **9**
Banks, Jeffrey **17**
Banks, William **11**
Barden, Don H. **9, 20**
Barrett, Andrew C. **12**
Bennett, Lerone, Jr. **5**
Bing, Dave **3**
Borders, James **9**
Boston, Lloyd **24**
Boyd, John W., Jr. **20**
Boyd, T. B., III **6**
Brimmer, Andrew F. **2**
Brown, Les **5**
Brown, Marie Dutton **12**
Brunson, Dorothy **1**
Burrell, Thomas J. **21**
Burroughs, Margaret Taylor **9**
Busby, Jheryl **3**
Cain, Herman **15**
CasSelle, Malcolm **11**
Chamberlain, Wilt **18**
Chapman, Jr., Nathan A. **21**
Chappell, Emma **18**
Chenault, Kenneth I. **4**
Clark, Celeste **15**
Clark, Patrick **14**
Clay, William Lacy **8**
Clayton, Xernona **3**
Cobbs, Price M. **9**
Colbert, Virgis William **17**
Coleman, Donald A. **24**
Connerly, Ward **14**
Conyers, Nathan G. **24**
Cornelius, Don **4**
Cosby, Bill **7**
Cottrell, Comer **11**
Daniels-Carter, Valerie **23**
Davis, Ed **24**
Delany, Bessie **12**
Delany, Sadie **12**
Divine, Father **7**
Dre, Dr. **14**
Driver, David E. **11**
Ducksworth, Marilyn **12**
Edelin, Ramona Hoage **19**
Edmonds, Tracey **16**
Elder, Lee **6**
Ellington, E. David **11**
Evans, Darryl **22**
Evers, Myrlie **8**
Farmer, Forest J. **1**
Farr, Mel Sr. **24**
Farrakhan, Louis **15**
Fauntroy, Walter E. **11**
Fletcher, Alphonse, Jr. **16**
Franklin, Hardy R. **9**
Friday, Jeff **24**
Fudge, Ann **11**
Fuller, S. B. **13**
Gaston, Arthur G. **4**
Gibson, Kenneth Allen **6**
Goldsberry, Ronald **18**
Gordon, Pamela **17**
Gordy, Berry, Jr. **1**

Goss, Tom 23
Graham, Stedman 13
Graves, Earl G. 1
Griffith, Mark Winston 8
Hale, Lorraine 8
Hamer, Fannie Lou 6
Hammer, M. C. 20
Handy, W. C. 8
Hannah, Marc 10
Hardison, Bethann 12
Harrell, Andre 9
Harris, Alice 7
Harris, E. Lynn 12
Harris, Monica 18
Harvey, Steve 18
Hawkins, La-Van 17
Henderson, Gordon 5
Henry, Lenny 9
Hightower, Dennis F. 13
Hill, Bonnie Guiton 20
Hill, Calvin 19
Hill, Janet 19
Hill, Jessie, Jr. 13
Holland, Robert, Jr. 11
Holmes, Larry 20
Houston, Whitney 7
Hudlin, Reginald 9
Hudlin, Warrington 9
Hudson, Cheryl 15
Hudson, Wade 15
Huggins, Larry 21
Ice Cube 8
Jackson, George 19
Jackson, Mannie 14
Jackson, Michael 19
James, Juanita 13
John, Daymond 23
Johnson, Eddie Bernice 8
Johnson, John H. 3
Johnson, Robert L. 3
Jones, Bobby 20
Jones, Carl 7
Jones, Ingrid Saunders 18
Jones, Quincy 8
Jordan, Michael 6, 21
Jordan, Montell 23
Julian, Percy Lavon 6
Kelly, Patrick 3
Kimbro, Dennis 10
King, Dexter 10
King, Don 14
Knight, Suge 11
Lane, Vincent 5
Langhart, Janet 19
Lawless, Theodore K. 8
Lawson, Jennifer 1
Leary, Kathryn D. 10
Leavell, Dorothy R. 17
Lee, Annie Francis 22
Leonard, Sugar Ray 15
Lewellyn, J. Bruce 13
Lewis, Byron E. 13
Lewis, Delano 7
Lewis, Edward T. 21
Lewis, Reginald F. 6
Lott, Ronnie 9
Louis, Errol T. 8
Lucas, John 7

Madhubuti, Haki R. 7
Malone, Annie 13
Marshall, Bella 22
Massenburg, Kedar 23
Master P 21
Maynard, Robert C. 7
McCabe, Jewell Jackson 10
McCoy, Elijah 8
McDonald, Erroll 1
Micheaux, Oscar 7
Morgan, Garrett 1
Morgan, Joe Leonard 9
Morgan, Rose 11
Nanula, Richard D. 20
Nichols, Nichelle 11
Parks, Gordon 1
Parsons, Richard Dean 11
Payton, Walter 11
Peck, Carolyn 23
Perez, Anna 1
Pleasant, Mary Ellen 9
Powell, Maxine 8
Price, Frederick K.C. 21
Price, Hugh B. 9
Procope, Ernesta 23
Queen Latifah 1, 16
Ralph, Sheryl Lee 18
Rand, A. Barry 6
Reeves, Rachel J. 23
Rhone, Sylvia 2
Rice, Linda Johnson 9
Rice, Norm 8
Richie, Leroy C. 18
Roberts, Roy S. 14
Robeson, Eslanda Goode 13
Robinson, Jackie 6
Robinson, Rachel 16
Robinson, Randall 7
Roche, Joyce M. 17
Rodgers, Johnathan 6
Rogers, John W., Jr. 5
Ross, Diana 8
Russell, Bill 8
Russell, Herman Jerome 17
Russell-McCloud, Patricia 17
Saint James, Synthia 12
Samara, Noah 15
Sanders, Dori 8
Sengstacke, John 18
Simmons, Russell 1
Sinbad, 1, 16
Smith, Barbara 11
Smith, Clarence O. 21
Smith, Jane E. 24
Smith, Joshua 10
Smith, Willi 8
Sneed, Paula A. 18
Spaulding, Charles Clinton 9
Stewart, Paul Wilbur 12
Sullivan, Leon H. 3
Taylor, Kristin Clark 8
Taylor, Susan L. 10
Terrell, Dorothy A. 24
Thomas, Franklin A. 5
Thomas, Isiah 7
Tribble, Israel, Jr. 8
Trotter, Monroe 9
Utendahl, John 23

Van Peebles, Melvin 7
VanDerZee, James 6
Walker, A'lelia 14
Walker, Cedric "Ricky" 19
Walker, Madame C. J. 7
Walker, Maggie Lena 17
Walker, T. J. 7
Ward, Lloyd 2
Washington, Val 12
Wasow, Omar 15
Watkins, Walter C. Jr, 24
Wattleton, Faye 9
Wek, Alek 18
Wells-Barnett, Ida B. 8
Wharton, Clifton R., Jr. 7
White, Walter F. 4
Wiley, Ralph 8
Williams, O. S. 13
Williams, Paul R. 9
Williams, Walter E. 4
Wilson, Phill 9
Wilson, Sunnie 7
Winfrey, Oprah 2, 15
Woodson, Robert L. 10
Yoba, Malik 11

Dance
Ailey, Alvin 8
Allen, Debbie 13
Baker, Josephine 3
Bates, Peg Leg 14
Beals, Jennifer 12
Byrd, Donald 10
Clarke, Hope 14
Davis, Sammy Jr. 18
Dove, Ulysses 5
Dunham, Katherine 4
Fagan, Garth 18
Glover, Savion 14
Guy, Jasmine 2
Hammer, M. C. 20
Hines, Gregory 1
Horne, Lena 5
Jackson, Michael 19
Jamison, Judith 7
Johnson, Virginia 9
Jones, Bill T. 1
McQueen, Butterfly 6
Miller, Bebe 3
Mills, Florence 22
Mitchell, Arthur 2
Moten, Etta 18
Muse, Clarence Edouard 21
Nicholas, Fayard 20
Nicholas, Harold 20
Nichols, Nichelle 11
Powell, Maxine 8
Primus, Pearl 6
Ribeiro, Alfonso, 17
Robinson, Bill "Bojangles" 11
Rolle, Esther 13, 21
Vereen, Ben 4
Walker, Cedric "Ricky" 19
Washington, Fredi 10
Williams, Vanessa L. 4, 17

Education
Achebe, Chinua 6

Cumulative Occupation Index

Adkins, Rutherford H. **21**
Alexander, Margaret Walker **22**
Archer, Dennis **7**
Aristide, Jean-Bertrand **6**
Asante, Molefi Kete **3**
Baker, Gwendolyn Calvert **9**
Baker, Houston A., Jr. **6**
Bambara, Toni Cade **10**
Baraka, Amiri **1**
Barboza, Anthony **10**
Bell, Derrick **6**
Berry, Bertice **8**
Berry, Mary Frances **7**
Bethune, Mary McLeod **4**
Biggers, John **20**
Black, Keith Lanier **18**
Bluitt, Juliann S. **14**
Bosley, Freeman, Jr. **7**
Boyd, T. B., III **6**
Brooks, Avery **9**
Brown, Sterling **10**
Brown, Wesley **23**
Burke, Selma **16**
Burroughs, Margaret Taylor **9**
Burton, LeVar **8**
Butler, Paul D. **17**
Callender, Clive O. **3**
Campbell, Bebe Moore **6, 24**
Cannon, Katie **10**
Carver, George Washington **4**
Cary, Lorene **3**
Catlett, Elizabeth **2**
Clark, Joe **1**
Clark, Kenneth B. **5**
Clark, Septima **7**
Clarke, John Henrik **20**
Clayton, Constance **1**
Clements, George **2**
Clifton, Lucille **14**
Cobbs, Price M. **9**
Cohen, Anthony **15**
Cole, Johnnetta B. **5**
Collins, Marva **3**
Comer, James P. **6**
Cone, James H. **3**
Cook, Samuel DuBois **14**
Cook, Toni **23**
Cooper, Anna Julia **20**
Cooper, Edward S. **6**
Cosby, Bill **7**
Cottrell, Comer **11**
Crew, Rudolph F. **16**
Cross, Dolores E. **23**
Crouch, Stanley **11**
Cullen, Countee **8**
Davis, Allison **12**
Davis, Angela **5**
Days, Drew S., III **10**
Delany, Sadie **12**
Delany, Samuel R., Jr. **9**
Dickens, Helen Octavia **14**
Diop, Cheikh Anta **4**
Dixon, Margaret **14**
Dodson, Howard, Jr. **7**
Douglas, Aaron **7**
Dove, Rita **6**
Dove, Ulysses **5**
Draper, Sharon M. **16**

Driskell, David C. **7**
Dyson, Michael Eric **11**
Early, Gerald **15**
Edelin, Ramona Hoage **19**
Edelman, Marian Wright **5**
Edley, Christopher **2**
Edwards, Harry **2**
Elders, Joycelyn **6**
Ellison, Ralph **7**
Fauset, Jessie **7**
Favors, Steve **23**
Franklin, John Hope **5**
Franklin, Robert M. **13**
Frazier, E. Franklin **10**
Freeman, Al, Jr. **11**
Fuller, Solomon Carter, Jr. **15**
Gaines, Ernest J. **7**
Gates, Henry Louis, Jr. **3**
Gates, Sylvester James, Jr. **15**
Giddings, Paula **11**
Giovanni, Nikki **9**
Golden, Marita **19**
Gomes, Peter J. **15**
Greenfield, Eloise **9**
Guinier, Lani **7**
Guy-Sheftall, Beverly **13**
Hale, Lorraine **8**
Handy, W. C. **8**
Hansberry, William Leo **11**
Harkless, Necia Desiree **19**
Harris, Alice **7**
Harris, Jay T. **19**
Harris, Patricia Roberts **2**
Harsh, Vivian Gordon **14**
Hayden, Robert **12**
Haynes, George Edmund **8**
Herenton, Willie W. **24**
Hill, Anita **5**
Hill, Bonnie Guiton **20**
Hine, Darlene Clark **24**
Hinton, William Augustus **8**
Holland, Endesha Ida Mae **3**
hooks, bell **5**
Hope, John **8**
Houston, Charles Hamilton **4**
Hrabowski, Freeman A. III **22**
Humphries, Frederick **20**
Hunt, Richard **6**
Hutson, Jean Blackwell **16**
Jarvis, Charlene Drew **21**
Jeffries, Leonard **8**
Jenifer, Franklyn G. **2**
Jenkins, Ella **15**
Johnson, Hazel **22**
Johnson, James Weldon **5**
Jones, Bobby **20**
Jones, Ingrid Saunders **18**
Jones, Lois Mailou **13**
Joplin, Scott **6**
Jordan, Barbara **4**
Jordan, June **7**
Josey, E. J. **10**
Just, Ernest Everett **3**
Karenga, Maulana **10**
Keith, Damon J. **16**
Kennedy, Florynce **12**
Kilpatrick, Carolyn Cheeks **16**
Kimbro, Dennis **10**

Komunyakaa, Yusef **9**
Kunjufu, Jawanza **3**
Lawrence, Jacob **4**
Lawrence-Lightfoot, Sara **10**
Lee, Annie Francis **22**
Leffall, LaSalle, Jr. **3**
Lester, Julius **9**
Lewis, David Levering **9**
Lewis, Shirley A. R. **14**
Lewis, Thomas **19**
Liberia-Peters, Maria Philomena **12**
Locke, Alain **10**
Lorde, Audre **6**
Lyttle, Hulda Margaret **14**
Madhubuti, Haki R. **7**
Major, Clarence **9**
Manley, Audrey Forbes **16**
Marable, Manning **10**
Marsalis, Wynton **16**
Marshall, Paule **7**
Masekela, Barbara **18**
Massey, Walter E. **5**
Maynard, Robert C. **7**
Maynor, Dorothy **19**
Mays, Benjamin E. **7**
McCarty, Oseola **16**
McKay, Nellie Yvonne **17**
McMillan, Terry **4, 17**
Meek, Carrie **6**
Meredith, James H. **11**
Millender-McDonald, Juanita **21**
Mitchell, Corinne **8**
Mongella, Gertrude **11**
Moore, Melba **21**
Morrison, Keith **13**
Morrison, Toni **15**
Moses, Robert Parris **11**
N'Namdi, George R. **17**
Norman, Maidie **20**
Norton, Eleanor Holmes **7**
Ogletree, Jr., Charles **12**
Onwueme, Tess Osonye **23**
Owens, Major **6**
Page, Alan **7**
Painter, Nell Irvin **24**
Patterson, Frederick Douglass **12**
Patterson, Orlando **4**
Payton, Benjamin F. **23**
Porter, James A. **11**
Poussaint, Alvin F. **5**
Price, Glenda **22**
Primus, Pearl **6**
Quarles, Benjamin Arthur **18**
Reagon, Bernice Johnson **7**
Reddick, Lawrence Dunbar **20**
Redmond, Eugene **23**
Reid, Irvin D. **20**
Ringgold, Faith **4**
Robinson, Sharon **22**
Robinson, Spottswood **22**
Russell-McCloud, Patricia **17**
Satcher, David **7**
Schomburg, Arthur Alfonso **9**
Shabazz, Betty **7**
Shange, Ntozake **8**
Shipp, E. R. **15**
Simmons, Ruth J. **13**
Sinkford, Jeanne C. **13**

Sisulu, Sheila Violet Makate 24
Smith, Anna Deavere 6
Smith, John L. 22
Smith, Tubby 18
Soyinka, Wole 4
Spikes, Dolores 18
Stanford, John 20
Steele, Claude Mason 13
Steele, Shelby 13
Stephens, Charlotte Andrews 14
Stewart, Maria W. Miller 19
Stone, Chuck 9
Sudarkasa, Niara 4
Sullivan, Louis 8
Swygert, H. Patrick 22
Taylor, Susie King 13
Terrell, Mary Church 9
Thomas, Alma 14
Thurman, Howard 3
Tribble, Israel, Jr. 8
Tucker, Rosina 14
Turnbull, Walter 13
Tutu, Desmond 6
Tyson, Neil de Grasse 15
Usry, James L. 23
Walcott, Derek 5
Wallace, Michele Faith 13
Wallace, Phyllis A. 9
Washington, Booker T. 4
Watkins, Shirley R. 17
Wattleton, Faye 9
Wells, James Lesesne 10
Wells-Barnett, Ida B. 8
Welsing, Frances Cress 5
Wesley, Dorothy Porter 19
West, Cornel 5
Wharton, Clifton R., Jr. 7
White, Lois Jean 20
Wilkins, Roger 2
Williams, Gregory 11
Williams, Patricia J. 11
Williams, Walter E. 4
Wilson, William Julius 22
Woodruff, Hale 9
Woodson, Carter G. 2
Worrill, Conrad 12
Young, Jean Childs 14

Fashion
Banks, Jeffrey 17
Banks, Tyra 11
Beals, Jennifer 12
Beckford, Tyson 11
Berry, Halle **4, 19**
Bailey, Xenobia 11
Barboza, Anthony 10
Campbell, Naomi 1
Davidson, Jaye 5
Henderson, Gordon 5
Iman 4
John, Daymond 23
Johnson, Beverly 2
Jones, Carl 7
Kani, Karl 10
Kelly, Patrick 3
Powell, Maxine 8
Robinson, Patrick 19
Rochon, Lela 16

Rowell, Victoria 13
Smaltz, Audrey 12
Smith, Barbara 11
Smith, Willi 8
Walker, T. J. 7
Webb, Veronica 10
Wek, Alek 18

Film
Amos, John 8
Baker, Josephine 3
Banks, Tyra 11
Bassett, Angela **6, 23**
Beals, Jennifer 12
Belafonte, Harry 4
Bellamy, Bill 12
Berry, Halle **4, 19**
Braugher, Andre 13
Brown, Jim 11
Brown, Tony 3
Burnett, Charles 16
Byrd, Michelle 19
Byrd, Robert 11
Calloway, Cab 14
Campbell, Naomi 1
Campbell, Tisha 8
Carroll, Diahann 9
Carson, Lisa Nicole 21
Cheadle, Don 19
Clash, Kevin 14
Cosby, Bill 7
Crothers, Scatman 19
Curry, Mark 17
Curtis-Hall, Vondie 17
Dandridge, Dorothy 3
Dash, Julie 4
Davidson, Jaye 5
Davidson, Tommy 21
Davis, Ossie 5
Davis, Sammy, Jr. 18
Dee, Ruby 8
Devine, Loretta 24
Dickerson, Ernest **6, 17**
Dr. Dre 10
Driskell, David C. 7
Duke, Bill 3
Dunham, Katherine 4
Dutton, Charles S. **4, 22**
Epps, Omar 23
Esposito, Giancarlo 9
Evans, Darryl 22
Everett, Francine 23
Fishburne, Larry 4
Fox, Vivica A. 15
Foxx, Jamie 15
Foxx, Redd 2
Franklin, Carl 11
Freeman, Al, Jr. 11
Freeman, Morgan **2, 20**
Friday, Jeff 24
Fuller, Charles 8
George, Nelson 12
Givens, Robin 4
Glover, Danny **1, 24**
Glover, Savion 14
Goldberg, Whoopi 4
Gooding, Cuba, Jr. 16
Gordy, Berry, Jr. 1

Gossett, Louis, Jr. 7
Gray, F. Gary 14
Grier, Pam 9
Guillaume, Robert 3
Gunn, Moses 10
Guy, Jasmine 2
Hampton, Henry 6
Hardison, Kadeem 22
Harris, Leslie 6
Harris, Robin 7
Hayes, Isaac 20
Hemsley, Sherman 19
Henry, Lenny 9
Hill, Lauryn 20
Hines, Gregory 1
Horne, Lena 5
Hounsou, Djimon 19
Houston, Whitney 7
Hudlin, Reginald 9
Hudlin, Warrington 9
Hughes, Albert 7
Hughes, Allen 7
Ice Cube 8
Iman 4
Ingram, Rex 5
Jackson, George 19
Jackson, Janet 6
Jackson, Samuel L. **8, 19**
Jean-Baptiste, Marianne 17
Johnson, Beverly 2
Jones, James Earl 3
Jones, Quincy 8
Julien, Isaac 3
King, Regina 22
Kirby, George 14
Kitt, Eartha 16
Kotto, Yaphet 7
Kunjufu, Jawanza 3
L. L. Cool J 16
La Salle, Eriq 12
LaBelle, Patti 13
Lane, Charles 3
Lawrence, Martin 6
Lee, Joie 1
Lee, Spike **5, 19**
Lemmons, Kasi 20
Lincoln, Abbey 3
Lindo, Delroy 18
Long, Nia 17
Love, Darlene 23
Lover, Ed 10
Mabley, Jackie "Moms" 15
Master P 21
McDaniel, Hattie 5
McKee, Lonette 12
McQueen, Butterfly 6
Micheaux, Oscar 7
Moore, Melba 21
Moore, Shemar 21
Morton, Joe 18
Moses, Gilbert 12
Moss, Carlton 17
Murphy, Eddie **4, 20**
Muse, Clarence Edouard 21
Nicholas, Fayard 20
Nicholas, Harold 20
Nichols, Nichelle 11
Norman, Maidie 20

Cumulative Occupation Index

Parks, Gordon **1**
Payne, Allen **13**
Pinkett, Jada **10**
Poitier, Sidney **11**
Prince **18**
Pryor, Richard **3**
Queen Latifah **1, 16**
Ralph, Sheryl Lee **18**
Randle, Theresa **16**
Reese, Della **6, 20**
Reuben, Gloria **15**
Rhames, Ving **14**
Riggs, Marlon **5**
Rochon, Lela **16**
Rock, Chris **3, 22**
Rolle, Esther **13, 21**
Rollins, Howard E., Jr. **16**
Ross, Diana **8**
Rowell, Victoria **13**
Rupaul **17**
Schultz, Michael A. **6**
Seal **14**
Sembène, Ousmane **13**
Shakur, Tupac **14**
Simpson, O. J. **15**
Sinbad **1, 16**
Singleton, John **2**
Smith, Anna Deavere **6**
Smith, Roger Guenveur **12**
Smith, Will **8, 18**
Snipes, Wesley **3, 24**
St. Jacques, Raymond **8**
Tate, Larenz **15**
Taylor, Meshach **4**
Taylor, Regina **9**
Thigpen, Lynne **17**
Thurman, Wallace **16**
Tillman, George, Jr. **20**
Townsend, Robert **4, 23**
Tucker, Chris **13, 23**
Turner, Tina **6**
Tyson, Cicely **7**
Uggams, Leslie **23**
Underwood, Blair **7**
Usher **23**
Van Peebles, Mario **2**
Van Peebles, Melvin **7**
Vance, Courtney B. **15**
Vereen, Ben **4**
Warfield, Marsha **2**
Warner, Malcolm-Jamal **22**
Warwick, Dionne **18**
Washington, Denzel **1, 16**
Washington, Fredi **10**
Waters, Ethel **7**
Wayans, Damon **8**
Wayans, Keenen Ivory **18**
Weathers, Carl **10**
Webb, Veronica **10**
Whitaker, Forest **2**
Whitfield, Lynn **18**
Williams, Billy Dee **8**
Williams, Samm-Art **21**
Williams, Vanessa L. **4, 17**
Williamson, Mykelti **22**
Winfield, Paul **2**
Winfrey, Oprah **2, 15**
Woodard, Alfre **9**

Yoba, Malik **11**

Government and politics–international
Abacha, Sani **11**
Abbott, Diane **9**
Achebe, Chinua **6**
Ali Mahdi Mohamed **5**
Annan, Kofi Atta **15**
Aristide, Jean-Bertrand **6**
Azikiwe, Nnamdi **13**
Babangida, Ibrahim **4**
Baker, Gwendolyn Calvert **9**
Banda, Hastings Kamuzu **6**
Bedie, Henri Konan **21**
Berry, Mary Frances **7**
Biko, Steven **4**
Bizimungu, Pasteur **19**
Bongo, Omar **1**
Bunche, Ralph J. **5**
Buthelezi, Mangosuthu Gatsha **9**
Charlemagne, Manno **11**
Charles, Mary Eugenia **10**
Chissano, Joaquim **7**
Christophe, Henri **9**
Conté, Lansana **7**
da Silva, Benedita **5**
Diop, Cheikh Anta **4**
Diouf, Abdou **3**
Eyadéma, Gnassingbé **7**
Fela **1**
Gordon, Pamela **17**
Habré, Hissène **6**
Habyarimana, Juvenal **8**
Haile Selassie **7**
Haley, George Williford Boyce **21**
Hani, Chris **6**
Houphouët-Boigny, Félix **4**
Ingraham, Hubert A. **19**
Jagan, Cheddi **16**
Jammeh, Yahya **23**
Jawara, Sir Dawda Kairaba **11**
Kabbah, Ahmad Tejan **23**
Kabila, Laurent **20**
Kabunda, Kenneth **2**
Kenyatta, Jomo **5**
Kerekou, Ahmed (Mathieu) **1**
Liberia-Peters, Maria Philomena **12**
Luthuli, Albert **13**
Mabuza, Lindiwe **18**
Machel, Samora Moises **8**
Mandela, Nelson **1, 14**
Mandela, Winnie **2**
Masekela, Barbara **18**
Masire, Quett **5**
Mbeki, Thabo Mvuyelwa **14**
Mbuende, Kaire **12**
Meles Zenawi **3**
Mkapa, Benjamin **16**
Mobutu Sese Seko **1**
Mogae, Festus Gontebanye **19**
Moi, Daniel **1**
Mongella, Gertrude **11**
Mugabe, Robert Gabriel **10**
Muluzi, Bakili **14**
Museveni, Yoweri **4**
Mwinyi, Ali Hassan **1**
Ndadaye, Melchior **7**

Nkomo, Joshua **4**
Nkrumah, Kwame **3**
Ntaryamira, Cyprien **8**
Nujoma, Samuel **10**
Nyanda, Siphiwe **21**
Nyerere, Julius **5**
Nzo, Alfred **15**
Obasanjo, Olusegun **5, 22**
Pascal-Trouillot, Ertha **3**
Patterson, P. J. **6, 20**
Perkins, Edward **5**
Perry, Ruth **15**
Pitt, David Thomas **10**
Pitta, Celso **17**
Ramaphosa, Cyril **3**
Rawlings, Jerry **9**
Rawlings, Nana Konadu Agyeman **13**
Rice, Condoleezza **3**
Robinson, Randall **7**
Sampson, Edith S. **4**
Sankara, Thomas **17**
Savimbi, Jonas **2**
Sawyer, Amos **2**
Senghor, Léopold Sédar **12**
Smith, Jennifer **21**
Soglo, Nicephore **15**
Soyinka, Wole **4**
Taylor, Charles **20**
Taylor, John (David Beckett) **16**
Toure, Amadou Toumani **18**
Touré, Sekou **6**
Tutu, Desmond **6**
Vieira, Joao **14**
Wharton, Clifton R., Jr. **7**

Government and politics–U.S.
Adams, Floyd, Jr. **12**
Alexander, Archie Alphonso **14**
Ali, Muhammad **2, 16**
Allen, Ethel D. **13**
Archer, Dennis **7**
Arrington, Richard **24**
Avant, Clarence **19**
Baker, Thurbert **22**
Barden, Don H. **9, 20**
Barrett, Andrew C. **12**
Barry, Marion S. **7**
Belton, Sharon Sayles **9, 16**
Berry, Mary Frances **7**
Bethune, Mary McLeod **4**
Blackwell, Unita **17**
Bond, Julian **2**
Bosley, Freeman, Jr. **7**
Boykin, Keith **14**
Bradley, Thomas **2**
Braun, Carol Moseley **4**
Brimmer, Andrew F. **2**
Brooke, Edward **8**
Brown, Corrine **24**
Brown, Elaine **8**
Brown, Jesse **6**
Brown, Lee Patrick **24**
Brown, Les **5**
Brown, Ron **5**
Brown, Willie L., Jr. **7**
Bryant, Wayne R. **6**
Buckley, Victoria (Vicki) **24**

Bunche, Ralph J. **5**
Burris, Chuck **21**
Caesar, Shirley **19**
Campbell, Bill **9**
Carson, Julia **23**
Chavis, Benjamin **6**
Chisholm, Shirley **2**
Christian-Green, Donna M. **17**
Clay, William Lacy **8**
Clayton, Eva M. **20**
Cleaver, Eldridge **5**
Cleaver, Emanuel **4**
Clyburn, James **21**
Collins, Barbara-Rose **7**
Collins, Cardiss **10**
Connerly, Ward **14**
Conyers, John, Jr. **4**
Cose, Ellis **5**
Crockett, George, Jr. **10**
Cummings, Elijah E. **24**
Cunningham, Evelyn **23**
Currie, Betty **21**
Davis, Angela **5**
Davis, Benjamin O., Jr. **2**
Davis, Benjamin O., Sr. **4**
Davis, Danny K. **24**
Days, Drew S., III **10**
Dellums, Ronald **2**
Diggs, Charles R. **21**
Dinkins, David **4**
Dixon, Julian C. **24**
Dixon, Sharon Pratt **1**
Du Bois, W. E. B. **3**
Edmonds, Terry **17**
Elders, Joycelyn **6**
Espy, Mike **6**
Farmer, James **2**
Farrakhan, Louis **2**
Fattah, Chaka **11**
Fauntroy, Walter E. **11**
Fields, Cleo **13**
Flake, Floyd H. **18**
Flipper, Henry O. **3**
Fortune, T. Thomas **6**
Franks, Gary **2**
Fulani, Lenora **11**
Gantt, Harvey **1**
Garvey, Marcus **1**
Gibson, Johnnie Mae **23**
Gibson, Kenneth Allen **6**
Gibson, William F. **6**
Goode, W. Wilson **4**
Gravely, Samuel L., Jr. **5**
Gray, William H., III **3**
Grimké, Archibald H. **9**
Guinier, Lani **7**
Haley, George Williford Boyce **21**
Hamer, Fannie Lou **6**
Harris, Alice **7**
Harris, Patricia Roberts **2**
Harvard, Beverly **11**
Hastie, William H. **8**
Hastings, Alcee L. **16**
Hayes, James C. **10**
Henry, Aaron **19**
Herenton, Willie W. **24**
Herman, Alexis M. **15**
Hernandez, Aileen Clarke **13**

Hill, Bonnie Guiton **20**
Hilliard, Earl F. **24**
Holder, Eric H., Jr. **9**
Irving, Larry, Jr. **12**
Jackson, George **14**
Jackson, Jesse **1**
Jackson, Jesse, Jr. **14**
Jackson Lee, Sheila **20**
Jackson, Maynard **2**
Jackson, Shirley Ann **12**
Jacob, John E. **2**
James, Sharpe **23**
Jarvis, Charlene Drew **21**
Johnson, Eddie Bernice **8**
Johnson, Harvey Jr. **24**
Johnson, James Weldon **5**
Johnson, Norma L. Holloway **17**
Johnson, Robert T. **17**
Jones, Elaine R. **7**
Jordan, Barbara **4**
Kennard, William Earl **18**
Keyes, Alan L. **11**
Kilpatrick, Carolyn Cheeks **16**
King, Martin Luther, III **20**
Kirk, Ron **11**
Lafontant, Jewel Stradford **3**
Leland, Mickey **2**
Lewis, Delano **7**
Lewis, John **2**
Mallett, Conrad, Jr. **16**
Marshall, Bella **22**
Marshall, Thurgood **1**
Martin, Louis E. **16**
McKinney, Cynthia Ann **11**
McKissick, Floyd B. **3**
Meek, Carrie **6**
Meredith, James H. **11**
Mfume, Kweisi **6**
Millender-McDonald, Juanita **21**
Morial, Marc **20**
Moses, Robert Parris **11**
Norton, Eleanor Holmes **7**
O'Leary, Hazel **6**
Owens, Major **6**
Page, Alan **7**
Patrick, Deval **12**
Payne, Donald M. **2**
Perez, Anna **1**
Perkins, Edward **5**
Pinchback, P. B. S. **9**
Powell, Adam Clayton, Jr. **3**
Powell, Colin **1**
Powell, Debra A. **23**
Raines, Franklin Delano **14**
Randolph, A. Philip **3**
Rangel, Charles **3**
Rice, Condoleezza **3**
Rice, Norm **8**
Robinson, Randall **7**
Rustin, Bayard **4**
Sampson, Edith S. **4**
Satcher, David **7**
Sayles Belton, Sharon **9**
Schmoke, Kurt **1**
Scott, Robert C. **23**
Sears-Collins, Leah J. **5**
Shakur, Assata **6**
Sharpton, Al **21**

Simpson, Carole **6**
Sisulu, Sheila Violet Makate **24**
Slater, Rodney E. **15**
Stanton, Robert **20**
Staupers, Mabel K. **7**
Stokes, Carl B. **10**
Stokes, Louis **3**
Stone, Chuck **9**
Street, John F. **24**
Sullivan, Louis **8**
Thomas, Clarence **2**
Towns, Edolphus **19**
Tribble, Israel, Jr. **8**
Tubbs Jones, Stephanie **24**
Tucker, C. DeLores **12**
Turner, Henry McNeal **5**
Usry, James L. **23**
Von Lipsey, Roderick K. **11**
Wallace, Phyllis A. **9**
Washington, Harold **6**
Washington, Val **12**
Waters, Maxine **3**
Watkins, Shirley R. **17**
Watts, J. C., Jr. **14**
Weaver, Robert C. **8**
Webb, Wellington **3**
Wharton, Clifton R., Jr. **7**
Wheat, Alan **14**
White, Jesse **22**
White, Michael R. **5**
Wilder, L. Douglas **3**
Wilkins, Roger **2**
Williams, Anthony **21**
Williams, George Washington **18**
Williams, Hosea Lorenzo **15**
Williams, Maggie **7**
Wilson, Sunnie **7**
Young, Andrew **3**

Law
Alexander, Joyce London **18**
Alexander, Sadie Tanner Mossell **22**
Archer, Dennis **7**
Banks, William **11**
Barrett, Andrew C. **12**
Baugh, David **23**
Bell, Derrick **6**
Berry, Mary Frances **7**
Bishop Jr., Sanford D. **24**
Bolin, Jane **22**
Bosley, Freeman, Jr. **7**
Boykin, Keith **14**
Bradley, Thomas **2**
Braun, Carol Moseley **4**
Brooke, Edward **8**
Brown, Lee Patrick **1, 24**
Brown, Ron **5**
Brown, Willie L., Jr. **7**
Bryant, Wayne R. **6**
Butler, Paul D. **17**
Campbell, Bill **9**
Carter, Stephen L. **4**
Chambers, Julius **3**
Cochran, Johnnie L., Jr. **11**
Conyers, John, Jr. **4**
Crockett, George, Jr. **10**
Darden, Christopher **13**
Days, Drew S., III **10**

Cumulative Occupation Index

Diggs-Taylor, Anna **20**
Dinkins, David **4**
Dixon, Sharon Pratt **1**
Edelman, Marian Wright **5**
Edley, Christopher **2**
Ellington, E. David **11**
Espy, Mike **6**
Fields, Cleo **13**
Freeman, Charles **19**
Gary, Willie E. **12**
Gibson, Johnnie Mae **23**
Glover, Nathaniel, Jr. **12**
Gomez-Preston, Cheryl **9**
Graham, Lawrence Otis **12**
Grimké, Archibald H. **9**
Guinier, Lani **7**
Haley, George Williford Boyce **21**
Hall, Elliott S. **24**
Harris, Patricia Roberts **2**
Harvard, Beverly **11**
Hastie, William H. **8**
Hastings, Alcee L. **16**
Hawkins, Steven **14**
Haywood, Margaret A. **24**
Higginbotham, A. Leon, Jr. **13**
Hill, Anita **5**
Hills, Oliver W. **24**
Holder, Eric H., Jr. **9**
Hooks, Benjamin L. **2**
Houston, Charles Hamilton **4**
Hunter, Billy **22**
Jackson Lee, Sheila **20**
Jackson, Maynard **2**
Johnson, James Weldon **5**
Johnson, Norma L. Holloway **17**
Jones, Elaine R. **7**
Jones, Star **10**
Jordan, Vernon E. **3**
Kearse, Amalya Lyle **12**
Keith, Damon J. **16**
Kennard, William Earl **18**
Kennedy, Florynce **12**
King, Bernice **4**
Kirk, Ron **11**
Lafontant, Jewel Stradford **3**
Lewis, Delano **7**
Lewis, Reginald F. **6**
Mallett, Conrad, Jr. **16**
Mandela, Nelson **1, 14**
Marshall, Thurgood **1**
McDonald, Gabrielle Kirk **20**
McDougall, Gay J. **11**
McKinnon, Isaiah **9**
McKissick, Floyd B. **3**
McPhail, Sharon **2**
Motley, Constance Baker **10**
Napoleon, Benny N. **23**
Norton, Eleanor Holmes **7**
O'Leary, Hazel **6**
Ogletree, Charles, Jr. **12**
Page, Alan **7**
Parks, Bernard C. **17**
Parsons, James **14**
Parsons, Richard Dean **11**
Pascal-Trouillot, Ertha **3**
Patrick, Deval **12**
Ramsey, Charles H. **21**
Richie, Leroy C. **18**

Robinson, Randall **7**
Russell-McCloud, Patricia **17**
Sampson, Edith S. **4**
Schmoke, Kurt **1**
Sears-Collins, Leah J. **5**
Stokes, Carl B. **10**
Stokes, Louis **3**
Stout, Juanita Kidd **24**
Taylor, John (David Beckett) **16**
Thomas, Clarence **2**
Thomas, Franklin A. **5**
Tubbs Jones, Stephaie **24**
Vanzant, Iyanla **17**
Wagner, Annice **22**
Washington, Harold **6**
Wilder, L. Douglas **3**
Wilkins, Roger **2**
Williams, Evelyn **10**
Williams, Gregory **11**
Williams, Patricia J. **11**
Williams, Willie L. **4**
Wright, Bruce McMarion **3**

Military
Abacha, Sani **11**
Adams Early, Charity **13**
Alexander, Margaret Walker **22**
Babangida, Ibrahim **4**
Bolden, Charles F., Jr. **7**
Brown, Erroll M. **23**
Brown, Jesse **6**
Bullard, Eugene **12**
Cadoria, Sherian Grace **14**
Chissano, Joaquim **7**
Christophe, Henri **9**
Conté, Lansana **7**
Davis, Benjamin O., Jr. **2**
Davis, Benjamin O., Sr. **4**
Europe, James Reese **10**
Eyadéma, Gnassingbé **7**
Flipper, Henry O. **3**
Gravely, Samuel L., Jr. **5**
Gregory, Frederick D. **8**
Habré, Hissène **6**
Habyarimana, Juvenal **8**
Harris, Marcelite Jordan **16**
James, Daniel, Jr. **16**
Johnson, Hazel **22**
Kerekou, Ahmed (Mathieu) **1**
Lawrence, Robert H., Jr. **16**
Nyanda, Siphiwe **21**
Obasanjo, Olusegun **5, 22**
Phelps, Shirelle **22**
Powell, Colin **1**
Pratt, Geronimo **18**
Rawlings, Jerry **9**
Reason, J. Paul **19**
Stanford, John **20**
Staupers, Mabel K. **7**
Stokes, Louis **3**
Touré, Amadou Toumani **18**
Vieira, Joao **14**
Von Lipsey, Roderick K. **11**
Watkins, Perry **12**
West, Togo, D., Jr. **16**

Music
Adams, Oleta **18**

Adams, Yolanda **17**
Albright, Gerald **23**
Anderson, Marian **2**
Armstrong, Louis **2**
Armstrong, Vanessa Bell **24**
Ashford, Nickolas **21**
Austin, Patti **24**
Avant, Clarence **19**
Ayers, Roy **16**
Badu, Erykah **22**
Baker, Anita **21**
Baker, Josephine **3**
Basie, Count **23**
Bechet, Sidney **18**
Belafonte, Harry **4**
Belle, Regina **1**
Blige, Mary J. **20**
Bonga, Kuenda **13**
Brandy **14**
Braxton, Toni **15**
Brooks, Avery **9**
Brown, Charles **23**
Bumbry, Grace **5**
Busby, Jheryl **3**
Caesar, Shirley **19**
Calloway, Cab **1**
Campbell, Tisha **8**
Carroll, Diahann **9**
Carter, Betty **19**
Carter, Regina **23**
Charlemagne, Manno **11**
Charles, Ray **16**
Cheatham, Doc **17**
Chuck D **9**
Clark-Sheard, Karen **22**
Cleveland, James **19**
Clinton, George **9**
Cole, Nat King **17**
Cole, Natalie Maria **17**
Collins, Albert **12**
Coltrane, John **19**
Combs, Sean "Puffy" **17**
Cooke, Sam **17**
Count Basie **23**
Crawford, Randy **19**
Crothers, Scatman **19**
Crouch, Stanley **11**
Crowder, Henry **16**
Davis, Anthony **11**
Davis, Miles **4**
Davis, Sammy, Jr. **18**
Dixon, Willie **4**
Donegan, Dorothy **19**
Dorsey, Thomas **15**
Downing, Will **19**
Dr. Dre **10**
Dre, Dr. **14**
Duke, George **21**
Dupri, Jermaine **13**
Edmonds, Kenneth "Babyface" **10**
Edmonds, Tracey **16**
Ellington, Duke **5**
Eubanks, Kevin **15**
Europe, James Reese **10**
Evans, Faith **22**
Evora, Cesaria **12**
Fats Domino **20**
Fela **1**

Fitzgerald, Ella **8, 18**
Flack, Roberta **19**
Foxx, Jamie **15**
Franklin, Aretha **11**
Franklin, Kirk **15**
Gaye, Marvin **2**
Gibson, Althea **8**
Gillespie, Dizzy **1**
Gordy, Berry, Jr. **1**
Graves, Denyce **19**
Gray, F. Gary **14**
Green, Al **13**
Hailey, JoJo **22**
Hailey, K-Ci **22**
Hammer, M. C. **20**
Hammond, Fred **23**
Hampton, Lionel **17**
Hancock, Herbie **20**
Handy, W. C. **8**
Harrell, Andre **9**
Hathaway, Donny **18**
Hawkins, Coleman **9**
Hawkins, Erskine **14**
Hawkins, Tramaine **16**
Hayes, Isaac **20**
Hayes, Roland **4**
Hendricks, Barbara **3**
Hendrix, Jimi **10**
Hill, Lauryn **20**
Hinderas, Natalie **5**
Holiday, Billie **1**
Horne, Lena **5**
House, Son **8**
Houston, Cissy **20**
Houston, Whitney **7**
Howlin' Wolf **9**
Humphrey, Bobbi **20**
Hyman, Phyllis **19**
Ice Cube **8**
Ice-T **6**
Jackson, George **19**
Jackson, Isaiah **3**
Jackson, Janet **6**
Jackson, Mahalia **5**
Jackson, Michael **19**
James, Etta **13**
James, Rick **17**
Jarreau, Al **21**
Jean, Wyclef
Jean-Baptiste, Marianne **17**
Jenkins, Ella **15**
Jimmy Jam **13**
Johnson, Beverly **2**
Johnson, James Weldon **5**
Johnson, Robert **2**
Jones, Bobby **20**
Jones, Elvin **14**
Jones, Quincy **8**
Joplin, Scott **6**
Jordan, Montell **23**
Joyner, Matilda Sissieretta **15**
Joyner, Tom **19**
Kelly, R. **18**
Kendricks, Eddie **22**
Khan, Chaka **12**
King, B. B. **7**
King, Coretta Scott **3**
Kitt, Eartha **16**

Knight, Gladys **16**
Knight, Suge **11**
Kravitz, Lenny **10**
L.L. Cool J **16**
LaBelle, Patti **13**
León, Tania **13**
Lester, Julius **9**
Levert, Gerald **22**
Lewis, Terry **13**
Lincoln, Abbey **3**
Little Richard **15**
Love, Darlene **23**
Lover, Ed **10**
Lymon, Frankie **22**
Madhubuti, Haki R. **7**
Makeba, Miriam **2**
Marley, Bob **5**
Marrow, Queen Esther **24**
Marsalis, Wynton **16**
Mase **24**
Masekela, Hugh **1**
Massenburg, Kedar **23**
Master P **21**
Mathis, Johnny **20**
Maxwell **20**
Mayfield, Curtis **2**
Maynor, Dorothy **19**
McDaniel, Hattie **5**
McKee, Lonette **12**
McKnight, Brian **18**
Mingus, Charles **15**
Monica **21**
Monk, Thelonious **1**
Moore, Melba **21**
Moses, Gilbert **12**
Moten, Etta **18**
Murphy, Eddie **4, 20**
Muse, Clarence Edouard **21**
N'Dour, Youssou **1**
Nascimento, Milton **2**
Ndegéocello, Me'Shell **15**
Neville, Aaron **21**
Nicholas, Fayard **20**
Nicholas, Harold **20**
Norman, Jessye **5**
Notorious B.I.G. **20**
O'Neal, Shaquille **8**
Ongala, Remmy **9**
Parker, Charlie **20**
Parks, Gordon **1**
Pendergrass, Teddy **22**
Peoples, Dottie **22**
Perry, Ruth **19**
Powell, Bud **24**
Powell, Maxine **8**
Price, Kelly **23**
Price, Leontyne **1**
Prince **18**
Pritchard, Robert Starling **21**
Queen Latifah **1, 16**
Ralph, Sheryl Lee **18**
Razaf, Andy **19**
Reagon, Bernice Johnson **7**
Reese, Della **6, 20**
Rhone, Sylvia **2**
Roach, Max **21**
Roberts, Marcus **19**
Robeson, Paul **2**

Robinson, Smokey **3**
Ross, Diana **8**
Rupaul **17**
Rushen, Patrice **12**
Sade **15**
Sangare, Oumou **18**
Seal **14**
Shakur, Tupac **14**
Simmons, Russell **1**
Simone, Nina **15**
Simpson, Valerie **21**
Sister Souljah **11**
Smith, Bessie **3**
Smith, Will **8, 18**
Sweat, Keith **19**
Sykes, Roosevelt **20**
Tamia **24**
Taylor, Billy **23**
Thomas, Rufus **20**
Tosh, Peter **9**
Turnbull, Walter **13**
Turner, Tina **6**
Uggams, Leslie **23**
Usher **23**
Vandross, Luther **13**
Vaughan, Sarah **13**
Vereen, Ben **4**
Walker, Albertina **10**
Walker, Cedric "Ricky" **19**
Wallace, Sippie **1**
Warwick, Dionne **18**
Washington, Dinah **22**
Washington, Grover, Jr. **17**
Waters, Ethel **7**
Watson, Johnny "Guitar" **18**
White, Barry **13**
Williams, Bert **18**
Williams, Joe **5**
Williams, Mary Lou **15**
Williams, Vanessa L. **4, 17**
Wilson, Cassandra **16**
Wilson, Nancy **10**
Wilson, Sunnie **7**
Winans, BeBe **14**
Winans, CeCe **14**
Winans, Marvin L. **17**
Winans, Vickie **24**
Wonder, Stevie **11**
Yoba, Malik **11**

Religion
Abernathy, Ralph David **1**
Adams, Yolanda **17**
Agyeman, Jaramogi Abebe **10**
Al-Amin, Jamil Abdullah **6**
Arinze, Francis Cardinal **19**
Aristide, Jean-Bertrand **6**
Armstrong, Vanessa Bell **24**
Banks, William **11**
Bell, Ralph S. **5**
Ben-Israel, Ben Ami **11**
Boyd, T. B., III **6**
Butts, Calvin O., III **9**
Caesar, Shirley **19**
Cannon, Katie **10**
Chavis, Benjamin **6**
Cleaver, Emanuel **4**
Clements, George **2**

Cumulative Occupation Index

Cleveland, James **19**
Colemon, Johnnie **11**
Cone, James H. **3**
Cook, Suzan D. Johnson **22**
Divine, Father **7**
Dyson, Michael Eric **11**
Elmore, Ronn **21**
Farrakhan, Louis **2, 15**
Fauntroy, Walter E. **11**
Flake, Floyd H. **18**
Foreman, George **15**
Franklin, Kirk **15**
Franklin, Robert M. **13**
Gomes, Peter J. **15**
Gray, William H., III **3**
Green, Al **13**
Grier, Roosevelt **13**
Haile Selassie **7**
Harris, Barbara **12**
Hawkins, Tramaine **16**
Hayes, James C. **10**
Hooks, Benjamin L. **2**
Jackson, Jesse **1**
Jakes, Thomas "T.D." **17**
Jones, Bobby **20**
King, Barbara **22**
King, Bernice **4**
King, Martin Luther, Jr. **1**
Lester, Julius **9**
Little Richard **15**
Lowery, Joseph **2**
Lyons, Henry **12**
Mays, Benjamin E. **7**
Muhammad, Elijah **4**
Muhammad, Khallid Abdul **10**
Murray, Cecil **12**
Pierre, Andre **17**
Powell, Adam Clayton, Jr. **3**
Price, Frederick K.C. **21**
Reese, Della **6, 20**
Riley, Helen Caldwell Day **13**
Rugambwa, Laurean **20**
Shabazz, Betty **7**
Sharpton, Al **21**
Somé, Malidoma Patrice **10**
Stallings, George A., Jr. **6**
Sullivan, Leon H. **3**
Thurman, Howard **3**
Turner, Henry McNeal **5**
Tutu, Desmond **6**
Vanzant, Iyanla **17**
Waddles, Charleszetta (Mother) **10**
Waters, Ethel **7**
West, Cornel **5**
White, Reggie **6**
Williams, Hosea Lorenzo **15**
Winans, BeBe **14**
Winans, CeCe **14**
Winans, Marvin L. **17**
X, Malcolm **1**
Youngblood, Johnny Ray **8**

Science and technology
Adkins, Rutherford H. **21**
Alexander, Archie Alphonso **14**
Allen, Ethel D. **13**
Auguste, Rose-Anne **13**
Banda, Hastings Kamuzu **6**
Benjamin, Regina **20**
Black, Keith Lanier **18**
Bluford, Guy **2**
Bluitt, Juliann S. **14**
Bolden, Charles F., Jr. **7**
Bullard, Eugene **12**
Callender, Clive O. **3**
Carson, Benjamin **1**
Carver, George Washington **4**
CasSelle, Malcolm **11**
Christian, Spencer **15**
Cobbs, Price M. **9**
Coleman, Bessie **9**
Comer, James P. **6**
Cooper, Edward S. **6**
Davis, Allison **12**
Delany, Bessie **12**
Dickens, Helen Octavia **14**
Diop, Cheikh Anta **4**
Drew, Charles Richard **7**
Dunham, Katherine **4**
Elders, Joycelyn **6**
Ellington, E. David **11**
Fisher, Rudolph **17**
Flipper, Henry O. **3**
Freeman, Harold P. **23**
Fulani, Lenora **11**
Fuller, Solomon Carter, Jr. **15**
Gates, Sylvester James, Jr. **15**
Gayle, Helene D. **3**
Gibson, Kenneth Allen **6**
Gibson, William F. **6**
Gregory, Frederick D. **8**
Hall, Lloyd A. **8**
Hannah, Marc **10**
Henson, Matthew **2**
Hinton, William Augustus **8**
Irving, Larry, Jr. **12**
Jackson, Shirley Ann **12**
Jawara, Sir Dawda Kairaba **11**
Jemison, Mae C. **1**
Jenifer, Franklyn G. **2**
Johnson, Eddie Bernice **8**
Julian, Percy Lavon **6**
Just, Ernest Everett **3**
Kountz, Samuel L. **10**
Latimer, Lewis H. **4**
Lawless, Theodore K. **8**
Lawrence, Robert H., Jr. **16**
Leffall, LaSalle, Jr. **3**
Lewis, Delano **7**
Logan, Onnie Lee **14**
Lyttle, Hulda Margaret **14**
Manley, Audrey Forbes **16**
Massey, Walter E. **5**
Mboup, Souleymane **10**
McCoy, Elijah **8**
McNair, Ronald **3**
Morgan, Garrett **1**
O'Leary, Hazel **6**
Person, Waverly **9**
Pitt, David Thomas **10**
Poussaint, Alvin F. **5**
Prothrow-Stith, Deborah **10**
Quarterman, Lloyd Albert **4**
Riley, Helen Caldwell Day **13**
Robeson, Eslanda Goode **13**
Robinson, Rachel **16**
Roker, Al **12**
Samara, Noah **15**
Satcher, David **7**
Shabazz, Betty **7**
Sinkford, Jeanne C. **13**
Staples, Brent **8**
Staupers, Mabel K. **7**
Sullivan, Louis **8**
Terrell, Dorothy A. **24**
Thomas, Vivien **9**
Tyson, Neil de Grasse **15**
Washington, Patrice Clarke **12**
Watkins, Levi, Jr. **9**
Welsing, Frances Cress **5**
Williams, Daniel Hale **2**
Williams, O. S. **13**
Woods, Granville T. **5**
Wright, Louis Tompkins **4**

Social issues
Aaron, Hank **5**
Abbott, Diane **9**
Abdul-Jabbar, Kareem **8**
Abernathy, Ralph David **1**
Abu-Jamal, Mumia **15**
Achebe, Chinua **6**
Agyeman, Jaramogi Abebe **10**
Al-Amin, Jamil Abdullah **6**
Alexander, Sadie Tanner Mossell **22**
Ali, Muhammad, **2, 16**
Allen, Ethel D. **13**
Andrews, Benny **22**
Angelou, Maya **1**
Annan, Kofi Atta **15**
Archer, Dennis **7**
Aristide, Jean-Bertrand **6**
Asante, Molefi Kete **3**
Ashe, Arthur **1, 18**
Auguste, Rose-Anne **13**
Azikiwe, Nnamdi **13**
Baker, Ella **5**
Baker, Gwendolyn Calvert **9**
Baker, Houston A., Jr. **6**
Baker, Josephine **3**
Baker, Thurbert **22**
Baldwin, James **1**
Baraka, Amiri **1**
Bates, Daisy **13**
Beals, Melba Patillo **15**
Belafonte, Harry **4**
Bell, Derrick **6**
Bell, Ralph S. **5**
Bennett, Lerone, Jr. **5**
Berry, Bertice **8**
Berry, Mary Frances **7**
Bethune, Mary McLeod **4**
Biko, Steven **4**
Blackwell, Unita **17**
Bolin, Jane **22**
Bond, Julian **2**
Bonga, Kuenda **13**
Bosley, Freeman, Jr. **7**
Boyd, John W., Jr. **20**
Boyd, T. B., III **6**
Boykin, Keith **14**
Braun, Carol Moseley **4**
Brooke, Edward **8**

Brown, Elaine 8
Brown, Jesse 6
Brown, Jim 11
Brown, Lee P. 1
Brown, Les 5
Brown, Tony 3
Brown, Zora Kramer 12
Bryant, Wayne R. 6
Bullock, Steve 22
Bunche, Ralph J. 5
Burroughs, Margaret Taylor 9
Butler, Paul D. 17
Butts, Calvin O., III 9
Campbell, Bebe Moore 6, 24
Canada, Geoffrey 23
Carmichael, Stokely 5
Carter, Mandy 11
Carter, Stephen L. 4
Cary, Lorene 3
Chavis, Benjamin 6
Chideya, Farai 14
Childress, Alice 15
Chissano, Joaquim 7
Christophe, Henri 9
Chuck D 9
Clark, Joe 1
Clark, Kenneth B. 5
Clark, Septima 7
Clay, William Lacy 8
Claytor, Helen 14
Cleaver, Eldridge 5
Clements, George 2
Cobbs, Price M. 9
Cole, Johnnetta B. 5
Collins, Barbara-Rose 7
Comer, James P. 6
Cone, James H. 3
Connerly, Ward 14
Conté, Lansana 7
Conyers, John, Jr. 4
Cook, Toni 23
Cooper, Anna Julia 20
Cooper, Edward S. 6
Cosby, Bill 7
Cosby, Camille 14
Cose, Ellis 5
Crockett, George, Jr. 10
Crouch, Stanley 11
Cummings, Elijah E. 24
Cunningham, Evelyn 23
da Silva, Benedita 5
Dash, Julie 4
Davis, Angela 5
Davis, Danny K. 24
Davis, Ossie 5
Dee, Ruby 8
Dellums, Ronald 2
Dickerson, Ernest 6
Diop, Cheikh Anta 4
Divine, Father 7
Dixon, Margaret 14
Dodson, Howard, Jr. 7
Dove, Rita 6
Drew, Charles Richard 7
Du Bois, W. E. B. 3
DuBois, Shirley Graham 21
Dunham, Katherine 4
Early, Gerald 15

Edelin, Ramona Hoage 19
Edelman, Marian Wright 5
Edley, Christopher 2
Edwards, Harry 2
Elder, Lee 6
Elders, Joycelyn 6
Ellison, Ralph 7
Esposito, Giancarlo 9
Espy, Mike 6
Europe, James Reese 10
Evers, Medgar 3
Evers, Myrlie 8
Farmer, James 2
Farrakhan, Louis 15
Fauntroy, Walter E. 11
Fauset, Jessie 7
Fela 1
Foreman, George 15
Forman, James 7
Fortune, T. Thomas 6
Franklin, Hardy R. 9
Franklin, John Hope 5
Franklin, Robert M. 13
Frazier, E. Franklin 10
Fulani, Lenora 11
Fuller, Charles 8
Gaines, Ernest J. 7
Garvey, Marcus 1
Gates, Henry Louis, Jr. 3
Gayle, Helene D. 3
Gibson, Kenneth Allen 6
Gibson, William F. 6
Gist, Carole 1
Goldberg, Whoopi 4
Golden, Marita 19
Gomez-Preston, Cheryl 9
Gossett, Louis, Jr. 7
Graham, Lawrence Otis 12
Gregory, Dick 1
Grier, Roosevelt 13
Griffith, Mark Winston 8
Grimké, Archibald H. 9
Guinier, Lani 7
Guy, Rosa 5
Guy-Sheftall, Beverly 13
Hale, Lorraine 8
Haley, Alex 4
Hall, Elliott S. 24
Hamblin, Ken 10
Hamer, Fannie Lou 6
Hampton, Fred 18
Hampton, Henry 6
Hani, Chris 6
Hansberry, Lorraine 6
Hansberry, William Leo 11
Harper, Frances Ellen Watkins 11
Harrington, Oliver W. 9
Harris, Alice 7
Harris, Leslie 6
Harris, Marcelite Jordan 16
Harris, Patricia Roberts 2
Hastings, Alcee L. 16
Hawkins, Steven 14
Haynes, George Edmund 8
Hedgeman, Anna Arnold 22
Height, Dorothy I. 2, 23
Henderson, Wade J. 14
Henry, Aaron 19

Henry, Lenny 9
Hernandez, Aileen Clarke 13
Hill, Anita 5
Hill, Jessie, Jr. 13
Hill, Lauryn 20
Hill, Oliver W. 24
Hilliard, David 7
Holland, Endesha Ida Mae 3
Hooks, Benjamin L. 2
hooks, bell 5
Horne, Lena 5
Houston, Charles Hamilton 4
Hughes, Albert 7
Hughes, Allen 7
Hughes, Langston 4
Hunter-Gault, Charlayne 6
Hutchinson, Earl Ofari 24
Hutson, Jean Blackwell 16
Ice-T 6
Iceberg Slim 11
Iman 4
Ingram, Rex 5
Innis, Roy 5
Jackson, George 14
Jackson, Janet 6
Jackson, Jesse 1
Jackson, Mahalia 5
Jacob, John E. 2
Jagan, Cheddi 16
James, Daniel, Jr. 16
Jean, Wyclef 20
Jeffries, Leonard 8
Johnson, Charles S. 12
Johnson, Earvin "Magic" 3
Johnson, James Weldon 5
Jones, Elaine R. 7
Jordan, Barbara 4
Jordan, June 7
Jordan, Vernon E. 3
Josey, E. J. 10
Joyner, Tom 19
Julian, Percy Lavon 6
Kaunda, Kenneth 2
Keith, Damon J. 16
Kennedy, Florynce 12
Khanga, Yelena 6
King, B. B. 7
King, Bernice 4
King, Coretta Scott 3
King, Dexter 10
King, Martin Luther, Jr. 1
King, Martin Luther, III 20
King, Yolanda 6
Kitt, Eartha 16
Lampkin, Daisy 19
Lane, Charles 3
Lane, Vincent 5
Lee, Canada 8
Lee, Spike 5, 19
Leland, Mickey 2
Lester, Julius 9
Lewis, Delano 7
Lewis, John 2
Lewis, Thomas 19
Little, Robert L. 2
Lorde, Audre 6
Louis, Errol T. 8
Lowery, Joseph 2

Lucas, John 7
Madhubuti, Haki R. 7
Madison, Joseph E. 17
Makeba, Miriam 2
Mandela, Nelson 1, 14
Mandela, Winnie 2
Manley, Audrey Forbes 16
Marable, Manning 10
Marley, Bob 5
Marshall, Paule 7
Marshall, Thurgood 1
Martin, Louis E. 16
Masekela, Barbara 18
Masekela, Hugh 1
Mathabane, Mark 5
Maynard, Robert C. 7
Mays, Benjamin E. 7
McCabe, Jewell Jackson 10
McCarty, Oseola 16
McDaniel, Hattie 5
McDougall, Gay J. 11
McKay, Claude 6
McKissick, Floyd B. 3
McQueen, Butterfly 6
Meek, Carrie 6
Meredith, James H. 11
Mfume, Kweisi 6
Micheaux, Oscar 7
Millender-McDonald, Juanita 21
Mkapa, Benjamin 16
Mongella, Gertrude 11
Morrison, Toni 2
Moses, Robert Parris 11
Mosley, Walter 5
Motley, Constance Baker 10
Moutoussamy-Ashe, Jeanne 7
Mowry, Jess 7
Muhammad, Elijah 4
Muhammad, Khallid Abdul 10
Ndadaye, Melchior 7
Nelson, Jill 6
Newton, Huey 2
Nkrumah, Kwame 3
Norman, Pat 10
Norton, Eleanor Holmes 7
Nzo, Alfred 15
O'Leary, Hazel 6
Obasanjo, Olusegun 5
Oglesby, Zena 12
Owens, Major 6
Page, Alan 7
Page, Clarence 4
Paige, Satchel 7
Parker, Pat 19
Parks, Rosa 1
Patterson, Frederick Douglass 12
Patterson, Orlando 4
Patterson, P. J. 6, 20
Perkins, Edward 5
Pitt, David Thomas 10
Pleasant, Mary Ellen 9
Poussaint, Alvin F. 5
Powell, Adam Clayton, Jr. 3
Pratt, Geronimo 18
Price, Hugh B. 9
Primus, Pearl 6
Pritchard, Robert Starling 21
Prothrow-Stith, Deborah 10

Quarles, Benjamin Arthur 18
Ramaphosa, Cyril 3
Ramsey, Charles H. 21
Rand, A. Barry 6
Randolph, A. Philip 3
Rangel, Charles 3
Rawlings, Nana Konadu Agyeman 13
Reagon, Bernice Johnson 7
Reed, Ishmael 8
Rice, Norm 8
Riggs, Marlon 5
Riley, Helen Caldwell Day 13
Ringgold, Faith 4
Robeson, Eslanda Goode 13
Robeson, Paul 2
Robinson, Jackie 6
Robinson, Rachel 16
Robinson, Randall 7
Robinson, Sharon 22
Robinson, Spottswood 22
Rowan, Carl T. 1
Rustin, Bayard 4
Sampson, Edith S. 4
Sané, Pierre Gabriel 21
Sapphire 14
Satcher, David 7
Savimbi, Jonas 2
Sawyer, Amos 5
Sayles Belton, Sharon 9, 16
Schomburg, Arthur Alfonso 9
Seale, Bobby 3
Senghor, Léopold Sédar 12
Shabazz, Attallah 6
Shabazz, Betty 7
Shakur, Assata 6
Sifford, Charlie 4
Simone, Nina 15
Simpson, Carole 6
Sister Souljah 11
Sisulu, Sheila Violet Makate 24
Sleet, Moneta, Jr. 5
Smith, Anna Deavere 6
Soyinka, Wole 4
Stallings, George A., Jr. 6
Staupers, Mabel K. 7
Steele, Claude Mason 13
Steele, Shelby 13
Stewart, Alison 13
Stewart, Maria W. Miller 19
Stone, Chuck 9
Sullivan, Leon H. 3
Tate, Eleanora E. 20
Taulbert, Clifton Lemoure 19
Taylor, Susan L. 10
Terrell, Mary Church 9
Thomas, Franklin A. 5
Thomas, Isiah 7
Thurman, Howard 3
Thurman, Wallace 16
Till, Emmett 7
Toomer, Jean 6
Tosh, Peter 9
Tribble, Israel, Jr. 8
Trotter, Monroe 9
Tubman, Harriet 9
Tucker, C. DeLores 12
Tucker, Cynthia 15

Tucker, Rosina 14
Tutu, Desmond 6
Tyree, Omar Rashad 21
Underwood, Blair 7
Van Peebles, Melvin 7
Vanzant, Iyanla 17
Vincent, Marjorie Judith 2
Waddles, Charleszetta (Mother) 10
Walcott, Derek 5
Walker, A'lelia 14
Walker, Alice 1
Walker, Cedric "Ricky" 19
Walker, Madame C. J. 7
Wallace, Michele Faith 13
Wallace, Phyllis A. 9
Washington, Booker T. 4
Washington, Fredi 10
Washington, Harold 6
Waters, Maxine 3
Wattleton, Faye 9
Wells, James Lesesne 10
Wells-Barnett, Ida B. 8
Welsing, Frances Cress 5
West, Cornel 5
White, Michael R. 5
White, Reggie 6
White, Walter F. 4
Wideman, John Edgar 5
Wilkins, Roger 2
Wilkins, Roy 4
Williams, Evelyn 10
Williams, George Washington 18
Williams, Hosea Lorenzo 15
Williams, Maggie 7
Williams, Montel 4
Williams, Patricia J. 11
Williams, Robert F. 11
Williams, Walter E. 4
Williams, Willie L. 4
Wilson, August 7
Wilson, Phill 9
Wilson, Sunnie 7
Wilson, William Julius 22
Winfield, Paul 2
Winfrey, Oprah 2, 15
Wolfe, George C. 6
Woodson, Robert L. 10
Worrill, Conrad 12
Wright, Louis Tompkins 4
Wright, Richard 5
X, Malcolm 1
Yoba, Malik 11
Young, Andrew 3
Young, Jean Childs 14
Young, Whitney M., Jr. 4
Youngblood, Johnny Ray 8

Sports
Aaron, Hank 5
Abdul-Jabbar, Kareem 8
Ali, Muhammad 2, 16
Allen, Marcus 20
Amos, John 8
Anderson, Jamal 22
Ashe, Arthur 1, 18
Ashford, Emmett 22
Ashley, Maurice 15
Baker, Dusty 8

Barkley, Charles 5
Barnes, Ernie 16
Baylor, Don 6
Belle, Albert 10
Bickerstaff, Bernie 21
Bing, Dave 3
Blanks, Billy 22
Bol, Manute 1
Bonaly, Surya 7
Bonds, Barry 6
Bowe, Riddick 6
Brandon, Terrell 16
Brock, Lou 18
Brown, James 22
Brown, Jim 11
Bryant, Kobe 15
Butler, Leroy, III 17
Carew, Rod 20
Carter, Anson 24
Carter, Cris 21
Chamberlain, Wilt 18
Christie, Linford 8
Coachman, Alice 18
Coleman, Leonard S., Jr. 12
Cooper, Cynthia 17
Cottrell, Comer 11
Cunningham, Randall 23
Davis, Piper 19
Davis, Terrell 20
Dawes, Dominique 11
Doby, Lawrence Eugene, Sr. 16
Drew, Charles Richard 7
Drexler, Clyde 4
Dumars, Joe 16
Duncan, Tim 20
Dungy, Tony 17
Edwards, Harry 2
Edwards, Teresa 14
Elder, Lee 6
Ellerbe, Brian 22
Erving, Julius 18
Ewing, Patrick A. 17
Farr, Mel Sr. 24
Fielder, Cecil 2
Flood, Curt 10
Foreman, George 1, 15
Frazier, Joe 19
Freeman, Marianna 23
Fuhr, Grant 1
Gaither, Alonzo Smith (Jake) 14
Garnett, Kevin 14
Garrison, Zina 2
Gentry, Alvin 23
Gibson, Althea 8
Gibson, Josh 22
Gilliam, Frank 23
Gooden, Dwight 20
Goss, Tom 23
Gourdine, Simon 11
Green, Dennis 5
Greene, Joe 10
Gregg, Eric 16
Grier, Roosevelt 1
Griffey, Ken, Jr. 12
Gumbel, Bryant 14
Gumbel, Greg 8
Gwynn, Tony 18

Hardaway, Anfernee (Penny) 13
Haskins, Clem 23
Hickman, Fred 11
Hill, Calvin 19
Hill, Grant 13
Holdsclaw, Chamique 24
Holmes, Larry 20
Holyfield, Evander 6
Howard, Desmond 16
Howard, Juwan 15
Hunter, Billy 22
Iverson, Allen 24
Jackson, Mannie 14
Jackson, Reggie 15
Johnson, Ben 1
Johnson, Earvin "Magic" 3
Johnson, Jack 8
Johnson, Michael 13
Jones, Cobi N'Gai 18
Jones, Marion 21
Jones, Roy Jr. 22
Jordan, Michael 6, 21
Joyner-Kersee, Jackie 5
Justice, David 18
King, Don 14
Lankford, Ray 23
Larkin, Barry
Lassiter, Roy 24
Lee, Canada 8
Leonard, Sugar Ray 15
Leslie, Lisa 16
Lewis, Carl 4
Lofton, Kenny 12
Lott, Ronnie 9
Louis, Joe 5
Love, Nat 9
Lucas, John 7
Malone, Karl A. 18
Manigault, Earl "The Goat" 15
Master P 21
Mays, Willie 3
McBride, Bryant 18
McCray, Nikki 18
McGriff, Fred 24
McKegney, Tony 3
McNair, Steve 22
McNeil, Lori 1
Milla, Roger 2
Miller, Cheryl 10
Moon, Warren 8
Moorer, Michael 19
Morgan, Joe Leonard 9
Moses, Edwin 8
Moss, Randy 23
Mourning, Alonzo 17
Murray, Eddie 12
Murray, Lenda 10
Mutola, Maria 12
Mutombo, Dikembe 7
Newcombe, Don 24
Noah, Yannick 4
O'Neal, Shaquille 8
O'Neil, Buck 19
O'Ree, Willie 5
Olajuwon, Hakeem 2
Owens, Jesse 2
Pace, Orlando 21
Page, Alan 7

Paige, Satchel 7
Patterson, Floyd 19
Payton, Walter 11
Peck, Carolyn 23
Peete, Calvin 11
Pelé 7
Perrot, Kim 23
Pickett, Bill 11
Pippen, Scottie 15
Powell, Mike 7
Puckett, Kirby 4
Quirot, Ana 13
Rashad, Ahmad 18
Rhodes, Ray 14
Ribbs, Willy T. 2
Rice, Jerry 5
Richardson, Nolan 9
Richmond, Mitch 19
Robinson, David 24
Robinson, Eddie G. 10
Robinson, Frank 9
Robinson, Jackie 6
Robinson, Sugar Ray 18
Rodman, Dennis 12
Rudolph, Wilma 4
Russell, Bill 8
Sampson, Charles 13
Sanders, Barry 1
Sanders, Deion 4
Scott, Wendell Oliver, Sr. 19
Sheffield, Gary 16
Shell, Art 1
Sifford, Charlie 4
Silas, Paul 24
Simpson, O. J. 15
Singletary, Mike 4
Smith, Emmitt 7
Smith, Tubby 18
Sosa, Sammy 21
Sprewell, Latrell 23
Steward, Emanuel 18
Stewart, Kordell 21
Stone, Toni 15
Strawberry, Darryl 22
Stringer, C. Vivian 13
Swoopes, Sheryl 12
Thomas, Frank 12
Thomas, Isiah 7
Thugwane, Josia 21
Unseld, Wes 23
Upshaw, Gene 18
Walker, Herschel 1
Washington, MaliVai 8
Watts, J. C., Jr. 14
Weathers, Carl 10
Webber, Chris 15
Westbrook, Peter 20
Whitaker, Pernell 10
White, Bill 1
White, Jesse 22
White, Reggie 6
Whitfield, Fred 23
Wilkens, Lenny 11
Williams, Doug 22
Williams, Serena 20
Williams, Venus Ebone 17
Wilson, Sunnie 7
Winfield, Dave 5

Cumulative Occupation Index

Woods, Tiger **14**

Television
Allen, Byron **3**
Allen, Debbie **13**
Allen, Marcus **20**
Amos, John **8**
Arkadie, Kevin **17**
Banks, William **11**
Barden, Don H. **9**
Bassett, Angela **6, 23**
Beaton, Norman **14**
Belafonte, Harry **4**
Bellamy, Bill **12**
Berry, Bertice **8**
Berry, Halle **4, 19**
Bowser, Yvette Lee **17**
Bradley, Ed **2**
Brandy **14**
Braugher, Andre **13**
Brooks, Avery **9**
Brown, James **22**
Brown, Les **5**
Brown, Tony **3**
Burnett, Charles **16**
Burton, LeVar **8**
Byrd, Robert **11**
Campbell, Tisha **8**
Carroll, Diahann **9**
Carson, Lisa Nicole **21**
Cheadle, Don **19**
Chideya, Farai **14**
Christian, Spencer **15**
Clash, Kevin **14**
Clayton, Xernona **3**
Cole, Nat King **17**
Cole, Natalie Maria **17**
Cornelius, Don **4**
Cosby, Bill **7**
Crothers, Scatman **19**
Curry, Mark **17**
Curtis-Hall, Vondie **17**
Davidson, Tommy **21**
Davis, Ossie **5**
Dee, Ruby **8**
Devine, Loretta **24**
Dickerson, Ernest **6**
Dr. Dre **10**
Duke, Bill **3**
Dutton, Charles S. **4, 22**
Erving, Julius **18**
Esposito, Giancarlo **9**
Eubanks, Kevin **15**
Fishburne, Larry **4**
Foxx, Jamie **15**
Foxx, Redd **2**
Freeman, Al, Jr. **11**
Freeman, Morgan **2**
Gaines, Ernest J. **7**
Givens, Robin **4**
Glover, Danny **3, 24**
Glover, Savion **14**
Goldberg, Whoopi **4**
Goode, Mal **13**
Gooding, Cuba, Jr. **16**
Gordon, Ed **10**
Gossett, Louis, Jr. **7**
Grier, Pam **9**
Guillaume, Robert **3**
Gumbel, Bryant **14**
Gumbel, Greg **8**
Gunn, Moses **10**
Guy, Jasmine **2**
Haley, Alex **4**
Hampton, Henry **6**
Hardison, Kadeem **22**
Harrell, Andre **9**
Harris, Robin **7**
Harvey, Steve **18**
Hayes, Isaac **20**
Hemsley, Sherman **19**
Henry, Lenny **9**
Hickman, Fred **11**
Hill, Lauryn **20**
Hinderas, Natalie **5**
Horne, Lena **5**
Hounsou, Djimon **19**
Hughley, D.L. **23**
Hunter-Gault, Charlayne **6**
Iman **4**
Ingram, Rex **5**
Jackson, George **19**
Jackson, Janet **6**
Jackson, Jesse **1**
Joe, Yolanda **21**
Johnson, Beverly **2**
Johnson, Robert L. **3**
Jones, Bobby **20**
Jones, James Earl **3**
Jones, Quincy **8**
Jones, Star **10**
King, Gayle **19**
King, Regina **22**
Kirby, George **14**
Kitt, Eartha **16**
Knight, Gladys **16**
Kotto, Yaphet **7**
L.L. Cool J **16**
La Salle, Eriq **12**
LaBelle, Patti **13**
Langhart, Janet **19**
Lawrence, Martin **6**
Lawson, Jennifer **1**
Lemmons, Kasi **20**
Lewis, Byron E. **13**
Lindo, Delroy **18**
Long, Nia **17**
Lover, Ed **10**
McDaniel, Hattie **5**
McEwen, Mark **5**
McKee, Lonette **12**
McQueen, Butterfly **6**
Miller, Cheryl **10**
Mitchell, Brian Stokes **21**
Mitchell, Russ **21**
Moore, Melba **21**
Moore, Shemar **21**
Morgan, Joe Leonard **9**
Morton, Joe **18**
Moses, Gilbert **12**
Moss, Carlton **17**
Murphy, Eddie **4, 20**
Muse, Clarence Edouard **21**
Nichols, Nichelle **11**
Norman, Maidie **20**
Payne, Allen **13**
Peete, Holly Robinson **20**
Perkins, Tony **24**
Pinkett, Jada **10**
Pinkston, W. Randall **24**
Price, Frederick K.C. **21**
Price, Hugh B. **9**
Queen Latifah **1, 16**
Ralph, Sheryl Lee **18**
Randle, Theresa **16**
Rashad, Ahmad **18**
Rashad, Phylicia **21**
Reese, Della **6, 20**
Reuben, Gloria **15**
Ribeiro, Alfonso **17**
Roberts, Robin **16**
Robinson, Max **3**
Rochon, Lela **16**
Rock, Chris **3, 22**
Rodgers, Johnathan **6**
Roker, Al **12**
Rolle, Esther **13, 21**
Rollins, Howard E., Jr. **16**
Ross, Diana **8**
Rowan, Carl T. **1**
Rowell, Victoria **13**
Rupaul **17**
Russell, Bill **8**
Schultz, Michael A. **6**
Shaw, Bernard **2**
Simpson, Carole **6**
Simpson, O. J. **15**
Sinbad **1, 16**
Smiley, Tavis **20**
Smith, Barbara **11**
Smith, Roger Guenveur **12**
Smith, Will **8, 18**
St. Jacques, Raymond **8**
Stewart, Alison **13**
Stokes, Carl B. **10**
Stone, Chuck **9**
Tate, Larenz **15**
Taylor, Meshach **4**
Taylor, Regina **9**
Thigpen, Lynne **17**
Townsend, Robert **4, 23**
Tucker, Chris **13, 23**
Tyson, Cicely **7**
Uggams, Leslie **23**
Underwood, Blair **7**
Usher **23**
Van Peebles, Mario **2**
Van Peebles, Melvin **7**
Vereen, Ben **4**
Warfield, Marsha **2**
Warner, Malcolm-Jamal **22**
Warwick, Dionne **18**
Washington, Denzel **1, 16**
Wattleton, Faye **9**
Watts, Rolonda **9**
Wayans, Damon **8**
Wayans, Keenen Ivory **18**
Weathers, Carl **10**
Whitfield, Lynn **1, 18**
Wilkins, Roger **2**
Williams, Billy Dee **8**
Williams, Montel **4**
Williams, Samm-Art **21**
Williams, Vanessa **4, 17**

Williamson, Mykelti **22**
Wilson, Flip **21**
Winfield, Paul **2**
Winfrey, Oprah **2, 15**
Yoba, Malik **11**

Theater
Ailey, Alvin **8**
Allen, Debbie **13**
Amos, John **8**
Andrews, Bert **13**
Angelou, Maya **1**
Arkadie, Kevin **17**
Armstrong, Vanessa Bell **24**
Baraka, Amiri **1**
Bassett, Angela **6, 23**
Beaton, Norman **14**
Belafonte, Harry **4**
Borders, James **9**
Brooks, Avery **9**
Calloway, Cab **14**
Campbell, Naomi **1**
Campbell, Tisha **8**
Carroll, Diahann **9**
Cheadle, Don **19**
Childress, Alice **15**
Clarke, Hope **14**
Cleage, Pearl **17**
Curtis-Hall, Vondie **17**
Davis, Ossie **5**
Davis, Sammy, Jr. **18**
Dee, Ruby **8**
Devine, Loretta **24**
Duke, Bill **3**
Dunham, Katherine **4**
Dutton, Charles S. **4, 22**
Esposito, Giancarlo **9**
Europe, James Reese **10**
Fishburne, Larry **4**
Freeman, Al, Jr. **11**
Freeman, Morgan **2, 20**
Fuller, Charles **8**
Glover, Danny **1, 24**
Glover, Savion **14**
Goldberg, Whoopi **4**
Gordone, Charles **15**
Gossett, Louis, Jr. **7**
Graves, Denyce **19**
Grier, Pam **9**
Guillaume, Robert **3**
Gunn, Moses **10**
Guy, Jasmine **2**
Hansberry, Lorraine **6**
Harris, Robin **7**
Hemsley, Sherman **19**
Holland, Endesha Ida Mae **3**
Horne, Lena **5**
Hyman, Phyllis **19**
Ingram, Rex **5**
Jackson, Samuel L. **8, 19**
Jamison, Judith **7**
Jean-Baptiste, Marianne **17**
Jones, James Earl **3**
Joyner, Matilda Sissieretta **15**
King, Yolanda **6**
Kitt, Eartha **16**
Kotto, Yaphet **7**
La Salle, Eriq **12**

Lee, Canada **8**
Lemmons, Kasi **20**
Leon, Kenny **10**
Lincoln, Abbey **3**
Lindo, Delroy **18**
Mabley, Jackie "Moms" **15**
Marrow, Queen Esther **24**
McDaniel, Hattie **5**
McDonald, Audra **20**
McKee, Lonette **12**
McQueen, Butterfly **6**
Mills, Florence **22**
Mitchell, Brian Stokes **21**
Moore, Melba **21**
Moses, Gilbert **12**
Moss, Carlton **17**
Moten, Etta **18**
Muse, Clarence Edouard **21**
Nicholas, Fayard **20**
Nicholas, Harold **20**
Norman, Maidie **20**
Payne, Allen **13**
Powell, Maxine **8**
Primus, Pearl **6**
Ralph, Sheryl Lee **18**
Randle, Theresa **16**
Rashad, Phylicia **21**
Reese, Della **6, 20**
Rhames, Ving **14**
Richards, Lloyd **2**
Robeson, Paul **2**
Rolle, Esther **13, 21**
Rollins, Howard E., Jr.
Rotimi, Ola **1**
Schultz, Michael A. **6**
Shabazz, Attallah **6**
Shange, Ntozake **8**
Smith, Anna Deavere **6**
Smith, Roger Guenveur **12**
Snipes, Wesley **3, 24**
Soyinka, Wole **4**
St. Jacques, Raymond **8**
Taylor, Meshach **4**
Taylor, Regina **9**
Thigpen, Lynne **17**
Thompson, Tazewell **13**
Thurman, Wallace **16**
Townsend, Robert **4, 23**
Tyson, Cicely **7**
Uggams, Leslie **23**
Underwood, Blair **7**
Van Peebles, Melvin **7**
Vance, Courtney B. **15**
Vereen, Ben **4**
Walcott, Derek **5**
Washington, Denzel **1, 16**
Washington, Fredi **10**
Waters, Ethel **7**
Whitaker, Forest **2**
Whitfield, Lynn **18**
Williams, Bert **18**
Williams, Billy Dee **8**
Williams, Samm-Art **21**
Williams, Vanessa L. **4, 17**
Williamson, Mykelti **22**
Wilson, August **7**
Winfield, Paul **2**
Wolfe, George C. **6**

Woodard, Alfre **9**

Writing
Abu-Jamal, Mumia **15**
Achebe, Chinua **6**
Al-Amin, Jamil Abdullah **6**
Alexander, Margaret Walker **22**
Andrews, Raymond **4**
Angelou, Maya **1, 15**
Ansa, Tina McElroy **14**
Aristide, Jean-Bertrand **6**
Arkadie, Kevin **17**
Asante, Molefi Kete **3**
Ashe, Arthur **1, 18**
Ashley-Ward, Amelia **23**
Azikiwe, Nnamdi **13**
Baker, Houston A., Jr. **6**
Baldwin, James **1**
Bambara, Toni Cade **10**
Baraka, Amiri **1**
Beals, Melba Patillo **15**
Bell, Derrick **6**
Bennett, Lerone, Jr. **5**
Berry, Mary Frances **7**
Bluitt, Juliann S. **14**
Bontemps, Arna **8**
Booker, Simeon **23**
Borders, James **9**
Boston, Lloyd **24**
Bradley, Ed **2**
Brimmer, Andrew F. **2**
Briscoe, Connie **15**
Brooks, Gwendolyn **1**
Brown, Elaine **8**
Brown, Les **5**
Brown, Marie Dutton **12**
Brown, Sterling **10**
Brown, Tony **3**
Brown, Wesley **23**
Bunche, Ralph J. **5**
Burroughs, Margaret Taylor **9**
Butler, Octavia **8**
Campbell, Bebe Moore **6, 24**
Carmichael, Stokely **5**
Carter, Stephen L. **4**
Cary, Lorene **3**
Chamberlain, Wilt **18**
Chase-Riboud, Barbara **20**
Chideya, Farai **14**
Childress, Alice **15**
Clark, Kenneth B. **5**
Clark, Septima **7**
Cleage, Pearl **17**
Cleaver, Eldridge **5**
Clifton, Lucille **14**
Cobbs, Price M. **9**
Cohen, Anthony **15**
Cole, Johnnetta B. **5**
Comer, James P. **6**
Cone, James H. **3**
Cook, Suzan D. Johnson **22**
Cooper, Anna Julia **20**
Cooper, J. California **12**
Cosby, Bill **7**
Cosby, Camille **14**
Cose, Ellis **5**
Crouch, Stanley **11**
Cullen, Countee **8**

Cumulative Occupation Index

Cunningham, Evelyn 23
Curry, George E. 23
Curtis-Hall, Vondie 17
Danticat, Edwidge 15
Davis, Allison 12
Davis, Angela 5
Davis, Miles 4
Davis, Ossie 5
Dawkins, Wayne 20
Delany, Samuel R., Jr. 9
Dickey, Eric Jerome 21
Diop, Cheikh Anta 4
Dodson, Howard, Jr. 7
Dove, Rita 6
Draper, Sharon M. 16
Driskell, David C. 7
Driver, David E. 11
Du Bois, W. E. B. 3
DuBois, Shirley Graham 21
Dunbar, Paul Laurence 8
Dunham, Katherine 4
Dyson, Michael Eric 11
Early, Gerald 15
Edmonds, Terry 17
Ellison, Ralph 7
Elmore, Ronn 21
Farrakhan, Louis 15
Fauset, Jessie 7
Feelings, Tom 11
Fisher, Rudolph 17
Forman, James 7
Fortune, T. Thomas 6
Franklin, John Hope 5
Franklin, Robert M. 13
Frazier, E. Franklin 10
French, Albert 18
Fuller, Charles 8
Gaines, Ernest J. 7
Gates, Henry Louis, Jr. 3
George, Nelson 12
Gibson, Althea 8
Giddings, Paula 11
Giovanni, Nikki 9
Goines, Donald 19
Golden, Marita 19
Graham, Lawrence Otis 12
Greenfield, Eloise 9
Griffith, Mark Winston 8
Grimké, Archibald H. 9
Guinier, Lani 7
Guy, Rosa 5
Guy-Sheftall, Beverly 13
Haley, Alex 4
Hamblin, Ken 10
Hamilton, Virginia 10
Hansberry, Lorraine 6
Harkless, Necia Desiree 19
Harper, Frances Ellen Watkins 11
Harrington, Oliver W. 9
Harris, Eddy L. 18
Harris, Jay 19
Harris, Leslie 6
Harris, Monica 18
Hayden, Robert 12
Hemphill, Essex 10
Henry, Lenny 9
Henson, Matthew 2
Hilliard, David 7

Holland, Endesha Ida Mae 3
hooks, bell 5
Hrabowski, Freeman A. III 22
Hudson, Cheryl 15
Hudson, Wade 15
Hughes, Langston 4
Hunter-Gault, Charlayne 6
Hurston, Zora Neale 3
Iceberg Slim 11
Jackson, George 14
Jackson, Sheneska 18
Jenkins, Beverly 14
Joe, Yolanda 21
Johnson, Charles 1
Johnson, Charles S. 12
Johnson, James Weldon 5
Johnson, John H. 3
Jordan, June 7
Josey, E. J. 10
Just, Ernest Everett 3
Karenga, Maulana 10
Kennedy, Adrienne 11
Kennedy, Florynce 12
Khanga, Yelena 6
Kimbro, Dennis 10
Kincaid, Jamaica 4
King, Coretta Scott 3
King, Yolanda 6
Kitt, Sandra 23
Komunyakaa, Yusef 9
Kotto, Yaphet 7
Kunjufu, Jawanza 3
Larsen, Nella 5
Lawrence, Martin 6
Lawrence-Lightfoot, Sara 10
Lemmons, Kasi 20
Lester, Julius 9
Lewis, David Levering 9
Little, Benilde 21
Locke, Alain 10
Lorde, Audre 6
Louis, Errol T. 8
Madhubuti, Haki R. 7
Major, Clarence 9
Makeba, Miriam 2
Marshall, Paule 7
Mathabane, Mark 5
Maynard, Robert C. 7
Mays, Benjamin E. 7
McCall, Nathan 8
McGruder, Robert 22
McKay, Claude 6
McMillan, Terry 4, 17
Meredith, James H. 11
Micheaux, Oscar 7
Mitchell, Russ 21
Morrison, Toni 2, 15
Mosley, Walter 5
Moss, Carlton 17
Moutoussamy-Ashe, Jeanne 7
Mowry, Jess 7
Myers, Walter Dean 8
Naylor, Gloria 10
Nelson, Jill 6
Newton, Huey 2
Nkrumah, Kwame 3
Onwueme, Tess Osonye 23
Owens, Major 6

Page, Clarence 4
Painter, Nell Irvin 24
Parker, Pat 19
Patterson, Orlando 4
Petry, Ann 19
Poussaint, Alvin F. 5
Powell, Adam Clayton, Jr. 3
Pryor, Richard 3
Quarles, Benjamin Arthur 18
Randall, Dudley 8
Raspberry, William 2
Reagon, Bernice Johnson 7
Reddick, Lawrence Dunbar 20
Redmond, Eugene 23
Reed, Ishmael 8
Riggs, Marlon 5
Ringgold, Faith 4
Robeson, Eslanda Goode 13
Rodman, Dennis 12
Rotimi, Ola 1
Rowan, Carl T. 1
Saint James, Synthia 12
Sanchez, Sonia 17
Sanders, Dori 8
Sapphire 14
Schomburg, Arthur Alfonso 9
Seale, Bobby 3
Sembène, Ousmane 13
Senghor, Léopold Sédar 12
Sengstacke, John 18
Shabazz, Attallah 6
Shakur, Assata 6
Shange, Ntozake 8
Shaw, Bernard 2
Shipp, E. R. 15
Simone, Nina 15
Simpson, Carole 6
Singleton, John 2
Sister Souljah 11
Smiley, Tavis 20
Smith, Anna Deavere 6
Smith, Barbara 11
Somé, Malidoma Patrice 10
Sowell, Thomas 2
Soyinka, Wole 4
Staples, Brent 8
Stewart, Alison 13
Stone, Chuck 9
Tate, Eleanora E. 20
Taulbert, Clifton Lemoure 19
Taylor, Kristin Clark 8
Taylor, Susan L. 10
Thurman, Howard 3
Toomer, Jean 6
Townsend, Robert 4
Trotter, Monroe 9
Tucker, Cynthia 15
Turner, Henry McNeal 5
Turner, Tina 6
Tutu, Desmond 6
Tyree, Omar Rashad 21
Tyson, Neil de Grasse 15
Van Peebles, Melvin 7
Walcott, Derek 5
Walker, Alice 1
Wallace, Michele Faith 13
Wallace, Phyllis A. 9
Washington, Booker T. 4

Washington, Laura S. **18**
Waters, Ethel **7**
Wattleton, Faye **9**
Wayans, Damon **8**
Webb, Veronica **10**
Wells-Barnett, Ida B. **8**
Wesley, Dorothy Porter **19**
Wesley, Valerie Wilson **18**
West, Cornel **5**
West, Dorothy **12**
Wharton, Clifton R., Jr. **7**
Whitaker, Mark **21**
White, Walter F. **4**
Wideman, John Edgar **5**
Wiley, Ralph **8**
Wilkins, Roger **2**
Wilkins, Roy **4**
Williams, George Washington **18**
Williams, Patricia J. **11**
Williams, Robert F. **11**
Williams, Samm-Art **21**
Wilson, August **7**
Wilson, William Julius **22**
Winans, Marvin L. **17**
Wolfe, George C. **6**
Woodson, Carter G. **2**
Worrill, Conrad **12**
Wright, Bruce McMarion **3**
Wright, Richard **5**
Young, Whitney M., Jr. **4**

Cumulative Subject Index

Volume numbers appear in **bold**.

AA
See Alcoholics Anonymous

AAAS
See American Association for the Advancement of Science

AARP
Dixon, Margaret **14**

ABC
See American Broadcasting Company

Academy awards
Austin, Patti **24**
Freeman, Morgan **2, 20**
Goldberg, Whoopi **4**
Gooding, Cuba, Jr. **16**
Gossett, Louis, Jr. **7**
Jean-Baptiste, Marianne **17**
McDaniel, Hattie **5**
Poitier, Sidney **11**
Prince **18**
Washington, Denzel **1, 16**
Wonder, Stevie **11**

A cappella
Cooke, Sam **17**
Reagon, Bernice Johnson **7**

ACDL
See Association for Constitutional Democracy in Liberia

ACLU
See American Civil Liberties Union

Acquired Immune Deficiency Syndrome (AIDS)
Ashe, Arthur **1, 18**
Gayle, Helene D. **3**
Hale, Lorraine **8**
Johnson, Earvin "Magic" **3**
Mboup, Souleymane **10**
Moutoussamy-Ashe, Jeanne **7**
Norman, Pat **10**
Riggs, Marlon **5**
Satcher, David **7**
Wilson, Phill **9**

Acting
Ailey, Alvin **8**
Allen, Debbie **13**
Amos, John **8**
Angelou, Maya **1, 15**
Armstrong, Vanessa Bell **24**
Baker, Josephine **3**
Banks, Tyra **11**
Bassett, Angela **6, 23**
Beals, Jennifer **12**
Beaton, Norman **14**
Berry, Halle **4, 19**
Blanks, Billy **22**
Blige, Mary J. **20**
Borders, James **9**
Braugher, Andre **13**
Brooks, Avery **9**
Brown, Jim **11**
Caesar, Shirley **19**
Calloway, Cab **14**
Campbell, Naomi **1**
Campbell, Tisha **8**
Carroll, Diahann **9**
Carson, Lisa Nicole **21**
Cheadle, Don **19**
Childress, Alice **15**
Clarke, Hope **14**
Cole, Nat King **17**
Cole, Natalie Maria **17**
Combs, Sean "Puffy" **17**
Cosby, Bill **7**
Crothers, Scatman **19**
Curry, Mark **17**
Curtis-Hall, Vondie **17**
Dandridge, Dorothy **3**
Davidson, Jaye **5**
Davis, Ossie **5**
Davis, Sammy Jr. **18**
Dee, Ruby **8**
Devine, Loretta **24**
Duke, Bill **3**
Dutton, Charles S. **4, 22**
Epps, Omar **23**
Esposito, Giancarlo **9**
Everett, Francine **23**
Fishburne, Larry **4, 22**
Fox, Vivica A. **15**
Foxx, Jamie **15**
Foxx, Redd **2**
Freeman, Al, Jr. **11**
Freeman, Morgan **2, 20**
Givens, Robin **4**
Glover, Danny **1, 24**
Goldberg, Whoopi **4**
Gooding, Cuba, Jr. **16**
Gossett, Louis, Jr. **7**
Grier, Pam **9**
Guillaume, Robert **3**
Gunn, Moses **10**
Guy, Jasmine **2**
Hammer, M. C. **20**
Hammond, Fred **23**
Hardison, Kadeem **22**
Harris, Robin **7**
Harvey, Steve **18**
Hayes, Isaac **20**
Hemsley, Sherman **19**
Henry, Lenny **9**
Hill, Lauryn **20**
Hines, Gregory **1**
Horne, Lena **5**
Hounsou, Djimon **19**
Houston, Whitney **7**
Hughley, D.L. **23**
Ice Cube **8**
Iman **4**
Ingram, Rex **5**
Jackson, Janet **6**
Jackson, Michael **19**
Jackson, Samuel L. **8, 19**
Jean-Baptiste, Marianne **17**
Jones, James Earl **3**
King, Regina **22**
Kirby, George **14**
Kitt, Eartha **16**
Knight, Gladys **16**
Kotto, Yaphet **7**
L. L. Cool J **16**
La Salle, Eriq **12**
Lane, Charles **3**
Lassiter, Roy **24**
Lawrence, Martin **6**
Lee, Canada **8**
Lee, Joie **1**
Lee, Spike **5, 19**
Lemmons, Kasi **20**
Lincoln, Abbey **3**
Lindo, Delroy **18**
Love, Darlene **23**
Mabley, Jackie "Moms" **15**

Marrow, Queen Esther **24**
Master P **21**
McDaniel, Hattie **5**
McDonald, Audra **20**
Mckee, Lonette **12**
McQueen, Butterfly **6**
Mitchell, Brian Stokes **21**
Moore, Melba **21**
Moore, Shemar **21**
Morton, Joe **18**
Moten, Etta **18**
Murphy, Eddie **4, 20**
Muse, Clarence Edouard **21**
Nicholas, Fayard **20**
Nicholas, Harold **20**
Nichols, Nichelle **11**
Norman, Maidie **20**
Notorious B.I.G. **20**
Payne, Allen **13**
Peete, Holly Robinson **20**
Pinkett, Jada **10**
Poitier, Sidney **11**
Prince **18**
Pryor, Richard **3, 24**
Queen Latifah **1, 16**
Randle, Theresa **16**
Rashad, Phylicia **21**
Reese, Della **6, 20**
Reuben, Gloria **15**
Rhames, Ving **14**
Ribeiro, Alfonso **17**
Richards, Lloyd **2**
Robeson, Paul **2**
Rock, Chris **3, 22**
Rolle, Esther **13, 21**
Ross, Diana **8**
Rowell, Victoria **13**
Shakur, Tupac **14**
Sinbad **1, 16**
Smith, Anna Deavere **6**
Smith, Barbara **11**
Smith, Roger Guenveur **12**
Smith, Will **8, 18**
Snipes, Wesley **3, 24**
St. Jacques, Raymond **8**
Tamia **24**
Tate, Larenz **15**
Taylor, Meshach **4**
Taylor, Regina **9**
Thompson, Tazewell **13**
Townsend, Robert **4, 23**
Tucker, Chris **23**
Turner, Tina **6**
Tyson, Cicely **7**
Uggams, Leslie **23**
Underwood, Blair **7**
Usher **23**
Van Peebles, Mario **2**
Van Peebles, Melvin **7**
Vance, Courtney B. **15**
Vereen, Ben **4**
Warfield, Marsha **2**
Washington, Denzel **1, 16**
Washington, Fredi **10**
Waters, Ethel **7**
Wayans, Damon **8**
Wayans, Keenen Ivory **18**
Weathers, Carl **10**
Webb, Veronica **10**
Whitaker, Forest **2**
Whitfield, Lynn **18**
Williams, Bert **18**
Williams, Billy Dee **8**
Williams, Samm-Art **21**
Williams, Vanessa L. **4, 17**
Williamson, Mykelti **22**
Wilson, Flip **21**
Winfield, Paul **2**
Winfrey, Oprah **2, 15**
Woodard, Alfre **9**
Yoba, Malik **11**

Active Ministers Engaged in Nurturance (AMEN)
King, Bernice **4**

Actuarial science
Hill, Jessie, Jr. **13**

ACT UP
See AIDS Coalition to Unleash Power

Acustar, Inc.
Farmer, Forest **1**

ADC
See Agricultural Development Council

Adoption and foster care
Baker, Josephine **3**
Clements, George **2**
Gossett, Louis, Jr. **7**
Hale, Clara **16**
Hale, Lorraine **8**
Oglesby, Zena **12**

Adventures in Movement (AIM)
Morgan, Joe Leonard **9**

Advertising
Barboza, Anthony **10**
Burrell, Thomas J. **21**
Campbell, E. Simms **13**
Coleman, Donald A. **24**
Johnson, Beverly **2**
Jordan, Montell **23**
Lewis, Byron E. **13**
Roche, Joyce M. **17**

Advocates Scene
Seale, Bobby **3**

AFCEA
See Armed Forces Communications and Electronics Associations

Affirmative action
Berry, Mary Frances **7**
Carter, Stephen L. **4**
Maynard, Robert C. **7**
Norton, Eleanor Holmes **7**
Rand, A. Barry **6**
Waters, Maxine **3**

AFL-CIO
See American Federation of Labor and Congress of Industrial Organizations

African/African-American Summit
Sullivan, Leon H. **3**

African American Catholic Congregation
Stallings, George A., Jr. **6**

African American folklore
Bailey, Xenobia **11**
Brown, Sterling **10**
Driskell, David C. **7**
Ellison, Ralph **7**
Gaines, Ernest J. **7**
Hamilton, Virginia **10**
Hughes, Langston **4**
Hurston, Zora Neale **3**
Lester, Julius **9**
Morrison, Toni **2, 15**
Primus, Pearl **6**
Tillman, George, Jr. **20**
Williams, Bert **18**

African American folk music
Handy, W. C. **8**
House, Son **8**
Johnson, James Weldon **5**
Lester, Julius **9**

African American history
Angelou, Maya **1, 15**
Ashe, Arthur **1, 18**
Bennett, Lerone, Jr. **5**
Berry, Mary Frances **7**
Burroughs, Margaret Taylor **9**
Camp, Kimberly **19**
Chase-Riboud, Barbara **20**
Cheadle, Don **19**
Clarke, John Henrik **20**
Cooper, Anna Julia **20**
Dodson, Howard, Jr. **7**
Douglas, Aaron **7**
Du Bois, W. E. B. **3**
DuBois, Shirley Graham **21**
Dyson, Michael Eric **11**
Feelings, Tom **11**
Franklin, John Hope **5**
Gaines, Ernest J. **7**
Gates, Henry Louis, Jr. **3**
Haley, Alex **4**
Harkless, Necia Desiree **19**
Hine, Darlene Clark **24**
Hughes, Langston **4**
Johnson, James Weldon **5**
Lewis, David Levering **9**
Madhubuti, Haki R. **7**
Marable, Manning **10**
Morrison, Toni **2**
Painter, Nell Irvin **24**
Pritchard, Robert Starling **21**
Quarles, Benjamin Arthur **18**
Reagon, Bernice Johnson **7**
Ringgold, Faith **4**
Schomburg, Arthur Alfonso **9**

Wilson, August **7**
Woodson, Carter G. **2**

African American Images
Kunjufu, Jawanza **3**

African American literature
Andrews, Raymond **4**
Angelou, Maya **1, 15**
Baker, Houston A., Jr. **6**
Baldwin, James **1**
Bambara, Toni Cade **1**
Baraka, Amiri **1**
Bontemps, Arna **8**
Briscoe, Connie **15**
Brooks, Gwendolyn **1**
Brown, Wesley **23**
Burroughs, Margaret Taylor **9**
Campbell, Bebe Moore **6, 24**
Cary, Lorene **3**
Childress, Alice **15**
Cleage, Pearl **17**
Cullen, Countee **8**
Dickey, Eric Jerome **21**
Dove, Rita **6**
Du Bois, W. E. B. **3**
Dunbar, Paul Laurence **8**
Ellison, Ralph **7**
Fauset, Jessie **7**
Feelings, Tom **11**
Fisher, Rudolph **17**
Fuller, Charles **8**
Gaines, Ernest J. **7**
Gates, Henry Louis, Jr. **3**
Giddings, Paula **11**
Giovanni, Nikki **9**
Goines, Donald **19**
Golden, Marita **19**
Guy, Rosa **5**
Haley, Alex **4**
Hansberry, Lorraine **6**
Harper, Frances Ellen Watkins **11**
Himes, Chester **8**
Holland, Endesha Ida Mae **3**
Hughes, Langston **4**
Hurston, Zora Neale **3**
Iceberg Slim **11**
Joe, Yolanda **21**
Johnson, Charles **1**
Johnson, James Weldon **5**
Jordan, June **7**
Kitt, Sandra **23**
Larsen, Nella **10**
Lester, Julius **9**
Little, Benilde **21**
Lorde, Audre **6**
Madhubuti, Haki R. **7**
Major, Clarence **9**
Marshall, Paule **7**
McKay, Claude **6**
McKay, Nellie Yvonne **17**
McMillan, Terry **4, 17**
Morrison, Toni **2, 15**
Mowry, Jess **7**
Naylor, Gloria **10**
Painter, Nell Irvin **24**
Petry, Ann **19**
Pinkney, Jerry **15**

Randall, Dudley **8**
Redmond, Eugene **23**
Reed, Ishmael **8**
Ringgold, Faith **4**
Sanchez, Sonia **17**
Schomburg, Arthur Alfonso **9**
Shange, Ntozake **8**
Thurman, Wallace **16**
Toomer, Jean **6**
Tyree, Omar Rashad **21**
Van Peebles, Melvin **7**
Walker, Alice **1**
Wesley, Valerie Wilson **18**
Wideman, John Edgar **5**
Wilson, August **7**
Wolfe, George C. **6**
Wright, Richard **5**

African dance
Ailey, Alvin **8**
Fagan, Garth **18**
Primus, Pearl **6**

African folk music
Makeba, Miriam **2**
Nascimento, Milton **2**

African history
Chase-Riboud, Barbara **20**
Clarke, John Henrik **20**
Diop, Cheikh Anta **4**
Dodson, Howard, Jr. **7**
DuBois, Shirley Graham **21**
Hansberry, William Leo **11**
Harkless, Necia Desiree **19**
Jawara, Sir Dawda Kairaba **11**
Madhubuti, Haki R. **7**
Marshall, Paule **7**

African Methodist Episcopal Church (AME)
Flake, Floyd H. **18**
Murray, Cecil **12**
Turner, Henry McNeal **5**
Youngblood, Johnny Ray **8**

African National Congress (ANC)
Baker, Ella **5**
Hani, Chris **6**
Kaunda, Kenneth **2**
Luthuli, Albert **13**
Mandela, Nelson **1, 14**
Mandela, Winnie **2**
Masekela, Barbara **18**
Mbeki, Thabo Mvuyelwa **14**
Nkomo, Joshua **4**
Nyanda, Siphiwe **21**
Nzo, Alfred **15**
Ramaphosa, Cyril **3**
Tutu, Desmond **6**

African Women on Tour conference
Taylor, Susan L. **10**

Afro-American League
Fortune, T. Thomas **6**

Afrocentricity
Asante, Molefi Kete **3**
Biggers, John **20**
Diop, Cheikh Anta **4**
Hansberry, Lorraine **6**
Hansberry, William Leo **11**
Sanchez, Sonia **17**
Turner, Henry McNeal **5**

Agency for International Development (AID)
Gayle, Helene D. **3**
Perkins, Edward **5**
Wilkins, Roger **2**

A. G. Gaston Boys and Girls Club
Gaston, Arthur G. **4**

A. G. Gaston Motel
Gaston, Arthur G. **4**

Agricultural Development Council (ADC)
Wharton, Clifton R., Jr. **7**

Agriculture
Boyd, John W., Jr. **20**
Carver, George Washington **4**
Espy, Mike **6**
Hall, Lloyd A. **8**
Masire, Quett **5**
Obasanjo, Olusegun **5**
Sanders, Dori **8**

AHA
See American Heart Association

AID
See Agency for International Development

AIDS
See Acquired Immune Deficiency Syndrome

AIDS Coalition to Unleash Power (ACT UP)
Norman, Pat **10**

AIDS Health Care Foundation
Wilson, Phill **9**

AIDS Prevention Team
Wilson, Phill **9**

AIDS research
Mboup, Souleymane **10**

AIM
See Adventures in Movement

ALA
See American Library Association

Alcoholics Anonymous (AA)
Hilliard, David **7**
Lucas, John **7**

All Afrikan People's Revolutionary Party
Carmichael, Stokely **5**
Moses, Robert Parris **11**

Alliance Theatre
Leon, Kenny **10**

Alpha & Omega Ministry
White, Reggie **6**

Alvin Ailey American Dance Theater
Ailey, Alvin **8**
Clarke, Hope **14**
Dove, Ulysses **5**
Faison, George **16**
Jamison, Judith **7**
Primus, Pearl **6**

Alvin Ailey Repertory Ensemble
Ailey, Alvin **8**
Miller, Bebe **3**

AME
See African Methodist Episcopal Church

AMEN
See Active Ministers Engaged in Nurturance

American Association for the Advancement of Science (AAAS)
Massey, Walter E. **5**

American Ballet Theatre
Dove, Ulysses **5**

American Basketball Association (ABA)
Chamberlain, Wilt **18**
Erving, Julius **18**

American Book Award
Baraka, Amiri **1**
Bates, Daisy **13**
Clark, Septima **7**
Gates, Henry Louis, Jr. **3**
Lorde, Audre **6**
Marshall, Paule **7**
Sanchez, Sonia **17**
Walker, Alice **1**

American Broadcasting Company (ABC)
Christian, Spencer **15**
Goode, Mal **13**
Jackson, Michael **19**
Joyner, Tom **19**
Roberts, Robin **16**
Robinson, Max **3**
Simpson, Carole **6**
Winfrey, Oprah **2, 15**

American Cancer Society
Ashe, Arthur **1, 18**
Leffall, LaSalle, Jr. **3**

American Civil Liberties Union (ACLU)
Baugh, David **23**
Norton, Eleanor Holmes **7**

American Community Housing Associates, Inc.
Lane, Vincent **5**

American Enterprise Institute
Woodson, Robert L. **10**

American Express Company
Chenault, Kenneth I. **4**

American Express Consumer Card Group, USA
Chenault, Kenneth I. **4**

American Federation of Labor and Congress of Industrial Organizations (AFL-CIO)
Randolph, A. Philip **3**

American Heart Association (AHA)
Cooper, Edward S. **6**

American Library Association (ALA)
Franklin, Hardy R. **9**
Josey, E. J. **10**

American Negro Academy
Grimké, Archibald H. **9**
Schomburg, Arthur Alfonso **9**

American Nurses' Association (ANA)
Kennedy, Adrienne **11**
Staupers, Mabel K. **7**

American Red Cross
Bullock, Steve **22**

American Red Cross blood banks
Drew, Charles Richard **7**

American Society of Magazine Editors
Curry, George E. **23**

ANA
See American Nurses' Association

ANC
See African National Congress

Anglican church hierarchy
Tutu, Desmond **6**

Anthropology
Asante, Molefi Kete **3**
Bunche, Ralph J. **5**
Cole, Johnnetta B. **5**
Davis, Allison **12**
Diop, Cheikh Anta **4**
Dunham, Katherine **4**
Hansberry, William Leo **11**
Morrison, Toni **2, 15**

Primus, Pearl **6**
Robeson, Eslanda Goode **13**

Antoinette Perry awards
See Tony awards

Apartheid
Ashe, Arthur **18**
Berry, Mary Frances **7**
Biko, Steven **4**
Luthuli, Albert **13**
Makeba, Miriam **2**
Mandela, Nelson **1, 14**
Mandela, Winnie **2**
Masekela, Hugh **1**
Mathabane, Mark **5**
Mbeki, Thabo Mvuyelwa **14**
Mbuende, Kaire **12**
McDougall, Gay J. **11**
Nyanda, Siphiwe **21**
Nzo, Alfred **15**
Ramaphosa, Cyril **3**
Robinson, Randall **7**
Sullivan, Leon H. **13**
Tutu, Desmond **6**

Apollo 13
Williams, O. S. **13**

Arab-Israeli conflict
Bunche, Ralph J. **5**

ARCH
See Argonne National Laboratory-University of Chicago Development Corporation

Architecture
Gantt, Harvey **1**
Williams, Paul R. **9**

Argonne National Laboratory
Massey, Walter E. **5**
Quarterman, Lloyd Albert **4**

Argonne National Laboratory-University of Chicago Development Corporation (ARCH)
Massey, Walter E. **5**

Ariel Capital Management
Rogers, John W., Jr. **5**

Arkansas Department of Health
Elders, Joycelyn **6**

Armed Forces Communications and Electronics Associations (AFCEA)
Gravely, Samuel L., Jr. **5**

Arthritis treatment
Julian, Percy Lavon **6**

Artists for a Free South Africa
Woodard, Alfre **9**

ASALH
See Association for the Study of

Cumulative Subject Index

Afro-American Life and History

ASH
See Association for the Sexually Harassed

Association for Constitutional Democracy in Liberia (ACDL)
Sawyer, Amos **2**

Association for the Sexually Harassed (ASH)
Gomez-Preston, Cheryl **9**

Association for the Study of Afro-American Life and History (ASALH)
Dodson, Howard, Jr. **7**
Woodson, Carter G. **2**

Astronauts
Bluford, Guy **2**
Bolden, Charles F., Jr. **7**
Gregory, Frederick D. **8**
Jemison, Mae C. **1**
Lawrence, Robert H., Jr. **16**
McNair, Ronald **3**

Atco-EastWest
Rhone, Sylvia **2**

Athletic administration
Goss, Tom **23**

Atlanta Baptist College
See Morehouse College

Atlanta Board of Education
Mays, Benjamin E. **7**

Atlanta Braves baseball team
Aaron, Hank **5**
Baker, Dusty **8**
Justice, David **18**
McGriff, Fred **24**
Sanders, Deion **4**

Atlanta Chamber of Commerce
Hill, Jessie, Jr. **13**

Atlanta City Council
Campbell, Bill **9**
Williams, Hosea Lorenzo **15**

Atlanta city government
Campbell, Bill **9**
Jackson, Maynard **2**
Williams, Hosea Lorenzo **15**
Young, Andrew **3**

Atlanta Falcons football team
Anderson, Jamal **22**
Sanders, Deion **4**

Atlanta Hawks basketball team
Silas, Paul **24**
Wilkens, Lenny **11**

Atlanta Life Insurance Company
Hill, Jessie, Jr. **13**

Atlanta Negro Voters League
Hill, Jessie, Jr. **13**

Atlanta Police Department
Brown, Lee Patrick **1, 24**
Harvard, Beverly **11**

Atlantic City city government
Usry, James L. **23**

Atlantic Records
Franklin, Aretha **11**
Rhone, Sylvia **2**

Aviation
Bullard, Eugene **12**
Coleman, Bessie **9**

"Back to Africa" movement
Turner, Henry McNeal **5**

Bad Boy Entertainment
Combs, Sean "Puffy" **17**
Notorious B.I.G. **20**

Ballet
Ailey, Alvin **8**
Allen, Debbie **13**
Dove, Ulysses **5**
Faison, George **16**
Johnson, Virginia **9**
Mitchell, Arthur **2**
Nichols, Nichelle **11**
Parks, Gordon **1**

Baltimore city government
Schmoke, Kurt **1**

Baltimore Colts football team
Barnes, Ernie **16**

Baltimore Orioles baseball team
Baylor, Don **6**
Jackson, Reggie **15**
Robinson, Frank **9**

Banking
Boyd, T. B., III **6**
Brimmer, Andrew F. **2**
Chapman, Jr., Nathan A. **21**
Chappell, Emma **18**
Griffith, Mark Winston **8**
Lawless, Theodore K. **8**
Louis, Errol T. **8**
Morgan, Rose **11**
Parsons, Richard Dean **11**
Utendahl, John **23**
Walker, Maggie Lena **17**
Watkins, Walter C. **24**

Baptist World Alliance Assembly
Mays, Benjamin E. **7**

Baptist
Gomes, Peter J. **15**

Barnett-Ader Gallery
Thomas, Alma **14**

Baseball
Aaron, Hank **5**
Ashford, Emmett **22**
Baker, Dusty **8**
Baylor, Don **6**
Belle, Albert **10**
Bonds, Barry **6**
Brock, Lou **18**
Carew, Rod **20**
Coleman, Leonard S., Jr. **12**
Cottrell, Comer **11**
Davis, Piper **19**
Doby, Lawrence Eugene **16**
Edwards, Harry **2**
Fielder, Cecil **2**
Flood, Curt **10**
Gibson, Josh **22**
Gooden, Dwight **20**
Gregg, Eric **16**
Griffey, Ken, Jr. **12**
Hammer, M. C. **20**
Jackson, Reggie **15**
Justice, David **18**
Lankford, Ray **23**
Larkin, Barry **24**
Lofton, Kenny **12**
Mays, Willie **3**
McGriff, Fred **24**
Morgan, Joe Leonard **9**
Murray, Eddie **12**
Newcombe, Don **24**
O'Neil, Buck **19**
Paige, Satchel **7**
Puckett, Kirby **4**
Robinson, Frank **9**
Robinson, Jackie **6**
Robinson, Sharon **22**
Sanders, Deion **4**
Sheffield, Gary **16**
Sosa, Sammy **21**
Stone, Toni **15**
Strawberry, Darryl **22**
Thomas, Frank **12**
Vaughn, Mo **16**
White, Bill **1**
Winfield, Dave **5**

Basketball
Abdul-Jabbar, Kareem **8**
Barkley, Charles **5**
Bing, Dave **3**
Bol, Manute **1**
Brandon, Terrell **16**
Bryant, Kobe **15**
Chamberlain, Wilt **18**
Cooper, Cynthia **17**
Drexler, Clyde **4**
Dumars, Joe **16**
Duncan, Tim **20**
Edwards, Harry **2**
Edwards, Teresa **14**
Ellerbe, Brian **22**
Ewing, Patrick A. **17**
Freeman, Marianna **23**
Garnett, Kevin **14**

Gentry, Alvin 23
Gossett, Louis, Jr. 7
Hardaway, Anfernee (Penny) 13
Haskins, Clem 23
Haynes, Marques 22
Hill, Grant 13
Holdsclaw, Chamique 24
Howard, Juwan 15
Hunter, Billy 22
Iverson, Allen 24
Johnson, Earvin "Magic" 3
Jones, Roy Jr. 22
Jordan, Michael 6, 21
Justice, David 18
Kelly, R. 18
Leslie, Lisa 16
Lofton, Kenny 12
Lucas, John 7
Malone, Karl A. 18
Manigault, Earl "The Goat" 15
Master P 21
Miller, Cheryl 10
Mourning, Alonzo 17
Mutombo, Dikembe 7
O'Neal, Shaquille 8
Olajuwon, Hakeem 2
Peck, Carolyn 23
Pippen, Scottie 15
Richardson, Nolan 9
Richmond, Mitch 19
Robinson, David 24
Russell, Bill 8
Silas, Paul 24
Smith, Tubby 18
Sprewell, Latrell 23
Stringer, C. Vivian 13
Swoopes, Sheryl 12
Thomas, Isiah 7
Unseld, Wes 23
Webber, Chris 15
Wilkens, Lenny 11

BCALA
See Black Caucus of the American Library Association

BDP
See Botswana Democratic Party

Bear, Stearns & Co.
Fletcher, Alphonso, Jr. 16

Beatrice International
See TLC Beatrice International Holdings, Inc.

Bebop
Carter, Betty 19
Coltrane, John 19
Davis, Miles 4
Fitzgerald, Ella 8, 18
Gillespie, Dizzy 1
Hancock, Herbie 20
Parker, Charlie 20
Powell, Bud 24
Roach, Max 21
Vaughan, Sarah 13

Bechuanaland Protectorate Legislative Council
Masire, Quett 5

Bedford-Stuyvesant Restoration Corporation
Thomas, Franklin A. 5

Ben & Jerry's Homemade Ice Cream, Inc.
Holland, Robert, Jr. 11

BET
See Black Entertainment Television

Bethann Management, Inc.
Hardison, Bethann 12

Bethune-Cookman College
Bethune, Mary McLeod 4

BFF
See Black Filmmaker Foundation

BGLLF
See Black Gay and Lesbian Leadership Forum

Billy Graham Evangelistic Association
Bell, Ralph S. 5
Waters, Ethel 7

Bing Steel, Inc.
Bing, Dave 3

Biology
Just, Ernest Everett 3

Birth control
Elders, Joycelyn 6
Williams, Maggie 7

Bishop College
Cottrell, Comer 11

BLA
See Black Liberation Army

Black Aesthetic
Baker, Houston A., Jr. 6

Black American West Museum
Stewart, Paul Wilbur 12

Black and White Minstrel Show
Henry, Lenny 9

Black Arts movement
Giovanni, Nikki 9

Black Cabinet
Hastie, William H. 8

Black Caucus of the American Library Association (BCALA)
Josey, E. J. 10

Black Christian Nationalist movement
Agyeman, Jaramogi Abebe 10

Black Coaches Association (BCA)
Freeman, Marianna 23

Black Consciousness movement
Biko, Steven 4
Muhammad, Elijah 4
Ramaphosa, Cyril 3
Tutu, Desmond 6

Black culturalism
Karenga, Maulana 10

Black Economic Union (BEU)
Brown, Jim 11

Black Enterprise
Brimmer, Andrew F. 2
Graves, Earl G. 1
Wallace, Phyllis A. 9

Black Entertainment Television (BET)
Gordon, Ed 10
Johnson, Robert L. 3
Jones, Bobby 20
Smiley, Tavis 20

Black Filmmaker Foundation (BFF)
Hudlin, Reginald 9
Hudlin, Warrington 9
Jackson, George 19

Black Gay and Lesbian Leadership Forum (BGLLF)
Wilson, Phill 9

Black Guerrilla Family (BGF)
Jackson, George 14

Black History Month
Woodson, Carter G. 2

Black Horizons on the Hill
Wilson, August 7

Black Liberation Army (BLA)
Shakur, Assata 6
Williams, Evelyn 10

Black literary theory
Gates, Henry Louis, Jr. 3

Black Manifesto
Forman, James 7

Black Muslims
Abdul-Jabbar, Kareem 8
Ali, Muhammad 2, 16
Farrakhan, Louis 2
Muhammad, Elijah 4
X, Malcolm 1

Black nationalism
Baker, Houston A., Jr. 6

Baraka, Amiri **1**
Carmichael, Stokely **5**
Farrakhan, Louis **2**
Forman, James **7**
Garvey, Marcus **1**
Innis, Roy **5**
Muhammad, Elijah **4**
Turner, Henry McNeal **5**
X, Malcolm **1**

Black Panther Party (BPP)
Abu-Jamal, Mumia **15**
Al-Amin, Jamil Abdullah **6**
Brown, Elaine **8**
Carmichael, Stokely **5**
Cleaver, Eldridge **5**
Davis, Angela **5**
Forman, James **7**
Hampton, Fred **18**
Hilliard, David **7**
Jackson, George **14**
Newton, Huey **2**
Pratt, Geronimo **18**
Seale, Bobby **3**
Shakur, Assata **6**

Black Power movement
Al-Amin, Jamil Abdullah **6**
Baker, Houston A., Jr. **6**
Brown, Elaine **8**
Carmichael, Stokely **5**
Dodson, Howard, Jr. **7**
Giovanni, Nikki **9**
McKissick, Floyd B. **3**
Stone, Chuck **9**

Blackside, Inc.
Hampton, Henry **6**

Black theology
Cone, James H. **3**

"Blood for Britain"
Drew, Charles Richard **7**

Blessed Martin House
Riley, Helen Caldwell Day **13**

Blood plasma research/preservation
Drew, Charles Richard **7**

Blues
Brown, Charles **23**
Collins, Albert **12**
Dixon, Willie **4**
Dorsey, Thomas **15**
Evora, Cesaria **12**
Handy, W. C. **8**
Holiday, Billie **1**
House, Son **8**
Howlin' Wolf **9**
Jean-Baptiste, Marianne **17**
King, B. B. **7**
Muse, Clarence Edouard **21**
Parker, Charlie **20**
Reese, Della **6, 20**
Smith, Bessie **3**
Sykes, Roosevelt **20**
Wallace, Sippie **1**
Washington, Dinah **22**
Waters, Ethel **7**
Watson, Johnny "Guitar" **18**
Williams, Joe **5**
Wilson, August **7**

Blues Heaven Foundation
Dixon, Willie **4**

Blues vernacular
Baker, Houston A., Jr. **6**

Bobsledding
Moses, Edwin **8**

Bodybuilding
Murray, Lenda **10**

Booker T. Washington Business College
Gaston, Arthur G. **4**

Booker T. Washington Insurance Company
Gaston, Arthur G. **4**

Boston Bruins hockey team
O'Ree, Willie **5**

Boston Celtics basketball team
Russell, Bill **8**
Silas, Paul **24**

Boston Red Sox baseball team
Baylor, Don **6**
Vaughn, Mo **16**

Botany
Carver, George Washington **4**

Botswana Democratic Party (BDP)
Masire, Quett **5**
Mogae, Festus Gontebanye **19**

Boxing
Ali, Muhammad **2, 16**
Bowe, Riddick **6**
Foreman, George **1, 15**
Frazier, Joe **19**
Holmes, Larry **20**
Holyfield, Evander **6**
Johnson, Jack **8**
Jones, Roy Jr. **22**
King, Don **14**
Lee, Canada **8**
Leonard, Sugar Ray **15**
Louis, Joe **5**
Moorer, Michael **19**
Patterson, Floyd **19**
Robinson, Sugar Ray **18**
Steward, Emanuel **18**
Whitaker, Pernell **10**

Boys Choir of Harlem
Turnbull, Walter **13**

BPP
See Black Panther Party

Brazilian Congress
da Silva, Benedita **5**

Breast Cancer Resource Committee
Brown, Zora Kramer **12**

British House of Commons
Abbott, Diane **9**
Pitt, David Thomas **10**

British House of Lords
Pitt, David Thomas **10**

British Parliament
See British House of Commons

Broadcasting
Allen, Byron **3, 24**
Ashley, Maurice **15**
Banks, William **11**
Barden, Don H. **9, 20**
Bradley, Ed **2**
Brown, Les **5**
Brown, Tony **3**
Brunson, Dorothy **1**
Clayton, Xernona **3**
Cornelius, Don **4**
Davis, Ossie **5**
Goode, Mal **13**
Gumbel, Bryant **14**
Gumbel, Greg **8**
Hamblin, Ken **10**
Hickman, Fred **11**
Hunter-Gault, Charlayne **6**
Johnson, Robert L. **3**
Jones, Bobby **20**
Jones, Star **10**
Joyner, Tom **19**
Langhart, Janet **19**
Lawson, Jennifer **1**
Lewis, Delano **7**
Madison, Joseph E. **17**
McEwen, Mark **5**
Miller, Cheryl **10**
Mitchell, Russ **21**
Morgan, Joe Leonard **9**
Pinkston, W. Randall **24**
Roberts, Robin **16**
Robinson, Max **3**
Rodgers, Johnathan **6**
Russell, Bill **8**
Shaw, Bernard **2**
Simpson, Carole **6**
Simpson, O. J. **15**
Smiley, Tavis **20**
Stewart, Alison **13**
Stokes, Carl B. **10**
Watts, Rolonda **9**
White, Bill **1**
Williams, Montel **4**
Winfrey, Oprah **2, 15**

Broadside Press
Randall, Dudley **8**

Brooklyn Academy of Music
Miller, Bebe 3

Brooklyn Dodgers baseball team
Newcombe, Don 24
Robinson, Jackie 6

Brotherhood of Sleeping Car Porters
Randolph, A. Philip 3
Tucker, Rosina 14

Brown v. Board of Education of Topeka
Bell, Derrick 6
Clark, Kenneth B. 5
Franklin, John Hope 5
Hill, Oliver W. 24
Houston, Charles Hamilton 4
Marshall, Thurgood 1
Motley, Constance Baker 10
Robinson, Spottswood W., III 22

Buffalo Bills football team
Simpson, O. J. 15

Bull-riding
Sampson, Charles 13

Busing (anti-busing legislation)
Bosley, Freeman, Jr. 7

Cabinet
See U.S. Cabinet

Cable News Network (CNN)
Chideya, Farai 14
Shaw, Bernard 2
Hickman, Fred 11

California Angels baseball team
Baylor, Don 6
Carew, Rod 20
Robinson, Frank 9
Winfield, Dave 5

California State Assembly
Brown, Willie L., Jr. 7
Dixon, Julian C. 24
Millender-McDonald, Juanita 21
Waters, Maxine 3

Calypso
Belafonte, Harry 4
Jean, Wyclef 20

Canadian Football League (CFL)
Gilliam, Frank 23
Moon, Warren 8
Weathers, Carl 10

Cancer research
Clark, Celeste 15
Freeman, Harold P. 23
Leffall, LaSalle, Jr. 3

Capital punishment
Hawkins, Steven 14

Cardiac research
Watkins, Levi, Jr. 9

CARE
Gossett, Louis, Jr. 7
Stone, Chuck 9

Caribbean dance
Ailey, Alvin 8
Dunham, Katherine 4
Fagan, Garth 18
Nichols, Nichelle 11
Primus, Pearl 6

Cartoonists
Armstrong, Robb 15
Brandon, Barbara 3
Campbell, E. Simms 13
Harrington, Oliver W. 9

Catholicism
See Roman Catholic Church

CBEA
See Council for a Black Economic Agenda

CBC
See Congressional Black Caucus

CBS
Pinkston, W. Randall 24
See Columbia Broadcasting System

CBS Television Stations Division
Rodgers, Johnathan 6

CDC
See Centers for Disease Control and Prevention

CDF
See Children's Defense Fund

CEDBA
See Council for the Economic Development of Black Americans

Celebrities for a Drug-Free America
Vereen, Ben 4

Censorship
Butts, Calvin O., III 9
Ice-T 6

Centers for Disease Control and Prevention (CDC)
Gayle, Helene D. 3
Satcher, David 7

CFL
See Canadian Football League

CHA
See Chicago Housing Authority

Challenger
McNair, Ronald 3

Chama cha Mapinduzi (Tanzania; Revolutionary Party)
Mkapa, Benjamin 16
Mongella, Gertrude 11
Nyerere, Julius 5

Chamber of Deputies (Brazil)
da Silva, Benedita 5

Chanteuses
Baker, Josephine 3
Dandridge, Dorothy 3
Horne, Lena 5
Kitt, Eartha 16
Moore, Melba 21
Moten, Etta 18
Reese, Della 6, 20

Che-Lumumba Club
Davis, Angela 5

Chemistry
Hall, Lloyd A. 8
Humphries, Frederick 20
Julian, Percy Lavon 6

Chemurgy
Carver, George Washington 4

Chesapeake and Potomac Telephone Company
Lewis, Delano 7

Chess
Ashley, Maurice 15

Chicago Bears football team
Page, Alan 7
Payton, Walter 11
Singletary, Mike 4

Chicago Bulls basketball team
Jordan, Michael 6, 21
Pippen, Scottie 15
Rodman, Dennis 12

Chicago city government
Washington, Harold 6

Chicago Cubs baseball team
Sosa, Sammy 21

Chicago Eight
Seale, Bobby 3

Chicago Housing Authority (CHA)
Lane, Vincent 5

Chicago Negro Chamber of Commerce
Fuller, S. B. 13

Chicago Reporter
Washington, Laura S. 18

Chicago Tribune
Page, Clarence 4

Chicago White Sox baseball team
Doby, Lawrence Eugene, Sr. 16
Thomas, Frank 12

Child abuse prevention
Waters, Maxine 3

Child psychiatry
Comer, James P. 6

Child psychology
Hale, Lorraine 8

Children's Defense Fund (CDF)
Edelman, Marian Wright 5
Williams, Maggie 7

Child Welfare Administration
Little, Robert L. 2

Choreography
Ailey, Alvin 8
Allen, Debbie 13
Brooks, Avery 9
Byrd, Donald 10
Dove, Ulysses 5
Dunham, Katherine 4
Fagan, Garth 18
Faison, George 16
Glover, Savion 14
Jamison, Judith 7
Johnson, Virginia 9
Jones, Bill T. 1
Miller, Bebe 3
Mitchell, Arthur 2
Nicholas, Fayard 20
Nicholas, Harold 20
Primus, Pearl 6

Christian Science Monitor
Khanga, Yelena 6

Chrysler Corporation
Colbert, Virgis William 17
Farmer, Forest 1
Richie, Leroy C. 18

Church for the Fellowship of All Peoples
Thurman, Howard 3

Church of God in Christ
Franklin, Robert M. 13
Hayes, James C. 10

Cincinnati Reds baseball team
Larkin, Barry 24
Morgan, Joe Leonard 9
Robinson, Frank 9

Cinematography
Dickerson, Ernest 6, 17

Citadel Press
Achebe, Chinua 6

Citizens Federal Savings and Loan Association

Gaston, Arthur G. 4

City government—U.S.
Archer, Dennis 7
Barden, Don H. 9, 20
Barry, Marion S. 7
Bosley, Freeman, Jr. 7
Bradley, Thomas 2, 20
Brown, Lee P. 1, 24
Burris, Chuck 21
Caesar, Shirley 19
Campbell, Bill 9
Clayton, Constance 1
Cleaver, Emanuel 4
Dinkins, David 4
Dixon, Sharon Pratt 1
Evers, Myrlie 8
Fauntroy, Walter E. 11
Gibson, Kenneth Allen 6
Goode, W. Wilson 4
Hayes, James C. 10
Jackson, Maynard 2
James, Sharpe 23
Jarvis, Charlene Drew 21
Johnson, Eddie Bernice 8
Johnson Jr., Harvey 24
Kirk, Ron 11
Mallett, Conrad, Jr. 16
McPhail, Sharon 2
Millender-McDonald, Juanita 21
Morial, Marc 20
Powell, Adam Clayton, Jr. 3
Powell, Debra A. 23
Rice, Norm 8
Sayles Belton, Sharon 9, 16
Schmoke, Kurt 1
Stokes, Carl B. 10
Street, John F. 24
Usry, James L. 23
Washington, Harold 6
Webb, Wellington 3
White, Michael R. 5
Williams, Anthony 21
Young, Andrew 3
Young, Coleman 1, 20

Civil rights
Abbott, Diane 9
Abernathy, Ralph 1
Agyeman, Jaramogi Abebe 10
Al-Amin, Jamil Abdullah 6
Ali, Muhammad 2, 16
Angelou, Maya 1
Aristide, Jean-Bertrand 6
Baker, Ella 5
Baker, Houston A., Jr. 6
Baker, Josephine 3
Bates, Daisy 13
Baugh, David 23
Beals, Melba Patillo 15
Belafonte, Harry 4
Bell, Derrick 6
Bennett, Lerone, Jr. 5
Berry, Mary Frances 7
Biko, Steven 4
Bishop Jr., Sanford D. 24
Bond, Julian 2
Booker, Simeon 23

Boyd, John W., Jr. 20
Brown, Elaine 8
Brown, Tony 3
Brown, Wesley 23
Campbell, Bebe Moore 6, 24
Carmichael, Stokely 5
Carter, Mandy 11
Carter, Stephen L. 4
Chambers, Julius 3
Chavis, Benjamin 6
Clark, Septima 7
Clay, William Lacy 8
Cleaver, Eldridge 5
Clyburn, James 21
Cobbs, Price M. 9
Cooper, Anna Julia 20
Cosby, Bill 7
Crockett, George, Jr. 10
Cunningham, Evelyn 23
Davis, Angela 5
Days, Drew S., III 10
Dee, Ruby 8
Diggs, Charles C. 21
Diggs-Taylor, Anna 20
Divine, Father 7
Dodson, Howard, Jr. 7
Du Bois, W. E. B. 3
Edelman, Marian Wright 5
Ellison, Ralph 7
Evers, Medgar 3
Evers, Myrlie 8
Farmer, James 2
Fauntroy, Walter E. 11
Forman, James 7
Fortune, T. Thomas 6
Franklin, John Hope 5
Gaines, Ernest J. 7
Gibson, William F. 6
Gregory, Dick 1
Grimké, Archibald H. 9
Guinier, Lani 7
Haley, Alex 4
Haley, George Williford Boyce 21
Hall, Elliott S. 24
Hamer, Fannie Lou 6
Hampton, Fred 18
Hampton, Henry 6
Hansberry, Lorraine 6
Harper, Frances Ellen Watkins 11
Harris, Patricia Roberts 2
Hastie, William H. 8
Hawkins, Steven 14
Hedgeman, Anna Arnold 22
Height, Dorothy I. 2, 23
Henderson, Wade J. 14
Henry, Aaron 19
Hill, Jessie, Jr. 13
Hill, Oliver W. 24
Hilliard, David 7
Holland, Endesha Ida Mae 3
Hooks, Benjamin L. 2
hooks, bell 5
Horne, Lena 5
Houston, Charles Hamilton 4
Hughes, Langston 4
Innis, Roy 5
Jackson, Alexine Clement 22
Jackson, Jesse 1

James, Daniel, Jr. **16**
Johnson, Eddie Bernice **8**
Johnson, James Weldon **5**
Johnson, Norma L. Holloway **17**
Jones, Elaine R. **7**
Jordan, Barbara **4**
Jordan, June **7**
Jordan, Vernon E. **3**
Julian, Percy Lavon **6**
Kennedy, Florynce **12**
Kenyatta, Jomo **5**
King, Bernice **4**
King, Coretta Scott **3**
King, Martin Luther, Jr. **1**
King, Martin Luther, III **20**
King, Yolanda **6**
Lampkin, Daisy **19**
Lee, Spike **5, 19**
Lester, Julius **9**
Lewis, John **2**
Lorde, Audre **6**
Lowery, Joseph **2**
Makeba, Miriam **2**
Mandela, Nelson **1, 14**
Mandela, Winnie **2**
Martin, Louis E. **16**
Mays, Benjamin E. **7**
Mbeki, Thabo Mvuyelwa **14**
McDonald, Gabrielle Kirk **20**
McDougall, Gay J. **11**
McKissick, Floyd B. **3**
Meek, Carrie **6**
Meredith, James H. **11**
Morrison, Toni **2, 15**
Moses, Robert Parris **11**
Motley, Constance Baker **10**
Mowry, Jess **7**
Ndadaye, Melchior **7**
Nelson, Jill **6**
Newton, Huey **2**
Nkomo, Joshua **4**
Norman, Pat **10**
Norton, Eleanor Holmes **7**
Nzo, Alfred **15**
Parks, Rosa **1**
Patrick, Deval **12**
Patterson, Orlando **4**
Perkins, Edward **5**
Pinchback, P. B. S. **9**
Pleasant, Mary Ellen **9**
Poitier, Sidney **11**
Powell, Adam Clayton, Jr. **3**
Price, Hugh B. **9**
Ramaphosa, Cyril **3**
Randolph, A. Philip **3**
Reagon, Bernice Johnson **7**
Riggs, Marlon **5**
Robeson, Paul **2**
Robinson, Jackie **6**
Robinson, Rachel **16**
Robinson, Randall **7**
Robinson, Sharon **22**
Robinson, Spottswood W. III **22**
Rowan, Carl T. **1**
Rustin, Bayard **4**
Sané, Pierre Gabriel **21**
Seale, Bobby **3**
Shabazz, Attallah **6**
Shabazz, Betty **7**
Shakur, Assata **6**
Simone, Nina **15**
Sisulu, Sheila Violet Makate **24**
Sleet, Moneta, Jr. **5**
Staupers, Mabel K. **7**
Sullivan, Leon H. **3**
Thurman, Howard **3**
Till, Emmett **7**
Trotter, Monroe **9**
Turner, Henry McNeal **5**
Tutu, Desmond **6**
Underwood, Blair **7**
Washington, Booker T. **4**
Washington, Fredi **10**
Weaver, Robert C. **8**
Wells-Barnett, Ida B. **8**
Wells, James Lesesne **10**
West, Cornel **5**
White, Walter F. **4**
Wideman, John Edgar **5**
Wilkins, Roy **4**
Williams, Evelyn **10**
Williams, Hosea Lorenzo **15**
Williams, Robert F. **11**
Williams, Walter E. **4**
Wilson, August **7**
Wilson, Sunnie **7**
Wilson, William Julius **22**
Woodson, Robert L. **10**
X, Malcolm **1**
Yoba, Malik **11**
Young, Andrew **3**
Young, Jean Childs **14**
Young, Whitney M., Jr. **4**

Classical singers
Anderson, Marian **2**
Bumbry, Grace **5**
Hayes, Roland **4**
Hendricks, Barbara **3**
Norman, Jessye **5**
Price, Leontyne **1**

Clergy
Caesar, Shirley **19**
Cleveland, James **19**
Cook, Suzan D. Johnson **22**
Gomes, Peter J. **15**
Jakes, Thomas "T.D." **17**
King, Barbara **22**
Reese, Della **6, 20**
Winans, Marvin L. **17**

Cleveland Browns football team
Brown, Jim **11**
Hill, Calvin **19**

Cleveland Cavaliers basketball team
Brandon, Terrell **16**
Wilkens, Lenny **11**

Cleveland city government
Stokes, Carl B. **10**
White, Michael R. **5**

Cleveland Indians baseball team
Belle, Albert **10**
Doby, Lawrence Eugene, Sr. **16**
Justice, David **18**
Lofton, Kenny **12**
Murray, Eddie **12**
Paige, Satchel **7**
Robinson, Frank **9**

Clothing design
Bailey, Xenobia **11**
Henderson, Gordon **5**
John, Daymond **23**
Jones, Carl **7**
Kani, Karl **10**
Kelly, Patrick **3**
Robinson, Patrick **19**
Smith, Willi **8**
Walker, T. J. **7**

CNN
See Cable News Network

Coaching
Ashley, Maurice **15**
Baylor, Don **6**
Bickerstaff, Bernie **21**
Carew, Rod **20**
Dungy, Tony **17**
Ellerbe, Brian **22**
Freeman, Marianna **23**
Gaither, Alonzo Smith (Jake) **14**
Gentry, Alvin **23**
Gibson, Althea **8**
Green, Dennis **5**
Greene, Joe **10**
Haskins, Clem **23**
Miller, Cheryl **10**
O'Neil, Buck **19**
Rhodes, Ray **14**
Richardson, Nolan **9**
Robinson, Eddie G. **10**
Russell, Bill **8**
Shell, Art **1**
Silas, Paul **24**
Smith, Tubby **18**
Stringer, C. Vivian **13**
White, Jesse **22**
Williams, Doug **22**

Coca-Cola Foundation
Jones, Ingrid Saunders **18**

COHAR
See Committee on Appeal for Human Rights

Collage
Andrews, Benny **22**
Bearden, Romare **2**
Driskell, David C. **7**

Colorado Rockies baseball team
Baylor, Don **6**

Columbia Broadcasting System (CBS)
Bradley, Ed **2**
McEwen, Mark **5**
Mitchell, Russ **21**

Rashad, Phylicia **21**
Rodgers, Johnathan **6**
Taylor, Meshach **4**

Comedy
Allen, Byron **3, 24**
Amos, John **8**
Beaton, Norman **14**
Bellamy, Bill **12**
Berry, Bertice **8**
Campbell, Tisha **8**
Cosby, Bill **7**
Curry, Mark **17**
Davidson, Tommy **21**
Davis, Sammy Jr. **18**
Foxx, Jamie **15**
Foxx, Redd **2**
Goldberg, Whoopi **4**
Gregory, Dick **1**
Harris, Robin **7**
Harvey, Steve **18**
Henry, Lenny **9**
Hughley, D.L. **23**
Kirby, George **14**
Lawrence, Martin **6**
Mabley, Jackie "Moms" **15**
McEwen, Mark **5**
Moore, Melba **21**
Murphy, Eddie **4, 20**
Pryor, Richard **3, 24**
Rashad, Phylicia **21**
Reese, Della **6, 20**
Rock, Chris **3, 22**
Schultz, Michael A. **6**
Sinbad **1, 16**
Smith, Will **8, 18**
Taylor, Meshach **4**
Townsend, Robert **4, 23**
Tucker, Chris **13, 23**
Warfield, Marsha **2**
Wayans, Damon **8**
Wayans, Keenen Ivory **18**
Wilson, Flip **21**

Comer Method
Comer, James P. **6**

Comic Relief
Goldberg, Whoopi **4**

Commission for Racial Justice
Chavis, Benjamin **6**

Committee on Appeal for Human Rights (COHAR)
Bond, Julian **2**

Communist party
Davis, Angela **5**
Du Bois, W. E. B. **3**
Jagan, Cheddi **16**
Wright, Richard **5**

Computer graphics
Hannah, Marc **10**

Computer science
Hannah, Marc **10**

Conceptual art
Allen, Tina **22**
Bailey, Xenobia **11**
Simpson, Lorna **4**

Concerned Black Men
Holder, Eric H., Jr. **9**

Conductors
Jackson, Isaiah **3**
Calloway, Cab **14**
León, Tania **13**

Congressional Black Caucus (CBC)
Christian-Green, Donna M. **17**
Clay, William Lacy **8**
Clyburn, James **21**
Collins, Cardiss **10**
Conyers, John, Jr. **4**
Dellums, Ronald **2**
Diggs, Charles C. **21**
Fauntroy, Walter E. **11**
Gray, William H. III **3**
Hastings, Alcee L. **16**
Johnson, Eddie Bernice **8**
Mfume, Kweisi **6**
Owens, Major **6**
Rangel, Charles **3**
Scott, Robert C. **23**
Stokes, Louis **3**
Towns, Edolphus **19**

Congressional Black Caucus Higher Education Braintrust
Owens, Major **6**

Congress of Racial Equality (CORE)
Dee, Ruby **8**
Farmer, James **2**
Innis, Roy **5**
Jackson, Jesse **1**
McKissick, Floyd B. **3**
Rustin, Bayard **4**

Connerly & Associates, Inc.
Connerly, Ward **14**

Convention People's Party (Ghana; CPP)
Nkrumah, Kwame **3**

Cook County Circuit Court
Sampson, Edith S. **4**

Cooking
Clark, Patrick **14**
Evans, Darryl **22**

CORE
See Congress of Racial Equality

Corporation for Public Broadcasting (CPB)
Brown, Tony **3**

Cosmetology
Cottrell, Comer **11**
Fuller, S. B. **13**

Morgan, Rose **11**
Powell, Maxine **8**
Roche, Joyce M. **17**
Walker, A'lelia **14**
Walker, Madame C. J. **7**

Council for a Black Economic Agenda (CBEA)
Woodson, Robert L. **10**

Council for Social Action of the Congregational Christian Churches
Julian, Percy Lavon **6**

Council for the Economic Development of Black Americans (CEDBA)
Brown, Tony **3**

Council on Legal Education Opportunities (CLEO)
Henderson, Wade J. **14**
Henry, Aaron **19**

Count Basie Orchestra
Williams, Joe **5**

Cow hand
Love, Nat **9**
Pickett, Bill **11**

CPB
See Corporation for Public Broadcasting

CPP
See Convention People's Party

Cress Theory of Color-Confrontation and Racism
Welsing, Frances Cress **5**

Crisis
Du Bois, W. E. B. **3**
Fauset, Jessie **7**
Wilkins, Roy **4**

Cross Colours
Jones, Carl **7**
Kani, Karl **10**
Walker, T. J. **7**

Crucial Films
Henry, Lenny **9**

Crusader
Williams, Robert F. **11**

CTRN
See Transitional Committee for National Recovery (Guinea)

Cubism
Bearden, Romare **2**

Culinary arts
Clark, Patrick **14**

Cultural pluralism
Locke, Alain 10

Cumulative voting
Guinier, Lani 7

Curator/exhibition designer
Camp, Kimberly 19
Golden, Thelma 10
Hutson, Jean Blackwell 16
Sanders, Joseph R., Jr. 11
Stewart, Paul Wilbur 12

Cytogenetics
Satcher, David 7

Dallas city government
Johnson, Eddie Bernice 8
Kirk, Ron 11

Dallas Cowboys football team
Hill, Calvin 19
Smith, Emmitt 7

Dance Theatre of Harlem
Johnson, Virginia 9
Mitchell, Arthur 2
Nicholas, Fayard 20
Nicholas, Harold 20
Tyson, Cicely 7

DAV
See Disabled American Veterans

David M. Winfield Foundation
Winfield, Dave 5

Daytona Institute
See Bethune-Cookman College

Dayton Philharmonic Orchestra
Jackson, Isaiah 3

D.C. Black Repertory Theater
Reagon, Bernice Johnson 7

Death Row Records
Dre, Dr. 14
Hammer, M. C. 20
Knight, Suge 11
Shakur, Tupac 14

De Beers Botswana
See Debswana

Debswana
Masire, Quett 5

Defense Communications Agency
Gravely, Samuel L., Jr. 5

Def Jam Records
Jordan, Montell 23
L.L. Cool J 16
Simmons, Russell 1

Democratic National Committee (DNC)
Brown, Ron 5
Brown, Willie L., Jr. 7
Dixon, Sharon Pratt 1
Fattah, Chaka 11
Hamer, Fannie Lou 6
Jordan, Barbara 4
Mallett, Conrad, Jr. 16
Martin, Louis E. 16
Waters, Maxine 3
Williams, Maggie 7

Democratic National Convention
Allen, Ethel D. 13
Brown, Ron 5
Brown, Willie L., Jr. 7
Dixon, Sharon Pratt 1
Hamer, Fannie Lou 6
Herman, Alexis M. 15
Jordan, Barbara 4
Millender-McDonald, Juanita 21
Waters, Maxine 3
Williams, Maggie 7

Democratic Socialists of America (DSA)
West, Cornel 5
Marable, Manning 10

Dentistry
Bluitt, Juliann S. 14
Delany, Bessie 12
Sinkford, Jeanne C. 13

Denver Broncos football team
Barnes, Ernie 16
Davis, Terrell 20

Denver city government
Webb, Wellington 3

Denver Nuggets basketball team
Bickerstaff, Bernie 21
Mutombo, Dikembe 7

Depression/The Great Depression
Hampton, Henry 6

Desert Shield
See Operation Desert Shield

Desert Storm
See Operation Desert Storm

Detective fiction
Himes, Chester 8
Mosley, Walter 5
Wesley, Valerie Wilson 18

Detroit City Council
Collins, Barbara-Rose 7

Detroit city government
Archer, Dennis 7
Crockett, George, Jr. 10
Marshall, Bella 22
Young, Coleman 1, 20

Detroit entertainment
Wilson, Sunnie 7

Detroit Golden Gloves
Wilson, Sunnie 7

Detroit Lions football team
Farr, Mel 24
Sanders, Barry 1

Detroit Pistons basketball team
Bing, Dave 3
Dumars, Joe 16
Gentry, Alvin 23
Hill, Grant 13
Thomas, Isiah 7

Detroit Police Department
Gomez-Preston, Cheryl 9
McKinnon, Isaiah 9
Napoleon, Benny N. 23

Detroit Tigers baseball team
Fielder, Cecil 2

Diamond mining
Masire, Quett 5

Dillard University
Cook, Samuel DuBois 14

Dime Savings Bank
Parsons, Richard Dean 11

Diplomatic Corps
See U.S. Diplomatic Corps

Directing
Thompson, Tazewell 13
Warner, Malcolm-Jamal 22

Disabled American Veterans (DAV)
Brown, Jesse 6

DNC
See Democratic National Committee

Documentary film
Byrd, Robert 11
Dash, Julie 4
Davis, Ossie 5
Hampton, Henry 6
Henry, Lenny 9
Hudlin, Reginald 9
Hudlin, Warrington 9
Julien, Isaac 3
Lee, Spike 5, 19
Riggs, Marlon 5

Donald Byrd/The Group
Byrd, Donald 10

Drug abuse prevention
Brown, Les 5
Clements, George 2
Hale, Lorraine 8
Harris, Alice 7

Lucas, John **7**
Rangel, Charles **3**

Drug synthesis
Julian, Percy Lavon **6**

DSA
See Democratic Socialists of America

Dunham Dance Company
Dunham, Katherine **4**

DuSable Museum of African American History
Burroughs, Margaret Taylor **9**

Earthquake Early Alerting Service
Person, Waverly **9**

East St. Louis city government
Powell, Debra A. **23**

Ebenezer Baptist Church
King, Bernice **4**

Ebonics
Cook, Toni **23**

Ebony
Bennett, Lerone, Jr. **5**
Johnson, John H. **3**
Rice, Linda Johnson **9**
Sleet, Moneta, Jr. **5**

Ebony Museum of African American History
See DuSable Museum of African American History

Economic Community of West African States (ECOWAS)
Sawyer, Amos **2**

Economic Regulatory Administration
O'Leary, Hazel **6**

Economics
Boyd, T. B. III **6**
Brimmer, Andrew F. **2**
Brown, Tony **3**
Divine, Father **7**
Dodson, Howard, Jr. **7**
Gibson, William F. **6**
Hamer, Fannie Lou **6**
Hampton, Henry **6**
Machel, Graca Simbine **16**
Masire, Quett **5**
Raines, Franklin Delano **14**
Robinson, Randall **7**
Sowell, Thomas **2**
Sullivan, Leon H. **3**
Van Peebles, Melvin **7**
Wallace, Phyllis A. **9**
Wharton, Clifton R., Jr. **7**
White, Michael R. **5**
Williams, Walter E. **4**

ECOWAS
See Economic Community of West African States

Edelman Public Relations
Barrett, Andrew C. **12**

Editing
Curry, George E. **23**

Edmonds Entertainment
Edmonds, Kenneth "Babyface" **10**
Edmonds, Tracey **16**
Tillman, George, Jr. **20**

Edmonton Oilers hockey team
Fuhr, Grant **1**

Educational Testing Service
Stone, Chuck **9**

EEC
See European Economic Community

EEOC
See Equal Employment Opportunity Commission

Egyptology
Diop, Cheikh Anta **4**

Elder Foundation
Elder, Lee **6**

Emerge magazine
Curry, George E. **23**

Emmy awards
Allen, Debbie **13**
Amos, John **8**
Ashe, Arthur **1, 18**
Belafonte, Harry **4**
Bradley, Ed **2**
Brown, James **22**
Brown, Les **5**
Clayton, Xernona **3**
Cosby, Bill **7**
Curtis-Hall, Vondie **17**
Dee, Ruby **8**
Foxx, Redd **2**
Freeman, Al, Jr. **11**
Goldberg, Whoopi **4**
Gossett, Louis, Jr. **7**
Guillaume, Robert **3**
Gumbel, Greg **8**
Hunter-Gault, Charlayne **6**
Jones, James Earl **3**
La Salle, Eriq **12**
McQueen, Butterfly **6**
Moore, Shemar **21**
Parks, Gordon **1**
Pinkston, W. Randall **24**
Robinson, Max **3**
Rock, Chris **3, 22**
Rolle, Esther **13, 21**
Stokes, Carl B. **10**
Taylor, Billy **23**

Thigpen, Lynne **17**
Tyson, Cicely **7**
Uggams, Leslie **23**
Wayans, Damon **8**
Whitfield, Lynn **18**
Williams, Montel **4**
Winfrey, Oprah **2, 15**
Woodard, Alfre **9**

Endocrinology
Elders, Joycelyn **6**

Energy studies
Cose, Ellis **5**
O'Leary, Hazel **6**

Engineering
Alexander, Archie Alphonso **14**
Gibson, Kenneth Allen **6**
Hannah, Marc **10**
McCoy, Elijah **8**
Williams, O. S. **13**

Environmental issues
Chavis, Benjamin **6**
Hill, Bonnie Guiton **20**

Epidemiology
Gayle, Helene D. **3**

Episcopal Diocese of Massachusetts
Harris, Barbara **12**

EPRDF
See Ethiopian People's Revolutionary Democratic Front

Equal Employment Opportunity Commission (EEOC)
Hill, Anita **5**
Lewis, Delano **7**
Norton, Eleanor Holmes **7**
Thomas, Clarence **2**
Wallace, Phyllis A. **9**

ESPN
Roberts, Robin **16**

Essence
Lewis, Edward T. **21**
Parks, Gordon **1**
Smith, Clarence O. **21**
Taylor, Susan L. **10**
Wesley, Valerie Wilson **18**

Essence Communications
Lewis, Edward T. **21**
Smith, Clarence O. **21**
Taylor, Susan L. **10**

Essence, the Television Program
Taylor, Susan L. **10**

Ethiopian People's Revolutionary Democratic Front (EPRDF)
Meles Zenawi **3**

Eugene O'Neill Theater
Richards, Lloyd **2**

European Economic Community (EEC)
Diouf, Abdou **3**

Executive Leadership Council
Jackson, Mannie **14**

Exiled heads of state
Aristide, Jean-Bertrand **6**

Exploration
Henson, Matthew **2**

***Eyes on the Prize* series**
Hampton, Henry **6**

Fairbanks city government
Hayes, James C. **10**

FAIRR
See Foundation for the Advancement of Inmate Rehabilitation and Recreation

Fair Share Agreements
Gibson, William F. **6**

Famine relief
See World hunger

Famous Amos Cookie Corporation
Amos, Wally **9**

FAN
See Forces Armées du Nord (Chad)

Fashion
Smaltz, Audrey **12**
Sade **15**

FCC
See Federal Communications Commission

Federal Bureau of Investigation (FBI)
Gibson, Johnnie Mae **23**
Harvard, Beverly **11**

Federal Communications Commission (FCC)
Barrett, Andrew C. **12**
Hooks, Benjamin L. **2**
Kennard, William Earl **18**
Russell-McCloud, Patricia A. **17**

Federal Energy Administration
O'Leary, Hazel **6**

Federal Reserve Bank
Brimmer, Andrew F. **2**

Fellowship of Reconciliation (FOR)
Farmer, James **2**
Rustin, Bayard **4**

Fencing
Westbrook, Peter **20**

Fiction
Alexander, Margaret Walker **22**
Ansa, Tina McElroy **14**
Briscoe, Connie **15**
Campbell, Bebe Moore **6, 24**
Chase-Riboud, Barbara **20**
Cleage, Pearl **17**
Danticat, Edwidge **15**
Harris, E. Lynn **12**
Jackson, Sheneska **18**
Jenkins, Beverly **14**
McMillan, Terry **4, 17**
Tate, Eleanora E. **20**

Figure skating
Bonaly, Surya **7**

Film direction
Allen, Debbie **13**
Burnett, Charles **16**
Byrd, Robert **11**
Curtis-Hall, Vondie **17**
Dash, Julie **4**
Davis, Ossie **5**
Dickerson, Ernest **6, 17**
Duke, Bill **3**
Franklin, Carl **11**
Freeman, Al, Jr. **11**
Gray, F. Gary **14**
Harris, Leslie **6**
Hudlin, Reginald **9**
Hudlin, Warrington **9**
Hughes, Albert **7**
Hughes, Allen **7**
Jackson, George **19**
Julien, Isaac **3**
Lane, Charles **3**
Lee, Spike **5, 19**
Lemmons, Kasi **20**
Micheaux, Oscar **7**
Morton, Joe **18**
Moses, Gilbert **12**
Moss, Carlton **17**
Poitier, Sidney **11**
Riggs, Marlon **5**
Schultz, Michael A. **6**
Sembène, Ousmane **13**
Singleton, John **2**
Smith, Roger Guenveur **12**
St. Jacques, Raymond **8**
Tillman, George, Jr. **20**
Townsend, Robert **4, 23**
Underwood, Blair **7**
Van Peebles, Mario **2**
Van Peebles, Melvin **7**
Wayans, Damon **8**
Wayans, Keenen Ivory **18**

Film scores
Hancock, Herbie **20**
Jean-Baptiste, Marianne **17**
Jones, Quincy **8**
Prince **18**

Finance
Banks, Jeffrey **17**
Chapman, Jr., Nathan A. **21**
Fletcher, Alphonse, Jr. **16**
Griffith, Mark Winston **8**
Lawless, Theodore K. **8**
Louis, Errol T. **8**
Marshall, Bella **22**
Rogers, John W., Jr. **5**

Fisk University
Johnson, Charles S. **12**
Smith, John L. **22**

Florida A & M University
Gaither, Alonzo Smith (Jake) **14**
Humphries, Frederick **20**

Florida Marlins baseball team
Sheffield, Gary **16**

Florida state government
Brown, Corrine **24**
Meek, Carrie **6**
Tribble, Isreal, Jr. **8**

Flouride chemistry
Quarterman, Lloyd Albert **4**

Folk music
Charlemagne, Manno **11**
Jenkins, Ella **15**
Wilson, Cassandra **16**

Football
Allen, Marcus **20**
Amos, John **8**
Anderson, Jamal **22**
Brown, James **22**
Brown, Jim **11**
Butler, LeRoy III **17**
Carter, Cris **21**
Cunningham, Randall **23**
Davis, Terrell **20**
Dungy, Tony **17**
Edwards, Harry **2**
Farr, Mel Sr. **24**
Gaither, Alonzo Smith (Jake) **14**
Gilliam, Frank **23**
Green, Dennis **5**
Greene, Joe **10**
Grier, Roosevelt **13**
Hill, Calvin **19**
Lott, Ronnie **9**
McNair, Steve **22**
Moon, Warren **8**
Moss, Randy **23**
Pace, Orlando **21**
Page, Alan **7**
Payton, Walter **11**
Rashad, Ahmad **18**
Rice, Jerry **5**
Robinson, Eddie G. **10**
Sanders, Barry **1**
Sanders, Deion **4**
Shell, Art **1**
Simpson, O. J. **15**
Singletary, Mike **4**

Smith, Emmitt **7**
Stewart, Kordell **21**
Upshaw, Gene **18**
Walker, Herschel **1**
Watts, J. C., Jr. **14**
Weathers, Carl **10**
White, Reggie **6**
Williams, Doug **22**

FOR
See Fellowship of Reconciliation

Forces Armées du Nord (Chad; FAN)
Habré, Hissène **6**

Ford Foundation
Thomas, Franklin A. **5**
Franklin, Robert M. **13**

Ford Motor Company
Goldsberry, Ronald **18**

Foreign policy
Bunche, Ralph J. **5**
Rice, Condoleezza **3**
Robinson, Randall **7**

Forest Club
Wilson, Sunnie **7**

40 Acres and a Mule Filmworks
Dickerson, Ernest **6, 17**
Lee, Spike **5, 19**

Foster care
Hale, Clara **16**
Hale, Lorraine **8**

Foundation for the Advancement of Inmate Rehabilitation and Recreation (FAIRR)
King, B. B. **7**

Freedom Farm Cooperative
Hamer, Fannie Lou **6**

Free Southern Theater (FST)
Borders, James **9**

FRELIMO
See Front for the Liberation of Mozambique

French West Africa
Diouf, Abdou **3**

FRODEBU
See Front for Democracy in Burundi

FROLINAT
See Front de la Libération Nationale du Tchad (Chad)

FRONASA
See Front for National Salvation (Uganda)

Front de la Libération Nationale du Tchad (Chad; FROLINAT)
Habré, Hissène **6**

Front for Democracy in Burundi (FRODEBU)
Ndadaye, Melchior **7**
Ntaryamira, Cyprien **8**

Front for National Salvation (Uganda; FRONASA)
Museveni, Yoweri **4**

Front for the Liberation of Mozambique (FRELIMO)
Chissano, Joaquim **7**
Machel, Graca Simbine **16**
Machel, Samora Moises **8**

FST
See Free Southern Theater

Funk music
Ayers, Roy **16**
Clinton, George **9**
Watson, Johnny "Guitar" **18**

Fusion
Davis, Miles **4**
Jones, Quincy **8**

Gary, Williams, Parenti, Finney, Lewis & McManus
Gary, Willie E. **12**

Gary Enterprises
Gary, Willie E. **12**

Gassaway, Crosson, Turner & Parsons
Parsons, James **14**

Gay Men of Color Consortium
Wilson, Phill **9**

Genealogy
Dash, Julie **4**
Haley, Alex **4**

General Motors Corporation
Roberts, Roy S. **14**

Geometric symbolism
Douglas, Aaron **7**

Geophysics
Person, Waverly **9**

George Foster Peabody Broadcasting Award
Bradley, Ed **2**
Hunter-Gault, Charlayne **6**
Shaw, Bernard **2**

Georgia state government
Baker, Thurbert **22**
Bishop Jr., Sanford D. **24**
Bond, Julian **2**
Williams, Hosea Lorenzo **15**

Georgia State Supreme Court
Sears-Collins, Leah J. **5**

Glaucoma treatment
Julian, Percy Lavon **6**

Glidden Company
Julian, Percy Lavon **6**

Golden Globe awards
Allen, Debbie **13**
Bassett, Angela **23**
Carroll, Diahann **9**
Freeman, Morgan **2, 20**
Taylor, Regina **9**

Golden State Warriors basketball team
Edwards, Harry **2**
Lucas, John **7**
Sprewell, Latrell **23**

Golf
Elder, Lee **6**
Gibson, Althea **8**
Peete, Calvin **11**
Richmond, Mitch **19**
Sifford, Charlie **4**
Webber, Chris **15**
Woods, Tiger **14**

Goodwill Games
Swoopes, Sheryl **12**

Gospel music
Adams, Oleta **18**
Adams, Yolanda **17**
Armstrong, Vanessa Bell **24**
Caesar, Shirley **19**
Clark-Sheard, Karen **22**
Cleveland, James **19**
Cooke, Sam **17**
Dorsey, Thomas **15**
Franklin, Aretha **11**
Franklin, Kirk **15**
Green, Al **13**
Hammond, Fred **23**
Hawkins, Tramaine **16**
Houston, Cissy **20**
Jackson, Mahalia **5**
Jakes, Thomas "T.D." **17**
Jones, Bobby **20**
Lassiter, Roy **24**
Little Richard **15**
Marrow, Queen Esther **24**
Mayfield, Curtis **2**
Monica **21**
Peoples, Dottie **22**
Reagon, Bernice Johnson **7**
Reese, Della **6, 20**
Walker, Albertina **10**
Washington, Dinah **22**
Winans, BeBe **14**
Winans, CeCe **14**
Winans, Marvin L. **17**
Winans, Vickie **24**

Grambling State University
Favors, Steve 23

Grammy awards
Adams, Oleta 18
Badu, Erykah 22
Belafonte, Harry 4
Blige, Mary J. 20
Brandy 14
Caesar, Shirley 19
Cleveland, James 19
Cole, Natalie Maria 17
Cosby, Bill 7
Davis, Miles 4
Edmonds, Kenneth "Babyface" 10
Ellington, Duke 5
Fitzgerald, Ella 8
Franklin, Aretha 11
Gaye, Marvin 2
Goldberg, Whoopi 4
Hammer, M. C. 20
Hathaway, Donny 18
Hawkins, Tramaine 16
Hill, Lauryn 20
Houston, Cissy 20
Houston, Whitney 7
Jackson, Michael 19
James, Etta 13
Jean, Wyclef 20
Jimmy Jam 13
Jones, Bobby 20
Jones, Quincy 8
Kelly, R. 18
Lewis, Terry 13
Makeba, Miriam 2
Murphy, Eddie 4, 20
Norman, Jessye 5
Price, Leontyne 1
Prince 18
Queen Latifah 1, 16
Reagon, Bernice Johnson 7
Redding, Otis 16
Robinson, Smokey 3
Sade 15
Smith, Will 8, 18
Turner, Tina 6
Warwick, Dionne 18
White, Barry 13
Wilson, Nancy 10
Winans, Marvin L. 17
Wonder, Stevie 11

Green Bay Packers football team
Butler, Leroy III 17
Howard, Desmond 16
White, Reggie 6

Groupe de Recherche Chorégraphique de l'Opéra de Paris
Dove, Ulysses 5

Guardian
Trotter, Monroe 9

Guitar
Hendrix, Jimi 10
House, Son 8
Howlin' Wolf 9
Jean, Wyclef 20
Johnson, Robert 2
King, B. B. 7
Kravitz, Lenny 10
Marley, Bob 5
Mayfield, Curtis 2
Ndegéocello, Me'Shell 15
Ongala, Remmy 9
Watson, Johnny "Guitar" 18
Wilson, Cassandra 16

Gulf War
Powell, Colin 1
Shaw, Bernard 2
Von Lipsey, Roderick K. 11

Gurdjieff Institute
Toomer, Jean 6

Gymnastics
Dawes, Dominique 11
White, Jesse 22

Hair care
Cottrell, Comer 11
Fuller, S. B. 13
Malone, Annie 13
Roche, Joyce M. 17
Walker, Madame C. J. 7

Haitian refugees
Ashe, Arthur 1, 18
Dunham, Katherine 4
Jean, Wyclef 20
Robinson, Randall 7

Hale House
Hale, Clara 16
Hale, Lorraine 8

Harlem Globetrotters
Chamberlain, Wilt 18
Haynes, Marques 22
Jackson, Mannie 14

Harlem Renaissance
Alexander, Margaret Walker 22
Cullen, Countee 8
Delaney, Beauford 19
Ellington, Duke 5
Fauset, Jessie 7
Fisher, Rudolph 17
Frazier, E. Franklin 10
Hughes, Langston 4
Hurston, Zora Neale 3
Johnson, James Weldon 5
Johnson, William Henry 3
Larsen, Nella 10
Locke, Alain 10
McKay, Claude 6
Mills, Florence 22
Petry, Ann 19
Thurman, Wallace 16
Toomer, Jean 6
VanDerZee, James 6
West, Dorothy 12

Harlem Writers Guild
Guy, Rosa 5
Wesley, Valerie Wilson 18

Harlem Youth Opportunities Unlimited (HARYOU)
Clark, Kenneth B. 5

Harmonica
Howlin' Wolf 9

Harriet Tubman Home for Aged and Indignet Colored People
Tubman, Harriet 9

Harvard Law School
Bell, Derrick 6
Ogletree, Charles, Jr. 12

HARYOU
See Harlem Youth Opportunities Unlimited

Head Start
Edelman, Marian Wright 5

Health care reform
Brown, Jesse 6
Cooper, Edward S. 6
Davis, Angela 5
Gibson, Kenneth A. 6
Norman, Pat 10
Satcher, David 7
Williams, Daniel Hale 2

Heart disease
Cooper, Edward S. 6

Heidelberg Project
Guyton, Tyree 9

HEW
See U.S. Department of Health, Education, and Welfare

HHS
See U.S. Department of Health and Human Services

Historians
Berry, Mary Frances 7
Chase-Riboud, Barbara 20
Cooper, Anna Julia 20
Diop, Cheikh Anta 4
Dodson, Howard, Jr. 7
Du Bois, W. E. B. 3
Franklin, John Hope 5
Gates, Henry Louis, Jr. 3
Giddings, Paula 11
Hansberry, William Leo 11
Harkless, Necia Desiree 19
Hine, Darlene Clark 24
Marable, Manning 10
Painter, Nell Irvin 24
Patterson, Orlando 4
Quarles, Benjamin Arthur 18
Reagon, Bernice Johnson 7
Reddick, Lawrence Dunbar 20

Schomburg, Arthur Alfonso **9**
Williams, George Washington **18**
Woodson, Carter G. **2**

Hockey
Brown, James **22**
Fuhr, Grant **1**
McBride, Bryant **18**
McKegney, Tony **3**
O'Ree, Willie **5**

Homosexuality
Carter, Mandy **11**
Delany, Samuel R., Jr. **9**
Gomes, Peter J. **15**
Harris, E. Lynn **12**
Hemphill, Essex **10**
Julien, Isaac **3**
Lorde, Audre **6**
Norman, Pat **10**
Parker, Pat **19**
Riggs, Marlon **5**
Rupaul **17**
Wilson, Phill **9**

Honeywell Corporation
Jackson, Mannie **14**

House of Representatives
See U.S. House of Representatives

Houston Astros baseball team
Morgan, Joe Leonard **9**

Houston Comets basketball team
Perrot, Kim **23**

Houston Oilers football team
McNair, Steve **22**
Moon, Warren **8**

Houston Rockets basketball team
Lucas, John **7**
Olajuwon, Hakeem **2**

Howard University
Jenifer, Franklyn G. **2**
Locke, Alain **10**
Mays, Benjamin E. **7**
Payton, Benjamin F. **23**
Porter, James A. **11**
Reid, Irvin D. **20**
Robinson, Spottswood W. III **22**
Swygert, H. Patrick **22**
Wells, James Lesesne **10**
Wesley, Dorothy Porter **19**

HRCF
See Human Rights Campaign Fund

Hubbard Hospital
Lyttle, Hulda Margaret **14**

HUD
See U.S. Department of Housing and Urban Development

Hugo awards
Butler, Octavia **8**
Delany, Samuel R., Jr. **9**

Hull-Ottawa Canadiens hockey team
O'Ree, Willie **5**

Human Rights Campaign Fund (HRCF)
Carter, Mandy **11**

Hurdles
Devers, Gail **7**

IBF
See International Boxing Federation

Ice skating
See Figure skating

Igbo people/traditions
Achebe, Chinua **6**

IHRLG
See International Human Rights Law Group

Illinois state government
Braun, Carol Moseley **4**
Washington, Harold **6**
White, Jesse **22**

Illustrations
Biggers, John **20**
Campbell, E. Simms **13**
Hudson, Cheryl **15**
Kitt, Sandra **23**
Pinkney, Jerry **15**
Saint James, Synthia **12**

Imani Temple
Stallings, George A., Jr. **6**

IMF
See International Monetary Fund

Indiana state government
Carson, Julia **23**

Indianapolis 500
Ribbs, Willy T. **2**

Information technology
Smith, Joshua **10**

In Friendship
Baker, Ella **5**

Inkatha
Buthelezi, Mangosuthu Gatsha **9**

Institute for Black Parenting
Oglesby, Zena **12**

Institute for Journalism Education
Harris, Jay T. **19**
Maynard, Robert C. **7**

Institute for Research in African American Studies
Marable, Manning **10**

Institute of Positive Education
Madhubuti, Haki R. **7**

Institute of Social and Religious Research
Mays, Benjamin E. **7**

Institute of the Black World
Dodson, Howard, Jr. **7**

Insurance
Hill, Jessie, Jr. **13**
Procope, Ernesta **23**
Spaulding, Charles Clinton **9**

International Boxing Federation (IBF)
Ali, Muhammad **2, 16**
Moorer, Michael **19**
Whitaker, Pernell **10**

International Free and Accepted Masons and Eastern Star
Banks, William **11**

International Human Rights Law Group (IHRLG)
McDougall, Gay J. **11**

International Ladies' Auxiliary
Tucker, Rosina **14**

International Monetary Fund (IMF)
Babangida, Ibrahim **4**
Chissano, Joaquim **7**
Conté, Lansana **7**
Diouf, Abdou **3**
Patterson, P. J. **6, 20**

Inventions
Julian, Percy Lavon **6**
Latimer, Lewis H. **4**
McCoy, Elijah **8**
Morgan, Garrett **1**
Woods, Granville T. **5**

Investment management
Procope, Ernesta **23**
Rogers, John W., Jr. **5**
Utendahl, John **23**

Jackie Robinson Foundation
Robinson, Rachel **16**

Jamison Project
Jamison, Judith **7**

Jazz
Albright, Gerald **23**
Armstrong, Louis **2**
Austin, Patti **24**
Ayers, Roy **16**
Basie, Count **23**
Bechet, Sidney **18**

Belle, Regina **1**
Brooks, Avery **9**
Calloway, Cab **14**
Carter, Betty **19**
Carter, Regina **23**
Charles, Ray **16**
Cheatham, Doc **17**
Cole, Nat King **17**
Coltrane, John **19**
Count Basie **23**
Crawford, Randy **19**
Crothers, Scatman **19**
Crouch, Stanley **11**
Crowder, Henry **16**
Davis, Anthony **11**
Davis, Miles **4**
Donegan, Dorothy **19**
Downing, Will **19**
Duke, George **21**
Ellington, Duke **5**
Ellison, Ralph **7**
Eubanks, Kevin **15**
Fitzgerald, Ella **8, 18**
Gillespie, Dizzy **1**
Hampton, Lionel **17**
Hancock, Herbie **20**
Hawkins, Coleman **9**
Holiday, Billie **1**
Hyman, Phyllis **19**
James, Etta **13**
Jarreau, Al **21**
Jones, Elvin **14**
Jones, Quincy **8**
Lincoln, Abbey **3**
Madhubuti, Haki R. **7**
Marsalis, Wynton **16**
Mills, Florence **22**
Mingus, Charles **15**
Monk, Thelonious **1**
Moore, Melba **21**
Muse, Clarence Edouard **21**
Nascimento, Milton **2**
Parker, Charlie **20**
Powell, Bud **24**
Reese, Della **6, 20**
Roach, Max **21**
Roberts, Marcus **19**
Ross, Diana **8**
Smith, Bessie **3**
Taylor, Billy **23**
Vaughan, Sarah **13**
Washington, Dinah **22**
Washington, Grover, Jr. **17**
Watson, Johnny "Guitar" **18**
Williams, Joe **5**
Williams, Mary Lou **15**
Wilson, Cassandra **16**
Wilson, Nancy **10**

Jet
Bennett, Lerone, Jr. **5**
Johnson, John H. **3**
Sleet, Moneta, Jr. **5**

John Lucas Enterprises
Lucas, John **7**

Johnson Publishing Company, Inc.
Bennett, Lerone, Jr. **5**
Booker, Simeon **23**
Johnson, John H. **3**
Rice, Linda Johnson **9**
Sleet, Moneta, Jr. **5**

Joint Chiefs of Staff
See U.S. Joint Chiefs of Staff

Journalism
Abu-Jamal, Mumia **15**
Ansa, Tina McElroy **14**
Ashley-Ward, Amelia **23**
Azikiwe, Nnamdi **13**
Barden, Don H. **9, 20**
Bennett, Lerone, Jr. **5**
Booker, Simeon **23**
Borders, James **9**
Bradley, Ed **2**
Brown, Tony **3**
Campbell, Bebe Moore **6, 24**
Chideya, Farai **14**
Cose, Ellis **5**
Crouch, Stanley **11**
Cullen, Countee **8**
Cunningham, Evelyn **23**
Dawkins, Wayne **20**
Dunbar, Paul Laurence **8**
Edmonds, Terry **17**
Forman, James **7**
Fortune, T. Thomas **6**
Giddings, Paula **11**
Goode, Mal **13**
Gordon, Ed **10**
Grimké, Archibald H. **9**
Gumbel, Bryant **14**
Gumbel, Greg **8**
Hansberry, Lorraine **6**
Harrington, Oliver W. **9**
Harris, Jay **19**
Hickman, Fred **11**
Hunter-Gault, Charlayne **6**
Johnson, James Weldon **5**
Khanga, Yelena **6**
Lampkin, Daisy **19**
Leavell, Dorothy R. **17**
Lewis, Edward T. **21**
Martin, Louis E. **16**
Maynard, Robert C. **7**
McCall, Nathan **8**
McGruder, Robert **22**
McKay, Claude **6**
Mitchell, Russ **21**
Mkapa, Benjamin **16**
Nelson, Jill **6**
Page, Clarence **4**
Parks, Gordon **1**
Perez, Anna **1**
Perkins, Tony **24**
Pinkston, W. Randall **24**
Price, Hugh B. **9**
Raspberry, William **2**
Reed, Ishmael **8**
Reeves, Rachel J. **23**
Roberts, Robin **16**
Robinson, Max **3**
Rodgers, Johnathan **6**
Rowan, Carl T. **1**
Shaw, Bernard **2**
Shipp, E. R. **15**
Simpson, Carole **6**
Smith, Clarence O. **21**
Sowell, Thomas **2**
Staples, Brent **8**
Stewart, Alison **13**
Stokes, Carl B. **10**
Stone, Chuck **9**
Tate, Eleanora E. **20**
Taylor, Kristin Clark **8**
Taylor, Susan L. **10**
Thurman, Wallace **16**
Trotter, Monroe **9**
Tucker, Cynthia **15**
Wallace, Michele Faith **13**
Watts, Rolonda **9**
Webb, Veronica **10**
Wells-Barnett, Ida B. **8**
Wesley, Valerie Wilson **18**
Whitaker, Mark **21**
Wiley, Ralph **8**
Wilkins, Roger **2**
Williams, Patricia J. **11**

Journal of Negro History
Woodson, Carter G. **2**

Just Us Books
Hudson, Cheryl **15**
Hudson, Wade **15**

Kansas City Athletics baseball team
Paige, Satchel **7**

Kansas City Chiefs football team
Allen, Marcus **20**
Dungy, Tony **17**

Kansas City government
Cleaver, Emanuel **4**

KANU
See Kenya African National Union

Karl Kani Infinity
Kani, Karl **10**

KAU
See Kenya African Union

KCA
See Kikuyu Central Association

Kenya African National Union (KANU)
Kenyatta, Jomo **5**

Kenya African Union (KAU)
Kenyatta, Jomo **5**

Kikuyu Central Association (KCA)
Kenyatta, Jomo **5**

King Center
See Martin Luther King Jr. Center for Nonviolent Social Change

Kraft General Foods
Fudge, Ann **11**
Sneed, Paula A. **18**

Kwanzaa
Karenga, Maulana **10**

Kwazulu Territorial Authority
Buthelezi, Mangosuthu Gatsha **9**

Ladies Professional Golfers' Association (LPGA)
Gibson, Althea **8**

LAPD
See Los Angeles Police Department

Latin American folk music
Nascimento, Milton **2**

Law enforcement
Alexander, Joyce London **18**
Bradley, Thomas **2, 20**
Brown, Lee P. **1, 24**
Freeman, Charles **19**
Gibson, Johnnie Mae **23**
Glover, Nathaniel, Jr. **12**
Gomez-Preston, Cheryl **9**
Harvard, Beverly **11**
Johnson, Norma L. Holloway **17**
Johnson, Robert T. **17**
Keith, Damon J. **16**
McKinnon, Isaiah **9**
Napoleon, Benny N. **23**
Parks, Bernard C. **17**
Ramsey, Charles H. **21**
Schmoke, Kurt **1**
Thomas, Franklin A. **5**
Williams, Willie L. **4**

Lawyers' Committee for Civil Rights Under Law
McDougall, Gay J. **11**

LDF
See NAACP Legal Defense Fund

Leadership Conference on Civil Rights (LCCR)
Henderson, Wade J. **14**

League of Nations
Haile Selassie **7**

Leary Group Inc.
Leary, Kathryn D. **10**

"Leave No Child Behind"
Edelman, Marian Wright **5**

Lee Elder Scholarship Fund
Elder, Lee **6**

Legal Defense Fund
See NAACP Legal Defense Fund

Les Brown Unlimited, Inc.
Brown, Les **5**

Lexicography
Major, Clarence **9**

Liberation theology
West, Cornel **5**

Library science
Bontemps, Arna **8**
Franklin, Hardy R. **9**
Harsh, Vivian Gordon **14**
Hutson, Jean Blackwell **16**
Josey, E. J. **10**
Kitt, Sandra **23**
Larsen, Nella **10**
Owens, Major **6**
Schomburg, Arthur Alfonso **9**
Wesley, Dorothy Porter **19**

Lincoln University
Randall, Dudley **8**
Sudarkasa, Niara **4**

LISC
See Local Initiative Support Corporation

Literacy Volunteers of America
Amos, Wally **9**

Literary criticism
Baker, Houston A., Jr. **6**
Brown, Sterling **10**
Reed, Ishmael **8**
Wesley, Valerie Wilson **18**
West, Cornel **5**

"Little Paris" group
Thomas, Alma **14**

"Little Rock Nine"
Bates, Daisy **13**

Lobbying
Brooke, Edward **8**
Brown, Elaine **8**
Brown, Jesse **6**
Brown, Ron **5**
Edelman, Marian Wright **5**
Lee, Canada **8**
Mallett, Conrad, Jr. **16**
Robinson, Randall **7**

Local Initiative Support Corporation (LISC)
Thomas, Franklin A. **5**

Long jump
Lewis, Carl **4**
Powell, Mike **7**

Los Angeles city government
Bradley, Thomas **2, 20**
Evers, Myrlie **8**

Los Angeles Dodgers baseball team
Baker, Dusty **8**
Newcombe, Don **24**
Robinson, Frank **9**
Strawberry, Darryl **22**

Los Angeles Galaxy soccer team
Jones, Cobi N'Gai **18**

Los Angeles Lakers basketball team
Abdul-Jabbar, Kareem **8**
Bryant, Kobe **15**
Chamberlain, Wilt **18**
Johnson, Earvin "Magic" **3**

Los Angeles Police Department (LAPD)
Parks, Bernard C. **17**
Williams, Willie L. **4**

Los Angeles Raiders football team
Allen, Marcus **20**
Lott, Ronnie **9**
Shell, Art **1**

Los Angeles Sparks basketball team
Leslie, Lisa **16**

Lost-Found Nation of Islam
Ali, Muhammad **2, 16**
Farrakhan, Louis **2, 15**
Muhammad, Elijah **4**
Muhammad, Khallid Abdul **10**
X, Malcolm **1**

Louisiana state government
Fields, Cleo **13**
Pinchback, P. B. S. **9**

Louisiana State Senate
Fields, Cleo **13**
Pinchback, P. B. S. **9**

LPGA
See Ladies Professional Golfers' Association

Lynching (anti-lynching legislation)
Johnson, James Weldon **5**
Till, Emmett **7**

Lyricist
Dunbar, Paul Laurence **8**
Fitzgerald, Ella **8**
Jean, Wyclef **20**
Johnson, James Weldon **5**

MacNeil/Lehrer NewsHour
Hunter-Gault, Charlayne **6**

Madame C. J. Walker Manufacturing Company
Walker, A'lelia **14**
Walker, Madame C. J. **7**

Major League Baseball Properties
Doby, Lawrence Eugene, Sr. **16**

Malawi Congress Party (MCP)
Banda, Hastings Kamuzu **6**

Manhattan Project
Quarterman, Lloyd Albert 4

MARC Corp.
See Metropolitan Applied Research Center

March on Washington/Freedom March
Baker, Josephine 3
Belafonte, Harry 4
Bunche, Ralph J. 5
Davis, Ossie 5
Fauntroy, Walter E. 11
Forman, James 7
Franklin, John Hope 5
Hedgeman, Anna Arnold 22
Horne, Lena 5
Jackson, Mahalia 5
King, Coretta Scott 3
King, Martin Luther, Jr. 1
Lewis, John 2
Meredith, James H. 11
Randolph, A. Philip 3
Rustin, Bayard 4
Sleet, Moneta, Jr. 5
Wilkins, Roy 4
Young, Whitney M., Jr. 4

Marie Brown Associates
Brown, Marie Dutton 12

Martin Luther King Jr. Center for Nonviolent Social Change
Dodson, Howard, Jr. 7
King, Bernice 4
King, Coretta Scott 3
King, Dexter 10
King, Martin Luther, Jr. 1
King, Yolanda 6

Marxism
Baraka, Amiri 1
Jagan, Cheddi 16
Machel, Samora Moises 8
Nkrumah, Kwame 3
Sankara, Thomas 17

Massachusetts state government
Brooke, Edward 8

Masters Tournament
Elder, Lee 6

Mathematics
Gates, Sylvester James, Jr. 15

MAXIMA Corporation
Smith, Joshua 10

Maxwell House Coffee Company
Fudge, Ann 11

McCall Pattern Company
Lewis, Reginald F. 6

MCP
See Malawi Congress Party

Medicine
Banda, Hastings Kamuzu 6
Benjamin, Regina 20
Black, Keith Lanier 18
Callender, Clive O. 3
Carson, Benjamin 1
Christian-Green, Donna M. 17
Comer, James P. 6
Cooper, Edward S. 6
Dickens, Helen Octavia 14
Drew, Charles Richard 7
Elders, Joycelyn 6
Fisher, Rudolph 17
Freeman, Harold P. 23
Fuller, Solomon Carter, Jr. 15
Gayle, Helene D. 3
Gibson, William F. 6
Hinton, William Augustus 8
Jemison, Mae C. 1
Kountz, Samuel L. 10
Lawless, Theodore K. 8
Leffall, LaSalle, Jr. 3
Logan, Onnie Lee 14
Pitt, David Thomas 10
Poussaint, Alvin F. 5
Satcher, David 7
Sullivan, Louis 8
Thomas, Vivien 9
Watkins, Levi, Jr. 9
Welsing, Frances Cress 5
Williams, Daniel Hale 2
Wright, Louis Tompkins 4

Meharry Medical College
Lyttle, Hulda Margaret 14

Melanin theory of racism
See also Cress Theory of Color Confrontation and Racism
Jeffries, Leonard 8

Men's movement
Somé, Malidoma Patrice 10

Merce Cunningham Dance Company
Dove, Ulysses 5

MESBICs
See Minority Enterprise Small Business Investment Corporations

Metropolitan Applied Research Center (MARC Corp.)
Clark, Kenneth B. 5

MFDP
See Mississippi Freedom Democratic Party

Miami Dolphins football team
Greene, Joe 10

Michael Jordan Foundation
Jordan, Michael 6, 21

Michigan House of Representatives
Collins, Barbara-Rose 7

Kilpatrick, Carolyn Cheeks 16

Michigan State Supreme Court
Archer, Dennis 7
Mallett, Conrad, Jr. 16

Michigan State University
Wharton, Clifton R., Jr. 7

Midwifery
Logan, Onnie Lee 14
Robinson, Sharon 22

Military police
Cadoria, Sherian Grace 14

Miller Brewing Company
Colbert, Virgis William 17

Millinery
Bailey, Xenobia 11

Million Man March
Farrakhan, Louis 15
Hawkins, La-Van 17
Worrill, Conrad 12

Milwaukee Braves baseball team
Aaron, Hank 5

Milwaukee Brewers baseball team
Aaron, Hank 5
Baylor, Don 6
Sheffield, Gary 16

Milwaukee Bucks basketball team
Abdul-Jabbar, Kareem 8
Lucas, John 7

Minneapolis City Council
Sayles Belton, Sharon 9, 16

Minneapolis city government
Sayles Belton, Sharon 9, 16

Minnesota State Supreme Court
Page, Alan 7

Minnesota Timberwolves basketball team
Garnett, Kevin 14

Minnesota Twins baseball team
Baylor, Don 6
Carew, Rod 20
Puckett, Kirby 4
Winfield, Dave 5

Minnesota Vikings football team
Carter, Cris 21
Cunningham, Randall 23
Dungy, Tony 17
Gilliam, Frank 23
Green, Dennis 5
Moon, Warren 8
Moss, Randy 23
Page, Alan 7
Rashad, Ahmad 18

Cumulative Subject Index

Walker, Herschel **1**

Minority Business Resource Center
Hill, Jessie, Jr. **13**

Minority Enterprise Small Business Investment Corporations (MESBICs)
Lewis, Reginald F. **6**

Minstrel shows
McDaniel, Hattie **5**

Miss America
Vincent, Marjorie Judith **2**
Williams, Vanessa L. **4, 17**

Mississippi Freedom Democratic Party (MFDP)
Baker, Ella **5**
Blackwell, Unita **17**
Hamer, Fannie Lou **6**
Henry, Aaron **19**
Norton, Eleanor Holmes **7**

Mississippi state government
Hamer, Fannie Lou **6**

Miss USA
Gist, Carole **1**

MLA
See Modern Language Association of America

Model Inner City Community Organization (MICCO)
Fauntroy, Walter E. **11**

Modeling
Banks, Tyra **11**
Beckford, Tyson **11**
Berry, Halle **4, 19**
Campbell, Naomi **1**
Hardison, Bethann **12**
Hounsou, Djimon **19**
Houston, Whitney **7**
Iman **4**
Johnson, Beverly **2**
Langhart, Janet **19**
Leslie, Lisa **16**
Powell, Maxine **8**
Rochon, Lela **16**
Smith, Barbara **11**
Tamia **24**
Tyson, Cicely **7**
Webb, Veronica **10**
Wek, Alek **18**

Modern dance
Ailey, Alvin **8**
Allen, Debbie **13**
Byrd, Donald **10**
Dove, Ulysses **5**
Fagan, Garth **18**
Faison, George **16**
Jamison, Judith **7**
Kitt, Eartha **16**

Miller, Bebe **3**
Primus, Pearl **6**
Vereen, Ben **4**

Modern Language Association of America (MLA)
Baker, Houston A., Jr. **6**

Montgomery bus boycott
Abernathy, Ralph David **1**
Baker, Ella **5**
Jackson, Mahalia **5**
King, Martin Luther, Jr. **1**
Parks, Rosa **1**
Rustin, Bayard **4**

Montreal Expos
Doby, Lawrence Eugene, Sr. **16**

Morehouse College
Hope, John **8**
Mays, Benjamin E. **7**

Morna
Evora, Cesaria **12**

Morris Brown College
Cross, Dolores E. **23**

Moscow World News
Khanga, Yelena **6**
Sullivan, Louis **8**

Mother Waddles Perpetual Mission, Inc.
Waddles, Charleszetta (Mother) **10**

Motivational speaking
Brown, Les **5**
Kimbro, Dennis **10**
Russell-McCloud, Patricia **17**

Motown Records
Bizimungu, Pasteur **19**
Busby, Jheryl **3**
Gaye, Marvin **2**
Gordy, Berry, Jr. **1**
Jackson, George **19**
Jackson, Michael **19**
Kendricks, Eddie **22**
Massenburg, Kedar **23**
Powell, Maxine **8**
Robinson, Smokey **3**
Ross, Diana **8**
Wonder, Stevie **11**

Mouvement Revolutionnaire National pour la Developpement (Rwanda; MRND)
Habyarimana, Juvenal **8**

MOVE
Goode, W. Wilson **4**
Wideman, John Edgar **5**

MRND
See Mouvement Revolutionnaire National pour la Developpement

MTV Jams
Bellamy, Bill **12**

Multimedia art
Bailey, Xenobia **11**
Simpson, Lorna **4**

Muppets, The
Clash, Kevin **14**

Murals
Biggers, John **20**
Douglas, Aaron **7**
Lee-Smith, Hughie **5**
Walker, Kara **16**

Music Television (MTV)
Bellamy, Bill **12**
Chideya, Farai **14**

Musical composition
Ashford, Nickolas **21**
Blige, Mary J **20**
Bonga, Kuenda **13**
Braxton, Toni **15**
Caesar, Shirley **19**
Charlemagne, Manno **11**
Charles, Ray **16**
Cleveland, James **19**
Cole, Natalie Maria **17**
Combs, Sean "Puffy" **17**
Davis, Anthony **11**
Davis, Miles **4**
Davis, Sammy Jr. **18**
Ellington, Duke **5**
Europe, James Reese **10**
Evans, Faith **22**
Fats Domino **20**
George, Nelson **12**
Gillespie, Dizzy **1**
Gordy, Berry, Jr. **1**
Green, Al **13**
Hailey, JoJo **22**
Hailey, K-Ci **22**
Hammer, M. C. **20**
Handy, W. C. **8**
Hathaway, Donny **18**
Hayes, Isaac **20**
Hill, Lauryn **20**
Humphrey, Bobbi **20**
Jackson, Michael **19**
James, Rick **17**
Jean, Wyclef **20**
Jean-Baptiste, Marianne **17**
Jones, Quincy **8**
Joplin, Scott **6**
Jordan, Montell **23**
Kelly, R. **18**
King, B. B. **7**
León, Tania **13**
Lincoln, Abbey **3**
Marsalis, Wynton **16**
Master P **21**
Maxwell **20**
Mitchell, Brian Stokes **21**
Monica **21**
Muse, Clarence Edouard **21**
Ndegéocello, Me'Shell **15**

Prince **18**
Pritchard, Robert Starling **21**
Reagon, Bernice Johnson **7**
Redding, Otis **16**
Roach, Max **21**
Rushen, Patrice **12**
Sangare, Oumou **18**
Simone, Nina **15**
Simpson, Valerie **21**
Sweat, Keith **19**
Usher **23**
Van Peebles, Melvin **7**
Warwick, Dionne **18**
Washington, Grover, Jr. **17**

Music publishing
Combs, Sean "Puffy" **17**
Cooke, Sam **17**
Edmonds, Tracey **16**
Gordy, Berry, Jr. **1**
Handy, W. C. **8**
Humphrey, Bobbi **20**
Ice Cube **8**
Jackson, George **19**
Jackson, Michael **19**
James, Rick **17**
Knight, Suge **11**
Master P **21**
Mayfield, Curtis **2**
Prince **18**
Redding, Otis **16**
Ross, Diana **8**

Muslim Mosque, Inc.
X, Malcolm **1**

Mysteries
Himes, Chester **8**
Mosley, Walter **5**
Wesley, Valerie Wilson **18**

NAACP
See National Association for the Advancement of Colored People

NAACP Legal Defense Fund (LDF)
Bell, Derrick **6**
Chambers, Julius **3**
Edelman, Marian Wright **5**
Guinier, Lani **7**
Jones, Elaine R. **7**
Julian, Percy Lavon **6**
Marshall, Thurgood **1**
Motley, Constance Baker **10**

NABJ
See National Association of Black Journalists

NAC
See Nyasaland African Congress

NACGN
See National Association of Colored Graduate Nurses

NACW
See National Association of Colored Women

NAG
See Nonviolent Action Group

NASA
See National Aeronautics and Space Administration

Nation
Wilkins, Roger **2**

Nation of Islam
See Lost-Found Nation of Islam

National Action Network
Sharpton, Al **21**

National Aeronautics and Space Administration (NASA)
Bluford, Guy **2**
Bolden, Charles F., Jr. **7**
Gregory, Frederick D. **8**
Jemison, Mae C. **1**
McNair, Ronald **3**
Nichols, Nichelle **11**

National Afro-American Council
Fortune, T. Thomas **6**

National Alliance Party (NAP)
Fulani, Lenora **11**

National Association for the Advancement of Colored People (NAACP)
Baker, Ella **5**
Bates, Daisy **13**
Bell, Derrick **6**
Bond, Julian **2**
Bontemps, Arna **8**
Brooks, Gwendolyn **1**
Bunche, Ralph J. **5**
Chambers, Julius **3**
Chavis, Benjamin **6**
Clark, Kenneth B. **5**
Clark, Septima **7**
Days, Drew S., III **10**
Dee, Ruby **8**
DuBois, Shirley Graham **21**
Du Bois, W. E. B. **3**
Edelman, Marian Wright **5**
Evers, Medgar **3**
Evers, Myrlie **8**
Farmer, James **2**
Fuller, S. B. **13**
Gibson, William F. **6**
Grimké, Archibald H. **9**
Hampton, Fred **18**
Harrington, Oliver W. **9**
Henderson, Wade **14**
Hooks, Benjamin L. **2**
Horne, Lena **5**
Houston, Charles Hamilton **4**
Johnson, James Weldon **5**
Jordan, Vernon E. **3**
Lampkin, Daisy **19**
Madison, Joseph E. **17**
Marshall, Thurgood **1**
McKissick, Floyd B. **3**
McPhail, Sharon **2**
Meredith, James H. **11**
Moses, Robert Parris **11**
Motley, Constance Baker **10**
Owens, Major **6**
Rustin, Bayard **4**
Terrell, Mary Church **9**
Tucker, C. DeLores **12**
White, Walter F. **4**
Wilkins, Roger **2**
Wilkins, Roy **4**
Williams, Hosea Lorenzo **15**
Williams, Robert F. **11**
Wright, Louis Tompkins **4**

National Association of Black Journalists (NABJ)
Curry, George E. **23**
Dawkins, Wayne **20**
Harris, Jay T. **19**
Shipp, E. R. **15**
Stone, Chuck **9**
Washington, Laura S. **18**

National Association of Colored Graduate Nurses (NACGN)
Staupers, Mabel K. **7**

National Association of Colored Women (NACW)
Bethune, Mary McLeod **4**
Harper, Frances Ellen Watkins **11**
Lampkin, Daisy **19**
Terrell, Mary Church **9**

National Baptist Convention USA
Lyons, Henry **12**

National Baptist Publishing Board
Boyd, T. B., III **6**

National Baptist Sunday Church School and Baptist Training Union Congress
Boyd, T. B., III **6**

National Bar Association
Alexander, Joyce London **18**
Alexander, Sadie Tanner Mossell **22**
Archer, Dennis **7**
McPhail, Sharon **2**

National Basketball Association (NBA)
Abdul-Jabbar, Kareem **8**
Barkley, Charles **5**
Bing, Dave **3**
Bol, Manute **1**
Brandon, Terrell **16**
Bryant, Kobe **15**
Chamberlain, Wilt **18**
Drexler, Clyde **4**
Duncan, Tim **20**
Erving, Julius **18**
Ewing, Patrick A. **17**

Garnett, Kevin **14**
Gourdine, Simon **11**
Hardaway, Anfernee (Penny) **13**
Hill, Grant **13**
Howard, Juwan **15**
Hunter, Billy **22**
Johnson, Earvin "Magic" **3**
Jordan, Michael **6, 21**
Lucas, John **7**
Mourning, Alonzo **17**
Mutombo, Dikembe **7**
O'Neal, Shaquille **8**
Olajuwon, Hakeem **2**
Pippen, Scottie **15**
Robinson, David **24**
Rodman, Dennis **12**
Russell, Bill **8**
Silas, Paul **24**
Sprewell, Latrell **23**
Thomas, Isiah **7**
Webber, Chris **15**
Wilkens, Lenny **11**

National Basketball Players Association
Erving, Julius **18**
Ewing, Patrick A. **17**
Gourdine, Simon **11**
Hunter, Billy **22**

National Black Arts Festival (NBAF)
Borders, James **9**
Brooks, Avery **9**

National Black Farmers Association (NBFA)
Boyd, John W., Jr. **20**

National Black Gay and Lesbian Conference
Wilson, Phill **9**

National Black Gay and Lesbian Leadership Forum (NBGLLF)
Boykin, Keith **14**
Carter, Mandy **11**

National Book Award
Ellison, Ralph **7**
Haley, Alex **4**
Johnson, Charles **1**
Patterson, Orlando **4**

National Broadcasting Company (NBC)
Allen, Byron **3, 24**
Cosby, Bill **7**
Gumbel, Bryant **14**
Hinderas, Natalie **5**
Jones, Star **10**
Rashad, Phylicia **21**
Reuben, Gloria **15**
Roker, Al **12**
Simpson, Carole **6**
Stokes, Carl B. **10**
Williams, Montel **4**
Wilson, Flip **21**

National Center for Neighborhood Enterprise (NCNE)
Woodson, Robert L. **10**

National Coalition of 100 Black Women
McCabe, Jewell Jackson **10**

National Coalition to Abolish the Dealth Penalty (NCADP)
Hawkins, Steven **14**

National Commission for Democracy (Ghana; NCD)
Rawlings, Jerry **9**

National Conference on Black Lawyers (NCBL)
McDougall, Gay J. **11**

National Council of Negro Women (NCNW)
Bethune, Mary McLeod **4**
Blackwell, Unita **17**
Cole, Johnnetta B. **5**
Hamer, Fannie Lou **6**
Height, Dorothy I. **2, 23**
Horne, Lena **5**
Lampkin, Daisy **19**
Sampson, Edith S. **4**
Smith, Jane E. **24**
Staupers, Mabel K. **7**

National Council of Nigeria and the Cameroons (NCNC)
Azikiwe, Nnamdi **13**

National Defence Council (Ghana; NDC)
Rawlings, Jerry **9**

National Democratic Party (Rhodesia)
Mugabe, Robert Gabriel **10**

National Earthquake Information Center (NEIC)
Person, Waverly **9**

National Endowment for the Arts (NEA)
Hemphill, Essex **10**
Serrano, Andres **3**
Williams, William T. **11**

National Equal Rights League (NERL)
Trotter, Monroe **9**

National Football League (NFL)
Allen, Marcus **20**
Brown, Jim **11**
Butler, Leroy III **17**
Cunningham, Randall **23**
Davis, Terrell **20**
Farr, Mel Sr. **24**
Gilliam, Frank **23**
Green, Dennis **5**
Greene, Joe **10**
Hill, Calvin **19**
Howard, Desmond **16**
Lott, Ronnie **9**
Moon, Warren **8**
Moss, Randy **23**
Pace, Orlando **21**
Page, Alan **7**
Payton, Walter **11**
Rhodes, Ray **14**
Rice, Jerry **5**
Sanders, Barry **1**
Sanders, Deion **4**
Shell, Art **1**
Simpson, O.J. **15**
Singletary, Mike **4**
Smith, Emmitt **7**
Stewart, Kordell **21**
Upshaw, Gene **18**
Walker, Herschel **1**
White, Reggie **6**
Williams, Doug **22**

National Hockey League (NHL)
McBride, Bryant **18**
Fuhr, Grant **1**
McKegney, Tony **3**
O'Ree, Willie **5**

National Information Infrastructure (NII)
Lewis, Delano **7**

National Institute of Education
Baker, Gwendolyn Calvert **9**

National League
Coleman, Leonard S., Jr. **12**

National Minority Business Council
Leary, Kathryn D. **10**

National Museum of American History
Reagon, Bernice Johnson **7**

National Negro Congress
Bunche, Ralph J. **5**

National Negro Suffrage League
Trotter, Monroe **9**

National Organization for Women (NOW)
Kennedy, Florynce **12**
Hernandez, Aileen Clarke **13**

National Political Congress of Black Women
Chisholm, Shirley **2**
Tucker, C. DeLores **12**
Waters, Maxine **3**

National Public Radio (NPR)
Early, Gerald **15**
Lewis, Delano **7**
Abu-Jamal, Mumia **15**

National Resistance Army (Uganda; NRA)
Museveni, Yoweri **4**

National Resistance Movement
Museveni, Yoweri **4**

National Revolutionary Movement for Development
See Mouvement Revolutionnaire National pour la Developpment

National Rifle Association (NRA)
Williams, Robert F. **11**

National Science Foundation (NSF)
Massey, Walter E. **5**

National Security Council
Powell, Colin **1**
Rice, Condoleezza **3**

National Union for the Total Independence of Angola (UNITA)
Savimbi, Jonas **2**

National Union of Mineworkers (South Africa; NUM)
Ramaphosa, Cyril **3**

National Urban Coalition (NUC)
Edelin, Ramona Hoage **19**

National Urban League
Brown, Ron **5**
Haynes, George Edmund **8**
Jacob, John E. **2**
Jordan, Vernon E. **3**
Price, Hugh B. **9**
Young, Whitney M., Jr. **4**

National Women's Political Caucus
Hamer, Fannie Lou **6**

National Youth Administration (NYA)
Bethune, Mary McLeod **4**
Primus, Pearl **6**

Nature Boy Enterprises
Yoba, Malik **11**

NBA
See National Basketball Association

NBAF
See National Black Arts Festival

NBC
See National Broadcasting Company

NBGLLF
See National Black Gay and Lesbian Leadership Forum

NCBL
See National Council of Black Lawyers

NCD
See National Commission for Democracy

NCNE
See National Center for Neighborhood Enterprise

NCNW
See National Council of Negro Women

NDC
See National Defence Council

NEA
See National Endowment for the Arts

Nebula awards
Butler, Octavia **8**
Delany, Jr., Samuel R. **9**

Negro American Labor Council
Randolph, A. Philip **3**

Negro American Political League
Trotter, Monroe **9**

Negro Digest
Johnson, John H. **3**

Negro Ensemble Company
Schultz, Michael A. **6**
Taylor, Susan L. **10**

Negro History Bulletin
Woodson, Carter G. **2**

Negro Leagues
Gibson, Josh **22**
O'Neil, Buck **19**
Paige, Satchel **7**
Davis, Piper **19**
Stone, Toni **15**

Negro Theater Ensemble
Rolle, Esther **13, 21**

Negro World
Fortune, T. Thomas **6**

NEIC
See National Earthquake Information Center

Neo-hoodoo
Reed, Ishmael **8**

Nequai Cosmetics
Taylor, Susan L. **10**

NERL
See National Equal Rights League

Netherlands Antilles
Liberia-Peters, Maria Philomena **12**

NetNoir Inc.
CasSelle, Malcolm **11**
Ellington, E. David **11**

Neurosurgery
Black, Keith Lanier **18**
Carson, Benjamin **1**

New Concept Development Center
Madhubuti, Haki R. **7**

New Dance Group
Primus, Pearl **6**

New Jersey Family Development Act
Bryant, Wayne R. **6**

New Jersey General Assembly
Bryant, Wayne R. **6**

New Jersey Nets
Doby, Lawrence Eugene, Sr. **16**

New Negro movement
See Harlem Renaissance

New York Age
Fortune, T. Thomas **6**

New York City government
Crew, Rudolph F. **16**
Dinkins, David **4**

New York Daily News
Cose, Ellis **5**

New York Drama Critics Circle Award
Hansberry, Lorraine **6**

New York Freeman
Fortune, T. Thomas **6**

New York Giants baseball team
Mays, Willie **3**

New York Globe
Fortune, T. Thomas **6**

New York Institute for Social Therapy and Research
Fulani, Lenora **11**

New York Jets football team
Lott, Ronnie **9**

New York Knicks basketball team
Ewing, Patrick A. **17**
Sprewell, Latrell **23**

New York Nets basketball team
Erving, Julius **18**

New York Public Library
Dodson, Howard, Jr. **7**
Schomburg, Arthur Alfonso **9**

New York Shakespeare Festival
Gunn, Moses **10**
Wolfe, George C. **6**

New York State Senate
Motley, Constance Baker **10**
Owens, Major **6**

New York State Supreme Court
Wright, Bruce McMarion **3**

New York Sun
Fortune, T. Thomas **6**

New York Times
Hunter-Gault, Charlayne **6**
Price, Hugh B. **9**
Wilkins, Roger **2**

New York Yankees baseball team
Baylor, Don **6**
Jackson, Reggie **15**
Strawberry, Darryl **22**
Winfield, Dave **5**

Newark city government
Gibson, Kenneth Allen **6**
James, Sharpe **23**

Newark Eagles
Doby, Lawrence Eugene, Sr. **16**

Newark Housing Authority
Gibson, Kenneth Allen **6**

NFL
See National Football League

Nguzo Saba
Karenga, Maulana **10**

NHL
See National Hockey League

Niagara movement
Du Bois, W. E. B. **3**
Hope, John **8**
Trotter, Monroe **9**

Nigerian Armed Forces
Abacha, Sani **11**
Babangida, Ibrahim **4**
Obasanjo, Olusegun **5, 22**

Nigerian literature
Achebe, Chinua **6**
Onwueme, Tess Osonye **23**
Rotimi, Ola **1**
Soyinka, Wole **4**

NII
See National Information Infrastructure

1960 Masks
Soyinka, Wole **4**

Nobel Peace Prize
Bunche, Ralph J. **5**
King, Martin Luther, Jr. **1**
Luthuli, Albert **13**
Tutu, Desmond **6**

Nobel Prize for literature
Soyinka, Wole **4**
Morrison, Toni **2, 15**
Walcott, Derek **5**

Nonviolent Action Group (NAG)
Al-Amin, Jamil Abdullah **6**

North Carolina Mutual Life Insurance
Spaulding, Charles Clinton **9**

North Pole
Henson, Matthew **2**

NOW
See National Organization for Women

NPR
See National Public Radio

NRA
See National Resistance Army (Uganda)

NRA
See National Rifle Association

NSF
See National Science Foundation

Nuclear energy
O'Leary, Hazel **6**
Quarterman, Lloyd Albert **4**

Nuclear Regulatory Commission
Jackson, Shirley Ann **12**

Nucleus
King, Yolanda **6**
Shabazz, Attallah **6**

NUM
See National Union of Mineworkers (South Africa)

Nursing
Auguste, Rose-Anne **13**
Johnson, Eddie Bernice **8**
Johnson, Hazel **22**
Larsen, Nella **10**
Lyttle, Hulda Margaret **14**
Riley, Helen Caldwell Day **13**
Robinson, Rachel **16**
Robinson, Sharon **22**
Shabazz, Betty **7**
Staupers, Mabel K. **7**
Taylor, Susie King **13**

Nutrition
Clark, Celeste **15**
Gregory, Dick **1**
Watkins, Shirley R. **17**

NYA
See National Youth Administration

Nyasaland African Congress (NAC)
Banda, Hastings Kamuzu **6**

Oakland Athletics baseball team
Baker, Dusty **8**
Baylor, Don **6**
Jackson, Reggie **15**
Morgan, Joe Leonard **9**

Oakland Raiders football team
Howard, Desmond **16**
Upshaw, Gene **18**

Oakland Tribune
Maynard, Robert C. **7**

OAU
See Organization of African Unity

OECS
See Organization of Eastern Caribbean States

Office of Civil Rights
See U.S. Department of Education

Office of Management and Budget
Raines, Franklin Delano **14**

Office of Public Liaison
Herman, Alexis M. **15**

Ohio House of Representatives
Stokes, Carl B. **10**

Ohio state government
Brown, Les **5**
Stokes, Carl B. **10**
Williams, George Washington **18**

Ohio State Senate
White, Michael R. **5**

OIC
See Opportunities Industrialization Centers of America, Inc.

Olympics
Ali, Muhammad **2, 16**
Bonaly, Surya **7**
Bowe, Riddick **6**
Christie, Linford **8**
Coachman, Alice **18**
Dawes, Dominique **11**
Devers, Gail **7**
Edwards, Harry **2**
Edwards, Teresa **14**
Ewing, Patrick A. **17**
Garrison, Zina **2**
Hardaway, Anfernee (Penny) **13**

Hill, Grant **13**
Holyfield, Evander **6**
Johnson, Ben **1**
Johnson, Michael **13**
Joyner-Kersee, Jackie **5**
Leslie, Lisa **16**
Lewis, Carl **4**
Malone, Karl A. **18**
Miller, Cheryl **10**
Moses, Edwin **8**
Mutola, Maria **12**
Owens, Jesse **2**
Pippen, Scottie **15**
Powell, Mike **7**
Quirot, Ana **13**
Rudolph, Wilma **4**
Russell, Bill **8**
Swoopes, Sheryl **12**
Thugwane, Josia **21**
Westbrook, Peter **20**
Whitaker, Pernell **10**
Wilkens, Lenny **11**

Oncology
Leffall, LaSalle, Jr. **3**

One Church, One Child
Clements, George **2**

OPC
See Ovambo People's Congress

Opera
Anderson, Marian **2**
Brooks, Avery **9**
Bumbry, Grace **5**
Davis, Anthony **11**
Graves, Denyce **19**
Hendricks, Barbara **3**
Joplin, Scott **6**
Joyner, Matilda Sissieretta **15**
Maynor, Dorothy **19**
McDonald, Audra **20**
Norman, Jessye **5**
Price, Leontyne **1**

Operation Desert Shield
Powell, Colin **1**

Operation Desert Storm
Powell, Colin **1**

OPO
See Ovamboland People's Organization

Opportunities Industrialization Centers of America, Inc. (OIC)
Sullivan, Leon H. **3**

Organization of African States
Museveni, Yoweri **4**

Organization of African Unity (OAU)
Diouf, Abdou **3**
Haile Selassie **7**
Kaunda, Kenneth **2**

Kenyatta, Jomo **5**
Nkrumah, Kwame **3**
Nujoma, Samuel **10**
Nyerere, Julius **5**
Touré, Sekou **6**

Organization of Afro-American Unity
X, Malcolm **1**

Organization of Eastern Caribbean States (OECS)
Charles, Mary Eugenia **10**

Orisun Repertory
Soyinka, Wole **4**

Orlando Magic basketball team
Erving, Julius **18**
O'Neal, Shaquille **8**

Orlando Miracle basketball team
Peck, Carolyn **23**

Osteopathy
Allen, Ethel D. **13**

Ovambo People's Congress (South Africa; OPC)
Nujoma, Samuel **10**

Ovamboland People's Organization (South Africa; OPO)
Nujoma, Samuel **10**

Page Education Foundation
Page, Alan **7**

Paine College
Lewis, Shirley A. R. **14**

Painting
Andrews, Benny **22**
Bailey, Radcliffe **19**
Barthe, Richmond **15**
Basquiat, Jean-Michel **5**
Bearden, Romare **2**
Biggers, John **20**
Campbell, E. Simms **13**
Cowans, Adger W. **20**
Delaney, Beauford **19**
Douglas, Aaron **7**
Driskell, David C. **7**
Ewing, Patrick A. **17**
Flood, Curt **10**
Gilliam, Sam **16**
Guyton, Tyree **9**
Harkless, Necia Desiree **19**
Hayden, Palmer **13**
Johnson, William Henry **3**
Jones, Lois Mailou **13**
Lawrence, Jacob **4**
Lee, Annie Francis **22**
Lee-Smith, Hughie **5, 22**
Major, Clarence **9**
McGee, Charles **10**
Mitchell, Corinne **8**
Pierre, Andre **17**

Pippin, Horace **9**
Porter, James A. **11**
Ringgold, Faith **4**
Tanner, Henry Ossawa **1**
Thomas, Alma **14**
Tolliver, William **9**
Wells, James Lesesne **10**
Williams, Billy Dee **8**
Williams, William T. **11**
Woodruff, Hale **9**

Pan-Africanism
Carmichael, Stokely **5**
Clarke, John Henrik **20**
Du Bois, W. E. B. **3**
Garvey, Marcus **1**
Haile Selassie **7**
Kenyatta, Jomo **5**
Madhubuti, Haki R. **7**
Marshall, Paule **7**
Nkrumah, Kwame **3**
Nyerere, Julius **5**
Touré, Sekou **6**
Turner, Henry McNeal **5**

Pan African Orthodox Christian Church
Agyeman, Jaramogi Abebe **10**

Parents of Watts (POW)
Harris, Alice **7**

Parti Démocratique de Guinée (Guinea Democratic Party; PDG)
Touré, Sekou **6**

Parti Démocratique de la Côte d'Ivoire (Democratic Party of the Ivory Coast; PDCI)
Houphouët-Boigny, Félix **4**

Parti Démocratique de la Côte d'Ivoire (Democratic Party of the
Bedie, Henri Konan **21**

Partido Africano da Independencia da Guine e Cabo Verde (PAIGC)
Vieira, Joao **14**

Party for Unity and Progress (Guinea; PUP)
Conté, Lansana **7**

PATC
See Performing Arts Training Center

Pathology
Fuller, Solomon Carter, Jr. **15**

Patriot Party
Fulani, Lenora **11**

Patriotic Alliance for Reconstruction and Construction (PARC)
Jammeh, Yahya **23**

PBS
See Public Broadcasting Service

PDCI
See Parti Démocratique de la Côte d'Ivoire (Democratic Party of the Ivory Coast)

PDG
See Parti Démocratique de Guinée (Guinea Democratic Party)

Peace and Freedom Party
Cleaver, Eldridge 5

Peace Corps
See U.S. Peace Corps

Peace Mission
Divine, Father 7

Pediatrics
Carson, Benjamin 1
Elders, Joycelyn 6

Peg Leg Bates Country Club
Bates, Peg Leg 14

Pennsylvania state government
Allen, Ethel D. 13

People Organized and Working for Economic Rebirth (POWER)
Farrakhan, Louis 2

People United to Serve Humanity (PUSH)
Jackson, Jesse 1
Jackson, Jesse, Jr. 14

People's Association Human Rights
Williams, Robert F. 11

People's Liberation Army of Namibia (PLAN)
Nujoma, Samuel 10

People's National Party (Jamaica; PNP)
Patterson, P. J. 6, 20

People's Progressive Party (PPP)
Jagan, Cheddi 16
Jawara, Sir Dawda Kairaba 11

Performing Arts Training Center (PATC)
Dunham, Katherine 4

PGA
See Professional Golfers' Association

Phelps Stokes Fund
Patterson, Frederick Douglass 12

Philadelphia City Council
Allen, Ethel D. 13

Philadelphia city government
Goode, W. Wilson 4
Street, John F. 24

Philadelphia Eagles football team
Cunningham, Randall 23
Rhodes, Ray 14
White, Reggie 6

Philadelphia Phillies baseball team
Morgan, Joe Leonard 9

Philadelphia public schools
Clayton, Constance 1

Philadelphia 76ers basketball team
Barkley, Charles 5
Bol, Manute 1
Chamberlain, Wilt 18
Erving, Julius 18
Iverson, Allen 24
Lucas, John 7

Philadelphia Warriors
Chamberlain, Wilt 18

Philanthropy
Cosby, Bill 7
Cosby, Camille 14
Golden, Marita 19
Malone, Annie 13
McCarty, Oseola 16
Pleasant, Mary Ellen 9
Reeves, Rachel J. 23
Thomas, Franklin A. 5
Waddles, Charleszetta (Mother) 10
Walker, Madame C. J. 7
White, Reggie 6
Wonder, Stevie 11

Philosophy
Baker, Houston A., Jr. 6
Davis, Angela 5
Toomer, Jean 6
West, Cornel 5

Phoenix Suns basketball team
Barkley, Charles 5

Photography
Andrews, Bert 13
Barboza, Anthony 10
Cowans, Adger W. 20
Lester, Julius 9
Moutoussamy-Ashe, Jeanne 7
Parks, Gordon 1
Robeson, Eslanda Goode 13
Serrano, Andres 3
Simpson, Lorna 4
Sleet, Moneta, Jr. 5
Tanner, Henry Ossawa 1
VanDerZee, James 6

Photojournalism
Ashley-Ward, Amelia 23
Moutoussamy-Ashe, Jeanne 7
Parks, Gordon 1
Sleet, Moneta, Jr. 5

Physical therapy
Elders, Joycelyn 6

Physics
Adkins, Rutherford H. 21
Gates, Sylvester James, Jr. 15
Jackson, Shirley Ann 12
Massey, Walter E. 5
Tyson, Neil de Grasse 15

Piano
Basie, Count 23
Cole, Nat King 17
Donegan, Dorothy 19
Duke, George 21
Ellington, Duke 5
Fats Domino 20
Hancock, Herbie 20
Hayes, Isaac 20
Hinderas, Natalie 5
Joplin, Scott 6
Monk, Thelonious 1
Powell, Bud 24
Pritchard, Robert Starling 21
Roberts, Marcus 19
Sykes, Roosevelt 20
Taylor, Billy 23
Vaughan, Sarah 13
Williams, Mary Lou 15

Pittsburgh Pirates baseball team
Bonds, Barry 6

Pittsburgh Steelers football team
Dungy, Tony 17
Greene, Joe 10
Stewart, Kordell 21

PLAN
See People's Liberation Army of Namibia

Planned Parenthood Federation of America Inc.
Wattleton, Faye 9

Playwright
Arkadie, Kevin 17
Baldwin, James 1
Cheadle, Don 19
Childress, Alice 15
Cleage, Pearl 17
Gordone, Charles 15
Hansberry, Lorraine 6
Hughes, Langston 4
Jean-Baptiste, Marianne 17
Kennedy, Adrienne 11
Moss, Carlton 17
Onwueme, Tess Osonye 23
Sanchez, Sonia 17
Thurman, Wallace 17
Walcott, Derek 5
Williams, Samm-Art 21
Wilson, August 7

PNP
See People's National Party (Jamaica)

Poet laureate (U.S.)
Dove, Rita **6**

Poetry
Alexander, Margaret Walker **22**
Angelou, Maya **1, 15**
Bontemps, Arna **8**
Cleage, Pearl **17**
Clifton, Lucille **14**
Dove, Rita **6**
Harkless, Necia Desiree **19**
Harper, Frances Ellen Watkins **11**
Hayden, Robert **12**
Hughes, Langston **7**
Lorde, Audre **6**
Parker, Pat **19**
Randall, Dudley **8**
Redmond, Eugene **23**
Sanchez, Sonia **17**
Sapphire **14**
Senghor, Léopold Sédar **12**

Politics
Alexander, Archie Alphonso **14**
Baker, Thurbert **22**
Belton, Sharon Sayles **9, 16**
Bishop Jr., Sanford D. **24**
Blackwell, Unita **17**
Brown, Corrine **24**
Buckley, Victoria (Vikki) **24**
Burris, Chuck **21**
Chideya, Farai **14**
Christian-Green, Donna M. **17**
Clayton, Eva M. **20**
Connerly, Ward **14**
Cummings, Elijah E. **24**
Currie, Betty **21**
Dixon, Julian C. **24**
Edmonds, Terry **17**
Gordon, Pamela **17**
Henry, Aaron **19**
Herenton, Willie W. **24**
Hilliard, Earl F. **24**
Ingraham, Hubert A. **19**
Jackson Lee, Sheila **20**
James, Sharpe **23**
Jammeh, Yahya **23**
Jarvis, Charlene Drew **21**
Johnson Jr., Harvey **24**
Kabbah, Ahmad Tejan **23**
Millender-McDonald, Juanita **21**
Morial, Marc **20**
Obasanjo, Olusegun **22**
Perry, Ruth **15**
Powell, Debra A. **23**
Scott, Robert C. **23**
Sisulu, Sheila Violet Makate **24**
Smith, Jennifer **21**
Touré, Amadou Toumani **18**
Watts, J. C., Jr. **14**
Wheat, Alan **14**
White, Jesse **22**
Williams, Anthony **21**
Williams, George Washington **18**

Pop music
Ashford, Nickolas **21**
Blige, Mary J. **20**
Cole, Nat King **17**
Combs, Sean "Puffy" **17**
Duke, George **21**
Edmonds, Kenneth "Babyface" **10**
Franklin, Aretha **11**
Franklin, Kirk **15**
Hailey, JoJo **22**
Hailey, K-Ci **22**
Hammer, M. C. **20**
Hayes, Isaac **20**
Hill, Lauryn **20**
Houston, Cissy **20**
Houston, Whitney **7**
Humphrey, Bobbi **20**
Jackson, Janet **6**
Jackson, Michael **19**
James, Rick **17**
Jarreau, Al **21**
Jean, Wyclef **20**
Jones, Quincy **8**
Jordan, Montell **23**
Kelly, R. **18**
Kendricks, Eddie **22**
Khan, Chaka **12**
Love, Darlene **23**
Massenburg, Kedar **23**
Mathis, Johnny **20**
Monica **21**
Neville, Aaron **21**
Prince **18**
Robinson, Smokey **3**
Rupaul **17**
Sade **15**
Seal **14**
Senghor, Léopold Sédar **12**
Simpson, Valerie **21**
Sweat, Keith **19**
Turner, Tina **6**
Usher **23**
Washington, Dinah **22**
Washington, Grover, Jr. **17**
Washington, Val **12**
White, Barry **13**
Williams, Vanessa L. **4, 17**
Wilson, Nancy **10**
Wonder, Stevie **11**

Portland Trail Blazers basketball team
Drexler, Clyde **4**
Wilkens, Lenny **11**

POW
See Parents of Watts

POWER
See People Organized and Working for Economic Rebirth

PPP
See People's Progressive Party (Gambia)

Presbyterianism
Cannon, Katie **10**

Pride Economic Enterprises
Barry, Marion S. **7**

Printmaking
Wells, James Lesesne **10**

Prison ministry
Bell, Ralph S. **5**

Pro-Line Corp.
Cottrell, Comer **11**

Professional Golfers' Association (PGA)
Elder, Lee **6**
Sifford, Charlie **4**

Progressive Labour Party
Smith, Jennifer **21**

Proposition 209
Connerly, Ward **14**

Psychiatry
Cobbs, Price M. **9**
Comer, James P. **6**
Fuller, Solomon Carter, Jr. **15**
Poussaint, Alvin F. **5**
Welsing, Frances Cress **5**

Psychology
Fulani, Lenora **11**
Staples, Brent **8**
Steele, Claude Mason **13**

Public Broadcasting Service (PBS)
Brown, Les **5**
Davis, Ossie **5**
Duke, Bill **3**
Hampton, Henry **6**
Hunter-Gault, Charlayne **6**
Lawson, Jennifer **1**
Riggs, Marlon **5**
Wilkins, Roger **2**

Public housing
Hamer, Fannie Lou **6**
Lane, Vincent **5**

Public relations
Barden, Don H. **9, 20**
Edmonds, Terry **17**
Graham, Stedman **13**
Hedgeman, Anna Arnold **22**
McCabe, Jewell Jackson **10**
Perez, Anna **1**
Pritchard, Robert Starling **21**
Rowan, Carl T. **1**
Taylor, Kristin Clark **8**
Williams, Maggie **7**

Public television
Brown, Tony **3**

Publishing
Achebe, Chinua **6**
Ashley-Ward, Amelia **23**
Barden, Don H. **9, 20**
Bates, Daisy **13**
Boston, Lloyd **24**
Boyd, T. B. III **6**

Brown, Marie Dutton **12**
Dawkins, Wayne **20**
Driver, David E. **11**
Ducksworth, Marilyn **12**
Giddings, Paula **11**
Graves, Earl G. **1**
Harris, Jay **19**
Harris, Monica **18**
Hill, Bonnie Guiton **20**
Hudson, Cheryl **15**
Hudson, Wade **15**
James, Juanita **13**
Johnson, John H. **3**
Jones, Quincy **8**
Kunjufu, Jawanza **3**
Lawson, Jennifer **1**
Leavell, Dorothy R. **17**
Lewis, Edward T. **21**
Lorde, Audre **6**
Madhubuti, Haki R. **7**
Maynard, Robert C. **7**
McDonald, Erroll **1**
Morgan, Garrett **1**
Myers, Walter Dean **8**
Parks, Gordon **1**
Perez, Anna **1**
Randall, Dudley **8**
Sengstacke, John **18**
Smith, Clarence O. **21**
Tyree, Omar Rashad **21**
Vanzant, Iyanla **17**
Walker, Alice **1**
Washington, Laura S. **18**
Wells-Barnett, Ida B. **8**
Williams, Patricia J. **11**

Pulitzer prize
Brooks, Gwendolyn **1**
Dove, Rita **6**
Fuller, Charles **8**
Gordone, Charles **15**
Haley, Alex **4**
Komunyakaa, Yusef **9**
Lewis, David Levering **9**
Morrison, Toni **2, 15**
Page, Clarence **4**
Shipp, E. R. **15**
Sleet, Moneta, Jr. **5**
Walker, Alice **1**
Wilkins, Roger **2**
Wilson, August **7**

PUP
See Party for Unity and Progress (Guinea)

Puppeteer
Clash, Kevin **14**

PUSH
See People United to Serve Humanity

Quiltmaking
Ringgold, Faith **4**

Race car driving
Ribbs, Willy T. **2**

Scott, Sr., Wendell Oliver **19**

Race relations
Abbott, Diane **9**
Achebe, Chinua **6**
Asante, Molefi Kete **3**
Baker, Ella **5**
Baker, Houston A., Jr. **6**
Baldwin, James **1**
Beals, Melba Patillo **15**
Bell, Derrick **6**
Bennett, Lerone, Jr. **5**
Bethune, Mary McLeod **4**
Booker, Simeon **23**
Bosley, Freeman, Jr. **7**
Boyd, T. B. III **6**
Brown, Elaine **8**
Bunche, Ralph J. **5**
Butler, Paul D. **17**
Butts, Calvin O., III **9**
Carter, Stephen L. **4**
Cary, Lorene **3**
Chavis, Benjamin **6**
Clark, Kenneth B. **5**
Clark, Septima **7**
Cobbs, Price M. **9**
Cochran, Johnnie L., Jr. **11**
Cole, Johnnetta B. **5**
Comer, James P. **6**
Cone, James H. **3**
Conyers, John, Jr. **4**
Cook, Suzan D. Johnson **22**
Cook, Toni **23**
Cosby, Bill **7**
Cunningham, Evelyn **23**
Darden, Christopher **13**
Davis, Angela **5**
Davis, Benjamin O., Sr. **4**
Davis, Benjamin O., Jr. **2**
Dee, Ruby **8**
Dellums, Ronald **2**
Divine, Father **7**
DuBois, Shirley Graham **21**
Dunbar, Paul Laurence **8**
Dyson, Michael Eric **11**
Edelman, Marian Wright **5**
Elder, Lee **6**
Ellison, Ralph **7**
Esposito, Giancarlo **9**
Farmer, James **2**
Farrakhan, Louis **2**
Fauset, Jessie **7**
Franklin, John Hope **5**
Fuller, Charles **8**
Gaines, Ernest J. **7**
Gibson, William F. **6**
Goode, W. Wilson **4**
Graham, Lawrence Otis **12**
Gregory, Dick **1**
Grimké, Archibald H. **9**
Guinier, Lani **7**
Guy, Rosa **5**
Haley, Alex **4**
Hall, Elliott S. **24**
Hampton, Henry **6**
Hansberry, Lorraine **6**
Harris, Alice **7**
Hastie, William H. **8**

Haynes, George Edmund **8**
Hedgeman, Anna Arnold **22**
Henry, Aaron **19**
Henry, Lenny **9**
Hill, Oliver W. **24**
Hooks, Benjamin L. **2**
hooks, bell **5**
Hope, John **8**
Ingram, Rex **5**
Innis, Roy **5**
Jeffries, Leonard **8**
Johnson, James Weldon **5**
Jones, Elaine R. **7**
Jordan, Vernon E. **3**
Khanga, Yelena **6**
King, Bernice **4**
King, Coretta Scott **3**
King, Martin Luther, Jr. **1**
King, Yolanda **6**
Lane, Charles **3**
Lee-Smith, Hughie **5, 22**
Lee, Spike **5, 19**
Lorde, Audre **6**
Mandela, Nelson **1, 14**
Martin, Louis E. **16**
Mathabane, Mark **5**
Maynard, Robert C. **7**
Mays, Benjamin E. **7**
McDougall, Gay J. **11**
McKay, Claude **6**
Meredith, James H. **11**
Micheaux, Oscar **7**
Mosley, Walter **5**
Muhammad, Khallid Abdul **10**
Norton, Eleanor Holmes **7**
Page, Clarence **4**
Perkins, Edward **5**
Pitt, David Thomas **10**
Poussaint, Alvin F. **5**
Price, Frederick K.C. **21**
Price, Hugh B. **9**
Robeson, Paul **2**
Robinson, Spottswood W. III **22**
Sampson, Edith S. **4**
Shabazz, Attallah **6**
Sifford, Charlie **4**
Simpson, Carole **6**
Sister Souljah **11**
Sisulu, Sheila Violet Makate **24**
Smith, Anna Deavere **6**
Sowell, Thomas **2**
Spaulding, Charles Clinton **9**
Staples, Brent **8**
Steele, Claude Mason **13**
Taulbert, Clifton Lemoure **19**
Till, Emmett **7**
Tutu, Desmond **6**
Tyree, Omar Rashad **21**
Walcott, Derek **5**
Walker, Maggie **17**
Washington, Booker T. **4**
Washington, Harold **6**
Wells-Barnett, Ida B. **8**
Welsing, Frances Cress **5**
West, Cornel **5**
Wideman, John Edgar **5**
Wiley, Ralph **8**
Wilkins, Roger **2**

Wilkins, Roy **4**
Williams, Gregory **11**
Williams, Hosea Lorenzo **15**
Williams, Patricia J. **11**
Williams, Walter E. **4**
Wilson, Sunnie **7**
Wright, Richard **5**
Young, Whitney M., Jr. **4**

Radio
Abu-Jamal, Mumia **15**
Banks, William **11**
Booker, Simeon **23**
Dee, Ruby **8**
Dr. Dre **10**
Fuller, Charles **8**
Goode, Mal **13**
Gumbel, Greg **8**
Hamblin, Ken **10**
Joe, Yolanda **21**
Joyner, Tom **19**
Keyes, Alan L. **11**
Lewis, Delano **7**
Lover, Ed **10**
Madison, Joseph E. **17**
Moss, Carlton **17**
Samara, Noah **15**
Smiley, Tavis **20**
Taylor, Billy **23**

Ragtime
Europe, James Reese **10**
Joplin, Scott **6**

Rainbow Coalition
Chappell, Emma **18**
Jackson, Jesse **1**
Jackson, Jesse, Jr. **14**

Rap music
Baker, Houston A., Jr. **6**
Butts, Calvin O., III **9**
Chuck D. **9**
Combs, Sean "Puffy" **17**
Dr. Dre **10**
Dre, Dr. **14**
Dupri, Jermaine **13**
Dyson, Michael Eric **11**
Gray, F. Gary **14**
Hammer, M. C. **20**
Harrell, Andre **9**
Hill, Lauryn **20**
Ice Cube **8**
Ice-T **6**
Jean, Wyclef **20**
Jones, Quincy **8**
Knight, Suge **11**
Lover, Ed **10**
Mase **24**
Master P **21**
Notorious B.I.G. **20**
O'Neal, Shaquille **8**
Queen Latifah **1, 16**
Shakur, Tupac **14**
Simmons, Russell **1**
Sister Souljah **11**
Smith, Will **8, 18**
Tucker, C. DeLores **12**

Rassemblement Démocratique Africain (African Democratic Rally; RDA)
Houphouët-Boigny, Félix **4**
Touré, Sekou **6**

Rastafarianism
Haile Selassie **7**
Marley, Bob **5**
Tosh, Peter **9**

RDA
See Rassemblement Démocratique Africain (African Democratic Rally)

Real estate development
Barden, Don H. **9, 20**
Brooke, Edward **8**
Lane, Vincent **5**
Marshall, Bella **22**
Russell, Herman Jerome **17**

Recording executives
Avant, Clarence **19**
Busby, Jheryl **3**
Combs, Sean "Puffy" **17**
Dupri, Jermaine **13**
Gordy, Berry, Jr. **1**
Harrell, Andre **9**
Jackson, George **19**
Jimmy Jam **13**
Jones, Quincy **8**
Knight, Suge **11**
Lewis, Terry **13**
Massenburg, Kedar **23**
Master P **21**
Mayfield, Curtis **2**
Queen Latifah **1, 16**
Rhone, Sylvia **2**
Robinson, Smokey **3**
Simmons, Russell **1**

Record producer
Albright, Gerald **23**
Ayers, Roy **16**
Blige, Mary J. **20**
Combs, Sean "Puffy" **17**
Dre, Dr. **14**
Duke, George **21**
Dupri, Jermaine **13**
Edmonds, Kenneth "Babyface" **10**
Hailey, JoJo **22**
Hailey, K-Ci **22**
Hammond, Fred **23**
Hill, Lauryn **20**
Ice Cube **8**
Jackson, George **19**
Jackson, Michael **19**
Jean, Wyclef **20**
Jimmy Jam **13**
Jones, Quincy **8**
Kelly, R. **18**
Lewis, Terry **13**
Master P **21**
Prince **18**
Queen Latifah **1, 16**
Sweat, Keith **19**

Vandross, Luther **13**
White, Barry **13**

Reggae
Marley, Bob **5**
Perry, Ruth **19**
Tosh, Peter **9**

Republican National Convention
Allen, Ethel D. **13**

Republic of New Africa (RNA)
Williams, Robert F. **11**

Restaurants
Cain, Herman **15**
Daniels-Carter, Valerie **23**
Hawkins, La-Van **17**
Smith, Barbara **11**

Revolutionary Party of Tanzania
See Chama cha Mapinduzi

Rheedlen Centers for Children and Families
Canada, Geoffrey **23**

Rhythm and blues/soul music
Adams, Oleta **18**
Ashford, Nickolas **21**
Austin, Patti **24**
Ayers, Roy **16**
Badu, Erykah **22**
Baker, Anita **21**
Belle, Regina **1**
Blige, Mary J. **20**
Brandy **14**
Braxton, Toni **15**
Brown, Charles **23**
Busby, Jheryl **3**
Campbell, Tisha **8**
Charles, Ray **16**
Clinton, George **9**
Combs, Sean "Puffy" **17**
Cooke, Sam **17**
Downing, Will **19**
Dre, Dr. **14**
Dupri, Jermaine **13**
Edmonds, Kenneth "Babyface" **10**
Evans, Faith **22**
Fats Domino **20**
Foxx, Jamie **15**
Franklin, Aretha **11**
Gaye, Marvin **2**
Green, Al **13**
Hailey, JoJo **22**
Hailey, K-Ci **22**
Hammer, M. C. **20**
Hathaway, Donny **18**
Hayes, Isaac **20**
Hill, Lauryn **20**
Houston, Cissy **20**
Houston, Whitney **7**
Hyman, Phyllis **19**
Jackson, Janet **6**
Jackson, Michael **19**
James, Etta **13**
James, Rick **17**

Jarreau, Al **21**
Jean, Wyclef **20**
Johnson, Robert **2**
Jones, Quincy **8**
Jordan, Montell **23**
Kelly, R. **18**
Kendricks, Eddie **22**
Knight, Gladys **16**
Levert, Gerald **22**
Little Richard **15**
Massenburg, Kedar **23**
Master P **21**
Maxwell **20**
Mayfield, Curtis **2**
McKnight, Brian **18**
Monica **21**
Moore, Melba **21**
Ndegéocello, Me'Shell **15**
Neville, Aaron **21**
Notorious B.I.G. **20**
Pendergrass, Teddy **22**
Price, Kelly **23**
Prince **18**
Redding, Otis **16**
Robinson, Smokey **3**
Ross, Diana **8**
Sade **15**
Simpson, Valerie **21**
Sweat, Keith **19**
Tamia **24**
Thomas, Rufus **20**
Turner, Tina **6**
Usher **23**
Vandross, Luther **13**
White, Barry **13**
Williams, Vanessa L. **4, 17**
Wilson, Cassandra **16**
Wilson, Nancy **10**
Wonder, Stevie **11**

RNA
See Republic of New Africa

Rock and Roll Hall of Fame
Brown, Charles **23**
Franklin, Aretha **11**
James, Etta **13**
Wonder, Stevie **11**

Rockefeller Foundation
Price, Hugh B. **9**

Rock music
Clinton, George **9**
Fats Domino **20**
Hendrix, Jimi **10**
Ice-T **6**
Kravitz, Lenny **10**
Little Richard **15**
Lymon, Frankie **22**
Prince **18**
Turner, Tina **6**

Rockets
Williams, O. S. **13**

Rodeo
Pickett, Bill **11**

Sampson, Charles **13**
Whitfield, Fred **23**

Roman Catholic Church
Arinze, Francis Cardinal **19**
Aristide, Jean-Bertrand **6**
Clements, George **2**
Guy, Rosa **5**
Rugambwa, Laurean **20**
Stallings, George A., Jr. **6**

Royal Ballet
Jackson, Isaiah **3**

Royalty
Christophe, Henri **9**

RPT
See Togolese People's Rally

Rush Artists Management Co.
Simmons, Russell **1**

Russell-McCloud and Associates
Russell-McCloud, Patricia A. **17**

St. Louis Rams football team
Pace, Orlando **21**

SAA
See Syndicat Agricole Africain

SACC
See South African Council of Churches

Sacramento Kings basketball team
Russell, Bill **8**

SADCC
See Southern African Development Coordination Conference

Southeastern University
Jarvis, Charlene Drew **21**

St. Louis Browns baseball team
Paige, Satchel **7**

St. Louis Cardinals baseball team
Baylor, Don **6**
Brock, Lou **18**
Flood, Curt **10**
Lankford, Ray **23**

St. Louis city government
Bosley, Freeman, Jr. **7**

St. Louis Hawks basketball team
See Atlanta Hawks basketball team

San Antonio Spurs basketball team
Duncan, Tim **20**
Lucas, John **7**
Robinson, David **24**

San Diego Chargers football team
Barnes, Ernie **16**

San Diego Conquistadors
Chamberlain, Wilt **18**

San Diego Gulls hockey team
O'Ree, Willie **5**

San Diego Hawks hockey team
O'Ree, Willie **5**

San Diego Padres baseball team
Gwynn, Tony **18**
McGriff, Fred **24**
Sheffield, Gary **16**
Winfield, Dave **5**

San Francisco 49ers football team
Edwards, Harry **2**
Green, Dennis **5**
Lott, Ronnie **9**
Rice, Jerry **5**
Simpson, O. J. **15**

San Francisco Giants baseball team
Baker, Dusty **8**
Bonds, Barry **6**
Mays, Willie **3**
Morgan, Joe Leonard **9**
Robinson, Frank **9**
Strawberry, Darryl **22**

Sankofa Film and Video
Julien, Isaac **3**

Saturday Night Live
Murphy, Eddie **4, 20**
Rock, Chris **3, 22**

Saxophone
Albright, Gerald **23**
Bechet, Sidney **18**
Coltrane, John **19**
Hawkins, Coleman **9**
Parker, Charlie **20**
Washington, Grover, Jr. **17**

Schomburg Center for Research in Black Culture
Andrews, Bert **13**
Dodson, Howard, Jr. **7**
Hutson, Jean Blackwell **16**
Reddick, Lawrence Dunbar **20**
Schomburg, Arthur Alfonso **9**

School desegregation
Fortune, T. Thomas **6**
Hamer, Fannie Lou **6**

Science fiction
Bell, Derrick **6**
Butler, Octavia **8**
Delany, Samuel R., Jr. **9**

SCLC
See Southern Christian Leadership Conference

Sculpture
Allen, Tina **22**

Barthe, Richmond **15**
Bailey, Radcliffe **19**
Biggers, John **20**
Brown, Donald **19**
Burke, Selma **16**
Catlett, Elizabeth **2**
Chase-Riboud, Barbara **20**
Edwards, Melvin **22**
Guyton, Tyree **9**
Hunt, Richard **6**
Lewis, Edmonia **10**
McGee, Charles **10**
Ringgold, Faith **4**
Saar, Alison **16**
Savage, Augusta **12**
Shabazz, Attallah **6**

Seattle city government
Rice, Norm **8**

Seattle Mariners baseball team
Griffey, Ken, Jr. **12**

Seattle Supersonics basketball team
Bickerstaff, Bernie **21**
Lucas, John **7**
Russell, Bill **8**
Silas, Paul **24**
Wilkens, Lenny **11**

Second Republic (Nigeria)
Obasanjo, Olusegun **5**

Seismology
Person, Waverly **9**

Senate Confirmation Hearings
Ogletree, Charles, Jr. **12**

Sesame Street
Clash, Kevin **14**
Glover, Savion **14**

Sexual harassment
Gomez-Preston, Cheryl **9**
Hill, Anita **5**
Thomas, Clarence **2**

Shrine of the Black Madonna
Agyeman, Jaramogi Abebe **10**

Sickle cell anemia
Satcher, David **7**

Sierra Leone People's Party (SLPP)
Kabbah, Ahmad Tejan **23**

Silicon Graphics Incorporated
Hannah, Marc **10**

Slavery
Asante, Molefi Kete **3**
Bennett, Lerone, Jr. **5**
Chase-Riboud, Barbara **20**
Cooper, Anna Julia **20**
Douglas, Aaron **7**
Du Bois, W. E. B. **3**
Dunbar, Paul Laurence **8**

Gaines, Ernest J. **7**
Haley, Alex **4**
Harper, Frances Ellen Watkins **11**
Johnson, Charles **1**
Morrison, Toni **2, 15**
Muhammad, Elijah **4**
Patterson, Orlando **4**
Pleasant, Mary Ellen **9**
Stephens, Charlotte Andrews **14**
Stewart, Maria W. Miller **19**
Taylor, Susie King **13**
Tubman, Harriet **9**
X, Malcolm **1**

SNCC
See Student Nonviolent Coordinating Committee

Soccer
Jones, Cobi N'Gai **18**
Milla, Roger **2**
Pelé **7**

Social disorganization theory
Frazier, E. Franklin **10**

Social science
Berry, Mary Frances **7**
Bunche, Ralph J. **5**
Clark, Kenneth B. **5**
Cobbs, Price M. **9**
Frazier, E. Franklin **10**
Harris, Eddy L. **18**
Haynes, George Edmund **8**
Lawrence-Lightfoot, Sara **10**
Marable, Manning **10**
Steele, Claude Mason **13**
Woodson, Robert L. **10**

Social work
Auguste, Rose-Anne **13**
Berry, Bertice **8**
Canada, Geoffrey **23**
Dunham, Katherine **4**
Hale, Clara **16**
Hale, Lorraine **8**
Harris, Alice **7**
Haynes, George Edmund **8**
King, Barbara **22**
Lewis, Thomas **19**
Little, Robert L. **2**
Robinson, Rachel **16**
Waddles, Charleszetta (Mother) **10**
Young, Whitney M., Jr. **4**

Socialist Party of Senegal
Diouf, Abdou **3**

Soledad Brothers
Jackson, George **14**

Soul City, NC
McKissick, Floyd B. **3**

Soul Train
Cornelius, Don **4**

South African Communist Party
Hani, Chris **6**

South African Council of Churches (SACC)
Tutu, Desmond **6**

South African Defence Force (SADF)
Nujoma, Samuel **10**

South African literature
Mathabane, Mark **5**

South African Students' Organization
Biko, Steven **4**

Southern African Development Community (SADC)
Mbuende, Kaire **12**

Southern African Development Coordination Conference (SADCC)
Masire, Quett **5**
Numjoma, Samuel **10**

Southern African Project
McDougall, Gay J. **11**

Southern Christian Leadership Conference (SCLC)
Abernathy, Ralph **1**
Angelou, Maya **1, 15**
Baker, Ella **5**
Chavis, Benjamin **6**
Dee, Ruby **8**
Fauntroy, Walter E. **11**
Hooks, Benjamin L. **2**
Jackson, Jesse **1**
King, Martin Luther, Jr. **1**
King, Martin Luther, III **20**
Lowery, Joseph **2**
Moses, Robert Parris **11**
Rustin, Bayard **4**
Williams, Hosea Lorenzo **15**
Young, Andrew **3**

South West African People's Organization (SWAPO)
Nujoma, Samuel **10**

Space Shuttle
Bluford, Guy **2**
Bolden, Charles F., Jr. **7**
Gregory, Frederick D. **8**
Jemison, Mae C. **1**
McNair, Ronald **3**

Spectroscopy
Quarterman, Lloyd Albert **4**

Spelman College
Cole, Johnnetta B. **5**
Price, Glenda **22**

Spingarn medal
Aaron, Hank **5**

Ailey, Alvin **8**
Anderson, Marian **2**
Angelou, Maya **15**
Bethune, Mary McLeod **4**
Bradley, Thomas **2, 20**
Brooke, Edward **8**
Bunche, Ralph J. **5**
Carver, George Washington **4**
Clark, Kenneth B. **5**
Cosby, Bill **7**
Davis, Sammy Jr. **18**
Drew, Charles Richard **7**
Du Bois, W. E. B. **3**
Ellington, Duke **5**
Evers, Medgar **3**
Grimké, Archibald H. **9**
Haley, Alex **4**
Hastie, William H. **8**
Hayes, Roland **4**
Hinton, William Augustus **8**
Hooks, Benjamin L. **2**
Horne, Lena **5**
Houston, Charles Hamilton **4**
Hughes, Langston **4**
Jackson, Jesse **1**
Johnson, James Weldon **5**
Johnson, John H. **3**
Jordan, Barbara **4**
Julian, Percy Lavon **6**
Just, Ernest Everett **3**
King, Martin Luther, Jr. **1**
Lawless, Theodore K. **8**
Lawrence, Jacob **4**
Marshall, Thurgood **1**
Mays, Benjamin E. **7**
Parks, Gordon **1**
Parks, Rosa **1**
Powell, Colin **1**
Price, Leontyne **1**
Randolph, A. Philip **3**
Robeson, Paul **2**
Robinson, Jackie **6**
Staupers, Mabel K. **7**
Sullivan, Leon H. **3**
Weaver, Robert C. **8**
White, Walter F. **4**
Wilder, L. Douglas **3**
Wilkins, Roy **4**
Williams, Paul R. **9**
Woodson, Carter **2**
Wright, Louis Tompkins **4**
Wright, Richard **5**
Young, Andrew **3**
Young, Coleman **1, 20**

Spirituals
Anderson, Marian **2**
Hayes, Roland **4**
Jackson, Mahalia **5**
Joyner, Matilda Sissieretta **15**
Norman, Jessye **5**
Reese, Della **6, 20**
Robeson, Paul **2**

Sports psychology
Edwards, Harry **2**

State University of New York System
Wharton, Clifton R., Jr. **7**

Stonewall 25
Norman, Pat **10**

Structural Readjustment Program
Babangida, Ibrahim **4**

Student Nonviolent Coordinating Committee (SNCC)
Al-Amin, Jamil Abdullah **6**
Baker, Ella **5**
Barry, Marion S. **7**
Blackwell, Unita **17**
Bond, Julian **2**
Carmichael, Stokely **5**
Clark, Septima **7**
Crouch, Stanley **11**
Davis, Angela **5**
Forman, James **7**
Hamer, Fannie Lou **6**
Holland, Endesha Ida Mae **3**
Lester, Julius **9**
Lewis, John **2**
Moses, Robert Parris **11**
Norton, Eleanor Holmes **7**
Poussaint, Alvin F. **5**
Reagon, Bernice Johnson **7**

Sundance Film Festival
Harris, Leslie **6**

Supreme Court
See U.S. Supreme Court

Supreme Court of Haiti
Pascal-Trouillot, Ertha **3**

Surrealism
Ellison, Ralph **7**
Lee-Smith, Hughie **5, 22**

SWAPO
See South West African People's Organization

Sweet Honey in the Rock
Reagon, Bernice Johnson **7**

Syndicat Agricole Africain (SAA)
Houphouët-Boigny, Félix **4**

Synthetic chemistry
Julian, Percy Lavon **6**

Tampa Bay Buccaneers football team
Dungy, Tony **17**
Williams, Doug **22**

Tanga Consultative Congress (Tanzania)
Nujoma, Samuel **10**

Tanganyikan African National Union (TANU)
Nyerere, Julius **5**

TANU
See Tanganyikan African National Union

Tanzanian African National Union (TANU)
See Tanganyikan African National Union

Tap dancing
Bates, Peg Leg **14**
Glover, Savion **14**
Hines, Gregory **1**

TBS
See Turner Broadcasting System

Teachers Insurance and Annuity Association and the College Retirement Equities Fund (TIAA-CREF)
Wharton, Clifton R., Jr. **7**

Teaching
Alexander, Margaret Walker **22**
Clarke, John Henrik **20**
Early, Gerald **15**
Gates, Sylvester James, Jr. **15**
Humphries, Frederick **20**
Norman, Maidie **20**
Redmond, Eugene **23**
Smith, John L. **22**

TEF
See Theological Education Fund

Television
Arkadie, Kevin **17**
Bowser, Yvette Lee **17**
Burnett, Charles **16**
Carson, Lisa Nicole **21**
Cheadle, Don **19**
Curtis-Hall, Vondie **17**
Eubanks, Kevin **15**
Hardison, Kadeem **22**
Hemsley, Sherman **19**
Hill, Lauryn **20**
Hughley, D.L. **23**
Jackson, George **19**
Joe, Yolanda **21**
Jones, Bobby **20**
Mitchell, Brian Stokes **21**
Mitchell, Russ **21**
Moss, Carlton **16**
Price, Frederick K. C. **21**
Rock, Chris **3, 22**
Rollins, Howard E. Jr., **17**
Smiley, Tavis **20**
Snipes, Wesley **3, 24**
Thigpen, Lynne **17**
Usher **23**
Williamson, Mykelti **22**

Tennessee Titans football team
McNair, Steve **22**

Tennis
Ashe, Arthur **1, 18**
Garrison, Zina **2**
Gibson, Althea **8**
Lucas, John **7**
McNeil, Lori **1**
Noah, Yannick **4**
Washington, MaliVai **8**
Williams, Samm-Art **21**
Williams, Serena **20**
Williams, Venus **17**

Texas House of Representatives
Johnson, Eddie Bernice **8**
Wilson, Flip **21**

Texas Rangers baseball team
Cottrell, Comer **11**

Texas State Senate
Johnson, Eddie Bernice **8**
Jordan, Barbara **4**

Theological Education Fund (TEF)
Gordon, Pamela **17**
Tutu, Desmond **6**

Theology
Franklin, Robert M. **13**

Third World Press
Madhubuti, Haki R. **7**

Threads 4 Life
Jones, Carl **7**
Kani, Karl **10**
Walker, T. J. **7**

TIAA-CREF
See Teachers Insurance and Annuity Association and the College Retirement Equities Fund

Time-Warner Inc.
Parsons, Richard Dean **11**

TLC Beatrice International Holdings, Inc.
Lewis, Reginald F. **6**

TLC Group L.P.
Lewis, Reginald F. **6**

Today
Gumbel, Bryant **14**

Togolese Army
Eyadéma, Gnassingbé **7**

Togolese People's Rally (RPT)
Eyadéma, Gnassingbé **7**

Tonight Show, The
Eubanks, Kevin **15**

Tony awards
Allen, Debbie **13**
Belafonte, Harry **4**
Carroll, Diahann **9**
Clarke, Hope **14**
Faison, George **16**
Fishburne, Larry **4, 22**
Horne, Lena **5**
Hyman, Phyllis **19**
Jones, James Earl **3**
McDonald, Audra **20**
Moore, Melba **21**
Richards, Lloyd **2**
Thigpen, Lynne **17**
Uggams, Leslie **23**
Vereen, Ben **4**
Wilson, August **7**
Wolfe, George C. **6**

Toronto Blue Jays baseball team
McGriff, Fred **24**
Winfield, Dave **5**

Toronto Raptors basketball team
Thomas, Isiah **7**

Track and field
Christie, Linford **8**
Devers, Gail **7**
Johnson, Michael **13**
Jones, Marion **21**
Joyner-Kersee, Jackie **5**
Lewis, Carl **4**
Moses, Edwin **8**
Mutola, Maria **12**
Owens, Jesse **2**
Powell, Mike **7**
Quirot, Ana **13**
Rudolph, Wilma **4**
Thugwane, Josia **21**

TransAfrica, Inc.
Robinson, Randall **7**

Transition
Soyinka, Wole **4**

Transitional Committee for National Recovery (Guinea; CTRN)
Conté, Lansana **7**

Transplant surgery
Callender, Clive O. **3**
Kountz, Samuel L. **10**

"Trial of the Century"
Cochran, Johnnie L., Jr. **11**
Darden, Christopher **13**
Simpson, O.J. **15**

Trinidad Theatre Workshop
Walcott, Derek **5**

Trumpet
Armstrong, Louis **2**
Davis, Miles **4**
Ellison, Ralph **7**
Gillespie, Dizzy **1**

Turner Broadcasting System (TBS)
Clayton, Xernona **3**

Tuskegee Airmen
James, Daniel, Jr. **16**
Patterson, Frederick Douglass **12**

Tuskegee Experiment Station
Carver, George Washington **4**

Tuskegee University
Payton, Benjamin F. **23**

U.S. Department of Agriculture
Watkins, Shirley R. **17**
Williams, Hosea Lorenzo **15**

U.S. Diplomatic Corp
Haley, George Williford Boyce **21**

U.S. District Court judge
Diggs-Taylor, Anna **20**
Keith, Damon J. **16**
Parsons, James **14**

UCC
See United Church of Christ

UFBL
See Universal Foundation for Better Living

UGA
See United Golf Association

Umkhonto we Sizwe
Hani, Chris **6**
Mandela, Nelson **1, 14**

UN
See United Nations

UNCF
See United Negro College Fund

Uncle Nonamé Cookie Company
Amos, Wally **9**

Underground Railroad
Cohen, Anthony **15**

Unemployment and Poverty Action Committee
Forman, James **7**

UNESCO
See United Nations Educational, Scientific, and Cultural Organization

UNIA
See United Negro Improvement Association

UNICEF
See United Nations Children's Fund

Cumulative Subject Index

Unions
Clay, William Lacy **8**
Crockett, George, Jr. **10**
Europe, James Reese **10**
Farmer, James **2**
Hilliard, David **7**
Ramaphosa, Cyril **3**
Randolph, A. Philip **3**
Touré, Sekou **6**

UNIP
See United National Independence Party

UNITA
See National Union for the Total Independence of Angola

United Bermuda Party
Gordon, Pamela **17**

United Church of Christ (UCC)
Chavis, Benjamin **6**

United Democratic Front (UDF)
Muluzi, Bakili **14**

United Golf Association (UGA)
Elder, Lee **6**
Sifford, Charlie **4**

United Methodist Church
Lewis, Shirley A. R. **14**

United National Independence Party (UNIP)
Kaunda, Kenneth **2**

United Nations (UN)
Annan, Kofi Atta **15**
Bunche, Ralph J. **5**
Diouf, Abdou **3**
Lafontant, Jewel Stradford **3**
McDonald, Gabrielle Kirk **20**
Mongella, Gertrude **11**
Perkins, Edward **5**
Sampson, Edith S. **4**
Young, Andrew **3**

United Nations Children's Fund (UNICEF)
Baker, Gwendolyn Calvert **9**
Belafonte, Harry **4**
Machel, Graca Simbine **16**

United Nations Educational, Scientific, and Cultural Organization (UNESCO)
Diop, Cheikh Anta **4**
Frazier, E. Franklin **10**
Machel, Graca Simbine **16**

United Negro College Fund (UNCF)
Boyd, T. B. III **6**
Edley, Christopher **2**
Gray, William H. III **3**
Jordan, Vernon E. **3**
Mays, Benjamin E. **7**

Patterson, Frederick Douglass **12**

United Negro Improvement Association (UNIA)
Garvey, Marcus **1**

United Parcel Service
Washington, Patrice Clarke **12**

United Somali Congress (USC)
Ali Mahdi Mohamed **5**

United States Football (USFL)
White, Reggie **6**
Williams, Doug **22**

United Workers Union of South Africa (UWUSA)
Buthelezi, Mangosuthu Gatsha **9**

Universal Foundation for Better Living (UFBL)
Colemon, Johnnie **11**
Reese, Della **6, 20**

University of California administration
Massey, Walter E. **5**

University of Colorado administration
Berry, Mary Frances **7**

University of Michigan administration
Goss, Tom **23**

UniverSoul Circus
Walker, Cedric "Ricky" **19**

Urban League (regional)
Clayton, Xernona **3**
Jacob, John E. **2**
Mays, Benjamin E. **7**
Young, Whitney M., Jr. **4**

Urban renewal
Archer, Dennis **7**
Barry, Marion S. **7**
Bosley, Freeman, Jr. **7**
Collins, Barbara-Rose **7**
Harris, Alice **7**
Lane, Vincent **5**
Waters, Maxine **3**

US
Karenga, Maulana **10**

U.S. Air Force
Davis, Benjamin O., Jr. **2**
Gregory, Frederick D. **8**
Harris, Marcelite Jordan **16**
James, Daniel, Jr. **16**

U.S. Armed Forces Nurse Corps
Staupers, Mabel K. **7**

U.S. Army
Cadoria, Sherian Grace **14**
Davis, Benjamin O., Sr. **4**
Flipper, Henry O. **3**
Johnson, Hazel **22**
Powell, Colin **1**
Stanford, John **20**
Watkins, Perry **12**
West, Togo D., Jr. **16**

U.S. Attorney's Office
Lafontant, Jewel Stradford **3**

U.S. Basketball League (USBL)
Lucas, John **7**

USBL
See U.S. Basketball League

USC
See United Somali Congress

U.S. Cabinet
Brown, Ron **5**
Elders, Joycelyn **6**
Espy, Mike **6**
Harris, Patricia Roberts **2**
Herman, Alexis M. **15**
O'Leary, Hazel **6**
Slater, Rodney E. **15**
Sullivan, Louis **8**
Weaver, Robert C. **8**

U.S. Circuit Court of Appeals
Hastie, William H. **8**
Keith, Damon J. **16**

U.S. Coast Guard
Brown, Erroll M. **23**

U.S. Commission on Civil Rights
Berry, Mary Frances **7**

U.S. Court of Appeals
Higginbotham, A. Leon, Jr. **13**
Kearse, Amalya Lyle **12**

USDA
See U.S. Department of Agriculture

U.S. Department of Agriculture (USDA)
Espy, Mike **6**

U.S. Department of Commerce
Brown, Ron **5**
Irving, Larry, Jr. **12**
Person, Waverly **9**
Wilkins, Roger **2**

U.S. Department of Defense
Tribble, Israel, Jr. **8**

U.S. Department of Education
Hill, Anita **5**
Hill, Bonnie Guiton **20**
Thomas, Clarence **2**
Tribble, Israel, Jr. **8**

U.S. Department of Energy
O'Leary, Hazel **6**

U.S. Department of Health and Human Services (HHS)
See also U.S. Department of Health, Education, and Welfare
Sullivan, Louis **8**

U.S. Department of Health, Education, and Welfare (HEW)
Bell, Derrick **6**
Berry, Mary Frances **7**
Harris, Patricia Roberts **2**
Johnson, Eddie Bernice **8**

U.S. Department of Housing and Urban Development (HUD)
Harris, Patricia Roberts **2**
Weaver, Robert C. **8**

U.S. Department of Justice
Bell, Derrick **6**
Campbell, Bill **9**
Days, Drew S., III **10**
Guinier, Lani **7**
Holder, Eric H., Jr. **9**
Lafontant, Jewel Stradford **3**
Lewis, Delano **7**
Patrick, Deval **12**
Wilkins, Roger **2**

U.S. Department of Labor
Crockett, George, Jr. **10**
Herman, Alexis M. **15**

U.S. Department of Social Services
Little, Robert L. **2**

U.S. Department of State
Bethune, Mary McLeod **4**
Bunche, Ralph J. **5**
Keyes, Alan L. **11**
Lafontant, Jewel Stradford **3**
Perkins, Edward **5**
Rice, Condoleezza **3**
Wharton, Clifton R., Jr. **7**

U.S. Department of the Interior
Person, Waverly **9**

U.S. Department of Veterans Affairs
Brown, Jesse **6**

U.S. Diplomatic Corps
Grimké, Archibald H. **9**
Harris, Patricia Roberts **2**
Stokes, Carl B. **10**

USFL
See United States Football League

U.S. Geological Survey
Person, Waverly **9**

U.S. House of Representatives
Bishop Jr., Sanford D. **24**
Brown, Corrine **24**
Carson, Julia **23**
Chisholm, Shirley **2**
Clay, William Lacy **8**
Clayton, Eva M. **20**
Clyburn, James **21**
Collins, Barbara-Rose **7**
Collins, Cardiss **10**
Conyers, John, Jr. **4**
Crockett, George, Jr. **10**
Cummings, Elijah E. **24**
Dellums, Ronald **2**
Diggs, Charles C. **21**
Dixon, Julian C. **24**
Espy, Mike **6**
Fauntroy, Walter E. **11**
Fields, Cleo **13**
Flake, Floyd H. **18**
Ford, Harold E., Jr., **16**
Franks, Gary **2**
Gray, William H. III **3**
Hastings, Alcee L. **16**
Hilliard, Earl F. **24**
Jackson, Jesse, Jr. **14**
Jackson Lee, Sheila **20**
Jordan, Barbara **4**
Kilpatrick, Carolyn Cheeks **16**
Leland, Mickey **2**
Lewis, John **2**
Meek, Carrie **6**
Mfume, Kweisi **6**
Millender-McDonald, Juanita **21**
Norton, Eleanor Holmes **7**
Owens, Major **6**
Payne, Donald M. **2**
Pinchback, P. B. S. **9**
Powell, Adam Clayton, Jr. **3**
Rangel, Charles **3**
Scott, Robert C. **23**
Stokes, Louis **3**
Towns, Edolphus **19**
Tubbs Jones, Stephanie **24**
Washington, Harold **6**
Waters, Maxine **3**
Wheat, Alan **14**
Young, Andrew **3**

U.S. Joint Chiefs of Staff
Powell, Colin **1**

U.S. Marines
Bolden, Charles F., Jr. **7**
Brown, Jesse **6**
Von Lipsey, Roderick K. **11**

U.S. Navy
Doby, Lawrence Eugene, Sr. **16**
Gravely, Samuel L., Jr. **5**
Reason, J. Paul **19**

U.S. Peace Corps
Days, Drew S., III **10**
Lewis, Delano **7**

U.S. Senate
Braun, Carol Moseley **4**
Brooke, Edward **8**
Dodson, Howard, Jr. **7**
Johnson, Eddie Bernice **8**
Pinchback, P. B. S. **9**

U.S. Supreme Court
Marshall, Thurgood **1**
Thomas, Clarence **2**

U.S. Surgeon General
Elders, Joycelyn **6**

U.S. Virgin Islands government
Hastie, William H. **8**

UWUSA
See United Workers Union of South Africa

Vaudeville
Bates, Peg Leg **14**
Davis, Sammy Jr. **18**
Johnson, Jack **8**
McDaniel, Hattie **5**
Mills, Florence **22**
Robinson, Bill "Bojangles" **11**
Waters, Ethel **7**

Veterinary science
Jawara, Sir Dawda Kairaba **11**
Patterson, Frederick Douglass **12**
Thomas, Vivien **9**

Vibe
Jones, Quincy **8**

Village Voice
Crouch, Stanley **11**

Virginia state government
Wilder, L. Douglas **3**

Virginia Squires basketball team
Erving, Julius **18**

Voodoo
Dunham, Katherine **4**
Guy, Rosa **5**
Hurston, Zora Neale **3**
Pierre, Andre **17**

Voting rights
Clark, Septima **7**
Forman, James **7**
Guinier, Lani **7**
Hamer, Fannie Lou **6**
Harper, Frances Ellen Watkins **11**
Hill, Jessie, Jr. **13**
Johnson, Eddie Bernice **8**
Lampkin, Daisy **19**
Mandela, Nelson **1, 14**
Moses, Robert Parris **11**
Terrell, Mary Church **9**
Trotter, Monroe **9**
Tubman, Harriet **9**
Wells-Barnett, Ida B. **8**
Williams, Hosea Lorenzo **15**
Woodard, Alfre **9**

Vulcan Realty and Investment Company
Gaston, Arthur G. **4**

Washington DC City Council
Jarvis, Charlene Drew **21**

WAAC
See Women's Auxiliary Army Corp

WAC
See Women's Army Corp

Walter Payton Inc.
Payton, Walter **11**

War Resister's League (WRL)
Carter, Mandy **11**

Washington Color Field group
Thomas, Alma **14**

Washington, DC City Council
Fauntroy, Walter E. **11**

Washington, DC city government
Barry, Marion S. **7**
Dixon, Sharon Pratt **1**
Fauntroy, Walter E. **11**
Jarvis, Charlene Drew **21**
Norton, Eleanor Holmes **7**
Williams, Anthony **21**

Washington Mystics basketball team
McCray, Nikki **18**

Washington Wizards basketball team
Bickerstaff, Bernie **21**
Howard, Juwan **15**
Lucas, John **7**
Unseld, Wes **23**
Webber, Chris **15**

Washington Post
Maynard, Robert C. **7**
McCall, Nathan **8**
Nelson, Jill **6**
Raspberry, William **2**
Wilkins, Roger **2**

WBA
See World Boxing Association

WBC
See World Boxing Council

WCC
See World Council of Churches

Weather
Christian, Spencer **15**
McEwen, Mark **5**

Welfare reform
Bryant, Wayne R. **6**
Carson, Julia **23**
Williams, Walter E. **4**

West Indian folklore
Walcott, Derek **5**

West Indian folk songs
Belafonte, Harry **4**

West Indian literature
Guy, Rosa **5**
Kincaid, Jamaica **4**
Marshall, Paule **7**
McKay, Claude **6**
Walcott, Derek **5**

West Point
Davis, Benjamin O., Jr. **2**
Flipper, Henry O. **3**

West Side Preparatory School
Collins, Marva **3**

White House Conference on Civil Rights
Randolph, A. Philip **3**

Whitney Museum of American Art
Golden, Thelma **10**

WHO
See Women Helping Offenders

"Why Are You on This Planet?"
Yoba, Malik **11**

William Morris Talent Agency
Amos, Wally **9**

WillieWear Ltd.
Smith, Willi **8**

Wilmington 10
Chavis, Benjamin **6**

WOMAD
See World of Music, Arts, and Dance

Women Helping Offenders (WHO)
Holland, Endesha Ida Mae **3**

Women's Auxiliary Army Corps
See Women's Army Corp

Women's Army Corps (WAC)
Adams Early, Charity **13**
Cadoria, Sherian Grace **14**

Women's issues
Allen, Ethel D. **13**
Angelou, Maya **1, 15**
Baker, Ella **5**
Berry, Mary Frances **7**
Brown, Elaine **8**
Campbell, Bebe Moore **6, 24**
Cannon, Katie **10**
Charles, Mary Eugenia **10**
Christian-Green, Donna M. **17**
Clark, Septima **7**
Cole, Johnnetta B. **5**
Cooper, Anna Julia **20**
Cunningham, Evelyn **23**
Dash, Julie **4**
Davis, Angela **5**
Edelman, Marian Wright **5**
Elders, Joycelyn **6**
Fauset, Jessie **7**
Giddings, Paula **11**
Goldberg, Whoopi **4**
Grimké, Archibald H. **9**
Guy-Sheftall, Beverly **13**
Hale, Clara **16**
Hale, Lorraine **8**
Hamer, Fannie Lou **6**
Harper, Frances Ellen Watkins **11**
Harris, Alice **7**
Harris, Leslie **6**
Harris, Patricia Roberts **2**
Height, Dorothy I. **2, 23**
Hernandez, Aileen Clarke **13**
Hill, Anita **5**
Hine, Darlene Clark **24**
Holland, Endesha Ida Mae **3**
hooks, bell **5**
Jackson, Alexine Clement **22**
Joe, Yolanda **21**
Jordan, Barbara **4**
Jordan, June **7**
Lampkin, Daisy **19**
Larsen, Nella **10**
Lorde, Audre **6**
Marshall, Paule **7**
McCabe, Jewell Jackson **10**
McMillan, Terry **4, 17**
Meek, Carrie **6**
Millender-McDonald, Juanita **21**
Mongella, Gertrude **11**
Morrison, Toni **2, 15**
Naylor, Gloria **10**
Nelson, Jill **6**
Nichols, Nichelle **11**
Norman, Pat **10**
Norton, Eleanor Holmes **7**
Painter, Nell Irvin **24**
Parker, Pat **19**
Rawlings, Nana Konadu Agyeman **13**
Ringgold, Faith **4**
Shange, Ntozake **8**
Simpson, Carole **6**
Smith, Jane E. **24**
Terrell, Mary Church **9**
Tubman, Harriet **9**
Vanzant, Iyanla **17**
Walker, Alice **1**
Walker, Maggie Lena **17**
Wallace, Michele Faith **13**
Waters, Maxine **3**
Wattleton, Faye **9**
Winfrey, Oprah **2, 15**

Women's National Basketball Association (WNBA)
Cooper, Cynthia **17**
Edwards, Teresa **14**
Holdsclaw, Chamique **24**
Leslie, Lisa **16**
McCray, Nikki **18**

Peck, Carolyn 23
Perrot, Kim 23
Swoopes, Sheryl 12

Women's Strike for Peace
King, Coretta Scott 3

Worker's Party (Brazil)
da Silva, Benedita 5

Workplace equity
Hill, Anita 5
Clark, Septima 7
Nelson, Jill 6
Simpson, Carole 6

Works Progress Administration (WPA)
Alexander, Margaret Walker 22
Baker, Ella 5
Douglas, Aaron 7
Dunham, Katherine 4
Lawrence, Jacob 4
Lee-Smith, Hughie 5, 22
Wright, Richard 5

World African Hebrew Israelite Community
Ben-Israel, Ben Ami 11

World beat
Belafonte, Harry 4
Fela 1
N'Dour, Youssou 1
Ongala, Remmy 9

World Bank
Soglo, Nicéphore 15

World Boxing Association (WBA)
Whitaker, Pernell 10

World Boxing Council (WBF)
Whitaker, Pernell 10

World Council of Churches (WCC)
Mays, Benjamin E. 7
Tutu, Desmond 6

World Cup
Milla, Roger 2
Pelé 7

World hunger
Belafonte, Harry 4
Iman 4
Jones, Quincy 8
Leland, Mickey 2
Masire, Quett 5
Obasanjo, Olusegun 5

World of Music, Arts, and Dance (WOMAD)
Ongala, Remmy 9

WPA
See Works Progress Administration

WRL
See War Resister's League

Xerox Corp.
Rand, A. Barry 6

Yab Yum Entertainment
Edmonds, Tracey 16

Yale Child Study Center
Comer, James P. 6

Yale Repertory Theater
Dutton, Charles S. 4, 22
Richards, Lloyd 2
Wilson, August 7

Yale School of Drama
Dutton, Charles S. 4, 22
Richards, Lloyd 2

YMCA
See Young Men's Christian Associations

Yoruban folklore
Soyinka, Wole 4
Vanzant, Iyanla 17

Young Men's Christian Association (YMCA)
Butts, Calvin O., III 9
Goode, Mal 13
Hope, John 8
Mays, Benjamin E. 7

Young Negroes' Cooperative League
Baker, Ella 5

Young Women's Christian Association (YWCA)
Baker, Ella 5
Baker, Gwendolyn Calvert 9
Clark, Septima 7
Hedgeman, Anna Arnold 22
Height, Dorothy I. 2, 23
Jackson, Alexine Clement 22
Jenkins, Ella 15
Sampson, Edith S. 4

Youth Pride Inc.
Barry, Marion S. 7

Youth Services Administration
Little, Robert L. 2

YWCA
See Young Women's Christian Association

ZANLA
See Zimbabwe African National Liberation Army

ZAPU
See Zimbabwe African People's Union

Zimbabwe African National Liberation Army (ZANLA)
Mugabe, Robert Gabriel 10

Zimbabwe African People's Union (ZAPU)
Mugabe, Robert Gabriel 10
Nkomo, Joshua 4

ZTA
See Zululand Territorial Authority

Zululand Territorial Authority (ZTA)
Buthelezi, Mangosuthu Gatsha 9

Cumulative Name Index

Volume numbers appear in **bold**.

Aaron, Hank 1934— **5**
Aaron, Henry Louis
  See Aaron, Hank
Abacha, Sani 1943— **11**
Abbott, Diane (Julie) 1953— **9**
Abdul-Jabbar, Kareem 1947— **8**
Abdulmajid, Iman Mohamed
  See Iman
Abernathy, Ralph David 1926-1990 **1**
Abu-Jamal, Mumia 1954— **15**
Achebe, (Albert) Chinua(lumogu) 1930— **6**
Adams Early, Charity (Edna) 1918— **13**
Adams, Floyd, Jr. 1945— **12**
Adams, Oleta 19(?)(?)– **18**
Adams, Yolanda 1961– **17**
Adkins, Rutherford H. 1924-1998 **21**
Adu, Helen Folasade
  See Sade
Agyeman, Jaramogi Abebe 1911— **10**
Agyeman Rawlings, Nana Konadu 1948— **13**
Aiken, Loretta Mary
  See Mabley, Jackie "Moms" **15**
Ailey, Alvin 1931-1989 **8**
Al-Amin, Jamil Abdullah 1943– **6**
Albright, Gerald 1947– **23**
Alcindor, Ferdinand Lewis
  See Abdul-Jabbar, Kareem
Alexander, Archie Alphonso 1888-1958 **14**
Alexander, Joyce London 1949– **18**
Alexander, Margaret Walker 1915-1998 **22**
Alexander, Sadie Tanner Mossell 1898-1989 **22**
Ali Mahdi Mohamed 1940— **5**
Ali, Muhammad 1942— **2, 16**
Allen, Byron 1961— **3, 24**
Allen, Debbie 1950— **13**
Allen, Ethel D. 1929-1981 **13**
Allen, Marcus 1960– **20**
Allen, Richard 1760-1831 **14**
Allen, Tina 1955– **22**
Amos, John 1941— **8**
Amos, Wally 1937— **9**
Anderson, Jamal 1972–**22**

Anderson, Marian 1902— **2**
Andrews, Benny 1930– **22**
Andrews, Bert 1929-1993 **13**
Andrews, Raymond 1934-1991 **4**
Angelou, Maya 1928— **1, 15**
Anna Marie
  See Lincoln, Abbey
Annan, Kofi Atta 1938— **15**
Ansa, Tina McElroy 1949— **14**
Archer, Dennis (Wayne) 1942— **7**
Arinze, Francis Cardinal 1932– **19**
Aristide, Jean-Bertrand 1953— **6**
Arkadie, Kevin 1957– **17**
Armstrong, (Daniel) Louis 1900-1971 **2**
Armstrong, Robb 1962— **15**
Armstrong, Vanessa Bell 1953– **24**
Arnold, Monica
  See Monica
Arrington, Richard 1934– **24**
Asante, Molefi Kete 1942— **3**
Ashe, Arthur Robert, Jr. 1943-1993 **1, 18**
Ashford, Emmett 1914-1980 **22**
Ashford, Nickolas 1942– **21**
Ashley, Maurice 1966— **15**
Ashley-Ward, Amelia 1957– **23**
Atkins, David
  See Sinbad
Auguste, (Marie Carmele) Rose-Anne 1963— **13**
Austin, Patti 1948– **24**
Avant, Clarence 19(?)(?)– **19**
Ayers, Roy 1940– **16**
Azikiwe, Nnamdi 1904-1996 **13**
Babangida, Ibrahim (Badamasi) 1941— **4**
Babyface
  See Edmonds, Kenneth "Babyface"
Badu, Erykah 1971(?)(?)– **22**
Bailey, Pearl Mae 1918-1990 **14**
Bailey, Radcliffe 1968– **19**
Bailey, Xenobia 1955(?)– **11**
Baker, Anita 1957(?)– **21**
Baker, Constance
  See Motley, Constance Baker
Baker, Dusty 1949— **8**
Baker, Ella 1903-1986 **5**
Baker, George
  See Divine, Father
Baker, Gwendolyn Calvert 1931— **9**

Baker, Houston A(lfred), Jr. 1943— **6**
Baker, Johnnie B., Jr.
  See Baker, Dusty
Baker, Josephine 1906-1975 **3**
Baker, Thurbert 1952– **22**
Baldwin, James 1924-1987 **1**
Bambara, Toni Cade 1939— **10**
Banda, (Ngwazi) Hastings Kamuzu 1898(?)— **6**
Banks, Jeffrey 1953– **17**
Banks, Tyra 1973— **11**
Banks, William (Venoid) 1903-1985 **11**
Baraka, Amiri 1934— **1**
Barboza, Anthony 1944— **10**
Barden, Don H. 1943— **9, 20**
Barkley, Charles (Wade) 1963— **5**
Barnes, Ernie 1938– **16**
Barrett, Andrew C. 1942(?)— **12**
Barrow, Joseph Louis
  See Louis, Joe
Barry, Marion S(hepilov, Jr.) 1936— **7**
Barthe, Richmond 1901-1989 **15**
Basie, Count 1904-1984 **23**
Basie, William James
  See Count Basie
Basie, William James
  See Basie, Count
Basquiat, Jean-Michel 1960-1988 **5**
Bassett, Angela 1959(?)— **6,23**
Bates, Clayton
  See Bates, Peg Leg
Bates, Daisy (Lee Gatson) 1914(?)— **13**
Bates, Peg Leg 1907— **14**
Baugh, David 1947– **23**
Baylor, Don(ald Edward) 1949— **6**
Beals, Jennifer 1963– **12**
Beals, Melba Patillo 1941— **15**
Bearden, Romare (Howard) 1912-1988 **2**
Beasley, Myrlie
  See Evers, Myrlie
Beaton, Norman Lugard 1934-1994 **14**
Bechet, Sidney 1897-1959 **18**
Beck, Robert
  See Iceberg Slim

Beckford, Tyson 1970— **11**
Bedie, Henri Konan 1934– **21**
Belafonte, Harold George, Jr.
  See Belafonte, Harry
Belafonte, Harry 1927— **4**
Bell, Derrick (Albert, Jr.) 1930— **6**
Bell, Ralph S. 1934— **5**
Bell, Robert Mack 1943– **22**
Bellamy, Bill 1967— **12**
Belle, Albert (Jojuan) 1966— **10**
Belle, Regina 1963— **1**
Belton, Sharon Sayles 1951– **9, 16**
Ben-Israel, Ben Ami 1940(?)— **11**
Benjamin, Regina 1956– **20**
Bennett, Lerone, Jr. 1928— **5**
Berry, Bertice 1960— **8**
Berry, Halle 1967(?)— **4, 19**
Berry, Mary Frances 1938— **7**
Betha, Mason Durrell 1977(?)– **24**
Bethune, Mary (Jane) McLeod 1875-1955 **4**
Bickerstaff, Bernard Tyrone 1944– **21**
Biggers, John 1924–**20**
Biko, Stephen
  See Biko, Steven (Bantu)
Biko, Steven (Bantu) 1946-1977 **4**
Bing, Dave 1943— **3**
Bishop, Eric
  See Foxx, Jamie
Bishop, Sanford D. Jr. 1947– **24**
Bizimungu, Pasteur 1951– **19**
Black, Keith Lanier 1955– **18**
Blackwell, Unita 1933–**17**
Blair, Maxine
  See Powell, Maxine
Blanks, Billy 1955(?)– **22**
Blige, Mary Jane 1971–**20**
Bluford, Guion Stewart, Jr.
  See Bluford, Guy
Bluford, Guy 1942— **2**
Bluitt, Juliann Stephanie 1938— **14**
Bol, Manute 1963— **1**
Bolden, Charles F(rank), Jr. 1946—**7**
Bolin, Jane 1908– **22**
Bonaly, Surya 1973— **7**
Bond, (Horace) Julian 1940— **2**
Bonds, Barry (Lamar) 1964— **6**
Bonga, Kuenda 1942— **13**
Bongo, (El Hadj) Omar 1935— **1**
Bongo, Albert-Bernard
  See Bongo, (El Hadj) Omar
Bontemps, Arna(ud Wendell) 1902-1973 **8**
Booker, Simeon 1918– **23**
Borders, James (Buchanan, IV) 1949— **9**
Bosley, Freeman (Robertson), Jr. 1954— **7**
Boston, Lloyd 1970(?)– **24**
Bowe, Riddick (Lamont) 1967– **6**
Bowser, Yvette Lee 1965(?)– **17**
Boyd, John W., Jr. 1965– **20**
Boyd, T(heophilus) B(artholomew), III 1947— **6**
Boykin, Keith 1965— **14**
Bradley, Ed(ward R.) 1941— **2**

Bradley, Thomas 1917— **2, 20**
Brandon, Barbara 1960(?)— **3**
Brandon, Thomas Terrell 1970– **16**
Brandy 1979— **14**
Braugher, Andre 1962(?)— **13**
Braun, Carol (Elizabeth) Moseley 1947— **4**
Braxton, Toni 1968(?)— **15**
Breedlove, Sarah
  See Walker, Madame C. J.
Brimmer, Andrew F(elton) 1926— **2**
Briscoe, Connie 1952— **15**
Brock, Louis Clark 1939– **18**
Brooke, Edward (William, III) 1919— **8**
Brooks, Avery 1949— **9**
Brooks, Gwendolyn 1917— **1**
Brown, Andre
  See Dr. Dre
Brown Bomber, The
  See Louis, Joe
Brown, Charles 1922-1999 **23**
Brown, Corrine 1946– **24**
Brown, Donald 1963– **19**
Brown, Elaine 1943— **8**
Brown, Erroll M. 1950(?)– **23**
Brown, H. Rap
  See Al-Amin, Jamil Abdullah
Brown, Hubert Gerold
  See Al-Amin, Jamil Abdullah
Brown, James Nathaniel
  See Brown, Jim
Brown, James 1933— **15**
Brown, James 1951– **22**
Brown, James Willie, Jr.
  See Komunyakaa, Yusef
Brown, Jesse 1944— **6**
Brown, Jim 1936— **11**
Brown, Lee P(atrick) 1937— **1, 24**
Brown, Les(lie Calvin) 1945— **5**
Brown, Ron(ald Harmon) 1941— **5**
Brown, Sterling (Allen) 1901— **10**
Brown, Tony 1933— **3**
Brown, Wesley 1945– **23**
Brown, William Anthony
  See Brown, Tony
Brown, Willie L., Jr. 1934— **7**
Brown, Zora Kramer 1949— **12**
Brunson, Dorothy 1938— **1**
Bryant, Kobe 1978— **15**
Bryant, Wayne R(ichard) 1947— **6**
Buckley, Victoria (Vikki) 1947-1999 **24**
Bullard, Eugene Jacques 1894-1961 **12**
Bullock, Anna Mae
  See Turner, Tina
Bullock, Steve 1936– **22**
Bumbry, Grace (Ann) 1937— **5**
Bunche, Ralph J(ohnson) 1904-1971 **5**
Burke, Selma Hortense 1900-1995 **16**
Burley, Mary Lou
  See Williams, Mary Lou
Burnett, Charles 1944– **16**
Burnett, Chester Arthur

  See Howlin' Wolf
Burnett, Dorothy 1905-1995 **19**
Burrell, Stanley Kirk
  See Hammer, M. C.
Burrell, Thomas J. 1939– **21**
Burris, Chuck 1951– **21**
Burroughs, Margaret Taylor 1917— **9**
Burton, LeVar(dis Robert Martyn) 1957– **8**
Busby, Jheryl 1949(?)— **3**
Buthelezi, Mangosuthu Gatsha 1928– **9**
Butler, Leroy, III 1968– **17**
Butler, Octavia (Estelle) 1947– **8**
Butler, Paul D. 1961– **17**
Butts, Calvin O(tis), III 1950— **9**
Byrd, Donald 1949— **10**
Byrd, Michelle 1965– **19**
Byrd, Robert (Oliver Daniel, III) 1952— **11**
Byron, JoAnne Deborah
  See Shakur, Assata
Cade, Toni
  See Bambara, Toni Cade
Cadoria, Sherian Grace 1940– **14**
Caesar, Shirley 1938– **19**
Cain, Herman 1945— **15**
Callender, Clive O(rville) 1936– **3**
Calloway, Cabell, III 1907-1994 **14**
Camp, Kimberly 1956– **19**
Campbell, Bebe Moore 1950— **6, 24**
Campbell, Bill 1954— **9**
Campbell, Charleszetta Lena
  See Waddles, Charleszetta (Mother)
Campbell, E(lmer) Simms 1906-1971 **13**
Campbell, Naomi 1970— **1**
Campbell, Tisha 1969— **8**
Canada, Geoffrey 1954– **23**
Canegata, Leonard Lionel Cornelius
  See Lee, Canada
Cannon, Katie 1950— **10**
Carew, Rod 1945–**20**
Carmichael, Stokely 1941— **5**
Carroll, Diahann 1935— **9**
Carson, Benjamin 1951— **1**
Carson, Josephine
  See Baker, Josephine
Carson, Julia 1938– **23**
Carson, Lisa Nicole 1969– **21**
Carter, Anson 1974– **24**
Carter, Ben
  See Ben-Israel, Ben Ami
Carter, Betty 1930– **19**
Carter, Cris 1965– **21**
Carter, Mandy 1946— **11**
Carter, Regina 1966(?)– **23**
Carter, Stephen L(isle) 1954— **4**
Carver, George Washington 1861(?)-1943 **4**
Cary, Lorene 1956— **3**
CasSelle, Malcolm 1970— **11**
Catlett, Elizabeth 1919— **2**
Chamberlain, Wilton Norman 1936– **18**
Chambers, Julius (LeVonne) 1936—

3

Chapman, Jr., Nathan A. 1957– **21**
Chappell, Emma C. 1941– **18**
Charlemagne, Emmanuel
　See Charlemagne, Manno
Charlemagne, Manno 1948– **11**
Charles, Mary Eugenia 1919– **10**
Charles, Ray 1930– **16**
Chase-Riboud, Barbara 1939– **20**
Chavis, Benjamin (Franklin, Jr.) 1948– **6**
Cheadle, Don 1964– **19**
Cheatham, Doc 1905-1997 **17**
Chenault, Kenneth I. 1952– **4**
Chesimard, JoAnne (Deborah)
　See Shakur, Assata
Chideya, Farai 1969– **14**
Childress, Alice 1920-1994 **15**
Chisholm, Shirley (Anita St. Hill) 1924– **2**
Chissano, Joaquim (Alberto) 1939– **7**
Christian, Spencer 1947– **15**
Christian-Green, Donna M. 1945– **17**
Christie, Linford 1960– **8**
Christophe, Henri 1767-1820 **9**
Chuck D 1960– **9**
Clark, Celeste (Clesteen) Abraham 1953– **15**
Clark, Joe 1939– **1**
Clark, Kenneth B(ancroft) 1914– **5**
Clark, Kristin
　See Taylor, Kristin Clark
Clark, Patrick 1955– **14**
Clark, Septima (Poinsette) 1898-1987 **7**
Clark-Sheard, Karen 19(?)(?)– **22**
Clarke, Hope 1943(?)– **14**
Clarke, John Henrik 1915-1998 **20**
Clarke, Patrice Francise
　See Washington, Patrice Clarke
Clash, Kevin 1961(?)– **14**
Clay, Cassius Marcellus, Jr.
　See Ali, Muhammad
Clay, William Lacy 1931– **8**
Clayton, Constance 1937– **1**
Clayton, Eva M. 1934– **20**
Clayton, Xernona 1930– **3**
Claytor, Helen 1907– **14**
Cleage, Albert Buford
　See Agyeman, Jaramogi Abebe
Cleage, Pearl Michelle 1934– **17**
Cleaver, (Leroy) Eldridge 1935– **5**
Cleaver, Emanuel (II) 1944– **4**
Clements, George (Harold) 1932– **2**
Cleveland, James 1932(?)-1991 **19**
Clifton, Lucille 1936– **14**
Clinton, George (Edward) 1941– **9**
Clyburn, James 1940– **21**
Coachman, Alice 1923– **18**
Cobbs, Price M(ashaw) 1928– **9**
Cochran, Johnnie (L., Jr.) 1937– **11**
Cohen, Anthony 1963– **15**
Colbert, Virgis William 1939– **17**
Cole, Johnnetta B(etsch) 1936– **5**
Cole, Nat King 1919-1965 **17**

Cole, Natalie Maria 1950– **17**
Coleman, Bessie 1892-1926 **9**
Coleman, Donald A. 1952– **24**
Coleman, Leonard S., Jr. 1949– **12**
Colemon, Johnnie 1921(?)– **11**
Collins, Albert 1932-1993 **12**
Collins, Barbara-Rose 1939– **7**
Collins, Cardiss 1931– **10**
Collins, Marva 1936– **3**
Coltrane, John William 1926-1967 **19**
Combs, Sean J. 1969– **17**
Comer, James P(ierpont) 1934– **6**
Cone, James H. 1938– **3**
Connerly, Ward 1939– **14**
Conté, Lansana 1944(?)– **7**
Conyers, John, Jr. 1929– **4**
Conyers, Nathan G. 1932– **24**
Cook, Sam 1931-1964 **17**
Cook, Samuel DuBois 1928– **14**
Cook, Suzan D. Johnson 1957– **22**
Cook, Toni 1944– **23**
Cook, Wesley
　See Abu-Jamal, Mumia
Cooks, Patricia 1944-1989 **19**
Cooper, Anna Julia 1858-1964 **20**
Cooper, Cynthia 1963– **17**
Cooper, Edward S(awyer) 1926– **6**
Cooper, J. California 19??– **12**
Cornelius, Don 1936– **4**
Cosby, Bill 1937– **7**
Cosby, Camille Olivia Hanks 1944– **14**
Cosby, William Henry, Jr.
　See Cosby, Bill
Cose, Ellis 1951– **5**
Cottrell, Comer 1931– **11**
Count Basie 1904-1984 **23**
Cowans, Adger W. 1936– **20**
Crawford, Randy 1952– **19**
Crawford, Veronica
　See Crawford, Randy
Crew, Rudolph F. 1950(?)– **16**
Crockett, George (William), Jr. 1909– **10**
Cross, Dolores E. 1938– **23**
Crothers, Benjamin Sherman
　See Crothers, Scatman
Crothers, Scatman 1910-1986 **19**
Crouch, Stanley 1945– **11**
Crowder, Henry 1895-1954(?) **16**
Cullen, Countee 1903-1946 **8**
Cummings, Elijah E. 1951– **24**
Cunningham, Evelyn 1916– **23**
Cunningham, Randall 1963– **23**
Currie, Betty 1939(?)– **21**
Curry, George E. 1947– **23**
Curry, Mark 1964– **17**
Curtis-Hall, Vondie 1956– **17**
da Silva, Benedita 1942– **5**
Dandridge, Dorothy 1922-1965 **3**
Daniels-Carter, Valerie 19(?)(?)– **23**
Danticat, Edwidge 1969– **15**
Darden, Christopher 1957– **13**
Dash, Julie 1952– **4**
Davenport, Arthur
　See Fattah, Chaka
Davidson, Jaye 1967(?)– **5**

Davidson, Tommy – **21**
Davis, Allison 1902-1983 **12**
Davis, Angela (Yvonne) 1944– **5**
Davis, Anthony 1951– **11**
Davis, Benjamin O(liver), Jr. 1912– **2**
Davis, Benjamin O(liver), Sr. 1877-1970 **4**
Davis, Danny K. 1941– **24**
Davis, Ed 1911-1999 **24**
Davis, Lorenzo "Piper" 1917-1997 **19**
Davis, Miles (Dewey, III) 1926-1991 **4**
Davis, Ossie 1917– **5**
Davis, Sammy, Jr. 1925-1990 **18**
Davis, Terrell 1972– **20**
Dawes, Dominique (Margaux) 1976– **11**
Dawkins, Wayne 1955– **20**
Days, Drew S(aunders, III) 1941– **10**
de Carvalho, Barcelo
　See Bonga, Kuenda
"Deadwood Dick"
　See Love, Nat
Dee, Ruby 1924– **8**
Delaney, Beauford 1901-1979 **19**
Delany, Annie Elizabeth 1891-1995 **12**
Delany, Samuel R(ay), Jr. 1942– **9**
Delany, Sarah (Sadie) 1889– **12**
Dellums, Ronald (Vernie) 1935– **2**
Devers, (Yolanda) Gail 1966– **7**
Devine, Loretta 1953– **24**
Devine, Major J.
　See Divine, Father
Dickens, Helen Octavia 1909– **14**
Dickerson, Ernest 1952(?)– **6, 17**
Dickey, Eric Jerome 19(?)(?)– **21**
Diggs, Charles C. 1922-1998 **21**
Diggs-Taylor, Anna 1932– **20**
Dinkins, David (Norman) 1927– **4**
Diop, Cheikh Anta 1923-1986 **4**
Diouf, Abdou 1935– **3**
Divine, Father 1877(?)-1965 **7**
Dixon, Julian C. 1934– **24**
Dixon, Margaret 192(?)– **14**
Dixon, Sharon Pratt 1944– **1**
Dixon, Willie (James) 1915-1992 **4**
do Nascimento, Edson Arantes
　See Pelé
Doby, Lawrence Eugene, Sr. 1924(?)– **16**
Dodson, Howard, Jr. 1939– **7**
Domini, Rey
　See Lorde, Audre (Geraldine)
Donegan, Dorothy 1922-1998 **19**
Dorsey, Thomas Andrew 1899-1993 **15**
Douglas, Aaron 1899-1979 **7**
Dove, Rita (Frances) 1952– **6**
Dove, Ulysses 1947– **5**
Downing, Will 19(?)(?)– **19**
Dr. Dre **10**
Dr. J
　See Erving, Julius Winfield, II
Draper, Sharon M. 1952– **16**

Dre, Dr. 1965?— **14**
Drew, Charles Richard 1904-1950 **7**
Drexler, Clyde 1962— **4**
Driskell, David C(lyde) 1931— **7**
Driver, David E. 1955— **11**
Du Bois, W(illiam) E(dward) B(urghardt) 1868-1963 **3**
DuBois, Shirley Graham 1907-1977 **21**
Ducksworth, Marilyn 1957— **12**
Duke, Bill 1943— **3**
Duke, George 1946– **21**
Dumars, Joe 1963– **16**
Dunbar, Paul Laurence 1872-1906 **8**
Duncan, Tim 1976– **20**
Dungy, Tony 1955– **17**
Dunham, Katherine (Mary) 1910(?)— **4**
Dupri, Jermaine 1972— **13**
Dutton, Charles S. 1951— **4, 22**
Dutton, Marie Elizabeth 1940— **12**
Dyson, Michael Eric 1958— **11**
Early, Deloreese Patricia
  See Reese, Della
Early, Gerald (Lyn) 1952— **15**
Edelin, Ramona Hoage 1945– **19**
Edelman, Marian Wright 1939— **5**
Edley, Christopher (Fairfield, Sr.) 1928— **2**
Edmonds, Kenneth "Babyface" 1958(?)— **10**
Edmonds, Terry 1950(?)– **17**
Edmonds, Tracey 1967(?)– **16**
Edwards, Eli
  See McKay, Claude
Edwards, Harry 1942— **2**
Edwards, Melvin 1937– **22**
Edwards, Teresa 1964— **14**
El-Hajj Malik El-Shabazz
  See X, Malcolm
El-Shabazz, El-Hajj Malik
  See X, Malcolm
Elder, (Robert) Lee 1934— **6**
Elders, Joycelyn (Minnie) 1933— **6**
Ellerbe, Brian 1963– **22**
Ellington, Duke 1899-1974 **5**
Ellington, E. David 1960— **11**
Ellington, Edward Kennedy
  See Ellington, Duke
Ellison, Ralph (Waldo) 1914-1994 **7**
Elmore, Ronn 1957– **21**
Epps, Omar 1973– **23**
Erving, Julius Winfield, II 1950– **18**
Esposito, Giancarlo (Giusseppi Alessandro) 1958– **9**
Espy, Alphonso Michael
  See Espy, Mike
Espy, Mike 1953– **6**
Eubanks, Kevin 1957– **15**
Europe, (William) James Reese 1880-1919 **10**
Evans, Darryl 1961– **22**
Evans, Faith 1973(?)(?)–**22**
Everett, Francine 1917-1999 **23**
Everett, Ronald McKinley
  See Karenga, Maulana

Evers, Medgar (Riley) 1925-1963 **3**
Evers, Myrlie 1933— **8**
Evora, Cesaria 1941— **12**
Ewing, Patrick Aloysius 1962– **17**
Eyadéma, (Étienne) Gnassingbé 1937— **7**
Fagan, Garth 1940— **18**
Faison, George William 1946– **16**
Farmer, Forest J(ackson) 1941— **1**
Farmer, James 1920— **2**
Farr, Mel 1944– **24**
Farrakhan, Louis 1933— **2, 15**
Fats Domino 1928– **20**
Fattah, Chaka 1956— **11**
Fauntroy, Walter E(dward) 1933— **11**
Fauset, Jessie (Redmon) 1882-1961 **7**
Favors, Steve 1948– **23**
Feelings, T(h)om(a)s 1933— **11**
Fela 1938— **1**
Fielder, Cecil (Grant) 1963— **2**
Fields, Cleo 1962— **13**
Fishburne, Larry 1962– **4, 22**
Fishburne, Laurence, III
  See Fishburne, Larry
Fisher, Rudolph John Chauncey 1897-1934 **17**
Fitzgerald, Ella 1918-1996 **8, 18**
Flack, Roberta 1940– **19**
Flake, Floyd H. 1945– **18**
Fletcher, Alphonse, Jr. 1965– **16**
Flipper, Henry O(ssian) 1856-1940 **3**
Flood, Curt(is) 1963— **10**
Folks, Byron
  See Allen, Byron
Forbes, Audrey Manley 1934– **16**
Ford, Harold Eugene, Jr. 1970– **16**
Foreman, George 1948– **1, 15**
Forman, James 1928— **7**
Fortune, T(imothy) Thomas 1856-1928 **6**
Fox, Vivica A. 1964— **15**
Foxx, Jamie 1967— **15**
Foxx, Redd 1922-1991 **2**
Franklin, Aretha 1942— **11**
Franklin, Carl 1949— **11**
Franklin, Hardy R. 1929— **9**
Franklin, John Hope 1915— **5**
Franklin, Kirk 1970— **15**
Franklin, Robert M(ichael) 1954— **13**
Franks, Gary 1954(?)— **2**
Frazier, Edward Franklin 1894-1962 **10**
Frazier, Joe 1944– **19**
Freeman, Al(bert Cornelius), Jr. 1934— **11**
Freeman, Charles Eldridge 1933– **19**
Freeman, Harold P. 1933– **23**
Freeman, Marianna 1957– **23**
Freeman, Morgan 1937— **2, 20**
French, Albert 1943– **18**
Fresh Prince, The
  See Smith, Will
Friday, Jeff 1964(?)– **24**
Fudge, Ann (Marie) 1951(?)— **11**

Fuhr, Grant 1962— **1**
Fulani, Lenora (Branch) 1950— **11**
Fuller, Charles (Henry) 1939— **8**
Fuller, S. B. 1895-1988 **13**
Fuller, Solomon Carter, Jr. 1872-1953 **15**
Gaines, Ernest J(ames) 1933— **7**
Gaither, Jake 1903-1994 **14**
Gantt, Harvey (Bernard) 1943— **1**
Garnett, Kevin 1976— **14**
Garrison, Zina 1963— **2**
Garvey, Marcus 1887-1940 **1**
Gary, Willie Edward 1947— **12**
Gaston, Arthur G(eorge) 1892– **4**
Gates, Henry Louis, Jr. 1950— **3**
Gates, Sylvester James, Jr. 1950— **15**
Gay, Marvin Pentz, Jr.
  See Gaye, Marvin
Gaye, Marvin 1939-1984 **2**
Gayle, Helene D(oris) 1955— **3**
Gentry, Alvin 1954– **23**
George, Nelson 1957– **12**
Gibson, Althea 1927— **8**
Gibson, Johnnie Mae 1949– **23**
Gibson, Josh 1911-1947 **22**
Gibson, Kenneth Allen 1932— **6**
Gibson, William F(rank) 1933— **6**
Giddings, Paula (Jane) 1947— **11**
Gillespie, Dizzy 1917-1993 **1**
Gillespie, John Birks
  See Gillespie, Dizzy
Gilliam, Frank 1934(?)– **23**
Gilliam, Sam 1933– **16**
Giovanni, Nikki 1943— **9**
Giovanni, Yolande Cornelia, Jr.
  See Giovanni, Nikki
Gist, Carole 1970(?)— **1**
Givens, Robin 1965— **4**
Glover, Danny 1948— **1, 24**
Glover, Nathaniel, Jr. 1943— **12**
Glover, Savion 1974– **14**
Goines, Donald 1937(?)-1974 **19**
Goldberg, Whoopi 1955— **4**
Golden, Marita 1950– **19**
Golden, Thelma 1965— **10**
Goldsberry, Ronald 1942– **18**
Gomes, Peter J(ohn) 1942— **15**
Gomez-Preston, Cheryl 1954— **9**
Goode, Mal(vin Russell) 1908-1995 **13**
Goode, W(oodrow) Wilson 1938— **4**
Gooden, Dwight 1964– **20**
Gooding, Cuba, Jr. 1968– **16**
Gordon, Ed(ward Lansing, III) 1960— **10**
Gordon, Pamela 1955– **17**
Gordone, Charles 1925-1995 **15**
Gordy, Berry, Jr. 1929— **1**
Goreed, Joseph
  See Williams, Joe
Goss, Tom 1946– **23**
Gossett, Louis, Jr. 1936— **7**
Gourdine, Simon (Peter) 1940— **11**
Graham, Lawrence Otis 1962— **12**
Graham, Stedman 1951(?)— **13**
Gravely, Samuel L(ee), Jr. 1922— **5**

Graves, Denyce Antoinette 1964– **19**
Graves, Earl G(ilbert) 1935– **1**
Gray, F. Gary 1969– **14**
Gray, Frizzell
  See Mfume, Kweisi
Gray, William H., III 1941– **3**
Green, Albert 1946– **13**
Green, Dennis 1949– **5**
Greene, Joe 1946– **10**
Greenfield, Eloise 1929– **9**
Gregg, Eric 1951– **16**
Gregory, Dick 1932– **1**
Gregory, Frederick D(rew) 1941– **8**
Grier, Pam(ala Suzette) 1949– **9**
Grier, Roosevelt (Rosey) 1932– **13**
Griffey, George Kenneth, Jr. 1969– **12**
Griffith, Mark Winston 1963– **8**
Grimké, Archibald H(enry) 1849-1930 **9**
Guarionex
  See Schomburg, Arthur Alfonso
Guillaume, Robert 1927– **3**
Guinier, (Carol) Lani 1950– **7**
Gumbel, Bryant Charles 1948– **14**
Gumbel, Greg 1946– **8**
Gunn, Moses 1929-1993 **10**
Guy, Jasmine 1964(?)– **2**
Guy, Rosa 1925(?)– **5**
Guy-Sheftall, Beverly 1946– **13**
Guyton, Tyree 1955– **9**
Gwynn, Anthony Keith 1960– **18**
Habré, Hissène 1942– **6**
Habyarimana, Juvenal 1937-1994 **8**
Haile Selassie 1892-1975 **7**
Hailey, JoJo 1971– **22**
Hailey, K-Ci 1969– **22**
Hale, Clara 1902-1992 **16**
Hale, Lorraine 1926(?)– **8**
Haley, Alex (Palmer) 1921-1992 **4**
Haley, George Williford Boyce 1925– **21**
Hall, Elliott S. 1938(?)– **24**
Hall, Lloyd A(ugustus) 1894-1971 **8**
Hamblin, Ken 1940– **10**
Hamer, Fannie Lou (Townsend) 1917-1977 **6**
Hamilton, Virginia 1936– **10**
Hammer, M. C. 1963– **20**
Hammer
  See Hammer, M. C.
Hammond, Fred 1960– **23**
Hampton, Fred 1948-1969 **18**
Hampton, Henry (Eugene, Jr.) 1940– **6**
Hampton, Lionel 1908(?)– **17**
Hancock, Herbie Jeffrey 1940– **20**
Handy, W(illiam) C(hristopher) 1873-1937 **8**
Hani, Chris 1942-1993 **6**
Hani, Martin Thembisile
  See Hani, Chris
Hannah, Marc (Regis) 1956– **10**
Hansberry, Lorraine (Vivian) 1930-1965 **6**
Hansberry, William Leo 1894-1965 **11**
Hardaway, Anfernee (Penny) 1971– **13**
Hardaway, Anfernee (Deon)
  See Hardaway, Anfernee (Penny)
Hardaway, Penny
  See Hardaway, Anfernee (Penny)
Hardison, Bethann 19??– **12**
Hardison, Kadeem 1966– **22**
Harkless, Necia Desiree 1920– **19**
Harper, Frances E(llen) W(atkins) 1825-1911 **11**
Harrell, Andre (O'Neal) 1962(?)– **9**
Harrington, Oliver W(endell) 1912– **9**
Harris, "Sweet" Alice
  See Harris, Alice
Harris, Alice 1934– **7**
Harris, Barbara 1930– **12**
Harris, E. Lynn 1957– **12**
Harris, Eddy L. 1956– **18**
Harris, James, III
  See Jimmy Jam
Harris, Jay **19**
Harris, Leslie 1961– **6**
Harris, Marcelite Jordon 1943– **16**
Harris, Monica 1968– **18**
Harris, Patricia Roberts 1924-1985 **2**
Harris, Robin 1953-1990 **7**
Harsh, Vivian Gordon 1890-1960 **14**
Harvard, Beverly (Joyce Bailey) 1950– **11**
Harvey, Steve 1957– **18**
Haskins, Clem 1943– **23**
Hastie, William H(enry) 1904-1976 **8**
Hastings, Alcee Lamar 1936– **16**
Hathaway, Donny 1945-1979 **18**
Hawkins, Adrienne Lita
  See Kennedy, Adrienne
Hawkins, Coleman 1904-1969 **9**
Hawkins, Erskine Ramsey 1914-1993 **14**
Hawkins, Jamesetta
  See James, Etta
Hawkins, La-Van 1960(?)– **17**
Hawkins, Steven Wayne 1962– **14**
Hawkins, Tramaine Aunzola 1951– **16**
Hayden, Palmer 1890-1973 **13**
Hayden, Robert Earl 1913-1980 **12**
Hayes, Isaac 1942– **20**
Hayes, James C. 1946– **10**
Hayes, Roland 1887-1977 **4**
Haynes, George Edmund 1880-1960 **8**
Haynes, Marques 1926– **22**
Haywood, Margaret A. 1912– **24**
Hedgeman, Anna Arnold 1899-1990 **22**
Hedgeman, Peyton Cole
  See Hayden, Palmer
Height, Dorothy I(rene) 1912– **2, 23**
Hemphill, Essex 1957– **10**
Hemsley, Sherman 1938– **19**
Henderson, Gordon 1957– **5**
Henderson, Natalie Leota
  See Hinderas, Natalie
Henderson, Wade **14**
Hendricks, Barbara 1948– **3**
Hendrix, James Marshall
  See Hendrix, Jimi
Hendrix, Jimi 1942-1970 **10**
Hendrix, Johnny Allen
  See Hendrix, Jimi
Henry, Aaron Edd 1922-1997 **19**
Henry, Lenny 1958– **9**
Henson, Matthew (Alexander) 1866-1955 **2**
Herenton, Willie W. 1940– **24**
Herman, Alexis Margaret 1947– **15**
Hernandez, Aileen Clarke 1926– **13**
Hickman, Fred(erick Douglass) 1951– **11**
Higginbotham, A(loysius) Leon, Jr. 1928– **13**
Hightower, Dennis F(owler) 1941– **13**
Hill, Anita (Faye) 1956– **5**
Hill, Beatrice
  See Moore, Melba
Hill, Bonnie Guiton 1941– **20**
Hill, Calvin 1947– **19**
Hill, Grant (Henry) 1972– **13**
Hill, Janet 1947– **19**
Hill, Jesse, Jr. 1927– **13**
Hill, Lauryn 1975(?)– **20**
Hill, Oliver W. 1907– **24**
Hill, Tamia
  See Tamia
Hilliard, David 1942– **7**
Hilliard, Earl F. 1942– **24**
Himes, Chester 1909-1984 **8**
Hinderas, Natalie 1927-1987 **5**
Hine, Darlene Clark 1947– **24**
Hines, Gregory (Oliver) 1946– **1**
Hinton, William Augustus 1883-1959– **8**
Holder, Eric H., Jr. 1951(?)– **9**
Holdsclaw, Chamique 1977– **24**
Holiday, Billie 1915-1959 **1**
Holland, Endesha Ida Mae 1944– **3**
Holland, Robert, Jr. 1940– **11**
Holmes, Larry 1949– **20**
Holte, Patricia Louise
  See LaBelle, Patti
Holyfield, Evander 1962– **6**
hooks, bell 1952– **5**
Hooks, Benjamin L(awson) 1925– **2**
Hope, John 1868-1936 **8**
Horne, Lena (Mary Calhoun) 1917– **5**
Hounsou, Djimon 1964– **19**
Houphouët-Boigny, Félix 1905– **4**
Houphouët, Dia
  See Houphouët-Boigny, Félix
House, Eddie James, Jr.
  See House, Son
House, Eugene
  See House, Son

House, Son 1902-1988 **8**
Houston, Charles Hamilton 1895-1950 **4**
Houston, Cissy 19(?)(?)– **20**
Houston, Whitney 1963– **7**
Howard, Corinne
  See Mitchell, Corinne
Howard, Desmond Kevin 1970– **16**
Howard, Juwan Antonio 1973– **15**
Howlin' Wolf 1910-1976 **9**
Hrabowski, Freeman A., III **22**
Hudlin, Reginald 1962(?)– **9**
Hudlin, Warrington, Jr. 1953(?)– **9**
Hudson, Cheryl 19(?)(?)– **15**
Hudson, Wade 1946– **15**
Huggins, Larry 1950– **21**
Hughes, (James Mercer) Langston 1902-1967 **4**
Hughes, Albert 1972– **7**
Hughes, Allen 1972– **7**
Hughley,, Darryl Lynn 1964– **23**
Humphrey, Bobbi 1950– **20**
Humphries, Frederick 1935– **20**
Hunt, Richard (Howard) 1935– **6**
Hunter, Billy 1943– **22**
Hunter, Charlayne
  See Hunter-Gault, Charlayne
Hunter-Gault, Charlayne 1942– **6**
Hunter, George William
  See Hunter, Billy
Hurston, Zora Neale 1891-1960 **3**
Hutchinson, Earl Ofari 1945– **24**
Hutson, Jean Blackwell 1914– **16**
Hyman, Phyllis 1949(?)-1995 **19**
Ice Cube 1969(?)– **8**
Ice-T 1958(?)– **6**
Iceberg Slim 1918-1992 **11**
Iman 1955– **4**
Ingraham, Hubert A. 1947– **19**
Ingram, Rex 1895-1969 **5**
Innis, Roy (Emile Alfredo) 1934– **5**
Irving, Clarence (Larry) 1955– **12**
Iverson, Allen 1975– **24**
Jackson, Alexine Clement 1936– **22**
Jackson, George Lester 1941-1971 **14**
Jackson, George 1960(?)– **19**
Jackson, Isaiah (Allen) 1945– **3**
Jackson, Janet 1966– **6**
Jackson, Jesse Louis, Jr. 1965– **14**
Jackson, Jesse 1941– **1**
Jackson Lee, Sheila 1950– **20**
Jackson, Mahalia 1911-1972 **5**
Jackson, Mannie 1939– **14**
Jackson, Maynard (Holbrook, Jr.) 1938– **2**
Jackson, Michael Joseph 1958– **19**
Jackson, O'Shea
  See Ice Cube
Jackson, Reginald Martinez 1946– **15**
Jackson, Samuel L. 1948– **8, 19**
Jackson, Sheneska 1970(?)– **18**
Jackson, Shirley Ann 1946– **12**
Jacob, John E(dward) 1934– **2**
Jagan, Cheddi 1918-1997 **16**
Jakes, Thomas "T.D." 1957– **17**
Jam, Jimmy
  See Jimmy Jam
James, Daniel "Chappie", Jr. 1920-1978 **16**
James, Etta 1938– **13**
James, Juanita (Therese) 1952– **13**
James, Sharpe 1936– **23**
Jamison, Judith 1943– **7**
Jammeh, Yahya 1965– **23**
Jarreau, Al 1940– **21**
Jarvis, Charlene Drew 1941– **21**
Jawara, Sir Dawda Kairaba 1924– **11**
Jean, Wyclef 1970– **20**
Jean-Baptiste, Marianne 1967(?)– **17**
Jeffries, Leonard 1937– **8**
Jemison, Mae C. 1957– **1**
Jenifer, Franklyn G(reen) 1939– **2**
Jenkins, Beverly **14**
Jenkins, Ella (Louise) 1924– **15**
Jimmy Jam 1959– **13**
Joe, Yolanda 19(?)(?)– **21**
John, Daymond 1969(?)– **23**
Johnson, "Magic"
  See Johnson, Earvin "Magic"
Johnson, Ben 1961– **1**
Johnson, Beverly 1952– **2**
Johnson, Carol Diann
  See Carroll, Diahann
Johnson, Caryn E.
  See Goldberg, Whoopi
Johnson, Charles Spurgeon 1893-1956 **12**
Johnson, Charles 1948– **1**
Johnson, Charles Arthur
  See St. Jacques, Raymond
Johnson, Earvin "Magic" 1959– **3**
Johnson, Eddie Bernice 1935– **8**
Johnson, Harvey Jr. 1947(?)– **24**
Johnson, Hazel 1927– **22**
Johnson, Jack 1878-1946 **8**
Johnson, James Weldon 1871-1938 **5**
Johnson, James William
  See Johnson, James Weldon
Johnson, John Arthur
  See Johnson, Jack
Johnson, John H(arold) 1918– **3**
Johnson, Marguerite
  See Angelou, Maya
Johnson, Michael (Duane) 1967– **13**
Johnson, Norma L. Holloway 1932– **17**
Johnson, Robert L. 1946(?)– **3**
Johnson, Robert T. 1948– **17**
Johnson, Robert 1911-1938 **2**
Johnson, Virginia (Alma Fairfax) 1950– **9**
Johnson, William Henry 1901-1970 **3**
Johnson-Brown, Hazel W.
  See, Johnson, Hazel
Jones, Bill T. 1952– **1**
Jones, Bobby 1939(?)– **20**
Jones, Carl 1955(?)– **7**
Jones, Cobi N'Gai 1970– **18**
Jones, Elaine R. 1944– **7**
Jones, Elvin 1927– **14**
Jones, Ingrid Saunders 1945– **18**
Jones, James Earl 1931– **3**
Jones, Le Roi
  See Baraka, Amiri
Jones, Lillie Mae
  See Carter, Betty
Jones, Lois Mailou 1905– **13**
Jones, Marion 1975– **21**
Jones, Quincy (Delight) 1933– **8**
Jones, Roy Jr. 1969– **22**
Jones, Ruth Lee
  See Washington, Dinah
Jones, Sissieretta
  See Joyner, Matilda Sissieretta
Jones, Star(let Marie) 1962(?)– **10**
Joplin, Scott 1868-1917 **6**
Jordan, Barbara (Charline) 1936– **4**
Jordan, June 1936– **7**
Jordan, Michael (Jeffrey) 1963– **6, 21**
Jordan, Montell 1968(?)– **23**
Jordan, Vernon E(ulion, Jr.) 1935– **3**
Josey, E. J. 1924– **10**
Joyner, Jacqueline
  See Joyner-Kersee, Jackie
Joyner-Kersee, Jackie 1962– **5**
Joyner, Matilda Sissieretta 1869(?)-1933 **15**
Joyner, Tom 1949(?)– **19**
Julian, Percy Lavon 1899-1975 **6**
Julien, Isaac 1960– **3**
Just, Ernest Everett 1883-1941 **3**
Justice, David Christopher 1966– **18**
Kabbah, Ahmad Tejan 1932– **23**
Kabila, Laurent 1939–**20**
Kamau, Johnstone
  See Kenyatta, Jomo
Kari, Karl 1968(?)– **10**
Karenga, Maulana 1941– **10**
Kaunda, Kenneth (David) 1924– **2**
Kearse, Amalya Lyle 1937– **12**
Keith, Damon Jerome 1922– **16**
Kelly, Patrick 1954(?)-1990 **3**
Kelly, R(obert) 1969(?)– **18**
Kelly, Sharon Pratt
  See Dixon, Sharon Pratt
Kendricks, Eddie 1939-1992 **22**
Kennard, William Earl 1957– **18**
Kennedy, Adrienne 1931– **11**
Kennedy, Florynce Rae 1916– **12**
Kennedy, Lelia McWilliams Robinson 1885-1931 **14**
Kenyatta, Jomo 1891(?)-1978 **5**
Kerekou, Ahmed (Mathieu) 1933– **1**
Keyes, Alan L(ee) 1950– **11**
Khan, Chaka 1953– **12**
Khanga, Yelena 1962– **6**
Kilpatrick, Carolyn Cheeks 1945– **16**
Kimbro, Dennis (Paul) 1950– **10**
Kincaid, Jamaica 1949– **4**
King, B. B. 1925– **7**
King, Barbara 19(?)(?)– **22**
King, Bernice (Albertine) 1963– **4**
King, Coretta Scott 1929– **3**
King, Dexter (Scott) 1961– **10**

King, Don 1931— **14**
King, Gayle 1956– **19**
King, Martin Luther, Jr. 1929-1968 **1**
King, Martin Luther, III 1957– **20**
King, Regina 1971–**22**
King, Riley B.
 See King, B. B.
King, Yolanda (Denise) 1955– **6**
Kirby, George 1924-1995 **14**
Kirk, Ron 1954— **11**
Kitt, Eartha Mae 1928(?)– **16**
Kitt, Sandra 1947– **23**
Knight, Gladys Maria 1944– **16**
Knight, Marion, Jr.
 See Knight, Suge
Knight, Suge 1966— **11**
Komunyakaa, Yusef 1941— **9**
Kotto, Yaphet (Fredrick) 1944— **7**
Kountz, Samuel L(ee) 1930-1981 **10**
Kravitz, Lenny 1964— **10**
Kravitz, Leonard
 See Kravitz, Lenny
Kunjufu, Jawanza 1953— **3**
Kuti, Fela Anikulapo
 See Fela
L. L. Cool J 1968– **16**
La Salle, Eriq 1962— **12**
LaBelle, Patti 1944– **13**
Lafontant, Jewel Stradford 1922— **3**
Lampkin, Daisy 1883(?)-1965 **19**
Lane, Charles 1953– **3**
Lane, Vincent 1942— **5**
Langhart, Janet 1941– **19**
Lankford, Raymond Lewis 1967– **23**
Larkin, Barry 1964– **24**
Larsen, Nella 1891-1964 **10**
Lassiter, Roy 1969– **24**
Latimer, Lewis H(oward) 1848-1928 **4**
Lawless, Theodore K(enneth) 1892-1971 **8**
Lawrence, Jacob (Armstead) 1917— **4**
Lawrence-Lightfoot, Sara 1944— **10**
Lawrence, Martin 1965— **6**
Lawrence, Robert Henry, Jr. 1935-1967 **16**
Lawson, Jennifer (Karen) 1946— **1**
Leary, Kathryn D. 1952— **10**
Leavell, Dorothy R. 1944– **17**
Lee, Annie Francis 1935– **22**
Lee, Canada 1907-1952 **8**
Lee, Don L(uther)
 See Madhubuti, Haki R.
Lee, Gabby
 See Lincoln, Abbey
Lee, Joie 1962(?)— **1**
Lee, Shelton Jackson
 See Lee, Spike
Lee-Smith, Hughie 1915— **5, 22**
Lee, Spike 1957– **5, 19**
Leffall, LaSalle (Doheny), Jr. 1930— **3**
Leland, George Thomas
 See Leland, Mickey
Leland, Mickey 1944-1989 **2**

Lemmons, Kasi 1961–**20**
Leon, Kenny 1957(?)— **10**
León, Tania 1943— **13**
Leonard, Sugar Ray 1956— **15**
Leslie, Lisa Deshaun 1972– **16**
Lester, Julius 1939— **9**
Levert, Gerald 1966– **22**
Lewellyn, J(ames) Bruce 1927— **13**
Lewis, (Frederick) Carl(ton) 1961— **4**
Lewis, (Mary) Edmonia 1845(?)-1911(?) **10**
Lewis, Byron E(ugene) 1931— **13**
Lewis, David Levering 1936— **9**
Lewis, Delano (Eugene) 1938— **7**
Lewis, Edward T. 1940– **21**
Lewis, John (Robert) 1940— **2**
Lewis, Reginald F. 1942-1993 **6**
Lewis, Shirley Ann Redd 1937– **14**
Lewis, Terry 1956– **13**
Lewis, Thomas 1939– **19**
Lincoln, Abbey 1930— **3**
Lindo, Delroy 1952– **18**
Little, Benilde 1958– **21**
Little, Malcolm
 See X, Malcolm
Little Richard 1932— **15**
Little, Robert L(angdon) 1938— **2**
Locke, Alain (LeRoy) 1886-1954 **10**
Lofton, Kenneth 1967— **12**
Lofton, Ramona 1950— **14**
Logan, Onnie Lee 1910(?)-1995 **14**
Long, Nia 1970– **17**
Lord Pitt of Hampstead
 See Pitt, David Thomas
Lorde, Audre (Geraldine) 1934-1992 **6**
Lott, Ronnie 1959— **9**
Louis, Errol T. 1962— **8**
Louis, Joe 1914-1981 **5**
Love, Darlene 1941– **23**
Love, Nat 1854-1921 **9**
Lover, Ed **10**
Lowery, Joseph E. 1924— **2**
Lucas, John 1953— **7**
Luthuli, Albert (John Mvumbi) 1898(?)-1967 **13**
Lyle, Marcenia
 See Stone, Toni
Lymon, Frankie 1942-1968 **22**
Lyons, Henry 1942(?)— **12**
Lyttle, Hulda Margaret 1889-1983 **14**
Mabley, Jackie "Moms" 1897(?)-1975 **15**
Mabuza, Lindiwe 1938– **18**
Machel, Graca Simbine 1945– **16**
Machel, Samora Moises 1933-1986 **8**
Madhubuti, Haki R. 1942— **7**
Madikizela, Nkosikazi Nobandle Nomzamo Winifred
 See Mandela, Winnie
Madison, Joseph E. 1949— **17**
Mainor, Dorothy Leigh 1910(?)-1996 **19**
Major, Clarence 1936— **9**
Makeba, (Zensi) Miriam 1932— **2**

Malcolm X
 See X, Malcolm
Mallett, Conrad, Jr. 1953– **16**
Malone, Annie (Minerva Turnbo Pope) 1869-1957 **13**
Malone, Karl A. 1963– **18**
Mandela, Nelson (Rolihlahla) 1918— **1, 14**
Mandela, Winnie 1934– **2**
Manigault, Earl "The Goat" 1943— **15**
Manley, Audrey Forbes 1934– **16**
Marable, Manning 1950— **10**
Marley, Bob 1945-1981 **5**
Marley, Robert Nesta
 See Marley, Bob
Marrow, Queen Esther 1943(?)– **24**
Marrow, Tracey
 See Ice-T
Marsalis, Wynton 1961– **16**
Marshall, Bella 1950– **22**
Marshall, Gloria
 See Sudarkasa, Niara
Marshall, Paule 1929— **7**
Marshall, Thurgood 1908— **1**
Marshall, Valenza Pauline Burke
 See Marshall, Paule
Martin, Louis Emanuel 1912-1997 **16**
Mase 1977(?)– **24**
Masekela, Barbara 1941– **18**
Masekela, Hugh (Ramopolo) 1939— **1**
Masire, Quett (Ketumile Joni) 1925— **5**
Massenburg, Kedar 1964(?)– **23**
Massey, Walter E(ugene) 1938— **5**
Master P 1970– **21**
Mathabane, Johannes
 See Mathabane, Mark
Mathabane, Mark 1960— **5**
Mathis, Johnny 1935– **20**
Mauldin, Jermaine Dupri
 See Dupri, Jermaine
Maxwell 1973– **20**
Mayfield, Curtis (Lee) 1942— **2**
Maynard, Robert C(lyve) 1937-1993 **7**
Maynor, Dorothy 1910-1996 **19**
Mays, Benjamin E(lijah) 1894-1984 **7**
Mays, William Howard, Jr.
 See Mays, Willie
Mays, Willie 1931– **3**
Mazrui, Ali Al'Amin 1933— **12**
Mbeki, Thabo Mvuyelwa 1942— **14**
Mboup, Souleymane 1951— **10**
Mbuende, Kaire Munionganda 1953— **12**
McBride, Bryant Scott 1965– **18**
McCabe, Jewell Jackson 1945— **10**
McCall, Nathan 1955— **8**
McCarty, Osseola 1908– **16**
McCoy, Elijah 1844-1929 **8**
McCray, Nikki 1972– **18**
McDaniel, Hattie 1895-1952 **5**
McDonald, Audra 1970– **20**
McDonald, Erroll 1954(?)— **1**

McDonald, Gabrielle Kirk 1942– **20**
McDougall, Gay J. 1947— **11**
McEwen, Mark 1954— **5**
McGee, Charles 1924— **10**
McGriff, Fred 1963– **24**
McGruder, Robert 1942– **22**
McIntosh, Winston Hubert
 See Tosh, Peter
McKay, Claude 1889-1948 **6**
McKay, Festus Claudius
 See McKay, Claude
McKay, Nellie Yvonne 194(?)– **17**
McKee, Lonette 1952— **12**
McKegney, Tony 1958— **3**
McKinney, Cynthia Ann 1955— **11**
McKinnon, Ike
 See McKinnon, Isaiah
McKinnon, Isaiah 1943— **9**
McKissick, Floyd B(ixler) 1922-1981 **3**
McKnight, Brian 1969– **18**
McMillan, Terry 1951— **4, 17**
McNair, Ronald (Ervin) 1950-1986 **3**
McNair, Steve 1973– **22**
McNeil, Lori 1964(?)— **1**
McPhail, Sharon 1948— **2**
McQueen, Butterfly 1911— **6**
McQueen, Thelma
 See McQueen, Butterfly
Meek, Carrie (Pittman) 1926– **6**
Meles Zenawi 1955(?)– **3**
Meredith, James H(oward) 1933— **11**
Messenger, The
 See Divine, Father
Meyer, June
 See Jordan, June
Mfume, Kweisi 1948— **6**
Micheaux, Oscar (Devereaux) 1884-1951 **7**
Milla, Roger 1952— **2**
Millender-McDonald, Juanita 1938– **21**
Miller, Bebe 1950— **3**
Miller, Cheryl 1964— **10**
Miller, Maria 1803-1879 **19**
Miller, Percy
 See Master P
Mills, Florence 1896-1927 **22**
Mingus, Charles Jr. 1922-1979 **15**
Mitchell, Arthur 1934— **2**
Mitchell, Brian Stokes 1957– **21**
Mitchell, Corinne 1914-1993 **8**
Mitchell, Russ 1960– **21**
Mkapa, Benjamin William 1938– **16**
Mobutu, Joseph-Desire
 See Mobutu Sese Seko (Nkuku wa za Banga)
Mobutu Sese Seko (Nkuku wa za Banga) 1930— **1**
Mogae, Festus Gontebanye 1939– **19**
Mohamed, Ali Mahdi
 See Ali Mahdi Mohamed
Moi, Daniel (Arap) 1924— **1**
Mongella, Gertrude 1945— **11**
Monica 1980– **21**

Monk, Thelonious (Sphere, Jr.) 1917-1982 **1**
Moon, (Harold) Warren 1956— **8**
Moore, Bobby
 See Rashad, Ahmad
Moore, Melba 1945– **21**
Moore, Shemar 1970– **21**
Moorer, Michael 1967– **19**
Morgan, Garrett (Augustus) 1877-1963 **1**
Morgan, Joe Leonard 1943— **9**
Morgan, Rose (Meta) 1912(?)— **11**
Morial, Marc 1958– **20**
Morris, Stevland Judkins
 See Wonder, Stevie
Morrison, Keith 1942– **13**
Morrison, Toni 1931— **2, 15**
Morton, Joe 1947– **18**
Moseka, Aminata
 See Lincoln, Abbey
Moseley-Braun, Carol
 See Braun, Carol (Elizabeth) Moseley
Moses, Edwin 1955— **8**
Moses, Gilbert, III 1942-1995 **12**
Moses, Robert Parris 1935— **11**
Mosley, Walter 1952— **5**
Moss, Carlton 1909-1997 **17**
Moss, Randy 1977– **23**
Moten, Emma Barnett 1901– **18**
Motley, Constance Baker 1921— **10**
Mourning, Alonzo 1970– **17**
Moutoussamy-Ashe, Jeanne 1951— **7**
Mowry, Jess 1960— **7**
Mugabe, Robert Gabriel 1928— **10**
Muhammad, Elijah 1897-1975 **4**
Muhammad, Khallid Abdul 1951(?)— **10**
Muluzi, Elson Bakili 1943— **14**
Murphy, Eddie 1961— **4, 20**
Murphy, Edward Regan
 See Murphy, Eddie
Murray, Cecil (Chip) 1929— **12**
Murray, Eddie 1956— **12**
Murray, Lenda 1962— **10**
Muse, Clarence Edouard 1889-1979 **21**
Museveni, Yoweri (Kaguta) 1944(?)— **4**
Mutola, Maria de Lurdes 1972— **12**
Mutombo, Dikembe 1966— **7**
Mwinyi, Ali Hassan 1925— **1**
Myers, Walter Milton
 See Myers, Walter Dean
Myers, Walter Dean 1937— **8**
N'Dour, Youssou 1959— **1**
N'Namdi, George R. 1946– **17**
Nanula, Richard D. 1960– **20**
Napoleon, Benny N. 1956(?)– **23**
Nascimento, Milton 1942– **2**
Naylor, Gloria 1950— **10**
Ndadaye, Melchior 1953-1993 **7**
Ndegeocello, Me'Shell 1968– **15**
Ndungane, Winston Njongonkulu 1941– **16**
Nelson, Jill 1952– **6**
Nelson, Prince Rogers

 See Prince
Nettles, Marva Deloise
 See Collins, Marva
Neville, Aaron 1941– **21**
Newcombe, Don 1926– **24**
Newton, Huey (Percy) 1942-1989 **2**
Ngengi, Kamau wa
 See Kenyatta, Jomo
Nicholas, Fayard 1914– **20**
Nicholas, Harold 1921– **20**
Nichols, Grace
 See Nichols, Nichelle
Nichols, Nichelle 1933(?)— **11**
Njongonkulu, Winston Ndungane 1941– **16**
Nkomo, Joshua (Mqabuko Nyongolo) 1917– **4**
Nkrumah, Kwame 1909-1972 **3**
Noah, Yannick (Simon Camille) 1960— **4**
Norman, Jessye 1945— **5**
Norman, Maidie 1912-1998 **20**
Norman, Pat 1939— **10**
Norton, Eleanor Holmes 1937— **7**
Norwood, Brandy
 See, Brandy
Notorious B.I.G. 1972-1997 **20**
Nottage, Cynthia DeLores
 See Tucker, C. DeLores
Ntaryamira, Cyprien 1955-1994 **8**
Nujoma, Samuel 1929– **10**
Nyanda, Siphiwe 1950– **21**
Nyerere, Julius (Kambarage) 1922– **5**
Nzo, Alfred (Baphethuxolo) 1925– **15**
O'Leary, Hazel (Rollins) 1937– **6**
O'Neal, Shaquille (Rashaun) 1972– **8**
O'Neil, Buck 1911– **19**
O'Neil, John Jordan
 See O'Neil, Buck
O'Ree, William Eldon
 See O'Ree, Willie
O'Ree, Willie 1935– **5**
Obasanjo, Olusegun 1937— **5, 22**
Oglesby, Zena 1947– **12**
Ogletree, Charles, Jr. 1933– **12**
Olajuwon, Akeem
 See Olajuwon, Hakeem (Abdul Ajibola)
Olajuwon, Hakeem (Abdul Ajibola) 1963– **2**
Ongala, Ramadhani Mtoro
 See Ongala, Remmy
Ongala, Remmy 1947— **9**
Onwueme, Tess Osonye 1955– **23**
Ousmane, Sembène
 See Sembène, Ousmane
Owens, Dana
 See Queen Latifah
Owens, J. C.
 See Owens, Jesse
Owens, James Cleveland
 See Owens, Jesse
Owens, Jesse 1913-1980 **2**
Owens, Major (Robert) 1936– **6**
Pace, Orlando 1975– **21**

Page, Alan (Cedric) 1945— **7**
Page, Clarence 1947— **4**
Paige, Leroy Robert
    See Paige, Satchel
Paige, Satchel 1906-1982 **7**
Painter, Nell Irvin 1942– **24**
Parker, Charlie 1920-1955 **20**
Parks, Bernard C. 1943– **17**
Parks, Gordon (Roger Alexander Buchanan) 1912— **1**
Parks, Rosa 1913– **1**
Parsons, James Benton 1911-1993 **14**
Parsons, Richard Dean 1948— **11**
Pascal-Trouillot, Ertha 1943– **3**
Patillo, Melba Joy 1941– **15**
Patrick, Deval Laurdine 1956– **12**
Patterson, Floyd 1935– **19**
Patterson, Frederick Douglass 1901-1988 **12**
Patterson, Orlando 1940— **4**
Patterson, P(ercival) J(ames) 1936(?)– **6, 20**
Payne, Allen 1962(?)— **13**
Payne, Donald M(ilford) 1934— **2**
Payton, Benjamin F. 1932– **23**
Payton, Walter (Jerry) 1954— **11**
Peck, Carolyn 1966(?)– **23**
Peete, Calvin 1943— **11**
Peete, Holly Robinson 1965– **20**
Pelé 1940— **7**
Pendergrass, Teddy 1950–**22**
Penniman, Richard Wayne
    See, Little Richard
Peoples, Dottie 19(?)(?)–**22**
Perez, Anna 1951— **1**
Perkins, Anthony 1959?– **24**
Perkins, Edward (Joseph) 1928— **5**
Perrot, Kim 1967-1999 **23**
Perry, Rainford Hugh
    See Perry, Lee "Scratch"
Perry, Ruth Sando 1939— **15**
Perry, Ruth 1936– **19**
Person, Waverly (J.) 1927— **9**
Peters, Maria Philomena 1941— **12**
Petry, Ann 1909-1997 **19**
Pickett, Bill 1870-1932 **11**
Pierre, Andre 1915– **17**
Pinchback, P(inckney) B(enton) S(tewart) 1837-1921 **9**
Pinkett, Jada 1971— **10**
Pinkney, Jerry 1939– **15**
Pinkston, W. Randall 1950– **24**
Pippen, Scottie 1965— **15**
Pippin, Horace 1888-1946 **9**
Pitt, David Thomas 1913-1994 **10**
Pitta, (do Nascimento), Celso (Roberto) 19(?)(?)– **17**
Pleasant, Mary Ellen 1814-1904 **9**
Poitier, Sidney 1927— **11**
Poole, Elijah
    See Muhammad, Elijah
Porter, Countee Leroy
    See, Cullin, Countee
Porter, James A(mos) 1905-1970 **11**
Poussaint, Alvin F(rancis) 1934— **5**
Powell, Adam Clayton, Jr. 1908-1972 **3**

Powell, Bud 1924-1966 **24**
Powell, Colin (Luther) 1937— **1**
Powell, Debra A. 1964– **23**
Powell, Maxine 1924– **8**
Powell, Michael Anthony
    See Powell, Mike
Powell, Mike 1963— **7**
Pratt Dixon, Sharon
    See Dixon, Sharon Pratt
Pratt, Geronimo 1947– **18**
Price, Frederick K.C. 1932– **21**
Price, Glenda 1939– **22**
Price, Hugh B. 1941— **9**
Price, Kelly 1973(?)– **23**
Price, Leontyne 1927— **1**
Primus, Pearl 1919— **6**
Prince 1958– **18**
Pritchard, Robert Starling 1927– **21**
Procope, Ernesta 19??– **23**
Prothrow, Deborah Boutin
    See Prothrow-Stith, Deborah
Prothrow-Stith, Deborah 1954– **10**
Pryor, Richard (Franklin Lennox Thomas) 1940– **3, 24**
Puckett, Kirby 1961— **4**
Quarles, Benjamin Arthur 1904-1996 **18**
Quarterman, Lloyd Albert 1918-1982 **4**
Queen Latifah 1970(?)— **1, 16**
Quirot, Ana (Fidelia) 1963— **13**
Raines, Franklin Delano 1949— **14**
Ralph, Sheryl Lee 1956– **18**
Ramaphosa, (Matamela) Cyril 1952— **3**
Ramsey, Charles H. 1948– **21**
Rand, A(ddison) Barry 1944— **6**
Randall, Dudley (Felker) 1914— **8**
Randle, Theresa 1967– **16**
Randolph, A(sa) Philip 1889-1979 **3**
Rangel, Charles (Bernard) 1930– **3**
Ras Tafari
    See Haile Selassie
Rashad, Ahmad 1949– **18**
Rashad, Phylicia 1948– **21**
Raspberry, William 1935– **2**
Rawlings, Jerry (John) 1947— **9**
Rawls, Lou 1936– **17**
Raymond IV, Usher 1978(?)– **23**
Razaf, Andy 1895-1973 **19**
Razafkeriefo, Andreamentania Paul
    See Razaf, Andy
Reagon, Bernice Johnson 1942— **7**
Reason, Joseph Paul 1943– **19**
Reddick, Lawrence Dunbar 1910-1995 **20**
Redding, Otis, Jr. 1941– **16**
Redmond, Eugene 1937– **23**
Reed, Ishmael 1938– **8**
Reese, Della 1931– **6, 20**
Reeves, Rachel J. 1950(?)– **23**
Reid, Irvin D. 1941– **20**
Reuben, Gloria 19(?)(?)– **15**
Rhames, Ving 1961— **14**
Rhodes, Ray 1950— **14**
Rhone, Sylvia 1952— **2**
Ribbs, William Theodore, Jr.
    See Ribbs, Willy T.

Ribbs, Willy T. 1956— **2**
Ribeiro, Alfonso 1971– **17**
Rice, Condoleezza 1954– **3**
Rice, Jerry 1962— **5**
Rice, Linda Johnson 1958– **9**
Rice, Norm(an Blann) 1943– **8**
Richards, Lloyd 1923(?)– **2**
Richardson, Elaine Potter
    See Kincaid, Jamaica
Richardson, Nolan 1941— **9**
Richardson, Pat
    See Norman, Pat
Richie, Leroy C. 1941– **18**
Richmond, Mitchell James 1965– **19**
Ridenhour, Carlton
    See Chuck D.
Riggs, Marlon 1957– **5**
Riley, Helen Caldwell Day 1926— **13**
Ringgold, Faith 1930– **4**
Roach, Max 1924– **21**
Roberts, James
    See Lover, Ed
Roberts, Marcus 1963– **19**
Roberts, Marthaniel
    See Roberts, Marcus
Roberts, Robin 1960– **16**
Roberts, Roy S. 1939(?)– **14**
Robeson, Eslanda Goode 1896-1965 **13**
Robeson, Paul (Leroy Bustill) 1898-1976 **2**
Robinson, Bill "Bojangles" 1878-1949 **11**
Robinson, David 1965– **24**
Robinson, Eddie G. 1919— **10**
Robinson, Frank 1935— **9**
Robinson, Jack Roosevelt
    See Robinson, Jackie
Robinson, Jackie 1919-1972 **6**
Robinson, Luther
    See Robinson, Bill "Bojangles"
Robinson, Max 1939-1988 **3**
Robinson, Rachel 1922– **16**
Robinson, Randall 1942(?)— **7**
Robinson, Sharon 1950– **22**
Robinson, Smokey 1940– **3**
Robinson, Spottswood W., III 1916-1998 **22**
Robinson, Sugar Ray 1921– **18**
Robinson, William, Jr.
    See Robinson, Smokey
Roche, Joyce M. 1947– **17**
Rochon, Lela 1965(?)– **16**
Rock, Chris 1967(?)– **3, 22**
Rodgers, Johnathan (Arlin) 1946— **6**
Rodman, Dennis Keith 1961— **12**
Rogers, John W., Jr. 1958– **5**
Roker, Albert Lincoln, Jr. 1954(?)— **12**
Rolle, Esther 1920-1998 **13, 21**
Rollins, Howard Ellsworth 1950-1996 **16**
Ross, Araminta
    See Tubman, Harriet
Ross, Diana 1944— **8**

Rotimi, (Emmanuel Gladstone) Ola(wale) 1938— **1**
Rowan, Carl T(homas) 1925— **1**
Rowell, Victoria 1962(?)— **13**
Rudolph, Wilma (Glodean) 1940— **4**
Rugambwa, Laurean 1912-1997 **20**
Rupaul 1960— **17**
Rushen, Patrice 1954— **12**
Russell, Bill 1934— **8**
Russell, Herman Jerome 1931(?)— **17**
Russell-McCloud, Patricia 1946— **17**
Russell, William Felton
  See Russell, Bill
Rustin, Bayard 1910-1987 **4**
Saar, Alison 1956— **16**
Sade 1959— **15**
Saint James, Synthia 1949— **12**
Samara, Noah 1956— **15**
SAMO
  See Basquiat, Jean-Michel
Sampson, Charles 1957— **13**
Sampson, Edith S(purlock) 1901-1979 **4**
Samuel, Sealhenry Olumide 1963— **14**
Sanchez, Sonia 1934— **17**
Sanders, Barry 1968— **1**
Sanders, Deion (Luwynn) 1967— **4**
Sanders, Dori(nda) 1935— **8**
Sanders, Joseph R(ichard, Jr.) 1954— **11**
Sane, Pierre Gabriel 1948– **21**
Sané, Pierre Gabriel -1998 **21**
Sanford, John Elroy
  See Foxx, Redd
Sangare, Oumou 1968– **18**
Sankara, Thomas 1949-1987 **17**
Satcher, David 1941— **7**
Satchmo
  See Armstrong, (Daniel) Louis
Savage, Augusta Christine 1892(?)-1962 **12**
Savimbi, Jonas (Malheiro) 1934— **2**
Sawyer, Amos 1945— **2**
Sayles Belton, Sharon 1952(?)— **9, 16**
Schmoke, Kurt (Lidell) 1949— **1**
Schomburg, Arthur Alfonso 1874-1938 **9**
Schomburg, Arturo Alfonso
  See Schomburg, Arthur Alfonso
Schultz, Michael A. 1938— **6**
Scott, Coretta
  See King, Coretta Scott
Scott, Robert C. 1947– **23**
Scott, Wendell Oliver, Sr. 1921-1990 **19**
Scruggs, Mary Elfrieda
  See Williams, Mary Lou
Seal **14**
Seale, Bobby 1936— **3**
Seale, Robert George
  See Seale, Bobby
Sears-Collins, Leah J(eanette) 1955— **5**
  See Williams, Billy Dee

Selassie, Haile
  See Haile Selassie
Sembène, Ousmane 1923— **13**
Senghor, Léopold Sédar 1906— **12**
Sengstacke, John Herman Henry 1912-1997 **18**
Serrano, Andres 1951(?)— **3**
Shabazz, Attallah 1958— **6**
Shabazz, Betty 1936— **7**
Shakur, Assata 1947— **6**
Shakur, Tupac Amaru 1971-1996 **14**
Shange, Ntozake 1948— **8**
Sharpton, Al 1954– **21**
Shaw, Bernard 1940— **2**
Sheffey, Asa Bundy
  See Hayden, Robert Earl
Sheffield, Gary Antonian 1968– **16**
Shell, Art(hur, Jr.) 1946— **1**
Sherrod, Clayton 1944— **17**
Shipp, E. R. 1955— **15**
Sifford, Charlie (Luther) 1922— **4**
Silas, Paul 1943– **24**
Simmons, Russell 1957(?)— **1**
Simmons, Ruth J. 1945— **13**
Simone, Nina 1933— **15**
Simpson, Carole 1940— **6**
Simpson, Lorna 1960— **4**
Simpson, O. J. 1947— **15**
Simpson, Valerie 1946– **21**
Sinbad 1957(?)— **1, 16**
Singletary, Michael
  See Singletary, Mike
Singletary, Mike 1958— **4**
Singleton, John 1968— **2**
Sinkford, Jeanne C. 1933— **13**
Sister Souljah 1964— **11**
Sisulu, Sheila Violet Makate 1948(?)- **24**
Slater, Rodney Earl 1955— **15**
Sleet, Moneta (J.), Jr. 1926— **5**
Smaltz, Audrey 1937(?)— **12**
Smiley, Tavis 1964– **20**
Smith, Anna Deavere 1950— **6**
Smith, Arthur Lee, Jr.
  See Asante, Molefi Kete
Smith, Barbara 1949(?)— **11**
Smith, Bessie 1894-1937 **3**
Smith, Clarence O. 1933– **21**
Smith, Emmitt (III) 1969— **7**
Smith, Jane E. 1946– **24**
Smith, Jennifer 1947– **21**
Smith, John L. 1938– **22**
Smith, Joshua (Isaac) 1941— **10**
Smith, Orlando
  See Smith, Tubby
Smith, Roger Guenveur 1960— **12**
Smith, Tubby 1951– **18**
Smith, Walker, Jr.
  See Robinson, Sugar Ray
Smith, Will 1968— **8, 18**
Smith, Willi (Donnell) 1948-1987 **8**
Sneed, Paula A. 1947– **18**
Snipes, Wesley 1962— **3, 24**
Soglo, Nicéphore 1935— **15**
Somé, Malidoma Patrice 1956— **10**
Sosa, Sammy 1968– **21**
Sowell, Thomas 1930— **2**

Soyinka, (Akinwande Olu)Wole 1934— **4**
Spaulding, Charles Clinton 1874-1952 **9**
Spikes, Dolores Margaret Richard 1936– **18**
Sprewell, Latrell 1970– **23**
St. Jacques, Raymond 1930-1990 **8**
Stallings, George A(ugustus), Jr. 1948— **6**
Stanford, John 1938– **20**
Stanton, Robert 1940– **20**
Staples, Brent 1951— **8**
Staupers, Mabel K(eaton) 1890-1989 **7**
Steele, Claude Mason 1946— **13**
Steele, Shelby 1946— **13**
Stephens, Charlotte Andrews 1854-1951 **14**
Stevens, Yvette
  See Khan, Chaka
Steward, Emanuel 1944– **18**
Stewart, Alison 1966(?)— **13**
Stewart, Kordell 1972– **21**
Stewart, Paul Wilbur 1925— **12**
Stokes, Carl B(urton) 1927— **10**
Stokes, Louis 1925— **3**
Stone, Charles Sumner, Jr.
  See Stone, Chuck
Stone, Chuck 1924— **9**
Stone, Toni 1921-1996 **15**
Stout, Juanita Kidd 1919-1998 **24**
Strawberry, Darryl 1962– **22**
Street, John F. 1943(?)– **24**
Stringer, C. Vivian 1948– **13**
Sudarkasa, Niara 1938– **4**
Sullivan, Leon H(oward) 1922— **3**
Sullivan, Louis (Wade) 1933— **8**
Sweat, Keith 1961(?)– **19**
Swoopes, Sheryl Denise 1971– **12**
Swygert, H. Patrick 1943– **22**
Sykes, Roosevelt 1906-1984 **20**
Tafari Makonnen
  See Haile Selassie
Tamia 1975– **24**
Tanner, Henry Ossawa 1859-1937 **1**
Tate, Eleanora E. 1948– **20**
Tate, Larenz 1975— **15**
Taulbert, Clifton Lemoure 1945– **19**
Taylor, Billy 1921– **23**
Taylor, Charles 1948– **20**
Taylor, John (David Beckett) 1952– **16**
Taylor, Kristin Clark 1959— **8**
Taylor, Meshach 1947(?)— **4**
Taylor, Regina 1959— **9**
Taylor, Susan L. 1946– **10**
Taylor, Susie King 1848-1912 **13**
Terrell, Dorothy A. 1945– **24**
Terrell, Mary (Elizabeth) Church 1863-1954 **9**
The Artist
  See Prince
"The Goat"
  See Manigault, Earl "The Goat"
Thigpen, Lynne 19(?)(?)– **17**
Thomas, Alma Woodsey 1891-1978

Cumulative Name Index • 259

Thomas, Clarence 1948— **2**
Thomas, Frank Edward, Jr. 1968— **12**
Thomas, Franklin A(ugustine) 1934— **5**
Thomas, Isiah (Lord III) 1961— **7**
Thomas, Rufus 1917— **20**
Thomas, Vivien (T.) 1910-1985 **9**
Thompson, Tazewell (Alfred, Jr.) 1954— **13**
Thugwane, Josia 1971– **21**
Thurman, Howard 1900-1981 **3**
Thurman, Wallace Henry 1902-1934 **16**
Till, Emmett (Louis) 1941-1955 **7**
Tillman, George, Jr. 1968– **20**
Tolliver, William (Mack) 1951— **9**
Toomer, Jean 1894-1967 **6**
Toomer, Nathan Pinchback
　See Toomer, Jean
Tosh, Peter 1944-1987 **9**
Touré, Amadou Toumani 1948?– **18**
Touré, Sekou 1922-1984 **6**
Towns, Edolphus 1934– **19**
Townsend, Robert 1957— **4**
Townsend, Robert 1957— **23**
Tribble, Isreal, Jr. 1940— **8**
Trotter, (William) Monroe 1872-1934 **9**
Trouillot, Ertha Pascal
　See Pascal-Trouillot, Ertha
Tubbs Jones, Stephanie 1949– **24**
Tubman, Harriet 1820(?)-1913 **9**
Tucker, C. DeLores 1927— **12**
Tucker, Chris 1973(?)— **13, 23**
Tucker, Cynthia (Anne) 1955— **15**
Tucker, Rosina Budd Harvey Corrothers 1881-1987 **14**
Ture, Kwame
　See Carmichael, Stokely
Turnbull, Walter 1944— **13**
Turner, Henry McNeal 1834-1915 **5**
Turner, Tina 1939— **6**
Tutu, Desmond (Mpilo) 1931— **6**
Tyree, Omar Rashad 1969– **21**
Tyson, Cicely 1933— **7**
Tyson, Neil de Grasse 1958— **15**
Uggams, Leslie 1943– **23**
Underwood, Blair 1964— **7**
Unseld, Wes 1946– **23**
Upshaw, Eugene, Jr. 1945– **18**
Usry, James L. 1922– **23**
Utendahl, John 1956– **23**
Van Peebles, Mario (Cain) 1957(?)— **2**
Van Peebles, Melvin 1932— **7**
Vance, Courtney B. 1960— **15**
VanDerZee, James (Augustus Joseph) 1886-1983 **6**
Vandross, Luther 1951— **13**
Vann, Harold Moore
　See Muhammad, Khallid Abdul
Vanzant, Iyanla 1953– **17**
Vaughan, Sarah (Lois) 1924-1990 **13**

Vaughn, Mo 1967– **16**
Vereen, Ben(jamin Augustus) 1946— **4**
Vieira, Joao 1939— **14**
Vincent, Marjorie Judith 1965(?)— **2**
Von Lipsey, Roderick 1959— **11**
wa Ngengi, Kamau
　See Kenyatta, Jomo
Waddles, Charleszetta (Mother) 1912— **10**
Waddles, Mother
　See Waddles, Charleszetta (Mother)
Wagner, Annice 1937– **22**
Walcott, Derek (Alton) 1930— **5**
Walcott, Louis Eugene 1933— **2, 15**
　See Farrakhan, Louis
Walker, Albertina 1929— **10**
Walker, Alice (Malsenior) 1944— **1**
Walker, Cedric "Ricky" 1953– **19**
Walker, Herschel (Junior) 1962— **1**
Walker, Kara 1969– **16**
Walker, Madame C. J. 1867-1919 **7**
Walker, Maggie Lena 1867(?)-1934 **17**
Walker, Nellie Marian
　See Larsen, Nella
Walker, T. J. 1961(?)— **7**
Walker, Thomas "T. J."
　See Walker, T. J.
Wallace, Michele Faith 1952— **13**
Wallace, Phyllis A(nn) 1920(?)-1993 **9**
Wallace, Ruby Ann
　See Dee, Ruby
Wallace, Sippie 1898-1986 **1**
Wamutombo, Dikembe Mutombo Mpolondo Mukamba Jean Jacque
　See Mutombo, Dikembe
Ward, Lloyd 1949– **21**
Warfield, Marsha 1955— **2**
Warner, Malcolm-Jamal 1970– **22**
Warwick, Dionne 1940– **18**
Washington, Booker T(aliaferro) 1856-1915 **4**
Washington, Denzel 1954— **1, 16**
Washington, Dinah 1924-1963 **22**
Washington, Fred(er)i(cka Carolyn) 1903-1994 **10**
Washington, Grover, Jr. 1943– **17**
Washington, Harold 1922-1987 **6**
Washington, Laura S. 1956(?)– **18**
Washington, MaliVai 1969— **8**
Washington, Patrice Clarke 1961— **12**
Washington, Valores James 1903-1995 **12**
Wasow, Omar 1970— **15**
Waters, Ethel 1895-1977 **7**
Waters, Maxine 1938— **3**
Watkins, Frances Ellen
　See Harper, Frances Ellen Watkins
Watkins, Gloria Jean
　See hooks, bell
Watkins, Levi, Jr. 1945— **9**
Watkins, Perry James Henry 1948-1996 **12**
Watkins, Shirley R. 1938– **17**

Watkins, Walter C. Jr. 1946– **24**
Watson, Johnny "Guitar" 1935-1996 **18**
Wattleton, (Alyce) Faye 1943— **9**
Watts, Julius Caesar, Jr. 1957— **14**
Watts, Rolonda 1959— **9**
Wayans, Damon 1961— **8**
Wayans, Keenen Ivory 1958– **18**
Waymon, Eunice Kathleen
　See Simone, Nina
Weathers, Carl 1948— **10**
Weaver, Robert C(lifton) 1907– **8**
Webb, Veronica 1965— **10**
Webb, Wellington, Jr. 1941— **3**
Webber, Chris 1973— **15**
Wek, Alek 1977– **18**
Wells-Barnett, Ida B(ell) 1862-1931 **8**
Wells, James Lesesne 1902-1993 **10**
Welsing, Frances (Luella) Cress 1935– **5**
Wesley, Valerie Wilson 194(?)– **18**
West, Cornel (Ronald) 1953— **5**
West, Dorothy 1907– **12**
West, Togo Dennis, Jr. 1942– **16**
Westbrook, Peter 1952– **20**
Wharton, Clifton R(eginald), Jr. 1926— **7**
Wheat, Alan Dupree 1951— **14**
Whitaker, "Sweet Pea"
　See Whitaker, Pernell
Whitaker, Forest 1961– **2**
Whitaker, Mark 1957(?)– **21**
Whitaker, Pernell 1964— **10**
White, Barry 1944— **13**
White, Bill 1933(?)— **1**
White, Jesse 1934– **22**
White, Lois Jean 1938– **20**
White, Michael R(eed) 1951— **5**
White, Reggie 1961— **6**
White, Reginald Howard
　See White, Reggie
White, Walter F(rancis) 1893-1955 **4**
White, William DeKova
　See White, Bill
Whitfield, Fred 1967– **23**
Whitfield, Lynn 1954– **18**
Wideman, John Edgar 1941– **5**
Wilder, L(awrence) Douglas 1931— **3**
Wiley, Ralph 1952— **8**
Wilkens, Lenny 1937— **11**
Wilkens, Leonard Randolph
　See Wilkens, Lenny
Wilkins, Roger (Wood) 1932– **2**
Wilkins, Roy 1901-1981 **4**
Williams, Anthony 1951– **21**
Williams, Bert 1874-1922 **18**
Williams, Billy Dee 1937– **8**
Williams, Carl
　See Kani, Karl
Williams, Daniel Hale (III) 1856-1931 **2**
Williams, Doug 1955– **22**
Williams, Evelyn 1922(?)— **10**
Williams, George Washington 1849-1891 **18**

Williams, Gregory (Howard) 1943— **11**
Williams, Hosea Lorenzo 1926— **15**
Williams, Joe 1918— **5**
Williams, Maggie 1954— **7**
Williams, Margaret Ann
　See Williams, Maggie
Williams, Mary Lou 1910-1981 **15**
Williams, Montel (B.) 1956(?)— **4**
Williams, O(swald) S. 1921— **13**
Williams, Patricia J. 1951— **11**
Williams, Paul R(evere) 1894-1980 **9**
Williams, Paulette Linda
　See Shange, Ntozake
Williams, Robert Peter
　See Guillaume, Robert
Williams, Robert F(ranklin) 1925— **11**
Williams, Samuel Arthur 1946– **21**
Williams, Serena 1981–**20**
Williams, Vanessa L. 1963— **4, 17**
Williams, Venus Ebone Starr 1980– **17**
Williams, Walter E(dward) 1936— **4**
Williams, William December
Williams, William T(homas) 1942— **11**
Williams, Willie L(awrence) 1943— **4**
Williamson, Lisa
　See Sister Souljah
Williamson, Mykelti 1957– **22**
Willis, Cheryl
　See Hudson, Cheryl
Wilson, August 1945— **7**
Wilson, Cassandra 1955– **16**
Wilson, Flip 1933-1998 **21**
Wilson, Nancy 1937— **10**
Wilson, Phill 1956— **9**
Wilson, Sunnie 1908— **7**
Wilson, William Julius 1935– **22**
Wilson, William Nathaniel
　See Wilson, Sunnie
Winans, Benjamin 1962— **14**
Winans, Marvin L. 1958– **17**
Winans, Priscilla 1964— **14**
Winans, Vickie 1953(?)– **24**
Winfield, Dave 1951— **5**
Winfield, David Mark
　See Winfield, Dave
Winfield, Paul (Edward) 1941— **2**
Winfrey, Oprah (Gail) 1954— **2, 15**
Wofford, Chloe Anthony
　See Morrison, Toni
Wolfe, George C. 1954— **6**
Wonder, Stevie 1950— **11**
Woodard, Alfre 1953— **9**
Woodruff, Hale (Aspacio) 1900-1980 **9**
Woods, Eldrick
　See Woods, Tiger
Woods, Granville T. 1856-1910 **5**
Woods, Tiger 1975— **14**
Woodson, Carter G(odwin) 1875-1950 **2**
Woodson, Robert L. 1937— **10**
Wooldridge, Anna Marie
　See Lincoln, Abbey
Worrill, Conrad 1941— **12**
Wright, Bruce McMarion 1918— **3**
Wright, Louis Tompkins 1891-1952 **4**
Wright, Richard 1908-1960 **5**
X, Malcolm 1925-1965 **1**
Yoba, (Abdul-)Malik (Kashie) 1967— **11**
Young, Andre Ramelle
　See Dre, Dr.
Young, Andrew (Jackson, Jr.) 1932— **3**
Young, Coleman 1918— **1, 20**
Young, Jean Childs 1933-1994 **14**
Young, Whitney M(oore), Jr. 1921-1971 **4**
Youngblood, Johnny Ray 1948—**8**